DEMANDING EQUALITY

DEMANDING EQUALITY

One Hundred Years of Canadian Feminism

Joan Sangster

UBCPress · Vancouver · Toronto

30 29 28 27 26 25 24 23 22 21 5 4 3 2 1

Printed in Canada on FSC-certified ancient-forest-free paper (100% post-consumer recycled) that is processed chlorine- and acid-free.

Library and Archives Canada Cataloguing in Publication

Title: Demanding equality : one hundred years of Canadian feminism / Joan Sangster.
Names: Sangster, Joan, 1952- author.
Description: Includes bibliographical references and index.
Identifiers: Canadiana (print) 20210105682 | Canadiana (ebook) 20210105712 | ISBN 9780774866064 (hardcover) | ISBN 9780774866088 (PDF) | ISBN 9780774866095 (EPUB)
Subjects: LCSH: Feminism—Canada—History—19th century. | LCSH: Feminism—Canada—History—20th century. | LCSH: Feminists—Canada—History—19th century. | LCSH: Feminists—Canada—History—20th century. | LCSH: Women—Canada—Social conditions—19th century. | LCSH: Women—Canada—Social conditions—20th century. | LCSH: Women—Canada—History—19th century. | LCSH: Women—Canada—History—20th century.
Classification: LCC HQ1453 .S26 2021 | DDC 305.420971—dc23

Canada

UBC Press gratefully acknowledges the financial support for our publishing program of the Government of Canada (through the Canada Book Fund), the Canada Council for the Arts, and the British Columbia Arts Council.

This book has been published with the help of a grant from the Canadian Federation for the Humanities and Social Sciences, through the Awards to Scholarly Publications Program, using funds provided by the Social Sciences and Humanities Research Council of Canada.

Printed and bound in Canada by Friesens
Set in Futura Condensed and Warnock by Artegraphica Design Co.
Copy editor: Barbara Tessman
Proofreader: Judith Earnshaw
Indexer: Noeline Bridge
Cover designer: Martyn Schmoll

UBC Press
The University of British Columbia
2029 West Mall
Vancouver, BC V6T 1Z2
www.ubcpress.ca

Contents

Acknowledgments

This is a book that seems decades in the making. It reflects years of teaching and researching women's history, as well as more recent research in and rethinking of that history. It also resonates with my own feminist history, since our intellectual and social positions are inevitably imprinted, in both conscious and unconscious ways, on what we create. It seemed ironic to me that one anonymous reviewer of the manuscript thought I should remove all "first person and personal" references in the book as they are "indulgent afterthoughts." After all, for decades feminists have said it is only right and proper to indicate where we have come from. Perhaps the reviewer's remark had something to do with their accompanying assumptions about, and criticisms of, "sixties feminists." However, a "sixties feminist" I am not: I wish I *had* been that politically aware in the sixties when I became a teenager. It took me longer, until the late 1970s, when I was a graduate student, to completely embrace feminism and other radical movements, though my curiosity and sympathies were already engaged.

You might characterize me as a "seventies socialist feminist," but my ideas, intellectual influences, and the causes I have cared about or been involved in have of course developed and shifted with changing theoretical and political concerns. Like many socialist feminists, I was shaped by my social origins, location, and the political times: I was a product of the post-war aspiring white middle-class but also, thankfully, of social movements, of challenges to my ideas, of new ways of seeing the world. If there is one constant since the seventies, it might be my love of history combined with the anticipation that rewriting our understanding of the past with attention to questions about power, exploitation, oppression, inequality, and resistance *matters,* and might even make a difference. This book is written as an introduction to the subject rather than a definitive statement, and I hope it encourages readers to see there is so much more to explore, to write, to question, to demand, in the multiple histories of women's equality seeking.

In putting this manuscript together, I received generous advice, encouragement, and aid. First, thanks go to the Social Science and Humanities Research Council and Trent University's internal research grants for financial support. Graduate students I worked with while writing the book provoked my thinking and some helped with research: thanks to Sean Antaya, Sean Carleton, Mason Godden, Sarah Jessup, Morgana Malyon, James Onusko, Julia Smith, and Christine Sy. While completing this book, Julia Smith and I were engaged in a concurrent labour history project that has stimulated my ideas on the history of feminism and also has been just plain fun. Colleagues writing in similar areas offered suggestions and shared their own writing with me; I am grateful to Penny Bryden, Lara Campbell, Lori Chambers, Sarah Carter, Meg Luxton, Kirk Niergarth, Ted McCoy, Lisa Pasolli, and Veronica Strong-Boag. Historians outside Canada also provided transnational, comparative feedback: thanks to Dorothy Sue Cobble, Lucy Delap, June Hannam, Alice Kessler-Harris, Silke Neunsinger, Ragnheiður Kristjánsdóttir, and Erla Hulda Halldórsdóttir. At the end of the project, when Covid-19 prevented me from travelling to archives to collect photos, Tarah Brookfield, Barbara Freeman, Andrée Lévesque, Mary Bissell, and Karen Teeple found and shared photos with me. Archives across the country have been critical to this project; I want to thank all of them collectively but give a special shout out to the great work done at Canadian Women's Movement Archives at the University of Ottawa and on the Rise Up! Feminism Digital archive website.

In crossing the country to collect research material and give talks, friends and colleagues have put me up and cheered me up: a special thanks to my long-standing Halifax confrères, Janet Guildford, Judith Fingard, and Frances Early, who provided solace and laughter when I broke my foot the first day at the archives, and also to Meaghan Beaton, Alvin Finkel, Betsy Jameson, Mark Leier, Linda and Greg Kealey, Valerie Korinek, Heather Murray, Karen Teeple, Kay Teschke, and Keith Walden. During my writing, Charles Smith, my coeditor at *Labour/Le Travail,* has made that collaboration thoroughly enjoyable, and members of my recent discussion group – Abbie Bakan, Elaine

Coburn, Sedef Arat-Koc, Meg Luxton, and Bonnie Fox – have prodded my thoughts on theoretical questions. I also want to acknowledge Trent friends who weathered some final storms with me: Dimitry Anastakis, Gillian Balfour, Molly Blyth, Caroline Durand, Winnie Lem, Barb Marshall, Janet Miron, Patricia Morton, Colleen O'Manique, and Elaine Stavro.

Working with UBC Press senior editor Randy Schmidt has been a pleasure, and other UBC staff, including Darcy Cullen, Carmen Tiampo, Michelle van der Merwe, and Barbara Tessman, have been professional, helpful, and supportive.

No one has been more present, intellectually and personally, throughout this project than my partner, Bryan Palmer, who has always challenged my thinking (and, I think, I have his), while offering unending love and support. As we begin a new life in the backcountry, I can only hope for many more years of the same. The isolation of the Covid-19 lockdown kept us from contact with our children and grandchildren, making us realize how important they are to our enjoyment of life. We both hold out hopes that the struggle for radical change might alter their futures and that of their generation. This book is dedicated to them: Kate, Beth, Laura, and Rob.

List of Abbreviations

ACVFQ	Alliance canadienne pour le vote des femmes du Québec
AHC	Ad Hoc Conference of Canadian Women on the Constitution
AOWSC	Association Opposed to Woman Suffrage in Canada
ASWAC	Alberta Status of Women Action Committee
BCIHA	British Columbia Indian Homemakers' Association
BPWC	Business and Professional Women's Club
CANEWA	Canadian Negro Women's Association
CBWC	Congress of Black Women of Canada
CCF	Co-operative Commonwealth Federation
CCYM	Co-operative Commonwealth Youth Movement
CEW	Committee for the Equality of Women in Canada
CFBPWC	Canadian Federation of Business and Professional Women's Clubs
CLAWF	Canadian League against War and Fascism
CLC	Canadian Labour Congress
CPC	Communist Party of Canada
CSA	Canadian Suffrage Association
CSL	Canadian Socialist League
CTCU	Canadian Textile and Chemical Union
CUPE	Canadian Union of Public Employees
CWSA	Canadian Women's Suffrage Association
CYC	Company of Young Canadians

DIA	Department of Indian Affairs
DLP	Dominion Labour Party
EYWA	East York Workers Association
FFQ	Fédération des femmes du Québec
FLFQ	Front de libération des femmes du Québec
FNSJB	Fédération nationale Saint-Jean-Baptiste
HCA	Housewives Consumers Association
ILGWU	International Ladies' Garment Workers Union
ILP	Independent Labour Party
IODE	Imperial Order Daughters of the Empire
IRIW	Indian Rights for Indian Women
IUNTW	International Union of Needle Trades Workers
IWD	International Women's Day
IWW	Industrial Workers of the World
JSM	Just Society Movement
LAR	Lesbians against the Right
LARA	Labour Advocacy and Research Association
LSA	League for Socialist Action
MA	mothers' allowances
NAC	National Action Committee on the Status of Women
NCWC	National Council of Women of Canada
NDP	New Democratic Party
NIB	National Indian Brotherhood
NSWAC	Nova Scotia Women's Action Committee
NWAC	Native Women's Association of Canada
OWW	Organized Working Women
PEL	Political Equality League
RCSW	Royal Commission on the Status of Women
RMG	Revolutionary Marxist Group
RWL	Revolutionary Workers League
SDPC	Social Democratic Party of Canada
SORWUC	Service, Office, Retail Workers Union of Canada
SOWC	Status of Women Action Committee
SPC	Socialist Party of Canada
SUPA	Student Union for Peace Action
SWW	Saskatchewan Working Women
TAC	therapeutic abortion committee
TLC	Trades and Labour Congress
TWLC	Toronto Women's Literary Club

UFC	United Farmers of Canada
UFO	United Farmers of Ontario
UFWO	United Farm Women of Ontario
UWEF	United Women's Educational Federation
VOW	Voice of Women
VWC	Vancouver Women's Caucus
WAB	Women against the Budget
WCTU	Woman's Christian Temperance Union
WI	Women's Institutes
WIL	Women's International League for Peace and Freedom
WJC	Women's Joint Committee
WL	women's liberation
WLL	Women's Labour League
WPU	Women's Peace Union
WSL	Women's Suffrage League
WSPU	Women's Social and Political Union
WUL	Workers Unity League
WWC	Western Women's Economic and Social Labour Conference
WWIW	Women Working with Immigrant Women

DEMANDING EQUALITY

Introduction

Nineteenth-century anti-slavery campaigner Mary Ann Shadd Cary, arguably the first woman newspaper editor in Canada, was a passionate abolitionist who believed African-Canadian women must join with their menfolk in the struggle against racism and white supremacy in all its ugly manifestations. Shadd Cary was one of the first African-Canadian women who publicly advocated for enhanced dignity for her racial community as well as equal education and rights for Black women.

Beginning in the 1930s, prairie activist Nellie Peterson devoted her political life to convincing others that cooperation should triumph over capitalism, peace over war. An Albertan farmer, teacher, and leader in the provincial Co-operative Commonwealth Federation (CCF), she saw socialism as the means to achieve a cooperative society, though she also identified women's legal and social inequality as an inexcusable blight on Canadian society.

Quebec trade union leader Madeleine Parent risked social ostracism, imprisonment, and denunciation as a supposed communist in the 1940s and 1950s to organize low-paid textile workers. As a socialist and trade unionist, Parent was committed to workers' self-organization and improvement of their working and living conditions. Through class struggle, she believed, women would also secure new dignity, rights, and equality, and, as her career evolved, she became more centrally involved in the women's movement.

An abolitionist, a cooperator, and a trade unionist: these women did not necessarily self-identify primarily as feminists. Yet I would argue that they were. Most women in this book would not have applied the term "feminist" to themselves: some employed vocabulary specific to their time, such as "equal rights" or "liberationists," but others avoided "feminist" because their concerns about women's oppression were expressed through and alongside other struggles, such as abolitionism, socialism, anti-militarism, or free thought. In fact, some argued that they were *for* women's equality but *against* feminism, as it was associated with a narrow group of women – more affluent or privileged – whose ideas were an impediment to the emancipation of all women.

What, then, is "feminism"? It has been categorized variously as theory, ideas, organizations, movements, sensibilities, feelings, even a way of living. It can be some and all of those. However, if we define it too expansively, it can dissolve into an amorphous description of all women's empowering political activity. Feminism is more specific: it questions, challenges, and hopes to alter women's subordination; it encompasses women's efforts to secure equality, autonomy, and dignity. Can we apply a "feminist" label to women in the past despite their seeming refusal of the term? If we redefine feminism, I think we can. Feminists understood women to be disadvantaged by their gender, but the origins and experience of disadvantage might be attributed to sexual oppression, patriarchy, class exploitation, racism, colonialism, heterosexism – or combinations of those. Some liberal definitions of feminism stress women's individual desire to throw off restrictive "encumbrances" as they seek "the self-determination of a freely choosing, autonomous person."[1] What this definition misses, however, is that autonomy and dignity may be expressed as collective ideals: women from subordinated groups saw women's emancipation as inseparable from the just treatment of their communities.

This book argues that Canadian feminism was polyphonic; it was a chorus of diverse political voices (not necessarily singing in harmony) rather than solos sung by a few women leaders. It is difficult to distinguish a singular feminist consciousness or movement: rather, groups of feminists fashioned different dreams of equality, freedom, and social transformation. Women pursued separate pathways to equality in parallel movements, sometimes mutually supportive, sometimes oppositional. If I had written a book concerning women who consciously endorsed the word "feminist" and were dedicated only to redressing women's inequality, it would have been a slim volume. Make no mistake: this is not just because terminology is historically specific; it is also because feminism was often a hybrid politics, in which women saw independence, equality, and dignity intertwined with struggles against related injustices, whether racism, war, colonialism, economic inequality, or homophobia. The political awakening of some feminists began in other movements as women "questioned the radical questioners,"[2] whether they were enlightenment philosophers, socialists, or liberal reformers. Other feminists began with gender equality but moved to a hybrid feminism.

Certainly, we should not underestimate women's oppression and their desire for freedom from a system of masculine dominance as incubators of feminism. It is undeniable that women's lives from the 1880s to the 1980s not only differed dramatically from men's but were valued less; women were more constrained than men and regulated and denigrated in ways men were not. For much of this time span, women were judged to be intellectually, physically, and/or psychologically inferior to men; therefore, their appropriate role was helpmate, follower, or subordinate. Women faced inordinate fear of sexual assault and violence, whether in familial or social surroundings. They had little control over their own reproduction – male doctors and politicians made the rules women had to live by. As a group, women earned less, had fewer opportunities for education and training, and faced a greater threat of poverty or economic dependence.

Women were also considered second-class citizens. For decades, they could not vote, sit on juries, run for office, have control over their wages, own their own property as married women, secure a divorce on the same terms as men, have custody of their children – the list goes on. Countless laws – such as those delineating self-defence, Indian status, sexual assault – were written in accordance with dominant ideals of patriarchy and masculinity. Social welfare policies similarly encoded gender and racial hierarchies.

Even when women secured citizenship rights, such as the ability to run for public office, gender norms, including women's responsibility for family care, worked against women making full use of those rights. What appeared to be victories for women's rights might also prove double-edged or ambiguous. Political recognition as voters did not produce economic equality, and reforms that benefited some women disadvantaged others. The ascendency of some feminist leaders silenced their counterparts, and, even after women secured formal legal equality, the archetypal "citizen" was still imagined as a white male. Formal citizenship is not necessarily "substantive citizenship" with equal rights, opportunities, treatment, and life conditions.[3]

All of these political, legal, and social inequalities were qualified and differentiated for women based on their social location: their class, race, ethnicity, sexual orientation, religion, place of origin. Because women's experiences diverged so dramatically, their understanding of feminism and (in)equality differed too. Women of Asian descent could not vote in British Columbia until long after white women secured the franchise; working-class women had fewer economic options and faced more acute economic deprivation than middle-class women; Quebec women struggled with intense clerical opposition to equal rights; Indigenous women were subject to the colonial violence of racism and sexism. As I argue in Chapter 3, the very meaning of democracy diverged between Indigenous and Eurocentric cultures, and the latter have dominated the history of feminism.

Nonetheless, there is a misperception that feminism involved only more affluent, white women anxious to overcome their social alienation and claim equal opportunity with men. That was one element of feminism, but so too were the human rights struggles of African-Canadian women determined that their daughters have equal access to education, and the organizing of labour feminists who believed the trade union movement was the best vehicle to secure gender equality. Since class, gender, and race are constituted together, not experienced as separate categories, women's politics might incorporate multiple, even contradictory, aspirations and feelings. Coalitions of politically diverse women determined to fix short-term crises, such as concerted attacks on women's right to work in the Great Depression, constituted another component of feminism.

Feminists were made as they witnessed what they or other women could not do, become, or enjoy, including the right to live without violence, poverty, and fear. While we are more cognizant of feminist struggles to change laws, politics, and institutions, women were also radicalized as they confronted the mundane injustices of daily life, from the employer who sexually harassed them to the fear of walking alone at night to anguish over their hungry children. Feminists questioned the recommended, assigned, or dictated place for women, rejecting admonitions that this was their fate and that the existing social order was reasonable, necessary, and inevitable, ordained by religion, reason, and science. Anti-feminism and outright misogyny were powerful constants in the history of feminism, even if their character shifted over time.

If some women concentrated on their individual freedom, in this volume I focus more on feminism as a collective project of resistance, since that is, ultimately, what galvanized social change. Not that the individual and the collective were mutually exclusive: they were reciprocal. Individual experience created pathways to feminism, and participation in the women's movement induced individual transformation, described by women as eye opening, life changing, spiritual, joyful, surprising, but also painful and difficult. Episodically, feminism elicited flashes of utopian desire and hope. Utopianism, a form of "social dreaming," signalled the transformation not just of societies, but also of consciousness, ideology, imagination, bodies, and the very definition of what is human and humanly possible. Feminists periodically imagined an almost unimaginable world of freedom, equality, and pleasure, the emancipation of those "designated 'other' by hegemonic cultures," the inversion of all dominant norms and ideas, including their own complicity in them.[4]

Broadening our definition of feminism, and recognizing that its political, cultural, and social dimensions are entangled, allows us to capture the heterogeneity of feminism and also destabilize the unfortunately tenacious model of feminist waves: the first encompassing suffrage campaigns circa 1900; the second emerging in the 1960s, with more emphasis on sexual liberation; the third taking shape in the 1990s. Despite many historical critiques, the "waves" concept has proven stubbornly popular. Although I occasionally fall back on this terminology, I believe the wave metaphor is a misleading template for women's history. Slotting feminism into waves is problematic not only because it falsely assumes these waves were followed by troughs of inactivity, but also because it obscures the feminist activism of left-wing, labour, ethnic, and racialized women. It reifies some struggles, such as those for suffrage or sexual autonomy, while ignoring other mobilizations as well as the continuities in women's activism. It also assumes waves are defined and driven by a peer group with a shared political agenda, and fails to acknowledge the ideological differences within feminism in all time periods.

Implicit in many wave accounts is the generational "matraphor" of mothers and daughters; feminism becomes a "family drama" (with noticeably absent fathers) in which each new generational wave measures its insights against the limitations of the previous one.[5] The result is a linear history of progress in which feminism is mapped as a chronological evolution of increasing sophistication and insight. This story of "maternal order and generational succession" has appealed to more than one cohort of feminist activists, especially in their coming-of-age years, to identify or disidentify themselves with feminists who came before.[6] However, the generational/wave metaphor camouflages as much as it illuminates: it suggests inevitable cross-generational tensions and obscures the continuities and heterogeneity in feminist history.

Feminism might be better characterized as political streams ebbing and flowing or as ever-present "radio waves" – multiple, overlapping, with different frequencies and channels.[7] In specific historical moments, certain streams of feminist thought and action find succor or, conversely, are suppressed. "Radical ruptures" may also occur, as feminism takes on new meanings, issues, or intensity, in the process shifting the very definition of concepts like equality, oppression, liberation.[8] Feminists inevitably carry the historical legacies of previous generations with them, but they may also perceive seemingly "spontaneous" shifts, eruptions, and inventions unique to their times.[9]

Remaining wary of a simple onward-and-upward progress narrative while still recognizing the significance of historical context is a delicate balancing act. Whatever the continuities in animating ideas, issues, and methods of organizing, feminist thought and action both shifted over time in relation to theoretical conversations about inequality, social and economic conditions, colonial and state institutions, political movements, diverse cultures, and unexpected events. What feminists reacted against and what they were determined to alter were products of changing global, national, and local environments. If talking about age-specific generations simplifies, we might still think about "political generations":[10] women of all ages struggling against worlds, large and small, that shaped their lives. The trauma of the First World War, for instance, produced new feminist theories about masculinist militarism; the Great Depression fostered critiques of gendered welfare policies and novel forms of socialist-feminist organizing; global anti-imperialist and liberation movements in the sixties inspired women's feminist consciousness and activism.

Feminism also had local and cultural specificity. Feminism in early twentieth-century Quebec was shaped by the dominant francophone, Catholic culture: some feminists aligned themselves with free thought advocates critical of the Catholic Church, while others worked with female religious orders to create a Catholic feminism. Early agrarian feminists on the Prairies argued that farm women's inequality was situated at the crossroads of eastern business domination, patriarchal laws, and a fundamental devaluation of women's labour on the family farm. Six Nations Indigenous women cast their demands for democracy and self-governance in the tradition of the longhouse, while left-wing Ukrainian women in the 1920s pursued an emancipatory project that wove together their ethnic identification, commitment to international communism, and critique of patriarchal norms.

Since the 1960s, feminist historians have criticized mainstream history for discounting or ignoring these women's struggles. The tendency of popular national histories is to focus on a progress narrative of gradual reform, often inspired by great leaders, as the best feminism has contributed to a very partial feminist history. So too has the view that organized feminism is a quaint relic, needed way back when women lacked rights, now relevant only in countries portrayed as backward compared to the West. Yet, if we misrepresent the present as a haven of equality, we may have a murky sense of the past. And feminist historians are not immune from our own misunderstandings and omissions. Sadly, feminists reminiscing about their past often claim historians, too, perpetuate "historical amnesia."[11] Even in a short space of time, some feminist ideas and movements are forgotten, misrepresented, distorted, airbrushed out of history.

If extending historical knowledge is an antidote for amnesia, we also have to be candid about the limitations of research. As feminist historians, we want to uncover voices hidden from history and question taken-for-granted definitions of what is historically significant. However, we may still inevitably privilege some voices, some perspectives, over others. We are always struggling to overcome the very history writing we critique – that is, a history of "winners and losers," a project that reinforces master narratives shaped by existing power relations.[12] Openness, reflection on our own intellectual standpoint, and willingness to rethink our assumptions are all vital as we balance analysis and sensibilities, frameworks and evidence, with an appropriate measure of humility.

Precisely because feminist historians began by questioning if prevailing theories and narratives were value-free, they have been forthright in acknowledging that how we tell our past is shaped by our own evolving perspectives, social location, and historical context. Writing women's history, suggests Susan Friedman, is a tug-of-war between two seemingly opposing impulses. On the one hand, we are trying to reclaim a forgotten, erased, trivialized, or ignored history. This compensatory project is inherently political, and it assumes that a more truthful rendition of history *is* possible. On the other hand, we worry our new histories will themselves be exclusionary or incomplete – we may ignore or misinterpret some women's lives, privileging those with class and race advantages.

We can be paralysed by these countervailing impulses or engage them in a productive dialogue. In a sense, this is an inevitable conundrum of *all* historians: we are always walking a tightrope between "objectivity and subjectivity."[13] We can acknowledge our own strong points of view while still "striving for dispassionate judgment."[14] We can engage in honest projects of historical retrieval while being self-critical of how we produce those very histories. While remaining wary of false notions of complete objectivity, we should not resign ourselves to relativism or pluralism, the former lacking a clear intellectual and moral compass, the latter masking inequalities by uncritically validating all points of view.

This book reads very much like a straightforward truth-telling narrative of historical recovery, but I acknowledge that it was shaped by available sources, feminist debates, and my own choices about which themes to highlight. After combing through archives, documentary, media, and cultural sources, as well as the interpretive works of other historians, I selected examples that typify or illustrate streams of feminist activism, including some individuals and stories already known, as well as others in need of more visibility. I only scratch the surface of a complex, rich history: recognizing that our historical work, like domestic labour, is "never done,"[15] is an acknowledgement that future historians will identify individuals, sources, and interpretations others have overlooked.

Navigating fragmentary and frustratingly incomplete sources detailing women's political activities is a perennial concern of feminist historians; every source has its own partialities and challenges, but, pieced together, counterposed to each other, they enable us to reconstruct a more fulsome account of multiple streams of feminist activity. Redefining what is "political" has been essential: rather than tallying up numbers of women successfully running for legislative office, historians have probed local and fleeting mobilizations, unpaid as well as paid work, and efforts to alter the "private" sphere of bodies, families, and relationships. We know that textual and visual records tend to favour the more literate, affluent, English and French speakers, and those with a leadership or public presence. Feminists were not always cognizant of the historical impact of their activities, they seldom left caches of personal papers, and they were less likely to be sought out by the government, media, or experts for their views. Some were just plain busy, doing the double or triple labour of family care, paid work, and politics, without the time or proclivity to document their political actions and reflections. This was especially so for working-class and racialized women, who often pursued their own pathways to equality, so it is particularly important to locate their equality-seeking efforts. Indigenous women also drew on different cultural practices of historical remembering that were not recorded in our colonial archive. After the 1970s, as a new women's history emerged, feminists have become far more committed to preserving an archive of their own movement, though much of that current history has yet to be written.

In this narrative, I have not hidden my own socialist feminist proclivities or concern with colonialism, already evident in my other writing, but an overview of multiple feminisms necessitated that I tell multiple stories. Feminists, after all, ranged from women with revolutionary hopes to those tinkering with the status quo, from women defying all gender norms to those who wanted women's "female" distinctness valued and given equal consideration. My intent is to show all these feminists "making their own history, but not always in conditions of their own choosing."[16] That well-worn Marxist axiom is not meant facetiously. It assumes that social context shapes but never determines the complexion of political movements: material conditions and social relations are a starting point to understand women's experiences, but culture and ideology are critical too. So too is human agency: after all, feminists "made" their own history through acts of courage, political stamina, innovative thinking, and leaps of the imagination, often defying entrenched ideas. We need to "always historicize,"[17] describing the environments women equality seekers lived in, the prevailing ideologies they encountered, and what they understood to be ideal, possible, and necessary, while also exposing their actions and ideas to critique nurtured by contemporary insights. Acknowledging the limits of their dreams of equality is but one step toward refashioning new ones.

Seventies feminists, who initiated the remarkable explosion of women's history upon which we have built, understood how "perilous and uncertain" efforts are to recover the history of women's lives and consciousness. Contemplating the historians' ongoing internal dialogue between analysis, reflection, and understanding, Sheila Rowbotham suggested we are always acting as intermediaries between the present and the past, using evidence and empathy to reconstruct feminist histories: "The act of analysis ... demands that in the very process of thinking, we transform the relation between thinker and thought about, theory and experience. Analysis is not alone enough for we enter the beings and worlds of other people through imagination and it is through imagination that we glimpse how things might change."[18]

Reclaiming feminist histories, then, is both a project of recovery and a political undertaking in which we are juggling our roles as feminist activists and creators of history, our commitment to uncover truths while recognizing those truths as circumscribed.[19] It is an undertaking in and of the present, predicated on the hope we may be acting on behalf of a better future. Since the eighteenth century, feminists have claimed we can never tackle the injustice of the present or create a more humane, egalitarian future without understanding the origins of inequality. We also need to appreciate how women's movements tried – successfully, partially, or not – to alter social and gender roles they were told were unalterable. That is the challenge of this feminist history.

1 Spreading the Word of Women's Emancipation

As a radical "free thinker," Quebec journalist Éva Circé-Côté was used to public criticism. She wrote for dissenting, liberal, secular publications, started her own independent journal, and delivered public lectures on social issues, including one on the "the causes of the inferiority of women." Defending herself against a male writer who denounced her "feminist" ideas, she responded indignantly that she was a "humanist," not a feminist. Her earliest writing disparaged feminism yet, at the same time, advocated equal education for girls. In a public lecture on women's equality, she reassured men of woman's role as helpmate: "Gentlemen do not think me a revolutionary because I put forward the educated woman as an ideal; the goal is your happiness ... Just like you sir, we have an immortal soul and an intelligence destined to the same end."[1]

How do we assess apparently contradictory impulses in her writing? Do we see her as an early feminist? The answer to the second question is yes; as to the first, she was not unusual in her ambivalent, changing, and, to our eyes, contradictory views. Indeed, she represents an essential beginning to the story of feminism: women who craved intellectual exploration, who questioned the masculine definition of humanity, who used the pen and press to ask if the condition of women was natural, moral, and just.

In the beginning was the printed word. Print culture was an incubator of early feminist thought, from late eighteenth-century Enlightenment treatises to women's columns in daily newspapers a century later. Pamphlets, books, newspapers, and magazines circulated across borders and oceans, conveying new questions, ideas, and visions of social life. The word "feminism" was not in common usage until the end of the nineteenth century, but the concept of women's rights, equality, emancipation, or even the "wrongs" visited upon women was transmitted through print culture prior to that. The electricity generated by these ideas was not the only incubator for feminism. It emerged, too, out of changing social and material conditions of life, both for more privileged women and the working classes, as household and paid labour changed significantly, as did women's social lives, cultural connections, and, for some women, educational prospects.

How feminist ideas took root in nineteenth-century Canada is the subject of this chapter. If we look only for writing tagged as being on the subject of feminism or women's rights, our discussion would be limited, at least until women's suffrage organizations emerged in the 1880s. However, from the mid-nineteenth century onwards, women were questioning their proscribed roles and status. Debates over the "condition of women" ranged from the fine points of political philosophy to practical issues of daily life. Was woman's subjection within the family decreed by nature or tradition? Could it be altered? Was woman's character shaped by biology or by society? Did women deserve an education that went beyond the arts of domesticity? Should women be allowed to work in professions or even in the most degraded of conditions – such as in mines – alongside men? Should they have a voice in politics?

Canadians consumed ideas published in Europe and the United States and gradually created their own print venues that interrogated the gender and social order. Some Canadian writers merely posed queries about the status quo or hinted at altering women's roles; others more forthrightly called for the extension of women's horizons, public engagement, and the means of economic survival. Whatever their approach, this "cultural front," and especially the rise of women's journalism, was a key medium for a feminist message. Percolating through newspapers and magazines, interwoven into women's novels and short stories, performed in plays, feminist ideas slowly took root. Discussion about women's roles also happened in women's literary study groups hungry for intellectual self-education.

The feminist impulse in print culture may seem understated to our eyes, especially compared to later, direct calls for equality. Yet women writers' gentle, probing queries about gender rights and wrongs did create questions that were subsequently taken up by women who were less interested in merely airing the issues and more committed to effecting social change. Print culture in combination with women's changed social and economic lives seeded dissenting ideas that germinated below the surface of social life, nurturing an incipient feminism that would become a powerful force in twentieth-century Canada.

Originating Ideas for the Rights of Women

We could locate the origins of feminism in centuries-old individual acts of rebellion or attempts to assert female autonomy. In early nineteenth-century Canada, an escaped slave's vocal resistance to brutal, forced deportation to the United States, an impoverished women's public denunciation of her punitive treatment for prostitution, or a woman's challenge to patriarchal child custody laws might all be read this way.[2] For Indigenous women, the dignity of cultural and social survival in the face of colonial assimilation was itself a form of resistance. However, if we are searching for the intellectual and political grounding of Western feminist movements, we also need to explore the Enlightenment, abolitionist, and free thought ideas that inspired Western women's collective search for equality.

The Enlightenment – a cluster of philosophies that explored the meaning of humanity, reason, science, progress, individual liberty, and secularism – held out immense possibilities for feminism. Although Enlightenment intellectual communities disagreed, debated, and changed over time, their discussions about the nature of humanity offered women an entrée to analysis of their own oppression. Ideas of universal humanity, freedom, and equality were never the preserve or property of European cultures; however, Enlightenment ideas were astutely adapted by white settler women for their own quest for emancipation.

Two philosophical Enlightenment traditions, John Stuart Mill's practical utilitarian liberalism and Mary Wollstonecraft's more religious egalitarian radicalism, echoed through the writing of nineteenth-century feminists. Canadian suffrage groups studied Mill's book *The Subjection of Women* (1869), which staked out classic liberal arguments for women's equality. Even anti-feminists such as Torontonian Goldwin Smith defined themselves *in opposition to* Mill, though the British-born Smith had once endorsed Mill's views. Fewer Canadian suffragists cited the earlier, pathbreaking writing of radical philosopher Mary Wollstonecraft, whose *A Vindication of the Rights of Woman* (1792), a passionate "insider's" view of women's oppression, was the opening salvo in the long nineteenth-century war of words over women's equality. Yet her ideas had an influence, especially on Quaker and abolitionist women in North America who saw her as the "spiritual mother" of feminism.[3]

Wollstonecraft's *A Vindication* was influenced by multiple traditions: the application of rational principles to religion, English "Jacobin" radicalism, Enlightenment philosophers, and the inspiring ideals of the French Revolution of 1789. Critical of despotism, social hierarchy, and injustice, Wollstonecraft assailed the evils of monarchy, the aristocracy, the excesses of private property, and the horrors of slavery. Ideally, she argued, there should be "no disparity between human souls; the qualities that matter are reason and the capacity for virtue."[4] She challenged not only the "divine right of kings," but also the "divine right of husbands" to rule tyrannically over their families.[5] Although her views influenced later utopian socialists, she is better known for her critique of patriarchal power and the impoverishment of women's minds and spirits through their stunted education.

Wollstonecraft believed women were trained into subordination; they become frivolous, mindless, weak, and manipulative through lack of education and their feminine socialization, though, like men, they had the potential to be intelligent and virtuous citizens. Inherently optimistic about human progress, she expressed her politics in a religious, spiritual language, stressing women's God-given capacities for reason and moral good, a prominent theme in nineteenth-century North American feminist writing. In more recent times, Wollstonecraft has been dismissed as a rather tame liberal feminist whose solution to inequality was merely the meritocracy provided by equal education. Yet her "radical imagination" was revolutionary in her time.[6] Writing at the end of the eighteenth century, she imagined an alternative society in which male-female relationships of respectful love replaced tyranny and hierarchy, and the human quest for intellectual freedom could thrive. Both she and Mill were advocating for the rights of individuals based simply on their humanity at a time when the concept of human rights barely existed.[7]

Wollstonecraft and Mill shared a devout belief in the transformative power of equal education, a cause taken up with fevour by nineteenth-century Canadian feminists. Education, Wollstonecraft and Mill determined, should not socialize boys and girls into rigidly different personalities, with girls encouraged to adopt an intellectually circumscribed, domestic, and emotional version of femininity. Anticipating later feminist views on the social construction of gender, as opposed to biological sex differences, Mill argued that women's minds were literally enslaved through a faulty socialization process, just as Wollstonecraft claimed that women's personalities were misshapen by the lack of education. For Mill, the attainment of individual potential through education was the pathway to a better, more useful society; for Wollstonecraft, the pathway to a higher plane of humanity. In a time of strictly separate, gendered education, with most institutions of higher education and professions closed to women, these ideas were remarkable. Feminists today might argue that we have yet to reach their vision, since many researchers contend that subconscious ideas about innate, natural sex differences guide society's socialization and education of girls and boys from the very moment of birth.

Both Wollstonecraft and Mill condemned laws that sanctioned "servitude" and patriarchal violence in marriage. Mill, strongly influenced by his feminist partner, Harriet Taylor, even condemned the "brute" violence of "marital rape," not an accepted legal concept until late in the twentieth century.[8] From our twenty-first-century perspective, of course, their views are limited. Mill did not critique a society based on private property; Wollstonecraft, sometimes labelled an early "maternal feminist,"[9] never doubted women's primary role as mother. More troubling, their conception of human development was predicated on assumptions of European cultural and racial superiority. Although British women lacked respect or power, Wollstonecraft believed they had a higher status than women in other inferior cultures, most especially in "savage, despotic" Muslim countries like Turkey.[10]

Wollstonecraft's ideas were disparaged immediately after her death in 1797, though one reason was her sexual non-conformity and two illegitimate children. Another was an emerging backlash against women's rights radicals, even from writers who claimed Enlightenment influences. But Wollstonecraft's ideas were resurrected some decades later by North American feminists impressed with the brilliance of her arguments questioning an immutable, natural gender hierarchy.

Enlightenment ideas have been subject to critical scrutiny more recently by some feminist and postmodern theorists who argue that these ideas claimed an interest in the "natural" rights of all humans yet ultimately sanctioned a dualistic equation of men with reason and intellect, and women with sentiment, emotion, and the body, while legitimating Western, white racial superiority and imperialism. There is some truth to these views. Influential Enlightenment philosophers such as Jean-Jacques Rousseau stressed the distinctions between the sexes and women's rightful place within the domestic sphere, ideas that were later clothed in scientific and medical imprimatur. Political thinkers such as Thomas Paine were keen on the inherent right of "the people" to self-governance – achieved by revolution, if necessary – but that meant the natural "rights of man," not the rights of women.[11] Some Enlightenment thinkers saw women as "barometers" of social progress:[12] the more economically and socially developed a society, the more elevated the status of women. This "stadial" theory of development presumed western European – especially English – superiority over other "rude economies" and cultures, whether "Native Americans, Highlanders, or Muslims."[13] Women's status was thus intertwined with a theory of cultural and racial hierarchy endorsing white supremacy.

Other feminist reconsiderations of the Enlightenment stress that it was never a "monolithic whole":[14] it left a complex intellectual legacy "littered with feminist possibilities" as well as problems.[15] The Enlightenment facilitated the inclusion of women in the public sphere of writing and debate; Scottish Enlightenment writers, including women literati, traced the positive female influence on history in their intellectual debates, poetry, fiction, essays, and personal letter writing.[16] Moreover, an early group of Enlightenment thinkers condemned slavery and critiqued European imperialism: they suggested an "environmental" view of progress in which different cultures were simply products of different social worlds. This anti-imperialist "ethic that gave dignity to every human being" was unfortunately overtaken by support for imperialism;[17] however, the malleability of Enlightenment ideas underlines their contradictory legacies, including both humanism and imperialism, egalitarianism and hierarchy.[18] Wollstonecraft's "orientalist" denigration of non-European cultures persisted as one element within nineteenth-century feminism, yet so too did her dissident condemnation of slavery.

Recent feminist criticisms of the Enlightenment are a cogent reminder of how historically contingent our judgments of feminist thinkers are: the feminist foremother praised by one generation may suddenly be deplored by the next. The contradictory dilemmas of "humanism" remain just as relevant in the twenty-first century as they were in the eighteenth: feminist philosophers now ask if Enlightenment assumptions are inherently tainted or can be employed to support human rights that are truly "universal." How, they ask, can we support "universalist" claims that all humanity deserves respect without being culturally oppressive, imposing one idea of humanity, culture, and rights – often a secular one – on other women? Is it possible to offer a critique of oppression *without* acknowledging the commonality of human needs, the dignity of the person, the right not to suffer violence?[19]

Nineteenth-century white, Euro-Canadian women welcomed Enlightenment ideas that offered them the "framework and vocabulary" to argue for

Figure 1.1 Emily Stowe, founder of the Toronto Women's Literary Club, drew on Enlightenment ideas articulated by Mary Wollstonecraft and John Stuart Mill | Photograph by Herbert Simpson, ca. 1880–1903. Wilfrid Laurier University Archives and Special Collections

their own inclusion into "humanity."[20] Wollstonecraft's dissenting, spiritual, humanist, optimistic views resonated with Emily Stowe, one of the earliest Canadian advocates for women's rights. Stowe's abolitionism and her Quaker upbringing, with its emphasis on the religious equality of men and women, corresponded with Wollstonecraft's ideas. Forced to attend medical school in the United States because Canadian universities did not admit women, she was also exposed to American feminist writers who read and cited Wollstonecraft. In one political speech reported in the American *Woman's Tribune,* Stowe exhorted men to recognize all women as "sovereign" beings just as men were, for they exhibited the same "intelligence" as men, and should therefore have the same citizenship rights.[21]

Like Wollstonecraft, Stowe described the possibilities of human progress and women's rights in religious, transcendental language: feminism would usher in a far better society by directly applying "the principle enunciated by the Divine Savior in the Golden Rule." Also like Wollstonecraft, she optimistically predicted the great potential of humanity, if only equality and justice were universalized: "Justice, the grandest, fullest and most beneficent attribute of the Deity has been fought for by nations, races, communities, peoples" and might also be extended to the struggle of men and women for equality. "Let justice be established between men and women," she wrote, and "every other Christian grace and virtue will follow."[22]

Stowe's emphasis on women's right to an education of the mind, her antipathy to social hierarchy, and her later interrogation of church doctrine, all echo Wollstonecraft. Her feminist protégée in Toronto, suffragist Flora MacDonald Denison, held similar views. Denison opted for a spiritual, though not Christian, view of the world, questioned confining sexual and marital mores for women, and believed women's character was the product of education, culture, and environment rather than biology. She praised Enlightenment radical Thomas Paine, whose invocation "my country is the world, and my religion is to do good," she adopted as her own motto.[23]

Canadian discussions of women's rights, however, more often referenced Mill's liberalism. Perhaps he was a more respectable oracle. Budding feminists studied Mill as a foundational text. One of the earliest British suffrage organizations, founded by Lydia Becker in the 1870s, sent copies of "Extracts of Mill's *The Subjection of Women*" to the Canadian Women's Suffrage Association (CWSA) for use in their Toronto study group.[24] Reference to Mill then made it into the CWSA constitution. Mill's arguments were also studied in the nineteenth-century Equal Suffrage Club in Winnipeg, a cross-class alliance of professional and trade union–affiliated women. Vancouver suffragists who founded the Vancouver Political Equality League in the early twentieth century likewise began their feminist journey by studying Mill, among other authors. If anti-feminist Goldwin Smith cited Mill negatively, male allies of the suffrage movement did the opposite, staking their political ideas on Mill's credentials. In British Columbia, pro-suffrage Liberal leader Harlan Brewster cited Mill when he told a public meeting that he trusted women to cast their ballots intelligently: sex differences should not determine who could vote.[25]

African-American Women's Community Organizing

Both Mill and Wollstonecraft were critics of slavery. So too were some American feminists who tried to fashion alliances between African-American and women's struggles for rights. While the entanglement of American feminism and abolitionism had a complex and increasingly tragic history, as post–Civil War suffragists turned to racist rationales for white women's suffrage,

Figure 1.2 An abolitionist and early advocate for women's rights, Mary Ann Shadd Cary edited the *Provincial Freeman* | LAC, C-029977

strong organizational links between abolitionism and feminism did not exist in Canada. However, abolitionist and feminist ideas did shape the writing of Mary Ann Shadd Cary, an African-Canadian educator, journalist, and advocate of women's and African-Canadian rights.

Shadd Cary might be designated Canada's first publishing feminist. She wrote about women's rights decades before suffragists organized in the 1880s, and her journalism deftly addressed the combined effects of race and gender inequality, offering insights largely ignored by many subsequent Canadian feminists. Shadd Cary, born a free Black in an educated and political family in Delaware, and employed as a teacher in New York, emigrated to Canada in 1851 after attending an anti-slavery convention in Toronto. She saw Canada as a haven for Blacks, but she was never under any illusions that it was free of bigotry and racism. Her 1857 pamphlet *A Plea for Emigration; or, Notes of Canada West,* promoted the emigration of African Americans, who came in waves across the border, as Loyalists – both free and slave – after the US war for independence, as escaped slaves, and, like Shadd Cary, as free men and women. Shadd Cary assumed her previous profession as a teacher in Windsor, Ontario, immediately encountering

Canada's racist reality: a segregated school system. She soon fell out with erstwhile abolitionist allies in the African-Canadian missionary community, such as Henry and Mary Bibb. Shadd Cary saw their support for separate settlements of Blacks, which were limited to former slaves, as "begging" efforts underpinned by the degrading implication that Blacks needed "protection" rather than equal integration into white society.[26]

Shadd Cary founded her own newspaper, the *Provincial Freeman,* in 1853, though she cautiously placed a sympathetic male abolitionist, Samuel Ringgold Ward, as the masthead editor, used male correspondents, and initially signed her articles with her initials. While recognized as a talented and dedicated advocate for abolition, Shadd Cary had to negotiate the social admonition that women's role should be primarily domestic and maternal, not public and political. Gender roles in the early African-Canadian community in Ontario were complicated: while somewhat flexible in terms of gender expectations, they were still influenced by a Victorian understanding of separate spheres for men and women.[27]

Given these constraints, Shadd Cary's writing is all the more courageous in its candour. An unwavering critic of white supremacy on both sides of the border, she advocated for land, decent schooling, and respect for Black Canadians. Shadd Cary also argued that women should have enhanced rights, including guardianship of their children (denied in law), control over their earnings, and the vote. "Some Men foolishly deny to a Woman the right to speak in public, to practice medicine, to vote," she wrote, but "the real question about a woman speaking in public was this: 'Has she anything to say? Does she say it with propriety? Does she mount the platform at the expense of the duties she owes her family?'"[28] Shadd Cary often wrote that women's highest, God-given calling was motherhood, and the *Provincial Freeman* counselled women on lady-like behaviour and finding a suitable husband. Yet it also argued that women should be permitted to secure a decent living and a "vigorous, practical and useful Education." Like Wollstonecraft, Shadd Cary saw education as a potent equalizer: it would endow a woman with the means "to get her own living, to make out her own course in life, to [countenance] any position she chooses to occupy."[29]

Above all, Shadd Cary believed that women should never be silent in the fight for racial equality. She encouraged the *Freeman*'s female readership to support the paper and raise funds, but also to engage with its ideas. When a timid reader, "Henrietta," asked in a letter to the editor if the *Freeman* would accept the views of a woman, a response, under a non de plume, came quickly. Was it not sad that a woman would have *to ask* if she could be heard?

No human should tell a woman not to use her God-given talents: "Would it not be preposterous" to ask the same of a man?[30]

The product of a more affluent background than some immigrants, Shadd Cary promoted "racial uplift": Blacks should improve their own lot in life through hard work, thrift, temperance, religion, and education. In order to secure respect, Blacks must change their "ill manners, coarse habits" and abandon their subservient "low cringing to negro haters."[31] Yet Shadd Cary's apparent middle-class moralism was combined with the recognition of the debilitating effects of racism on Black lives and the need for social supports for a community that was beleaguered and poor. Running the *Provincial Freeman* itself was a challenging financial enterprise, as well as a taxing personal one, not the least because Shadd Cary never shied away from a political fight, one of which resulted in a libel suit. A variety of factors contributed to the paper folding in 1860. Shadd Cary, married in 1859 and then soon widowed, had to support her stepchildren and two of her own through a return to teaching; moreover, her attention was increasingly focused on the American Civil War. She left Canada to recruit for the Union Army and remained in the United States after the war, taught school, and earned a law degree at age sixty. She continued to advocate for both African-American and women's rights. Unlike many Black women who were disillusioned with the intensified racism of many suffrage organizations after the war, she kept her political feet in both camps.

Shadd Cary saw herself as a feminist trailblazer. When she temporarily removed her name from the masthead of the *Provincial Freeman,* she explicitly encouraged other Black women to step into the breach: "To colored women we have a word – we have broken the Editorial Ice ... so go to Editing as many of you are willing, as soon as you may if you think you are able."[32] While Shadd Cary was unusually outspoken and public, other African-Canadian women in Ontario were quietly laying the groundwork for equal rights advocacy through collective study, work, and organization for African-Canadian needs and social recognition.[33] Like their male family members, they negotiated life in a racist society that advertised legal equality while it practised denigration and segregation.

Canadian women drew inspiration from transnational ideas associated with African-American self-help, abolitionist, and anti-slavery movements. Canadians were acquainted with and sometimes travelled to American "negro" meetings that included women as participants in anti-slavery work. Cognizant of the need for racial solidarity, African-American organizations, argue some historians, were more supportive of women's political participation than were white organizations. Moreover, even those who embraced the ideal of separate spheres acknowledged women's "right" to public participation: since moral and religious issues were part of women's sphere, and slavery was a moral issue, women's public role in the movement was more than justified.[34]

By mid-century, African-Canadian women in Ontario were active in benevolent societies dedicated to community welfare and women's auxiliaries linked to Black male fraternal orders such as the Oddfellows and Masons, as well as in supporting their churches, a long-standing focus for the African-Canadian community. Anxious to rise above an image of "begging" Black immigrants, they used community self-betterment as evidence of Black dignity, equality, and respectability. Even in smaller towns and rural areas where travel was difficult, women's organizations flourished. Attuned to racial prejudice against impoverished African Canadians, these community organizations tried to "look after their own." Women's benevolent groups, some called True Bands, provided charity to those in need, instructed new refugees, and encouraged school attendance. Women's auxiliaries also became avenues for young women's socialization in motherhood, domesticity, and respectable femininity. In the United States, class distinctions characterized such community engagement: as a more educated Black middle class emerged, these women attempted to "uplift" poorer women with moral instruction, fearful that they would reinforce racist images of "debased" Black womanhood. Given Mary Ann Shadd Cary's lectures to poorer Blacks, such divisions no doubt existed in Canada, though they may have been less sharp in a smaller, less differentiated community, especially in rural areas.

Black civil society organizations like women's benevolent societies, argues Lorene Brigden, were "schools of self-governance" where women learned leadership and organizational skills "and gained the confidence to challenge the status quo." Women's volunteer work was a natural outcome of their close encounters with families in need, but it was also shaped by the painful legacies of slavery. The pernicious racist ideologies justifying slavery not only deemed all Blacks inferior, but also characterized Black women as oversexualized, immoral, and promiscuous "Jezebels." Overcoming that image was one objective of women's community work. By showcasing a respectable Black community, women believed, they might "wear away the prejudices" of the white community.[35]

One avenue to dignity, equality, and respect was education for girls as well as boys. Women helped organize youth groups to pass on Black cultural traditions, encourage formal schooling, and develop the skills necessary for future advancement. Sunday schools and literary, temperance, and debating societies for youth were organized, both as mixed-gender and separate groups. Named after a leading American abolitionist, the Frederick Douglass Self-Improvement Club for girls in Amherstburg, Ontario, combined etiquette and manners with discussions of literature. Education was to provide the next generation with the means to advance socially, counteracting the racism and limited opportunities African Canadians faced. Indeed, it was also the avenue to adult self-advancement and the advancement of "the race." Writing in the abolitionist *Voice of the Fugitive,* Samuel Ringgold Ward emphasized this priority with the same fervent idealism of Wollstonecraft: "with education we can be strengthened and elevated – without it we shall be ignorant ... and degraded." With it, we will be able to "command respect"; without it, we will be "forever oppressed and enslaved."[36]

It is not surprising, then, that African-Canadian women were the first to organize women's "literary societies" in Ontario. In 1854, Mary Bibb formed the Windsor Ladies Club, also called the Mutual Improvement Society, followed by the Ladies Society of Chatham, established by Mary Ann Shadd Cary's sister-in-law, Amelia Freeman Shadd. Canadian women were inspired by similar abolitionist educational societies in the United States. African-American literary societies, never restricted to literature in our sense of the word, were dedicated to the pursuit of knowledge and self-betterment through reading, discussion, performance, and recitation. Such groups flourished in large and small centres, from Toronto (the Provincial Union) to Amherstburg (the Cheerful Workers). The Toronto Provincial Union had a separate Ladies Committee, which raised funds for and promoted the *Provincial Freeman,* but also mixed-gender meetings where men and women read aloud, debated, and recited their own original writing. Its organizational pledge captures the multiple hopes for self-improvement, community betterment, and the pursuit of emancipation: "each member pledges to endorse literature, general intelligence, active benevolence and the principles of universal freedom."[37]

Women's literary societies, perhaps even more than benevolent organizations, captured women's fervent hope that education might usher in recognition of African-Canadian dignity and equality. In contrast to the pronouncements of Emily Stowe, such groups pursued "rights" primarily on the basis of "race," not gender. African-Canadian women were building a community in which they had influence and respect, but both groups drew on an Enlightenment language of "humanity," universalism, and the capacity for citizen virtue.

The Cultural Front

Women's literary societies also nurtured white women's interest in equality. Early nineteenth-century men's literary clubs, Heather Murray suggests, may have been unwelcoming to women, who were seen as selfish or flighty bluestockings for daring to announce their intellectual aspirations. Separate women's societies were born of this disparagement; women-only groups offered the promise of reassuring homosociability, self-improvement, and knowledge. Never strictly literary, these clubs provided opportunities for women to participate in performance, music, discussion, elocution, and the study of both fiction and non-fiction texts. The emphasis on secular topics, including philosophy and science, was freedom in itself, setting literary societies apart from the intellectual constraints of religious and church groups. Ethelwyn Wetherald, the editor of *Wives and Daughters,* a late nineteenth-century Ontario women's magazine, recommended "half hour a day" reading projects in history, philosophy, and science for women confined to the home. A passionate advocate of women's empowerment through self education, Wetherald drew up a reading list that initially suggested women switch from novels to science and philosophy, including authors such as Carlyle, Mill, Macaulay, Ruskin, Spencer, and Darwin, a hefty intellectual list. Judging by letters to the editor, however, women were hungry for new ideas.[38]

One of the best-documented women's literary societies, the Toronto Women's Literary Club (TWLC), was likely inspired by similar American groups; in 1877, Emily Stowe attended meetings of the American Association for the Advancement of Women, which coordinated US women's study groups. She founded the TWLC the same year. Women's literary societies might look to us like rather comfortable spaces of middle-class "book club" sociability, but they could unsettle taken-for-granted ideas about gender. Participants who read philosophy, history, and political theory might develop more critical views of women's place in society, not unlike study and consciousness-raising groups later in the twentieth century. As one fictional character in a contemporary novel about a women's literary group explained, women who were confined to the domestic sphere craved a wider window on the world: "we are women of culture ... we want to learn about ourselves and about others. We want to understand changing social patterns and world events that shape our destiny."[39]

The TWLC was likewise oriented to "knowing the world better." It incorporated existing adult education techniques as well as novel means of self-improvement. Like the earlier Ontario Mechanics Institutes providing adult education for working people, the group invited experts and speakers to share their knowledge, and, like other women's literary groups, their reading lists included an eclectic blend of subjects, from poetry to science, drama to philosophy. Self-study and the sharing of knowledge replaced the university education women were denied, at a time when even women's colleges (more like high schools) downplayed scholarly subjects, opting instead to train young women in the feminine arts necessary for them to become marriageable ladies.

In order to better understand feminism, TWLC members read classic feminist texts by Elizabeth Cady Stanton and Margaret Fuller, and the club soon turned its attention to studying and improving social conditions for women in the city. First on its agenda was a survey of health conditions, including women's washrooms, in the city's factories and workshops; it then sought the municipal franchise for women property holders and the reform of universities. Accompanied by an ally, reformer William Houston, they sent a delegation to University of Toronto president Daniel Wilson in 1882 asking that women be allowed to enroll for degrees. In 1883, the group made a transition to a more concentrated focus on women's rights when it changed its name to the Canadian Women's Suffrage Association. Yet as Heather Murray notes, seeing the literary society as a mere "preface or pretext" in relation to the more important political story misses the way in which culture and politics were closely linked, with the former providing the knowledge that motivated political work.[40]

The TWLC's effort to dislodge University of Toronto's stubborn ban on women students was aided by a satirical play written by one of its members, amateur historian Sarah Anne Curzon. Her short drama, *The Sweet Girl Graduate,* used a cultural pulpit to make a feminist statement. Using the tale of Katie Blaggs, an aspiring scholar denied entrance to university, it mocked the justifications used to bar women from higher education. Katie's father is a successful Scugog merchant, who is quite sure his daughter has had sufficient schooling to find a husband. Her mother is even more perturbed by Katie's educational ambitions, suggesting that women who "put themselves forward like impudent minxes," studying side-by-side with men, encourage immorality. Katie points out that she sits beside men at local church picnics without incurring disaster, and she tries to persuade her parents that "better education" will make her a "better mother." When reason and persuasion fail, she hatches a plan to attend University College dressed as a man, Tom Christopher. At a final banquet celebrating Tom's intellectual achievements – gold medals in the "masculine" subjects of mathematics and natural sciences, no less – she unmasks her true self, converting the attendees to women's right to attend university.[41] Curzon's play helped to secure 1,600 signatures of men on a petition protesting the "unjust" exclusion of women from University of Toronto; it was then presented to the provincial legislature – as well as the president of the university – by a sympathetic Liberal member.[42]

The play appeared in the *Grip Sack,* an annual journal of "fun, fancy and fiction" published by J.W. Bengough, writer, editor, and cartoonist for the progressive magazine, the *Grip*. Bengough also used satire and humour to advance feminist ideas. In his essay, "Mr Stotinbottle on Woman Suffrage," Bengough assumes the voice of an "everyman," an anti-suffragist who comes to see the error of his ways. Stotinbottle admits he was quite sure of his own intellectual superiority, only to find he was mistaken. The ridiculous arguments used by anti-feminists are then marshalled one by one, only to be pilloried with humour. The equation of men's "heavier brains" with more intelligence was nothing more than a myth; after all, the "average man occasionally carries a brick in his hat." Stotinbottle reassures his fellow men that women will use the vote wisely (which, he reminds them, all men don't), and that home duties will not suddenly be abandoned for discussions of the latest fishery policy. Don't worry, he adds, "only the occasional spinster voter will be disposed to lead a gang of roughs on the hustings to interrupt speakers." Exposing men's bad political behaviour and foibles to satirical scrutiny mocked those who would deny women the same rights as men.[43]

Curzon and Bengough's contributions were didactic, if humorous, pieces about women's rights. Drama, fiction, and journalism all became venues for discussions of the rights and wrongs of women. While didactic suffrage fiction was more plentiful in the United States and Britain, there were a few examples in Canada, including the later, well-known Pearlie Watson trilogy by Nellie McClung and Francis Marion Beynon's moving wartime novel, *Aleta Dey,* discussed in Chapter 7. By 1883, women's suffrage was supported by the temperance movement,[44] and at least one nineteenth-century Canadian temperance novel addressed women's rights. Lottie McAllister's *Clipped Wings,* published and endorsed by the Methodist Church, uses the story of a farm family torn apart by alcohol to draw a moral and feminist lesson. Bright and ambitious daughter Agnes is denied a chance to become a teacher by her domineering father, who tells her "you are worth more to me [as a worker] on the farm." Agnes "repeatedly heard stock valued in similar terms" to her. She eventually escapes to study nursing while her no-good brother Henry, who is to inherit all, avoids farm work, lollygags in the saloon, and destroys himself and the family with drink, with the father and mother dying soon after him. Agnes moves to the city, where temperance and reform work lead to her conviction that women must not only "rock the cradle for the world, but rock the world for the cradle." She embraces women's suffrage not only to stop "the demon drink" from "destroying homes," but because the current, male-dominated government does not represent the "consent of the governed." Romance also blooms. Agnes meets an earnest minister, whom she converts to women's suffrage; they marry and live happily ever after on the family farm, with Agnes caring for their children and the reverend giving sermons on suffrage. McAllister's primary goal is to promote temperance, but there are markers of feminism in her story: the critique of patriarchal families, the right of women to education and work, and the importance of women's public voice on issues of social morality.[45]

In contrast to this didactic suffrage fiction, more women writers skirted around issues of equal rights, discussing the social context of women's lives, their aspirations, social disadvantages, and the possibilities of female independence. Some gingerly tendered an alternative picture of male-female relationships that were not characterized by overbearing patriarchy. Others innovated by stressing women's intelligence and value as individuals, discounting assumptions of women's inferiority. Sara Jeannette Duncan would have recoiled at the label "women's" or "feminist" novelist.[46] She was known better as a commentator on imperialism, social norms, and cultural identity. Yet her female characters were unusually cerebral and adventurous: they contradicted prevailing, negative constructions of capricious femininity, and their lives elicited discussions of women's independence and intellectually egalitarian relationships with men.

In *A Social Departure,* Duncan used the popular travelogue to tell the semi-fictional story of her trip with another woman around the world "the wrong way," from East to West. The travellers lacked a chaperone, got by on their own, and reported with delight on their daily cross-cultural encounters. Duncan's take on non-Western societies fit neatly into Enlightenment stadial versions of progress, displaying a racist orientalism embraced by many nineteenth-century Canadian feminists. Japanese culture was not as advanced as Western cultures, signified by the lower status of women, but this might change as Japan was evolving, "beginning to take women into account."[47]

Her heroines, suggests literary scholar Misao Dean, "secured their own self-definition" through travel, writing, work, and their intellect.[48] Occasionally, her fictional female characters stepped outside convention, as did an American would-be artist and writer living abroad, Elfrida Bell in *Daughter of Today.* Having been told in Paris that she would never be a great, but merely a "female," artist, Elfrida turned her hand to writing in London, courageously going undercover to work in a burlesque troupe for one article, to the moralistic disgust of her respectable friends. Elfrida wrestled with questions of sexuality, marriage, and career, eventually facing her own demons: unpleasant jealousy and unsatiated ego. Many critics found Elfrida an unpleasant character, and her final end, suicide, was hardly a rousing endorsement of women's search for fulfilment, but Duncan was raising difficult questions about the struggles of the modern woman as aspiring artist.

Duncan, like many nineteenth-century women writers, apprenticed as a journalist. Journalism provided women with a decent living and promised a pathway into a literary career, and changes in the newspaper industry in the late nineteenth century dramatically improved the prospects of women writers. As newspapers abandoned their role as primarily partisan political organs and attempted to build mass-circulation dailies supported by advertising, editors sought out new groups of readers, including women. Women's columns, topics of interest to women, and women writers were suddenly a commercial plus for papers.[49] Duncan began writing a column for women in the *Toronto Globe* and *Montreal Star* in the 1880s. Though her topics ranged across many social issues, women's rights were among them. She covered a suffrage convention in Washington, weighed in on the debate about women's municipal right to vote (which she endorsed), and wrote about the benefits of training women as doctors. Duncan supported expanded education and rights for women, but she believed these should be extended on the basis of women's intelligence and responsibilities as citizens. She disliked emotional appeals to feminine sentimentality and morality, scornfully dismissing feminist views she deemed too "extreme, strident, rhetorically overdone with metaphors of oppression and female slavery." Reason, wit, and intellect should prevail over the emotional performance of "damp females."[50] When it came to feminism, as Janice Fiamengo aptly notes, Duncan was ambivalent, "prickly, ironic, elitist, combative."[51] She brooked little sympathy for working-class women, once dismissing their unionization: they had "no skills" to speak of and nothing to bargain with, much like the lowly male "hodcarrier."[52] Duncan likely saw women's rights through the liberal utilitarian eyes of John Stuart Mill, "within a political economy of competition."[53] Women who had the intelligence to compete in the world of men should be allowed to do so, unfettered by mistaken notions of their limited capacities. They should not need special privileges.

Not all women writers were as caustic as Duncan about female sentimentality; some embraced the idea of "feminine" personality traits in their verse and short stories. The short story was an especially popular format for women: it could be written (and read) in snatches around other duties, and many magazines and newspapers welcomed their submissions, a trend that increased in the early twentieth century.[54] Although many women stuck to romantic and melodramatic templates, there were "New Woman" writers who wrestled with changing gender relations, challenging ideas about marriage, education, autonomy, and women's work in the modern world. Women in these stories were rarely radicals or revolutionaries, and the denouement of some came with a traditional, heterosexual romance. Yet the questions raised suggested feminism was in the air. In "The Experiences of a Woman Bachelor," Jean Blewett explored women's choice of marriage or career. Two close friends, on very different life pathways, write back and forth about their lives and dreams. One chose homemaking, while the other opted for education and living autonomously away from her family. Rather than romance, she seeks out intellectual relationships with men. Instead of chastising the unmarried woman, the homemaker expresses wistful admiration and longing for a life of independence and intellect. "Leave all this foolishness [marriage] to us," she writes, we "who know nothing of the delights of brand new womanhood, who can't write books, speak on platforms, box, fence, run, row or analyze our emotions, [while we] hang on to our embroidery frames ... and hug our chains."[55]

Other short story writers tackled issues of overbearing husbands, violence, and women's lack of economic and property rights, especially in farm families. A few attempted to address the intersection of gender, race, and class inequalities. In "The Assimilation of Christina," Jean McIlwraith described an unfolding romance between a working-class Scottish domestic and an Ojibway man; she works for an upper-class family at their summer retreat, and he lives nearby, sometimes working for the family. Both are marginalized and looked down on: she because of class, he because of race. Like many white women writers, McIlwraith tends to portray the male "Indian" as a romanticized "noble savage," but he is still more likeable and honourable than Christina's snobby, stuffy (and useless) white, upper-class employers, something that Christina comes to understand only by confronting her own racial prejudices.[56]

Race and colonialism were considered far less than gender in these New Woman stories, but some biracial authors, such as Mohawk-English poet Pauline Johnson and Sui Sin Far (Edith Eaton), a Chinese-English immigrant to Montreal, wrote about the experiences of "mixed-race" women in racist and patriarchal cultures. The complex plot in Eaton's "Story of One

White Woman Who Married a Chinese" includes a white working-class woman named Minnie, her domineering white husband, his middle-class, white "suffragette" friend, and Minnie's second husband, a Chinese man who comes to her aid after her first husband abandons her. Told from Minnie's view, the story explains why she preferred her Chinese husband's respectful, quiet manliness to her white husband's patriarchal control – despite the latter's claim to support women's rights. Class, race, and gender relations are all questioned in this story: there are tense interactions between a middle-class suffragist and a working-class woman, between the aggressive version of white manhood and more gentle Chinese manhood, and between Minnie and her progressive white husband. Some characters are rather one-dimensional gender and racial stereotypes, but the story nonetheless reminds us that some writers were wrestling with multiple oppressions of race and gender.[57]

Short story writers often turned to journalism to support their writing habit, using both genres to question women's social roles. Raised in a Quaker family and given an extended education away from home, Ethelwyn Wetherald was encouraged by her father to pursue journalism; he purchased a local Ontario newspaper and arranged for her to learn how to use a printing press. Wetherald worked as printer and writer on the paper, while publishing poems, book reviews, and short commentaries for literary journals. Succeeding Duncan as women's columnist for the *Globe* under the nom de plume Bel Thistlewaite, Wetherald offered up the expected fare of decorating, food, and fashion, but she also discussed current social issues. Women's newspaper columns offered equal-rights-minded women a propitious opportunity to introduce their readers to the world and, by doing so, to pose questions about "the condition of women." Wetherald, for instance, penned a column, "Queer Husbands," which did not question marriage itself but rather proposed more respectful, egalitarian relations between husband and wife. She asked critically why some husbands dominated their wives so unremittingly, ordering them around, demanding they wait on them like servants. Women, she concluded, should avoid being "soft" and malleable to such demands; instead, they should stand up for themselves, developing "stout hearts and muscles and (dare I say it) strong minds."[58]

Wetherald was subsequently recruited in 1890 by a London, Ontario, publisher to start a new women's magazine, *Wives and Daughters*. It featured anecdotes of daily life and domestic advice, from training household help to the dos and don'ts of etiquette, but it also included a hefty dose of serious social commentary on topics ranging from capital punishment to animal cruelty (advising against the seal hunt), dress reform (corsets were assailed), and women's rights. Wetherald was an all-purpose editor and writer, producing a children's column, articles, book reviews, and a letters section, "Five O'Clock Tea," overseen by her alter ego Aunt Barbara. Aunt Barbara answered readers' queries, both about domestic issues and reform topics, throwing out questions to encourage divergent reader views on gender relations: "what do you think are the most attractive and most repellant" qualities in a man, she asked, eliciting a range of earnest responses from homemakers and a "working woman."[59]

Wetherald had been a sick, "bookish" youth, devouring whatever books she could find. Equipped with a remarkably broad-ranging intellectual archive, she was an erudite, adaptable writer and editor, able to comment on an extraordinary range of authors and issues. The "Women in Fiction" section of the paper encouraged readers to analyse novels according to how women characters were portrayed, a forerunner to later feminist literary criticism. Wetherald's brilliance was the way she infused a traditional women's magazine with intellectual debate and feminist questions, discussing the vote, sexual purity, and the right of women to education and the professions, among other issues. Her readers were assumed to be thinking, curious women with concerns about the world; the most important advice she gave was to read widely and respond critically. In her "Browsing in the Library" section, Wetherald compared those who did *not* read to prisoners in a "penitentiary."[60]

Countering anti-feminists, Wetherald insisted the problem was not giving women too much education, but too little: "education is harmful to women administered in too small quantities ... It is a little learning that is a dangerous thing ... It is absurd that the accident of birth should prevent human beings from making the most and best of themselves."[61] J.S. Mill's liberalism echoed through her views, though one suspects she shared much with the Quaker-educated Stowe. In one piece dissecting men's "excuses" for women's inequality, she challenged the cultural equation of womanhood with the home: many women had to "earn a living," and all women should not be defined by domesticity but by their "noble, gentle, brave generous qualities." The real excuse for denying women equal pay, she concluded (citing Mill), amounted to men claiming the "lion's share" of society's rewards.[62]

Imaginative, prolific, and hardworking, Wetherald was eventually enticed away to work at a larger American women's magazine. Her first love may have been writing verse, but her career captures the eclecticism and literary range of the nineteenth-century cultural feminist front. While not remembered primarily as a women's rights author, she wove questions about equality into her journalism. Slipping such topics into a "traditional" women's magazine was an especially important way of seeding feminist ideas – not unlike what was done at *Chatelaine* in the 1960s. In the early twentieth century, a new cohort of journalists assumed the mantle of these pioneering women's columnists, pushing the feminist envelope much further. Bertha Merrill Burns, Flora MacDonald Denison, Violet McNaughton, Francis Marion Beynon, all discussed later in this book, more forthrightly promoted feminist ideas developed by the burgeoning women's movement.

Québécoises

Journalism was also critical to the seeding of feminism in Quebec. At the turn of the century, only 5 percent of the journalists in Quebec were women, but their influence outweighed their numbers.[63] This small group of female journalists initially made their names writing for daily newspapers, *rouge* (liberal), free thought, nationalist, and other reform publications. Some began as newspaper "women's columnists," though they cleverly turned this space into a "salon littéraire public," which combined literary and domestic discussions, encouraging readers' intellectual self-exploration.[64] The leading lights of female journalism, including Éva Circé-Côté, Robertine Barry, and Joséphine Dandurand, created their own Association des femmes journalistes canadiennes-françaises (much like the English-Canadian Women's Press Club) and became part of a larger women's reform community. Barry joined the Catholic women's reform group the Fédération Nationale Saint-Jean-Baptiste (FNSJB), while Joséphine Dandurand was vice-president of the bicultural National Council of Women of Canada. Their writing raised women's stature as public intellectuals and initiated questions about women's abilities, social role, education, and work. Not unlike later farm journalists discussed in Chapter 3, they saw their newspaper writing as a "mission," bringing ideas to women denied a formal education, isolated in the home: "the woman's page" in newspapers, noted Robertine Barry, "is our university."[65]

Like Ethelwyn Wetherald, many of these writers were extremely well-read intellectuals who used multiple modes of communication, including poetry, short stories, drama, non-fiction commentary, and historical writing. They were not cut from an identical political cloth. Circé-Côté's political evolution over decades, charted by her biographer, Andrée Lévesque, took her from nineteenth-century radicalism and free thought to the labour movement and feminism after the First World War, even though, early in her career, she disparaged feminism, which she associated with "Anglo-Saxon,

Figure 1.3 Poet, playwright, and journalist Éva Circé-Côté espoused Enlightenment ideas about free thought as well as promoting women's right to education | Laprès and Lavergne. Courtesy of Andrée Lévesque

Protestant, puritanism."[66] Barry was associated with *rouge* newspapers, and Dandurand, with her ties to the federal and Quebec Liberal elite, reflected more establishment thinking in her reform ideas and associations.

In 1900, Circé-Côté began contributing to *Les Debats,* an anti-imperialist, dissenting, "free thinking" paper, and radical thorn in the side of the Catholic Church. Her work was eclectic in theme and presentation: she wrote poems, drama, "lyrical moralizing essays," and pieces about history, particularly the 1837 rebellion, which she celebrated as the foundation of Quebec democracy.[67] She was an astute observer of current events, offered commentary on issues of cultural taste, surveyed the urban landscape of Montreal, and discussed the latest books. The sheer breadth of her intellectual work was astounding. Like Barry, she took the education of her readers seriously. Journalism, she once wrote, was "the sweetest profession ... the only one to which an educated *canadienne* can aspire." For these women, it was a career, a calling, "a way to create a better world."[68] All three of these women published their own magazines: Circé-Côté founded *Étincelle,* Barry, *Le journal de Françoise,* and Dandurand, *Le coin du feu.*

Barry and Circé-Côté often wrote under noms de plume, Circé-Côté under many. Anonymity offered them the freedom to speak more openly and some protection against censure and reprisals, something Circé-Côté increasingly faced after her marriage to a doctor who was a Freemason (an organization condemned by the Catholic Church) solidified her reputation as a "freethinker." Circé-Côté and her husband were part of a bohemian circle whose members consciously embraced secular lives devoted to political debate, art, and literature. To reject religion as *the* guiding force for personal and social life exposed them to the condemnation of the church and its political allies. When Circé-Côté's husband refused to take the last rites on his deathbed and was cremated, a furor ensued, one paper announcing that these acts were nothing less than a "shocking scandal."[69] One can see why Circé-Côté's dedication to free thought and unfettered access to knowledge, especially secular knowledge, was so keenly held. The mere right to read was an integral part of her political project; she was for many years the librarian at the municipal library, an institution that democratized knowledge for people.

The right to read was a pathway to feminism. Books shunned by the church included Enlightenment writing about science, politics, and philosophy, including those addressing human equality. These ideas were importance influences on Circé-Côté: she quoted John Stuart Mill, Olympe de Gouges (the French counterpart to Mary Wollstonecraft), and the French utopian socialist Charles Fourier. Scientific research, she believed, would lead to social progress; improvement could be attained through reason, free intellectual debate, and changes to the social environment. Circé-Côté's debt to Enlightenment traditions was evident in her angst at the suffocating role of religion in stifling intellectual debate: "to be well regarded here [in Quebec]," she complained sardonically, "one must say Voltaire is a second-rate writer, Rousseau a figure of depravity."[70]

Circé-Côté, like Wollstonecraft, did see the *mentalités* and social roles of men and women as distinct, not the least because of women's maternal role, but she also believed that all humans were endowed with intelligence and should be offered educational opportunities. She collaborated with other women to open a secular, modern "lycée pour jeunes filles inc.," acting as a volunteer principal. Even Circé-Côté's views on immorality and prostitution embraced education rather than mere punishment; contradicting the

Catholic reformers in the FNSJB, she suggested that society "educate young women about the dangers in life rather than seeking to spare their innocence for as long as possible."[71] Throughout her writing career, Circé-Côté's hope in education – the Enlightenment legacy of Wollstonecraft and Mill – as a means to both women's and social emancipation never wavered.

Circé-Côté represented a "rebel, avant-garde" wing of women journalists. Barry was closely associated with radical and *rouge* newspapers of the time, such as *La Patrie,* which published her first article in 1891. From a relatively well-off family, she was formally educated in a convent but broke away from the expectations of traditional marriage and maternity to become a self-supporting journalist. To some clerical writers, her dangerous Enlightenment views made her the antithesis of a role model for Québécoises. The Catholic conservative paper *La Vérité,* edited by anti-suffragist Jules-Paul Tardivel, attacked Barry's writing in *La Patrie,* charging her with the high crime of reiterating the views of Enlightenment philosopher Jean-Jacques Rousseau.

Women's education was a cause close to Barry's heart: she too supported the *lycée* for young women and even the "revolutionary" idea of women attending university. While she lived and worked in a "bourgeois milieu," she also spoke publicly of the reforms badly needed to improve the living conditions of urban working-class women and children. Like Circé-Côté, she was well read and prolific, writing for many publications and working in multiple genres. Women journalists might campaign for women's educational opportunities but also get their bread and butter from more traditional feminine forms. Barry, for instance, penned a column "Reponses aux correspondants," a lonely-hearts column. Yet her overall journalist contribution was decidedly feminist, pushing the boundaries of the reigning ideology of separate spheres, emphasizing women's economic independence, and challenging the weight of unjust traditions. For Barry, "il y a un lien étroit entre les préjugés ou injustices subie par les femmes et lois faites par les hommes" (there's a close link between prejudices or injustices suffered by women and laws made by men).[72]

In 1900, Robertine Barry and Joséphine Dandurand were appointed to represent Canadian women at the universal exposition in Paris. Both were associated with reform causes, although, in contrast to the emerging cadre of English-Canadian journalists, they did not publicly devote their energies to suffrage. Moreover, Dandurand's feminism fit more comfortably within the ideal of separate spheres than did Barry's. While Barry spoke of women's "rights," argues Diane Thibeault, Dandurand spoke of their "duties."[73] Like many other journalists, Dandurand wrote in multiple genres, publishing short stories, plays, and journalistic pieces. As the daughter of a premier and the wife of a federal senator, Dandurand's elite, Liberal background ensured her the time and financial resources to write and links to the mainstream publishing world. Her social world was quite distant from the nationalist, free-thinking, bohemian and *rouge* circles of Circé-Côté and Barry. As a result, she was less vocal about a woman's right to be a self-supporting writer, and was more deeply invested in rhetoric that invoked women's special maternal knowledge as a rationale for their social engagement outside the home.

Still, Dandurand insisted that women had a duty to serve both the family *and* humanity. The women's movement, she believed, allowed women to extend their important familial roles to much-needed improvements in Quebec's social and cultural life. Women could engage in "good works," discuss social issues, and develop their own intellect – the latter was crucial for Dandurand, whose chosen charity involved dispensing free books to those who could not afford them. She used *Le coin du feu* to spark a conversation that circled *around* issues of feminism, including articles on social reform, suffrage, and culture, while maintaining the traditional women's magazine topics of childrearing, fashion, health, and cooking. Despite her place in the ruling class, Dandurand's cultural work was viewed warily by religious and conservative elites, who fretted about the negative effects on Quebec society of any hint of women's intellectual independence.[74]

Conclusion

All three of the Québécoises writers discussed above encouraged women to gain more knowledge, take up social issues, and express themselves intellectually. Barry and Circé-Côté were far more committed to a woman's right to a journalistic career and equal education; their writing was more strongly inflected with liberal Enlightenment notions of equality, humanity, and freedom. Initially, none of these Québécoises assumed the label "feminist," but then neither did many of the English-Canadian authors discussed in this chapter, with the exception of Emily Stowe. That said, Quebec women did write within a distinct linguistic, religious, and cultural context, resulting in different preoccupations: the Quebec nation, the struggle for secularism and free thought, and identification with France.

Still, nineteenth- and early twentieth-century women literati in both cultures shared something that was potentially unsettling to the gender order: a commitment to the intellect, to reading, to thinking critically about the world. In a society that told women they could not think rationally, did not have important thoughts, and should be satisfied with a limited education, this commitment mattered. In recommending women's autonomy and independence, they also held out the prospect of life choices most women lacked. In validating women's morality and intellect, in establishing women's worth as "human souls," in Wollstonecraft's words, they prepared the ground for political and social movements to come. Women, as Heather Murray puts it so well, searched first for "intellectual enfranchisement," later political enfranchisement.[75]

Ideas about equality were percolating below the surface of social life, in both subtle and direct ways, but each community of women lived this project differently. Black women identified the importance of building up their intellectual confidence as women, but this was also linked to their status as African Canadians in a racist society that accepted white supremacy and denigrated their communities. Using their own literary and benevolent organizations as tools of emancipation, they too emphasized the potential, indeed, the absolute necessity, of education, but different goals – respect and equality for African-American women *and* men – lay at the heart of their organizational work.

Canadian women had other intellectual options to choose from when contemplating their inequality. By the late nineteenth century, Marxists and socialists were competing for the ear of women dissatisfied with their second-class citizenship, patriarchy, and the class divisions that many of these English- and French-Canadian writers did not emphasize. British, American, and European socialist ideas about women's inequality permeated Canadian left-wing circles, sparking both debate and efforts to translate socialist feminism into organizational practice.

2

The Origins of Socialist and Labour Feminism

In the late 1890s, Bertha Merrill travelled from Ontario to British Columbia on a mission of political and self-discovery. The early life of Merrill, who was the child of German Baptist immigrants, offered lessons in working-class survival. Widowed young, her mother struggled to make ends meet in Brantford, Ontario; Bertha became an economic mainstay for the family, working as a teacher, then as a journalist for the *Brantford Expositor*. Later, Bertha and her mother moved to Nelson, British Columbia, where they operated a boarding house and Bertha became involved in socialist politics.

While she had enjoyed some occupational independence as a newspaperwoman, Bertha was incensed at the treatment of the printing "girls" in the mechanical department of her newspaper. "Indignation led to investigation," research that sparked "her first encounter with socialism," which she embraced wholeheartedly.[1] In British Columbia, she threw herself into the movement; in 1901, she was elected vice-president of the new Socialist Party of Canada (SPC). She helped to run the party's paper, the *Western Clarion*, and subsequently married a fellow SPCer, Ernest Burns. Together they created a dynamic partnership of socialist activism.

Bertha Merrill Burns represented a stream of feminism in which socialist and feminist ideas intersected, usually in mutual reinforcement, though sometimes in tension. Burns saw this ideological pairing as women's only hope for emancipation. "What will socialism do for women?" she asked, answering, with a utopian flourish, that it would endow them with "free womanhood, freedom to love unashamed, to work honourably, and to become a co-partner in the building of a true home." Women wage-earners would be liberated from theft of their wages and health; women homemakers from constant drudgery. Even affluent women would discover the rewards of "honest work" under socialism.[2]

Burn's socialist-feminist world view was grounded in a critique of private property and wealth inequality. Capitalism was a system of profit making that usurped the fruits of workers' labour, sanctioned private ownership of resources that should be for collective use, and created economic crises and dependencies that undermined marriages and families. Capitalism struck at the core of family life, abetting tragedies such as infant and maternal mortality, which women experienced with heart-felt intensity. Socialism would rectify these travesties, but it was not enough: women were also shackled by gender inequalities, especially their economic dependency on men. Only when women secured economic autonomy could one talk of true freedom for women.[3] Seizing the "the means of production," she warned fellow socialists, was not enough. The "sex struggle" existed and had to be addressed now, not after the revolution. Unless women secure their "political and economic freedom while the battle for [socialist] freedom is on," Burns warned, "men would continue to treat women as a subordinate sex even in a socialist future."[4]

How do we situate Burn's feminist politics? Her vision of emancipation blended feminism and socialism in various measures, depending on the political context. As a member of the SPC, she might insist that socialism was the foundation for women's equality, yet, writing as a feminist, she declared herself in favour of women's rights, including suffrage. Socialist feminists like Burns explained women's oppression drawing on an eclectic blend of utopian and ethical socialism, Marxism, and labourism, while also insisting that socialist-feminist politics should be grounded in the real-life experiences of working-class women. Although their emphasis on social cooperation and critique of capitalism differed from the liberal individualism of John Stuart Mill, some socialist feminists drew on a similar language of liberalism and democracy.

This chapter traces the intersections of feminist, socialist, and labour ideas through intellectual debates, political parties, the labour movement, and the cultural front. Placing feminists in distinct streams like "socialist feminism" is both necessary and problematic: necessary because socialist feminists did see the world differently from liberal reformers, but problematic if we assume socialists never collaborated with reform feminists, incorporated other radical ideas, or even felt the tug of complicated political loyalties to more than one cause. Moreover, socialist women were not a unitary group with a common program; they belonged to different parties and movements, debating among themselves the best pathway to equality. Despite problems with categorization, labour and socialist feminists deserve their own narrative, not the least because they were consciously fashioning an interpretation of humanity that was distinct from liberalism. Their day-to-day political organizing also centred on the mobilization of "the masses"; they believed the poor, workers, and rural producers – all those who were not owners or managers – had the most to gain from socialism and feminism.

Socialist feminism, like liberal, Enlightenment feminism, materialized through novel, inspiring ideals combined with shifts in social and economic life precipitated by industrial capitalism. Both race and colonialism were underdeveloped or ignored in these critiques of capitalism. Few adherents reflected critically on their use of the metaphor of wage slavery, employed since the nineteenth century by socialists to describe exploitation, but absolutely different from the actual coercive sale of humans. While some socialist feminists called for a global "brotherhood of man," irrespective of race, religion, and caste, and some derided the divisiveness of ethnocentrism or "nativism" in Canada, they did not see how their own movements replicated notions of British, Eurocentric, and white superiority. Racial inequality, whether legally encoded or ideologically reproduced, did not figure in their critiques of capitalism as crucially as gender and class did.

Utopian Ideals

Socialist feminists like Burns drew in part on utopian socialist traditions imported from Britain, Europe, and the United States. Nineteenth-century utopian socialists confronted a perplexing problem in a time of intensified capitalist and industrial development: How do you emancipate women in the face of seemingly insurmountable ideological and social obstacles? Utopian socialists' answer was to create functioning egalitarian communities that modelled cooperation and equality and, at the same time, to spread the message of socialism far and wide. Only a few years after Mary Wollstonecraft's death, French utopian socialists Henri de Saint-Simon and Charles Fourier, along with British factory owner Robert Owen, laid out intellectual foundations for utopian socialism, addressing both the social blight of a competitive economic system and the sexual oppression of women. Fourier, who claimed that the more advanced a society, the more emancipated women were, published his first book in 1808 and soon had a following among working women in France for his collectivist and emancipatory ideals.[5] Fourier's ideas, along with Saint-Simon's writing on women's enfranchisement, international peace, and the antithetical interests of the producing and the idle upper classes, were transplanted to receptive audiences in Britain and North America.[6]

Owen began his political odyssey as a paternalist factory owner experimenting with housing and welfare programs for his workers but moved beyond this partial measure, creating communal living experiments where people shared all economic resources and social responsibilities. In Owenite communities, economic, personal, and gender hierarchies were contested, private property abolished, and the nuclear single-family dwelling questioned. For Owenites, competitive capitalism and patriarchy were twin obstacles to women's equality and communal well-being; both had to be challenged in these experimental "co-operative commonwealths" that aspired to eradicate all hierarchical relationships.[7]

Utopian thinking spread beyond these communal experiments, generating a political tradition that connected women's oppression and their potential liberation to the fate of some other subordinated groups, including peasants or workers. Nineteenth-century socialists William Thompson and Anna Wheeler assailed not only the failings of competitive capitalism but also the confining patriarchal norms that turned women into the "property" of men.[8] Wheeler was a rebel who read Mary Wollstonecraft and the French utopian socialists and then, disenchanted with an oppressive marriage, fled her upper-class home to live a life of radical politics. She attributed women's subjection to their inadequate education and a hypocritical double standard of sexual morality. Thompson's famous treatise on women's emancipation, dedicated to Wheeler, referred to patriarchal marriage as nothing less than a "rod of domestic despotism" that forced wives into total "sexual subordination."[9]

By introducing a critique of capitalism into discussions of women's rights, socialists shifted the intellectual terrain of debate. Their solutions often placed hope in the transformation of beliefs, consciousness, and morality, sometimes through small-scale experiments. Utopian-socialist communes were far less numerous in Canada than in the United States, but there were a few. Perhaps the best known, Sointula (Place of Harmony), was inspired by the writing of a Finnish socialist feminist, Minna Canth, who advocated for women's political rights and sexual emancipation. Her ideas were admired

Figure 2.1 Sointula (Place of Harmony), a Finnish utopian settlement on Malcolm Island, British Columbia, was established on the basis of the full equality of men and women | Courtesy of the Royal BC Museum and Archives, E-03019

by journalist Matti Kurikka, who was invited to Canada in 1901 by Finnish immigrants to set up a model utopian community on Malcolm Island, just off the coast of mainland British Columbia. Given to the Finnish Kalevan Kansa Colonisation Company by the provincial government to encourage white settlement, Malcolm Island was designated by Kurikka a "refuge for Finnish socialists persecuted in Finland ... and for the whole working class."[10] Like other utopian experiments, it was committed to peaceful and equal coexistence, pooled profits, shared domestic labour, free schooling for all children, women's right to participate in governance, and equal remuneration of men and women.

Sointula abided by two principles, "natural law" and gender equality: women should be "free citizens in free bodies," with the right to choose their partners, have control over their bodies, and be released from legal and religious marriage contracts that affirmed women's subordination to men. The idea of women's choice in sexual partnerships, without the ties of religious or legal validation, was far more radical than most early feminists countenanced, and it quickly earned Sointula the reputation as a scandalous bastion of promiscuous free love, sparking outrage from BC clergymen.

The colony's demise a few years later, however, had much more to do with the harsh conditions of life, lack of economic sustainability, and a devastating fire that killed many settlers.[11] While Finnish women in Canada and the United States eagerly promoted Sointula's ideals, not all women settlers experienced "free love" as liberating.[12] If critics at the time focused their fire on free love, a present-day critique of the scheme might be different: utopian socialists in North America did not consider that their utopian settlement was a dystopia for Indigenous peoples facing dispossession of their ancestral lands. Sadly, white settlers committed to utopianism did not explore the communal social norms of Indigenous peoples as existing models of collectivism.

However rare utopian-socialist communes were in Canada, some radical reformers idealized the values associated with them long after they folded. Alice Amelia Chown, a well-educated, middle-class writer and reformer, gave voice to both utopian-socialist and more liberal Christian social gospel ideas in her semi-autobiographical book, *The Stairway*. Chown describes her geographical and intellectual journeys through Canada, the United States, and Britain as she searched for like-minded idealists. She was deeply disappointed with the milieu of middle-class Toronto feminists, who recoiled at the suggestion that they support working-class women on strike. She sought out something better: a more radical politics of heightened moral accountability and socialist-feminist camaraderie. Chown visited cooperative-living experiments in the United States, such as settlement houses; in Britain, she declared she had finally discovered her "own utopia" at Letchworth, a planned community with shared social responsibilities and socialist ideals. Increasingly influenced by British sex radical and socialist Edward Carpenter, Chown never abandoned her utopian belief that "truth in the individual soul" and the "innate goodness" of humans would lead to social and sexual emancipation.[13]

By the early twentieth century, many socialists no longer saw islands of communalism as a viable challenge to the triumphant behemoth of industrial capitalism. Mass mobilization, social movements, and political parties seemed more sensible means of political combat. Yet utopian-socialist ideas did persist, reformulated into late nineteenth- and early twentieth-century ethical socialism. Like the utopians, ethical socialists articulated an optimistic faith in the possibilities of the intellectual, personal, and social transformation of humanity, without resorting to the violence of revolution. Eschewing the more technocratic, state-planned socialism espoused by British Fabian socialists, ethical socialists stressed the combined power of moral awakening and social action. Women's equality would be integrated into a future socialist world built on cooperation, love, truth, and universality.

The earlier utopian socialists' critique of the patriarchal nuclear family and marriage faded, but their moral call to work collaboratively for a better version of humanity remained strong. Ethical socialists sometimes drew on Christian language of doing unto others as they would do unto to you, but they were critical of organized religion: in their minds, Christian churches were complicit in a class society. Ethical socialists embraced late nineteenth-century utopian literature – like Edward Bellamy's famous novel of an imaginary future, *Looking Backward* (1889) – which asserted that rationality and humanity could triumph over the irrationality, competition, and inefficiency of capitalism. A more equitable, cooperative commonwealth was possible if socialists committed themselves to a project of intellectual, personal, and social transformation.

Ethical socialist ideas, along with a commitment to exposing social inequality and documenting the experiences of working-class life, created new articulations of socialist feminism in newspapers like *Citizen and Country* and the *Western Socialist,* as well as in a new party, the Canadian Socialist League (CSL). Founded in 1899, the CSL was committed to co-operation, education, and political agitation as the peaceful pathway to socialism. Sixty-two locals across Canada established a set of principles that included female enfranchisement, and the CSL newspaper, *Citizen and Country,* tried to recruit members from women's moral reform groups such as the Woman's Christian Temperance Union (WCTU). A women's column in *Citizen and Country,* "The Kingdom of the Home," penned by Sarah Wrigley, urged women to translate their domestic and maternal concerns into a politics of social improvement; the column's name encapsulated socialists' hope that "home and family" might become the rudder for a reformed nation in which the values of "love and collective responsibility" would impel social transformation.[14]

Women columnists in both *Citizen and Country* and the subsequent *Western Socialist* posited socialism as a moral answer to immoral practices oppressing women, such as the "white slave trade," abuse of alcohol, and the sexual double standard. Christian-infused language of salvation, reclamation, and the need to build a caring, spiritual "brotherhood" of humanity was common: Christ was, after all, the "model Socialist."[15] These early socialist women combined their commitment to working-class and women's emancipation in different measures, but they all saw an intersectional connection between gender and class inequality.

The Lasting Imprint of Marx and Engels

Bertha Merrill Burns employed the language of ethical socialism, but her writing also reflected the socialism of Marx and Engels. More than any other set of ideas, writing by Marxists on the "woman question" – their term for queries about the origins and meaning of women's oppression – had a lasting imprint on socialists' understanding of women's inequality over the entire twentieth century. What Marxists texts said, and how they were interpreted over time, could be quite different, leaving us with significant interpretive quandaries, but the global intellectual impact of Marxism on the women's movement should not be underestimated.

The starting point for Marx's theory of historical materialism was an explication of production and reproduction: the production of things necessary for survival and the reproduction of human and social life – both were indispensable and intertwined. Marx's analysis dissected the commodification of human labour under capitalism, challenging prevailing arguments of classical liberal economists that the competitive market economy was superior, progressive, and inevitable. The *historical* side of historical materialism suggested that neither the social relations of capitalism nor women's subordination were natural, unchanging, and inevitable. History was not predetermined. Human agency – humans creating their own history, though not in conditions of their choosing – could play a decisive role in developing working-class consciousness and opposition to capitalism's rapacious search for profit.[16]

Marx's analyses of gender and the family traced women's changing economic roles in the emergence of capitalist production: over the nineteenth century, the production of goods needed for survival – from soap to clothing – moved from the home to the workplace, a route children and women followed, since most families needed multiple earners to survive. Many working-class women still laboured in the home, as homemakers or domestic servants, but capitalism profoundly altered women's arduous day-to-day experience of both productive work and unpaid reproductive labour. Marx was also cognizant of the links between material shifts and changing cultural ideals, pointing to the ideological oppression of women within the family and in popular and medical discourses.

The unremittingly harsh conditions of working-class life Marx described in outraged detail corroborated his critique of capitalism: it was a system of vast inequality in wealth; the vagaries of the market economy exposed working-class families to periodic want, ill health, and insecurity; wage labour for profit was alienated labour, and, for women, it entailed added risks of workplace harassment and violence, low pay, and marginality. Marx inferred the possibility of a different kind of human progress, just as utopian socialists did, but his analysis stressed changing the economic structure rather than altering human ideals. His outrage at the human costs of capitalist accumulation, the conditions of working-class poverty and insecurity, spoke directly to women who lived these conditions on a daily, grinding basis.

While Marx's analysis of women's labour was influential, many early twentieth-century socialists looked to his collaborator, Friedrich Engels, for a more specific analysis of gender and the family. Engels's theories became "accepted thinking," if not established doctrine, in socialist parties and global organizations like the socialist Second International.[17] Like Marx, Engels's interpretation of women's oppression in his classic book, *Origin of the Family, Private Property, and the State* (1884), offered hope for a different future. The subordination of women, he reasoned, going against much Victorian writing, was not natural, incontrovertible, or biological; it was rooted in history, the product of changing social and economic forces and familial organization. Engels's arguments drew heavily on anthropological writing about past "primitive" societies organized on collective principles, including research on the Iroquois (Haudenosaunee) by American amateur anthropologist Lewis Henry Morgan. Extrapolating from Morgan, Engels posited that class society and women's oppression had the same origin: the emergence of private property. Women's "world historic defeat" occurred when the accumulation of private wealth became ascendant; men then used monogamy and sexual repression to ensure their property would go to their heirs.[18] As women became subject to patriarchal ownership, rather than equal contributors to the common welfare, their status plunged and their dependence was assured.

Like Wollstonecraft, Engels believed women were socialized into feminine behaviour designed to assure their place in the marriage market while men became more sexually aggressive, enjoying the masculine privileges associated with the Victorian double standard. Since this contemporary "battle of the sexes" was historically generated,[19] only a fundamental transformation in economic and social relations offered the prospect of a different future; in a non-class society, real love between the sexes, unfettered by economic dependence and material need, could thrive. Like most socialists of the time, his ideal family was a heterosexual couple in a nuclear household, based on love not economic power.

August Bebel's *Woman under Socialism,* originally published in 1879, was also widely read by Canadian socialist feminists. Associated with the German Social Democratic Party, Bebel argued that women's oppression occurred along the axis of both class and sex, necessitating struggles against capitalism and patriarchal ideas. Unlike many socialists, he did not promote the idea of women's natural calling as mothers, arguing instead for their right to work and the need for socialized, collective domestic labour. Social change was not inevitable. It would emerge through human action and resistance, but there was hope for future sexual relationships built on love rather than economic dependence if the reign of private property sustaining class inequality was abolished.[20]

These Marxist classics provided the core of socialist women's political education: women in Socialist Party of Canada study groups read Bebel, Engels, and Morgan's *Ancient Society,* as well as Canadian, American, and British socialist writing that discussed these texts. Lecture tours of socialist speakers, political pamphlets, and discussions in socialist newspapers popularized these ideas. However, texts were reinterpreted over time, and not always to the benefit of women. Both Bebel and Engels saw women's work outside the home as a positive trigger for their class consciousness, yet this idea was not welcomed by all male socialists, many of whom remained wedded to the ideal of a male breadwinner earning enough to support his dependent wife and family. Socialist feminists also searched for answers from other socialist thinkers, from sex-positive radicals who challenged heteronormativity and monogamy, like Edward Carpenter, to anarchist and birth-control advocate Emma Goldman. Socialist women concurred with their male comrades that socialism would give the working class freedom, but their politics were also shaped by day-to-day dilemmas men could not imagine: unwanted pregnancies, physical and sexual violence, and the threat of the loss of respectability associated with sexual "downfall."

Socialist-Feminist Journalism

Marxist socialism – labelled "scientific socialism" – eventually overshadowed utopian or ethical socialism, but Canadian socialist feminists often combined ethical concepts with Marxism; eclecticism rather than orthodoxy characterized their politics. Feminist Mary Cotton Wisdom, who wrote a women's column in her brother's socialist paper, *Cotton's Weekly,* combined moral critique – often bordering on outrage – with a more analytic Marxist political economy. Decrying false images of socialists as "bomb-throwing" radicals, Wisdom argued that they were engaged in the moral, spiritual, and economic transformation of humanity: "They are working to help the weak to rise, the fallen to lift the burden of oppression, to overthrow crime and bind up the broken hearts, striving to fulfill the teaching of Christ in truth."[21]

Edging closer to Engels, she told her readers that women's subordination and their "low status" in marriage had a materialist basis in property relations, with women "bound" to men in the "marriage market": the only way to liberate women from this legal "concubinage" was to allow them to "become economically free."[22] When it came to describing the legal system, Wisdom inclined toward a feminist critique of patriarchy, pure and simple. She was infuriated with a judicial system that "punished women" yet "let men go free" for exactly the same crime (prostitution); she asserted that, after women had the vote, they would "see to it that some of the infamous man-made laws now in force are abolished in short order ... We are heartily sick of being governed, ruled, judged, sentenced, imprisoned and even hanged by men and man-made laws."[23] Mary Cotton Wisdom's column mixed Marxist ideas, feminist conviction, and social reform rhetoric, including support for temperance. Her views did not match the platform of any one socialist party, but they mirrored the broader intellectual ferment of the times: Marxist debates about capitalism; the proliferation of women's organizations parallel to socialist parties; and a women's reform movement intent on curing social ills.[24]

For her part, Bertha Merrill Burns wrote extensively in the *Canadian Socialist,* the *Western Socialist,* and the *Western Clarion,* combining journalistic reportage, analytic insight, moral protest, and Marxist analysis. Merrill Burns never wavered in her search for the right recipe for an integrated feminist socialism that would transform the lives of both women in the workforce and homemakers. The housewife was "most in need of what socialism could do for her," and, at the same time, due to her "potent" influence on the family, she was badly needed in the fight for socialism. Burns imagined a socialism that would completely reorganize the home with "food laboratories," socialized domestic work, kindergartens, and free schooling.[25] She enthusiastically embraced Bebel's suggestion of socialized domestic labour, done scientifically and collectively, freeing women from dependence on the patriarchal nuclear family household. At that time, most socialist feminists did not entertain the possibility of men doing housework. When Mary Cotton Wisdom suggested that instead of "discussing their own woes [men] should pitch in after their day's work and help their wives," she faced an angry tirade from readers, including one woman who wrote that her husband would divorce her before following this advice.[26]

Unlike many male Marxists, Burns and fellow socialist feminists were attuned to the constraints and undervaluing of women's domestic labour; in fact, domestic responsibility might be the spark that made women into socialists. When a "woman buys sugar and finds it half sand, [when] she buys milk made of half chalk and water," Burns asked, "how then is a woman to provide pure food for her family? She can never do so as long as the present profit system prevails ... These adulterations are made for profit – that some man or corporation of men may make money."[27] Countless other socialist feminists echoed Burns's critique and hope. Capitalism was structured and controlled by men who were all too happy to sacrifice women's needs on the "alter" of profit,[28] wrote suffragist, socialist, and feminist Nora Tutty; but women's caregiving roles might open their eyes to the menace of profit making as they struggled to feed and protect their children.

Discussing the wage-earning woman, Burns again deviated from the usual socialist script. Although most socialists promoted the male breadwinner or "family wage" ideal, Burns found it suspect, since it still left women economically subject to male power. "If socialists don't believe in property rights in human beings," she wrote, "then they should not allude to their wives and children" in this way.[29] When employers used women to undercut male wages, she added, the solution was equal pay, not banishing women from the workforce. Like labour feminist Helena Gutteridge, Burns defended the rights of *all* working women and was remarkably sensitive to even the most marginalized. Few socialists imagined domestic servants as revolutionary prospects, yet Burns devoted attention to their travails: they faced hard physical work and endless hours, were at the beck and call of a mistress, and their subservient role robbed them of the basic dignity enjoyed by other working women. The working-class woman forced to perform this arduous work, she reminded readers, had fundamentally different interests than the bourgeois woman, that "useless, ill-bred, supercilious creature, living in luxury and idleness off the toil of her fellows."[30]

Burns supported unconventional ideas, even for socialists, such as sex education for children, but she found common ground with many socialist feminists on the issue of prostitution. Their discussion of prostitution and "white slavery" – that is, the trickery, kidnapping, and coercive capture of innocent white women into prostitution – was coloured by their abiding moral anger at the sexual double standard and the criminalization of prostitutes, not the men who used them. They rejected the claims by some anti-prostitution social purity campaigners that feminine moral weakness and women's search for easy money contributed to prostitution. No, they replied: prostitution was the product of economic desperation, low wages, and capitalism. By 1909, many women's reform organizations likewise stressed that "trafficking" in women had roots in women's low wages, but, as

Figure 2.2 Socialist and labour feminists saw prostitution as an economic issue, caused by low wages, poverty, and capitalism | *Industrial Banner*, 9 May 1913

Lara Campbell points out, this insistence on women's economic victimization denied poor and working-class sex workers, who chose this work among few choices, any agency and ignored issues of their immediate safety.[31] Most socialist feminists also shared the racist suppositions of reform feminists who expressed colonial and racial anxieties about white slavery: the notion that "foreign," especially Asian, men were amoral procurers and that Asian and Indigenous girls were sold into slavery within their own (more brutal) cultures.[32] Socialists might publicly criticize racist and nativist attitudes that divided the working class, but, when it came to prostitution, they succumbed to prevailing racist and orientalist tropes, reinforcing fears that whiteness was imperiled by "foreign" immigration.

Reflecting the ideological norms of the time, socialist feminists also assumed that mothering was a woman's primary, natural, desired calling. Although distorted and limited by capitalism, motherhood would be elevated to its rightful place under socialism. State support for women's material well-being, health care, and child welfare would relieve women of worries about their children's needs, leaving women free to embrace fully the true joys of domesticity.

Placing Feminist Hopes in Socialist Parties

Many socialist women like Burns invested hope in parties like the SPC and its later breakaway, the Social Democratic Party of Canada (SDPC), as vehicles for social transformation. Socialist feminists sought a like-minded community of organized comrades, working together for the greater good, even if they found parties frustrating when male comrades disparaged women for their "backwardness" or theoretical ineptitude. Nonetheless, women used party circles and newspapers to initiate debates about women's subordination, insisting this issue not be relegated to the back burner of socialist politics. Conversely, they urged socialist women to become more involved in feminist causes like suffrage. Vancouver socialist feminist Nora Tutty acknowledged it was tempting to see socialism as the "greater cause," but women's enfranchisement would give women the power to make socialism a reality. Invoking *The Communist Manifesto,* she issued a call to women's action: "To quote ... Marx: You have a world to win; you have nothing to lose but your chains."[33]

To focus only on Mary Cotton Wisdom or Bertha Merrill Burns can be misleading, as women socialists were not of one mind: they mixed and matched strands of Marxism, feminism, ethical socialism, and occasionally sex radicalism. Some found feminism a misguided effort that would enhance the power of propertied, middle-class women: like other piecemeal, parliamentary demands, it lulled workers into the mistaken belief that capitalism could be reformed. Manchester-born Ruth Lestor, who gave public lectures for the SPC, did not describe women as hopelessly backward, but she believed feminism and suffrage could not vanquish the true enemy of humanity, namely capitalism. The influence of Engels was always prescient: socialists replicated much of the social and evolutionary writing of the time that considered males and females biologically and socially distinct, yet they referred to the existence of a matriarchal past and stressed the fluidity of historical change.[34] Women's oppression was not fixed forever; it might end, but only if the curtain fell on private property.

The negative characterizations of feminism by Lestor and many members of the SPC had a dogmatic and derogatory ring; however, socialists' suspicions about middle-class feminists were not entirely unfounded. Feminists who came from more privileged backgrounds often displayed little understanding of working-class women, spent an inordinate amount of time talking about the problem of finding good servants, and were hostile to socialism. Some vocally opposed strikes involving women workers. They also denigrated working-class eastern and southern European immigrants in socialist parties, assuming the superiority of Anglo-British culture and the need to assimilate these "dangerous foreigners."[35]

Lestor actually shifted her views on the woman question over time; most socialist women did, too, though they consistently embraced *some* version of women's equality, and a few harboured unconventional views on sexuality and the family. Socialist Party supporter Dora Forster Kerr, one of a few sex radicals writing in Canada, supported suffrage, birth control, and "free marriage" – similar to utopian socialist definitions – which anti-socialist commentators equated with licentious free love, promiscuity, and sin. Public hostility to her writing (which was censored in the United States) reminds us that socialist women, particularly sex radicals, faced a deeply antagonistic social climate. The mainstream press was not just unsympathetic, they were sometimes hysterically condemnatory, claiming socialists wanted to destroy the family and throw decent civilization to the dogs.

An immigrant from Britain, Kerr was influenced by Fabian socialism but modified her ideas once in Canada. She represented a host of positions, some radical, some contradictory, some antithetical to how we define feminism today. She belonged to the SPC but challenged the party's rejection of alliances with non-socialist suffragists. She collaborated with middle-class feminists but denounced their punitive, reactionary views on crime and punishment, especially the flogging of prisoners. She endorsed class struggle and socialism but critiqued man-made laws on sexual issues, child custody, and the family as patriarchal and oppressive to women. She courageously defended her unconventional views about egalitarian marriage but promoted prevailing eugenic theories that implicitly endorsed "better breeding."[36]

It was not uncommon for socialist parties to offer contradictory views about the woman question. In British Columbia, where these debates were especially intense, party women like Bertha Merrill Burns were committed suffragists, yet the SPC leadership contemptuously informed one suffrage group seeking the party's endorsement that, while it was not "violently opposed" to women's enfranchisement, "we simply don't care a cuss ... We know only two kinds of people. Not men and women but masters and (wage) slaves."[37] When Burns's column in the *Western Clarion* was cancelled in 1903, she was suspicious that her feminist criticisms of the party leadership were not welcomed by the paper's doctrinaire editors. Similarly ambivalent were SPC members of the BC legislature, J.H. Hawthornthwaite and John Thomas Place, who put forward five women's suffrage bills between 1906 and 1916, yet warned that such legislation could never deliver true equality. Hawthornthwaite contended that women must "have some means of combating the economic conditions of the modern world where man-made laws offered them small protection,"[38] but added that the franchise could not free any woman or man from economic dependence on the master class – only socialism could.[39] He also thought women might be a "civilizing force" to counter the influence of racialized – especially Asian – immigrants, echoing the racist rationale used by other BC labour feminists, such as Susie Lane Clark.[40]

Conflicting views also surfaced over separate women's columns in socialist newspapers and women's role in the party. In 1908, the *Western Clarion* published an article that discussed the stereotype of women as inherently conservative, citing a party member who flippantly claimed "most women became a socialist because of some man." Incenced readers defended women comrades against socialist men who acted like patriarchal "tyrants."[41] One letter writer warned that narrow-minded egotism and "intolerant" attitudes toward women would solidify a limited "man's movement ... Women cannot recognize themselves only under the name of men; it would be equally ridiculous only to speak to miners and no one else." Taking the high road, another respondent asked how male socialists could advocate the emancipation of only half of the human race, while a more sarcastic critic recommended role reversal: if women needed political education, perhaps men should look after the home, so that women could attend socialist meetings.[42] Why do women become socialists, Edith Wrigley asked, offering a Marxist *and* feminist answer: "Not just because of a man, unless it is some man she is working for ... She wishes the emancipation and freedom of the sex from economic slavery." One angry reply concluded that both equality and solidarity were needed: "Our work is to arouse the workers to revolt ... [so] let us arouse the workers, not one sex; let us have more equality and democracy in our work."[43]

Socialist men and women might spar over tactics, but most agreed that stand-alone feminism was inadequate. The notion that equality could rest on bourgeois legal rights within a liberal capitalist state met with scepticism. Canadians were not alone in this view. Similar questions about the relationship between socialism and feminism preoccupied socialism internationally, including within the Second International (1889–1916), which represented most European and American socialist parties. At precisely this time, a resurgent wave of international socialist-feminist organizing brought women into the socialist fold and contributed to the vigour of the global suffrage movement.

Fed up with the SPC's view of suffrage and immediate reform, Burns and other disgruntled party members established a new socialist party, the SDPC in 1907, which placed women's suffrage, along with other immediate reforms, in its platform and encouraged the participation of socialist feminists. The party was also more welcoming to immigrant groups, including Finnish Canadians who had already established language-based locals and separate socialist study groups for women. Burns believed the party's openness to women was one of its great strengths. Writing to Margaret MacDonald, wife of the future leader of the British Labour Party, in 1907, she noted her determination to conduct party business so that women would stay involved.[44] When the First World War broke out seven years later, the SDPC newspaper made good on this promise, publishing the views of anti-war socialist feminists when both mainstream and feminist newspapers refused to do so.

Labouring for Feminism

Like the SDPC, labour movement activists sometimes entertained alliances with feminist organizations to promote women's suffrage, although their primary concerns were trade unions, labour parties, and labour newspapers. Labour support for feminism was highly differentiated: it was less visible in trade unions, which were preoccupied with seeking a family wage for working men, but more apparent in labour newspapers and Independent Labour Parties, which encouraged discussion of gender equality.

The material reality and conceptualization of labour, however, were central to many varieties of feminist thought and organizing as women responded to transformations in daily life wrought by industrial capitalism. Women's changing labour inside and outside the home was the animating theme in influential international feminist writing, which was consumed by Canadians and then featured prominently in their own rationalizations for feminism. At the time, a progressive reform movement debated the "labour question": Were workers justly treated, and what was the proper relationship between employers, the state, and workers? For feminists, the labour question was also a gender question. If the production of goods is taken outside the home, what was the role of homemakers? If women workers –

like the "girl printers" who so moved Burns – were exploited, whose responsibility was it to take up their cause?

The issue of wage-earning women generated more widespread public debate. Intensified immigration, almost entirely from preferred "white" European countries, the spread and growth of cities, and increased female employment in factories, stores, and offices all sparked anxieties about the "working girl adrift" in the city. Although many working women handed over their wages to their families, disproportionate anxiety focused on self-supporting single women, presumed to be vulnerable to both sexual harassment and their own descent into sexual misconduct. Living outside of the moral surveillance of family, partaking in new urban pleasures like dance halls, they might be corrupted by "foreign'" men, be they Asian or Eastern European – concerns highlighting the underlying nativist, racist subtext to these anxieties.

The labour movement discussed women's rights from the 1880s onwards, but progressive ideas did not necessarily emerge in a linear fashion. Some nineteenth-century groups were more forward thinking than twentieth-century ones. The Knights of Labor, founded in 1869 in the United States, was committed to organizing all workers irrespective of gender, skill, or religion; the Canadian Knights endorsed equal pay for women and universal suffrage for all citizens instead of a male, property-based franchise. As much a social movement as a trade union, the Knights used grassroots mobilizations, cultural events, workplace unions, and participation in elections to promote their distinctive vision of working-class dignity and solidarity. Since workers produced the wealth of society, the Knights believed, they merited social respect and a fair wage. Dignity, however, was not due all workers; in British Columbia especially, racism undergirded the Knights' hostility to Chinese labour, which they claimed threatened the earning power and respectability of the white working class.

The Knights' insistence on the worth of women workers encouraged a wider debate about gender equality. Toronto Knights of Labor journalist T. Phillips Thompson used his pen to promote "equal citizenship" for women: they merited the right "to be regarded in all matters of citizenship and all relations between the government and the people as the equal of men." Denying women a political voice, he wrote in the Knights' *Palladium of Labor*, was just as "stupid and unreasonable" as the arbitrary distinctions made between men according to "race, creed, birth or property" and just as unfair as the past exclusion of working men from political life by the wealthy few.[45] He rejected the popular notion that women were naturally inferior and the property of their husbands or fathers as faulty ideas and disturbing residue from the prehistoric past. Thompson's support for feminism was tied to his ethical socialist perspective: capitalism not only devalued women's labour, but also put the working-class home in jeopardy through its cheapening of all paid labour.

Although the Knights promoted a chivalrous Victorian image of pure and virtuous working-class womanhood in need of protection, its female members insisted on their right to fair compensation and protection from sexual harassment. Katie McVicar, who began work as a teenager in a Hamilton shoe factory, was an impassioned advocate of working women's empowerment under the Knights banner. Organization was the only hope for women workers, she wrote, and not just for factory operatives like herself, but for clerical and especially domestic workers, who were the most "underpaid" and "underfed drudges" in the workforce.[46] The Knights' enticing message of respectable femininity, citizen equality, and working-class solidarity brought many women into the organization; they created eight all-female assemblies across Ontario, with Katie McVicar elected the first "directoress" of the Hamilton women's Excelsior Assembly. McVicar's early death silenced her remarkable voice, and the Knights themselves faded away by the 1890s, supplanted by the Trades and Labour Congress, which was dominated by craft-based (skilled) unions, with a predominantly male membership largely uninterested in women's equality.[47] Over the next decades, the labour movement did slowly shift its view, at least on suffrage, as feminists worked to secure trade union support, often union by union, city by city, by pointing to labour and feminists' common goals, such as the "protection" of wage-earning women.

By the early twentieth century, labour feminists found new homes in local Labour Parties or Independent Labour Parties (ILPs), which were springing up across Canada. "Labourism" was a distinct, if somewhat amorphous set of ideas and political practices that varied with each local organization, though most shared ideals imported from Britain. Like the British ILP, Canadian "labourite" parties were deeply critical of capitalism, but they still placed their hopes in change through parliamentary democracy. Both Labour Parties and new labour newspapers reflected the workplace experiences of their proletarian membership, and they drew intellectually on nineteenth-century English "radicalism" and ethical socialism, with an infusion, too, of Marxism. Theirs was a moral and economic critique of the moneyed and political interests that stood in the way of the equality, democracy, and dignity the working class deserved.[48]

The line between socialist and labour feminists could be blurred, as women moved between or embraced both causes, and there was also cross-fertilization of labourite and feminist ideas, particularly for more intellectually venturesome radical women. Emily Stowe, along with T. Phillips Thompson, founded a free-thinking Toronto Theosophy Society; Toronto journalist Flora MacDonald Denison joined with Labour Party leader Jimmy Simpson to fight puritanical city ordinances prohibiting leisure pursuits on Sunday; and Winnipeg feminist journalist Francis Marion Beynon found intellectual friendship with ILP leader Fred Dixon, joining him in anti-war activities during the First World War.

Two examples of labour feminists offer a glimpse of the varying strategies they used to tackle women's inequality. Labour movement activist May Darwin began her political life in 1902 in the Toronto Union Label League, an organization that encouraged the household purchase of union-made "label" goods to ensure decent wages for workers. Like working-class women in the Label Leagues first established in the United States, Darwin saw an opportunity to draw working-class women into the labour movement through their role as household budgeters, work she recognized as undervalued but essential to family survival. When the Label League floundered from a lack of Labour Council support, Darwin diverted her energies to the Trades and Labour Council's educational committee and initiated a column "Of Interest to Women," for its paper, the *Toronto Tribune*, mixing commentary on domesticity, romance, motherhood, and femininity with invocations of class solidarity and the importance of women joining the Label League and trade union auxiliaries.

In Darwin's view, the improvement of working-class life required more than women's mobilization behind the labour movement: socialism was also necessary. She was a member of the CSL, assuming a visible role in the 1902 election campaign of Toronto socialist Margaret Haile for the provincial legislature. Although women could not vote, no law restricted women from running for office, a loophole feminist and socialist supporters cleverly exploited: they nominated Haile and used the election campaign to publicize their ideas. In a public lecture in 1901, Darwin laid out her case for the indispensable connections between women's emancipation and socialism. Asking "why women should be socialists," she optimistically predicted that women should be in the "vanguard" of socialism, since they had the most to

Figure 2.3 Labour feminist May Darwin worked for the Toronto Union Label League. Its Labour Day souvenir reflects Darwin's idealized hope for a more economically secure working-class family | Russell Hann, Tom Reid, and New Hogtown Press

gain from "equality of the sexes": women and children suffered more than men from "the competitive system," and mothers would benefit since they would not have to send their children out to factories at an early age. Even "society" women, she added, would gain: under socialist egalitarianism, they would no longer feel that they had to rub shoulders with their "social inferiors" – they would have none![49]

A decade later in British Columbia, Helena Gutteridge, a British working-class immigrant, became a leading advocate for women's rights as a union representative on the Vancouver Trades and Labour Council and a columnist for the labour paper the *British Columbia Federationist.* Gutteridge

Figure 2.4 Suffragist Helena Gutteridge was a feminist, socialist, trade unionist, and peace advocate. From 1937 to 1940, she was a CCF city councillor in Vancouver, the first woman to serve in that position | Major Mathews Collection, Vancouver City Archives, AM54-S4-2 CVA371-2693-HG

arrived in Vancouver in 1911, armed with knowledge of unions from her work in the London tailoring industry and political experience from her participation in the Women's Social and Political Union (WSPU), representing the militant suffragette movement in Britain. She promoted unions as crucial means of protecting and improving the lives of working-class women, but she went beyond mere reformism, indicting capitalism as the cause of working women's exploitation. Sweatshops and unhealthy factory conditions provoked her passionate denunciation, as did bosses who profited from the employment of women in low-wage job ghettos.

Her *British Columbia Federationist* column shunned domestic advice in favour of political news on prostitution, suffrage, and other reform issues. It provided hard-hitting commentary, not only on the exploitation of working women, but also on working-class men's failure to support fellow women workers. Unlike many other female trade unionists, she fearlessly took on working-class men who were apathetic about the plight of super-exploited working women: "The history of women in industry ... is the story of struggle against not only the capitalist class who have exploited them mercilessly, but also against the men of their own class who said because they were women they must not expect to be looked on as co-workers or receive the same pay."[50]

Gutteridge was even more scathing about middle-class anti-feminist men, who wielded their social influence in the campaign against women's rights. After an anti-suffrage priest gave a public lecture in Vancouver, in which he extolled the virtue of "feminine helplessness," she exploded in print: "Does the Reverend Father walk around Vancouver with his eyes closed? Perhaps [he] will devise some means of keeping the bodies and souls of women together without food, and their bodies warm without clothes or shelter that they may remain feminine and charming."[51] In concert with many other early twentieth-century labour feminists, however, Gutteridge was little concerned with racial inequality, repeating trade unions' suggestion that anti-Asian, "white preference" hiring might solve the unemployment problem.[52] While socialist feminists were critical of the gendered division of labour, they were less concerned with the racial division of labour and racism, although, in subsequent decades, Gutteridge changed her views with respect to the latter.

As a feminist, Gutteridge joined Vancouver's main suffrage organization, the Pioneer Political Equality League, and advocated an alliance of all suffrage groups in the province. As a labour activist, she promoted unionization and founded a working women's group, the Women's Suffrage League, discussed in the next chapter. Gutteridge, like May Darwin, was grounded in the labour movement, although Darwin focused on women's work in the home and Gutteridge on wage earners. For both women, unionization, labour education, and political action were all strategic imperatives, but so too was the mobilization of women, both as members of the working class and as women who deserved equal citizenship rights. Feminism and labour action were linked, as strategy, as organization, and in a vision of a better future.

Labour and the Cultural Front

Women's work was also a recurring theme in the cultural front of feminist dissent, as early twentieth-century journalists, poets, artists, and novelists tackled thorny issues of working women's autonomy, rights, and social roles, critiquing both outdated patriarchal ideas and industrial capitalism. Influential international feminist thinkers shaped these debates. American Charlotte Perkins Gilman's 1898 book, *Women and Economics,* heralded as a brilliant feminist milestone and equated with John Stuart Mill's *The Subjection of Women*, was read by Canadian reform and socialist feminists alike. The "staggering" breadth of her vision, enthused one Canadian journalist, likely makes her "the greatest woman writer of the day."[53] Initially interested in ethical, cooperative socialism, Gilman developed a "humanist" theory explaining women's subordination that drew on Marx, Darwin, and Thorstein Veblen, a critic of conspicuous capitalist consumption. Melding these influences, her writing fundamentally rethought women's relationship to family, children, and domestic labour.[54]

Like Marx, Gilman assumed that work was central to social life, but she focused on reproductive labour in the home, using her own experience of stultifying domesticity as a springboard to analyse the ideological imperatives that confined all wives and mothers to domesticity. Why, she asked, did women have to choose between public life and a home life, while men did not? Biology did not drive women's capabilities; rather, their socialization did, and that could be altered. Her argument that women's homemaking labour was undervalued was appreciated by many feminists, but her solution was more radical than most countenanced: domestic work and child care should be collectivized and professionalized, done by experts who were paid for their labour.

Gilman's economic theory seemed to suit the needs of women who could have careers, not those in low-paid work, and she was primarily concerned with the lives of white women, displaying nativism and anti-Semitism in her other writing. Socialist feminists, however, were intrigued by her critique of capitalist consumption and her collectivist solutions, often pairing her book with Olive Schreiner's *Woman and Labour* (1911), a collection of the South African writer's essays from the late nineteenth century. *Woman and Labour* was a similarly influential feminist text cited by Canadian feminists; journalist Flora MacDonald Denison called it "the most remarkable and instructive book I've ever read."[55] Like Gilman, Schreiner addressed women's narrow socialization to domesticity and their need for meaningful work: women's dependence on men, she argued, created a form of "parasitism" that was dangerous not only to women but to all of society.[56] Women's autonomy, their right to their share of "socially useful, honest toil outside the home,"[57] was the answer to their sexual subordination.

Woman and Labour minimized the predicament of working-class women, who might have preferred one job to a double day, and, in the tradition of Enlightenment orientalism, assumed white, European women were in the vanguard of social and moral progress. Canadian feminists, including

Dora Forster Kerr and Flora MacDonald Denison, were primarily swayed by Schreiner's relentless critique of women's enforced "idleness" and their consequent subservience to men.[58] Neither Gilman nor Schreiner disputed that motherhood was one of women's highest callings, but they questioned whether motherhood should be their *only* calling, a view echoed by Canadian suffragist Augusta Stowe-Gullen, discussed in the next chapter. These feminists' intellectual challenge to the apparently iron-clad claim that women were destined for domestic labour encouraged labour feminists to challenge the sexual division of labour outside the home too. At a time when the largest group of women worked as servants scrubbing floors and doing laundry by hand, Helena Gutteridge ridiculed the notion that men's superior physical abilities determined their monopoly on both taxing and skilled work. "If the world's work were divided on the principle of giving men the heavier tasks and women the lighter and more pleasant duties, the male clerk should at once change places with the housemaid and the ticket-collector with the laundress."[59]

Flora MacDonald Denison also promoted the novel concept that the gendered division of labour was ideological, not natural, and was fundamental to women's inequality. In an extended essay on men, women, and work, she argued, following Engels, that matriarchy once "held sway" across the globe, but was replaced by patriarchy, which was found in its most extreme form in the Western white slave trade, Turkish harems, and Chinese footbinding. Denison thus embraced the orientalism that had pervaded feminism since the time of Wollstonecraft. Most of the essay, however, explained why patriarchy produced an artificial gendered division of labour. Custom and prejudice, not abilities, determined the work women did. Women had proven they could excel at fields previously closed to them, such as medicine, without jeopardizing their motherly roles. More controversially, she asked, "when will women get rid of the idea that it is their holy mission in life to be caterers and cleaners? For heaven's sake, women, hire some man who is fitted for nothing more than dusting pictures and polishing floors."[60] This comment was unusual for Denison, who usually invoked the dignity of all labour, but her point was that gender should not determine one's occupation. In other columns, Denison extolled the value of the most "lowly" labour and supported – unlike some suffragists – trade unions for women, from charwomen to tobacco strippers.[61]

Women poets and novelists also linked women's equality to the labour question. Few came from the working classes, though Marie Joussaye was a notable exception. A feisty, aspiring writer with a "chequered" life, including two run-ins with the law and two months in a Yukon prison for economic offences, Joussaye began publishing poetry in the 1880s.[62] Her well-known "signature" verse, "Only a Working Girl," was penned in 1886 when she was a twenty-two-year-old domestic servant. The poem is a plea for the dignity and worth of women workers whose abilities and right to "earn their daily bread" should garner them social recognition, not the social disdain they faced from hypocritical "upper class" ladies.[63] Strength, skill, and independence are all virtues of the "working girl" to be celebrated. Like some labour reformers, Joussaye invoked religious imagery, pointing to Christ as the original lowly toiler:[64]

Only a Working Girl

I know I am only a working girl,
And I am not ashamed to say
I belong to the ranks of those who toil
For a living, day by day ...

I belong to the "lower classes;"
That's a phrase we often meet.
There are some who sneer at working girls;
As they pass us on the street,
They stare at us in proud disdain
And their lips in scorn will curl,
And oftentimes we hear them say:
"She's only a working girl." ...

O working girls! Remember,
It is neither crime nor shame
To work for honest wages,
Since Christ has done the same,
And wealth and high position
Seem but of little worth
To us, whose fellow laborer
Is King of Heaven and Earth.

So when you meet with scornful sneers,
Just lift your heads in pride;
The shield of honest womanhood

Can turn such sneers aside,
And some day they will realize
That the purest, fairest pearls
'Mid the gems of noble womankind
Are "only working girls."[65]

"Only a Working Girl" was reprinted in Joussaye's first collection of poems, *Songs That Quinte Sang*, self-published in her hometown of Belleville, Ontario. She subsequently worked as a domestic in Toronto, where she joined suffragists in a delegation to the Ontario legislature.[66] She also tried to organize other domestics into a union and get her foot in the door as a journalist. The first project faltered in the face of the logistical nightmare of organizing such a dispersed workforce. The second also disappointed: Joussaye blamed the masculine domination of the newspaper world for her exclusion, though one suspects her lowly origins also counted against her. Writing to *Globe* editor John Willison of her attempt to promote herself, she complained: "The worst was scandal. If I spoke to an editor or haunted a newspaper office, there was an evil construction put on it. Young men pushed themselves forward by their sheer persistence ... but what was permitted to them, was resented in my case."[67]

Joussaye moved to British Columbia and then Yukon, first on her own and later with her husband, a former North West Mounted Police officer. She nurtured her writing ambitions while patching together a scant living, and, in 1920, she published a second collection, *Selections from Anglo-Saxon Songs*, with labour themes as well as odes to individual suffering, love, and admiration for the British Empire in wartime. Her poem "Labour" again spoke to the dignity of the working class in the face of upper-class denigration: "preachers and politicians," she wrote, offered up public praise for labour's "holy" role, when in fact their words were nothing more than shallow, cynical rhetoric. One poem, anticipating the language of Occupy Wall Street, condemned the "ninety and nine who must live and die in hunger and want and cold, that one may revel in luxury, enwrapped in its silken fold." The 99 percent experience greed, oppression, and wrong, filling the coffers of the rich 1 percent, but when "greed is overthrown, labour will have its own."[68] Joussaye was no revolutionary, but her transcendent language captured her hope for the emancipation of working-class women.

Joussaye's equation of autonomy, independence, and respect with women's emancipation echoed in other fiction, including books penned by educated middle-class reformers who believed the more affluent had a moral, Christian duty to "help" working-class women. Feminist author and social gospel reformer Agnes Maule Machar, for example, addressed the "labour question" through a gendered lens, expressing horror at women's exploitative working conditions and hope that women reformers would play a key role in the creation of a more humane and just society. Not to take this reform work seriously, she argued rather idealistically, was to abandon any hope of a true feminist sisterhood of women that crossed the boundaries of class.

In her journalism, Machar denounced the discipline, abuse, and "inhumane conditions" associated with women's paid work that resulted from capital's quest for material gain,[69] but she also saw the labour question as a moral, Christian dilemma, not the least because women's work environment exposed them to sexual risk. Machar's best-known novel, *Roland Graeme, Knight,* addressed the labour question through the prism of moral conscience, with women taking a central role in the reclamation of humanity. Set in a mill town severely divided between owners/managers and workers who toiled long hours in the mill, the novel's hero, Roland Graeme, a Knight of Labor, fights to improve working conditions and wages. Yet the true heroine might be Nora Blanchard, a well-to-do young woman whose personal contact with downtrodden mill girls leads to her saintly efforts to aid them through a combination of good works and advocacy. Feminists like Machar acknowledged their own class privilege but rationalized that it could be parlayed into service and solidarity with working-class women.[70]

In other novels and short stories by feminists, work is a potential pathway to emancipation, offering the tantalizing prospect of economic independence, including independence from men: "work is viewed as a way to level women's relationships with men, to make women serious participants in public and political life," and, for middle-class authors, as a means to improve a woman's class status.[71] Equality was not only about legislative reform, such as equal pay, but also about self-respect: the "means to earn one's daily bread" was essential to autonomy, dignity, and a better life for women.[72] In *House of Windows,* a Canadian novel written about a "shop girl" labouring in a large department store, the heroine comes home, elated after securing her first position, announcing to her sisters: "I've done it ... Let's celebrate! ... I've got a place, a position, a job, a 'sit'! I'm an independent working person. Votes for women!"[73] Women's rights and economic self-sufficiency were two sides of the same coin. The popular appeal of *House of Windows* also rested on its mimicry of the melodramatic plot lines of the romantic formula fiction that working-class women consumed. Less interested in earnest political messages, they appreciated novels in which the virtuous working-class working girl is rewarded with marriage to the boss's son.

By the First World War, some fiction writers were discussing women's labour in more daring forms of feminist dissent. No author provided a more jarring break with the past than J.G. (Georgina) Sime. A Scottish immigrant to Montreal, Sime was an accomplished, erudite editor and writer when she arrived; she worked for a time as a secretary but was well off enough to have time to develop her craft. Despite her highly educated, middle-class background, her life was quite unconventional: she came to Canada as a thirty-nine-year-old single woman in order to live close to a married Montreal professor of medicine with whom she had a lasting relationship until his death in 1950.[74]

Sime's *Sister Woman,* published in 1919, turned Machar's middle-class moralism on its head. This collection of twenty-eight snappy stories about urban, modern working women confounded critics as it was so alien to previous sentimental renditions of womanhood, and, not surprisingly, it did not sell well. Drawing on social realism, *Sister Woman* suggests ways that women, as workers, mothers, lovers, might live in the world differently. Titles like "The Char Lady," "The Bachelor Girl," and "Divorced" announced Sime's thorough rethinking of morality, family, love, and work. Her female protagonists, ranging from lowly charwomen to more respectable "business girls," questioned or defied sexual and marital conventions, though not without anxious reflection about the consequences.

Economic independence, dignity, and self-respect, even in the face of social approbation, were important to these women. In "An Irregular Union," a secretary had a long-time affair with her boss but refused to become a "kept" woman, dependent on him.[75] "The Bachelor Girl" featured a woman who refused to marry and carved out a life as a masseuse. In that story, men were simply superfluous to a good life: "Men for Tryphena really don't exist. She does not so much dislike them – she simply feels an absolute indifference for and about them."[76] Significantly, though, Tryphena does adopt a child. Mother love was still a fundamental part of the definition of womanhood for Sime; still, in "Motherhood," the unmarried female character has a child with her lover, outside of marriage, and manages to find the same joys in motherhood, without the harsh shame of Victorian morality.[77]

In one story ("Munitions") set during the First World War, the heroine, Bertha, escapes the personal subservience of domestic service for a job in a munitions factory that finally allowed her to be the mistress of her own fate.

Sime's description of Bertha's rowdy co-workers on a streetcar was exactly the scene many social reformers feared: they were "loud, noisy, forever talking, unseemly," as they enjoyed their close camaraderie. Factory work is far from idealized. Bertha is "worn out" from working ten hours a day in "noise and grime and wet," but she is buoyed by a new sense of self: she is "capable, strong, earning good money" and is "free" to live in her own room, make her own choices, enjoy her life.[78] *Sister Woman,* representing a "socialist-realist" interlude in Sime's writing, was a "messy, provocative, unsettling, wonderful modernist text."[79] It validated women's work, economic independence, and sexual autonomy while also posing rebellious alternatives to the social norms that constrained women's happiness. Sime ushered in the "New Woman" of the 1920s, even if Canadians were not ready to embrace her.

Conclusion

Bertha Merrill Burns died at fifty-one in 1917, two years before *Sister Woman* was published. One imagines she might have enjoyed it, since she thought discussions of sexuality should be more open, with shibboleths challenged, and that women must, above all, secure their economic independence. Burns's socialist-feminist voice – analytic, compassionate, honest – and her vision of a collective and egalitarian future represented a pioneering effort to develop a theory and praxis that connected gender and class inequality and that might emancipate women working in the home and outside of it. Before the First World War, there were multiple entry points to politics for women who were committed to feminism, socialism, and labour organizing: socialist organizations with utopian or ethical ideals, parties indebted to Marx and Engels, ILPs and labour newspapers, journalism and cultural production. At the heart of their politics was a critique of the destructive social relations that defined capitalism, but many also had a deep aversion to the patriarchal ideas that constrained women's lives. They shared an embryonic awareness that class relations and gender ideology were connected, that both had to be altered if socialists were to tackle the conditions and consequences of working-class life that so incensed them: poverty, prostitution, ill health, low wages, and unsavory workplaces. As Burns told her SDPC comrades, fighting on the economic front was not enough; sex inequality must be part of the socialist struggle if women's emancipation was to become part of the socialist future.[80]

Even socialist feminists were not of one ideological mind: ethical socialists might place more hope in transforming human morality, Marxists on transforming economic structures. Marxist socialist feminists did have a finely developed theoretical explanation for women's oppression, rooted in the writing of Engels, who explained the precise moment of the "world historic defeat" of women. It may seem perplexing that women cast their lot with socialist parties that seemed to exude masculinist intellectual superiority and could not shake off ideas of natural sexual difference. However, one reason Marxist theories appealed was their grounding in history: they promised women hope, since social and gender relations were not ordained by God or fixed in time but rather evolved historically and might be altered by human agency.

Few socialist and labour feminists clung to one undeviating political groove; more often, their ideas evolved as they read, organized, and rethought positions. Some collaborated with other feminists on select issues: Mary Cotton Wisdom endorsed temperance, and Burns was active in the suffrage movement, even though the SPC rejected both of these causes. Socialist and labour feminists did often stress issues of women's work, defining feminism *as* a labour question: women's right to economic self-sufficiency, to live with their families decently and with dignity, was central to their vision of emancipation. For women, earning respect through labour was emancipating, if not emancipation, a view not unlike the thinking of Enlightenment feminists.

Like Enlightenment feminists, too, labour and socialist feminists' thinking betrayed a deep-seated orientalism, assumptions of white, British superiority, and a complete lack of interest in addressing the dispossession of Indigenous women. A minority spoke out against the nativism directed against maligned "foreigners," but many others did not challenge the dominant image of nation that marginalized women of colour and exalted white, settler, Eurocentric government. For socialist women, like the suffragists discussed in the next chapter, racialized women were primarily objects of charity, aid, or assimilation, not sisters in a struggle for a transformed world.

3 Women, Democracy, and Suffrage

In 1898, women from the Akwesasne and Caughnawaga reserves petitioned the federal government to restore their democratic rights. The Department of Indian Affairs was determined to institute Western-style elections for reserve band councils. In Akwesasne, Ottawa resorted to force to impose its policy: police were brought onto the reserve, and an Indigenous protester was killed. Calling on "our noble and gracious mother, the Queen of England," Haudenosaunee women pleaded with the federal government and the governor general to recognize their communities' existing expression of democracy: the ancient rights of clan mothers to appoint and depose life chiefs, based on assessments of their moral and political behaviour. Akwesasne women pointed to the destructive "ill feeling" the government had caused within the reserve, and, well aware of Western patriarchal ideals, asked that they not be dismissed as "mere women":

> We have considered the elective system as not being intended for us Indians and we would therefore return to our old method of selecting our life chiefs according our Constitution of Iroquois Government. As your Excellency must know, the ancient custom of creating life chiefs is that they are selected according to the different clans ... [by clan mothers] ... But if any misdemeanor shall offend their clans, these women first hold council with the women of their own clan, and if they find his offense of sufficient strength

> to warrant his resignation, these women will call upon the men members of their clan and they meet and select another member to represent them.[1]

It will not surprise any reader that their voices went unheeded, but their petition reminds us that the concepts of democracy and good governance have been defined differently by women from distinct cultures. Many settler women brought with them western European, Enlightenment-influenced ideals of rights, citizenship, and equality. Indigenous women and men had pre-existing ideals and practices of governance, though both settler and Indigenous traditions changed over time. This chapter's exploration of democracy, women's rights, and suffrage reveals both parallel and distinct experiences of colonized and settler women as well as interconnected relations of colonial, racial, gender, and class power that divided these groups.

By the late nineteenth and early twentieth centuries, settler women measured democracy by their access to, or denial of, economic and legal rights. The vote became the ultimate symbol of women's dignity, equality, and autonomy, and of their valued integration into the Canadian polity, as well as a marker of their sovereign personhood. Women's suffrage was an ideal shared across class and race divisions, although there were significant ideological rifts in the movement, with each group embracing different definitions of citizenship, rights, and democracy. Feminism and democracy were not automatic allies – their relationship constituted an ongoing debate.

Indigenous Women and Democratic Governance

Aboriginal rights, James Henderson reminds us, are grounded in Indigenous peoples' own jurisprudence, world views, and moral reasoning, all distinct from Eurocentric discourses. Emanating from relationships with families, communities, and the land, Indigenous jurisprudence draws on cumulative Indigenous knowledge systems and epistemologies, and is expressed through culture, language, ceremony, and practice. When Europeans arrived, Indigenous nations were self-governing sovereign entities, although, across Canada, Indigenous cultures were (and are) multiple and variable. Still, scholars point to some commonalities in their jurisprudence: law is interactive and cumulative, relies heavily on oral traditions, is intertwined with spirituality, and incorporates a belief in the practice of consent and participation.[2] Also, First Nations jurisprudence, like Indigenous Knowledge, is rooted in an ecology that takes into account "the relationship of living beings (including humans) with one another and the environment."[3]

Enlightenment feminist understandings of rights, grounded in individual equality, autonomy, and freedom, and increasingly encoded in "legalistic and adversarial theories" of law,[4] were different from the conceptualization of individual responsibilities and collective reciprocities in Indigenous jurisprudence. Overgeneralization is, of course, risky. As Mohawk scholar Marlene Brant Castellano reminds us, Indigenous gender roles and governance were far from uniform across Canada: it is erroneous to assert a blanket "myth of female dominated matriarchy."[5] Different forms of kin organization (patrilineal and matrilineal) and social organization existed, ranging from the Mohawk Confederacy described above to Pacific West Coast societies where Indigenous women's access to status and sexual autonomy far "exceeded" that of settler women, though it still depended on their high or low rank in hierarchically ordered societies. Even within the Haudenosaunee (Six Nations), different spiritual traditions evolved, with Christian Indigenous women leading distinct projects of community building.[6]

Although gender roles differed across Indigenous nations, women's active participation in governance, ranging from formal decision making to informal advising, was often commented on as unusual, remarkable, or abnormal by settler newcomers. On the West Coast, as Jean Barman observes, Nootka and Kwantlen women expressed their agency in ways "not incompatible with what we call feminism": these women "took themselves seriously, acted independently, valued their roles as comparable or equal to men's."[7] Other Indigenous women were similarly vocal in the public sphere of politics, defending their communities and protesting colonial rule. In mid-nineteenth-century Ontario, Anishinaabe writer, teacher, and advocate Catherine Sutton (Nahneebahwequa) counselled Indigenous bands about their rights as well as petitioning the queen to protest her own family's dispossession.[8] At the turn of the century, Jane Constance Cook was a formidable political presence within her Gixsam (British Columbia) community, making repeated remonstrations to the federal government about issues related to land, law, and marriage. Cook demanded justice from colonial powers for "taking the land away from us without proper compensation," and protested what she saw as the local Indian agent's unjust decisions on Gixsam marriage practices. Cook was, at the time and historically, admonished for supporting the colonizers' ban on the potlatch, but, as a recent reappraisal shows, she was animated by her concern for the negative effects of "male customary power" in potlatch practices on women and children.[9]

Figure 3.1 Jane Constance Cook was an advocate for her Gixsam community, protesting to the federal government about various issues affecting the community | Courtesy of the Royal BC Museum and Archives, H-07220.

Indigenous women's independence and sexual autonomy were deeply threatening to the Eurocentric world view vigorously promulgated by missionaries and the state, both of whom were engaged in efforts to impose more "civilized" Christian patriarchal laws on Indigenous nations. The clan mothers' role in selecting Haudenosaunee chiefs was a continual thorn in the side of colonial and Canadian authorities, who contemptuously referred to women's leadership as "petticoat government."[10] Despite the creeping influence of Western gender ideals in their community, Six Nations women of the longhouse defended their right to select and "dehorn" (remove) male leaders, appealing directly to the king in 1909 to preserve this right. They preferred their Confederacy governance to Western democracy: "we are not seeking a white man's Government, with its annual Scramble for place, position and power and the incidents of bargaining, vain promises and corruption."[11]

Haudenosaunee traditional governance fascinated a small enclave of nineteenth-century American feminists on the Eastern Seaboard, in part because it seemed to substantiate what *they* wanted to prove: the historical existence of matriarchal societies, evidence of women's equal community power, and the harmful impact of patriarchal Christianity on women's status. Indigenous governance buttressed the "natural rights" argument for suffrage: that "women were equally human and equally entitled to a voice in government."[12] Drawing on historical and anthropological writing as well as their own connections to Indigenous peoples in upstate New York, suffragists Lydia Maria Child, Matilda Joslyn Gage, and Elizabeth Cady Stanton published laudatory descriptions of "Iroquois" (Haudenosaunee) gender relations and government, claiming "the division of power between the sexes" in their society "was nearly equal."[13] Women ruled over the longhouse in large part because they oversaw food production and councils of war; property and descent were "traced fully through the mother."[14]

In contrast to American women, Iroquois women could divorce, had control over their bodies, and rarely experienced domestic violence. Gage placed the blame for white American women's downfall squarely on institutionalized religion, particularly Western Christianity, for promulgating degrading, misogynist doctrines of women's inherent sinfulness and inferiority. Of course, feminists' praise for Indigeneity was contradictory. Stanton was no anti-racist – she was later unsympathetic to African-American voting rights – and Gage situated matrilineal governance in the past, believing Indigenous women now needed the helping hand of their white colonial sisters.

In 1900, Mohawk–English-Canadian poet Pauline Johnson tried to enlighten Canadian women about Six Nations women's political leadership in order to contradict the misconception that "Indian men look down on and belittle" First Nations women. Haudenosaunee women's role in their "great council and public affairs" showed the esteem they commanded. "Not all civilized races honour their women as highly as do the stern old chiefs, warriors and braves of the Six Nations Indians,"[15] wrote Johnson, although she situated Haudenosaunee women's cultural "superiority" over that of their "less fortunate [Indigenous] sisters." After Pauline's death, her sister Evelyn similarly defended the Confederacy, claiming it was "rapacious greed" for Indigenous land that led to the federal attacks on traditional governance.[16]

Canadian suffragists may have admired Pauline Johnson's poetry, but they were disinclined to heed her political views. They rarely, if ever, alluded to the Six Nations Confederacy – or any other Indigenous nation – as an example of women's equality, past or present. Most shied away from a forceful critique of patriarchal Christianity implied by a matriarchal past, and few drew attention to Gage's theories. Moreover, an organized suffrage movement emerged in Canada in the 1880s as white settlement, Indigenous dispossession, and racism intensified in the aftermath of the 1885 rebellion. Although few white women could legally claim western homesteads of their own, they nonetheless benefited from the overall dispossession of Indigenous land. They shared with settler men a colonial view of "progress": superior, white, European and British rural settlements should naturally replace backward transient "Indian tribes."

More contemporary feminist and socialist appraisals of Canadian law have developed strong critiques of European rights-based equality premised on individual freedom or liberty; they argue that liberating the individual from unfair, discriminatory constraints does not generate substantive equality since oppression is never just "individual" but rather is the product of social relations of power often ignored or masked in formal law.[17] However, late nineteenth-century thinking was different. The suffrage movement looked primarily to Eurocentric concepts of individual rights, and the colonial context militated against the coexistence of two equal, parallel concepts of good governance, one Indigenous, one Western. Politicians of the time believed Western notions of rights and governance were more advanced – both more civilized and more democratic. Ironically, settler men decreed Western gender ideology to be superior, even as they withheld political and legal rights from all women. In 1885, during the first substantial parliamentary debate about extending a limited vote to Indigenous peoples and women, politicians voiced both of these contradictory colonial and patriarchal views.

Colonialism, Gender, and Limited Democracy

In the public eye, voting rights became mediations on women's proper social role. Women's suffrage had been debated before 1885, not only by abolitionist Mary Ann Shadd Cary but also by politicians establishing the limited democracy of responsible government. In Upper and Lower Canada and the Maritimes, a few intrepid women attempted to vote in nineteenth-century elections. In Canada West (Ontario), Laura Secord's daughter and six other widowed landholders cast ballots in West Halton in 1845, though their votes were successfully challenged by the defeated Reform candidate.[18] Women voting attracted critical attention. Often it was assumed they were political naïfs, easily manipulated by men; in such cases, politicians objected to what they saw as the unscrupulous exploitation of the weaker sex. In Nova Scotia, an outraged candidate complained contemptuously that his opponent was "getting up all the old women and old maids and everything in the shape of petticoats to the hustings" to defeat him.[19] Lower Canadian (Quebec) women also voted, and in significant numbers; in 1832, in Montreal women property owners made up 14 percent of the electorate, though many had to defend their credentials in the face of criticism.

By 1849, provincial legislatures had closed off the constitutional loopholes women voters had slipped through.[20] Constitutions had referred to electors as "persons" with property; legislation now explicitly banned women from voting. These changes sailed through legislatures without controversy, but it seemed especially ironic that the 1837 rebellion and Patriote leader, Louis-Joseph Papineau, whose own mother had once voted, avidly promoted women's exclusion from the "public display" associated with rowdy electioneering. It was "odious," he wrote, "to see wives dragged to hustings by their husbands, daughters by their fathers, often against their wishes. The public interest, decency, and the natural modesty of the female sex demands these scandals not be repeated."[21] Rather than address the violence, bribery, drunkenness, and riots associated with the worst of electioneering, legislators' solution was to restrict women to the privacy of the home.

Women had other avenues for political participation. In New Brunswick, petitioning the legislature was common; soldiers' widows petitioned for pensions and teachers for their salaries, and, once women organized collectively, they petitioned en masse for reforms such as temperance. Women were hardly the manipulated political naïfs of some men's imaginings: they read newspapers, attended political rallies, and discussed politics with male kin and confidants, sometimes lobbying them to take a particular stance.[22] Those who commanded power because of their connections, wealth, and influence were known to use the same back channels of influence that men did. Poor, farm, and working-class women were more likely to join their menfolk in public demonstrations, rallies, and marches, as they demanded bread for their families' survival, rent relief, or even revolution.

Nineteenth-century debates about the vote were shaped by these same wealth differentials, particularly property ownership. Extending the vote was part of a British strategy to establish imperial ownership over Indigenous land, thus aiding white settlement. In mid-nineteenth-century British Columbia, a very small white settler minority voted, but the Indigenous majority did not: cheap land and the franchise for settlers (though initially excluding the "lower-class" gold miners) ensured white-dominated settlement geared toward the "proper" economic development of land and resources. The same connection emerged on the Prairies – as a mark of a citizen's stake in society, property ownership bestowed the right to vote.

Yet, property ownership was constructed upon the bedrock of Indigenous dispossession.[23]

In the nineteenth century, property ownership, income level, or payment of a certain level of rent gave most men the right to vote across the country, prompting suffragists to ask: If property was the key to political rights, did it matter whether a woman or a man owned it? Property ownership was a foot in the door for suffragists, who claimed some victories by the early twentieth century as certain provices and municipalities gave single and widowed female property owners municipal voting rights – even though, in Ontario, this was linked to the Protestant majority's fear of Catholic voting power. Still, local victories provoked women to demand more. In 1902, a highly organized English-French coalition in Montreal, led by Marie Lacoste Gérin-Lajoie, stymied a campaign to disenfranchise tax-paying women tenants who, along with widows and single women property owners, had voted since the late nineteenth century. Their subsequent successful mobilization of women voters for municipal reforms spurred new efforts to secure federal and provincial voting rights.[24]

Property was also important to the 1885 parliamentary debate initiated when Prime Minister John A. Macdonald proposed expanding the electorate to include widowed and single women property holders and Indigenous men who owned individual property and had made improvements on it.[25] Neither the Liberals nor the Conservatives suggested universal suffrage (one person one vote). In the earlier Confederation debates, both parties had rejected this dangerous concept, warning that such unchecked or "unbridled" democracy would engender "mob rule" and disorder, and lay behind the "sad spectacle" of civil war in the United States.[26]

The prospect of women voters found limited support from both parties. The small group of Conservatives who favoured suffrage reform saw distinctions between the propertied and the non-propertied as more critical than gender ideology, while some Liberals, in contrast, supported the idea as a corrective to "injustice" and part of the natural march of Enlightenment progress and the expansion of "natural rights" to women.[27] One member of Parliament asked how the vote could be given to "one half the human race but not to the other half."[28] Moral reformers also hoped women voters might help to purify politics, pressing for temperance and "moral, social and religious reform."[29]

Far more MPs of both parties found the idea disturbing. They feared that allowing "spinster" voters might be the thin edge of the wedge, opening the door to the calamity of full female suffrage or, even more unimaginable, women running for office. One MP asked incredulously whether legislators could really fathom extending the vote to "squaws" and Chinese women who owned property but not to the white "mothers of this country." Clearly, he posed the question for shock value, projecting his idealized, racist image of white mothers of the nation.[30] Some men had no desire to see moral purity and temperance intrude in the House of Commons, while many opponents argued that even a restricted female electorate was a slippery slope that would destabilize the family, endanger marital relations, and invert the God-given order of society. Men, as heads of households, spoke for and "protected" women, who did not need, or even want, voting rights. Social catastrophe loomed in some men's minds. One MP fretted that the vote would "unsex" and masculinize women, turning them into unattractive "Amazons,"[31] while a Quebec MP prophesied "indescribable trouble and social disorder," like that unleashed by the ungodly female insurgents in the French Revolution.[32]

Given the vociferous objections, especially from Quebec, Macdonald quickly abandoned this proposal. Debate over an expanded Indigenous vote was more heated. At the time, most provinces prohibited "Indian" people, though not Métis, from voting. Most Indigenous people were disqualified because they did not hold the required individual property but rather held property collectively on reserves. Indigenous leaders were of two views: Peter Jones, an Ontario Ojibway minister and chief, supported the legislation, while the Six Nations, cognizant of their autonomy and nationhood, did not. Since the time of the Gradual Civilization Act of 1857, status Indians were enfranchised as British subjects only if they gave up their Indian status – that is, their right to live on reserves, collect treaty payments, and endow their children with Indian rights. Enfranchisement was a synonym for cultural obliteration.[33] Wives had no choice in the matter: if their husbands became enfranchised, they and their children lost their status too.

The enfranchisement bill that Macdonald's government proposed allowed enfranchised Indigenous men to keep their Indian status, primarily as a long-term strategy for assimilation. Macdonald, like many other politicians, believed that the "Indian problem" would be solved if Indigenous people adopted the values of white civilization, exemplified by their accumulation of property. "Indians" had to replace their "nomadic habits" with "industry and ambition."[34] If they insisted on laying claim to their communal lands, they could simply be starved into submission, as the government was doing in the prairie West.[35]

A few unusual political voices advocated humane treatment of Indigenous people or suggested the vote might be restitution for their loss of land, but they were drowned out by claims that Indigenous people were wards of the state; "primitives" without morality, government, and laws, in contrast to white men, who were modern, rational, and educationally and intellectually advanced. The recent Indigenous rebellion in the West exacerbated this hostility, as the English-Canadian press tended to portray all "Indians" as disloyal and violent.[36] Although Macdonald's reform passed, the western provinces lobbied successfully to limit new Indigenous voters to men living east of Manitoba. The project of a white settler Canada was thus safeguarded.

The debate about votes for women and Indigenous men proceeded along parallel lines, though there were connected concerns. Both status Indians and women were deemed minors, in reality if not in the eyes of the law; in the eyes of the state, they were dependent, child-like, incapable of knowledgeable participation, and perhaps uninterested in the vote. Status Indians were wards of the state; women wards of the paternal familial order. Race and gender were also intertwined in the indignant arguments of MPs who queried why less civilized Indigenous people should vote, when some of our "noble [white] young men" and "our intelligent women" could not.[37] Moreover, the treatment of women in white settler communities was deployed as evidence of the superiority of their civilization, in comparison to the practices of "bloodthirsty barbarians."[38] MPs ignored or misrepresented Indigenous gender relations, including the participatory role women assumed in their own governance, claiming instead that Indigenous men were guilty of "brutal" mistreatment and exploitation of "their" women.[39] One BC MP cited the horror of "orgies" at potlatch ceremonies in the province – ceremonies banned by the state the year before – as confirmation of the familial and sexual perversity and backwardness in Indigenous cultures.[40]

Voting rights were the subject of parliamentary debate again in 1898, when the Liberal government revised the franchise in favour of provincially based eligibility criteria that created an even more limited racial order; Indigenous men with status were now disqualified by provincial voting restrictions. Women's suffrage was not even given serious consideration. Political conflicts over whether federal or provincial electoral eligibility rules should govern voting were, on one level, partisan divisions between Conservative centralizers and Liberal decentralizers. However, both sides presumed some underlying cultural assumptions about good government. Both parties favoured a restrictive, not full democracy, and the ruling elites assumed that capitalism and the individual accumulation of wealth drove economic progress. Indigenous life, stressing communal landholding and the redistribution of wealth, was thus a deterrent to development. Both Liberals and Conservatives envisioned a state that would legislate to protect values they held dear, relating to white settlement, economic development, morality, gender roles, and the patriarchal family. These shared cultural assumptions about state formation resulted in the political exclusion of newcomers of Asian descent, women, and most Indigenous people.

The Alliance of Anti-Feminism and Anti-Democracy

By the mid-1880s, working- and middle-class women were congregating in organizations to secure enhanced legal, occupational, and economic rights, such as access to higher education and the professions, the right to their own wages and property, and custody of their own children. Women's demands for formal democratic rights, most notably the vote, marked a new chapter in feminist history. Their political work required resilience and courage to endure public ridicule and sometimes family disapproval. Anti-feminism was a robust ideological force that portrayed women equality seekers as unreasonable, unknowledgeable, even unbalanced; they were overturning the gender order, rejecting their prescribed feminine roles, and endangering the very existence of the family. Although anti arguments were varied, and sometimes contradictory, they focused on five overarching rebuttals of feminist claims: innate sex differences required separate spheres for men and women; women should concentrate solely on maternity, domesticity, and family care; tradition and order (and, for Anglos, the British Empire) must be preserved; only men could wage war; and culture and religion (especially Catholicism, for francophones) decreed women's proper role. Antis were often fearful of challenges not only to gender relations but also to existing class and racial hierarchies: they abhorred the idea of unrestricted democracy for all. Anti-feminism, in short, was a repudiation of full democracy.

Arguments against suffrage – indeed against all manner of women's rights – drew on prevailing ideals of femininity and masculinity, which antis interpreted as naturally ordained rather than culturally constructed: the existing gender order was the inevitable consequence of religion, biology, psychology, and tradition. Since women's natural functions were childbearing and childrearing, their social roles dictated domesticity and maternity. Citing science as their guide, antis drew on medical and psychiatric experts who claimed that women's reproductive systems and their psychologies shaped personalities that were sentimental, emotional, and less rational and inductive than men's. Some suffragists also accepted the idea that the home was women's primary domain; by character and inclination, women were innately suited to maternity and family care. However, suffragists turned separate spheres to their ideological advantage, claiming that women's familial responsibilities gave them important social insights that should inform public governance.

The most vocal and powerful English-Canadian antis were men of political influence and immense cultural capital: members of legislatures, intellectuals, university professors.[41] McGill university professor of the history of medicine Andrew Macphail backed up his anti-feminism with "science," while anti Stephen Leacock taught the "rational" discipline of political economy in the same institution. Known for his witty social commentary, Leacock used his acerbic pen to lampoon women reformers, whom he portrayed as bossy, puritanical, and controlling "Awful Women." His humour took a misogynist turn when he described what medieval society did with uppity women: drowned them in ponds and burned them at the stake.[42] Like many antis, Leacock saw women as intellectually inferior, unwelcome intruders in political life; they could not think creatively or lead others. Public intellectual Goldwin Smith, an Oxford historian and former member of the British Parliament who had relocated to Toronto, was slightly more generous, acknowledging women's "superior, angelic" moral character, but he nonetheless believed "perfect equality" was impossible as men's and women's worlds had to be "complementary" but resolutely separate.[43]

For Anglo imperialists such as Macphail and Leacock, women's suffrage was also incompatible with Canada's role in the British Empire. Men had to speak for the Empire, making all military decisions, and, since women did not take up arms, why did they deserve political rights? This version of empire also incorporated notions of white superiority. It was not only women who were unwelcome in antis' social Darwinist limited democracy: non-white "lesser races" (and for Smith, Jews) and the most impoverished, who were the authors of their own poverty, were also not fit to wield political rights.

Suffrage was a fundamental threat to a Catholic, French Quebec for French-Canadian antis such as Henri Bourassa, a member of Parliament; Jules-Paul Tardivel, editor of *La Vérité;* and Monsignor Louis-Adolphe Paquet, a clerical author. Religion and a conservative nationalism rather than Anglo imperialism shaped their anti-feminism. The arguments of clerics, intellectuals, and politicians stressed the potentially destructive impact of women's enfranchisement on the social order and the French nation more

Figure 3.2 One version of Stephen Leacock's reforming "Awful Woman." Anti-suffrage cartoons invariably compared overbearing feminists to hen-pecked men | *Toronto Daily Mail and Empire,* July 1899, in Charles Hou, *Great Canadian Political Cartoons* (Vancouver: Moody's Place Press, 1997)

than doctrine or principle. For many prominent French-Canadian antis, feminism was a foreign import to Quebec, a Trojan horse importing Protestant, individualistic, materialistic, Anglo-Saxon values. Both feminism and its political progeny, suffrage, were a "deviation from the Christian spirit" that would prove fatal to the traditional family, itself an anchor of the nation.[44] Feminism encouraged women's perverse and deluded "false ambition" to compete with men, wrenching them from their natural role as guardians of the home. As a "crime against nature," the vote would turn women into men: "the woman man, the hybrid and repugnant monster who will kill the woman-mother and woman-woman."[45] "Fadette," a woman columnist in the influential *Le Devoir* and cousin of Bourassa, echoed this fear that feminism transformed women into the hostile rivals of men. Better they should embrace their honoured separate sphere of familial care.

English-Canadian female anti-suffragists were similarly well situated socially, able to trade on their respectability, affluence, or connections to elites. Like Fadette, Cleminda Fessenden, the wife of an Anglican minister and an ardent supporter of the Imperial Order Daughters of the Empire (IODE), claimed in her newspaper columns that the Christian-directed "divinity" of motherhood would be degraded by women's political participation. She did depart from the views of male antis, in that she supported women's local reform efforts and did not ridicule and denigrate suffragists as did Leacock and others. However, she shared these men's imperialist and anti-democratic impulses: she warned of "race suicide" if white, middle-class women, distracted by politics, remained childless, and she saw poor women, more prone to neglectfulness and drunkenness, as incapable of making sound political decisions.[46]

Dissecting Fessenden's arguments helps explain the attraction of anti-feminism to women as well as men. References to the glory of empire were politically appealing for some white, middle-class settler women, and, perhaps most important, Fessenden stressed the under-recognized social value of women's motherwork and reassured women that the traditional male-headed family offered them protection from economic vulnerability and destitution. This pitch was not unlike that of reformer and crusader for domestic science education Adelaide Hunter Hoodless, who also opposed suffrage; she used her public profile to persuade women that their true influence and prestige lay in their essential familial roles.[47]

The Association Opposed to Woman Suffrage in Canada (AOWSC), a Toronto organization of primarily upper-class women, also shared the antis' anxiety about full democracy.[48] Though AOWSC women reiterated the separate spheres argument, they were not home bound, as servants did their domestic labour, leaving them time for social rounds and philanthropic endeavours. For women who might already have the ear of male elites, suffrage did not hold the same appeal as it did for middle-class women intent on expanding their opportunities for work and education or building a more caring welfare state in which they could play a prominent role. Affluent anti-suffrage women, in contrast, had a clear sense of their gender and class interests and were intent on protecting the privilege they had.

Given that legislatures across the country routinely defeated suffrage bills for over thirty years, the appeal of anti-democratic, anti-suffrage arguments should not be underestimated. Newspaper editors and journalists used the highly partisan press to mould public opinion. In Halifax, the provincial attorney general and editor of the *Acadian Recorder,* James Wilberforce Longley, utilized both his paper and his political office to promote his claims that suffrage would spell the end of the family. This "destruction of the family" argument was one of the most popular scare tactics in legislative debates, often coupled with a paternal version of a chivalrous democracy in which men spoke for and offered protection to the entire family. In New Brunswick, for example, Liberal premier William Blair adamantly opposed an 1894 suffrage bill promoted by pro-suffrage men, claiming suffrage violated the "laws of nature," and women themselves would be most injured: they would lose their gentle attributes if they were forced out of the family into the public fray.[49]

Inspiring the Suffrage Movement

Some suffragists shared the antis' distrust of full democracy, accepting restrictions on the vote based on property ownership, literacy, ethnicity, or race. A common lament was the unfair exclusion of white, Anglo-Celtic, *competent* women from the vote when non-British European immigrant men – who were illiterate, did not speak English, and came from backward cultures in which, according to common assumptions, women were treated poorly – had this right. While many suffragists accepted limited, property-based voting as a pragmatic foot in the door to a wider franchise for women, at the other end of the suffrage spectrum, some women advocated a more Enlightenment-inspired democracy in which *all* citizens had the "natural" right to participate in their self-governance. As the Canadian Suffrage Association wrote to the Ontario premier, no state could be called "democratic where half the community is governed and punished according to laws which they have neither helped to make nor agreed to submit to ... The vote is a right acquired through centuries of struggle for the recognition of human liberties and human self respect."[50] Suffragists also disagreed on the nature of human nature: some saw fixed biological and psychological differences between the sexes; others were eager to upend those cultural constructions.

Capturing the essence of such an intellectually diverse movement, especially one that changed significantly over a thirty-year period, is near impossible, but we can appraise a range of suffragist ideas about rights and democracy, asking what led women to a movement that their opponents claimed was extreme, foolish, and dangerous. By the turn of the century, suffrage support came from overlapping circles of ideas and people: a circle of feminists primarily devoted to women's intellectual, social, and economic equality; an overlapping circle of social reformers for whom the vote was a means to improve the lives of women, children, and families; and a third circle comprising the women's club and reform movement, including the umbrella organization that tried to knit all these disparate women together, the National Council of Women of Canada (NCWC). The NCWC grew stronger and more reform-minded in the early twentieth century; by 1912, it endorsed suffrage. The boundaries between these groups were porous, as women moved from one cause to another, altered their goals, or embraced multiple objectives.

Suffrage was, concurrently, a local, national, and international movement. Intellectually, Canadians were animated by religious, Enlightenment, democratic, temperance, and socialist ideas that circulated internationally, with some also influenced by transnational imperialist notions of white supremacy that urged the maintenance of a "colour line" between white and racialized peoples.[51] Organizationally, the Canadian movement was decentralized, reflecting regional economic, cultural, and linguistic differences within the nation; in contrast to the United Kingdom and the United States, one or two powerful national suffrage organizations did not dominate. Almost all Canadian suffragists, though, were influenced by transnational feminism: they followed international suffrage developments; were inspired by women's rights movements in Britain, Australia, New Zealand, continental Europe, and the United States; and claimed political sisterhood with suffragists elsewhere. Indeed, suffragists in the British colony (by 1907 Dominion) of Newfoundland looked eastwards, across the Atlantic for allies, orienting to the British Dominion Women's Suffrage Union and sending updates on their progress to *Jus Suffragii,* the newspaper of the European-based International Woman Suffrage Alliance.

However divergent women's intellectual and social backgrounds, their conversion to suffrage usually emerged from experience, conscience, and ideas: their witness to, or personal experience of, oppression and inequality; inspiring feminist ideas; and religious and moral commitments to social betterment. Suffragists were often made in struggles over discrimination and exclusion, as women experienced what they were *not* allowed to do, by law, convention, or force: attend university, become doctors, control their own bodies, earn equal pay, claim custody of their children, avoid, or have legal recourse to address, marital violence, choose work over marriage, keep their own wages, or simply assert their individuality. Feminists, as Australian historian Marilyn Lake puts it, "began to demand self possession."[52] Whether it was due to personal experience or witnessing discrimination, women became dissatisfied, outraged, and determined to change society.

Novel ideas inspired. The original impetus for suffrage organizations often came from working, educated, or intellectual women roused by international suffrage publications, political and philosophical writing, or visiting feminist lecturers. Although socialism was one route to suffrage, liberal Enlightenment ideas celebrating individual liberty, rights, and freedom were also important, not least because they fit well with the dominant ideals of the time. The constitution of the Toronto Suffrage Association anchored its founding principles in the writing of John Stuart Mill. Moreover, one rights struggle led to another; suffragists moved between campaigns for the vote, married women's right to own their own property, university education, access to professions, a living wage, and equal pay. Inspiring ideas were not always imbibed through dry treatises of political philosophy; women were moved to action through public performances, speakers, or their reading of fiction, journalism, drama, and humour. One of the most popular means of conveying feminist ideas was the mock parliament, a public performance in which women used irony and parody to portray a parliament in which roles were reversed, with men pleading with women legislators for equal rights. Clearly this form of propaganda worked, as suffragists replayed them across the country to enthusiastic crowds.

Suffragists were also impelled by commitments of conscience to collective social betterment: women spoke of their civic responsibility, public duty, and religious devotion in efforts to uplift, improve, or bring justice to the community. Violet McNaughton, Saskatchewan farmer, political organizer, and journalist, saw the vote as "our inalienable right as human beings" *and* as a means to improve farm women's lives.[53] Suffrage was inseparable from efforts to lighten the load of women's agricultural work, ensure the equitable distribution of marital property, and improve social supports to farm families.

Marie Gérin-Lajoie, founder of the Quebec reform coalition the Fédération nationale Saint-Jean-Baptiste (FNSJB), expressed a Catholic feminism that extolled women's duty to the less fortunate, combined with their maternal obligation to protect the family from social harm.[54] Like many Quebec suffragists, she concurred with nationalist anti-suffragists that women's familial role was their most cherished and important contribution, essential to the well-being of the Quebec nation: "La vie familiale reste pour la femme la vocation humaine la plus propre à lui procurer le bonheur," she wrote. "Ni la vie professionnelle ni la vie ouvrière ne peuvent satisfaire la coeur de la femme" (Family life is the most suitable human vocation for women to bring them happiness. Neither a working nor a professional life can satisfy the heart of women).[55] However, antis thought women should not cross the boundary between the private sphere of the family and the public sphere of politics, while Gérin-Lajoie believed the boundary was "artificial" and must be breached so that women could bring their maternal insight to bear upon political decisions.[56]

Conscience, experience, and novel ideas were intersecting motivations behind the suffrage activism of the remarkable "Misses Ritchie," three sisters – Ella, Mary, and Eliza – from a middle-class Halifax family whose single status and a small family bequest allowed them to devote their lives to cultural and educational causes, such as the local art college and public library; social reform, including public health, playgrounds, and child welfare; and women's rights. All three lived their lives within religious, cultural, and homosocial networks of women; all three laboured for charitable and reform causes, though Eliza left temporarily to attend Cornell, get a PhD, and teach at women's colleges in the United States. Not surprisingly, it was Eliza, who knew the limitations on professional women's lives first-hand, who was the most outspoken on women's employment issues, suggesting equal pay for teachers, better remuneration for workers, and reform of domestic servants' working conditions. All three were commited suffragists. Ella, who declared she was converted in 1868, helped found the first Halifax suffrage group in 1895; Eliza worked strenuously at the end of the Nova Scotia suffrage campaign in 1918.[57]

In contrast to the inspiration the Ritchies derived within a social improvement milieu, the commitment of labour and socialist suffragists to the vote emanated from their Marxist, ethical socialist, and labourite critiques of women's inequality and their profound disgust with the conditions of life for working-class women. Democracy was no less important to them, but their definition of democracy was premised on social and economic, as well as political, equality. Separating socialists from other feminists is especially fraught when discussing suffrage. Cross-class alliances and collaboration between socialist and reform suffragists did exist, apparently more in urban centres in Ontario, Manitoba, and British Columbia. In Winnipeg, the first English-Canadian suffrage group, the Equal Suffrage Club, included professional women and wives of trade unionists. These women made presentations to the local Labour Council, secured its support, and scored coverage for their ideas in the labour paper the *Voice*. In some cities, labour feminists were bridge builders, connecting unions and suffragists, helping to persuade the labour movement to support women's enfranchisement.

Cross-fertilization of ideas occurred, as many socialist feminists shared the maternalist view that women's familial concerns needed representation in politics: the vote was a means to tackle working-class women's problems, whether of low wages or lack of mothers' (widows') pensions. Moreover, socialist feminists' emphasis on women's economic autonomy resonated with some self-supporting professional women such as teachers or middle-class homemakers who understood that their lives might be suddenly rendered precarious through widowhood, family disinheritance, or an unemployed husband.

Socialist and labour organizing also bolstered the suffrage movement, especially in British Columbia. As Lara Campbell shows, BC socialist feminists were key movers and shakers in the "revolutionary wave" of suffrage organizing in that province. Support for suffrage extended from coal-mining communities on Vancouver Island to working-class communities in Vancouver, which had the only Canadian suffrage group led by and for working-class women, with its own identity, goals, and methods of agitating. The BC Women's Suffrage League (WSL), initiated by Helena Gutteridge, Bertha Merrill Burns, Nora Tutty, and Susie Lane Clark, included neighbourhood-based groups that met at night in venues like the Labour Temple, a space and time frowned upon by some middle-class suffragists, but fitting for women who worked during the day and did not have comfortable parlours to meet in. Children were welcome, a recognition that working-class women had no access to child care. Everything from local transit fares to critiques of the wage system was on the table for political discussion.

The WSL sponsored open-air meetings and pamphleted on street corners, with some members delivering "soapbox" suffrage speeches, a tactic that had a long socialist pedigree and was imitated by the British WSPU – though avoided by middle-class Canadian suffragists. An attempt to create a WSL newspaper faltered for financial reasons, but Susie Lane Clark, a former teacher, used her suffrage column in the *Vancouver Daily World* to highlight working-class activism and socialist ideas. Clark's critiques of capitalism and male domination were linked: profit-making compromised the health of women and children and was the cause of working women's "starvation wages," precisely the reason that male capitalists, the "moneyed interests" who benefitted from low wages, opposed women's equality.[58] Racial inequality, however, was not a concern; like many labour suffragists, she ignored Indigenous dispossession and opposed Asian immigration.

Early Suffrage Stirrings

Experience, intellect, and conscience were not discreet motivations: they might overlap, take on various accents, or occasionally be in tension. Women's conceptions of equality and democracy were also shaped by their class, ethnic, and religious backgrounds. Emily Stowe, her daughter Augusta Stowe-Gullen, and Maria Pollard Grant, who were drawn to suffrage in the late nineteenth century, are good examples of the motivational "messiness" of suffrage.

As we saw in Chapter 1, Dr. Emily Stowe's interest in suffrage was sparked by her Quaker upbringing, stressing the spiritual equality of men and women, and her own experience of discrimination in education and work. Barred from Canadian medical schools, she trained in the United States, where she encountered inspiring suffragist ideas and speakers. Returning to Canada, Stowe opened a practice in Toronto that ministered to women and children, often from the working classes, sharpening her consciousness of the desperate conditions of the urban poor. Stowe shared her intellectual feminist metamorphosis with like-minded company in the Toronto Women's Literary Club, which in 1883 became the Canadian Women's Suffrage Association (CWSA).

Stowe is often memorialized for her challenge to professional barriers, yet her ideas were more broadly unconventional, radical, and democratic. Sceptical of organized Christianity, she eventually embraced Theosophy, an alternative spiritual perspective based on religious equality, optimistic idealism, and an inclusive, universal humanity. She was also critical of extreme income inequality, undoubtedly influenced by friends in Toronto's radical intellectual elite, including Knights of Labor journalist T. Phillips Thompson. Stowe spoke of women's commitment to social betterment, organizing efforts to improve the working conditions in shops and factories, yet she also spoke in a liberal language of individual opportunity, particularly with respect to women's right to education. She helped organize the campaign to force the University of Toronto to open its classes to women, including her daughter, Augusta Stowe-Gullen, who trained as a doctor in Toronto and became a leading suffragist.

Advocating for suffrage, Stowe highlighted the unique moral insights of mothers, yet maternity was not everything: she blended motherhood with a radical democratic view of individual rights. Appealing for the vote before the Ontario legislature in 1889, Stowe combined multiple justifications: "as educated citizens and moral and loving women, we desire to be placed in the position to impress directly our thoughts on our nation. The invidious distinction of sex is an arbitrary and artificial one, having no foundation in reason or common sense. Motherhood should leave the woman free to choose her vocation as does her brother man."[59]

Although able to access medical school, Augusta Stowe-Gullen faced the disparaging rebukes of her fellow male medical students, who teased and "hated her unmercifully."[60] Coming from a family that valued political courage and feminist activism, she had the stamina to persist with unusual life choices and the confidence to speak in public. Stowe-Gullen stepped into the Toronto suffrage leadership after her mother died. At first glance, she seemed not to gravitate toward any one political philosophy: she was active in the very respectable liberal reform group the Local Council of Women but was also one of the first to endorse Socialist Party candidate Margaret Haile in the 1902 provincial election. Like many suffragists across these political boundaries, she claimed women would use their votes to address urgent social and moral problems.

Her most passionate words described a more egalitarian social order in which women could exercise intellectual freedom and pursue education and meaningful work. It is ironic, she wrote, that men were quite content to see women labour at back-breaking jobs like farming but then suddenly invoked women's weaker biological nature when denying them access to professions. While not critical of marriage as were some sex radicals, Stowe-Gullen was critical of marriage as women's *only* goal in life: "all girls should be taught some avocation in life, whether it be as housewives, doctors, lawyers, ministers, artists, farmers or dressmakers, depending upon the desires and intelligent capabilities of the individual ... Do not educate your daughters to think that marriage is the Alpha and Omega of their earthly career, but rather a happy incident in their life's work, and then women will only marry from the highest and purest motives."[61] Stowe-Gullen put her words into action. Elected to the Toronto School Board in 1892, she pursued a forthright feminist agenda on women's work. She and a fellow female trustee scotched a resolution that barred women from the position of principal in larger schools, called for equal pay for teachers, and opposed the moralistic efforts of male trustees to dictate female teachers' dress by banning the popular bloomer.

If Stowe-Gullen was an advocate for professional and working women, Maria Pollard Grant represented social conscience and maternal duty, though she also voiced liberal, egalitarian, and democratic values. Grant also began her suffrage journey in the 1880s. Brought up in a family of reform-minded Methodists, she listened to American suffragist Susan B. Anthony lecture in Victoria in 1871, but it was the visit of the founder of the Woman's Christian Temperance Union (WCTU) in the United States, Frances Willard, in 1883 that encouraged Grant, her mother, and others to form a chapter of WCTU and begin women's suffrage agitation. Within two years, members were petitioning the legislature for women's voting rights, and Grant's WCTU work eventually led to her prominent role in the more broadly based suffrage organization the Political Equality League (PEL), established in 1910.

Many suffragists shared Grant's commitment to the WCTU. Whether they advocated for individual abstinence or outright banning of the sale of alcohol, anti-alcohol politics were a direct pathway to suffrage. Explaining the immense popularity of the WCTU has generated historical contention. While some point to the movement's penchant for white women's middle-class moralizing about the drinking habits of immigrant and working-class men, others take at face value the WCTU claim that they were combating women's economic vulnerability and the scourge of domestic violence. Alcohol, the WCTU claimed, was at the root of family destruction; men squandered their wages at the saloon and returned home to batter their wives and children.[62]

As a respectable moral crusade, the WCTU gave women permission to criticize the male-dominated family, the sexual double standard, and women's subordination in political decision making; however, multiple motives characterized this international movement, which took on different regional and religious hues across urban and rural spaces. The WCTU's working-class opponents understandably resented the class-biased portrayal of violence and drunkenness as working-class, immigrant vices. Yet, the WCTU platform also elicited some trade union support; both temperance and labour advocates agreed that women needed a living wage to prevent prostitution, and, in British Columbia, both endorsed anti–Chinese immigration positions. Sympathy for temperance as a form of "family protection" came from many quarters: socialists such as Mary Cotton Wisdom endorsed it, and, as Lara Campbell shows, those signing WCTU petitions in Victoria included African Canadians, Métis descendants of fur traders, and Jews, as well as the more predominant white, Protestant, middle-class membership.[63] Temperance also generated male support for enfranchisement; suffrage legislation was tabled in British Columbia and Nova Scotia by legislators sympathetic to temperance – in Nova Scotia, six bills were attempted in the 1890s, some reaching the second-reading stage.

Maria Grant initially developed her suffrage convictions through temperance, religion, reform, and social betterment; for her, using the vote was a moral imperative as much as a political right. Like many social gospel Christians, her faith stressed social, not simply individual, salvation; the "Kingdom of God" had to be built on earth through human compassion and social

Figure 3.3 There was a direct pathway from the WCTU to the suffrage movement. Male temperance allies often supported women's suffrage bills in provincial legislatures | University of Calgary Archives and Special Collections

justice.[64] While most social gospel feminists favoured respectable charity or ameliorative reforms, the more radical few were critical of capitalism. Grant's friend and fellow suffragist Florence Hall, who worked as a PEL organizer in the BC interior and penned a column, "Suffragette Sermons" for a Methodist newspaper, stressed the spiritual equality of men and women before God but also condemned the destructiveness of capitalism, which "cheapened humanity because it valued profit more than human lives."[65]

Like many suffragists who saw the vote as a means to social reform, Grant was devoted to causes intended to aid the less fortunate, including day nurseries, children's aid societies, and homes for unwed mothers. However middle-class women's social reform goals were often elitist and class inflected; these women were more intent on instructing than emancipating working-class women and tended toward critical "moralizing" about the working-class family. Their notion of social betterment might also involve the "uplift" of non-Anglo immigrants, whom they believed should (and could) assimilate into the more progressive, democratic values of British culture. "Conscience," in other words, could be a synonym for superior moral regulation.

Yet social reform might also lead some women to point to the inadequacies or corruption of Canada's much vaunted democracy. Grant spoke of women's right to representation as citizens, and she ran for election as a school trustee, winning twice. When provincial legislation later rescinded some women's right to run for school boards, she and other members of the PEL mobilized, expressing their righteous feminist indignation, declaring that "justice cannot be left in the hand of men."[66] While she usually opted for respectable, gradualist reform, Grant expressed sympathy for the British suffragettes, refusing to "censure" their militant tactics despite the sharp disapproval of her views by both fellow suffragists and the public.[67]

Grant was a founder and editor of the PEL newspaper, *The Champion*. It provided a list of reasons why women should vote, beginning with the most basic egalitarian argument, asserting women were "human beings" just as men were, but then adding a multitude of diverse rationales. Canadian women were as "intelligent, virtuous and public spirited" as they were in countries where they had the vote; they paid taxes; they were wealth creators, mothers of citizens, well educated; they understood the home; they would introduce equal pay; and, of course, their moral intentions meant that

Figure 3.4 The cover of *The Champion*, a newspaper published by BC suffragists, used a British image that reflected feminist reformers' belief that they were aiding and uplifting less fortunate women | *The Champion*, August, 1912

"women's ballots are feared by evil doers" (presumably liquor and other corrupt interests).[68] Much PEL writing in *The Champion* drew on maternal feminist and reform arguments, but it also embraced liberal-egalitarian rationales, including the classic "British liberty" line of reasoning – that is, that Britain had birthed a unique parliamentary democracy in which arbitrary power was in check and citizens were equal before the law. Women – white British women, that is – had a claim on this "natural" right to liberty: "Is it [not] a question of mere justice that women who bear their part in the burdens and responsibilities of citizenship should not share its privileges and its scope?" the newspaper asked rhetorically.[69] Like the movement, then, *The Champion* employed an assemblage of suffrage arguments – maternal, liberal, religious, radical – in attempting to create an alliance of many voices, though these invariably excluded racialized and non-Anglo immigrant women.

Suffrage Ideas in Twentieth-Century Canadian Journalism

As social reformers swelled the ranks of the suffrage movement in the first decade of the twentieth century, its ideological tenor shifted. The more audible public voices were increasingly those of women with education, class confidence, and access to social and professional networks of influence. Their employment of domestic servants also gave them the time to "do" politics. Political declarations about women's moral and maternal duty to clean up corruption, combat social decay, and act as "social housekeepers" became more voluble, not the least because the women's club movement, exemplified by the NCWC, was becoming more influential.

This social maternalism adroitly incorporated the dominant gender ideology into its progressive platform, but was still limited by a rigid race- and class-based view of gender roles and ideals. Appeals to women's individual, democratic rights were sometimes drowned out by claims that women voters would help construct a more moral, productive, vigorous nation in which "British" values – and, implicitly, a white population – prevailed. Efforts to aid working-class women with refuges, mothers' allowances, and day nurseries were justified with a discourse of moral uplift rather than one promulgating the rights of all women.

Nowhere was this tendency toward elitism more troubling than in the promotion of eugenics, a notion of "better breeding" that called for limitations on the reproduction of the "unfit." Eugenics was not a unilateral feminist aim; it was a debate. Catholic French-Canadian suffragists did not embrace it; some English-Canadian suffragists were sceptical; and socialist feminists worried about its links to elite men's railings against "race suicide" – that is, the fear that middle-class, white, Anglo, Protestant women were not reproducing as rapidly as "undesirable" populations. Yet eugenics had many suffragist proponents. One of the most vociferous was Emily Murphy, a popular writer and later magistrate, who successfully lobbied with others for legislation to prevent the "unfit" from having children. In Murphy's mind, forced sterilization was an unquestioned social good: it would protect society from the promiscuous and irresponsible sexual reproduction of the infirm, criminals, and those who were a financial burden on society.[70] The targets of such eugenic regulation were inevitably racialized, poor, and working class.

Despite this trend toward social reform, the suffrage movement still had ideological breadth: there was no one feminist point of view. The work of early twentieth-century suffragist journalists reveals how, even as social reform rhetoric ramped up, democratic, radical, and socialist ideas were still in play. The printed word was fundamental to the spread of feminism. The initiated read suffrage newspapers from Britain and the United States, but many women discovered suffrage through "women's columns" in local, mainstream papers. Much like the talented Ethelwyn Wetherald, featured in Chapter 1, suffragists injected political commentary into a medium – the women's page – that was previously associated with fashion, romance, personal advice, and recipes.

Suffrage journalists often spoke for and to distinct occupational groups, ethnic communities, and regional readerships. Icelandic immigrant Margret Benedictsson edited and wrote for the longest-running pro-suffrage newspaper in Canada, *Freyja* (Woman), from 1898 to 1910. Born into rural poverty in Iceland, Benedictsson was fostered out at a young age, earning her keep through farm and domestic labour; in search of opportunity, she immigrated to the United States, where she laboured as a domestic and attended school. She became increasingly interested in progressive causes, including "free thought," which elevated rationalism, science, and humanism over accepted religious doctrine. After she moved to Winnipeg, she and her husband, Sigfus Benedictsson, a writer, publisher, and suffrage supporter, launched *Freyja,* which included news from Iceland and United States but also cultivated a feminist presence in the local Icelandic women's community. In 1908, Margret Benedictsson was named president of the new Icelandic women's suffrage association, Tilraum (Endeavour),[71] founded before the better-known Anglo-Canadian suffrage organization, the Political Equality League. Benedictsson, well aware that immigrant women's voices were overshadowed by those of Anglo-Celtic women, lamented the ethnocentric erasure of Icelandic women's political labour: "These highly esteemed ladies have considered it below their dignity to see the co-operation of the Icelandic nationality ... These English ladies no doubt expect little appreciation of a matter like this from a foreign nationality which has come from a remote and poor country."[72]

Benedictsson's own experience of economic struggle shaped her politics; she insisted, for instance, on better working conditions for labouring women and the need for adequate welfare so impoverished women could be self-sufficient. While she acknowledged the importance of women's maternal role, she was critical of the family as an institution, casting a more discerning eye than many other suffragists on its patriarchal underpinnings. Drawing on her unique blend of "liberalism, anti-clerical free-thought, anarchism and sex radicalism,"[73] she advocated for marriages built on cooperation and equality, even down to sharing domestic labour. And if marriages failed, women should have access to divorce (which she secured for herself). Along with socialist Dora Forster Kerr, Benedictsson was one of the very few free thinkers in Canada with unconventional views on women's right to sexual and marital equality. With no Canadian publication advocating these ideas, they read and occasionally contributed to the American anarchist magazine *Lucifer*, known for its "free love" views.

Benedictsson also dabbled in fiction. Her short stories expressed a decidedly working-class, immigrant understanding of multiple inequalities. In "The Widow," Benedictsson explores the agonizing choices faced by an impoverished mother who is unable to feed her children after the death of her husband. When she tries to give away his political book on human rights, hoping for some compassion at the very least, she encounters the mean-spirited hypocrisy of the affluent and respectable, including the local Christian minister. Class is determining for this mother, and religion is neither a refuge nor an expression of social conscience: it is part of a system of oppression.[74]

Women's rights and democracy were also debated in the prairie farm newspaper the *Grain Growers' Guide* (*GGG*), which endorsed women's suffrage from its inception in 1908. However, the first *GGG* women's columnist, Isabelle Beaton Graham, had a highly restrictive view of who deserved democratic rights. She led a call for homesteads for women, but only the "British born"; her campaign was scaffolded on xenophobic fear mongering about "ignorant, uncouth, lawless [male] foreigners"[75] securing homesteads in the West. Francis Marion Beynon, a subsequent editor of the *GGG* women's page, did not share Graham's discriminatory views of the "foreign born," but she initially appeared to be a conventional suffragist: she supported the WCTU, and her column relayed advice on women's farm and domestic work. However Beynon's column also offered more unconventional ideas. She shied away from the idealized picture of rural family contentment promoted in countless immigration recruitment posters for the West, instead pointing to the undervaluing of women's farm labour and their second-class legal status. She also raised controversial, often ignored, issues such as masculine violence in the family, as well as the perennial complaint that converted a number of prairie women into suffragists: a woman's lack of legal dower right to any share of the farm should her husband die. Indeed, a husband could sell the farm that family labour built without even consulting his wife. *GGG* cartoons and text lampooning John Tightwad, a patriarchal tyrant who owned the farm and excluded his wife from all financial decisions, elicited intense debate among *GGG* readers, not the least because it spoke directly to feminists' condemnation of this form of discrimination.[76] No matter how geographically isolated, correspondents to the *GGG* aired their views on legal reform, suffrage, and women's inequality in the family; their stream of letters became a form of "radical democracy" in action.[77]

If Beynon's rural upbringing shaped her world view, the lessons of earning a wage moulded the feminism of journalist Flora MacDonald Denison. Born in Belleville, Ontario, to a middle-class family that valued education but fell on hard times, she left school at fifteen to earn her keep. She experimented with a number of occupations – teaching, office work, and journalism – and sojourned in Detroit before returning to Toronto, where she set up her own small dressmaking business. Because Denison knew the hard knocks of earning a living, she sympathized with working women, including their unionization. She also had a son to support; her husband was often absent, her marriage of murky legal validity, likely one reason she was looked down on by some "society" suffragists. However, Denison was one of the most indefatigable suffrage builders, thinkers, and publicists. She nurtured strong international connections and was one of the few Canadian suffragists who philosophized about the meaning of democracy. First brought into the movement by Emily Stowe, Denison and Stowe's daughter, Dr. Augusta Stowe-Gullen, revived the flagging suffrage organization in Toronto in 1907, rebranding it the Canadian Suffrage Association (CSA). Denison served as president, travelled to promote it, and financially subsidized the Toronto office.

Denison's column "Under the Pines" in the *Toronto World* presented a lively dialogue about women's domestic and social roles, reform, and suffrage through a mélange of reporting, autobiographical anecdotes, storytelling, and opinions. Her writing was "personal, emotional, direct," conveying passion and idealism, including her fervent belief that a "revolutionary sisterhood of women," without divisions of "race, colour, caste or creed," could transform humanity.[78] When speaking about her international connections especially, Denison conveyed a sense of "radical happiness," a term later feminists used to convey the "joy of collective energy" binding women together in a common cause of social transformation.[79]

Both Enlightenment-inflected natural rights and maternal-based arguments structured her feminism. Democratic rights were the foundation for all "political liberty," as "those who obey the law should be able to have a voice in choosing those who make the law."[80] Women's "rightful inheritance" was that of all of humanity: "the opportunity to live their life to the fullest and highest extent and the right to earn a decent living."[81] Denison accented a woman's right to meaningful work, autonomy, and freedom, sharing with Benedictsson and Kerr a critique of patriarchal Christian dogma that subordinated women, denying them any right to divorce and birth control. Yet, she also believed that women were a "civilizing" force and that their "mother-hearted" concerns for women and children underwrote their political activism;[82] issues such as safe food, pure milk, urban sanitation, and the white slave trade necessitated that women have a voice in government. Denison urged women to use the vote to transform the conditions of motherhood for all, providing state-funded pensions for widows and child care centres for working mothers.

In 1911, Denison's renamed column, "The Open Road to Democracy," extended her discussion of the meaning of democracy. Women's vote must be the route to a greater end – not just a political democracy, but a "*social democracy* based on equal opportunity and justice ... [and] equality between the sexes."[83] Intellectually adventurous and well-read, Denison devised her political philosophy from radical texts on democracy such as Thomas Paine's *The Rights of Man* and the feminist theories of women's labour penned by Charlotte Perkins Gilman and Olive Schreiner. Denison was also deeply moved by poetry. She lamented that the world was still "trying to catch up" with the inspirational eighteenth-century Scottish poet of democracy and the common people, Robbie Burns, who "believed in the sacred rights of men, and if he were living today, he would be fighting women's battles."[84] Her most important influence, however, was nineteenth-century American poet Walt Whitman, whose writing on religion, humanity, and democracy spawned a cult-like Whitmanite following in North America and Britain.[85]

Figure 3.5 President of the Canadian Suffrage Association from 1911 to 1914, journalist Flora MacDonald Denison represented Canada at international suffrage events. Her photo was signed at "Bon Echo," where literati gathered to celebrate the work of poet Walt Whitman | Photograph by E. Lyont, Library of Congress, Manuscript Division, National Woman's Party Records, group 1, container I:149

Denison hosted Whitman-inspired retreats at the wilderness resort she ran at Bon Echo, north of Belleville. There, radical literati gathered to share poetry readings, listen to speakers, and talk of progressive politics; some, like Denison, were spiritualists, so séances might have transpired. "The stupidly respectable," Denison warned, tongue in cheek, "will not be at home in Bon Echo."[86] Her Bon Echo newsletter, *The Sunset of Bon Echo,* ruminated on Whitman's "divine democracy," which was to be constructed on the basis of dignity and respect for all souls. Rejecting organized religion in favour of a "pantheistic" spiritualism,[87] Whitman celebrated nature, human "empathy, love and compassion," brotherhood, and equality. His women followers were entranced with not only his feminist insistence on equality but also his sensuous, positive celebration of female sexuality and the body.[88] This was not the way of most suffragists, who still stressed the dangers, not the pleasures, associated with sexuality.

In Whitman-like fashion, Denison hoped that a democratic sensibility might transform personal as well as social relations. She often decried the snobbery associated with a "caste" (or class) society, undoubtedly having been on the receiving end of such snobbery. The family should become a "democracy of the home": parents should teach dignity and equality in everyday life so that children might be raised without any sense of superiority, never making others feel inferior.[89] Reflecting ideas animating multiple radical movements of the time, Denison's writing incorporated flashes of utopian hope and desire. Feminism and the "Great Spirit of Democracy," she surmised, might be the means to regenerate society entirely, a revolutionary solution to the spiritual alienation, material deprivation, and violence that plagued her own society.

Denison was more engaged with discussions of democracy than were other feminists, but all suffrage journalism in farm, labour, and more mainstream papers contributed to a dialogue about gender roles, equality, and representative democracy. Explicitly suffrage newspapers like *The Champion* (1912–14), published by the Victoria PEL, were rare and had a relatively small readership, but they nonetheless fashioned a feminist public sphere and space for debate, cultivating a feminist counterculture that sustained suffragists' sense of purpose, resolve, and optimism. Along with mock parliaments, cartoons, pageants, music, film, and fiction writing, feminist journalism created an oppositional ethos that both reflected and quickened suffragists' changing consciousness, cultivating a deep emotional feeling for the movement. *The Champion*'s international coverage reminded Canadians they were connected to a noble, international movement of like-minded (and not unreasonable, unbalanced) women. News from abroad showcased suffrage "success stories" from American states, Australia, and New Zealand, offering proof that peaceful suffrage organizing worked and that, once women voted, the "moral atmosphere had been purified" and countless reforms "dear to women's hearts" were enacted, from "Children's Courts ... to the Suppression of Indecent Advertising."[90]

The Champion covered employment, education, legal issues, PEL organizing in the BC hinterland, and suffrage events ranging from Halloween parties to public debates. Poems, editorials, letters to the editor, and a mock

Figure 3.6 Political Equality League float in Victoria. Canadian suffragists rarely organized demonstrations, though they participated in some civic parades | Courtesy of the Royal BC Museum and Archives, D-03976

men's column, "Our Men's Cozy Corner," with hints for men's attire, manners, and deportment, rounded out the content. Controlling the media message offered suffragists a delicious opportunity to turn the tables on anti-feminist, condescending, and sometimes misogynistic views of women in the mainstream press, cultivating a feeling of camaraderie that might push women into more daring public display. While Canadian suffragists were less demonstration-oriented than their British or American sisters, they edged toward more visible forms of dissent; PEL women staged controversial public debates, set up soapboxes at fairs, and held open-air meetings. In 1913, the PEL created a float for a parade in Victoria. It deployed suffrage symbolism to create a message of moral authority and optimism: led by women on white horses with trumpets, the float was flanked by male allies walking in suffragette colours while, on the float, a woman symbolizing "Liberty" held a laurel for victory, while other women draped in white represented countries and states where suffrage was a reality. Symbolism was a form of storytelling used by suffragists to create their own self-image, but their narratives also exposed their own prejudice and exclusionary perspectives. In *The Champion* and other western papers, suffragists often positioned themselves as white settler nation builders, heroic pioneers doing equal work with men opening up the frontier – simultaneously a story of Indigenous dispossession and supposedly superior British values.[91]

Milestones of Limited Democracy

In January 1916, Manitoba became the first province to pass women's suffrage legislation, followed by the other western provinces and Ontario in 1916–17. The Maritime provinces and Newfoundland followed suit between 1918 and 1925. Quebec was an outlier, waiting until 1940 (that struggle is discussed in the next chapter). Contrary to patriotic hype, in part encouraged by suffragists themselves, the vote was not "given" to women in recognition of their wartime loyalty and work. The First World War hastened this legislation in some contexts, but decades of suffrage organizing ensured that the foundation was already in place. As Beynon reminded her readers, this was no "easy victory" but rather the outcome of years of political "drudgery" by tireless workers who slowly but surely shifted public opinion and made strategic allies, including political parties that traded women's campaign support for the promise that they would introduce suffrage legislation when elected.[92] Once the first few provinces conceded, other premiers who were long-time antis followed suit, anxious to be on the right side of history. The federal vote was a more complicated wartime story, discussed in Chapter 7.

Suffrage was a significant legal advance, not because it provided a smooth avenue to social equality, but rather because it was a symbol of citizenship for women who had been relegated to the private sphere, told that their menfolk should speak for them, and lectured that they were not rational, worthy, or knowledgeable enough to participate in politics. Still, it was a partial victory. Rights were doled out incrementally, sometimes resentfully so, and democratic ideals had long been constrained by a class system and discourses of white, British superiority. A step forward could be simultaneously a step back. The 1920 Dominion Election Act secured the federal vote for most women, along with their right to run for parliament, yet it also solidified provincial racial exclusions for Chinese-, Japanese-, and South Asian–Canadian voters.

To be enfranchised, "Indians" were still required to give up their status and treaty rights. A few women did, notably during the Great Depression, when they left reserves in search of a living wage, but the vast majority understood that this was not a fair bargain.[93] After the extension of the federal franchise, Indigenous women's relationship to democracy was complicated by the state's ongoing efforts to assimilate Indigenous nations to western European concepts of good governance, insisting on elected band councils, subject, of course, to local Indian agents appointed by the state. Because the Indian Act allowed only men to run for the band councils, women were caught in a no woman's land: traditional governance in which they played a role was discouraged and band councils were men only. Subject to the constant pressure of Western patriarchal ideals, some members of Indigenous communities began to support these arrangements. Yet Indigenous women resisted: they pursued political issues informally and sometimes protested formally. When the federal government moved to unseat the Six Nations Confederacy council and replace it with a band council in 1923–24, women were active in the protest against this political usurpation. Ironically, even after settler women secured the vote, both the government and the local newspaper adjacent to the Six Nations reserve ridiculed elections of chiefs by "women folk" as "backward," misrepresenting the Confederacy's forms of accountability.[94] Democracy and equality were imagined one way: Western style. Indigenous women did not give up. In 1930, two women were part of a Six Nations delegation of protest to the League of Nations in Geneva; women again joined a protest to the United Nations in the late 1940s.[95]

Between the 1940s and 1960s, provinces and territories enfranchised Indigenous residents, and, in 1948, Parliament again debated adding "status Indians" to the voting lists.[96] Some arguments that had been forwarded in 1885 reappeared. Politicians warned that "Indians," still referred to as "dependants," could not expect to hold on to their treaty rights if they joined the Canadian polity. Assimilation was also lauded; in fact, democracy was the route *to* assimilation as it would teach "the Indian ... to help himself" and "train him in [our] democratic practices."[97] There were, however, indications of a more liberal, rights discourse, promoted by a minority of Canadians. Liberal MP David Croll, for example, denounced Canada's history of white paternalism, insisting that, far from Indigenous peoples being backward, whites were truly the "backward" ones.[98]

After the 1948 legislation was withdrawn, it took eleven more years until all Indignenous Canadians were finally included in the federal vote. By 1960, a human rights discourse and a sense of international embarrassment shaped MPs' responses. Introducing the bill, Conservative Minister of Citizenship and Immigration Ellen Fairclough noted that extending the vote to Indigenous people was a "long overdue" matter of "democratic principles" and "fundamental rights." It was also a corrective: "removing the eyes of the world" on Canada's record on racial equality – perhaps seen as less than ideal.[99]

Still, First Nations were not of one mind. While the Six Nations expressed ambivalence, the Native Brotherhood of British Columbia did not: its newspaper, the *Native Voice,* referred optimistically to the extension of the federal vote as "the Indian Magna Carta." Yet there were divergent views, even within British Columbia. An eastern Indigenous commentator in the *Native Voice* asked how Indigenous people could possibly trust that their treaty rights would be respected after years of being "cheated, robbed, fleeced, despised and trampled on."[100] He had a point.

In the House of Commons, a softer language of "integration" rather than "assimilation" was used in the debate (though it sometimes meant the same thing) and an older style of dismissive, blatant racism was tolerated less. Indigenous women were now mentioned as exemplars of progress, not as downtrodden "primitives." But when it came to characterizing democracy and governance, racism and paternalism persisted. Just as in 1885, some MPs in 1960 saw British-European institutions as higher on an evolutionary political scale. One Quebec MP noted that the Maniwaki "Indians" in his riding were "more highly developed" than others as they had benefitted from living among "civilized (white) people."[101] Others pointed to the educative value of the vote, as it would encourage "Indians to take a more direct interest in their own affairs."[102] Indigenous peoples seemingly knew nothing of self-governance. The clan mothers might have told him differently.

Conclusion

During the 1960 parliamentary debate, Liberal influencer Jack Pickersgill told fellow MPs that "the vote is the most priceless of all the possessions of a citizen."[103] No mention was made of the fact that it had taken over a hundred years for the state to extend this "priceless possession" to everyone in the country. Until well into the second half of the twentieth century, one could not equate the exercise of suffrage with full democracy: property qualifications as well as exclusions relating to religion, place of origin, "race," and gender all limited who voted. Even today, many feminists argue that we still suffer from a "democratic deficit": economic inequalities and social prejudices discourage the political participation of women, especially less affluent and racialized women, thus skewing decision making in favour of those with power.

What Fairclough had in mind was a western European model of citizenship rights; Anglo-British forms of parliamentary democracy were still seen as superior to Indigenous governance practices, even though the latter had included women's voices in meaningful ways. It would take many more decades for some limited recognition by Canadian courts of Indigenous jurisprudence. Notions of democracy were bound by culture and time, and settler struggles over the franchise existed parallel to Indigenous governance, but they also intersected because debates about the vote were part of a process of state formation in which private property, a patriarchal gender order, and a racial hierarchy figured prominently. Gender and race, especially misconceptions about Indigenous gender relations, were the basis for rationales about why Indigenous people were not advanced enough to participate in politics. Ironically, in the early 1920s, when Duncan Campbell Scott was decrying Indigenous "petticoat rule," Canadian newspapers were celebrating a "first": a single woman elected to the federal Parliament.

Even within settler society, democracy was a contested concept. It was not naturally and completely aligned with feminism: there was debate, not only between opponents and supporters of equal gender rights, but also within feminist circles. Suffragist motivations in particular were not tidily boxed up into maternal versus equal rights feminism, though some suffragists did stress one or the other, and only the bravest directly challenged the prevailing familial and sexual norms. Some feminists accepted limited and piecemeal inclusion into democracy; others had a more open, expansive understanding of citizen democracy. Most tied the vote to a broader vision of social change. For some women, that meant joining the ruling elite; for others, it meant abolishing a class society. For some, it meant giving women the power to regulate other women, curing social ills and disorder. For others, the more pressing issue was women's freedom and personal autonomy. For some, the vote was an instrument to ensure the nation remained British and white, though others advocated a more ethnically tolerant democracy.

Canadian suffragists are sometimes portrayed as so politically respectable that they verged on boring. During the campaign, and even to this day, commentators were inordinately obsessed with militant British suffragettes, igoring other strains of suffragism. A more serious critique focuses on the limitations of their democratic discourse, which was tied to Eurocentric notions of governance and compromised by the class and race biases of some suffragists' exclusionary, regulatory goals. Anti-suffragist *and* suffragist imperialists shared an overlapping ideal of a white, settler British nation, although their views were not identical. Committed to equal opportunity and critical of patriarchy, suffragists did not scoff at the idea of violence against women, as did Goldwin Smith. Some suffragists were also suspicious of anti-feminist warnings of race suicide, and many embraced a more evolutionary optimism about human change. The antis, in contrast, upheld social

Darwinism, "innate" hierarchies of sex and race, a patriarchal family, a paternalist social order, and a deep suspicion of democracy. Acknowledging the immense influence of anti-feminists is important, a reminder of suffragists' uphill battle. Suffragists created a countercultural social movement that was, in some respects, quite conventional, but it could also be unconventional, passionate, creative, and joyful, offering utopian glimpses of a radically different gender and social order.

4 Reform Feminism and Women's Right to Work

In 1938, Halifax secretaries, journalists, and health care and clerical workers in the local Business and Professional Women's Club (BPWC) organized a study group on the constitution, inviting newspaperman John Dafoe to enlighten them on the Royal Commission on Dominion-Provincial relations.[1] However bone-dry the topic, their earnest self-education signalled a desire to deepen their political awareness and help make social change. Aspiration for knowledge about the world, a sense of shared work experience, a search for female company, and a commitment to new ideas about women's equality were all part of the club experience. Equal pay was one such idea. Married women's right to work was another. The feminism of the BPWCs was muted, fundamentally "small l" liberal in its orientation, sometimes invisible at the grassroots level; however, the clubs helped to keep pragmatic, reform feminism alive. Ideas forwarded by the suffragists were diffused and popularized through the BPWCs, and, like the earlier feminist movement, the clubs reflected a certain political heterogeneity – they made common cause with some CCF women on the right to work but shared conservative feminists' aversion to socialism and reverence for the British Empire.

After most women secured the federal vote in 1918, reform feminism was represented through multiple campaigns, personalities, and events. Some women were involved in the Liberal and Conservative Parties – usually in an auxiliary, not decision making, capacity – but these parties' commitment to gender equality was weak in the Liberal case, almost non-existent among Tories.[2] While a few groups like the National Council of Women claimed to represent "the" women's movement, their white, upper- and middle-class base and concentration on morality and motherhood belied this claim. After the dissolution of the tenuous alliance for suffrage, feminist vitality was more often located in grassroots, local, regional, issue-based causes. Women's interwar advocacy for gender rights and opportunities echoed continuity with past values but also incorporated new ideals, reflecting a changing economy, cultural mores, and political circumstances.

Silent, however, women were not. Equality demands, often designated as "women's rights" or sometimes under the rubric of "feminism," did not disappear after suffrage activism. If pessimistic commentators claimed the movement was now passé, feminists responded that struggle was only beginning: a burst of reform optimism followed the First World War, though it was increasingly tempered with time. In this chapter, I explore a few feminist causes: the Quebec struggle for the provincial vote, mother citizens promoting a welfare state, the BPWCs and women's right to paid work, and anti-racist efforts to equalize employment opportunities. There were many more – campaigns for access to professions and higher education, preserving citizenship rights of Canadian women married to non-Canadians, securing access to birth control – simply proving the point that, after the federal vote was won, women did not languish in a non-political trough but took many roads in search of equality.

Reform feminists engaged in the narration of their own history often claimed the extension of the federal vote to the majority of women in 1918 as a victorious, progressive milestone. However, new rights were tempered by persisting inequalities. Immigrant, colonized, and racialized women in Canada's white settler nation were still considered less than full-fledged citizens. The Dominion Election Act of 1920 sanctioned provincial voting exclusions based on race and ethnicity.[3] Economic and social changes were also doubled-edged. Steadily increasing numbers of young single women worked outside the home, yet they encountered limited job prospects in a labour force segregated by gender, race, and ethnicity. Women's access to sports, leisure, and urban public spaces expanded, but always within the boundaries of gendered moral surveillance. Popular culture expressed in film, fashion, and print culture implied women's enhanced sexual autonomy; at the same time, women remained subject to patriarchal laws, violence, and social ostracism if they stepped across proscribed moral lines.

The interwar period was also a rollercoaster of crises, most notably the Great Depression – the world economy crashed in 1929, leaving economic disruption and suffering in its wake. Immigration, still possible in the 1920s, was suddenly restricted, and forced deportations based on political and economic criteria increased. A slowly climbing birth rate in the 1920s reversed as families responded to the crisis by not having children. Birth control, though more openly discussed, was also promoted by some eugenic-minded economic and political leaders as a means of solving the Depression poverty of the despised "lower classes," who supposedly reproduced indiscriminately.

Feminists and Anti-Feminists Debate "This New Freedom"

The termination of English-Canadian suffrage organizations did not conclude debates about feminism. *This Freedom,* a controversial 1922 British novel featuring an unappealing, selfish, self-absorbed "New Woman," was one of many cultural interventions portraying the "new" post-war woman.[4] She was imagined – positively or negatively – as free from the confining sexual and social strictures of the past. Yet, as Canadian novelist Martha Ostenso's shockingly frank *Wild Geese* pointed out, the new and the old were both part of women's post-war world.[5] Ostenso's "modern realist" novel was more open than other Canadian writing about the expression of female sexuality, but it also discussed women's continuing subjection to patriarchal violence. Her stark realism did not sit well with Canadian readers, who were perhaps looking for more sentimental fare. Ostenso and other modernist artists, some of whom are discussed in Chapter 6, nonetheless represented a changing cultural landscape animated by feminist questions: What should women do with their new political freedom?

The Canadian mainstream media echoed transnational conversations about women's "new freedom," yet there was no consensus on whether women now *had* freedom, were still seeking it, or even wanted it. While the word "freedom" had liberal, individualist connotations, it might also suggest collective action: would women's new freedom lead to mobilizations for a more egalitarian social order? Some feminists recognized "freedom" had incongruous, contradictory meanings. A writer in the left-wing magazine *Canadian Forum* mused that working women's "new freedom" to earn their own wages was cancelled out by intensified consumerist pressure for them to use their paltry pay to "buy, buy, buy" beauty and fashion products, as women were told that their sole means of validation was attractive femininity.[6]

The implications of women's enhanced political rights were the stuff of many articles by writers eager to deflate this accomplishment. The "long shadow" of anti-feminist prejudice pervaded politics, even if women were treated with "benign bigotry" rather than the bald language of female inferiority that had been used by anti-suffragists.[7] Dismissive assessments of the newly enfranchised "woman citizen" were common: women simply imitated their husbands' political choices, made no impact on society, and, in any case, should remain primarily home-based wives and mothers. In 1930, Conservative senator Gratton O'Leary penned one of these countless negative post-mortems on suffrage, arguing that women had failed to make their mark on politics. In doing so, he used one measurement: few women were elected to political office. Suffragists, he asserted, had been wrong: women's votes had not dispelled all "evil things" from society; women voted "much like men." Gratton infantilized women; they were still political neophytes "in rompers," largely used as "window dressing" in the recent federal election.[8]

Anti-feminism, then, did not disappear: it simply changed its clothes. It ridiculed feminism as passé, and continued to stress women's inherent intellectual and psychological limitations. In most newspapers, "feminism" was reduced to a joke: about women drivers being required to post a "W" on the car (as they were substandard drivers) or about classic tropes such as the female (now "feminist") gold-digger.[9] Experts who declared feminism "spent" were cited with authority; one doctor announced that college-educated women were having more children, indicating that "the fight for a position of equality is mostly over."[10] When the famous American pilot Amelia Earhart rejected the feminist label, the press jumped on her remark as proof of feminism's irrelevance.[11]

The ideology of separate spheres, though modified to allow some women enhanced access to the public sphere of education and work, was still powerful. Women's ultimate goal should be marriage and family; their primary métier was caring and nurturing. Popular culture looked suspiciously on single "career" women: in anti-suffragist Andrew Macphail's terms, they were failures at husband getting. The only woman elected to Parliament in 1921, Agnes Macphail, responded to insinuations she was unfeminine and "mannish" by reassuring the public that she had marriage offers – she just turned them down.[12]

Although she did not begin her political career as a self-named feminist, Macphail became outspoken about the misogyny she experienced. In her feisty article "Men Want to Hog Everything," she listed ridicule, heckling, marginalization, and stereotyping as part of her daily experience as a parliamentarian. I was a "curiosity, a freak," she said, "and you know the way the world treats freaks."[13] Other women who dipped their toes in the political

Figure 4.1 Agnes Macphail entering Parliament, 1922 | *Toronto Star* Photo Archive, Toronto Public Reference Library, TS_1_B_347

realm recalled the discouragement of similar old boys' networks and the routinely dismissive press coverage of their hats, not their policies. An anonymous "she-politician" writing in *Maclean's* magazine faulted women for their own failures in language so derisive that Nellie McClung and others suspected that the writer was not a "she" at all but yet another contemptuous man. When feminist Farmer-Labour candidate Beatrice Brigden explained her defeat in the 1930 federal election for *Chatelaine* magazine readers, she proffered a different interpretation of women's political "failures": nine out of the ten female candidates in that election, she noted, ran for independent, labour, and farmer parties, a much harder electoral slog than running for the Liberals or Conservatives. Rather than abandoning suffrage goals, these women were faithful to more radical visions of change rather than the "old line parties."[14] She had a point: the Conservatives could not bring themselves to nominate a single female candidate in the decade after the war, and remained resistant to women's equal participation in the Party.[15]

Feminists in the 1920s and 1930s debated whether they should join these old-line parties, set up new ones, or try non-partisan activism; this choice between partisanship and independence was a recurring dilemma for feminists over the twentieth century.[16] After decades of disappointment with anti-suffragist Liberals and Conservatives, some looked for new political homes. A small group of Ontario (largely Toronto) women proposed a Woman's Party after the war, modelled on a short-lived effort by Emmeline Pankhurst in Britain. Even after they scrambled to clarify that this was a lobby group, not an electoral party, it was treated with derision by labour and prairie feminists, who saw it as a front for imperialist, conservative politics (which it was, in part). Middle-class Vancouver women contemplated a Woman's Party too, using the unfortunately coy language of flirtation to explain how they would court all male politicians: "like a girl with two beaux we could keep both political parties guessing."[17] Neither proposal lasted long.

More influential were cross-party post-suffrage "schools," civic forums, and other momentary coalitions set up to acquaint the new woman voter with her rights and to discuss the next steps for social reform. Though critical of a gender-based party, some Saskatchewan suffragists experimented with a "Non-Partisan League," emulating an attempt at non-partisanship from the American Midwest. Exasperated with corrupt parties that failed to serve the needs of rural people, suffragist Zoa Haight ran as a Non-Partisan League candidate in Saskatchewan in 1917, though she was defeated. Other women combined independent and partisan political connections. Mary Ellen Smith, who in 1918 became the first woman elected to the BC legislature, fashioned a coalition from her association with the Liberal Party and suffrage, temperance, social reform, and British imperialist organizations. A working-class English immigrant, Smith had built a dynamic political partnership with her husband, Ralph, a "Lib Lab" (Liberal-Labour) MP and later a Liberal MLA. Widowed in 1917, she ran successfully for the provincial legislature. Although liberalism increasingly overrode her labourism, her feminist commitments to the vote, equal pay, mothers' pensions, and other "women and children" reforms earned her cross-party women's votes. Yet, as Veronica Strong-Boag's biography shows, Smith represented both the success and tragedy of post-war reform feminism. Smith was used by, but increasingly marginalized within, a male-dominated Liberal Party little interested in feminists' agenda. Moreover, her racist calls for Asian exclusion and eugenicist views on sterilization also remained fixed, tied to the white, British settler imperialism that had shaped her early politics.[18]

Some former suffragists expressed frustration with women's (mis)use of their new freedom – in their view, they were not political enough. Journalist Anne Anderson Perry claimed that Canadian women lacked gender solidarity, as they elected fewer women to Parliament than their British counterparts. United Farmers of Alberta MLA Irene Parlby identified a generational problem, lamenting that "girls of today are rather too prone to take their political equality with men too casually."[19] This dynamic of mother-daughter disappointment and misunderstanding was a recurring theme in the history of feminism. The priorities of Parlby's generation, such as temperance, were rejected by younger women, who appeared to have imbibed the consumerist message on display in popular Hollywood films: that dancing, drinking, and smoking were the "new freedom." Suffragists mourned deflated feminist momentum: "our forces so well organized [for suffrage] began to dwindle," wrote Nellie McClung in a rare moment of pessimism. "We had no constructive program for making a new world ... so the enfranchised women drifted."[20]

Yet, some suffrage alliances were recast as new projects, such as the Persons Case. Although that case became a symbol of women's political equality, its origins lay in Emily Murphy's interest in a Senate seat and the legal uncertainty unleashed when an Alberta lawyer claimed in a lower court that women were not "persons" under the constitution. Five prominent former suffragists (the "Famous Five") petitioned Ottawa for a legal decision on women's personhood and eligibility for appointment to the Senate. The Department of Justice refused to acknowledge women's political personhood, as did the Supreme Court of Canada; after all, the learned judges opined, the Fathers of Confederation had never *intended* women to be office holders. The final court of appeal, the British Judicial Committee of the Privy Council, reversed the Canadian judgment in 1929, reminding the narrow-minded Canadian judges that the constitution was a "living tree" that evolved over time and noting that the view that women could not hold office was a relic of the "barbarous" past. While the notion that women were not "persons" was galling and insulting, a sign of continuing sexist denigration, the decision did not, ironically, result in substantial political or legal advances for all women, only the appointment of a few women senators. Nonetheless, the campaign proved the possibility of feminist reform alliances, though women on the far left saw the campaign as irrelevant and elitist.[21]

If the Persons Case seemed to belie McClung's lament about the feminist doldrums, in reality, a condescending anti-feminism persisted throughout the 1930s. Journalists lavished attention on Margaret Lawrence's 1936 book *The School of Femininity,* one reporter declaring hyperbolically that it was the "most distinguished book ever written by a Canadian woman author."[22] Lawrence went on the lecture circuit for the Canadian Club, giving speeches on women's rights. True, the book had a veneer of feminist sensibility, showcasing famous women writers from pioneering feminist Mary Wollstonecraft to Finnish modernist Minna Canth. However, Lawrence maintained that women's maternal, biological clock ultimately shaped their destiny; those who denied this impulse were deluding themselves, doomed to personal unhappiness.[23] No wonder the mainstream press was so positive: the author reinforced anti-feminist views, telling a Windsor audience that "women owe more to advertising than all the feminist leaders," since the "glamour girl" in magazines gave them a vision of beauty to aspire to.[24]

Feminists' alternative view of womanhood was usually given voice in smaller, progressive cultural venues. A reviewer of *The School of Femininity* in the *Canadian Forum* threw up her hands in dismay at Lawrence's "modern" resurrection of a "traditional" view of women as a "deep sexual being ... a biological force under a compelling instinct to find a safe place to lay her babes."[25] Judge Helen Gregory MacGill, a former suffragist, also took on anti-feminism, insisting that women were shut out of political life not because they were inferior but because men fiercely protected their own power. She lamented women's difficulty in shaking off the dominant ideological assumptions of men's assumed superiority and their own internalized inferiority, what later feminists summed up as female socialization. Her pragmatic, humanist, reform perspective was unwavering: women's special knowledge was required in public life more than ever if Canada was to solve the urgent issues of the day. Both sexes, "mothers and fathers," should be creating a better civilization.[26]

Debates over women's "new freedom" kept feminism in the public eye in the twenties and thirties, but there was no consensus on what women's equality meant. Definitions of women's autonomy and freedom did shift. Discourses about more egalitarian, companionate marriage validated mutual sexual expression within marriage; single women's paid work was accepted more readily; and more women accessed higher education. As women's experience during the First World War proved, middle-class women could be drawn into networks of political influence, in limited but, to them, edifying ways. Many social reform suffragists claimed victory as token women were selected for movie censor boards, consumer organizations, and mothers allowance boards, appointments that shrewdly incorporated a limited group of white, middle-class women into bureaucratic circles of influence and expertise.

The Struggle in Quebec Continues

Canadian feminists were little concerned with persisting racial voting exclusions, though they were with the last provincial suffrage straggler: Quebec. In the influential Fédération nationale Saint-Jean-Baptiste (FNSJB) and its newspaper, *La bonne parole,* maternalist social reform prospered after the war, but equal rights feminism was still a debate. As a medium for many political voices, *La bonne parole* published positive commentary on feminist reforms, including the vote, but other authors, including the president of the Ligue catholique féminine, voiced concerns about women's "emancipation" based on "democratic" principles that contradicted Catholic Christian morality.[27] Women and men had God-given, complementary, but distinct social responsibilities; women's "primary and natural" role was motherhood, the education of the young, and the inculcation of feminine morality in girls.[28] Maternalism still defined the FNSJB's reform agenda, but it should be activated "in the service of society": woman's feminine nature, moral superiority, and knowledge of the family made her public voice unique and essential.[29]

If the FNSJB did not always go out on a limb for political rights, new organizations stepped into the breach. The FNSJB initiated the Comité provincial pour le suffrage féminin in 1921, with English and French co-chairs. Buoyed by the fact that Quebec women overwhelmingly voted in the 1921 federal election (without any violence or familial fallout, Marie Gérin-Lajoie pointed out), suffragists in Quebec optimistically mobilized to demand the provincial vote. Four to five hundred suffragists converged on Quebec City in 1922 to present their case to the legislative assembly, only to be disappointed. Liberal premier Louis Taschereau announced his government would never accede to their demands. The government's flat-out refusal contrasted with the placatory presentations of suffragists Lady Julia Drummond and Marie Gérin-Lajoie, who reassured politicians that they had no intention of "destroying" the home – indeed, they just wanted to protect it. Younger suffragists such as Thérèse Casgrain and Idola Saint-Jean shared the view that women had unique maternal, moral, and familial insights on politics; Casgrain implied that women would continue the pronatal project of Quebec: "we promise ... that homes will be looked after, that dinner will not be late, that families ... will at least be as numerous as before."[30] However these emerging leaders, suggests Denyse Baillargeon, also took a more direct, "rebellious tack," advocating for equal rights by strongly refuting anti-suffrage arguments.[31]

Disappointed but not defeated, suffragists regrouped in a few years, establishing new organizations: in 1927, the Alliance canadienne pour le vote des femmes du Québec (ACVFQ), led by Saint-Jean, and, two years later, the Ligue des droits de la femme, under the direction of Casgrain. Both organizations were bicultural and situated within a reform tradition, though they veered away from earlier suffragists' efforts to align their struggle with Quebec nationalism and the Catholic Church. Together, representatives of the two suffrage groups made annual pilgrimages to Quebec City to present petitions, support private-members' suffrage bills, and meet with politicians.[32] They encountered more than rejection, enduring ridicule, misogynist remarks, and "vulgar" jokes, often directed at Saint-Jean, a single woman with a more radical persona. Even the anti-suffrage newspaper *Le Devoir* finally felt compelled to call out politicians' insults as unbecoming.[33]

The two groups did differ. The ACVFQ focused more on grassroots mobilizations, trying to reach working women often ignored by middle-class suffragists. Idola Saint-Jean, a writer who had studied in France and circulated in radical artistic circles in Montreal, was a self-supporting teacher closely attuned to the world of work. The ACVFQ called for adequate welfare and an enforced mimimum wage for women: women's economic autonomy, the organization believed, was the bedrock of women's social equality. Saint-Jean even supported a strike of garment workers led by a left-wing union, a brave stance in a climate of intense anti-communism. Rather than drawing solely on maternalism, Saint-Jean emphasized natural rights, democracy, egalitarianism, and republicanism. Women should not receive the vote as a "favour," she argued, but because they were an integral part of society, intelligent and free, as men were.[34] Her words would have resonated with Mary Wollstonecraft.

Casgrain, a well-connected Liberal through her husband, a federal MP, initially positioned her feminist politics with cautious compromise: while arguing the vote should be extended as a "right" not a "favour", she reassured *La bonne parole* readers that she was no radical "suffragette." In making their demands, feminists needed to use "moderation and a measure of serenity," stressing women's "inherent maternal qualities" as well as their citizenship rights.[35] Casgrain was nonetheless an articulate and effective leader. A clever public advocate, private lobbyist, and person of immense persistence, she used her ties to the establishment to change the minds of those in power while concurrently building an effective lobby that tackled the multiple legal disabilities of women. Like English-Canadian suffragists, Quebec women saw legal, political, and social rights as interconnected; struggles on one legal front often led to, and buttressed, other struggles. Both the ACVFQ and the Ligue des droits de la femme participated in hearings of the provincial Dorion commission of inquiry examining the modernization of family law; they used this public platform to indict egregious examples of outdated laws condoning a sexual double standard and denying women equal guardianship of their children. They also advocated for the most basic of economic rights: women's control of their bank accounts and wages and access to work in the professions.

Figure 4.2 (A, B) Interwar Quebec suffrage leaders: writer and teacher Idola Saint-Jean led the the Alliance canadienne pour le vote des femmes du Québec, while Thérèse Casgrain was president of the Ligue des droits de la femme | A) Idola Saint-Jean: Photograph by Garcia Studio, ca. 1940–45, LAC, C-009482; B) Thérèse Casgrain: Photograph by Yousuf Karsh, 1937, LAC, PA-178196

(B)

(A)

Saint-Jean's blunt support for equal rights, argues Diane Lamoureux, stood in contrast to Casgrain's "seduction" of the ruling elites, but both were deemed the leading "women warriors" of the Quebec suffrage battle.[36] Quebec suffragists did not simply opt for maternalist or equal rights feminism. Marie Gérin-Lajoie was perhaps the archetypal maternalist reformer who connected Quebec feminism before and after the First World War, consistently arguing that women's heightened moral sensibility and familial responsibilities necessitated their voice in politics. First associated with the National Council of Women of Canada, and then a founder of the FNSJB, she campaigned for social reforms intended to protect the family but also for the expansion of women's education, associations (though not unions) for working women, and married women's rights, which were circumscribed by Quebec's civil code. If Gérin-Lajoie emphasized maternalism, she also drew on a language of rights. Taking note of suffrage extended to women in other countries, she reasoned that women earned the vote because of faith in the "justice of their judgment" and their experience in domestic problems – in short, the merit and the dignity of their social function.[37]

The complicated landscape of Quebec Catholicism resulted in Gérin-Lajoie's move away from suffrage activism in the mid-1920s. At a conference for Catholic women in Rome in 1922, she was elated to hear that the church was about to accept a resolution allowing women to vote, but furious when a last-minute clause was added – due to the lobbying of Henri Bourassa – that they must obey the wishes of their *local* clergy: in Quebec, that meant abandoning the suffrage struggle. Gérin-Lajoie remained a suffragist but focused her considerable political energies on the FNSJB and combating other forms of legal discrimination. She may not have relished opposing the church, but her reformist inclinations likely also shaped her decision to put suffrage activism aside temporarily: feminists, she believed, should avoid "upheavals," opting instead to "let new ideas infiltrate" society, slowly but surely.[38]

Even when they invoked respectable maternalism, Quebec suffragists faced intractable obstacles. In some European countries, the Catholic Church made peace with women's suffrage, hoping to garner newly enfranchised women's support in their fight against their enemies, both secularists and communists. The Quebec Catholic Church, which commanded formidable influence as an integral element of French-Canadian history, culture, education, welfare, and daily family life, was not similarly conciliatory. Although the Quebec clergy's views on suffrage differed somewhat, the conservative, anti-suffrage position dominated by the end of the twenties. Cloaked in the church's moral authority, the press and politicians held their anti-suffrage ground. The cultural, religious, and political male elite feared that women's suffrage would undermine Quebec's distinct society in which "the mother absorbed in household and children" was a pillar of the nation. One cannot understand the opposition to suffrage in Quebec, argues Denyse Baillargeon, without "considering the national question and the roles nationalists assigned to men and women to safeguard the nation." As in the earlier period, French-Canadian antis argued less about the principles involved and more about what would be "lost" to the nation if mothers "abandoned" the private sphere.[39]

The provincial government, for its part, tried to steer women away from suffrage. In 1915, it launched the Cercles de Fermières du Québec, which gently urged farm women to devote their primary efforts to the family, not the vote. Other organizations, sponsored by the church, were also antidotes to the evils of feminism, including auxiliaries for Catholic boarding school graduates and the Ligue catholique féminine, which took up the church's campaigns to stave off the perils of dancing, "immodest clothing" (sleeveless dresses), *garçonism* in fashion (the boyish flapper style), and, of course, sex outside of marriage.[40] Anti-suffragists were able to secure signatures of large numbers of women on petitions against the vote and had considerable support from the French-language press. When a federal bill to equalize grounds for divorce for men and women was presented in the early 1920s, *Le Devoir* offered Henri Bourassa a chance to re-sharpen his anti-feminist pen. Bourassa resolutely rejected all disruption to the traditional gender order; indeed, the inherent differences between the sexes justified a patriarchal order in which women should be punished more severely for any lapses in the marriage vows.[41] Well into the 1930s, Fadette, his anti-suffragist cousin and *Le Devoir* columnist, warned young Quebecers against imitating English Protestant values, including feminism: to do so would threaten not just the family, but cultural, national, and linguistic survival as well.

The last line of defence of the status quo was the legislative assembly. In his arguments against suffrage, Premier Taschereau appealed to his imagined French-Canadian nation: suffrage was negatively equated with Anglo-Saxon culture, which he contrasted to Quebec's "Latin mentality." In line with other "Latin" European nations (or, in his terms, "races") a francophone, Catholic Quebec should act as a bulwark against feminism and suffrage. This argument especially riled English-Canadian suffragists. Isabella Scott, associated with the Montreal Women's Club, ridiculed Taschereau's boasts of a "Latin" temperament, suggesting Quebec's sense of "difference" included "practically medieval" ideas about women's equality.[42]

Given these formidable barriers, perhaps we should ask why suffragists finally succeeded in 1940. The fact that Quebec women voted federally helped; thousands of women went to the polls to cast their votes without undermining the family and the nation. Quebec suffragists had the advantage of communication strategies unavailable to earlier suffragists; both suffrage organizations used the radio, attempting to reach rural women, who often expressed little interest in the vote. In 1931, the Ligue initiated a fifteen-minute show discussing women's issues, while the ACVFQ sponsored *Les droits des femmes* and, later, *L'actualité,* broadcast in both French and English. Casgrain's CBC program *Fémina,* started in 1937, offered women-centred news with a pro-suffrage slant. Casgrain reminded women that their lives were shaped within a male-dominated system over which they had no say; the vote was the only "logical" means of giving them that say.[43] Idola Saint-Jean's radio addresses cleverly cast suffrage in nationalist terms: modern feminists were part of the long lineage of Quebec heroines and early white settlers, including Madeleine de Verchères and the mother of Louis-Joseph Papineau.[44]

As in other provinces, suffragists sought out allies. Trade unionists associated with the Trades and Labour Congress (though not the Catholic unions) brought three suffrage spokeswomen to their lobby meeting with the premier to make the point that they too supported women's suffrage. Labour journalist Éva Circé-Côté also chimed in: writing in *Le monde ouvrier,* she pointed to the career of Canada's only female MP, Agnes Macphail, as "la preuve vivante" that women were the equal of men.[45] Circé-Côté's views on anti-suffragists echoed her earlier Enlightenment-inspired feminism: "objecting to women's right to vote," she wrote in disgust, "is to take us back to the shadowy ages when it was seriously wondered if they [women] had a soul."[46]

Allies, publicity, lobbying, and political connections: in a sense, the vote was achieved in Quebec in a manner not unlike that of other provinces. In Quebec, too, a political party that was out of power – the Liberals, in the mid-1930s – added suffrage to its election platform, and when the party defeated the incumbent Union nationale in 1939, it made good on its promise, though the church was still opposed. Victory was achieved through a coalition of English and French suffragists, but there were tensions. English-Canadian feminists blamed the predicament of Quebec women on an unprogressive, "backward" French Catholic culture, and, within Quebec, Anglo suffragists thought the French element was "holding back" the struggle.[47] In regular updates to the International Women's Suffrage Alliance newspaper,

Jus Suffragii, Isabella Scott claimed women were virtually "slaves" in the family due to Quebec's "unjust, humiliating and degrading" laws.[48] Scott and other English Quebecers attended London meetings of the British Dominion Women's Citizen Union, a Commonwealth group dedicated to equal citizenship, using this venue to pass resolutions urging the Quebec government to join other "civilized" countries by giving women the vote.[49] Pragmatically, though, Scott conceded that resolutions attempting to shame the Quebec government, if passed at a British conference, might make English-speaking suffragists unpopular in the province. International support may have lifted the spirits of these anglophone women, but victory ultimately came from francophone and anglophone women's hard political work on the home front.

Mother Citizens and the Welfare State

In the 1920s and 1930s, reform feminists in both English and French Canada still believed that their special knowledge about mothers, children, and families should be the basis for new state policy. Embracing their role as "mother citizens," they laid the groundwork for the welfare state, though one deeply marred by race and class inequalities. Their hopes were conveyed in a cartoon penned by artist Emily Carr in the *Western Woman's Weekly* in 1918. Reminiscent of an endearing Peter Rabbit story, it showed a mother rabbit surrounded at the kitchen table with her contented little rabbits. Titled "When We Have Mother's Pensions," the cartoon symbolized feminists' intense optimism about the potential of new maternalist social policies. "I can stay at home with you my dears," announces the mother rabbit, while the seven little ones add "hurrah" and "more carrots please."[50]

Echoing Judge Helen Gregory MacGill's claim that feminists' political battles had just begun, reformers merged pre-war suffragists' hope in women's collective, maternal political power with commitment to using their voting power to press for social reforms. Newfoundland suffragists transitioned into a new League of Women Voters, designed to lobby for legislation relating to women and children, while Saskatchewan's Political Equality League developed a far-reaching reform platform including equal pay, the nationalization of public utilities, international arbitration to end all wars, changes to the *Criminal Code,* and education reform. In Vancouver, Political Equality League members merged into the New Era League (the very title reflecting feminist post-war optimism), a non-partisan feminist education and lobbying organization. The New Era League discussed almost every issue imaginable, including drugs, civic reform, equal pay, and peace,

Figure 4.3 "When We Have Mother's Pensions" | *Western Woman's Weekly*, 10 January 1918

and, though members were not always in full agreement, they did agree on one long-cherished feminist reform, mothers' allowances.

Across Canada, goals that had been articulated in suffrage organizations were pursued: female judges and probation workers for women and juveniles; equal custody rights for mothers; maternal and baby health clinics; a minimum wage for women; and protection from sexual violence for girls. The more exaggerated suffragist claims that women's votes would eradicate crime, violence, and poverty had always been unrealistic, but feminists in British Columbia claimed that the legal landscape was so transformed that a book on women and the law had to be completely rewritten by 1924.[51] When sceptics challenged the president of the New Era League, Susie Lane Clark, about suffragists' failures in 1937, she was affronted by their ignorance of feminists' actual goals: "those who sought the suffrage had not in mind glorified seats in parliament – the last thought was self-aggrandizement. Rather ... [we] carried the vision of a deserted wife or needy mother with a flock of little ones."[52]

Many successes, including provincial minimum wages for women, were designed to "protect" the vulnerable, and were celebrated as such.[53] Few

Canadian feminists advocated the abandonment of such protective legislation in favour of equality of economic competition between women and men, as did one group of American feminists. Some suffragist reforms seem unquestionably progressive, such as free maternal and baby health care or custody rights for mothers. Yet, the implementation of everything from minimum wage to mothers' allowance legislation held intractable contradictions: as Elizabeth Kalmakoff puts it, suffragists' "motherhood" demands were often translated into "minimum legal remedies."[54]

Mothers' allowances (also called mothers' pensions), paid by governments to widows with young children, was a case in point. Intended to alleviate the worst stresses of familial poverty, mothers' allowances (MA) were promoted by feminists as recognition that motherwork was socially valuable work, a position that, if it had been applied to all women, was ahead of the times. Women reformers pointed out that women's low wages could not possibly sustain families, protect child health, and prevent the scourge of the poor: child delinquency. International examples were mobilized to prove similar schemes elsewhere saved children from orphanages, keeping the nuclear family intact. Child saving was also a form of nation building: healthy families meant a healthy country.

However, as provinces implemented mothers' allowances, most designated only widows morally worthy of support; deserted wives and, of course, unmarried mothers were left out, despite contrary pressure from the labour movement.[55] In retrospect, welfare state historians such as Margaret Little contend, mothers' allowances were a "bourgeois" project that reinforced a male-breadwinner ideology and sustained a "two-tiered welfare state," one stream for men as earners, another for women as mothers.[56] The allowance was so meagre that women often had to supplement it with part-time wage work and return to the workforce as soon as they could – or remarry a new male breadwinner. The welfare of children, not women, was the real concern of the state, although it also assumed that working-class children should leave school and begin earning their keep as young as possible.

Perhaps most damning, MAs were a privilege for women of good moral standing, not a right of all widows. Provinces set up regulatory processes to monitor women's cleanliness, housekeeping, leisure, child-rearing practices, character, and intimate relationships. Government investigators inspected recipients' homes to ascertain that recipients were not consorting with men or luxuriating on the taxpayers' dime – wasting their allowance on movies, booze, cigarettes, or radios. In Quebec, the 1937 Needy Mothers Assistance Act required women to demonstrate their "good conduct" and have a local religious minister or other designated official countersign the cheque.[57] The Quebec allowance was so meagre that orphanages continued to fill up with the children of impoverished mothers. Intrusive moral regulation, in short, was integral to this reform; like some earlier suffragists, middle-class feminists saw some mothers as more worthy than others. A partial exception was the mothers' pension program in British Columbia. While its more "inclusive, rights-based" definition of eligibility was less concerned with morality, the program was profoundly racist, excluding women of Asian background as a means of bolstering a white province.[58] While provincial mothers allowances were not implemented on federal reserves, DIA policies were similarly racialized, blaming familial ill health on Indigenous women's inadequate mothering.

Maternalism was never an undifferentiated, universal ideology that respected all women's caring labour: it underwrote political agendas ranging from the redistribution of economic resources to the promotion of racism and class hierarchies. Mothers' allowances both challenged and preserved the dichotomous good mother versus bad mother discourse already embedded in Canadian feminism. Although intended to respect motherwork, MA programs were constructed with middle-class norms in mind, preserving the existing wage structure and gendered and racial hierarchies. Negative outcomes were in part the unintended consequences of feminists' honest hopes for family preservation and child protection. But this victory was nonetheless a sharp reminder of the persisting ideological and class differences within feminism.

Mothers' allowances made some women clients of the welfare state; others became its architects, either as social reformers or social work professionals. The suffrage and social reform movements did open up new career opportunities for professional women in social (or "welfare") work. Both English- and French-Canadian feminists, for instance, promoted separate courts for children, probation systems, and training (or reform) schools for criminalized girls, to be managed by women. Women court workers were supposed to offer "applied maternalism"; they would provide caring insight and professional guidance to young women in trouble with the law. Those "delinquents," however, were usually poor and working-class girls apprehended for vague, gender-specific offences: being "incorrigible," sexually active, running away, engaging in immoral leisure, refusing parental control. Feminist Rose Henderson believed her job as a Montreal probation officer was to expose the environmental causes of crime, protect girls, and treat them with "mercy not punishment." In practice, argues Tamara

Myers, such laudable goals often turned into intrusive moral regulation and old-fashioned mother-blaming, as working-class mothers were held accountable when their daughters fell into bad company and bad ways.[59]

Educated, professional welfare workers increasingly stressed objective casework rather than their innate maternal insights, but they were nonetheless symptomatic of the contradictions of the "mother citizen" feminist agenda. In Toronto, for instance, reform feminists celebrated two victories: first, they lobbied successfully for a separate women's court where female defendants might be shielded from leering onlookers, rescued from the streets, and offered alternatives to a life of crime. Second, feminists secured the appointment of a woman magistrate, Margaret Patterson, to oversee the court. Patterson was the beneficiary of the maternal feminist agenda, but the women who appeared before her, argues Amanda Glasbeek, were not. The feminism animating this "feminized justice" became "statements of authority" of some women over others. Criminalized women, invariably poor, addicted, and sexually suspect, were assessed according to bourgeois moral and economic standards; as a result, they encountered the punitive side of middle-class feminist ideas.[60]

Finding Common Cause in Work: The Business and Professional Women's Clubs

Reform feminism also found an outlet in the BPWCs. Some of the first clubs, like the Toronto's Business Girls Club, founded in 1910, were social reform efforts by middle-class women to protect vulnerable working women. By 1921, the Toronto club changed its name to the Canadian Business and Professional Women's Club, later relinquishing its claim to the national name.[61] Clubs multiplied in the 1920s and especially the 1930s, promoted by enthusiastic local advocates, a national BPWC, and a growing international BPWC movement. Each club had its own distinct personnel, character, chosen pastimes, and issues, but they were uniformly for women who worked outside the home: secretaries, stenographers, doctors, bank workers, bookkeepers, social workers, retail workers, small business owners, and more. Larger urban clubs were more likely to have an agenda of legislative reform, and, as one climbed the ladder of the organization, national leaders were more assertively concerned with women's rights.

When "the National" sent out surveys to gather material on women's economic status, it gently admonished locals not to bask only in pleasures of club social life but to contemplate the importance of political change. It is no accident that suffragist Nellie McClung initiated a Calgary "current affairs luncheon group" that grew into a BPWC,[62] and that suffragists Thérèse

Casgrain and Isabella St. John were featured as club speakers in Quebec. Suffragists had long understood women's paid labour to be central to feminism, and the middle-class and white-collar women who gravitated to the BPWCs were likely comfortable with McClung and Casgrain's gradualist, pragmatic reform agenda – and vice versa.

The shift in nomenclature from business "girls" to "women" had symbolic importance, signifying increased acceptance of single wage-earning women in the interwar period. Working women, BPWC members claimed, were "dissatisfied with the part they were playing in social life outside the home" after the war, many recognizing that "a generation of men was wiped out" and that single women needed to support themselves, perhaps moving into jobs previously done by men.[63] Explaining the club's origins, one speaker at the 1931 BPWC convention reminded attendees that women had always worked, though this shifted with industrialization as women moved into the public sphere.[64] They were now here to stay. Nothing irritated club women more than hearing the nineteenth-century dictum that women worked only for pin money. They knew otherwise, and they wanted to realign societal expectations with that reality.

The BPWC was not, however, a working-class project. This is not to say that the membership was solidly middle-class and affluent; members included lawyers, doctors, and journalists isolated in their respective professions, but also secretaries, clerks, bank tellers, and retail workers, some of whom might survive on salaries as meagre as the wages of factory workers. When the Hamilton, Ontario, club was founded, it announced its cross-class intentions by inviting women from the Labour, Liberal, and Conservative Parties to the podium.[65] Over time, however, the clubs became composed primarily of professional and white-collar women who shied away from the label "working class." Some were likely intent on climbing out of the insecurity of working-class life. Not only did the early clubs stress the respectability of white-collar work, but they were quite deferential to employers. One wonders what Toronto women bank clerks thought when a Royal Bank manager told the local BPWC meeting that a mere 25 percent of them had skills equal to those of male bank workers. He added the patently untrue statement that their pay was equal – and that, in any case, no one should expect high salaries from bank clerking.[66] Nor did the clubs necessarily embrace solidarity with all other working women. When faced with an invitation from the Toronto YWCA to contribute to an "impartial inquiry" into the 1931 dressmakers' strike, the BPWC demurred that "it was not wise" to even "investigate this matter."[67]

Figure 4.4 The BPWC represented working women in white-collar as well as professional occupations. During the Depression, the national BPWC advocated against firing married women working for pay | LAC, Business and Professional Women's Clubs fonds

Local clubs were also wary of the "f word." They reassured the public that they were not radical, "bad" feminists: "We are not moving to turn women into men. Reasonable women are not pressing the woman question in this direction; we are simply trying to recognize that many women can play useful roles in public and government bodies."[68] A tension existed between a liberal individualist emphasis on bootstrapping and a shared understanding of structural inequalities women faced. On one hand, BPWC women advocated self-improvement through training and education; on the other, they admitted that the world of work was not always hospitable or fair to women.

In the twenties, clubs moved cautiously into politics by resolving to study "the common problems of our occupations." By the 1930s, they were "fashioning a machine" to confront those problems.[69] National and international links facilitated this shift. In 1929, local clubs met in Vancouver to discuss a national federation, which they finalized with a founding convention and constitution in Winnipeg in 1930. Canadian members also took advice and heart from a growing International Federation of Business and Professional Women, whose leadership included Canadian Dorothy Heneker, a lawyer whose residency in Quebec barred her from practising law. The international federation professed a sense of sisterhood across nations, though, in reality, it was dominated by federations in the Americas and Europe, reflecting the colonizing, not the colonized, world.

Initially, the new Canadian Federation of Business and Professional Women's Clubs (CFBPWC) stressed cooperation and mutual aid, promoting the value of women's paid work and enhancing women's educational opportunities. Raising funds for scholarships was an important goal, and local clubs engaged in respectable charitable work, from collecting shoes for school children to supporting the Red Cross. Local minutes spent more time discussing banquets, sports, travel talks, and amateur plays, a sign that many members were simply seeking friendship and fun. Yet the efforts of the CFBPWC to encourage social action did gradually bear some fruit. The establishment of a national magazine, *The Business and Professional Woman,* helped this consciousness-raising project by situating the clubs' work in the lineage of feminist struggles. The magazine, for instance, lauded the CFBPWC's efforts to commemorate the Persons Case. Aided by Co-operative Commonwealth Federation MP Agnes Macphail and Liberal senator Cairine Wilson, the CFBPWC successfully lobbied for a bronze tablet on the walls of Parliament, unveiled in 1938 by Prime Minister Mackenzie King and the surviving "Famous Five" and their descendants.

Key equal rights issues came to define the CFBPWC: equal pay for equal work; the appointment of women senators from every province; the appointment of qualified women to boards and commissions; allowing women to serve on juries; and women's access to administrative jobs in the public service. Married women's lack of municipal voting rights in some cities (due to property qualifications) and women's forfeiture of Canadian citizenship on marriage to an "alien" (i.e., a non-Canadian) also registered protest. Local clubs were encouraged to study the status of women in their own locale, though "rights" were defined solely through the prism of gender, not race or ethnicity, something that would only slowly change in the years after the Second World War.

The Depression accentuated the urgency of addressing working women's precarious economic position. Some clubs collaborated with the YWCA to examine the need for urban housing for poorly paid or out-of-work women; others advocated welfare provision for the unemployed single women who had almost no access to relief (welfare) from municipalities, which prioritized male breadwinner and family needs. Some clubs called for shorter hours and a higher minimum wage, and a few outspoken leaders decried "fascistic" speeches by politicians determined to send women "back to the home."[70]

In 1931, the CFBPWC urged the federal government to include women in its employment emergency plans, a recommendation that was ignored. Some locals called on women from all walks of life to stand together during a time of hardship, and they urged the CFBPWC to enlighten the public about women's need to work, pushing back against those demanding that married women be fired to make room for unemployed men.

In 1931, the CFBPWC went on record in support of the controversial right of married women to work. How to justify this demand was a delicate issue, since some leaders believed the federation should use the language of needs – that is, that married women needed to work to support themselves or their families – while others thought the more egalitarian language of women's right to work should be defended. Trepidation about using the language of "rights" was in part a fear of being labelled extreme feminists: "We are all over women's rights," wrote one of these more timid BPWC leaders. "That sort of thing is out of date. The feminist movement terminated at the time of the war, and our goal is not obtaining rights, but helping to create a new society with a woman's point of view."[71]

Despite this declaration of feminism's decline, women's right to employment gained momentum as a key CFBPWC demand during the 1930s and especially in the 1940s and 1950s. When the federation later constructed its own history, its narrative was predicated on its quest for women's economic equality. Campaigns for federal and provincial equal pay laws, realized only in the 1950s, were a central part of this story, but some clubs ventured criticisms of a gendered division of labour that barred women from "men's" jobs. The BPWCs' feminist legacy was not just their public advocacy but also the manner in which ideas about equality percolated through local clubs, emboldening women who felt their labour was essential to the social good but lacked the language and courage to speak up. By creating a supportive women-only occupational group, the BPWCs modelled self-organization by and for women.

The CFBPWC was a complicated organization: its ideals were shaped by local needs, its leadership might differ from the grassroots, and its feminism was circumscribed by its overwhelming white, aspiring middle-class clientele. On workplace issues, the federation found allies on the left, such as Agnes Macphail. When it came to welfare or mothers' pensions, it veered toward the right. When the national convention discussed mothers' pensions, for instance, derogatory views of welfare recipients as wasteful spenders surfaced. Western clubs also applauded speakers who endorsed sterilization legislation.

The CFBPWC's choice of convention speakers reveals much: they included the progressive Nellie McClung, but also the conservative Hamilton city councillor Nora Henderson and even the upper-class Lady Eaton, not known for her defence of working women. Interviewed at the 1930 convention, Eaton voiced her disdain for democracy, saying "the extension of the franchise has not been of much benefit" since it doubled an electorate that was "not overly intelligent."[72] While her snooty superiority did not reflect CFBPWC politics, her imperialist sentiments were echoed in clubs before and during the Second World War. Like other reform feminists, members took for granted the benefits of the British Empire and the privileges associated with white, Anglo-Celtic superiority. That said, this outlook did shift after the Second World War, when the federation supported a broader understanding of human rights.

Women's Right to Work

The BPWCs' defence of married women's right to work took courage, but they had allies. If there was one issue that drew politically disparate women together in the thirties, it was opposition to demands that married women quit their jobs to make way for men. Some right-wing commentators even argued that *all* working women should be sent back to the home. No national group was created specifically to defend women's right to work; rather, different organizations, parties, and individuals constituted an informal united front of refusal. Advocacy for women's right to work was a stream of reform feminism – short lived, issue based, sometimes with multiple rationales – but it nonetheless was one of the most important issues generating feminist opposition to patriarchal thinking since the suffrage struggle.

Public commentary on women's right to work was intense and passionate. As Margaret Hobbs shows, local newspapers erupted into antagonistic debates about working wives in which the battlelines were not only set on the basis of gender.[73] Still, married women workers were always those assailed most viciously. Single women as well as full-time homemakers railed against working wives, claiming they were selfishly working for luxuries, taking jobs away from father-earners as well as needy single jobless women, who might be forced to sell their bodies for sustenance. The most vitriolic denunciations came from men who claimed married women workers were snatching the bread from the mouths of children by denying male breadwinners a job; they were undermining the family, Canadian manhood (since masculinity was measured by earning), and even the manhood of the nation.[74] Critics admitted that there might be a few needy widows or deserted mothers, but they were not the norm. Single working women who lived with their families were also suspect. They were working only for pin money, charged one unemployed veteran writing to Prime Minister R.B. Bennett: "They always spend their money on shows, besides having some Sugar Daddy to take them out."[75] Accusations against women often descended into hyperbole: people claimed they knew a woman came to work in a limo, threw luxurious dinner parties, bought fur coats, took extravagant holidays, and on and on.

The context – massive unemployment, human suffering, and a persisting ideal of separate spheres – made arguing for *all* women's right to work an uphill struggle. Individual working women pleaded their case privately to friends and families and publicly in letters to local newspapers. Many claimed wage earning was an extension of their maternal role; it was the only means to ensure their family's survival. They challenged stereotypes about the working wife with evidence that they supported desperate families and were hardly contemplating their next luxury cruise; in any case, they pointed out, most women did not usurp men's jobs, since they were relegated to domestic and other "feminine" work.

Where could individual women find support? Some women's reform organizations equivocated. The National Council of Women of Canada (NCWC) put its political head in the sand on this issue, not even following the progressive lead of its international parent organization (though some local councils, like the one in Montreal, diverged from this apathy). In contrast, the CFBPWC, influenced by its international parent, increasingly stood up for women's right to work. In 1933, the national president denounced attempts to replace women with men and lower women's salaries, undermining suffrage-era gains, which were "ours by right of a difficult conquest and painstaking labour."[76] However, some members continued to voice a "needs-based" argument; in a time of crisis, they ventured, women who did not absolutely need to work for self or family survival should leave the workforce.

Other women's reform organizations were similarly conflicted. Should they stress that women worked for self and family support, likely because there was no male breadwinner, or should they emphasize all women's equal right to work and economic independence? Feminist historians have characterized these two contenting arguments about work and welfare as the difference versus sameness debate: should feminists acknowledge women's biological and social differences or equate their needs and rights directly with those of men?[77] Both arguments were used during the Depression, sometimes within one organization or even by the same person. American historians have argued that the Depression undermined egalitarian feminist arguments for the right to work, but in Canada they did not disappear, and sometimes became more vigorous.

Like the NCWC, the trade union movement was ambivalent about married women's right to work. The influential craft trade union organization, the Trades and Labour Congress (TLC), editorialized that it had some sympathy for the "business girl" working for pay, but women's paid labour was an unfortunate byproduct of a disintegrating economy. If all men could earn a decent wage, marry, and establish homes, a wife would not want to work outside the home – a view some working-class women supported. The "Home" column for women in the TLC's *Canadian Congress Journal* (*CCJ*) made it clear that a male breadwinner was the true ideal.

Kathleen Derry, a labour feminist and occasional *CCJ* columnist, expressed sympathy for the forgotten unemployed woman, who faced social stigma as well as dire health consequences of low-paid labour. However, her arguments stressed the single unemployed "girl" while avoiding the contentious question of married women's work.[78] While the *CCJ* did not openly blame working wives, some local unions did, passing resolutions calling for their return to the home, even though their actual numbers in the workforce were small.[79] In 1931, the Toronto District Labour Council urged the city to fire married women, and the national TLC passed a similar resolution against working wives, thus making common cause with conservative women's auxiliaries of the Canadian Legion.

Federal, provincial, and municipal politicians usually acceded to these requests; they reassured – even boasted to – the voting public that *their* governments fired all women employees once they married. As late as 1939, labour feminist and Vancouver city coucillor Helena Gutteridge was still battling the city's efforts to limit the employment of wives.[80] Single unemployed women also garnered scant sympathy from welfare officials who assumed they should either retreat to their family home or find domestic jobs. The YWCA, long concerned with the working woman "adrift" in the city, stood out by advocating for these women's housing and welfare needs. Yet many middle-class women's reform groups, even if they supported the unemployed woman, were uninterested in other maligned groups such as immigrants and the racialized, scapegoated as women were – for high unemployment and 'taking jobs away' from more deserving men – but treated more punitively, threatened with deportation.

A feminist defence of *all* women's unambiguous right to work fell to a few brave feminist organizations, writers, and politicians, as well as the socialist left (discussed in the next chapter). The progressive magazine *Canadian Forum* published articles lamenting the "retroactive movement" against women and the "persecution of married women." Should not women, Gwethalyn Graham asked, be able to "work for the sake of work itself?"[81] Those who thought that earlier feminists had thrown in the towel were proven wrong, as former suffragists took up the cause of women's right to work and welfare. Helen Gregory MacGill took on the back-to-the-home advocates in *Chatelaine,* reminding readers that women's wages kept some families afloat after a husband deserted them, died, or was disabled. But she also went beyond familial need, challenging the double standard about wage earning: being jobless, she warned, "is not a matter of sex, and suffering caused by hunger and cold is not limited to either men or women."[82]

As fascism gained ground in Europe, some politically minded women warned that a "fascistic" ideology, in which women were limited to "Kinder, Küche, Kirche," was seeping into Canada; critics equated anti-feminist Montreal mayor Camillien Houde with "Mussolini and Hitler."[83] No one was more prominent in defence of working women than Canada's only female MP. Agnes Macphail knew first-hand the antipathy directed at women in non-traditional work, and she jumped into the fray, deriding the argument that married women should be confined to housework, which, in any case, she did not see as particularly fulfilling. She marshalled economic arguments about women's role as worker and consumer in the evolution of industrialism, but, unlike many feminists, she suggested work was integral to human life: in order to be "spiritually happy, [a woman] must work, must make her contribution to the highest good."[84]

Macphail took on some of the most vocal anti-feminists of the time, including Médéric Martin, a former Montreal mayor and member of Quebec's legislative upper house, who published a deliberately provocative piece, "Go Home Young Woman," in *Chatelaine,* arguing that all women should do the patriotic thing and vacate their jobs for male earners.[85] In *Le Devoir,* too, Martin insisted unequivocally, "il va failloir remettre la femme à sa place, à la maison" (we will have to put women back in their place, in the home).[86] The current economic crisis, he argued, was caused not only by overproduction but by the substitution of women's for men's labour in various occupations since the nineteenth century. Society was now reaping the disastrous consequences. While he recognized that women's immediate removal from the workforce might seem impossible, he suggested an international conference to work out a gradual withdrawal – say 5 percent a year – to turn back the clock to a sound male-breadwinner economy.[87]

Macphail ridiculed Martin's outlandish call to abolish all women's paid work, yet Martin gave voice to widespread fears across English and French Canada of an imperilled patriarchal family, menacing gender-role reversal, and threats to masculine dignity. He was not the only politician to blame working women for the crisis. Joseph-Napoléon Francoeur, a Liberal member of the Quebec legislative assembly, tabled a motion to restrict women's paid labour unless they could prove it necessary for their own or their family's survival. It was defeated in 1935.[88] Leaders of the Quebec suffrage campaign provided powerful counter-arguments, with Idola Saint-Jean making the radical claim that women had an unequivocal right to work. In her radio addresses and in *La sphère féminine*, published by the Alliance canadienne pour le vote des femmes du Québec, she defied Francoeur with resolutely feminist rhetoric: "Prétend-on refuser aux femmes le droit de vivre et de jouir de la dignité et de l'indépendance que le travail confère à tout être?" (Do we pretend to refuse women the right to live and enjoy the dignity and independence that work confers on all beings?)[89]

Quebec's maternalist reformers had – perhaps inadvertently – facilitated social approbation of working wives. *La bonne parole* acknowledged that the single woman working for wages was an inevitable necessity, though one requiring moral vigilance, but a married working woman was a serious social problem. Married women's paid labour was an affront to social life: it was outside the bounds of normalcy, "en soi contra nature ... une conception erronée de la vie sociale" (in itself against nature ... a misconception of social life).[90] In reports on conferences abroad about mothers' industrial work outside the home, various remedies were offered, but always with the view to keep mothers in the home. Even long-time rights advocate Marie Gérin-Lajoie had shied away from demanding rights for working mothers, suggesting that married women working were an exception, not the ideal.[91]

Protesting Racial Workforce Exclusions

English-Canadian feminists assumed that Quebec women had to contend with a backward culture, nurtured by the Catholic Church. While the church's antipathy to feminism was indisputable, working wives faced opposition across the country. Moreover, few feminists who opposed gender discrimination in the workforce acknowledged persisting racial and ethnic discrimination. Racial and ethnic divisions of labour were ideologically normalized as natural, and some racialized women were barred from higher education and certain occupations.

The First World War exacerbated ethnic tensions between preferred British and non-preferred Asian and European immigrants, and these divisions persisted in the interwar period. Some former suffragists remained committed to a project of assimilation. Augusta Stowe-Gullen, often a progressive voice, was not so on immigration. Non-English speaking immigrants, she believed, must assimilate: they should "adopt our habits, customs, language," otherwise "Canada will have foreign nations in our dominion and we will be in danger of being overthrown by people in her midst."[92] In equating "Canadianess" with "Britishness," she was far from alone. Southern and eastern European women found their employment opportunities limited by prejudice as well as language barriers. Women of colour were often targeted most openly. Organizations like the newly formed Native Daughters of British Columbia promoted a virulent anti-Asian agenda and the BC women's reform paper, the *Western Woman's Weekly*, published racist suggestions to segregate "Oriental" children in their own schools and boycott businesses of "foreigners."[93]

In the 1930s, women of colour spoke out against persisting racial discrimination at work, taking their struggle into the 1940s and 1950s, when they finally received a somewhat better hearing. Anti-racist women often battled alone as they fought for better lives and opportunities for themselves and especially for their daughters: this too was part of the quest for women's equality, even if it was not lauded as such at the time. In Ontario, for instance, the Depression put pressure on African-Canadian women's wages and solidified their limited occupational choices, which, since the nineteenth century had focused primarily on domestic and service work. As one woman remembered, "Depression" was only a word she heard from her parents: for most struggling Black families, economic insecurity defined their lives throughout the 1920s and 1930s. African-Canadian women in Toronto vividly recalled the boundaries of work: "Domestic work – there was no other work Black women could get in those days." Women worked for as little as "five dollars a week and old clothes"; those who wanted to train for white-collar work were dismissively asked, "who would hire you?"[94] Some occupations were simply out of bounds: no nursing schools in Canada admitted African-Canadian students.

African-Canadian women's grassroots groups in both Ontario and Nova Scotia took up the cause of access to nursing education. Even after the Canadian Nurses Association passed a resolution against all discrimination in 1944, schools might disregard this policy, continuing to tell Black applicants to go to the United States.[95] In Windsor, in the 1930s, the Hour-a-Day

Club organized by local African-Canadian women wrote to the provincial government and the University of Toronto, protesting this blatant discrimination. Founded in 1935, the Hour-a-Day Study Club had evolved from an earlier Motherhood Club and was closely linked to the Black churches, as well as being affiliated with the Local Council of Women. "Community development and self-improvement" lay at the heart of the club's early volunteer work. Dedicated to maternal self-education to benefit the family, as well as charitable and social service work for their own community, the Hour-a-Day women also confronted educational discrimination, initiating, for instance, scholarships for local Black students. They addressed racism in the local community by working with white women's reform groups such as the YWCA and, increasingly, by demanding legislative and social change. When local groups suggested banning all Blacks from the nearby Boblo Island amusement park in 1944, the club wrote to the *Windsor Daily Star*, calling for a new municipal bylaw banning racial discrimination.[96]

Supporting and recognizing Black culture was an important element of Black women's equality agenda: African-Canadian history had to be preserved and valued, not only as a matter of dignity, but in order to spark a change in white consciousness. And there could be no equality for African-Canadian women without dignity for their community. Their cultural and political efforts went hand-in-hand with efforts to open up better economic opportunities for their children. This was true as well for the Nova Scotia Association for the Advancement of Coloured People, an organization that supported Viola Desmond's famous court case against discrimination and nurtured the efforts of Pearleen Oliver to end racist discrimination in education, including nursing education.

Raised in the mining community of New Glasgow, Nova Scotia, by the widow of a miner, Oliver knew the sting of poverty and the limited job opportunities for African-Canadian women. She put herself through high school by doing housework and was the first African-Canadian woman to graduate from that school; she was not "segregated," she remembered, just "ignored."[97] Even though she was relatively well educated for the time, her ambition to attend nursing school was thwarted: no Canadian schools would train Black nurses. After marriage to a minister also deeply involved in the African-Canadian community, she moved to Halifax, where she spearheaded anti-discrimination protests through the courts, public education, and local institutions. Oliver encouraged Viola Desmond to mount a legal defence after she was ejected from a "white" section of a movie theatre in New Glasgow, and she lobbied the Halifax School Board to remove racist books like *Little Black Sambo* from the curriculum. She was also critical of discrimination within her own community, lamenting the Baptist Church's refusal to allow the ordination of women ministers.[98]

Known in the Black community for her equal rights work, Oliver was contacted by women who were denied entry to nursing schools. She took the issue public, speaking out and writing about it in local newspapers. During the Second World War, she pointed out that her brothers were serving overseas, fighting against Hitler, supposedly for "democracy," a word that seemed rather shallow to those who did not experience it at home. After considerable public effort, Oliver saw nursing open up, first with two Black women admitted to the Nova Scotia Children's Hospital and then the Victoria General Hospital. One nursing student came from Ontario through Oliver's contacts with women fighting the same battle there. Oliver's efforts to address discrimination were not unlike those of the Hour-a-Day Club. She spoke publicly about racist discrimination to social service organizations, newspapers, and on radio. At the same time, she put her faith in community self-development through women's institutes, girls' clubs like Canadian Girls in Training, and camps for African-Canadian youth: these, she felt, would nurture Black leadership, education, and pride.[99] Like the Windsor women, Oliver understood that the concept of equality was meaningless while racism persisted; only by challenging both racial and gender barriers could African-Canadian mothers and their daughters secure the social and economic opportunities they had long been denied.

Conclusion

While both Pearleen Oliver and the Hour-a-Day Club attempted to cooperate with white women's service organizations like the YWCA, racial and ethnic differences directed women into different pathways to equality. Take the example of the Halifax BPWC opening this chapter. In that group, local minutes show no concern with racial discrimination until well into the period after the Second World War. Even then, the club's understanding of cultural and racial diversity was to discuss different "international" groups and promote the ideals of the United Nations. Discrimination on their home turf was not on the agenda. In 1956, in recognition of "brotherhood" week, they invited women from the Second Baptist Church to sing "negro spirituals."[100] This attempt at cultural outreach was a far cry from an understanding that African-Canadian women in the city had a distinct history, their experiences shaped by multiple inequalities of gender, class, and race.

The Halifax BPWC was not unusual; other women's reform organizations were also composed primarily of white professional and working women pursuing equality of opportunity in politics, education, and the workforce. Despite its limitations, their activism did shatter the myth that suffrage-era feminists suddenly dropped the ball after they won their "new freedom." "Mother citizens" lobbied for welfare measures for vulnerable women, and working women resisted efforts to limit or remove their right to work for pay, while Quebec women campaigned for suffrage and other legal rights. Like other Canadian suffragists, francophone women met with ingrained patriarchal ideas about gender and the family, but, in Quebec, these were closely interwoven with discourses about nationalism and the survival of French Canada.

Armed with new political rights, women's equality seekers were now demanding enhanced economic rights. Feminist pushback against those who demanded that women workers return to their proper place in the home led to perhaps the most amorphous, decentralized, and ideologically diverse alliance of all, interesting precisely for that reason. It symbolized a united front of refusal: a defence of women's right to economic survival and independence and, indirectly, a critique of a falsely idealized domesticity for women.

Most women's rights and reform organizations, however, did not consider, let alone reach out to, ethnic and racialized groups, including non-Anglo, white working-class women immigrants, and certainly not to Indigenous women, save to see them as subjects for assimilation. In the era after the Second World War, this would slowly shift. There were, however, other feminist streams of activism in the 1920s and 1930s more inclusive of immigrant women, as well as new political parties more acutely aware of the needs of working-class women. Labour and socialist feminists also regrouped after the First World War. If some made common cause with other feminists to defend all women's right to work, they nonetheless had a different vision of equality, tied to human liberation from class exploitation and the competitive ethos of capitalism.

5 Agrarian, Labour, and Socialist Feminism after the First World War

In 1980, I asked Sophia Dixon, former Woman President of the United Farmers of Canada (UFC), Saskatchewan Section, if socialism might change women's lives. "Yes [it would]," she shot back tersely. "We'd be equal." Her rapid-fire repartee had something to do with Dixon's prickly character, but, when given the chance to elaborate, she had an acute analysis of the bodily, social, and political inequality experienced by women under capitalism. Discussing her campaign for legal birth control in the thirties, she identified the heart of the matter: "without [reproductive] control, you are not free; you are simply not a person." She was decades ahead of her time.[1]

Nellie Peterson, also a farmer, expressed her socialism and feminism differently. Peterson was acutely aware of gender inequality, even within her own party, the Co-operative Commonwealth Federation (CCF), yet she stressed her hopes for a society based on peace and cooperation: social resources should be shared so all human needs were taken care of, an impossibility in any society beholden to the profit motive of competitive capitalism. For Peterson, cooperation meant that "people with varying needs" would come together "to solve common problems, such as making the economic system work for everyone, or choosing peace over war. Competition aligns one against the other. There is a winner and loser. With cooperation, we can all be winners. Maybe that's a dream. But it's my dream."[2]

Dixon and Peterson were products of radical farmers' movements, their politics shaped by the Depression experience, ethical and materialist socialist ideas, and the brand of agrarian feminism first articulated by suffragists such as Violet McNaughton, who was an essential link between suffragists and interwar feminism. In the two decades after the First World War, agrarian, labour, and socialist feminism flourished; these overlapping currents of "progressive" feminism sometimes existed in tension but, as much as possible, sought mutual alliances. Women expressed their hopes for equality and improved lives for rural and working-class women through farm, labour, and socialist newspapers, movements, political parties, fleeting campaigns, and temporary coalitions. This chapter highlights the social conditions and ideas shaping their feminism, their political concerns, and their modalities of organizing.

Since I interviewed Dixon and Peterson in 1980, scholarship on these currents of feminism has changed dramatically. Sources previously hidden have come to light, oral histories have been completed, government surveillance records have been uncovered, and interpretive paradigms have come and gone. The expanse of new writing includes biographies of socialist and communist women and studies of women's farm and anti-war movements, labour socialism, the CCF and the Communist Party of Canada (CPC), left-wing unions, anti-poverty campaigns, communist culture, socialist feminist female friendships, political tourism, consumer activism, and more. If I could barely scratch the surface of left-wing feminism in one book in the 1980s, it is even more difficult to do so in the following two chapters: inevitably, my scope is narrowed to a few people, issues, and organizations; however, the plethora of unexplored topics simply reinforces the point that no trough followed the wave of suffrage activism.[3]

Categorization – just like waves – plagues our history writing. "Progressive" might be an appropriate umbrella term for agrarian, labour, and socialist women, though it lacks some precision; after all, many were, or became, left leaning and had some critique of capitalism and Canada's class system. The label "feminist" is also contentious. Some socialist women embraced it; others recoiled from it. Annie Hollis, a former British suffragette who became a suffragist and then agrarian feminist in Saskatchewan, did not describe herself as a feminist, believing this term implied women's separateness or superiority rather than a political partnership of women and men. Other feminist socialists were similarly averse to the word, but, because they critiqued women's exploitation and oppression and advocated measures to tackle gender equality, they deserve representation in the history of feminism.

Like reform-minded feminists, agrarian and labour feminists were deeply affected by the economic crisis of the Depression, though working-class and farm women did not recall the twenties as a period of "roaring" affluence. A recession after the First World War led to job losses and wage cuts, and the labour movement was weakened after the 1919 Winnipeg General Strike. The mass action in Winnipeg and solidarity strikes across Canada laid bare class divisions between feminists: women had no option but to choose sides in this defining historical moment. While Nellie McClung denounced the arrogance of the workers' tactics, Winnipeg socialist and pacifist Helen Armstrong mobilized women's strike support – spending time in jail as a result.

Blacklisting, deportations, and firings occurred in the wake of this Canadian-wide workers' revolt. If the Bolshevik-led Russian Revolution of 1917 inspired workers, it cast fear into boardrooms and cabinet offices, intensified in the wake of 1919. The state reacted quickly, using censorship, legislation limiting political dissent, political trials, and deportations to contain the "scourge" of anarchism, communism, and socialism.[4] In the United States, an intense Red Scare after 1919 galvanized conservative women against any version of feminism linked to working-class and socialist politics. They denounced "Miss Bolsheviki" as the female version of the dreaded male revolutionary but also claimed that socialist and pacifist women were a mortal danger to America. Conservative women's campaigns to cast these women as "un-American" were so successful that even reform feminists backtracked on their moderate political agenda, fearing they would be tarred with the socialist brush.[5]

Anti-socialist ideas always spilled over the border, and, while a similar backlash was less thoroughgoing in Canada, it did occur. Conservative women's organizations incorporated anti-socialism into their post-war politics of conservatism, tradition, empire, and anti-immigrant rhetoric. The immediate post-war years were not ideologically welcoming to socialist-feminist ideas – though, in some ways, no time had been. Nonetheless, over the next two decades, new feminist organizing thrived in multiple venues, often focused either on agrarian or labour organizing, although some women bravely tried to create an alliance of the two.

Agrarian Feminism

Agrarian feminism had roots in the suffrage struggle but was refashioned in the interwar period in radical women's farm organizations and later the CCF. Agrarian feminism was grounded in women' day-to-day experience of, and concerns about, family farm production, but it also encompassed a critique of unequal gender relations, both in society and underpinning farm life. Agrarian feminists, as Georgina Taylor observes, had "two identities": as farmers who needed a square deal in the face of a rigged economic system and as farm women who simultaneously suffered inequalities and disabilities specific to their sex.[6] Agrarian feminists often invoked the need for democracy, egalitarianism, and cooperation, but some also referred to themselves as part of an oppressed "farming class."

Not all organized farm women followed this path. Across the country, Women's Institutes (WI), Cercles de fermières, and Homemakers Clubs were more inclusive and non-partisan avenues for farm women's organizing. These voluntary organizations brought to light the undervaluing of women's farm work, promoted rural reforms to improve the lives of farm families, and facilitated invaluable social connections for isolated women.[7] The Ontario Women's Institutes, initially funded by the Ontario government (and overseen by a male government official) as a "non-political" project for women's education and farm betterment, included many small-town members as well as farmers who benefited from the organization's sociability, charity, and reform work. Despite the group's non-political designation, WI women gained leadership acumen as they mobilized to secure better social services for rural families.[8]

Agrarian feminist groups like the United Farm Women of Ontario (UFWO), United Farm Women of Alberta, and United Farm Women of Manitoba shared many of these concerns, and sometimes had overlapping memberships, but also developed a more ambitious political agenda for social change.[9] The years immediately after the First World War saw a flurry of agrarian feminist organizing as newly enfranchised women raised their political voices, not only about the oppression of the farming class but also about women's disadvantaged position in farm families and rural communities. In theory, agrarian feminists in the UFWO had allies in the parent United Farmers of Ontario (UFO), whose platform trumpeted support for "absolute equality of the sexes socially, politically, economically."[10]

The UFWO attempted to juggle separate organizing of women, to address their specific concerns, with participation in the UFO. It was not easy. Emma Griesbach, UFWO columnist in the *Farmers' Sun,* vowed to create a women's column for "thinking" feminist farm women that jettisoned recipes in favour of serious economic and gender issues, discussing women's undervalued labour and suggesting radical alternatives, such as cooperative laundries and kitchens. Aghast at the UFO's lack of interest in welcoming women into its ranks, she also critiqued the patriarchal ideology that licensed men to "ride their high horses" over the needs of women and children.[11]

While almost all farm women's organizations talked about protecting the viability of the family farm during the Depression, agrarian feminists were ready to contemplate radical solutions to do so. The United Farmers of Canada in Saskatchewan, for example, discussed common ownership of the land and a "use lease policy," a fundamental challenge to the sacred liberal belief in private property.[12] Although the United Farmers of Ontario had a testy relationship with socialists in the CCF, some Prairie farm women threw their lot in with the new socialist party. Margaret McClelland, a farmer from Letellier, Manitoba, initially tried to build the radical Independent Farmers Party, and then acted as president of the United Farm Women of Manitoba before shifting her allegiance to the CCF. As the Depression took its toll, agrarian socialist feminists assailed the profit motive of capitalism and advocated for the nationalization of resources, railways, and banks, as well as demanding a radically comprehensive, universal welfare state. They also named farm women's specific oppression: their unrecognized labour, heavy work load, lack of reproductive control, and vulnerability to patriarchal legal norms.

Sophia Dixon exemplified this stream of agrarian feminism, rooted in the material realities of farmwork, cemented through cooperative community activism, yet also attuned to women's specific needs and disadvantages. Dixon's Danish parents immigrated to the Prairies in 1915 when she was eleven. Barely eking out a living on a homestead, they placed Sophia out as a domestic servant before she had learned English. The experience of denigration at the hand of her employers, all too common for domestics, was not something she forgot. Dixon knew the feel of farm poverty intimately, but, as a voracious reader and autodidact, she excelled at school, even while simultaneously working as a domestic to aid her struggling parents. After training at a normal school and working as a teacher, she married and became a farmer herself.

Dixon was an early convert to farm activism, first joining the Saskatchewan Grain Growers Association in 1919 when she was a rural teacher, then supporting the Progressive Group, the more radical of whom, like member of Parliament William Irvine, encouraged her activism. Her correspondence with Violet McNaughton and subsequent involvement in the Women's International League for Peace and Freedom sharpened her sense that women had a qualitatively different view of politics. She was politically active both in her own community and provincially, first on the UFC executive and later as a CCF organizer. Activism was labour in itself, not always easily accommodated to farm women's work schedules. In Dixon's case, four

Figure 5.1 Sophia Dixon combined a socialist and feminist analysis of agrarian women's labour and advocated for the legalization of birth control information | Saskatchewan Archives Board, S-B5517

young children born in quick succession and inescapable farm labour often temporarily circumscribed her political activities during the early 1930s.

Dixon was intellectually engaged and politically astute, even if she was not always comfortable bending her principles in pursuit of political power. Politics may have been her métier, but she disliked politicking, and, as the CCF increasingly engaged in the latter by the late 1940s, she became disenchanted, though she remained loyal to the party she helped build. As an agrarian socialist feminist, Dixon twinned her analysis of the social problems of farmers with the specifics of women's oppression. She conveyed her political ideals in maternal terms, arguing that socialist women had to build a better future for their children, yet she was equally animated by economic debates about monetary reform, social credit, and agricultural cooperation. Her farm activism was impelled by an anti-capitalist critique that saw maldistribution of goods as responsible for rampant economic inequality. At the same time, her feminism was sharpened by her abhorrence of war and her courageous campaign for women's reproductive rights – women, she believed, had to "own their own bodies."[13]

The birth control issue was buffeted about by the UFC with little regard for women's needs, teaching Dixon and other farm feminists a bitter lesson. In 1930, a resolution advocating changes in the law and stating that physicians should be free to offer birth control advice was approved at the UFC annual convention, strongly supported by women attendees. It was undermined later by a male-dominated executive, anxious lest it alienate the electorate, including Catholics. A compromise resolution proposed by Dixon a year later was also rescinded by the executive. She acquiesced, promising to back the "economic" platform of the UFC, but privately voiced her feminist disappointment: "I cannot forgive him [the male president] for saying that there is 'no principle involved' in asking doctors to dispense [birth control] advice to needy cases ... There's just as much principle involved in saving a woman's life as there is in saving the buildings which constitute the shell of a home ... to prevent evictions, foreclosures and seizures."[14]

The birth control defeat went to the heart of farm women's dilemma: they felt kinship with male farmers, with whom they shared economic uncertainty and hard labour, but they were aggrieved when the same men failed to comprehend women's specific hardships. A politics of collaboration and critique was their solution: collaboration with men in radical farm organizations but selective criticism of patriarchal ideas and traditions that circumscribed farm women's lives. In a similar fashion, they cooperated with other feminist groups on issues of mutual benefit but did not hesitate to criticize middle- and upper-class women who aligned themselves with the power-brokers propping up an unjust economic system.

Across the country, agrarian feminism took on different political hues, but it was especially strong on the Prairies, where the devastation of the Depression – plummeting wheat prices, drought, farms lost to foreclosure – sparked an openness to rethinking the entire economic system.[15] As Sophia Dixon told me, it seemed that "capitalism was crumbling and it was up to us to find an alternative." Her alternative was "production for use not for profit," the ethical socialist proposal that resources be used for the well-being of all, not corralled for the profit of the very few.[16] In the eyes of agrarian feminists, land was more than a private commodity: it was also home, a place of work, a locus of family, and the means of survival. It held out potential rewards, but, for impoverished farm women, it could also be a prison of incessant demands.

Figure 5.2 Agrarian feminist Violet McNaughton linked the suffrage and post-war women's movement | University of Saskatchewan Archives, S-B 2048

Politicized rural women contributed to mixed-gender farm groups, but many built autonomous organizations dedicated to women's issues, such as the Women's Section of the UFC. For Violet McNaughton, a UFC supporter and editor of the women's page of the *Western Producer* (*WP*), gender and class inequality could not be disentangled. A self-named "ardent feminist, farm woman and radical" on the left,[17] McNaughton believed that rural women and men were drawn together by virtue of their ties to the land, but that women were subject to unequal familial and social power, lacking full control over their productive and reproductive labour. Fighting eastern corporate interests, tariffs, and an unsympathetic state was one battle. Another, though more quietly stated, was to end women's subjection to the "benevolent patriarchs" running most farms.[18]

Like Dixon, McNaughton was a strong advocate of accessible birth control, sometimes privately sending information to desperate women who begged for advice. Her politics veered toward social democracy, advocating reform of the capitalist system, but she also expressed a socialist commitment to cooperation rather than competition and to full social and economic security for small producers. Free, universally accessible rural medical care "within the reach of all" was one of McNaughton's cherished goals, twinning class and gender concerns.[19] Universal health care would aid all rural families, but it particularly addressed the unequal burden of women's labour; women cared for the sick, injured, and elderly, and the lack of prenatal, birthing, and postnatal care left women vulnerable to ill health and death. McNaughton could recite rural statistics on high infant and maternal mortality rates, but she knew they could never capture the fear, anxiety, and pain of isolated farm women suffering miscarriages and difficult births or desperately seeking medical care for ill children. Her solution was democratic and socialist medicine: local communities would have control over medical provision, which would be fully funded by all levels of government. Arguably, the ideological work of her campaign paved the way for the Saskatchewan CCF's later, historic enactment of medicare.

McNaughton had her finger on the pulse of many political issues, from tariffs and international peace to medical care, women's right to work, and birth control. By the time she began editing the *WP* women's page in 1925, she had carved out a reputation as an astute organizer in the Saskatchewan Women's Grain Growers and a talented "bridge builder" between feminist organizations.[20] Yet, providing a welcoming virtual space in the *WP* for farm women to voice their problems and advocate social solutions proved to be one of her most enduring contributions. While travel and communication were easier for interwar than nineteenth-century feminists, the circulation of print culture remained critical to the popularization of feminist ideas. Most people did not have radios, farm women were geographically isolated, and they, like most working-class women, could not afford to travel. Print culture was a form of community building; as UFC activist Lori Jones recalls, *WP* letters often came from repeat correspondents, and "one began to feel" they were one's "neighbours" in print.[21]

McNaughton also nurtured a vibrant feminist network through her vast personal correspondence. With a keen eye for political talent, she cultivated many Saskatchewan women leaders, including Annie Hollis, Sophia Dixon, and Dorise Nielsen (later a communist MP). In 1924, she invited Hollis, a former president of the women's section of the Saskatchewan Grain Growers Association, to author a *WP* column. Hollis had been both a suffragette and an admirer of Owenite cooperative socialism in England before she immigrated to Saskatchewan. She incorporated both ideals into her agrarian socialist feminism. Although she did not use the label "feminist," when some politicians called for the dismissal of working women during the Depression, she stood resolutely on the side of feminism, denouncing reactionary attempts to "blame" married women workers for unemployment.[22]

The advantage of cooperation over the disasters of competitive capitalism was one theme in Hollis's writing, but so too was women's second-class citizenship. As an Owenite, she placed her faith in a changed environment, culture, and education to address women's oppression and build a more co-operative humanity. As a feminist, she tried to nurture women's political consciousness and translate their daily discontents into activism. No issue was more galling to her than the discounting of women's unpaid farm labour. Anticipating later feminist critiques, she pointed out that the census legitimated this ideological slight of hand: farm wives were advised to write "no occupation" when, in fact, they were "cooks, housemaid, nurse, seamstress ... to which could be added gardening, poultry raising, dairy work."[23]

For Hollis and other agrarian feminists, the discounting of women's farm labour mirrored their legal and social inequality. Often farm women "pulled a double harness," sharing the field work while being solely responsible for domestic labour.[24] Yet they had little say in financial decisions, minimal rights to the farm property, and were vulnerable to abusive partners. The downgrading of women's rural labour was a lament heard across the country. "Feminism in the city may mean ... equal pay for equal work," wrote an Ontario farmer, "but on the farm ... it means a power-machine for the house for every tractor bought for the farm. A bathtub in every house for a binder on the farm."[25] A survey by the United Farm Women of Manitoba concluded women's "unrelenting" labour stretched across field and household, but power machinery was not considered for the home, even for "woman killing" chores like hauling water.[26]

Both Hollis and McNaughton used the *Western Producer* as a tool for collective consciousness raising among farm women. Their outreach had limits. Despite the intent to create a space for all "creeds, races and religions," the women's page was read primarily by English-speaking, Anglo-Celtic white settlers.[27] McNaughton promoted ethnic tolerance toward often-maligned non-Anglo settlers, such as the Ukrainians, but the paper did not reflect their input. The "mail bag" was intended to be a cooperative project, with women readers determining what was discussed, but McNaughton censored submissions if she felt they were factually inaccurate, inflammatory, or incited religious hatred.[28]

Nonetheless, women's grievances, political commentary, and hopes for a transformed society, expressed with insight and emotion, made their way into *WP* pages. Readers wrote about birth control (usually demanding it, with justifications that ran the gamut from eugenics to women's rights), the need to avoid wars, better education and medical care, economic reform, marriage, and all manner of domestic and child care issues. Farm women's strategy of critique and collaboration was often apparent, sometimes in the same letter. While advocating cooperative ideals, women also vented about gender inequality. "It is rather incongruous to see a man smarting with a sense of capitalist injustice, trying to snatch his purse from the capitalist with one hand while he holds it out of his partner's reach with the other," commented one correspondent in a critique of patriarchal control of the household.[29] The privacy of pseudonyms allowed letter writers to speak their feminist minds: "slavery starts with marriage," said one letter writer, reminding *WP* readers that, legally, a husband "controls the property ... that you may both have worked for – you own nothing. Because a man and woman decide to live together it should not mean that he is head of the house and chancellor of the exchequer."[30]

Hollis and McNaughton were suffragists who redefined their agrarian feminism after the First World War. Nellie Peterson represented a new generation of agrarian feminists, though it is likely significant that her mother was a suffragist. Peterson's parents, active in the farm movement, introduced her to the United Farmers of Alberta and to socialist William Irvine, her life-long mentor and political comrade. A Scottish immigrant, Irvine came to Alberta as a minister but, after resigning from his church position in the wake of the 1919 workers' revolt, devoted his life to journalism and politics, initially elected to Parliament for the Progressive Party before breaking off as part of the independent "Ginger Group." Irvine combined a materialist analysis of capitalism's waste and irrationality with an optimistic faith in popular democracy and a social gospel abhorrence of injustice. While he worked for evolutionary change, Irvine was also critical of the "half way house" of piecemeal, social democratic reform,[31] believing socialists should always keep their eye on the ultimate goal: the end of the competitive, capitalist system.

Nellie Peterson, Sophia Dixon, and Amelia Turner Smith (discussed below) were all encouraged by Irvine to become politically active. An only child, Peterson was able to attend normal school; her experience teaching across Alberta offered a front-row seat on rural poverty, as she witnessed farm families reduced to "little more than potatoes, rhubarb and salt pork."[32] She too became a farmer, marrying and settling near Mayerthorpe, north of Edmonton. While both she and her husband Roy were United Farmers of Alberta and later CCF supporters, Nellie was the family politician, one of the most talented, persuasive, and passionate of her generation. She was a strong advocate of rural co-ops, the nationalization of resources, and a

Farmer-Labour alliance, running for office more than once, always in lost-cause constituencies.

Peterson was not known primarily as a feminist yet, when campaigning for the CCF, it was expected that women candidates would address female voters' concerns about family care, and Peterson did so in her radio addresses.[33] She did see women's economic independence as the bedrock of a socialist, egalitarian society. When she married in the 1930s, she was horrified to find "she owned nothing of her own." Without basic legal and property rights, she argued, women would never achieve economic equality.[34] For someone who likely identified first as a socialist, she had innovative feminist ideas. In the 1950s, she ushered a resolution on "wages for housework" – a feminist concept ahead of its time – through the Alberta CCF convention, even cajoling cautious social democrat Grant Notley into voting for it (though the national party never allowed it to go further).[35]

Dixon, McNaughton, and Peterson were on-the-ground architects of an agrarian socialist feminism, conditioned by women's labour on the land, forged in economic adversity, and fashioned within women's collective search for an alternative to capitalism that went beyond rural cooperation to encompass a radical redistribution of wealth, social ownership of resources, and a universal welfare state. Unlike earlier agrarian feminists, they more forthrightly called for women's reproductive autonomy, and some challenged inequality within the family, community, and radical movements, or, as one UFC woman put it succinctly, the way "[women] were always overpowered by the men in the room."[36]

They had political weaknesses. The pre-eminence of white, Euro-Canadian men and women in political life was rarely questioned. Though some advocated tolerance toward "outsider" non-Anglo settlers, they did not see colonialism on their own doorstep. Few were concerned with Indigenous women, yet many farmed on land previously cared for by Indigenous people. This profound settler myopia makes it seem incongruous to talk about women's land-based politics when they did not consider whose land they were on. Many accepted the mythology that "Indians" never wanted to farm so had signed treaties consigning them to reserves. Ironically, socialists praised collectivity and cooperation, yet knew little about the importance of these concepts in Indigenous communities. Agrarian feminists also seemed unacquainted with Indigenous women's own maternal organizing in homemakers clubs, initiated by the state, but increasingly conduits for Indigenous activism – discussed in Chapter 9.

This political deficiency was not unique to rural feminists. Urban socialist feminists also tended to see class as critical; they put less emphasis on race and ethnic oppression, and remained insensible to Canada's own brand of internal colonialism.

Labour and Socialist Feminism

When Beatrice Brigden ran for federal election in Brandon, Manitoba, in 1930 as a Farmer-Labour candidate, she was convinced these two disadvantaged groups could unite to challenge capitalism. Not all socialist feminists shared her optimism about this alliance, but many agreed on the importance of "labour" to socialist politics: the task at hand was to mobilize workers' conscious of their own economic interests, which were inevitably different from those of capital. Working-class people could be roused to fight for the redistribution of wealth, the sharing of resources, economic security for all, true democracy unencumbered by the power of money, and the dignity of the "common people." "Labour socialism" has been suggested as one label for their ideals.[37] Whether they called themselves labourites, syndicalists, or socialists, these women developed a thoroughgoing critique of the inhumanity of capitalism and a vision of society without class and gender exploitation.

Yet how to get to this utopia on earth – the "New Jerusalem" – was a point of disagreement. The 1919 workers' revolt had a profound impact on socialists, but they subsequently experimented with different strategies, making a linear genealogy, or even a comprehensive account, of socialist feminism almost impossible. In the 1920s, women were active in Labour Parties and Independent Labour Parties (in the British mode); Socialist Parties, especially in British Columbia and Ontario; the syndicalist One Big Union; Industrial Workers of the World (IWW) unions; labour and socialist publishing; anti-poverty and unemployment work; and coalitions of socialist and feminist women, both long term and fleeting, local and regional. There was no one socialist-feminist home base.

It is also difficult to disentangle the feminist side of socialist feminism in organizations whose raison d'être was socialism. Women worked with male comrades on a common anti-capitalist project, but it is a mistake to think that socialist politics were gender neutral or that women's issues were completely inconsequential. Labour socialism was decidedly gendered, though in a masculine mould: the images and metaphors used by socialists echoed a virile masculine radical manhood; those workers deemed most important to recruit were wage-earning men; there was an assumption of superior male leadership; and, in some cases, women's discussion of their oppression or calls to organize women autonomously were scornfully dismissed.[38] Yet some women came to socialism through feminism. Like Laura Jamieson, they might be inspired by the "zest of the suffrage fight" to pursue their equality-seeking goals within the socialist movement.[39] They saw women's equality as integral to their brand of socialism, a reason to be, or to remain, socialists. Autonomous women's groups were also part of labour socialism; in the 1920s, they were often amorphous, decentralized, local, sometimes short lived, and quite unlike political parties in their eschewal of strict membership criteria. Yet, women's separate organizing created important networks, which acted as political incubators for socialist-feminist ideas.

In the aftermath of suffrage, the war, and the turmoil of 1919, working-class women in English Canada regrouped. In southern Ontario, a Women's Independent Labour Party and a United Women's Educational Federation (UWEF) were established, the latter advertised as the "working-class version" of the middle-class National Council of Women of Canada. Although meant as an antidote to the bourgeois women's movement, the UWEF shared the council's maternalist hopes to "champion womanhood, children, and the home." The UWEF pursued issues relating to the home and wage work, advocating for a comprehensive safety net for the working-class family, equal pay for women, and the unionization of underpaid female workers. The federation hoped that "capitalism would pass peacefully into oblivion," but, on the way to this rather utopian goal, more immediate demands arose: free health care, school meals for children of the unemployed, and healthy, public leisure for working-class children.[40] In northern Ontario, the post-war organization of socialist-feminist women took a region-specific, ethnic turn. Finnish socialist women mobilized both on their own and with male workers in IWW ("Wobbly") lumber unions to sustain the project of rank-and-file labour organizing: socialist women were the "backbone of an oppositional Wobbly culture" in Thunder Bay and environs.[41]

In the 1920s, socialist and labour newspapers were an important conduit for feminist discussions. By 1918, Rose Henderson had her own column in the Ontario-based *Labor News,* in which she argued that women and labour must "join forces ... to attain the emancipation of the toiling masses." Her theorization of class and gender even recognized the liberation of women in the household: "Freeing women from domestic slavery," she told the labour movement, "was the last link in the chain for the emancipation of the workers of the world."[42] Travelling and reporting internationally over the next decade, Henderson published articles in many Canadian and British newspapers – the *Maritime Labor Herald, One Big Union Bulletin,* the *Daily Herald,* the *British Columbia Federationist,* the *Canadian Farmer-Labor Advocate* – underscoring how important print culture was to the dissemination of socialist-feminist ideas.

Henderson's ability to weave together an analysis of the suffering and struggles of women, children, and the working class was unusually sophisticated for the time. Other women journalists concentrated on specific equality issues. In Quebec, the labour newspaper of the Montreal Trades and Labour Council, *Le monde ouvrier,* featured writing by Julien Saint-Michel, another nom de plume of Éva Circé-Côté. During the interwar period, she wrote both about the exploitation of women workers and attacks on women's right to work. Women's labour, she wrote, might be a "sad necessity of the times," but it could not be abolished, nor should it be. Would banning women from workshops and offices send women back to the home, she asked, then answered rhetorically, "No, it will drive them to the gutter, the streets, La Maternité [home for unwed mothers], the prison." Yet Circé-Côté did equivocate on this issue: she saw no reason for well-off bourgeois daughters to take jobs badly needed by others, but she routinely defended the legitimacy of women's paid labour.[43] Another Quebec newspaper further to the left, the communist *Ouvrier canadien,* discussed the struggles of women workers and supported the right of Quebec women to vote.[44]

Florence Rowe, writing for the syndicalist *One Big Union Bulletin,* took on another cause: motherhood and birth control. Rowe criticized the meagre mothers' allowance in Manitoba, asking how any mother could feed and clothe her family on such a pittance. She referred with disdain to the indifference of middle-class reformers who responded without compassion that the amount allotted was "more than the wives of working men can get for themselves." Not good enough, replied Rowe indignantly. Their comments simply confirmed that working-class wives "did not have anything like enough to make things decent."[45] Why, she asked, did working-class women have children at all when they knew the owning class would "grind them out in drudgery or slaughter them wholesale in wars engineered by those who have the power."[46] Worn down mentally and physically, working-class women could not support the unhealthy children they had. Birth control was an immediate necessity; women needed to move beyond "superstition and tradition," demanding birth control clinics so they could control their own fertility. Rowe matched her rhetoric with action: the paper announced she was available every Tuesday at the Winnipeg Plebs League "to be consulted on any matter relating to women and girls."[47] Such "matters" undoubtedly included birth control advice.

In the same manner, labour and socialist women often set their sights on local issues, crafting feminist solidarities in one community. In Calgary, Dominion Labour Party (DLP) women made public education one of their priorities; they supported teachers' collective-bargaining rights, equal pay for women educators, and free school clinics offering children medical and dental care. DLP activist Amelia Turner Smith ran successfully in 1926 for the local school board in a recall election precipitated by a controversy over free school texts, at the time a fundamentally working-class demand. Without free books, she argued in her speeches, we "condemn the working class to leave school" at an early age and go into "a blind alley and poorly paid work."[48]

Amelia Turner Smith proudly declared that she became an agnostic, socialist, and feminist as a teenager, after reading British socialists Keir Hardie and Robert Blatchford, and attending rural political gatherings near the family home. After a move to Calgary, she was influenced by William Irvine and mentored by a group of seasoned feminists in the Calgary DLP, many former suffragists. Shaped by the recent labour revolt, the DLP emphasized working-class mobilization through the ballot box, in contrast to the local Women's Labour League, a non-partisan (though communist leaning) militant advocate for working-class women's needs.[49]

Women constituted about half of the DLP membership, an indication of the appeal of labour socialism for feminists looking for a left alternative in the wake of the suffrage movement. They established a women's section of the party, studying and advocating for "women's issues" such as education, social welfare, and birth control. Because she worked as a journalist on the United Farmers of Alberta newspaper, Turner Smith became a staunch advocate of a Farmer-Labour alliance, describing her socialist vision in affective and millenarian language: "I am fortunate to be part of a great human movement, the onward march of progress, the march of humanity to a new day of freedom."[50]

If the DLP women in Calgary focused on the ballot box, other socialist feminists shifted their energies from one grassroots social movement to another, depending on the economic context and their own search for social and gender justice. Edith Hancox, whose political evolution is traced by David Thompson, is a good example. A former domestic servant and British immigrant, Hancox settled in Winnipeg with her husband and children in

1904, where she and her family eked out a difficult working-class existence. She discarded her original loyalty to the Salvation Army, critical of its empty rhetoric about the poor, aligning herself with the "revolutionary humanism" of the Labor Church, and also passing through the One Big Union, the Women's Labour League, and the Communist Party. Her trajectory represented neither indecision nor opportunism, but rather her search for the best means to defend the dispossessed: the working class and the poor, women, the homeless, immigrants, and the unemployed.

A formidable labour movement orator during the Winnipeg General Strike, Hancox subsequently organized countless municipal mobilizations to secure adequate relief for the destitute jobless and their families. Especially attuned to women's sexual oppression and the economic exploitation of working-class women, Hancox's socialism was "suffused with feminism."[51] Like some suffragists, her politics were also imbued with the power of emotion as she expressed pure outrage at wealth inequality and the cruel discrimination experienced by many immigrants. Hancox's retreat into private life in the later 1930s due to familial financial needs – though also differences with the Communist Party – was common for working-class women, who had to put daily survival first. Her life story speaks to the difficulty of retrieving socialist feminists from the silence of history: their activism was localized, changing, spread across multiple causes, ignored in the mainstream media, and less likely to be memorialized even in histories of labour.[52]

When local labour- and socialist-feminist efforts shifted organizationally, faded, or lost their radical edge, other women's organizations, dotted across the Canadian map, took up the slack. The Western Women's Economic and Social Labour Conference (WWC), the brainchild of Beatrice Brigden, was one attempt to create socialist-feminist regional connections. Brigden's political evolution demonstrated the powerful transformative influence of the 1919 labour revolt: in a moment of a cataclysmic social upheaval, utopian change could be imagined. Women like Brigden took to heart Methodist minister J.S. Woodsworth's speech during the strike: "In the coming day, women will take their place side by side with men not as dependents or inferiors but as equals ... This strike was part of the great movement for the emancipation of women."[53]

Raised on a prosperous farm by socially conscious parents, and with some postsecondary education, Brigden was employed before the First World War by the Methodist Church to travel across Canada, lecturing to girls and women on social purity, a synonym for sex education designed to prevent premarital sex, sexually transmitted diseases, promiscuity, and

Figure 5.3 Beatrice Brigden founded the Western Women's Economic and Social Labour Conference, ran for the Farmer-Labour Party, and was later active in the CCF | Brigden Beatrice Collection, Manitoba Archives

prostitution. Although her heroine was American Jane Addams, who lived in a Chicago settlement house amid the immigrant poor, Brigden's class prejudices are evident in her early writing, even though she also reflects critically on her own limited perspectives as she confronted the material realities of working-class survival.[54]

After 1919, Brigden became disillusioned with the Methodist Church's disavowal of ministers who supported the Winnipeg General Strike. "Ashamed and disgusted" with the church's decision to align itself with the more prosperous rather than the disadvantaged, Brigden resigned and became a youth worker in Rev. A.E. Smith's breakaway labour-oriented Peoples Church in Brandon, Manitoba.[55] Youth education remained a project dear to her heart. She later established youth groups in which boys and girls developed their socialist skills with mock parliaments, debates, and the performance of plays, and, once the CCF was formed, she wrote a "Boys and Girls" column for the party newspaper, putting basic themes such as "the production of food" into common-sense socialist language.[56]

When A.E. Smith left Brandon and joined the Communist Party, Brigden threw herself into new projects: a Speakers Bureau to tour progressive lecturers across Canada and the WWC. Brigden identified herself as a "pioneer for the labour movement," yet her political vision was socialist and feminist: it encompassed a critique of male domination and women's economic inequality, as well as a deep belief in the possibilities of human cooperation – not unlike earlier ethical and utopian socialists. Production for use, not for profit, was the motto of the Women's Conference, as it was Brigden's own.

The WWC, remembers Brigden's sister-in-law, was labour in name, but "we always knew we were socialists and we'd always keep in the foreground that we had to go by the principles of socialism."[57] It created a feminist space to link women's equality to the labour-socialist agenda. Given its decentralized nature, the WWC's longevity – about a decade – was remarkable. On the Prairies, women set up local groups, which concentrated on their own political study and advocacy, then met once a year in different cities to debate resolutions, share political concerns, and foster a sense of political hope and solidarity. Brigden was particularly concerned that women, accustomed to men assuming the right to lead, gain the confidence to become leaders themselves.

The WWC required no dictum of belief, but rather incorporated a vision of women bound together by common desire for radical change. As a result, the conference was a venue where divisive issues were thrashed out, but not always solved: a motion supporting eugenics was defeated one year yet endorsed the next. The 1931 Edmonton meeting produced no less than twenty-five resolutions on everything from disability to cadet training to deportations, an impressive product of collaborative political work.[58] The WWC's political heterogeneity allowed many progressive women to participate, though, in 1929, Communist women were directed by their party to disaffiliate. Until then, the WWC's non-partisanship facilitated solidarity on some issues; in 1928, it passed a motion supporting Toronto Communists who were being incarcerated because of their campaign for "free speech" on the streets. If differences existed, delegates hammered out some common positions. Among these were the need for a comprehensive welfare state, including free dental and health care; unemployment insurance; better working conditions and rights for women, such as equal pay; and cooperation between farm and labour women to build a new society. Birth control resolutions were always strongly endorsed, sometimes pursued as action items by women who set up their own local clinics, as the Winnipeg women did.

Searching for a means to express her feminist, egalitarian commitment to the "dignity and equality" of all women and men, Brigden later joined the CCF. Rose Henderson followed a similar trajectory. Her evolution from reforming suffragist, who offered up a heavy dose of middle-class moralism to working-class families, to outspoken socialist-feminist after the First World War, is chronicled by Peter Campbell. Henderson too was radicalized by the 1919 labour revolt; her politics led to dismissal from her job as a probation officer with the Montreal juvenile court, propelling her into a new career as a political writer, activist and speaker across Canada and abroad. Henderson, Campbell argues, was developing what was later called an "intersectional" analysis, exploring not one, but all hierarchies of power connected to capitalist society. Her exaltation of women's mothering role and her passionate call for men and women to construct a new social, moral, and spiritual order bore a remarkable resemblance to the ideas of Wollstonecraft.[59] Henderson's socialist metamorphosis also unsettled her earlier middle-class moralism. In a piece on the "modern girl" in the *One Big Union Bulletin,* Henderson rejoiced in young women's rejection of the old shackles of passivity and their questioning of all "the underlying hypocrisies of our civilization." "Blazing a trail into the future," the modern woman is challenging the church, politicians, morality, tradition, "daring to kick holes in the paper partition between what is termed 'moral' and 'immoral.'"[60]

Henderson, along with Jean Laing, Alice Loeb, and Elizabeth Morton, built another non-partisan socialist feminist group, the Toronto CCF Women's Joint Committee (WJC), established in 1935. Though its founders were associated with the CCF, their goal was a grassroots movement stretching across party lines that would educate women and inspire them to political action. Organizing women separately, they reasoned, enabled women's distinct work and world view to be validated, and they would come to see the connection between their arduous daily labour and the need for socialism. Homemakers were assumed to be the primary target group, but connections were made to workplace issues, through proposed boycotts of non-union businesses and solidaristic support for striking women garment workers.

The WJC resolved to reach out personally to women in community groups in working-class neighbourhoods, creating an organization from the bottom up. Generating women leaders was also a goal; the WJC rotated leadership positions, giving women the space to develop their political voices, often silenced in mixed-gender meetings. Laing called the WJC a "training school for speakers," but it was much more. It focused on the working-class family in the economic crisis, demanding more generous relief rates and supporting unemployed men who went "on strike" to secure cash payments instead of food vouchers in exchange for their free labour on local public works. As household budgeters, women wanted cash to make the purchases they deemed necessary for their families rather than the assigned goods they were allowed to buy.[61] As collective "mothers," WJC members visited the imprisoned relief strikers in jail. The WJC also denounced wage cuts singling out women workers and promoted access to birth control for married women. Women's right to work, economic security, housing, birth control, and support for the union label: these were all on the WJC agenda, served up in a blend of maternalism, feminism, and socialism.

The WJC's plan to build a united front of progressive women eventually landed it in disciplinary hot water with the CCF, which insisted that the committee renounce all contact with Communist women, not even marching in the same May Day parade. After disregarding this order, Laing and Morton were expelled by the CCF and Henderson was reprimanded, and it was left to Loeb to rally supporters to their defence. Laing and Morton were eventually taken back, but the non-partisan WJC did not survive.

Elizabeth Morton's disinclination to hew to partisan politics and her uncompromising belief in working-class unity reflected her own social beginnings. The daughter of a coal miner and a factory worker, she emigrated from Britain with her parents in 1910 and worked in various factory jobs in Toronto. Once married, she joined the Amalgamated Carpenters of Canada Women's Guild, linked to the All Canadian Congress of Labour; through the guild, she met Communist leader and editor of the *Woman Worker*, Florence Custance. By the 1930s, Morton was known for her work in the East York Workers' Association (EYWA), a community organization committed to militant organizing against evictions, inadequate relief, and unemployment. Her EYWA activism was so dynamic it incurred the "jealousy" of male leaders, who worried she might snag the nomination to run locally for the CCF (she did not).[62]

Morton was convinced that socialism had to be built by and for the working class. Yet if her class identity took precedence, it was inflected with a feminist sensibility; she believed women should be organized around their own workplace issues (including the home) and mobilized as a distinct interest group. Within the EYWA, Morton organized a women's Marxist study group and set up an East York Parents Clinic to provide women with birth control information, a plan, she soon discovered, that incurred strong support from the women but not all men. As fascism became an international threat, she warned that what little equality women had was under threat: "a thinking woman is a dangerous thing to the ruling class," she warned. Only in the Soviet Union had women found true "equality, whereas in fascist countries" they are transformed into "blind, unquestioning creatures."[63]

Morton's "Labour Woman" column in the *Trade Unionist,* incorporating her own and reprinted material, combined a critique of capitalism with attention to women's specific political needs and views. Women were a marginalized but important constituency in the class struggle: they might be less knowledgeable about politics, even susceptible to "superstition and charlatan" views, but, as "a reasoning being," every woman must learn "to think for herself ... to emancipate her thought."[64] Socialism was the answer to women's exploitation; those facing wage cuts must not be satisfied with the sop of "half a loaf" but should see that "the defects of the capitalist system" were structural. "Surplus profits for a privileged few and starvation wages for the workers," she lectured, were simply "not acceptable ideals for the twentieth century."[65] Yet, while stressing class, the column also encouraged feminist voices: one contribution named patriarchal capitalism as the problem, paraphrasing George Bernard Shaw: "Capitalism made a man a slave, and by paying a woman through him, made her a slave of the slave."[66]

Conclusion

Elizabeth Morton, in contrast to Beatrice Brigden and Amelia Turner Smith, had little faith in a labour-farmer alliance. In Ontario, the farm movement lacked the radical edge of some Prairie groups and seemed to labour socialists more of a millstone around their necks than an ally. These different views underscore the ideological diversity of agrarian, labour, and socialist feminists across the country. These progressive feminists had intellectual links to earlier strands of feminism; however, they also charted unfamiliar political waters, both tactically and philosophically, building innovative strategies of political resistance. These were highly local: city, regional, and provincial organizations, newspapers, and political clusters were shaped by different histories, economic contexts, and political cultures, though Depression conditions had a common radicalizing effect. Agrarian feminists' concerns were grounded in their farm experiences and labour, and, while they sometimes collaborated with reform-minded feminists, by the 1930s, a significant enclave of farm women developed an affinity for anti-capitalist, anti-war politics, voicing emphatic calls for large-scale social transformation.

Progressive women did share some common concerns. Birth control was one, an issue noticeably avoided in the pre-war women's movement, but now more courageously championed by most agrarian, labour, and socialist feminists. Nevertheless, women's investment in feminism diverged. As socialists, almost none singularly blamed male domination for gender inequality, but, beyond that principle, the way in which their feminism and socialism intersected differed. Most women saw connections between class and gender inequality; many endorsed the benefit of addressing women's distinct familial and labour experiences, including their domestic labour. A smaller, but hardly insignificant, group argued that feminism and socialism were interdependent – both were written into their hopes for a new social and gender order.

Brigden, for instance, stressed the importance of women's motherwork and the connection between women's domestic and political consciousness, but she also supported a more egalitarian view of women's right to self-determination, whether at work or in her reproductive choices. Without a transformation in capitalism, she believed, women would remain socially and economically oppressed, but, without the mobilization of women and feminist ideals, capitalism could not be challenged. The socialist feminist discussions begun in small circles, coalitions, and organizations scattered across the country continued in the CCF and Communist Party, each party claiming that it represented the true pathway to social and gender equality.

6 Feminism and the Party Question

Elizabeth Morton, feminist anti-fascist and fiery defender of working-class rights, joined the Co-operative Commonwealth Federation (CCF) after attending its founding convention in Regina in 1933. Over the rest of the decade, she periodically disagreed with party priorities. She was briefly expelled for cooperating with other leftists, and, in her later years, was more inclined towards communism. Morton's rocky relations with the party leadership indicate the paradoxes women faced when they put their political apples in a party basket. Parties appealed: they offered women a community, a set of principles, and the inescapable logic that collectivity, rather than disparate groups, would bring social change. On the other hand, parties were confining: they limited women's sphere of action, had set platforms, imposed discipline, and told members with whom they could form alliances. They might institutionalize rather than unsettle established masculine power structures.

By the 1930s, the "woman question" was also a party question, resurrecting a feminist strategic quandary: is partisanship or independence the best way to secure equality? The CCF and the Communist Party of Canada (CPC), both claiming a solution to gender inequality, dominated left-wing discussion, while reform feminists such as Nellie McClung and Thérèse Casgrain maintained their allegiance to the Liberal Party – an alliance discussed in Chapter 8. Drawing on different intellectual traditions, though sometimes overlapping in their activities, the CCF and Communists fought for different versions of socialism but occasionally agreed on a common enemy. Understanding left-wing women's equality seeking in their own parties, as well as in the workplace, anti-poverty mobilizations, ethnic organizations, and on the cultural front, is the goal of this chapter.

Women's Political Labour and Autonomous Organizing within the CCF

Socialists had long claimed gender equality was hard-wired into socialism, yet a gendered division of political labour and a predominantly male leadership were realities in both the CCF and Communist Party. Pictures of delegates at the CCF founding convention capture the contradiction associated with women in socialist parties. Women were a minority of those assembled, though still a more substantial, active contingent compared to women in the Liberal and Conservative Parties, which relegated most women to auxiliaries. Feminists pointed out that the CCF's Regina Manifesto called for "equal services irrespective of sex," but its most rousing appeal for new members was the demand that capitalism be "eradicated" and replaced with a cooperative commonwealth.[1]

A coalition of diverse ideological interests, the CCF included women from Marxist socialist parties, trade unions, farm organizations, and the League for Social Reconstruction, a group of progressive intellectuals with no mass base. Political tensions simmered for years between these different factions, each with competing interpretations of socialism. Gender equality was not a priority in these tussles, which is not to say the issue was never raised. The Saskatchewan Farmer-Labour Group proposed in 1933 that women, perennially unrepresented in politics, should have two assured positions on CCF national and provincial executives until "the economic emancipation of women was secured."[2] No such practice was adopted. Nonetheless, some women at the Regina convention were already committed feminists. Beatrice Brigden believed that women's labour and socialist groups, like the earlier Working Women's Conference she created, gave voice to women routinely marginalized by male politicians; socialism, she stated, meant "striving for equality on all fronts," with "no suppression of one sex for the benefit of the other."[3] Other attendees, including Agnes Macphail, the adamant defender of women's right to work, disdained separate women's organizing, fearing this would relegate women to the political wilderness.[4] For Brigden, autonomous women's organizing and feminism intersected; for Macphail, they might be counterproductive.

Divergent views on feminism were not surprising, given the diversity of CCF women's backgrounds, motivations, and ideas. Women's experience of farm and working-class life, or their witnessing of social inequality, radicalized many party members, but class background was not a perfect predictor of ideology. Some middle-class women attendees, like Mildred Fahrni, attributed their political awakening to the Christian social gospel; another participant from Vancouver, Dorothy Steeves, who was middle class and university educated, came from the resolutely Marxist wing of the Socialist Party.

Whatever their intellectual motivations, women CCFers were often concentrated in "female" areas of political work within the party, though there were always exceptions, including Steeves, an accomplished speaker and leader who "loved the public platform."[5] More often, women's grassroots electioneering, local organizing, educational work, and fundraising provided essential domestic labour for the movement. Echoing Annie Hollis's complaint about unrecognized domestic labour, one woman recalled that "the CCF was made in the kitchen and you didn't find too many men in the kitchen."[6] Political life replicated women's occupational roles outside the party. Many CCF women were teachers, and educational work for the party was a natural extension of their profession. In Saskatchewan, Gertrude Telford organized the annual Crystal Lake summer camp that socialized new CCFers with lectures, visiting speakers, economics lessons, and debates. This was not inconsequential work; in a movement battling the dominant social ideology of free enterprise, education was critical to a committed membership. Moreover, the camp was run on shared, non-gendered labour, not unlike earlier utopian communes. The cooperative commonwealth was made "real" in daily life. At least for a week, the men washed the dishes too.[7]

Women's political labour was shaped by their caregiving, familial roles. Few could go far afield as organizers or leaders if they had a farm or family to care for. This was an economic reality, but women also knew they were judged harshly for "abandoning" their families for party business. Most women combined domestic and political labour when engaging in grassroots organizing. A "life in the day" report from a CCF activist in Fort William, Ontario, captured this well:

> Up at 8, feed family of 5, make lunch send boy to school, do report on meetings, draw up ads, numerous phone calls. 9 o'clock dress baby, wash dishes, answer phone, make beds, sweep and dust, answer phone. Sell potatoes donated by country CCF units. Write letters and notes for tonight's speech. Dishwashing, cleaning, calls, dress baby for outdoors. Shop for supper, prepare kids for bed, go to meeting.[8]

Figure 6.1 As in this CCF brochure, left-wing parties often appealed to women based on their household labour | *Women, in Peace as in War, Protect Your Home* [1947?]. University of Saskatchewan Archives, Sophia Dixon fonds, series 4, vol. 29

Women's responsibility for domestic labour was one rationale for separate CCF women's groups. Intentionally renamed "committees" or "councils," to replace the more handmaiden-ish "auxiliary," they addressed women's distinct homemaking labour, social experiences, and family obligations, as well as gender equality issues such as women's right to work and equal pay. Separate committees were advertised as a first step toward women's full integration into party structures, leadership, and decision making. The notion that women needed extra confidence-building may seem condescending until we recall that, in the 1960s and 1970s, separate women's groups were again created to construct a safe space apart from male dominance and derision. And masculinist exclusion in the CCF was amazingly resilient. After a complaint by the Ontario women's committee, the provincial executive warned the Keewatin CCF local that it had to stop denying women memberships. Not only did this contravene the party's principles concerning "sex discrimination," but discouraging new members was rather short-sighted politically.[9]

Almost every regional and local CCF organization experimented at some point with autonomous women's groups. In the Saskatchewan CCF, even women leaders who did not self-identify as feminists recommended that women's CCF study clubs have the same voting rights at conventions as all clubs, resulting in an ongoing tussle with the male leadership. The latter prevailed but offered a concession – a women's organizer, Minerva Cooper, who criss-crossed the province setting up women's CCF clubs, assuming these might develop into mixed CCF clubs in which women would no longer take a backseat role in the party.[10] The clubs carried on traditional fund-raising for socialist causes like the Mackenzie-Papineau Battalion fighting fascism in Spain, but they also discussed current events, reviewed socialist literature, examined newspapers, and practised their political rhetoric.

The Saskatchewan clubs – like other efforts across the country – created a critique of capitalism in the context of women's daily homemaking labour, whether on farms or in urban homes. Women's unpaid domestic labour might be undervalued, but it was also imagined as a means to convert women to socialism. Politics involves government decisions about whether your husband will work, how much you will pay for milk, what kind of education your children receive, and if you will get medical care for the family, the CCF again and again reminded women. Beatrice Brigden's column in *Manitoba Commonwealth* underlined this connection: "Mrs Housewife," she wrote concerning a federal inquiry into consumer prices, "you must see that bonds, interests and profits are not merely words, but they are your daily concerns – food, clothing and shelter."[11]

Assuming women were primarily maternal and domestic had a disadvantage: rather than questioning gender roles, it reaffirmed them. Women's wage earning was downplayed, and the prevailing gendered division of political labour that kept women out of party decision making left intact. Similar concerns were raised about women's columns in CCF newspapers. The sceptical feared they narrowed women's intellectual horizons and risked replicating women's pages in the bourgeois press featuring the frivolities of fashion and food. The women's columnist in the Ontario *CCF Commonwealth* was herself ambivalent, assigning her column a name with a "double meaning: Fairly Feminine." She disapproved of women's pages because "women should read all the articles in the paper," but thought women needed special encouragement because they "are rather backward about expressing their ideas in print especially in competition with the masculine point of view."[12] Her solution: she adroitly turned traditional bourgeois topics on their head, questioning women's earning and consumption under capitalism, describing, for instance, a strike of the women workers who sewed the fashionable "Paris gown."

Like the message of earlier suffragists, this women's column combined maternal and egalitarian rhetoric; women were needed in politics because of their gendered insights and familial roles, but also because they are "intelligent, wise and socially minded citizens." Also like her feminist predecessors, she believed women needed to conquer their timidity about public activism, rejecting the "backward" prejudices of those who "look in horror" on women participating in the affairs of the state.[13] That her advice was so similar to that of the suffragist generation spoke volumes about the untractable misogynist barriers women faced in political life.

Women's columns appeared and disappeared in almost all the provincial CCF newspapers, taking on a different flavour according to the paper, time period, and writer. Dorothy Blair's short-lived column for the early *BC Commonwealth* included domestic hints but also promoted socialist women's involvement in politics. Taken over briefly in the renamed *The Federationist* by Marxist Eve Grey Smith, the column examined the specific contours of women's exploitation within capitalism. "My main attitude," Smith remembered, "was that women shouldn't be separated from men. The problem is not a sexual one but an economic one and the economic problem makes a sexual one."[14] Only through revolutionary change, she cautioned, "can [women's] emancipation come."[15]

Later in the decade, Elizabeth (Betty) Kerr's column, "Women's Views," was forthrightly socialist feminist. A Scottish immigrant who had tried to organize her fellow nurses in support of an eight-hour day before the First World War, she had roots both in the suffrage movement and the Socialist Party of Canada. Along with Steeves and other Vancouver CCF women, she organized the Women's Lyceum to encourage women to hone their political skills. Kerr's column featured class issues and struggles, especially as they affected the household, but she also tackled gender inequalities: the need for better divorce laws and birth control and the right of married women to work. Her writing on gender socialization anticipated feminists in the 1960s. Appalled by women who felt they must act the "coquette," flattering men rather than reasoning with them, she looked forward to a time when femininity was not used as a bargaining tool: "only when women are free from the petty tyranny to flatter and wheedle men will there be complete freedom for them."[16]

After the 1938 provincial CCF convention, Kerr decried the small numbers of women present, blaming sexism and women's constraining family obligations, and she objected strenuously to the rumours that the election of three women to the executive spelled "feminist control" of the party. The very left-leaning Kerr distanced herself from bourgeois feminism, yet her sentiments were clearly feminist: "we have not shown feminist views, but we have examined a broad range of problems from a human perspective ... But even if we were stay-at-home types, why should that womanly view not be expressed in our movement? For a movement boasting no difference in sex, race and creed, some of our Marxian socialists are pitifully mid Victorian."[17]

From unthreatening domestic hints to strong feminist statements: this was the range of views on women in just one provincial CCF paper. Discussion of gender equality was usually relegated to the marginality of the women's column, but even some who saw class struggle as primary gave it attention. Self-taught Marxist and railway worker George Weaver drew heavily on Engels's *Origin of the Family, Private Property and the State* to analyse women's oppression: "it has been a man's world," he concluded, "since matriarchy died an economic death." He criticized "age old assumptions of male dominance" but suggested women's increasing waged labour and access to birth control spelled a possible end to their economic subservience and dependence on men. A "rural housewife" wrote in to second his views. For some women, socialism appealed as the best prospect for gender equality, despite the party's masculinist flaws. Women are currently "slaves and parasites ... with little freedom for creative living," she lamented. "This degrades us and it degrades those who bind us ... My only reason to remain a socialist is the hope that, along with benefits conferred on others, women will finally be given a place of equality in the new cooperative social order."[18]

Anti-Poverty Organizing

When it came to unemployment, relief, and poverty, the CCF addressed women primarily as homemakers; as mothers caring for families on limited budgets, they should intuitively understand economic precariousness and the value of socialism. However, like liberal, reform-minded feminists, CCF women did not entirely ignore the self-supporting jobless woman, routinely victimized by discriminatory welfare policies. Yet labour, socialist, and liberal reformers all differed on how to solve the problem of the unemployed woman. At a Toronto meeting of charitable, women's, and labour groups, CCFer Elizabeth Morton clashed with both reformers and a more moderate trade unionist, Mary McNab. While they could all agree the government should introduce unemployment insurance, McNab wanted a committee to look after "fallen girls" – a code for promiscuity and prostitution – "who could come to us for sympathy and help." Having none of this moralism, Morton countered that unemployment was a structural issue, linked to workers' inability to consume under capitalism. A labour-socialist government was the real answer, but, more immediately, they should demand a six-hour day, immediate increases in women's wages, and unemployment insurance. Her radical demands seemed to irritate some present, but she did neatly sum up the socialist position on women's unemployment: it could not be dealt with effectively through "half-loaf" measures or gendered moralism.[19]

CCF women joined broadly based demonstrations and delegations calling for both unemployment insurance and more generous local relief, but they also built new anti-poverty groups and strategies. Meagre relief allocations, often doled out with restrictive regulations, vouchers, and humiliating lectures, were a particular focus of women's ire. CCFers' participation in solidaristic actions with the poor and unemployed proved a strategy more effective than mere speeches and petitions. In Ontario, CCFers provided stopgap charitable aid to those in need, brought food to relief workers on strike, and arranged for strikers' bail when they were arrested.[20] CCF women in the East York Workers' Association participated in anti-eviction struggles in which residents mobilized on the streets to prevent bailiffs from evicting families, as well as selling CCF literature, organizing a library of radical books, and doing traditional fundraising. When men became overbearing, telling them how to allot the funds, the women asserted their right to make their own decisions, "calling [the men] to order."[21]

Vancouver CCF women, including former suffragist Helena Gutteridge, established an unemployment action group to tackle joblessness. In one deputation to the provincial government, Sarah Colley, who had lost her infant son to pneumonia, argued for a universal prenatal allowance for pregnant women and infant bottles and nipples: "the very first thing [a child] needs is warm clothing," she told the assembled politicians. "It is for you to make this better" for struggling mothers. CCF party secretary Mary McCormack warned the assembled legislators that working-class women were delaying marriage due to widespread poverty and that mothers' ill health was jeopardizing future generations: "We are the mothers of tomorrow and unless we are properly nourished, our children will be poor wretched creatures."[22]

This maternal appeal was used for symbolic effect during the On-to-Ottawa Trek of unemployed men in 1935. Vancouver CCF women led marches of strikers, and "Mothers Committees," composed of all manner of left-wing women, were formed to support the trek, both in Vancouver and in Regina after the trekkers were stopped short by a police-initiated riot.[23] Yet, how different was this maternalism from suffrage-era discourses, or even from that of women in other political parties? CCF women thought it was. They looked at the Liberals and Conservatives and saw women confined to "social" events, shut out of the "inner councils" of policy-making. They believed their critique of capitalism and embrace of direct action made their "militant mothering" distinct. The CCF woman, Beatrice Brigden asserted, does "differ" from other reformers: "she has separated herself very largely from the prejudices and fallacies of the capitalist order. She repudiates the system of competition ... She has accepted the cooperative principle, the well-tested recipe for success in her own homemaking: each giving according to her ability and each receiving according to their need."[24]

Socialist women's definition of "women's issues" as maternal and familial seems limited and essentialist to us, their relegation to women's committees a form of gender sidelining – just as Agnes Macphail feared. Their definition of "women's issues" appears less "feminist" than a new incarnation of maternalism. Yet women's separate organizing implied a critique of masculinist politics that failed to take women's lives into account and make good on socialism's promise of egalitarianism for all. Marginalized by party men, occupying second-class status in society, women could focus on their most direct concerns, including household labour, in more hospitable separate groups. Their insistence on the worth of motherwork would be echoed by later feminists across subsequent decades.

Imagining the "New Jerusalem"

Socialist feminism needed more than skilful organizing; it also required imagination and hope. Challenging the exaltation of competitive individualism and fashioning resistance to it required "dreamers who could imagine the undoubted benefits that would flow from a future socialist society."[25] Cultural creations that critiqued capitalism but also offered glimpses of what socialism might offer were important conduits for the utopian desire to create a "New Woman," a new social order, a "New Jerusalem." The Co-operative Commonwealth Youth Movement (CCYM), for instance, put on plays, created song books, crafted political banners, and even composed its own anthem. In British Columbia, some CCF clubs devoted themselves entirely to "play reading," creating original scripts and putting on performances. A province-wide workers' drama festival was established in 1936, although there was no money for a prize: the winning group, remembered an organizer, "took the deficit."[26]

Progressives who were part of this movement culture injected feminist ideas into their artistic creations. Playwright Elsie Park Gowan immigrated to Alberta from Scotland and began teaching in rural schools at sixteen, then attended the University of Alberta, where she began her career as a playwright. Finding the Edmonton theatre scene more interested in bourgeois escapist fare than socially conscious drama, she wrote for the CCF and other progressive audiences. Her play *The Hungry Spirit* explored women's struggle for higher education; many other creations were anti-imperialist and anti-war statements. Turning to radio drama, Gowan was able to reach a larger audience for her progressive ideas. Her 1936 script for a CBC series, *New Lamps for Old,* used historical dramatic fiction to bring to life the ideas of Mary Wollstonecraft. Gowan's smart, crisp dialogue between Wollstonecraft and other historical characters deftly explores the early feminist's personal and political life, her championship of women's equality, and her struggle against restrictive eighteenth-century sexual conventions. With insight and empathy, Gowan captured Wollstonecraft's dislike of arbitrary authority and her fervent belief in women's education. She clearly intended a contemporary message. The announcer's introduction reminds the audience of current feminist issues – the rise of fascism, efforts to push women out of employment – and notes that the "situation today" should "re-awaken our interest in the girl who declared herself champion of half the human race."[27]

Gowan's 1936 play *You Can't Do That,* co-written with former member of Parliament William Irvine (though her name was originally left off the play by the publisher), also had a feminist subtext. Performed in Alberta towns by touring CCYM members, who made do with makeshift stages and sheets for curtains, the play had the imprint of Irvine's Fabian socialism and Gowan's playful feminism. Like many earlier suffrage dramas, it involved a plucky heroine and a reversal of gender roles. Belinda, whose stodgy uncle is prime minister, is frustrated with the "pussy-footed old politicians doing nothing" about the Depression,[28] so she concocts a scheme to isolate most of the cabinet on an island and surreptitiously issue policy directives under her uncle's name. Her initiatives provide funds for the jobless and take on the big banks, curing the economic crisis. Belinda's pluckiness also earns her the affection of the minister of labour, a reformer now ashamed of his previous political paralysis. While Belinda's intelligence, pragmatism, and humanity are contrasted with ineffective, self-promotional male politicians, the play closes with her finding heterosexual happiness in the arms of the minister of labour.

Other progressive women writers concentrated more on the differences between working-class and more affluent women. Of sixty-seven entries in a national contest for progressive "social drama," the winning entry, *And the Answer Is ...*, written by Mary Reynolds, contrasted Lilli, a working-class, immigrant singer and music teacher with a group of affluent women "bridge club" players for whom she performed. Far from oppressed, these bourgeois women are the oppressors. Their well-educated, privileged daughters have respectable jobs; one was a "social service" worker overseeing welfare recipients whom the mother fretted would pass their "infections" on to her daughter.[29] Lilli pleads with the bourgeois women to lend out their club room for a concert so she can raise funds for medical care for her homeless friends. They refuse, in part because they suspect her of flimsy sexual morals, as she lives in the same rooming house as her boyfriend. She, in turn, suspects their "unwomanly" avoidance of mothering. Reynolds's exploration of class divisions drew on some tired tropes of the spoiled, bridge-playing female bourgeoisie, but it was unusual in exploring the ubiquitous sexual stereotyping and suspicions of working-class women's loose morals.[30]

As in the nineteenth century, many feminists used the short story format to convey their criticisms of society. Mary Quayle Innis's stories, many published in the *Canadian Forum*, explored themes of power, oppression, and inequality in women's lives. Like Reynolds, she also drew attention to the chasm between affluent women and their working-class counterparts, between Anglo elites and immigrants. In "Schooling," she captures the sentient feel of poverty – bodies shivering without blankets, a diet of fried potatoes, the incessant tiredness – as a young farm woman strives to stay in school to secure her teaching credentials in the hope that she can pull her family out of their hopelessness and destitution.[31]

Class division is the theme of her "Two Ears," as the narrator listens to the conversations on either side of her while on a tram. On one side, two affluent women breeze on about their chauffeurs, gardens, clothes, and social events, while on the other side a forlorn couple with a baby discuss their forced separation. Broke and homeless, they have made the agonizing decision to separate; the woman and young child are going to live with her father while the husband continues to look for work.[32] Innis's socialist sensibilities permeated these short stories, but, as Donica Belisle shows, they were also infused with feminist themes, including the patriarchal limitations on women's lives, their social alienation, and the undervaluing of their domestic labour.[33]

Portraits of selfish bourgeois women and selfless working-class women played on long-standing, simplistic tropes in socialist popular culture in which class trumped gender oppression. However, unambiguously feminist creations in which male domination and patriarchy were blamed for the world's problems would not have been true to these women's socialist-feminist politics. Gender and class themes were intertwined in their writing, but, ultimately, no emancipation was possible for all women as long as some women faced homelessness and hunger.

Communism and Women's Inequality

Like the CCF, the CPC also claimed to understand the origins of women's inequality and have the only solution: communism modelled on the Soviet Union (USSR). Until 1935, communists disdained the word "feminism" for its correlation with "bourgeois" feminism. Yet, the CPC was a vociferous critic of women's exploitation, advocated for accessible birth control, and mobilized women based on their domestic labouring roles. If feminism was a disparaged word, women's equality was claimed as a communist goal.

The contradictions betweeen communism and "the woman question" are complicated by the relationship between Canadian communism and the Communist International or Comintern, a global organization inspired by the 1917 Bolshevik Revolution in Russia but, by the 1930s, under Soviet control, rendering the Comintern an instrument of Stalinist brutal suppression, centralized control, and the USSR's perceived needs. Accordingly, the Comintern's advice to the CPC on how to address women's inequality shifted significantly over time. Historical debates about the extent to which North American communists followed these Comintern directives or created a modified "local" communism are voluminous. While more nuanced histories show both international and local influences at play, to overstress North American communists' local autonomy obscures the destructive impact of Stalinism on the history of the left.[34] Indeed, after 1956, when the USSR exposed Stalin's crimes and the CPC imploded, some asked why communists had accepted this advice so uncritically for so long.

The example of women's equality offers a small clue. Communism offered women an imagined transnational community based on shared ideals of socialist transformation and class and gender equality. In the 1920s and 1930s, in the face of unrelenting anti-communist propaganda from Western governments and the mainstream press, Canadian communist women chose instead to believe Soviet propaganda. Many working-class Canadians saw the Bolshevik Revolution as an inspiring "first" socialist experiment, and countless political tourists to the USSR in these years had much to praise about Soviet women's new freedom. Even liberals and social democrats, including CCF columnist Elizabeth Kerr and Toronto social worker and League for Social Reconstruction member Margaret Gould, publicly lauded the remarkable Soviet progress on child care, family welfare, women's labour, and gender equality. Gould's very positive observations on her "visit to the Soviets" were featured in a series in the *Toronto Star*.[35] The Communist Party also spoke a language of class that resonated meaningfully with working-class women, including immigrants who came from ethnic and cultural communities that were socially maligned and were unwelcome in traditional political parties, even the CCF, with its overwhelming Anglo-British character. This was evidence enough for many women that the CPC was the best option for socialist transformation and socialism was the only answer to working-class women's inequality.

Women's Labour Leagues and the *Woman Worker*

Despite the shifting strategies of the CPC, there was continuity in its belief that Marx and Engels offered the most compelling explanations for women's inequality. The CPC was even more indebted than earlier socialists to Engels's *Origin of the Family:* since women's inequality originated in capitalist private property relations, it could be rectified only under Soviet-style communism. Soviet policies seemed to offer compelling proof of this theory. After the revolution, women were given property rights, equal citizenship, and legal rights to divorce, birth control, abortion, and equal pay. Illegitimacy was abolished, and new sexual freedoms initially instituted; women's paid labour was welcomed as the path to economic independence; and socialized domestic labour – communal kitchens, laundries, and crèches – were established to overcome women's oppression within the family. The Soviets had done in a few years what other Western countries had not achieved in hundreds; it is easy to see why Canadian women were intrigued and impressed.[36]

The Soviet equality agenda was promoted by *Zhenotdels,* women's sections of the party, which instructed women on their new rights and attempted to make these rights "a key element of the revolution."[37] Of particular concern was the problematic *baba,* the backward, conservative, and superstitious homemaker (especially peasant women) isolated in her kitchen. Although later abolished by Stalin, the *Zhenotdel* model was initially adopted by the Canadian Communist Party. The CPC set up a women's department to oversee the organization of women and reinvigorated and refashioned the Women's Labour Leagues (WLLs) – originally founded during the First World War by labour movement women – into a communist-led organization. Many local WLLs had a distinct linguistic, ethnic, and regional character, with Finnish, Jewish, and Ukrainian leagues predominating. Despite a lack of interest within the male-dominated party leadership, the WLLs thrived. Party leader Florence Custance shared apprehensions about "backward" housewives who predominated in the WLLs; they were "almost entirely under capitalist class influence via the church and newspapers," but she believed they could be radicalized through their domestic labour, family care, and maternal concerns.[38]

Custance almost single-handedly oversaw the WLLs and edited their newspaper, the *Woman Worker*. Her opening editorial promised not to publish "sickly love stories" and recipes but rather explore the realities of working-class women's lives.[39] She was true to her promise, publishing articles on Marxist theories of gender inequality, women's wage labour, prostitution, gender relations within the family, and activities of local leagues across the country. Her aim – to offer working-class women the knowledge to comprehend their own female experience within a Marxist understanding of class – succeeded remarkably well, in part because she allowed space for women readers to express their views, even in disagreement.

Custance might warn readers not to attribute women's oppression solely to male dominance, but she included submissions about patriarchal laws, violence against women, and discriminatory court decisions that reinforced women's subjection within the family.[40] WLL correspondents were allowed to vent about women's sexual oppression, some espousing the same racialized panic about the "white" slave trade as reform feminists.[41] Custance did have the last word: if men were overbearing dictators, or women were pressed into prostitution, the real problem was the economic system, and the only transformative solution was communism. In the USSR, women's new equality meant men were "no longer the privileged sex," and loving and truly equal partnerships were possible. Engels's predictions, in other words, had come true.

The *Woman Worker* also fostered a sense of international sisterhood in struggle. Articles traced communist women's strikes and struggles, reported on anti-war and anti-colonial mobilizations around the world, and celebrated the multicultural, multilingual character of the movement. Within Canada, the WLLs tried to fashion alliances with other socialist and labour women but drew the line at a "bourgeois" feminist politics of individual

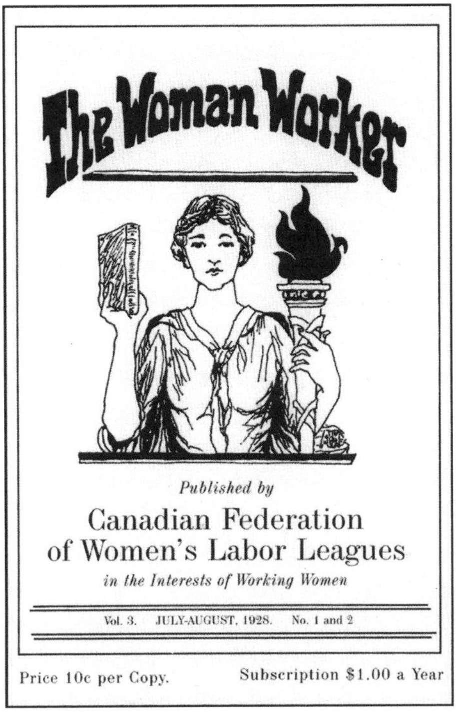

Figure 6.2 The *Woman Worker*, edited by Florence Custance, provided left-wing commentary on women's equality within a class perspective. The book represents knowledge; the flame, liberty | Canadian Federation of Women's Labor Leagues, July–August, 1928, vol. 3, 1/2

advancement. Securing women's right to sit in the Senate, for example, was undemocratic, elitist, and of little use to working-class women.[42] Similarly, reforms intended to ameliorate working women's exploitation, such as minimum wage laws, were well meaning but inherently inadequate. Custance aided some Toronto factory workers who appealed to the new Minimum Wage Board to secure their rightful wages, but their unsuccessful case became a lesson in the pitfalls of liberal reform: these laws were ineffective, laced with loopholes, and unable to fully address the exploitation of women earners.[43]

Communists might critique "bourgeois" feminism, but the *Woman Worker*, reflecting transnational influences on the party in the twenties, encouraged discussion of sexual and familial oppression. One of the most popular issues discussed was birth control. Inspired by the Soviet Union, the WLLs called for free birth control clinics for working-class women. Letters from readers poured in on this topic, and some women joined the leagues because of it, mobilizing locally to secure "Mothers Clinics" dispensing birth control advice. While readers had different justifications for birth control, ranging from women's reproductive rights to more disturbing eugenic rationales, Custance consistently made socialist arguments: birth control should be accessible to working-class women as a health benefit, but limiting family size should never be seen as a solution to poverty. By even raising the issue, however, communists stood out. Many feminists, CCFer Laura Jamieson admitted, would not sponsor a visit to Vancouver by American birth control advocate Margaret Sanger, as they worried it would ruffle the feathers of their husbands. In the twenties, communist women were braver.

Unionizing Exploited Women: Garment Work

Custance's plan to mobilize working-class wives and working daughters through the WLLs ended in 1929, when the Comintern announced a shift in tactics to the "Third Period" of intense class struggle across the globe. The leagues were criticized as reformist auxiliaries, disparaged as ghettos for housewives. The ethnically and linguistically based WLLs were also suspect as an impediment to the recruitment of highly desired Anglo-Saxon and French-Canadian party members. Publicly chastised (though not always privately repentant), the WLLs were merged into the newly established Workers Unity League (WUL), concerned primarily with the mobilization of workers.

The unionization of women was a long-standing socialist-feminist goal. From the time of Bertha Merrill Burns, socialists argued that unionization would enhance working-class women's autonomy, dignity, and equality. The CPC's strategic shift to an emphasis on wage labour, unionization, and militant job action held out the possibility that women workers might secure attention they had never received from the conservative, craft-based Trades and Labour Congress (TLC). To some extent, this was true. Propelled by political fervour, communists and their allies on the left aided the unionization of long-ignored women, whether domestic servants or low-paid textile workers.

However, the WUL leadership believed that male-dominated workplaces were more important sites of class conflict, and the revolutionary zeal of the Third Period produced a decidedly gendered union politics. The idealized unencumbered male organizer who could travel at the drop of a hat, organize at all hours, and go to jail if necessary, did not fit well with women's lives, save a few single leaders or those with stand-in child care. Party leaders

Becky Buhay, Annie Buller, and Jeanne Corbin fit this bill; they were held up as evidence of communist gender equality. It is no coincidence that younger women often assumed the risk of arrest and jail during the free-speech fights that pitted police against radicals on Toronto streets in 1931–32. Seventeen-year-old "Red Lilly" Himmelfarb was arrested and served jail time after being dragged off a soapbox.[44] Her courage notwithstanding, other party women had to go home to make dinner rather than go to jail.

Communists did acknowledge the gendered experiences of Canadian working women who were super-exploited, subject to lower pay, harassment, and insecure employment. The Soviets' radical transformation of women's paid labour thus "held incontestable attraction for Canadian women comrades."[45] Becky Buhay, who took over the Women's Department after Custance's death in 1929, led a women's delegation to the Soviet Union so five carefully chosen Canadian comrades could witness equality at work in the socialist motherland. On their return, they gave speeches and published a statement about Soviet women's new freedoms, pointing out that socialism provided remedies to problems that had long confounded Canadian feminism. In the French-Canadian communist press, for instance, the delegation wrote about "profilectories," which offered former prostitutes education, jobs, and freedom instead of the moralizing criminalization they faced in capitalist countries.[46]

What underpaid working women needed in Canada, communists claimed, were "revolutionary" unions that would not bend and scrape to employers. Revolutionary unions had to be led by revolutionaries, not lacklustre socialists, so the WUL began to organize its own "dual" unions, sometimes competing with existing unions. The ensuing battle between communist and non-communist unions ultimately divided women workers, benefiting the employers far more than the workers.[47] However, dual unions made sense to left-wing women who were blacklisted, expelled from their unions because of their assumed communist politics. However reckless and wrong-headed the dual union strategy was, the WUL made some bold efforts to organize unskilled, immigrant, and women workers in food, footwear, fur, textile, and garment industries – precisely those ignored by the TLC.

Garment-making factories were one organizing target. Even though some unions already existed in this sector, the odds against successful organizing during the Depression were immense. The industry was characterized by countless small factories, intense competition, seasonal shifts, piecework, and contracting out. A gendered division of labour relegated women to jobs considered less skilled, their low wages justified by their presumed domestic future. But there was also reason for organizing optimism: many workers were Jewish, with left-wing sympathies forged through their immigrant, class, and ethnic experiences. Accustomed to playing a role in the public sphere, some Jewish women eschewed middle-class notions of passive femininity and embraced union militancy.

A new communist union, the International Union of Needle Trades Workers (IUNTW), proclaimed its intent to unionize underpaid women garment workers. Prominent women trade unionists, including fur worker Pearl Wedro, a member of the CPC's women's delegation to the Soviet Union, sat on the IUNTW executive. Labour historians are divided on whether the union's rhetoric about addressing women's special needs matched the reality of its organizing efforts, though some conclude the IUNTW did encourage women to fight for their workplace rights.[48] The Montreal dressmaker strikes offer some confirmation. In Montreal, French-Canadian women, invariably infantilized as "girls," were the majority of the garment workforce. Jewish fellow workers and organizers in the IUNTW saw them as timid, "backward," always susceptible to the Catholic clergy's vociferous anti-unionism and anti-socialism. The existing rival union, the International Ladies' Garment Workers Union (ILGWU), had all but given up organizing. The IUNTW persevered, leading a brief, unsuccessful strike in 1930–31, a limited walkout in 1933, and a general strike of 125 garment shops in 1934. Organizers and workers faced formidable obstacles: employer-hired thugs, church and press opposition, and orchestrated anti-communism, as well as the linguistic, ethnic, and craft loyalties dividing the workforce.[49]

The egregious conditions of labour for women did spur unionization in Montreal. Women's salaries were as low as five or six dollars a week (even lower than other cities); workers claimed that minimum wage laws were skirted by employers who had more than one family member punch in as one person. The IUNTW drew on the organizing talents of Jewish women communists, including rank-and-file activists Rose Myerson (who, fortuitously, spoke French) and Eva Shanoff, who, locked out of their jobs the previous year, had picketed their employer for a further three months, despite repeated arrests.[50] The IUNTW organized social clubs for French-Canadian women, met them at home, and spoke out against the practice of paying French-Canadian women less than other workers. The strike was nonetheless defeated; both the union's decision to settle each factory separately and their rejection of arbitration proposed by the Quebec government proved disastrous.[51]

Why, then, did organizers claim some success? The IUNTW disproved the myth that French-Canadian women could not be organized and showed the benefit of cross-ethnic female alliances in the workplace. When organizer Leah Roback tried later to organize the same women into the ILGWU, she acknowledged that the IUNTW had paved the way, developing a union consciousness and the "militancy" of the "French girls" in spite of the clergy's anti-unionism.[52]

Where it was successful in other cities, the IUNTW set up "shop floor delegates committees," which encouraged women's grassroots participation in the day-to-day affairs of the union. When the IUNTW, influenced yet again by Comintern advice, abruptly switched strategies and told its members to join the rival ILGWU in 1935, women's voices were lost, muted by the ILGWU's more bureaucratic union structure.[53] That union's subsequent decision to pursue state-regulated wage agreements further exacerbated the marginalization of women. The rigid sex typing of jobs, differential pay, and the male breadwinner ideal were solidified even more firmly in agreements hammered out by (male) union leaders, employers, and the state. It appears that earlier communist suspicions of state-sanctioned reform and regulation had some merit.

Ethnicity, Culture, and Gender Consciousness

Jewish garment workers' activism emerged out of their experiences of family, community, work, class, and culture, as well as their investment in socialist ideals. As with African-Canadian women organizing in the nineteenth century, non-Anglo-Celtic women articulated a desire for equality, dignity, and respect related not only to gender but also to their class and ethnicity, experienced as intertwined identities. Jewish immigrants, for example, were viewed suspiciously, subject to housing, educational, social, and job discrimination, symbolized evocatively by beach signs in Toronto reading "No Jews or Negroes allowed."[54] Women's work and family lives were filtered through these experiences, and many were drawn to communism precisely because it offered a transnational ideal of socialist solidarity that defied race and ethnic prejudice.

Ethnicity shaped women's understandings of equality as well as the organizations they created – this was true of the predominantly Anglo women's reform and club movement as well as for socialists. Even within the left, ethnic identification differentiated communist and CCF women. With its strong ILP and British émigré background, the CCF was not only English speaking but often articulated a British identity. Communists from eastern European Jewish, Ukrainian, and Finnish backgrounds were shaped by their own cultural traditions and their experience of exclusion and discrimination in Canada. Unlike the British, they were not preferred newcomers.

The political and cultural mobilization of Ukrainian women makes this point well. In the interwar period, Ukrainians faced discrimination in the workplace and nativist attitudes perpetuated by journalists, writers, and politicians who portrayed Ukrainians as ignorant, backward peasants in need of assimilation and anglicization. Indeed, a pejorative language of "race" was still employed to describe their shortcomings and need for cultural uplift. In this inhospitable context, left-wing Ukrainian women created a movement culture that addressed ethnic exclusion, class exploitation, and gender inequality.

The Women's Section of the Ukrainian Labour-Farmer Temple Association, founded in 1922, with strong communist sympathies, requested its own women's organizer and a "women's journal that would represent their interests."[55] *Robitnytsia* (Working Women), established two years later, fulfilled the latter demand, though it had male editors, most notably Myroslav Irchan, the pen name of Andriy Babiuk, an internationally known poet, dramatist, and writer who was persuaded to immigrate from the Ukraine to oversee a number of Canadian communist publications.[56] The intellectual leadership of men was unsurprising, since communists themselves often claimed that Ukrainian women were isolated in the kitchen and less politically knowledgeable than men – another version of the backward *baba*. This stereotype may have had its origins in the material reality of women's unending domestic work, but Ukrainian women countered that they faced prejudice and censure from their own communities when they dared to speak out publicly.

Robitnytsia spoke to women's connected experiences of gender, ethnic, and class inequality. It was just as innovative as the *Woman Worker*, although discussion of abortion and birth control was noticeably absent. Articles covered religious belief versus science, women's wage labour, female health and hygiene, popular science, and many issues relevant to homemakers' daily domestic labour and child care. Coverage of International Women's Day at home and abroad and profiles of European leaders such as Rosa Luxemburg created a message of women's empowerment within the international communist left. Irchan's credentials meant that cultural offerings were particularly rich, including poems, fiction, commentary on movies (American and

Soviet), and many excerpts from Ukrainian literature, appreciated by an émigré community deeply invested in its own heritage and history.

Robitnystia's intent was to educate women, but it also tried to enlighten less than enlightened men, pointing to the chauvinist prejudices that hampered socialist unity. Emboldened women, the editors hoped, might "gradually educate" men stuck in "dark" ways, who abuse their wives "savagely," clearly a reference to domestic violence.[57] To hurry along this re-education project, the editors encouraged a debate about gender equality by publishing a contemptuous article on women under the pen name Tymko Izhak, the last name a play on the word "porcupine." The porcupine claimed women were backward, ignorant, dependent, unsalvageable, and not in need of organization for they had no "solid convictions" and did not even know how to "use [their] rights."[58]

Reader responses flooded in. Some male writers endorsed the porcupine's claim that women were merely men's "slaves,"[59] but more women took him on. One replied that she could no longer contain her "silence and anger": she had been "ordered" home from a political meeting by her overbearing husband who was convinced she should remain in the kitchen.[60] Other readers called for a separate organization for women to address their political ignorance, noting that men purposely kept women isolated.[61] Some of the strongest responses discussed women's domestic labour: unpaid, unrecognized contributions routinely denigrated by men. As in the *Woman Worker*, discussions of patriarchal authoritarianism and gender inequality surfaced in these raw but insightful letters. If you compared the work of men and women, a reader argued, men are actually "the appendages of women." Her husband, a miner, returns home "bellowing" for his supper, then smokes and gossips afterwards with neighbours. But her work is never done: "You, husband, have worked your shift and for this you have your pay, but you woman, where is your pay?"[62]

Working-class wives' material and social standpoint produced a nascent understanding of what Marxist feminists would later refer to as social reproduction. If domestic issues were supposed to radicalize women, working-class homemakers knew that domestic work was undervalued and limited their ability to be politically active. Women's backtalk to the porcupine suggests not ignorance, but women brave enough to identify gender oppression, if always framed within a robust class politics wrapped up in ethnic identification. Sadly, *Robitnystia*'s promise was curtailed. The paper survived through the Third Period by toeing the party's political line, but its innovative editor returned to the Ukraine, where he was incarcerated, executed by Stalin in 1937, along with hundreds of thousands of other communists.

Imagining Women's Emancipation

Communist cultural producers like Irchan understood that working people might readily identify the lived exploitation of capitalism, but they also needed to imagine the possibility of a different future. Culture was one way to make this revolution in the mind. Culture was initially an integral part of the Bolshevik Revolution; intense debates about art, politics, and socialism raged within the Soviet Union and throughout international communism in its aftermath. Free debate was increasingly silenced by the Stalinist state, but, within the Canadian party and its sympathetic left-wing milieu, there was some political latitude for cultural creators, if only because culture – like gender equality – was a low priority compared to other party endeavours.

Cultural work was also an area of significant female involvement, from working-class Jewish women who created Yiddish-language socialist theatre to middle-class, university-educated intellectuals such as Jean ("Jim") Watts and Dorothy Livesay. Livesay is perhaps better known, as she became a leading Canadian poet, but, in the thirties, Watts was the critical cultural linchpin in the creation of a left-wing arts scene. A talented, charismatic networker, Watts, along with other comrades, founded a Progressive Arts Club in Toronto to nurture socialist art, writing, and drama. She helped sustain the Canadian cultural magazine *Masses* (dubbed the first "Canadian proletarian art monthly"), co-directed a performance of the wildly popular socialist play *Waiting for Lefty,* and toured political plays across Ontario's small towns, transporting cast and crew in her old Chrysler. In other cities too, Progressive Arts Clubs sprang up as incubators for cultural production and the socialist imagination.[63]

In the early 1930s, communist intellectuals challenged bourgeois culture by staging plays at factory gates, in the streets, or in makeshift theatres. Although women writers and actors participated in this "agit prop" theatre, dramas usually stressed class conflict and men's experiences.[64] Similarly, in the raw representation of class in *Masses,* women were portrayed as either downtrodden victims of exploitation or salt-of-the-earth revolutionaries, both one-dimensional polarities.[65] Working-class women, *Masses* articles warned (in terms not unlike those applied to the *baba*), had to be weaned from the "sickly reformism" peddled by middle-class feminists like Nellie

McClung, who wrote about working-class women without any real understanding of proletarian life. Women must not be taken in by her moralistic, "insipid burbling," good only for the "tea sipping, coupon clipping strata of society."[66]

After 1935, the Comintern drastically shifted its advice to communists around the world, urging them to create a "Popular Front": protecting democracy from fascism was paramount, and, to do so, communist women should forge alliances with all manner of liberal, social democrat, and socialist feminists. Cultural strategies shifted accordingly. Feminism was no longer bad-mouthed, and a more expansive definition of women's issues included peace, health, children, homemaking, schooling, unionization, and consumer prices. Efforts to address the daily burdens of working-class women's work, inside and outside the home, created a political culture more welcoming to women, but there were trade-offs. If the Popular Front jettisoned the "proletarian masculinism" of the early 1930s,[67] women's interests were now often portrayed within the confines of a conventional, heterosexual family. In order to be "popular," communist writing often replicated prevailing gender ideology.

Still, women's lives and gender inequality often came to the forefront, especially in left-wing cultural magazines like *Masses* and *New Frontier*. In the latter, Marjorie King's essay "Women Are Mugs" explored the "social conditioning" of middle-class women, "brought up to believe they must marry and keep house for a living." Cut off from the world in "unhealthy lives" of confining domesticity, their "urge to work" was channelled by society into "home, clothes and food." King's claim that women needed to rid themselves of this "claptrap" read surprisingly like Betty Friedan's famous 1963 book, *The Feminine Mystique*.[68] *New Frontier* articles addressed gender inequality in the workforce, debunking the notion that women's occupational and social roles were innate or "natural." Feminists were reminded that their hopes for "emancipation" after suffrage became a mirage in the face of Depression economic instability. Wage work, wrote social worker Margaret Gould, offered women the tantalizing hope of economic independence, yet their reality was "slavish working conditions" justified with false "myths" of female inferiority.[69]

Gould called not only for "new economic opportunities" for women but also for "a new morality of marriage, education against idleness, and a social conscience."[70] In *New Frontier* pieces describing her trip to the Soviet Union, Gould laid out her vision of an emancipated female future. She repeated the usual positive claims that the USSR had vanquished gender inequality and racial prejudice, but admitted that women still faced "shabby" living conditions, attributed to a country still struggling to develop after a bruising civil war. What was important, however, was the pervasive character of communist transformation, the connection between the political and personal. For Gould, economic freedom would permeate everyday life, transforming women's economic, social, reproductive choices and engendering a new female subjectivity as well as sexual and intimate relationships: "the Russian woman appears to have freed herself from many of the inhibitions that warp the personalities of women in most countries."[71]

Fiction was an appealing métier for left-wing activists imagining women's emancipation, including new sexual freedoms. Even in the Third Period, Livesay was toying in her writing with themes of love, sexuality, and (in)egalitarian relationships;[72] her story "A Girl Sees It!" in *Masses,* for example, acknowledged women's sexual autonomy as well as her class exploitation. Livesay depicts the life of a young female domestic who becomes pregnant by her employer, is pressed into poverty, but eventually finds her way to the class struggle. In contrast to the writing of many early socialists, the story explores the domestic's sexual choices and desire rather than creating a simplistic "victim story."[73]

For left-wing women, communism meant hopes for new personal relationships of esteem and equality between men and women. Yet there was glaring disjuncture between the sexual freedom women carved out for themselves in communist artistic circles and the party's public adulation of the traditional family. Livesay's memoirs recounts her love affairs, an abortion, and sexual experimentation by women intellectuals on the left, while she claims that working-class housewives married to party members were mired in traditionalism, "tied to the kitchen sink."[74] Watts's rejection of monogamy, her reputed bisexuality, and her androgynous dress marked out her sexual difference, seemingly tolerated in left-wing artistic circles. For good reason, Livesay later referred to Watts as the "New Woman" of her time.[75]

Personal experimentation was tolerated, but sexual liberation was not announced openly, and homophobia was rampant in the party. Issues like birth control became examples of tortured party doublespeak, as Canadian communists struggled to justify why the Soviet Union backtracked on women's reproductive freedom in 1936 when it discouraged birth control and banned abortion. The communist newspaper, the *Daily Clarion,* had to reassure its readers that birth control clinics were still necessary in Canada – or lose all credibility on women's equality.

Eugenia "Jim" Watts, 1940

Figure 6.3 Jean Watts led efforts to create a left-wing culture that questioned class exploitation and gender conventions | Courtesy of Elinor (Fen) Taylor, LAC, Frederick B. Taylor fonds, R3299-0-8-E

Communist concessions to traditional gender and familial ideology have been attributed to Stalinism and the party's lazy acquiescence to masculinist, patriarchal ideas, but Barbara Foley has an intriguing argument that communists were not Marxist *enough*. The party's reformist rhetoric in the late 1930s and repetition of simplistic solutions suggested by Engels's theories obviated a truly innovative Marxist critique of class and gender inequality. If there was a ray of hope for innovation, it lay in women's cultural production. By paying heed to everyday, familial, sexual, as well as productive forces, communist women may have come closest to imagining both "women's liberation and class emancipation."[76]

Watts, perhaps more than anyone else on the Canadian cultural scene, symbolized the emancipated communist woman. Traditional gender roles were there to be challenged. In 1936, Watts went to Spain, ostensibly as a correspondent to cover the civil war, but in reality hoping to fight for the Republican side. She sent back reports to *New Frontier* and the *Daily Clarion* and later managed to secure a job driving an ambulance for the

British volunteers. Back in Canada, she went into hiding in 1939 at the outbreak of the Second World War to prevent her internment by the state but resurfaced in 1941 after the Soviet Union joined the war, and she joined the armed forces.[77] Both she and Livesay moved away from communism by the late 1940s. Although Livesay's offered a more public "self fashioning" narrative that disavowed her youthful political choices,[78] Watts did not renounce her past.

Conclusion

Left-wing politics as a path to gender equality was both an encouraging promise and a deep disappointment. The CPC's largely male leadership, tied to Comintern advice, downplayed the separate mobilization of women and conveniently promised gender equality "after the revolution." Even in the Popular Front, when women's concerns were more adequately addressed, women's issues were equated with a heteronormative, traditional, male-breadwinner family.

Yet the communist movement spoke meaningfully to women's class consciousness, working-class experiences, ethnic exclusion, and hopes for social transformation, especially in the face of economic crisis and widespread immiseration. The principles, discipline, and sense of collectivity offered by the party seemed the most effective strategy to challenge entrenched power and secure some dignity for women workers, mothers, comrades. Women who believed there was no path to gender equality other than through socialism accepted political trade-offs as they struggled for a collective future. Moreover, membership in a left-wing movement nurtured women with a gendered comradeship; their socialist politics was tied up with female friendships and loyalties based on shared working-class, ethnic, family, and mothering roles.[79]

Like Margaret Gould, some believed that communism would spark a transformation in personal relations between men and women. For a very few like Jean Watts, a left-wing cultural milieu was an opportunity to challenge gender norms and heteronormativity while working for social justice. In retrospect, of course, hard questions need to be asked: why was women's misplaced belief in the Soviet miracle of gender equality so strong? Why did women fail to question wholesale executions in the Soviet Union – including of Irchan – and the confining rigidities of Stalinism in their own party?[80]

For women in the CCF orbit, party life also signified promise and disappointment, comradeship and second-class roles. Women's oppression may have been a non-existent or minor issue for most male socialists leading the CCF, but not for women who came to socialism through feminism or who assimilated women's equality into their vision of socialism. Like the earlier suffrage movement – and some CCF women were former suffragists – the party appealed to women primarily as mothers, homemakers, and caregivers, reproducing its own version of maternalism. Women's columns and separate groups within the party reflected this ideology, but were these efforts merely pragmatic strategies to recruit women and harness their unpaid labour or did they also nurture a feminist consciousness? A minority of women in separate groups were feminist socialists, some very vocally so, some more circumspectly. Even feminists such as Agnes Macphail sensed the catch-22 of women's groups: in a male-dominated party, women could become stuck in an auxiliary rut. Still, feminists' political presence within the CCF, however compromised, should dispel the wave/trough model that assumes that, post-suffrage, there were simply "no feminist agitators" within political parties until the 1970s.[81]

Beatrice Brigden was unashamedly feminist, condemned gender inequality, and endorsed women-only organizing because she saw women marginalized in the real world of male-dominated politics. She too was sustained in life's exhausting political battles by close female friendships with fellow socialist feminists.[82] Dorothy Steeves, in contrast, challenged sexist stereotypes and discrimination all her life and put forward feminist legislation yet was not very interested in the autonomous women's sphere of "co-operative feminism."[83] CCF women did privately lament the sidelining of equality issues and the way that, as candidates, they were shunted into unwinnable ridings. However, those who believed that women's equality was not possible within capitalism, or that emancipation was not possible for *all* women as long as *some* women faced homelessness and hunger, could not abandon the socialist project even when it sometimes disappointed them as feminists.

7 Feminism, War, and Peace

Laura Hughes grew up surrounded by middle-class privilege and possibilities. The daughter of James and Adeline Hughes, respectively Toronto's chief inspector of schools and an educational expert on kindergartens, Laura talked over the dinner table with Toronto's reform-minded intellectual elite. Her family had solid Conservative connections too: her uncle Sam Hughes was the minister of munitions in the Robert Borden cabinet during the First World War. Laura might have married well and settled down to a middle-class life of good works. She did not.

We might blame her parents, both suffragists. They cultivated her social conscience and activism; for her eighteenth birthday, her father gave her a membership in a suffrage society. Laura, however, moved beyond reputable suffrage campaigning. During the First World War, she threw away respectability by joining a group of international feminists preaching peace, disarmament, and an end to the war. She then turned to labour and socialist causes. By 1917, she would no longer have been welcome in the salons of Toronto's Anglo-British elite.

The experience and analysis of war had a profound influence on Canadian feminism, extending from Hughes's pacifism in the First World War to anti–Vietnam War protests in the 1960s, and beyond. This chapter traces the connections between feminism, war, and peace until the end of the Second World War, suggesting how life changing war was for many feminists, how it transformed their notions of equality, and how peacemaking became hyphenated with feminism in a politics of hope that was often defeated by the reality of war. Feminist organizing might be encouraged in a war environment, but might just as easily be crushed by it. Feminists invariably bemoaned the violence of war, but some accepted armed combat as the only means of defending principles or nations. Many argued that women had a uniquely gendered perspective on war and peace that needed to be heard by the nation and might even change the world. While most feminists agreed that war *was* a feminist issue, they disagreed on why and on how to respond to it.

Peaceful Platitudes and Hopes

Most late nineteenth- and early twentieth-century feminists claimed world peace as a political aspiration. Yet it became a lot harder to stay the course in a time of war. Religious groups associated with pacifism, such as Quakers, Mennonites, and Hutterites, were a constant presence from the nineteenth century onwards, though, save for the Quakers, their pacifism did not cross over into feminist politics. Two other streams of anti-war thought conditioned feminist views. In the late nineteenth century, liberal pacifism, associated with Christian churches and women's reform groups, decried war an anathema to Christianity and promoted international arbitration as its antidote.[1] Shared with the women's reform movement by social gospel advocates, these ideas were echoed in the National Council of Women of Canada (NCWC), which established a peace and arbitration committee, though only a minority of NCWC locals participated.[2]

Second, labour and socialist groups critiqued war as an outgrowth of capitalism and imperialism, claiming that the working class became little more than cannon fodder in military escapades, which benefited the ruling class. Socialist feminists added a gendered analysis: wars inevitably impoverished working-class women and children, and, as mothers, women should argue for the preservation of life, rather than its wanton destruction. Although labour newspapers like the Winnipeg *Voice* succumbed to British imperialist thinking – supporting the 1899 Boer War, for example – the labour movement harboured suspicions that war usually benefited moneyed interests, not workers. Even the timid Trades and Labour Congress passed a resolution in 1911 declaring it would support a general strike if war was declared – though it backtracked in 1914. Socialists sustained a more unrelenting critique, arguing wars were fought for profits, control of trade, and land for the elites. War was also the antithesis of the internationalist tradition of universal working-class solidarity. The Second International promised to unite all its national members against global conflicts – though it too reneged in 1914.

Before the First World War, feminists of many political hues shared a rhetorical aversion to war, a stance cited by anti-suffragists to prove women were not equipped to make rational decisions about armed conflict. Woman's domestic role and emotional, sentimental nature rendered her incapable, by inclination and knowledge, of judging war and foreign relations. Nor did women serve in the military; men's ultimate sacrifice justified their entitlement to citizenship. While anti-suffragist Goldwin Smith claimed women were likely to march men off to war without thinking twice, other antis claimed they would be too hesitant to do so. Either way, they were not fit to make such decisions.

Feminists countered that women's social perspective and critical stance on war was the very reason they should vote. Laura Hughes's father argued in his pro-suffrage book that "anti-suffragists feared a transfer of power from the military to the unmilitary sex ... changing the very character of the nation." Serving in the military, he added, was no rationale for political rights: the logical conclusion was that only soldiers could vote.[3] It would be women's public political participation, James Hughes predicted overly optimistically, which would quell future wars.

The pre-war women's movement routinely criticized the cultivation of militaristic masculinity, especially in school lessons that equated prestige with military achievement. "The soldier remains the hero of civilization," lamented Nellie McClung. "We inculcate the love of battle ... in boys" by putting "miniature weapons of warfare into their little hands ... rewarding them with accolades when they march home from war." Rather than a masculinity associated with force, competitiveness, and authority, suffragists idealized the "New Man" of virtue, compassion, and physical/sexual restraint. Even after the First World War began, McClung bemoaned male "statecraft" as its cause: "women have had nothing to say about war except pay the price of war" – namely mothers' painful loss of their sons on the battlefield. Once enfranchised, she predicted, women would inject a pragmatic perspective to governing that valued human life over militarism.[4]

Other feminists similarly predicted peace would follow the achievement of women's rights. Flora MacDonald Denison's long-standing links to feminists from other nations was likely one factor shaping her aversion to war. Having basked in the feeling of sisterhood in the International Woman Suffrage Association, she may have been horrified by the ferocious, irrational anti-German sentiment whipped up in Canada at the outbreak of war. Her 1914 pamphlet "Women and War" warned of the impending tragedy of the "deadly" current conflict but claimed war could be purged or "evolved out of" human life. Men had been socialized to support "combat and dominance through force," while women were more "constructive" in their thought. But, she reminded readers, these roles were not biologically predestined; men had the intellectual and moral capacity to build for peaceful co-existence, even if women had to lead the way.[5]

While feminists' arguments seemed to lean on an essentialist view of women's innate maternal instincts, some attributed women's abhorrence of war to their "social motherhood." Following the influential American pacifist and feminist Jane Addams, they admitted that not all women opposed war and, conversely, that men could be socialized to non-violence. Nonetheless, women's social experience of motherhood and caring labour produced "a unique standpoint" that might spark their revulsion at the destruction of humanity and encourage anti-war views.[6]

Wartime Feminism

When war was declared in 1914, the pacifism of Christian churches and the NCWC quickly evaporated. The Trades and Labour Congress also endorsed the nation's war aims, though it demanded that the rich pay their fair share of the economic burden. Although labour parties with a strong British émigré membership often supported the war, socialists, in concert with a small enclave of feminists, became the minority opposition. It may seem hypocritical that feminists like McClung kept sermonizing about women's propensity for peace while supporting the war. However, McClung was also a British imperialist, liberal, nationalist, and the mother of an enlistee. All these identities conditioned her views. She rationalized that women, had they been international players, might have prevented the war (though, ultimately, she laid all blame on German "expansionism"). Her views were further characterized by a moralistic and eugenics streak: war, she feared, would lead to the inevitable fraying of the "moral fabric" of Canada, and, if the better class of men were volunteering, society would be left with "the unfit, the epileptic, the consumptive, the inebriate."[7]

McClung's views help explain why most suffragists who had critiqued militarism suddenly became recruiters for the military. First, despite their self-proclaimed role as "guardians of the race," they claimed they had no choice but to take a stand on men's fateful decisions about war.[8] Second, they claimed that Christianity was equated with Canada's goal of defeating militaristic, totalitarian "Prussianism" – and, indeed, many Christian churches promoted this view. Third, McClung and other suffragists never questioned the state's version of German dictatorship and cruelty. It was

Germany's nefarious sinking of the passenger ship *Lusitania,* she claimed, that opened her Christian eyes to the necessity of defeating the dark "Prince of Evil." By the time she wrote *Next of Kin* in 1917, she was even critical of the "slackers" who avoided active military service.[9]

Other pro-war suffragists' ethnic and cultural loyalty to Britain and their class association with the leaders of the Canadian wartime state influenced their loyalties, as did the unprecedented government propaganda campaign – posters, newspapers, and public events – about enemy atrocities against women and children. International feminist sisterhood was only one part of their identity; another was Britishness, whiteness, and the global good of the British Empire. They did not see the contradiction of imperialism: empires were built upon wars, including dispossession and violence against Indigenous populations. Finally, the cumulative personal loss and family grief for soldiers who died in combat, memorialized daily in press casualty lists and worn on women's bodies as mourning attire, undoubtedly had an impact on their political choices.[10]

If feminists admitted war was a tragedy, they also saw it as an opportunity. Suffrage and reform feminists threw themselves into fundraising and recruiting; politically, they shored up the wartime state and urged the substitution of women for men in munitions work in the hopes the latter would enlist. War was integrated into reform feminism: it was an opportunity to remake the nation in crisis – hurrying along national "purification" through legislation such as prohibition – and, perhaps most important, to confirm women's equality, loyalty, and right to citizenship.[11] When the government convened a Women's War Conference in 1918 in Ottawa, the invitees claimed their importance as nation builders: they were now "moulding the destinies of the nation," as the "Mothers of Consolidation" following the "Fathers of Confederation."[12] Women passed resolutions for equal pay and a minimum wage as well as endorsing various government "win the war" measures. Politicians were astutely using middle-class female allies to secure their war agenda; meanwhile, the women anticipated that their presence would advance their reform demands. This was not, however, an alliance of equals: the advantages accrued disproportionately to the government.

While the majority of Anglo-Canadian suffragists saw the war as a necessary, patriotic endeavour, they did differ on whether they should temporarily halt or continue suffrage campaigns. The Toronto-based Canadian Suffrage Association kept up its activities and advocated for the international arbitration of disputes between nations. Even mentioning arbitration smacked of unacceptable pacifism to other suffragists who criticized the association's misplaced priorities. How can we possibly do suffrage work, asked suffragist Constance Hamilton, when "the freedom of the whole Empire is at stake?"[13] By 1917, lines hardened. Pro-war suffragists deemed arbitration and discussion of peace a betrayal: opposition to any form of "pacifism" was equated with the fight against "ignorance, cowardice and treason."[14] Constance Boulton and other suffragists established a "suffragist war auxiliary" to exhibit the worthiness of those women who were solidly behind the government. Emmeline Pankhurst, who abandoned the British suffrage campaign to support the war, was an ideal role model; feminists who opposed the war, including her socialist daughter, Sylvia, were dismissed as wrong-headed and disloyal.

Anti-War Feminism

Feminists who took the more unpopular path of anti-war politics were a beleaguered minority, but they found solace in their Christian faith, transnational feminist allies, and socialist organizations. Some feminists moved from scepticism to staunch anti-war politics; their experience of wartime intolerance, censorship, and rabid militarism pushed them into the pacifist camp. Others equivocated. Their sympathies rested with the peace movement, but they were persuaded of German atrocities and the need to defend democracy. Flora MacDonald Denison's ambivalence was apparent in her geographical mobility. Although she wrote disapprovingly of German "autocracy," she moved to her hometown, Napanee, to work as a seamstress to put her son through school, thus avoiding the political nastiness of hyperpatriotic Toronto. Denison withdrew periodically to her nearby wilderness retreat at Bon Echo, and in 1916 worked as a travelling organizer for the New York State suffrage campaign.[15]

Other anti-war feminists spoke up periodically, albeit forcefully. Social gospel reformer Alice Chown publicly defended visiting Scottish feminist pacifist Chrystal Macmillan in 1915 against charges of disloyalty. The NCWC had reluctantly given Macmillan, known for other feminist legal campaigns, three minutes to speak at its convention, during which she expressed her anti-war views. Self-appointed patriots within the NCWC promptly denounced her, echoing the newspapers' view she was "under the influence of ... German plotters." Chown defended Macmillan's freedom of speech (surely this is what democracy stands for, she said) but also pointed out that Christians who believed in the teachings of Jesus Christ had long opposed militarism. Paraphrasing playwright George Bernard Shaw, she admonished pro-war advocates to concede they were not true Christians but

Figure 7.1 The international meeting at The Hague in 1915 led to the founding of the Women's International League for Peace and Freedom. Laura Hughes is third from left | London School of Economics Library, WILPF/2011/18

rather "pagans." Readers responded with "trolling" – at that time, through letters to the newspaper, not social media – suggesting Chown be sent to an asylum or, better, deported to German-occupied Belgium.[16]

A small group of determined women organized openly against the war, holding meetings, circulating anti-war material, and writing for the very few newspapers that would publish their views. Many were inspired by transnational feminist pacifism. In 1915, Laura Hughes attended the International Women's Peace Conference in The Hague, led by American pacifist Jane Addams. Conference speakers drew on established arguments about social motherhood but added prescient warnings about the terrifying destructiveness of modern warfare and the danger war posed to democratic "free speech."[17] For men, the conference heard, wars were "contests for economic and political power," while women were the inevitable victims of wartime violence, including rape. Hughes returned home fired up for peace. Perhaps losing her brother Chester in battle in 1915 sharpened her anti-war beliefs. Sadly, her suffragist father was torn on the war question, remarking that he was "trying in two ways to end the war and bring peace by sending my boy to the trenches and my girl to the peace conference."[18]

Another Canadian woman was influential to The Hague conference. The conference's peace proposal was drafted by Julia Grace Wales, a Canadian teaching English at an American university (opportunities for such women being nil in Canada). Wales's reform and social gospel leanings, as well as her transnational education, sparked her interest in international affairs, inspiring her to pen a pamphlet "Continuous Mediation without Armistice," endorsed by the meeting in The Hague. Wales joined conference leaders who travelled across Europe to promote the plan in neutral countries as well as among ambassadors from combatant nations, none of whom had time for these upstart female diplomats. Wartime travel was hazardous. As a British subject, Wales could not traverse Germany, so she took passage to Denmark as the only woman on a small freighter heading through the North Sea, a recipe for sea sickness and isolation. Despite the difficult conditions and illness, Wales returned to Europe the following year on a second peace mission, financed by industrialist Henry Ford. Her activism, however, was limited to the international scene. In Canada, other women took the lead.[19]

Inspired by the pacifist idealism and international sisterhood of the meeting in The Hague, Laura Hughes, Alice Chown, and Elsie Charlton founded the short-lived Canadian Women's Peace Party in the inhospitable political climate of Anglo Toronto. Hughes was such an embarrassment to her Tory uncle Sir Sam Hughes that he offered to buy her a plot of Saskatchewan land if she would just disappear into rural ignominy. Routinely accused of traitorous disloyalty, anti-war women and men faced denigration and violence. In Winnipeg, anti-war protests were attacked by vigilantes; labour feminist Helen Armstrong, remembered her granddaughter, returned home from these protests "covered in bruises from head to toe."[20] Socialists claimed the mainstream press encouraged militarist vigilantes to break up anti-war meetings; in Guelph, local police watched as speakers were dragged from the platform and beaten.[21]

Women might face more subtle intimidation. A Toronto public school teacher, Frieda Held, was forced by the school board to resign due to rumours (later retracted) that she was not "loyal" enough to Britain, based on her parents' German heritage and some second-hand conversation about her views on the national anthem. Cognizant of Held's fate, teachers avoided talking politics or attending meetings outside school hours.[22] Anti-war feminist Gertrude Richardson closed her column in the socialist *Canadian Forward* by acknowledging how hard pacifism was: "Let us be brave and fearless. We shall be called traitors, but we are the true patriots, uplifting humanity."[23]

Gertrude Richardson did her anti-war organizing from the kitchen table of her farmhouse in northern Manitoba; using letter writing and journalism, she created far-reaching national and transnational networks of feminist-pacifist discussion. Richardson had emigrated from Britain only a few years earlier, with well-formulated social gospel, suffragist, anti-imperialist, and pacifist sympathies. In Britain, her family had opposed the Boer War, with her father suffering a fatal beating by a pro-war vigilante mob after a pacifist meeting. After emigrating, Richardson married a farmer and quickly threw herself into suffrage work, becoming vice-president of the Manitoba Political Equality League. In between farm chores, she wrote prodigiously on feminism and suffrage for newspapers in Britain and Canada.

When the war broke out, she initially focused on humanitarian aid and exposés of the abuse of conscientious objectors (including her imprisoned brother) by the army, but her anti-war writing became more politically focused, impassioned, and socialist. In 1917, her column in *Women's Century,* a magazine endorsed by the NCWC, disappeared. All pacifist literature, the pro-war editors admitted, goes to the "waste paper basket."[24] Richardson switched to the *Canadian Forward,* published by the socialist Social Democratic Party, although it was under siege by state censors, its editor imprisoned for anti-war views.

Richardson's feminist-pacifist writing was imbued with maternalist rhetoric. The last cry of dying soldiers of all nationalities, she wrote, is for their mothers, as the men pleaded "why did you do nothing to stop the war?"[25] She believed women's "mother hearts" shaped their pacifism, though this was not simply a matter of biology. Motherhood is "more than physical" she wrote. "It is a deep spiritual possession, a love for humanity, a longing to protect, conserve, guard and save."[26] Richardson began a "write-in" women's crusade against the war – women sent her letters pledging to "oppose all war, conscription and slavery, a pledge to support those who work for freedom of peace, the suppression of militarism under all forms, and to support the struggles of workers and international socialism."[27]

Richardson's Christian and feminist beliefs were both elements of her opposition to the "cruel militarism" of war. Socialism was another: militarism was a product of capitalism and imperialism, which conquered and enslaved subject populations across the globe. The enemy, she said in words that likely horrified pro-war suffragists, "is neither Germany nor Austria" but the "spirit of cruelty and conquest in the conditions of war and militarism, the oppression of the other and all of the weak, and the institutions of slavery in every form." Moreover, war left shattered women in its wake: both bereft mothers and those women pushed into prostitution, "sacrificed to crime wherever there is an army."[28] What began as a maternalist aversion to war became an integrative critique of capitalism, patriarchy, and empire.

Although Richardson had not previously criticized Canada's treatment of Indigenous peoples, she now began to question Canada's internal empire.

Similarly, Harriet Prenter, a member of the Toronto Equal Franchise League who marched with Canadian feminists of all political persuasions in the 1913 Washington suffrage parade, increasingly condemned pro-war feminists' British "jingoism," anti-immigrant fervour, and class prejudice. Not only will "industrial workers shoulder the financial burden of war," she warned, but working-class boys will be groomed for military service, while affluent private school students will "escape" it. When Ontario women obtained the provincial vote in 1917, she warned that "society ladies" were contemplating how to disenfranchise "foreigners" (which had some truth) and countered that these "patriotic pagans were far more detrimental to the future of democracy" than so-called "foreigners ... Let us gather [together] those of every race ... The only enemies are the militarists, profiteers, exploiters."[29]

Prenter's fears about the unequal burden of war were echoed by labour feminists who lamented worsening economic conditions shouldered by the working class as wartime inflation ate away at household budgets and soldiers' pensions barely supported working-class families. Helen Armstrong initiated a "Next of Kin" organization in Winnipeg, not to knit socks for soldiers, but to protest the worsening wartime conditions for working-class families. With the local Women's Labour League, she lobbied for better support for war widows and protested the treatment of imprisoned immigrant "aliens" from enemy nations whose impoverished families had no means of support.[30]

Labour feminist Helen Gutteridge combined trade union, socialist, and feminist arguments in her *British Columbia Federationist* column, arguing that the war was a product of both hyper-masculinity and capitalist monopoly. War abroad and the "starvation" of working-class families at home were two sides of the same coin: a system geared toward profit, not people. If the war represented the best "male statescraft" can offer, she wrote sarcastically, it was time for women to become involved in the "councils of the nations." Women's experience as mothers might act as an "antidote to the false conception of man that places property and possessions at a higher value than human welfare."[31]

Laura Hughes's anti-war politics propelled her from suffrage into the labour movement; she went to work undercover in a factory producing soldier's clothing, then exposed the substandard, sweated working conditions, writing in a Toronto labour newspaper. Her investigative mission was characterized by some as a middle-class do-gooder effort, but it was true to her belief that war was sustained by a ruling elite who profited economically from the control of working people and the suppression of opposition politics. In one speech, she traced the links between an "international armament ring" tying together politicians in Germany, England, and Canada, concluding "the war is kept alive by those interested in the making of arms."[32] In the parlance of the 1970s, war was the product of the military-industrial complex, propped up by a sympathetic state.

Feminism and Political Rights in War

Public condemnation of Hughes's anti-war activism may explain her move to Chicago, where she married a conscientious objector and remained connected to the women's international peace movement. Gertrude Richardson, physically exhausted and mentally despairing by the end of the war, had a breakdown and was committed to an asylum, where she later died. Francis Marion Beynon, suffragist columnist for the *Grain Growers Guide,* also paid a price for her growing opposition to the war. Soldiers, she wrote in one column, were being sacrificed for the profits of "gun-making corporations." Anticipating feminist anti-war slogans of the 1970s ("It will be a great day when our schools get all the money they need and the air force has to hold a bake sale to buy a bomber"), she argued that funding for the war should be redirected to the social good, such as the "education of the entire population of Western Canada."[33] Under suspicion by the federal war censor, she lost her job, then moved to New York City to join her sister and brother-in-law, also journalist exiles from Canada's wartime intolerance. In New York, Beynon penned a thinly disguised autobiographical novel, *Aleta Dey,* which laid bare wartime divisions within Canadian feminism.

Part melodrama, part memoir of the movement, part feminist rallying call, *Aleta Dey* uses the romantic relationships and friendships of her fictional heroine as plot devices to explore the tragedies and contradictions of feminist and pacifist politics. Beynon wrestles with questions almost no other Canadian writers tackled at the time: How do we reconcile our romantic attraction to men who don't share our politics? How do we work with suffragists whose middle-class privilege we abhor? How do we confront feminists who have seemingly abandoned pacifism? How do we conquer our own feminine fears of speaking out in public when women who march for suffrage, let alone against the war, are denounced as "disgustingly unwomanly?"[34]

Beynon satirized suffragists who hastily abandoned their claims about women's pacifist nature and called for the obliteration of the "evil" Germans, and she exposes the racial and ethnic intolerance fostered by war. A "society woman" suffragist corners Aleta at an event, horrified that she has become a pacifist: "She leveled her lorgnette at me fearsomely. 'But the atrocities my dear, the atrocities ... Surely people who do things like that ought to be exterminated.'" Aleta reminds the woman of the atrocities against African Americans in the United States and against Africans in the Belgian Congo. "As I remember it those were only coloured people" responds her adversary. "There is a vast difference between crucifying a white man and hanging a coloured one." Yes, Aleta replies sarcastically, "I have no doubt their naked bodies have quite a different effect against the sky."[35]

In the denouement of the novel, Aleta's participation in an anti-conscription rally results in her being badly beaten by soldiers. She dies a martyr to the cause of freedom of speech and a pacifism aligned with social justice, feminism, and the Christian spirit. Beynon's anguished examination of wartime feminism exposed divisions within the movement over democratic rights, liberties, and nationalism. Even feminists supporting the war disagreed on the meaning of democratic rights. In 1917, controversies over conscription and federal voting rights in the Wartime Elections Act (WEA) and Military Voters Act (MVA) brought these differences to a head. At loggerheads were two different views of democratic rights, one seeing the vote as a privilege for select women, the other stressing the vote as an inalienable right for all women.

Conscription divided suffragists. The francophone Fédération nationale Saint-Jean-Baptiste opposed the Conservative government's effort to compel men to join the military, seeing it as an undemocratic, coercive measure infringing on the rights of Quebecers. Even the moderate, reformist National Council of Women of Canada was torn: with eight local councils in favour of conscription and seven against, it avoided a national statement. After conscription was passed, Prime Minister Borden's government faced a December election, which his party feared losing. The Conservatives were already wrestling with a suffrage dilemma: since the federal vote was determined by provincial voting lists and many women had recently won the provincial franchise, could these women vote federally?

This question was obviated by the WEA. Its purpose was straightforward: enfranchise people likely to support conscription and therefore re-elect Borden and his "Union" government, which had taken in some Liberal deserters, and disenfranchise those unlikely to support it. The WEA was massive gerrymandering on an unprecedented scale. Women who had family members – sons, brothers, fathers – serving in the British and Canadian forces, as well as widows of soldiers, could vote. Conscientious objectors could not. Especially devastating in the immigrant, prairie West, men born in nations under the control of Austria and Germany who had become "naturalized" Canadians after 1902 had their vote taken away, unless they had a close male relative serving in the military. Even those speaking one of these "enemy" languages could be disenfranchised!

While the assignment of voting rights was complex, the bill revealed its ethnocentric and corrupt purpose in one of many minor provisions: immigrant women whose family members from "enemy" nations were serving in the Canadian military could still be disenfranchised if provincial voting rules barred them from the vote. As Lyndsay Campbell concludes in her dissection of the bill, "the WEA meticulously sliced up the electorate, enfranchising and disenfranchising on the basis of gender, race, ethnicity, language, Indigeneity, property and income, and relationship to the military."[36] A sister act to the WEA, the MVA used complex regulations to enlarge the numbers of soldiers voting, assigning overseas soldier votes to certain ridings and also enfranchising nurses serving in the military. Rife with corruption in its implementation, the MVA solidified the gerrymander.

To strip away someone's existing rights based on their place of origin and ethnicity was unprecedented, yet Borden had the support of suffragists who believed that conscription would end the war more quickly and that women's "sacrifice" of male family members to the war entitled them to a say in government. Underneath these rationales, of course, were also long-standing prejudices against French Canadians and non-British immigrants. In a private meeting, Nellie McClung suggested to Prime Minster Borden that he give Canadian and English, but not "foreign," women the vote. Faced with howls of protest, McClung later recanted, but her suggestion reassured Borden that the WEA, crafted in all its mendacity by Solicitor General Arthur Meighen, would secure suffragist support. Francis Marion Beynon, once McClung's protégée, was horrified. She denounced the WEA as a "monstrous act of injustice" and "threefold betrayal, first, to the democratic right to vote free of political tampering"; second, of immigrants "lured to Canada to build the country" and now denied their rights; and finally, of soldiers who thought they were fighting for "a free and honourable Canada" rather than for politicians and financiers who had made Canada "into a little Germany."[37]

The Wartime Elections Act exposed divisions within feminism between pacifists and war supporters, English and French, socialists and liberals, equal rights and social reform advocates. It also reflected the legacy of long-standing suffrage rhetoric that had questioned whether non-Anglo immigrants merited the vote when upstanding British women were denied it: the message had sunk in. Suffragists supporting the act claimed that women with relatives serving in the forces had the privilege of a more deserving political "stake" in this national decision, having made the ultimate sacrifice of their sons and husbands, unlike the "slackers" who remained behind. The WEA's "selective draft" of women voters, wrote one supporter, was bestowed on "true patriots," those who could be "trusted" to understand the politics of conscription.[38] Some supporters simply resorted to characterizations of the "foreign" and "Quebec" vote as disloyal and unpatriotic. This was an instrumental argument about how voting rights would likely be used, not entirely out of line with earlier feminist arguments that women needed the vote to clean up society. It was also a nationalist argument in which feminism played second fiddle to ethnic-racial identification, a more selective than universal understanding of rights.

English-Canadian feminists who opposed the WEA called for universal, democratic rights. The Manitoba Political Equality League (in defiance of McClung) objected to the act's denial of democracy, as did Prairie journalist Violet McNaughton, who opposed the disenfranchisement of the foreign born. Socialist-feminist opponents, already critical of wartime assaults on workers' rights, knew their ranks included many of the despised "foreigners" who were disenfranchised. Labour movement leader Helena Gutteridge, backed by a coalition of BC suffragists, telegraphed Borden, demanding that all women be enfranchised on the same terms as men.[39]

In Quebec, where the war was unpopular and riots followed conscription, Marie Gérin-Lajoie opposed rights for women based on their male family members' military service, particularly when all women had made contributions to the war effort. Women loyal to anti-conscriptionist Liberal Party leader Wilfrid Laurier believed the law affronted the "minority" rights of Quebecers. Montreal Liberal and suffragist Dr. Grace Ritchie-England claimed the act's undemocratic nature defied "every fundamental of British justice,"[40] putting her out of step with most English-speaking Quebecers. Her outspoken opposition resulted in her impeachment as president of the Montreal Council of Women.

Both the state and pro-war women's organizations defined women's worth in relation to their "patriotic motherhood," but this also cast their opponents as unpatriotic, disloyal or undeserving of rights. In the United States, trials of anti-war women charged under wartime emergency laws revealed this same dichotomy: pro-war, "patriotic" mothers claimed they nurtured the "social fabric" of the nation and that pacifists undermined it. The latter were portrayed by prosecutors as unpatriotic, unwomanly, disorderly, unwanted foreigners, immoral, or dangerous Bolsheviks.[41]

While debates about the vote as a privilege or a right, and efforts to disenfranchise "dangerous foreigners," may seem remote to us, they have current implications. The incarcerated in Canada secured the right to vote only relatively recently, scuttling the notion of the vote as a privilege relinquished by incarceration. Feminists debate whether "universalist" rights mean tolerance for all ethnic and cultural differences, even if they seem to conflict with other definitions of equality. Perhaps most important, debates about the hijab and immigration suggest that some still see rights as "selective" or contingent, with acceptable limitations based on language, culture, ethnicity, or religion. Sadly, some women claiming to support equal gender rights still use ethnocentric suspicion and fear to curtail the rights of *other* women to advance their own political careers – just as they did in the First World War.[42]

Interwar Feminist Pacifism and the Women's International League for Peace and Freedom

The drama of feminist wartime dissent was a dress rehearsal for feminist pacifism in the 1920s and 1930s. In the wake of such horrific loss of life, many women were determined to prevent another war. They created new organizations such as the Women's International League for Peace and Freedom (WIL), fashioned novel international coalitions, and developed a more sophisticated theoretical understanding of women, war, and peace.

Both the First World War and the 1919 labour revolt, as we have seen, pushed reformers such as Beatrice Brigden and Rose Henderson leftwards. Henderson, who became one of the most prominent standard-bearers for peace, developed a critique of war that linked socialism, feminism, and anti-imperialism. She believed that women had a special role in leading peace politics due to their maternalist concern for human life, but that class nonetheless differentiated women's experience of war. On the home front, more privileged women were swept up in the "blind and senseless" patriotism of military balls, while "women of the masses were used to do the meanest work ... while the blood of their men folk was being coined into profits on the battle fields."[43] Henderson's most scathing condemnation was directed at economic elites, whose patriotism was simply a "cloak for profit": wars were about "oil wells, coal fields, new markets and to plunder new spheres of influence."[44] She condemned British imperialism, rooted in "the power of the banks and trusts," and called for an anti-war internationalism of working people across the globe.

Henderson's writing was impassioned, angry, and graphic: there was visceral disgust in her descriptions of the horror of trench warfare, millions of senseless deaths, and the false promises of a reconstructed economic democracy when working men and women returned to the same hopeless "slum shacks and tenements."[45] She did see a way forward: gender equality was a necessary first step, along with the global eradication of all social inequality, and religious and racial prejudices. Although her writing excelled at describing the interlocking power relations of gender and class, she was inconsistent on issues of race. Like American feminist pacifists in the WIL, she called out racism as a problem and advocated solidarities across racial, ethnic, and religious differences, but in practice she succumbed to racist stereotypes.[46]

At war's end, new women's anti-war organizations flourished, including the Women's Peace Union (WPU), which Henderson joined. The first meeting in Niagara Falls, Ontario, initiated by Canadian peace activist Christine Ross Barker, tried to unite like-minded feminist pacifists in the "Western Hemisphere," though the WPU was soon dominated by US leaders. Its "absolutist" platform had strong appeal – members pledged never to support any war, even performing humanitarian relief work. While seemingly idealistic, the American WPU pursued a concrete amendment to the US constitution that would outlaw future wars. Henderson explored a similar idea for the Canadian Parliament, writing to the prime minister and others, though the plan floundered in a parliamentary political structure that the American WPU leadership seemingly did not understand.

A more respectable option for liberal-minded reformers was the League of Nations Society, which had its own women's committee and enjoyed tacit government support for its educational efforts to foster international knowledge and cooperation. Social gospel feminist Alice Chown promoted the league's agenda of disarmament as both a symbolic and real hope for international cooperation,[47] while MP Agnes Macphail supported the league, the WIL, and temporary coalitions such as the "No More War" march co-sponsored by the United Farmers of Ontario. Macphail's multiple loyalties were grounded in a pragmatic assessment of the political landscape and strategic alliances. While she went out on a political limb to support the more radical WIL, she took a more traditional stance in her refusal to sit on the "women's committee" when she went to Geneva to represent Canada at the League of Nations. Macphail was well aware that, at this level of power, "women's" concerns were hived off as inconsequential in the arena of global politics.[48]

Of all these new anti-war organizations, the WIL was the most consciously feminist, its members including social gospel, reform, social democratic, and socialist women. Emerging from women's peace organizing during the war, it evolved in fits and starts in the 1920s, primarily in western Canada and Ontario. In 1919, Toronto's Women's Peace Party became a branch of the WIL, and, in 1921, Lucy Woodsworth, wife of Labour MP J.S. Woodsworth, established a WIL in Vancouver. With former suffragist Laura Jamieson as its president, the Vancouver group fostered branches across British Columbia and the Prairies. Jamieson had an invaluable ally in Violet McNaughton, who used her extensive feminist network and *Western Producer* women's page to alert women to the cause. Jamieson began her own column in that paper in 1929, taking the WIL's message to thousands of rural women.

Led internationally by European and American feminists involved in the 1915 conference in The Hague, the WIL inspired Canadian women precisely because of its transnational reach, which extended even across recent enemy lines. When male Allied leaders met at Versailles in 1919 to impose a bruising peace treaty on Germany, the WIL countered with a meeting in Zurich, developing a "Women's Charter" predicated on internationalism rather than destructive nationalism. The WIL rejected the allies' plan of costly reparations to punish Germany, predicting that it would be a recipe for future wars. They were not wrong.[49] Global social justice, equality, and humanitarianism were the WIL's suggested foundation for lasting peace. They demanded equality for women, including suffrage, citizenship, property, and child custody rights; protection against slavery, especially the white slave trade; an end to prostitution and the illegitimate status of children; food for those in need; and economic aid for pregnant women and mothers. Their laundry list of feminist demands was never taken seriously by the Versailles group. After cultivating women's support for the war, Prime Minister Borden dismissed the notion that they had anything useful to say about peace.

International connections were utilized to help build the Canadian organization. In 1924, following a WIL meeting in Washington attended by Agnes Macphail, European and American leaders returned with her to Toronto for a "Pax Special" campaign of public speeches. Despite community interest, conservative papers equated the visit of German and Austrian women with a "sinister attempt to undermine British patriotism."[50] If world peace now sounds like a motherhood issue, the WIL platform was a hard sell in a country where "Britishness" and the empire still commanded loyalty. In Vancouver, Jamieson organized public speeches on independence for India and a "Hands off China" campaign, both indicting British imperialism, to the consternation of some local newspapers. Likewise, Macphail was routinely denounced in the House of Commons for her anti-war views. Opposing the government's annual grant for military cadet training in schools, she asked, with biting sarcasm, "Why should we take young boys, dress them in uniforms and teach them to strut along to martial strains with their foolish little guns and swords?" "Go back to Russia," hooted the Opposition, informing her that she had failed the test of "fine Canadian womanhood."[51]

Transnational ties aided the WIL, but local chapters developed their own strategies. The Toronto WIL believed it was resolute in "clinging" to its absolutist "pacifist principles," in contrast to western Canadian locals, which cooperated with liberal-minded League of Nations proponents of disarmament.[52] Across the country, though, education was a shared concern, with the goal of changing hearts and minds both through public discussion and through the school system. The WIL had a near "millenarian faith" that progressive education might replace militaristic, competitive values with co-operative ones, wiping away the "hatred" toward other nations that had fuelled the last war.[53] Visiting speakers, petitions, and newspaper columns were used; in Vancouver, Jamieson pioneered day-long conferences on global affairs that created connections to other disarmament and women's groups.

Reform of the school system was of particular concern to the WIL: it developed new teacher-training materials, sponsored extracurricular events, and advocated a revision of propagandistic school texts that glorified war. WIL women wanted a full-scale rethinking of education to "create a new attitude of mind," stressing the "prevention of war, international goodwill and the economic and spiritual unity of mankind."[54] WILers also organized anti-war student-produced plays and pageants, as well as essay and poster competitions, often coinciding with Armistice Day. Inevitably, these ruffled the patriotic feathers of more conservative women's organizations; in Vancouver, Laura Jamieson ran afoul of the Imperial Order Daughters of the Empire (IODE) when she protested the "war pictures" they donated to the Vancouver School Board.[55]

Eliminating cadet training in the schools became a cause for almost every local WIL. Initiated in 1907 with a donation from railway magnate Lord

Strathcona, cadet training received federal funding that more than quadrupled from 1913 to 1926. Like pre-war feminists, the WIL equated cadet training with the cultivation of militaristic masculinity and the idealization of war. As more and more women ran for municipal office, WILers campaigned for seats on local school boards, promising to end cadet training. In 1933, Rose Henderson, by then a WILer, and Ida Siegel were elected to the Toronto board but, not surprisingly in imperialist-minded Toronto, faced opposition to calls for a ban on cadet training. However, after Siegel publicized the unsavoury practice of rewarding Toronto teachers financially for every cadet they recruited, the program was temporarily halted. In Vancouver and Regina too, the WIL celebrated when they vanquished cadet training.

Although there was considerable public sympathy for the League of Nations Society, the WIL's criticisms of capitalism and the British Empire made it more highly suspect. Yet it was precisely the WIL's integration of socialism, pacifism, and feminism that galvanized a new cohort of interwar feminists. The organization claimed more political breadth than the one-issue pacifism of the WPU, and it also went beyond the tamer liberalism of the League of Nations Society. The WIL's indictment of militarism grew out of new wartime feminist theories that linked militarism to anti-feminism. As an expression of force, domination, and a system of institutionalized masculine violence, pacifist women argued, militarism was the antithesis of feminism; indeed, the core ethos of militarism presumed and demanded the "subjection of women."[56]

Grounded in reason and sentiment, logic and emotion, the WIL platform incorporated feminist demands for women's equality, the elimination of racial, ethnic, and religious prejudices, and solidarity with the working-class – addressing those who benefited least from war. Although many WILers contended that war was facilitated by economic inequality, they also rallied their members using maternalist and feminist ideas, drawing in women who could identify with any, or all, of these ideas. The WIL's maternalism reiterated Jane Addams's concept of social motherhood – women's domestic, caring labour should be extrapolated to the international sphere, too often seen as the purview of men. It was not necessarily women's moral superiority but their moral *authority* that determined they should organize autonomously for peace.[57] In *Peace and Bread in the Time of War,* Addams used food as a symbol of women's nurturing labour and their capacity for empathy across borders. Ensuring that women and children did not starve, that everyone had bread, might "enlarge women's conception of duty" from the home and community to "international activities."[58] The WIL's emphasis on both gender equality and gender difference appealed to feminists who felt that women could invoke their maternal moral authority yet still campaign for women's rights.

Arguing that peace rested upon social justice, and social justice upon the elimination of race and religious prejudice, the American WIL addressed racism at home and abroad; it critiqued American imperialism in Latin America, promoted anti-racist education, and countered biologically determinist ideas about race with cultural pluralism. Its efforts to create a racially integrated organization, however, were stymied by lingering racism within the organization.[59] Nonetheless, new attention to racial prejudice clearly affected the Canadian WIL. Laura Jamieson became a critic of racist voting laws in British Columbia; both she and Violet McNaughton supported the cultural pluralism and feminist cooperation promoted by the interracial and transnational Pan-Pacific Women's Organization. Since internationalism was equated with a cultural tolerance, Jamieson, Betty Kerr, and other Vancouver WIL women worked on folk festivals and other cultural events intended to foster more accepting attitudes toward racialized and denigrated non-British immigrants.

But ethnocentrism and racism were not fully addressed: while the Canadian WIL was critical of colonialism abroad, its members seemed undisturbed about colonialism at home. Like other feminists of the time, they seldom discussed Canada's dispossession of Indigenous peoples. One might expect feminist pacifists suspicious of European imperial conquests to see parallels in Canada, but most did not. Violet McNaughton admired Gandhi's efforts to secure Indian independence from Britain, yet in the 1920s she still imbibed the dominant version of white settler progress in Canada in which Indigenous peoples, uninterested in farming, were inevitably displaced by white settlers.[60] On this account, the WIL was more in tune with mainstream women's politics, and its silence contrasts with a cadre of Australian feminists who, in the same time period, protested the forced removal of Indigenous children from their families and violence against Indigenous women. While couched in a superior language of paternalistic concern for the "less advanced races," the Australian women's organizing did tackle violence and forced family breakup, practices that were still being ignored, justified, and normalized in Canada.[61]

Confronting Fascism

The WIL expanded in the early 1930s, its anti-war message resonating in an international context of rising tensions, armed clashes in Asia and Africa, and rearmament. Yet, it also faced moral dilemmas. In 1934 a new left-wing organization emerged, the Canadian League against War and Fascism (CLAWF), which urged the WIL to join it in a "united front" against war. The CLAWF was a communist-initiated, Popular Front organization, which the Communist Party of Canada astutely understood could claim to be "popular" only if it welcomed participants of all political persuasions and did not dominate the leadership. With 315 delegates representing 203 organizations at its founding congress, the CLAWF seemed to guarantee unified political clout in the face of both European fascism and Canada's home-grown variety.

Feminists in the WIL were both encouraged by and worried about the CLAWF. Some were suspicious of communists, who had only recently denounced all other socialists and feminists as "social fascists," but others welcomed the league, believing fascism posed a greater threat than political differences. The CLAWF adopted the WIL's language of feminism and social motherhood, though, ironically, it became less overtly anti-capitalist, given its Popular Front craving for respectability. The CLAWF argued it was important to appeal to women workers who might be drawn into war industries, but it increasingly stressed maternalist and feminist arguments. It equated women's interests with protection of the family and of human life, but it also warned that fascism was a direct assault on the equal rights women had only recently secured. Progressive newspapers carried articles on the degraded status of women in fascist countries, especially Germany, where the slogan *Kinder, Küche, Kirche* signalled a new-pronatalism, a focus on "selected" breeding, and the oppression of women. Fascism, declared Rose Henderson at the founding CLWAF convention, "enslaves women and it is impossible to do this without also enslaving men."[62]

A "Women's Commission" was set up within the CLAWF, though some female executive members stressed that women must be "integral," not an auxiliary appendage to the organization, just as there should be no segregated "women's page" in the CLAWF newspaper.[63] At the founding convention, trade union organizer Jean Laing recommended a cross-country "caravan" to recruit working-class women who might otherwise be enticed into "patriotic" and bourgeois organs like the IODE.[64] Elizabeth Morton, fresh from attending the Paris Congress against War and Fascism, gave a rousing feminist speech stressing the dehumanization of Italian and German women under fascist rule: "They are relegated to the position of blind, unquestioning creatures, even classified in Germany for breeding purposes."[65] At the end of the founding congress, an elected women's section from across the country was tasked with broadening the anti-fascist fight by addressing women's issues. A Windsor delegate from a local "Mothers Club," the only African-Canadian woman present, vowed to contact "other women of her race" and mothers in the border cities to drum up support.[66]

WILers Anna Sissons, Rose Henderson, Ida Siegal, Alice Loeb, and Elizabeth Morton were vocal on the CLAWF national bureau, urging more concerted attention to women in the CLAWF paper, *Action*. By the second CLAWF congress, feminist rhetoric was front and centre, as speakers linked fascism abroad to those opposed to women's rights at home. Communist Annie Buller equated the struggle against fascism with campaigns to drive Canadian women out of "the professions, out of industry, back to the kitchen there to rank as man's slave."[67] Siegel, a Toronto School Board member, outlined discrimination against women teachers, and Henderson addressed the unholy alliance of church and state to "ensure the subjection of women and the [church] dogma that woman owes man unqualified obedience."[68] Fascism, in short, was a feminist issue.

This broad alliance for peace could not withstand differences over war. In 1936, the CLAWF helped to create the Mackenzie-Papineau Battalion, a volunteer force of Canadian men who went to Spain to fight the fascists trying to topple the democratically elected government. The Spanish Civil War defined a generation of progressive youth, symbolizing a brave stand against fascism as Western governments sat on the sidelines. However, the war posed an existential crisis for the WIL, an "agonizing choice" between their commitment to non-violence and their commitment to anti-fascism and social justice.[69] When the CLAWF changed its name to the Canadian League for Peace and Democracy in 1937, it no longer endorsed unconditional non-violence. At its own national convention in 1937, the WIL backed away from the new League for Peace and Democracy and renewed its own feminist and pacifist credentials with resolutions demanding women's access to birth control and a national referendum before any war could be declared.

Locally, WILs continued in the late 1930s to press their feminist, pacifist, and social democratic agenda, organizing protests against military expenditures and international aggression, bringing in international speakers, and aiding refugees fleeing Nazism, but international events sapped away any optimism that war might be avoided. In 1939, when Canada declared war on Germany, decisions had to be made: Should feminist pacifists persist with an absolutist anti-war stance or accept that some wars were more virtuous than others?

Figure 7.2 Women's International League for Peace and Freedom demonstrate in 1938, calling for a boycott of Japanese goods after it invaded China | Toronto City Archives, Globe and Mail Collection, 53041

Feminism and Pacifism in the Second World War

Many WIL women also belonged to the Co-operative Commonwealth Federation (CCF). Already an ideologically balkanized party, the CCF had difficulty developing a coherent statement on the Second World War; internal discussions were less about the absolutist pacifism later associated with J.S.Woodsworth and more about whether the war was essentially imperialist.[70] WIL feminists were also divided. Take the example of four prominent Vancouver feminists: Dorothy Steeves, Laura Jamieson, Mildred Fahrni, and Elizabeth Kerr. Dorothy Steeves condemned the imperialist nature of the war, locating its origins in economic inequality, poverty, and the "privileged group that profits from war." The British Empire, so lauded in Canada, she noted, was not to be equated with democracy: "Empire means imperialism and the apostles of imperialism are the arms manufacturers." As a member of the BC legislature, she called for "human welfare not warfare," and was promptly denounced as a traitor: one Conservative said she should be "whipped so she cannot sit down."[71] Laura Jamieson concurred with elements of Steeves's anti-war analysis but believed the threat of fascism overshadowed idealistic pacifism. The fight against Hitler was an unavoidable choice, even though she despaired that the war "marks the complete bankruptcy of our civilization."[72]

WILer Mildred Fahrni, inclined toward absolute pacifism and Christian socialism, did not support the war. Defending her unpopular stance, she explained in the *Vancouver Daily Province* that she endorsed the practice of "active non-violence" she had learned from Gandhi, and concluded that "democracy cannot be saved by war ... [There will be] tremendous losses to all participants, great destruction and demoralization of all mankind. No wrong will be righted. No peace established."[73] Opposed to the forced internment of Japanese Canadians, Fahrni volunteered to work during the war as a teacher in the New Denver internment camp in the interior of the province for a nominal twenty-five dollars a month.[74]

Elizabeth Kerr sought a middle ground. Like Jamieson, she accepted the need to wage war against fascism, but she tried to sustain a socialist feminist critique of war even during war. Many of her CCF newspaper columns focused on the home front, deploring wartime economic deprivations of working-class women and their families, as well as women's impossible task of picking up the pieces of shattered lives.[75] She brooked little patience with gung-ho war promoters who spouted pure "hatred" for the German people and denounced the shaming of men who did not enlist, as if manliness and citizenship were to be equated with armed combat.[76] She relayed one anecdote to register her disgust: a single mother, denied a job because she was a woman, was told by the employer they might reconsider if her sons signed up![77] If war encouraged suspicion and hatred, it also threatened democracy. Critical of the federal Defence of Canada (DOC) regulations putting severe limits on political dissent, Kerr used her "Women's Views" column in the CCF paper to raise the alarm about the DOC, chastising communist Dorise Nielsen for claiming that she had led the resistance against the DOC, when other socialist feminists, including Agnes Macphail, had too.[78]

Like Flora MacDonald Denison during the First World War, some feminists claimed that an aggressive, militaristic world still suffered from a lack of women's political participation, but, more often, WIL women pointed their finger at the economic conflict, clash of empires, and obscene profits underlying war. As one feminist declared succinctly in the CCF *Manitoba Commonwealth,* until "the profit motive" is removed from war and we have "world socialism," we will have war.[79] Kerr concurred: "War will go on, somewhere, until capitalism is done."[80] Her pessimism was shaped by her memory of the First World War, which resulted in the deaths of millions of soldiers but also civilian "death, mutilation and rape."[81] She was also suspicious of wartime platitudes coming from Canadian politicians. Having seen women welcomed into non-traditional jobs and praised for their contributions during the First World War, then quickly ignored, Kerr predicted the same might happen again.[82]

While feminists like Kerr warned against wartime nativism, their cautions were not particularly effective, and the CCF paid an electoral price in British Columbia for its unpopular defence of Japanese-Canadians' civil rights. The ideology of patriotic motherhood, though perhaps not as vociferous as in the First World War, resurfaced, and its most conservative versions connected war, patriotism, and racism. Club women who were not feminists and some reformers who claimed to be promoted a wartime nationalism that lauded Canada's British heritage and cast suspicion on "enemy aliens" and "disloyal" Quebecers. The IODE not only supported Japanese internment but propagated virulent racist, gendered stereotypes about the Japanese. As Muriel Kitagawa remembered, the IODE portrayed all Japanese Canadians as potential "spies and saboteurs," but women posed a special reproductive threat: "Why is it IODE women," she wrote, create "fear and ill will ... [claiming] our numbers have doubled in the last ten years – a biological absurdity." Moreover, Kitigawa added, this racism sanctioned intensified violence against Japanese women: "the horrors young [Japanese] girls have faced from men in uniform. We are prey for wolves in democratic clothing."[83]

War as Opportunity – Again

More than one of Elizabeth Kerr's columns in *The Federationist* dealt with the critical value of women's domestic labour to the nation, but, for many feminists, paid labour became the issue of the day during the war. In comparison to the First World War, far more women were now entering paid labour, including non-traditional work; women worked in the armed forces for the first time; and new industrial-based unions, more inclusive than craft unions, were recruiting women workers. Women's right to paid labour, so important to many brands of feminism in the interwar period, seemed ripe for positive change. The flush wartime economy, constantly in need of workers, offered an opportunity to make the case for both the needs- and rights-based arguments for women workers.

Women's right to employment irrespective of marital status, equal pay, and child care became a troika of demands, raised repeatedly by women's rights advocates, club women, and some unions. Women's reform groups like the NCWC promoted women's integration into war production, although its members did not usually engage in this type of work; women in war industries were working-class earners seeking decent pay to support

Figure 7.3 A 1943 American comic book series celebrated Elsie Gregory MacGill, an aeronautics engineer who oversaw the Hurricane airplane manufactured in Thunder Bay, Ontario, during the Second World War. MacGill later served on the Royal Commission on the Status of Women | "Queen of the Hurricanes: Elsie MacGill," *True Comics*, no. 8, January 1942

themselves and their families. Women in these jobs also found new allies in the labour movement. When unions supported equal pay in the past (including during the First World War), it was often to protect men's jobs and wages from employers who replaced men with lower-paid women. Unions' discussion of equal pay began to shift, if only slightly. Twenty-seven women at a Ford plant in Windsor, Ontario, whose union supported their demand for equal pay, were likely shocked when hundreds of men staged a wildcat strike for eleven days to support them. As Wendy Cuthbertson shows, old views of equal pay as a strategy to protect men's jobs did not entirely disappear, but unions developed a new wartime rationale: women deserved equal pay as equal citizens in a democracy supposedly fighting for democracy.[84] If this argument was not robustly defended by all unions, working women nonetheless embraced it, and it would become a useful tool for them in the post-war period. Incorporated into the surge in unionization during the war, women discovered other union tools to advance their equality demands: grievance systems, collective bargaining, and membership in a movement that, at least in rhetoric, claimed to symbolize democracy, equality, and solidarity.

Equal treatment of all workers, though, was sorely lacking in wartime; employment discrimination, excused by the state, pervaded the workforce. Indigenous, Jewish, Asian, and African Canadians were denied jobs, as were some racialized whites whose last names suggested non-Anglo backgrounds – Shostakovitch instead of Smith. These "minority" groups and a small group of white allies protested vigorously, leading to small changes in rights discourse and, after the war, some anti-discrimination legislation.[85] During the war, racialized women encountered entrenched barriers in the workplace; well-educated Jewish women were denied white-collar jobs and African Canadians struggled to secure factory positions, up the ladder from domestic work. Indigenous women were discouraged from travelling to work in war industries by local Indian agents convinced they were suited only for casual and domestic labour. Discussion of gender and race discrimination, however, operated on parallel tracks, with the latter given priority. When anti-discrimination legislation was crafted, it invariably dealt with race not sex discrimination.

Another avenue for wartime feminist demands for equality was the state's post-war planning process. Magazines were full of stories asking if the woman in overalls would happily retreat to the kitchen after the war. Feminists had a firm answer: no, they should have choices and opportunities. In the *Canadian Forum,* Helen Forsey warned that women might not "win the peace," as a government "controlled by capitalists" was uninterested in gender equality. Post-war reaction was likely: women will be "pushed out of jobs," "justified by appeals to the moral and religious sanctions of the past." She set out two socialist principles on gender equality: first, "all human resources" should be used by the state, and, second, women should be recognized as "persons with all the rights and freedoms of men."[86]

Forsey chastised the CCF for its lack of interest in gender equality, as did other disgruntled members, weary of the party's superficial claim to equality and its habit of male dominance. In Ontario, Avis McCurdy privately told the provincial executive in 1945 that she was "appalled" that the recent convention would "ignore what ought to be one of our major concerns." Headlines in the press should read "CCF stands for women's equality," especially when women were being pushed out of jobs. Other parties, other countries, were recognizing women as "free persons," yet the lacklustre CCF offered "an inadequate report" on women, and female members who did the research were asked "not to speak" to the convention![87]

Feminists of many political views agreed the war was an opportunity to hurry along new social and labour rights for women. Vancouver women, including Laura Jamieson, created a non-partisan think tank, the Vancouver Women's School for Citizenship, to debate policy solutions and offer political newcomers lessons in speaking and organizing. Some feminists prodded the state to take the lead in policy development. A federal subcommittee on the Postwar Problems of Women was established, a concession thrown to women who protested when the "real" Reconstruction Committee completely ignored women's issues. Led by long-time Winnipeg Liberal Margaret McWilliams, the committee provided equality-seeking women with some ammunition, recommending "full employment" for women who chose paid labour, along with their enhanced education and training. But the report also took some of the wind out of feminist sails, for it assumed most women would choose homemaking, suggested new training for traditionally "feminine" jobs, and endorsed only "nursery schools," the proverbial part-time "aid" to middle-class women rather than the child care desperately needed by working women.[88]

Controversies around child care at war's end reveal the ideological hurdles faced by reform and left-wing feminists alike. A limited number of wartime "day nurseries" were funded by the federal government; their closure at war's end elicited a public debate about women's rights, labour, and child care. Working women desperately wanted wartime day nurseries to stay open and, indeed, to expand. Childhood educators favoured limited nurseries to aid child development, while social welfare experts advocated for child care as a "welfare" investment for mothers who "needed" to work and their at-risk children (always in danger of becoming juvenile delinquents). Many progressive organizations, including unions, supported child care, but they ultimately failed to challenge the larger social consensus framing state policies – namely, that the ideal post-war family consisted of breadwinning fathers and domestic mothers. The "needs" argument for child care came to dominate public discussion: child care became a "welfare" issue, disengaged from women's right to work.

Figure 7.4 Three CCF members of the BC legislature – Laura Jamieson, Dorothy Gretchen Steeves, and Grace MacInnis, elected in 1941 – put forward women's equality legislation and supported voting rights for Canadians of Asian descent. They also supported child care for working mothers | Courtesy of the Royal BC Museum and Archives, E-00046

But there was another political argument, bubbling up from below. In the wake of wartime day nursery closures, the first grassroots movement for child care emerged in some cities. A cross-class coalition, it noisily lobbied governments, pointing to the social and economic needs of single working mothers and working-class families, while also supporting women's right to work. The latter stance was strongly promoted by women in the CCF and the Communist Party of Canada.[89] Laura Jamieson captured the hopes that the war could be an opportunity to build a more feminist future for working women when she declared that Canadian women did not want to return to the "barbarism" of the past in which children were not "properly cared for ... and homes economically unstable." Day nurseries allowed women to have "earnings of their own" and "go home, after work, to pleasant children."[90] If her vision remained marginal in the 1950s, the incipient ideal of child care as a right for children and families, and necessary to women's full emancipation, would re-emerge in future feminist discourse.

Conclusion

War transformed feminists. The social upheaval and losses of war shaped women's political and emotional reactions to armed violence, and in the process encouraged feminist reflections about gender and militarism, human nature, violence, citizenship rights, and women's role in society. Feminist theorizing about war accrued systematically and was seldom only about gender; it was linked to interpretations of universal or selective civil rights, ethnicity and race, capitalism and imperialism. If the First World War did not transform women's economic and social roles, it did mark a watershed in feminist theorizing, as the relationship between militarism and masculinity, war and global inequalities, was probed in novel ways. In the writing of Rose Henderson and other WILers, there was an inkling of late twentieth-century feminist arguments that "militarized masculinity has a strategic function" in the reproduction of gender hierarchies within nations and "imperialism" across the globe.[91]

Maternalism was a common but highly malleable thread in feminist thinking about war and peace. Nineteenth-century reform feminists could comfortably muse on women's maternal propensity for preserving life, but their full-throttle support for the First World War shattered such notions. Many feminists drew on concepts of maternalism or social motherhood, but they disagreed on when, why, and if war was a necessity. Maternalism might be used, on the one hand, to buttress an exclusive, xenophobic, racist patriotic notion of motherhood or, on the other, to support Gertrude Richardson's socialist, anti-imperialist "mother hearts" in rebellion against all wars – and many permutations of such ideas in between.

Theory was tied to praxis. Hoping never to see another cataclysm like the First World War, women created new peace organizations, of which the WIL, which connected war to social and gender inequality, was the most resolutely feminist. Its success lay in its combination of sentiment and logic, maternalism and materialism, and feminism and humanism, as well as in its international connections to a sisterhood of peace activists. Some WILers were motivated by social motherhood, others convinced by its anti-capitalist message, still others encouraged by its ongoing commitment to women's equal rights. In the face of fascism's direct assault on women's equality and racialized others, though, the WIL faced an impossible moral dilemma. When many WIL allies promoted armed resistance to fascist violence in Spain, the organization was torn between its commitment to social justice and its commitment to peace, an existential crisis it faced again when the Second World War began.

Internationally, the WIL edged toward a fledging rights discourse of opposition to racial, ethnic, and religious prejudice in the interwar years. In Canada, these ideas were tenuous; like socialist feminists of the time, the WIL focused on the connections between class and gender inequality but was less attuned to racism. Regional context did matter: WIL feminists in British Columbia were confronted with the egregious exclusion of Asian Canadians from the vote and, like the CCF, advocated for their political rights. Former suffragist Helena Gutteridge, who during the First World War had supported Asian exclusion in employment, had by the early 1940s shifted her position, advocating for democratic rights for Asian Canadians. Nonetheless, it is revealing that, during the Second World War, WIL women involved in anti-racist work defending Japanese Canadians gravitated toward civil rights groups and were less likely to look for support from the women's movement.

Feminist pacifists were not the only group of equality seekers claiming insight on war. The majority of suffragists supported the First World War, rationalizing that the means, violence, justified the ends of the preservation of empire, British global power, and British "democracy and values." Ironically, some then supported the Wartime Elections Act, which undermined democracy by assigning the vote as a privilege based on ethnicity, gender, language, place of origin, and relationship to the military. Many pro-war suffragists also claimed a connection between patriotic motherhood and their feminist agenda; war was an opportunity to establish their worth as citizens and hurry along their reform agenda. Differences within feminism became extraordinarily raw, as pro-war suffragists denounced anti-war suffragists, whom they had previously collaborated with, as traitors and less than patriotic mothers. Francis Marion Beynon literally fled the country to escape what she perceived as a political tragedy, her exit a permanent loss for Canadian feminism. Conscription and the Wartime Elections Act became touchstones for different views on civil liberties, democracy, and ethnic exclusion as much as debates about women's suffrage. In retrospect, women who claimed *their* equality at the expense of the rights of other women and racialized immigrants have not fared well in assessments of feminist history.

During the Second World War, some women's organizations – though not feminist ones – replicated the racism unleashed in 1914, but the division between those claiming patriotic womanhood and anti-war feminists was less starkly drawn. War again became a feminist "opportunity" to prove women's equal citizenship, turning the state's rhetoric about fighting for democracy to political service. Feminists of all varieties wanted to seize the day, but their definitions of opportunity varied. Some reform feminists sought equality of opportunity, the "right to compete" with men, while socialist feminists envisioned a transformed economic democracy in which women's rights were combined with an all-encompassing social welfare state.

Feminists such as Elizabeth Kerr, who were opposed to Nazism but critical of persisting class inequality and women's oppression, tried to reconcile the war against fascism with hopes for enhanced social justice. In the First World War, "equality" had signalled equal voting rights and selective moral and social reforms such as temperance. By 1945, a broader group of feminists scattered across political parties and lobby groups, and in unions, promoted women's right to work, equal pay, and, for socialists, a comprehensive, caring welfare state. Those same issues defined post-war feminism.

8 Feminism in a Cold War Climate

Muriel Duckworth was a woman of faith – religious, humanitarian, pacifist, feminist faith that war might be eradicated, human equality achieved. As a university student in the 1930s, she joined the McGill Student Christian Movement, an organization in the social gospel tradition. After marrying a like-minded religious social worker, she attended theological classes in the United States and, on her return to Montreal, joined the socialist League for Social Reconstruction. Duckworth and her husband settled in Halifax after the Second World War, where Muriel was involved in adult education, human rights, and other social causes. In 1960, she and anti-nuclear campaigner Peggy Hope-Simpson drew together twenty-three women in Duckworth's living room to discuss organizing women for peace. They became a local of the newly established Voice of Women (VOW), which mushroomed to 5,000 national members within three years.

Duckworth's experience of an all-women's organization as well as her analysis of violence, war, and militarism was her "springboard" to feminism. Her pacifist feminism incorporated strains of social motherhood, the understanding that women's maternal standpoint gave them insight and reason to oppose human destruction. War was also the ultimate "instrument of violence against women": rape, civilian death, refugees followed in its wake.[1] Nor could there be a foundation for peace without human rights and equality. Her recollection of taking the first steps into VOW activism are reminiscent of Francis Marion Beynon's fictional feminist pacifist, Aleta

Dey, who worried she would become a public target of derision. "Some VOW women," Duckworth recalled, "were afraid to speak out. There was a strong fear of communism and there was a Cold War ... and to go out on the street and make people pay attention to you is not an easy decision to make."[2]

The end of the Second World War did not spell the end of war as a defining influence on Canadian and international feminism. The ensuing Cold War, and terrifying new nuclear reality after the atomic bomb was used by the United States in August 1945, profoundly shaped feminist organizing in the 1950s and 1960s. The prospect of a catastrophic nuclear war drew a new cohort of women to pacifism, and the VOW created a pathway from maternalist peace work to women's equality seeking. The Cold War between the Soviet and American power blocs also resulted in an anti-communist red scare of immense proportions: McCarthyism, though an American term, was also a Canadian reality. The climate of political fear sparked by the Cold War inhibited left-wing feminist politics and dampened prospects of collaborations across political lines. It did not, however, change a new economic reality that created fertile ground for equality mobilizing. Increasing numbers of women working for pay led to new demands for workplace rights, and international and national conversations about human rights encouraged organizing against racism and, later, gender discrimination.

Our image of the post-war era, once associated with female domesticity, has been substantially revised: June Cleaver, a symbol of women's retreat to suburban, apolitical domesticity, was more prescribed ideal than lived reality. Persisting ethnic, racial, class, and linguistic fault lines in Canadian society belied the image of affluent suburbs; citizenship was still defined in gendered and racialized ways; and more women were working outside the home. Nor did women go into political hibernation. They were active in educational, social policy, workplace, political party, and cultural contexts, imbibing progressive ideas that led some to move gingerly toward feminism. In popular culture, too, below the surface of advertised domestic bliss, the "seeds of [female] revolt" were slowly germinating in Hollywood film, beat poetry, and rebellious rock-and-roll teen music.[3]

Post-war Canada, of course, was more than the Cold War: it was also characterized by a nascent welfare state, a new brand of Canadian nationalism, intensified urbanization and suburbanization, increased affluence and consumption associated with a "Fordist" economy, the baby boom, and reinvigorated immigration, though one still favouring "preferred" white newcomers until the late 1960s.[4] All of these framed feminist organizing. This contradictory period is aptly characterized by American historian Alice

Kessler-Harris as a time of "incremental change with radical consequences."[5] This chapter charts three sites of Cold War activism: peace, paid labour, human rights and anti-racist organizing. It ends with the memories of four women who emerged as postwar feminists and the Royal Commission on the Status of Women, the culmination of much post-war organizing.

Feminism, Media Debates, and Partisan Politics

In 1960, the CBC in Quebec refused to broadcast an interview with Simone de Beauvoir, the renowned French author of a groundbreaking feminist classic, *The Second Sex* (1949), which famously argued that one is not "born" a woman, but "becomes" one – through cultural and social ideas and practices. In the interview, de Beauvoir's cavalier dismissal of marriage as "obscene" was too much in a province yet to experience the full implications of the Quiet Revolution. When *Chatelaine* editor Doris Anderson suggested that women should judge the interview rather than have censors decide for them, the majority of reader responses supported the CBC, pointing to de Beauvoir's denial of God and her "crackpot" views on marriage.[6] The censoring of de Beauvoir accords with the image of post-war Canada as ideologically conservative, bound to traditional gender roles. Yet in the mid-1960s, the French-language version of *Chatelaine* sponsored a forum on *The Second Sex,* "notre bible," printing both critical and laudatory opinions. De Beauvoir, the magazine observed, perhaps had a more profound impact on women in the home, since career women were already thinking about "emancipation." The forum was a far cry from CBC's fearful censorship.[7]

This de Beauvoir debate suggests the complicated views on feminism in the post-war period stretching from 1945 to the mid-1960s. Feminists who saw the Second World War as a chance to break down barriers to opportunity believed women should have access to new life choices, but far more media commentators assumed the post-war woman wanted the reassuring normalcy of a male breadwinner/female homemaker family. A *Maclean's* journalist admitted that opinion polls showed many women wished to continue working, but, undeterred by evidence, she declared women *really* wanted to be homemakers.[8] In contrast, the alternative press defended women's right to work; the progressive *Canadian Forum* and, further left, the communist-influenced *UE News* stressed *all* women's right to paid labour. "Winning the peace," said the *UE,* meant "full freedom in job opportunity and advancement for women, subsidized child care, equal wages and earnings."[9]

Yet Canada's mainstream magazine for women, *Chatelaine*, still published male journalists who vented "pervasive contempt" for women; one panned all women in politics as "parrots" with little to say.[10] There was no shortage of commentary claiming that girls should be educated for housewifery and that married career women inevitably had unsuccessful marriages. Psychological experts, including the guru of child health, Dr. Spock, claimed stay-at-home moms produced well-adjusted children. Only a few journalists offered a reality check, acknowledging that working-class, immigrant wives had to work to sustain the family economy. While many magazines featured stories of professional career women, wage-earning women were the stuff of real life.

The word "feminism" still sparked heated debate, usually about married women's work outside the home. Defences of married women's paid work gained ground by the mid-1960s as other equality issues – divorce, birth control, education, women in politics – were increasingly raised in *Chatelaine*, both the English and French versions. English editor Doris Anderson considered the magazine a "closet feminist" publication by the 1960s.[11] Still, closet feminism might be an apt moniker for the Cold War environment. Since the nineteenth century, women journalists were the harbingers of novel feminist ideas, but Anderson's cohort still faced overt discrimination and outright misogyny.[12] Feminist journalists such June Callwood questioned gender roles, but gingerly so. In "Let's End the Battle of the Sexes" in *Maclean's*, she suggested that rigid male and female roles were not "innate" but socialized (in de Beauvoir's terms, made not born), and she stressed that relaxing them would aid both men and women: these "cast iron" expectations led to unhappy lives for all.[13]

Feminists continued to talk about equality, but they faced a Cold War context of "fear, conformity, consensus and denial."[14] In 1958, a male speaker told Toronto women prominent in politics and social services that he longed for the time past when a woman was a "chattel which [sic] stayed at home and took a definite second place to the man who was the head of the home." Surprisingly, an Elizabeth Fry representative at the meeting claimed she too was no advocate for "women's emancipation."[15] Mass culture, humour, romance fiction, movies, and advertising coupled femininity with domesticity and beauty; sexuality was men's to explore, women's to protect; and social policy still condemned unmarried mothers and discriminated against unemployed married women workers trying to collect unemployment insurance. Trade union newspapers reflected the contradictions of the period.

They extolled women's social activism and promoted their unionization but also idealized the male breadwinner; they called for equal pay laws but featured sexy pin-ups and sponsored beauty contests.[16]

Women's equality-seeking often reinvented tried and true methods of mobilization, a sign of activism sustained but in a holding pattern. Some women continued to organize through political parties, echoing concerns expressed since the 1930s. Women's committees in the post-war Co-operative Commonwealth Federation (CCF), for instance, tried to interest women in socialism, aid their move from the margins to the mainstream of the party, and sharpen their awareness of women's issues, including rising consumer prices, child welfare, peace, and equal pay. Organizing differed regionally, as provincial parties varied in strength, but many CCF women's committees addressed domestic labour in an effort to convince women that social democracy provided the best protection for the working-class family. Invoking women's roles as mothers was a plea for class and community betterment, suggesting a vision of a more just society geared toward human needs, not business profit.[17]

Stressing the importance of women's daily motherwork might be implicitly feminist, but limiting women's political sphere to family welfare and consumer activism also reified existing gender and family norms. Still, the Ontario CCF women's committee also called for women's right to work, equal pay, vocational training, and an advocacy-oriented Women's Bureau at the federal level.[18] In British Columbia, CCF feminists lobbied for daycare for working mothers and equal pay. Laura Jamieson battled Vancouver city hall to secure municipal voting rights for all women and racial minorities; many cities were the last bastion of a restrictive, property-based "taxpayer" franchise favouring men – or, in British Columbia, white men.[19]

Other parties also picked up threads of pre-war organizing using activist maternalism, always an ideologically flexible political strategy. During the Depression, the Housewives Consumers Association (HCA), with many communist members, had mobilized homemakers against rising prices on essentials such as milk. Maternalism drew on homemakers' occupational sense of self-worth, though the HCA's militant boycotts and demonstrations contradicted traditional gender roles. After the war, the HCA carried on with campaigns against rising prices, using petitions, marches, and lobbying to insist on government controls on food prices. In order to support the working-class family, it also advocated for subsidized housing, a desperate need in post-war Canada. Its success was circumscribed by the organization's obvious communist connections.[20] Communists had a powerful advocate in Dorise Nielsen, an independent Saskatchewan MP elected in 1940, who switched her allegiance to the renamed communist Labour Progressive Party. Nielsen promoted women's right to employment, equal pay, and state-funded daycare, but an increasingly intolerant Cold War atmosphere ensured her electoral defeat and sidelined her progressive voice.[21]

After the war, Liberal Party women began to gradually alter course, querying their auxiliary role in the party. In the interwar years, the Liberals, with their "big tent" politics, extending from corporate Canada on the right to social reformers on the left, had attracted prominent feminists (and suffragists) Mary Ellen Smith, Nellie McClung, and Thérèse Casgrain, who placed their hopes for women's equality in pragmatic, gradualist parliamentary reform of social welfare, family law, and employment regimes. Liberal women had drawn on the ideals of nineteenth-century "new liberalism," which combined equality of opportunity with a social conscience, and they too invoked maternalist activism. They had some successes, especially with welfare measures like mothers' allowances. For these "big L" Liberal feminists, a modern, interventionist state might "serve as an instrument of justice for white women and workers," avoiding the collectivist, class-struggle solutions of socialists.[22] When partisanship challenged their feminist principles, some had put women's rights before party loyalty. As a member of the Alberta legislature, McClung had collaborated with feminists in other parties, and she had angered the BC Liberals in the 1930s by refusing to endorse their anti-Asian platform.

Notables such as Smith and McClung had run for elected office, but most Liberal women had been assigned to auxiliary work. The Women's Liberal Federation of Canada (WLF), founded in 1928 as a parallel but decidedly secondary organization to the men's National Liberal Federation (NLF), claimed it would study social issues and acclimitize women to politics, but locals were usually confined to organizing teas and scrutineering at election time. Some provinces had no women's organization, women's policy recommendations were discouraged, and they had no channel to the leadership; between 1937 and 1948, the WLF did not meet.

After the Second World War, women began to chafe at these limitations. Perhaps, the WLF asked deferentially, women could be informal advisers on issues such as social welfare and offer input on the party platform, candidate selection (women were usually discouraged from running for office), and government appointments. The leadership baulked; one power-broker agreed that women might have a distinct "familial" point of view, but the WLF was not there to "promote the interests of women" but rather to offer the "real" politicians support.[23]

Educated, professional women who imagined a career in policy-making or politics, not tea pouring, were in the vanguard of small changes in the 1950s and 1960s. Like McClung, they saw liberal reform as a pragmatic politics combining social conscience, individual liberty, and equality of opportunity, but, unlike McClung, they did not necessarily move from the women's movement to the Liberal Party. Casgrain was an exception, but she absconded to the CCF in the 1950s. By the late 1960s, a renewed feminist movement outside the Liberal Party and a small core of determined women inside the party shifted attitudes; after years of debate, a new Women's Liberal Commission, part of, not parallel to, the parent NLF, was established in 1973. High-profile Liberals such as Monique Bégin, a research director for the Royal Commission on the Status of Women (RCSW), were encouraged to run for office, though the savvy Bégin insisted she be placed in a winnable constituency. The Women's Liberal Commission may have come late to the feminist table, but by the 1970s, Liberal feminists exerted more influence on mainstream politics, as advocates for the Royal Commission on the Status of Women and in policy debates on gender equality. Still, old attitudes of male superiority were hard to shake.[24] In 1963, Pauline Jewett, a high-profile Liberal MP with a doctorate, expressed some hope that she might eventually move into cabinet. Prime Minister Lester Pearson was not really interested: after all, he already had a woman (Judy LaMarsh) in cabinet. Who needed two?[25]

The VOW: From Maternalism to Feminism

The Women's International League for Peace and Freedom (WIL) outlived the war, but only just. Its European branches were decimated; in fascist countries, its leaders were threatened, jailed, sent to concentration camps. In North America, too, it lost members. Four Canadian branches survived, still faithful to the ideals of socialism, internationalism, feminism, and maternalism. WILers continued to argue that social equality was foundational to peace: they called for a Canadian Bill of Rights, better housing, and employment for poor Canadians, immigrants, and refugees. Committed to direct action, the Vancouver WIL supported a longshoreman's picket of the city harbour to block arms shipments abroad.[26] Internationally, the WIL stood for universal disarmament, a strong United Nations with communist China included as a member, and dialogue between the United States and the

Soviet Union. In a Cold War context, these seemingly sensible ideas were unwelcome: the WIL was suspect for its socialism and "traitorous" favouring of "international over national interests."[27]

Pacifism as a women's issue, however, was reinvented in new forms. In the 1950s, women's concerns about nuclear war were expressed through Ban the Bomb groups, anti–nuclear testing campaigns, and the most mainstream option, United Nations Associations. CCF anti-war feminists such as Dorothy Steeves and Nellie Peterson opposed Canadian membership in NATO – in their view, a military alliance led by an imperialist United States – calling instead for universal disarmament and Canadian neutrality. They were on the losing end of this battle: the CCF, anxious to distance itself from communism, supported NATO.[28]

Another option was the Canadian Congress of Women, which also advanced an internationalist, maternal peace message, working in tandem with the Canadian Peace Congress, founded by former missionary James Endicott. Both groups, however, had obvious communist connections and struggled with Cold War accusations that their definition of "peace" meant sympathy for Canada's communist enemies. Anti-communism was not new, but its post-war version was particularly virulent. Justified with government claims that Soviet spies were undermining the country's safety, and a powerful narrative portraying communism as the antithesis of all "democratic" values, anti-communism seeped into educational, cultural, associational, family, and workplace life. It was also internalized by individuals: those who saw others disciplined, shamed, ostracized – or worse – self-silenced, hiding ideas and associations that might incriminate them. The repression of communists, real and imagined, was aided by a surveillance state cavalier about civil rights, accomplished through purges (often behind closed doors) of known and "fellow traveller" communists from governments, the National Film Board, unions, and even volunteer agencies.[29] Business interests, patriotic organizations, some conservative ethnic associations, and CCF union leaders either applauded or remained silent.

The Cold War concurrently fostered a patriarchal ideal of retrenched gender relations in the "warm hearth" of the family.[30] Father-headed, heteronormative families were reified as a bulwark against communism; women and children, "contained" within the home, would be "protected" by husbands and fathers.[31] A generalized fear of "untoward" sexuality was also fostered. Gays and lesbians were the antithesis of this familial ideal and were driven out of government employment, their dismissals justified with the rationale they were potential security risks.[32] The intensified anti-communist climate was reflected in women's political tourism. In the interwar period, Canadian visitors who sang the praises of women's equality in the Soviet Union received some hearing in the press. By the 1950s, visitors sponsored by the new Canadian-Soviet Friendship Society brought back similar stories of gender equality, but their claims were a harder sell, convincing only those "already sympathetic" to communism.[33]

Given this Cold War climate, the meteoric rise of a new, unifying women's peace organization, the Voice of Women, or the "Voices," was all the more remarkable. In May 1960, after the failure of international disarmament talks, a *Toronto Star* women's columnist, Lotta Dempsey, published a heartfelt appeal to women, urging them to speak out against the threat of nuclear war. Dempsey made the classic maternalist assumption that women had a natural disposition toward peace: "I have never met a woman who did not hate fighting and killing and the loss of husbands and the terrible tragedy of children dead, maimed or homeless."[34] She was immediately deluged with letters from women responding positively to her message. Let's look at war and peace as we would "our housekeeping," wrote one reader, by tallying up the costs of war versus the costs of housing, education, and so on. Another urged women to join with Chinese, African, and other women "to scream for the preservation of children all over the world ... The men seem to have lost sight of the fact that the first – the only important thing to do now, is to feed and shelter the hungry, and to get rid of these dangerous weapons of war."[35]

The publicity stimulated a broader public conversation, and a group of savvy women met with Dempsey over the summer to kick-start a new organization. A mass meeting in July at Toronto's Massey Hall launched the Voice of Women; within a few years it had 5,000 members, a national office, regional branches, and connections to other international groups like Women Strike for Peace in the United States. The detailed history of the VOW has been told elsewhere.[36] What is germane here is its progression from popular maternalism to anti-war feminism, and its "bridging" role between past incarnations of feminist pacifism and a future anti-imperialist feminism.[37]

For the first few years, the Voices focused primarily on international dialogue and nuclear disarmament. The organization's spectacular growth had much to do with its non-threatening self-presentation as "civic-minded homemakers" on a moral mission.[38] Maternalism shielded members from the negative image of Ban-the-Bomb radical "peaceniks" – as founders Kay Macpherson and Meg Sears reflected, tongue-in-cheek, "What could be

Figure 8.1 Silent peace vigils were one method of protest for the early Voice of Women | Clara Thomas Archives and Special Collections, York University Libraries, Toronto Telegram fonds, ASC 04608

more pleasing than women raising their voices in hymns to peace, international understanding and goodwill towards men?"[39] Through their dress, demeanour, language, and polite lobbying, the Voices were the incarnation of respectable Canadian motherhood. They asked for government advice and conducted silent Mother's Day vigils; sporting gloves, hats, and purses, they did not look like rabble-rousing radicals. Their maternal message was so appealing that it earned them endorsements from women senators and the honorary patronage of Maryon Pearson, the prime minister's wife.

Their image was not entirely out of step with VOW membership. Many were young homemakers with families, and an estimated 80 percent were newcomers to social activism. Though linguistically and religiously diverse, the Voices were overwhelmingly white, with a few significant exceptions such as African-Canadian human rights crusaders Kay Livingstone and Pearleen Oliver. Nor was their maternalism only public relations: it came from a wellspring of deep feeling. Macpherson recalled that the VOW was founded on a "tidal wave of emotion" in the midst of nuclear uncertainty.[40] When members claimed that love for their children, not politics, was their motivation, they spoke with sincerity. Some believed mothers' anti-war inclinations were "natural" and innate, others stressed women's socialization, but almost all embraced a version of Jane Addams's social motherhood – the notion that women's unique standpoint gave them the desire, obligation, and moral authority to speak on behalf of the world's children. Stressing women's impulse to protect human welfare, the VOW followed in the lineage of earlier feminist pacifists, Flora MacDonald Denison and Helena Gutteridge.[41] The Voices also deployed tactics reminiscent of the interwar WIL. In Saskatoon, for example, they invited school children and university students to paint "a picture of world peace" on public boarding as means of personal and public education.[42]

Cautious humanitarian positioning on peace, an appealing image, and honest emotion were all important to the VOW's growth. So too was its delicate navigation of the Cold War. Especially after some Voices travelled to Moscow for a peace conference, the RCMP and that bastion of female patriotism, the Imperial Order Daughters of the Empire, expressed fears the Voices were dominated by "reds." One Quebec VOW member of the Moscow delegation remembers horrified denunciations of her trip by her parents and parish priest.[43] However, no prominent communists were VOW leaders (though some past and current communists, including Jean Watts, were members), and the VOW resisted all "partisan" labels. Facing down a television interviewer who grilled her about communist infiltrators, VOW leader Thérèse Casgrain averred, with her usual grace under fire, that members should not be asked their political or religious affiliation, only if they upheld VOW peace goals.[44] The Voices' strategic use of motherhood also helped calm concerns. A popular child-centred campaign, for instance, was the baby-tooth project: women sent their children's baby teeth to scientist Ursula Franklin for testing to see if radiation in the atmosphere was having a deleterious effect on their health.

The VOW shifted course in 1963, although tensions between those advising caution and those favouring more activist tactics were already simmering. A national debate about whether Canada should accept nuclear warheads for NORAD (North American Aerospace Defense Command) missiles on Canadian soil forced the VOW to take a stand. The Quebec Voix des Femmes chartered a train to Ottawa for four hundred women demanding a "nuclear-free" Canada. Government leaders heard them out, but the male press gallery dismissed the Voices as "pathetically foolish matrons," much like "hens running around with their heads cut off."[45] When Liberal prime minister Lester Pearson reversed his position and agreed in 1962 to have Canada take nuclear missiles, the VOW opposed the Liberals. Disenchanted with this "partisan" decision, some members left.

After a partial test-ban treaty in 1963 assuaged nuclear tensions, the Voices shifted their focus to the Vietnam War. Motherhood remained a dominant motif in their organizing, but they insisted sides had to be taken: they were critical of the Canadian state's complicity in the war and the raw brutality of American aggression, waged with chemical weapons and the merciless bombing of civilians. VOW members welcomed American draft resisters into their homes and organized tours and peace conferences of combatant women from the United States and both North and South Vietnam. Their new child-centred project involved knitting dark-coloured baby clothes for Vietnamese children, forced to live in tunnels and in need of camouflage from American bombers. This project was wildly successful, including with American anti-war women who sent their knitting to Canada to be shipped to Vietnam. The knitting project, like the teeth collection, was an ingenious call to motherhood: using women's and children's "bodies" as symbols of the indiscriminate ravages of war, as Frances Early notes, was a long-standing theme in feminist pacifism.[46]

Two other political shifts demonstrated the Voices' increased embrace of feminism. The organization sharpened its critique of male domination and expanded its peace agenda to encompass other equality and human rights issues. The former was implicit in the ideological roots of the VOW, founded to counteract male-dominated governments and militaries, which had played the politics of nuclear brinkmanship so recklessly. Militarism had led to obscene spending on arms and neglect of human social needs such as education and health – precisely the argument of Francis Marion Beynon during the First World War. "The world," according to the Victoria VOW, "is more likely to be saved from nuclear disaster, pollution, starvation and overpopulation if women are given a real voice."[47]

The definition of "peace" also broadened. Rather than simply "the absence of war," peace meant to be "free to think, free of fear, of unemployment, of being beaten by one's husband, of losing one's land, like the Inuit."[48] By 1967, VOW briefs to the Royal Commission on the Status of Women incorporated a range of feminist arguments. The Victoria Voices argued that women were needed in public life to offset male-dominated governance, as women were "more inclined towards practical solutions, less likely to use violence and force."[49] The Edmonton VOW decried patriarchal ideas, the view that women are mere "chattel" and appendages of men,[50] while the Montreal branch condemned the endlessly derogatory constructions of women in popular culture. Not only did the media dismiss women's peace politics as unimportant "feminine news," but it denigrated, dismissed, and mocked all women. "Must they stand like dummies, poor dears, beside their husband on [the] front page of the newspaper," the Montreal Voices wrote about the "good wife."[51] Another branch gave a detailed analysis of the mass media's "insulting" sexism in its promotion of consumption, in which women are depicted as "non-persons, caricatures, a bit of fluff ... given to flights of fancy ... spending time in pursuit of men, dirt and recipes."[52] Though reformist in tone and always hopeful of gradualist, democratic methods, VOW briefs insisted on significant legislative change, advocating for child-care funding, access to birth control, and opening up all occupations to women.

The connection between war and economic, racial, and gender inequality took on more salience in VOW work. The reasoning was not unlike that of Rose Henderson and the WIL: class, colonial, and gender oppressions were underlying causes of violence, along with racial, national, and religious hatred. Global inequality, the immorality of First World affluence and Third World poverty, was assailed by the VOW, but so too was poverty and racism at home. From its inception, the Halifax branch addressed racial inequality in the city. Overlapping membership and common concerns shared by the VOW and the Nova Scotia Association for the Advancement for Coloured People led to efforts to document discrimination in African-Canadian women's employment in order to expose racism in hiring. Other branches stressed the needs of Indigenous women: the Regina VOW told the RCSW that poverty was a most urgent issue for "Indian and Metis" women, "triply disadvantaged" by gender, race, and birth. Gender discrimination in the Indian Act had to be rectified and support given to Indian women as they mobilized around issues such as child welfare.[53]

Equal Rights at Work

Federal policies at the end of the Second World War were designed to push married women out of the workforce: child care was cut, favourable tax policies for working wives abandoned, and the civil service "re-established as a male domain," as the government heeded calls for preferential hiring for male veterans.[54] The idealized male breadwinner family model had some appeal for working- and middle-class families; given how time consuming domestic labour was, not to mention a soaring birth rate, women welcomed doing one job, not two. New hopes for economic stability emerged with the post-war "Fordist accord," an economy premised on increased production and consumption, a interventionist Keynesian state managing the economy, a social safety net, and, for many unionized workers, a full-time, steady income in exchange for contracts that subdued workplace protest. Fordism did not spell affluence for all. Poor, Indigenous, racialized, and immigrant families relied on multiple wage earners; this "second tier" of workers was less likely to benefit from Fordism and union protection.[55]

Although women's participation in the workforce dipped shortly after the war, the long-term story was the real story: the number of married women working for pay multiplied exponentially. In 1931, only 10 percent of working women were married; by 1971, that had soared to 56 percent.[56] Despite much public hand-wringing over this change, women were not usurping men's jobs; they were relegated to female blue- and white-collar occupations, teaching and nursing. The family economy needed their wages,[57] but businesses also welcomed a flexible, cheap workforce, especially for the expanding service and clerical sector, including the "temp" industry: the "Kelly Girls" temporary help agency was referred to as a "halfway house for housewives."[58]

Married women workers were under the microscope, assessed as good or bad mothers, the latter producing "latch-key kids" and juvenile delinquents. Working women, however, recognized the new normal, and were not quiescent in the workplace. There were flashes of rebellion: they went on spontaneous wildcat strikes, walked away from jobs, complained to management, unionized, and coordinated informal protests. While some women rebelled individually, collectively their voices were stronger. Two issues became lightning rods for feminist discontent: equal pay to combat women's lower wages and legal protections for married women and working mothers, including maternity leave.

By 1949, the Business and Professional Women's Clubs (BPWC) referred to equal pay as the unofficial "slogan" of their organization. Other organizations and parties, including the National Council of Women of Canada, the YWCA, and the CCF, vigorously promoted equal pay laws, as did reform feminist, BPWC member and Conservative member of Parliament Ellen Fairclough. In response to pressure from women's organizations, eight provinces and the federal government passed equal pay laws in the fifties. The concept was hardly novel. It had been advanced by suffragists and the Trades and Labour Congress in the First World War, and was promoted anew during the Second World War by labour and women's reform groups. By the 1950s, it was pursued by women across the political spectrum as a "simple matter of justice."[59] Yet there were limits to collaboration. While some CCF women had collaborated with communists in the 1930s, the Cold War and the CCF's rightward trajectory (though not without internal battles) now discouraged such alliances. CCF women were more inclined to join forces with the BPWC. Communist-led unions were some of the most vocal advocates of equal pay, but they were isolated from other labour feminists.

Firmly situated in a liberal rights discourse, equal pay laws varied to a small degree across provincial jurisdictions. The most promising legislation, passed by the CCF government in Saskatchewan, defined equal work as "comparatively" equal. The Ontario CCF's proposal for a similar bill was defeated; in its place, Conservative legislation in 1952 required proof women were performing exactly the same work down to every detail, and workers were required to brave a bureaucratic process to lay complaints against potentially punitive employers who had already made their enmity to equal pay known.[60] The Ontario CCF Status of Women Committee dismissed this narrow law as a "toothless ghost of a real equal pay bill."[61]

Advocates of equal pay hoped it would correct wage disparities between women and men and have an educational impact, discouraging gender discrimination at work. Ultimately it paid modest, if any, economic dividends. Focusing only on individual cases of discrimination obscured the structural causes of women's lower wages, particularly a labour force segregated by gender and race, and hope for any educational benefit relied on employers changing their minds on unequal wages. Few did. The very profitable Campbell's Soup Company, to note only one example, responded by hiring men rather than giving female employees equal pay.[62] While one study suggested the Ontario law modestly increased women's wages over time, more probing research suggests it was a well-intentioned reform that papered over economic inequality and had unintended "regressive" effects.[63] A BC equal pay law was ultimately deemed "a dismal failure."[64] Even the cabinet minister who guided the federal equal pay bill through Parliament recognized it was little more than a "do good" measure "appeasing" women voters.[65]

In 1953, the federal government also established a Women's Bureau within the Department of Labour in response to lobbing by liberal and labour feminists. Some provinces followed suit. Politicians hoped these bureaus would accrue female votes for their parties, while pitching them to business as smart economic planning to aid the "efficient integration of women into the workforce."[66] Often directed by well-educated feminists acutely aware of workforce discrimination, women's bureaus did useful research that was turned into advocacy for equality legislation. Drawing on allies from the labour movement and the BPWC, for instance, the Ontario Bureau developed the

Women's Equal Employment Opportunity Act in 1969; it forbade separate job advertising by sex, eliminated male and female seniority lists (a significant victory for many blue-collar women), and established unpaid maternity leave.

Even these small reforms incurred employer hostility. One lectured the Ontario Bureau about women workers' many failings, a reminder of a thriving anti-feminism: women did not produce "equal output ... They do not think like a man ... They should demonstrate value rather than complaining." In legislatures, male politicians guffawed that some jobs – like being a Playboy "bunny" – could never be done by men.[67] Men had little reason to worry. Such incremental reforms were premised on individual rights thinking; they did not challenge structural economic inequality, and women's bureaus answered to the state, not the women's movement. Still, less than satisfying incremental change can result in a flood of complaints directed at governments, as women demand more effective equality measures.

Equal pay legislation highlighted women's sameness with men. The right to work when pregnant and maternity leave recognized their biological difference, though it acknowledged that women needed protection from reprisal, since work for pay was now a reality for many married women.[68] Maternity leave sparked even stronger antipathy than equal pay; businesses moaned that it would encourage women to get pregnant with abandon, and even some working women, having absorbed a self-help ideology, grumbled that children were an individual, not a state, responsibility. Federal and provincial women's bureaus began researching legal protections for married women workers in the late 1950s, but women were already engaged in grassroots, informal resistance to the status quo. Women refused to quit their jobs, hiding marriages and pregnancies; others claimed unemployment insurance after childbirth, though state policy did not allow them to do so.[69]

Unionized women had an additional valuable tool at their disposal: collective agreements. Occasionally, left-wing and communist union leaders defended both married women's right to work and maternity leave as non-negotiable basics of gender equality. More often, unions invoked principles of union fairness to defend women fired because of marriage or pregnancy: seniority, without attention to marital status, had to be defended; the company could not arbitrarily impose discriminatory policies outside of the collective agreement; and union solidarity meant fighting for men and women alike. Women drew on these discourses of fairness, equality, and solidarity in individual grievances that became collective victories. In 1953, Rosina Saxby,

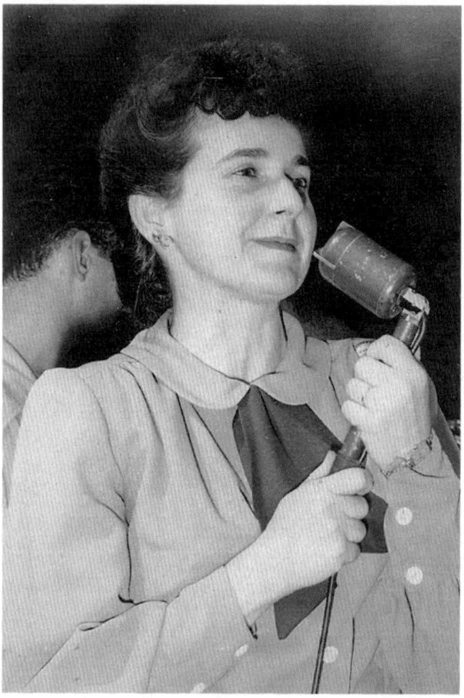

Figure 8.2 Madeleine Parent organized women textile workers in Quebec and Ontario after the Second World War. She believed the labour movement was an avenue to pursue women's equality | LAC, PA 120397

a married woman laid off from an auto plant, protested when single women with less seniority were given priority in re-employment. Her complaint reached the ears of the union's American head office, which pressed the less-than-sympathetic Canadian union to resist discrimination against married women. "Will we give single men different seniority rights because they don't support children?" they asked rhetorically. Saxby won her case based on the principle of fair seniority, but her victory had feminist repercussions, setting an inspiring precedent for other women. The company, however, refused to rehire her – such was the price for being a progressive troublemaker.

Similar protests bubbling up from the grassroots pushed other unions to fight women's dismissals for marriage, pregnancy, or maternity. Women demanded to know why men had sick leave but they had no maternity leave; why they could not return to work when the family needed their wages; why they could not judge when a pregnancy inhibited their work. Employers, from school boards to factories, cited tradition, past practice, and management policy as a rationale for dismissal; some paternalistically claimed they were acting in the best interests of the woman or protecting "the family."

Employer policies were wrapped up in discriminatory sexual and moral regulation. Flight attendants, for instance, were dismissed on marriage or at age thirty-two; divorcees were not hired. In 1965, their union, the Canadian Airline Flight Attendants Association, vigorously supported a flight attendant's effort to challenge the marriage rules in court. A CCF member of Parliament urged the federal government, which regulated air travel, to object to this "shameful" practice. Despite political pressure and the union's public campaign, she lost her case; labour arbitrators assumed that firing married women was the company's right. The same union later launched human rights and courts cases against women's dismissal for pregnancy, arguing that these regulations had little to do with safety or women's physical well-being and far more to do with the airlines' marketing of women's bodies as young, single, and attractive.[70]

Women workers often faced paternalistic lectures about their proper place in the family when they tried to secure rights as pregnant or married workers. In 1960, the Quaker Oats factory in Peterborough, Ontario, dismissed "Doris" for being pregnant, although management conceded they *might* keep on or rehire a widow or single mother – if they deemed her deserving. Their message: women workers did not have rights – only privileges, if they were judged morally upright. Doris's union filed a grievance and, although she lost, the dissenting opinion in the grievance, written by Mary Eady, was symbolically significant. One of a small group of labour feminists in the union movement, she opposed the dismissal and criticized the invasive, moralistic discussion of Doris's sex life in the hearing – questions about whether she was married or in a common law relationship and whether the child was legitimate – as completely "irrelevant."[71]

Labour feminists rejected outdated moralism and arbitrary rules about pregnancy and maternity, calling instead for contract and legislated protections. Deeply committed to a working-class project, Mary Eady, Eileen Suffrin (who led efforts to unionize bank and Eaton's workers), and other female CCF union leaders often avoided the label feminist, associated with women "only" concerned with gender discrimination. However, they were working behind the scenes, discussing women's role in unions, and pressing unions to consider contract and legislated equality provisions. It is revealing that Suffrin's personal correspondence with labour feminists abroad was more openly feminist in tenor than her public comments at home, perhaps one more indication of feminism in a Cold War holding pattern.

Human Rights and Women's Rights

Equal rights legislation introduced in the late 1960s was justified with human rights ideals – that is, women citizens, like men, had an inherent right to life, dignity, and equality. Until then, sex discrimination had been absent from human rights discussions; legislation barring discrimination in employment passed in the 1950s and human rights commissions set up in the 1960s did not consider "sex discrimination" important.

Many scholars contend that the concept of human rights took on new importance after the Second World War. The horrific disclosure of the Holocaust and the newly founded United Nations' 1948 Declaration of Human Rights signified a shift in international discourse. Canada's own sordid history of anti-Semitism and its wartime repression of Japanese-Canadian citizens, including government efforts to deport them, encouraged the creation of new civil rights organizations. The labour movement was a key player, establishing the Jewish Labour Committee to monitor and combat anti-Semitism and racism. Public education, court challenges to racist laws, and on-the-ground actions such as sit-ins in white-only restaurants were all in their tactical tool kit.

If this new concern with discrimination did not address gender, it did encourage African-Canadian women to continue their efforts to combat racism and lobby for equality for the Black community. Canada may have lacked the Jim Crow laws of the American South, but it had Jim Crow practices of segregation. In the 1930s, African-Canadian newspapers and the Union of Sleeping Car Porters and its women's auxiliary opposed these practices. They were tackled anew after 1945.[72] Halifax community activist Pearleen Oliver, who had campaigned for African-Canadian women's admission to nursing schools, took up new challenges. Oliver was a critical influence on Viola Desmond, who was dragged from a New Glasgow, Nova Scotia, movie theatre in 1946 when she sat in the "white" section; she was incarcerated overnight and convicted of a "tax offence" in local court. A humiliated and distraught Desmond came to see Oliver, who urged her to secure legal advice. Oliver also helped persuade the Nova Scotia Association for the Advancement of Coloured People to back Desmond's court case – though some members feared it would spark a racist backlash.

Desmond's legal challenge to Jim Crow practices was aided by Carrie Best, the editor of the Nova Scotia newspaper the *Clarion*, a Black community voice for racial uplift, the celebration of Black achievement, and a long-time critic of racial discrimination. Indeed, Best was forceably removed from the same theatre by the police in 1941 for sitting in a "white" section; her protest,

Figure 8.3 Pearleen Oliver, shown here with her family in 1954, campaigned for decades for civic, employment, and legal rights for African Canadians in Nova Soctia | *Chatelaine*, June 1954

taken to the courts, failed in the face of business' established legal "right" to discriminate.[73] Best advertised for donations for a Desmond defence fund in the *Clarion*, urging supporters not to "take the line of least resistance" but to join this principled fight. Unless people opposed this kind of "religious and racial hatred ... born of fear and ignorance," it could develop into an "uncontrollable catastrophe" like Hitler. Human "freedom," she wrote, was supposedly what "all men" had recently laid down their lives to protect.[74] Pearleen Oliver also referenced Hitler in her rationale for her human rights work: her brothers "fought in the war, over there for democracy ... yet we don't live in a democracy." It was now time to defeat racism on the home front.[75]

Gender, as Constance Backhouse notes, was a significant element of Desmond's legal fight.[76] Desmond, Best, and Oliver were educated, middle-class African Canadians who were admired as role models and advocates of equality; they also symbolized women's central role in community building – in Oliver's words, the "matriarchal" Black culture.[77] Desmond, a poised, refined, successful business woman symbolized the "essence of middle-class Black femininity," and her manhandling by the theatre manager, coupled with her incarceration in a men's jail cell, reminded African-Canadian women of the gendered racial denigration of Black women rooted in the history of slavery. If Desmond, a cultured and respectable woman, could be so targeted, this "crushed any hope of ever achieving an egalitarian society."[78]

Not unlike labour feminists, anti-racist women used individual cases to pursue collective ends. African-Canadian women's post-war organizing did not focus on gender discrimination per se, as much as it used gender as a mobilizing tool to counter racism, both by making statements of women's worth, respectability, and equality, and by organizing against egregious examples of racism. In Ontario, a social club – the Dilettantes – transformed into the Canadian Negro Women's Association (CANEWA) in 1951; it sponsored events marking Black culture and achievement, and raised money for scholarships for African-Canadian students to counteract the racism they faced in the school system. Education and history were closely correlated in women's equality struggles: documenting Black women's history as "worthy," as CANEWA member Rella Braithwate did in *The Black Woman in Canada,* was itself considered "a political act."[79] Civil rights struggles also crossed borders: CANEWA women attended a Toronto speech by Martin Luther King Jr.; some also picketed the visit of racist Alabama governor George Wallace.

Women in CANEWA were sensitive to mutually reinforcing racist and sexist stereotypes; in a group letter to *Chatelaine* in 1973, they protested an article on Caribbean immigrant women that, in their view, reflected the "ignorance of the white community." They criticized the article for its stereotypical gendered physical depiction: "Why the necessity to describe the physical characteristics of the woman, and that in such a way to convey the impression that all immigrant women are big, buxom and gentle – for which we could read simple?"[80] Other African-Canadian women objected to the equation of all Black women with domestic service.[81] CANEWA women were well aware of the gendered and racialized division of labour that limited their employment options, but they did not necessarily see a common bond with white working women. Pointing to the endless media debate about married women workers, one member observed that "no husband told us not to go to work. In order for us to survive, we had to go to work. We didn't have to fight our husbands to do certain things; we had to fight society in order to make our mark."[82]

By the early 1970s, there were tenuous links between CANEWA and other feminist groups, especially through CANEWA president Kay Livingstone, an accomplished radio interviewer and actress. Livingstone's biography connected the earlier history of African-Canadian protests against racism to Black women's post-war community activism and to new feminist groups. Raised by parents who founded the *Dawn of Tomorrow,* a London, Ontario, newspaper celebrating Black culture and opposed to racial discrimination, she was attuned to the history of resistance to Jim Crow in Canada.[83] Like other CANEWA women, she saw the need for a separate African-Canadian women's movement that spoke to their history, social roles, and experience of discrimination. Yet she also wanted CANEWA to speak out on social issues of relevance to a broad range of women, and she was an early member of the Toronto Voice of Women. No doubt Livingstone welcomed the provocative speech of politician Rosemary Brown at the annual CANEWA banquet in 1973: Brown spoke from the perspective of a "Black woman, a feminist and a socialist,"[84] encouraging listeners to connect anti-racism with socialism and women's equality.

CANEWA subsequently became the Congress of Black Women of Canada, which engaged in human rights advocacy for race- and gender-based discrimination. The shift from human rights without women to women using human rights was an uphill struggle throughout the 1950s and 1960s. The head of the Jewish Labour Committee, Kalmen Kaplansky, admitted later that "women were just not considered equal [in employment]; they were expected to be mothers and look after their families." Post-war human rights discourse was governed by "conventional beliefs about women's fundamental nature that made politicians blind to the discrimination women faced."[85] Even the labour movement's human rights educational work ignored women. The annual institutes of the Labour Committee for Human Rights in Vancouver, for instance, addressed religion, race, and Indigenous issues, but not women. When a Canadian Labour Congress official mused that "human rights was a man to man affair," he inadvertently summed up this view.[86]

Feminists were increasingly dismayed by their non-inclusion in the definition of "human." Given the labour movement's purported support for human rights, labour and socialist feminists were disturbed by the silence of male allies when it came to gender discrimination. When the Conservative Ontario government tabled a Fair Employment Practices Act in 1948 to ban discrimination in hiring, CCF member of the Ontario legislature Agnes Macphail was appalled by the omission of sex: "What are women to think?" she asked. Anybody of "any creed, colour, nationality, religion ... so long as they are male, will get equal treatment," but a woman "can be discriminated against."[87] The predicament of Saskatchewan CCF women was perhaps worse. Once elected in 1944, their own party reneged on gender equality, allowing married women to be fired from the public service and omitting sex discrimination from their much-vaunted 1947 *Bill of Rights.* Women inside and outside the party mobilized in opposition. Beatrice Trew wrote to fellow CCF women in Saskatchewan urging them to support a party resolution that forbade discrimination against married women, reminding her comrades that "socialism will not be based on discrimination."[88] The 1947 *Bill of Rights* betrayal incurred protest beyond Saskatchewan's borders from CCF women in Manitoba and Ontario. Manitoba CCF activist Margaret Mann was assured paternalistically by a Saskatchewan CCF leader that it was all for the better: "There are some rights like jury duty, women did not want."[89] She immediately organized Manitoba women to challenge their exclusion from juries.

Women across the political spectrum lobbied to have sex discrimination added to human rights thinking and legislation. By late 1960s, they finally succeeded. Public discourse on gender discrimination had shifted in the wake of Royal Commission on the Status of Women hearings that recounted gender inequities, international discourses on human rights, and a more enlightened stance within the Canadian labour movement.[90] By 1968, sex discrimination was no longer an outlandish idea. Provincial and federal human rights legislation began to take women into account; however, when "sex" was added to these codes, the investigation process and narrowness of the law often worked against women complainants. What changed by the early 1970s, as Dominique Clément has shown, was not only discourse, but action. Feminists schooled in the women's movement brought cases to human rights tribunals, made public education a priority, and called for a more robust complaint process. They came to human rights work as feminists, determined to use liberal rights discourse as one more strategic device in a much larger equality project.[91] By the time they did so, other competing feminisms were claiming attention, some of which looked sceptically on liberal and reform feminism.

Feminists Reflect on Post-War Culture

Some historians suggest that one can trace remarkably strong continuities in Canadian social life and movements from the post-war 1950s through the 1970s. Yet, women who lived through these years identify jarring discontinuities: their own stories contrast the highly restrictive cultural context of the Cold War in the late 1950s and early 1960s with the enticing possibilities that began to open up in the very late 1960s and the 1970s.[92]

Rosemary Brown remembers a speech she gave to CANEWA in 1973 as the "most important of her life" because she expressed all three elements of her political identity as a "feminist, socialist and Black woman." Brown

Figure 8.4 Rosemary Brown | From the website of the Department of Gender, Sexuality and Women's Studies at Simon Fraser University; photographer unknown

feared that a "Black audience" might be unsympathetic to "women's liberation," yet she yearned to say something politically "important," making a convincing rationale for the political solidarity of Black Canadians and feminists. "Unless all of us are free," she told the audience, "none of us will be free."[93] By 1973, Brown was nationally known as a human rights advocate and New Democratic member of the BC legislature, the first African-Canadian woman ever to be elected in that province. Her memoir of her journey from a relatively privileged childhood in Jamaica to the BC legislature describes university life at McGill, her work as a homemaker and social worker, and her political involvements.

While her most painful memories are the unrelenting racism she encountered, her memoir also reveals the highly circumscribed gender order of the fifties, one in which the career interests of husbands were always expected to take priority. Her African-American husband, she suggests, was unusual, as he encouraged her to study and work after marriage and children. She cites her reading of Betty Friedan's *The Feminine Mystique* (1963) as an "aha" feminist moment, even though later critiques of the book claim it addressed only white, middle-class women. Friedan's indictment of a domesticity that imprisoned women in mind and body resonated for Brown: "Suddenly it was all there, the story of my life ... I realized I was not unique, that there were women all over America of all colours, who were experiencing the same sense of being unfulfilled."[94]

Pauline Jewett eventually joined Brown in the New Democratic Party (NDP), but she began her political life as a Liberal. After securing a doctorate in political science from Harvard, she returned to her undergraduate alma mater, Queen's University, hoping to teach, only to discover that universities were old boys' clubs inhospitable to women. After countless applications for university positions, she worked for the Canadian Nurses Association; the dynamic women she met there were her "first introduction to feminism," but she continued her efforts to make a difference in the male-dominated world of academe and party politics. While she was teaching at Carleton University in 1963, Jewett ran successfully as a federal Liberal candidate in the rural Ontario riding of Northumberland. Her parliamentary experience confirmed that the doors to political success were closed to women. She was treated as an "oddity" when campaigning; she was kept off a parliamentary committee on prisons, told the shocking issues might offend her sensibility; and she knew advancement would be stalled by the masculine culture of political life.[95]

Defeated in the next election, she returned to university life, serving as president of Simon Fraser University, and she switched her allegiance to the NDP, a better fit with her ideas on civil liberties and the needs of the "average person."[96] In 1979, she was elected as a NDP federal member from New Westminster, British Columbia.[97] Jewett's own experiences, coupled with a reinvigorated women's movement, led her to champion feminist positions, addressing unequal pay for women in the university and urging equality legislation in Parliament. Her biography underscores the social climate of the 1970s and its differences from the 1950s, when women and men were to inhabit separate spheres of work, professional women had limited opportunities, and women in politics faced inflexible barriers.

The memoir of Jewett's close friend, *Chatelaine* editor Doris Anderson, is a self-portrait of a girl who was a feminist in spirit long before she acknowledged the label as an adult. Jewett came from a middle-class family that had the resources to send her to university; Anderson did not, but she was determined to secure an education and fulfill her dream of being a writer. Anderson's mother felt that the best option for any young woman after the Second World War was to marry well. Yet Anderson looked at the marriages all around her and saw only stultifying confinement: women were expected to subordinate their needs to their husbands; careers were a non-starter.

Anderson was eventually successful in the publishing world, but she conveys how difficult it was for women to buck gender expectations, challenges sometimes internalized as anxiety and self-doubt. The moral norms of the fifties punished women, not men, for exploring their sexuality, and the publishing world took for granted sexual harassment, demeaning jokes, and a glass ceiling for women. Women who combined work with children were viewed sceptically as bad mothers well into the 1960s. Even her own magazine, she concedes, printed such claims about maternal deprivation, though they contradicted what she believed in. Nonetheless, Anderson made *Chatelaine* into a venue for feminist discussion and later was a mover and shaker in the women's movement, also running for the Liberal Party. The contrast between the confining ideology she battled in the 1950s, when feminism was not even named, and her later advocacy of child care, reproductive rights, and equal economic opportunity is striking.[98]

Anderson had a personal and political understanding of the need for child care for working mothers. The life story of daycare activist Pat Schultz

Figure 8.5 Doris Anderson | LAC R2770-1-3-E

offers a final glimpse of transformations in post-war culture and women's lives. Schultz came from an immigrant, working-class background, though one steeped in a sense of pride in the dignity of labour. It was a short step to socialist politics: in 1952, at eighteen, she joined the CCF but within a few years moved leftwards, becoming active in a revolutionary socialist group, the League for Social Action. In 1972, she joined the feminist Toronto Women's Caucus.

Asked in a documentary film to describe life in the 1950s and early 1960s, she recalled both the political repression of the Cold War and the overwhelming assumption of male superiority, simply taken for granted and internalized by women. "Heterosexuality" was also assumed to be the only conceivable choice; she did not see bisexual and lesbian relations in the realm of possibility. Women imagined themselves "as second best" she remembers; even if they secretly thought women should be equal, "our important relationships were with men ... In fact, it was better to be a man. Why relate to women when they were second best?"[99] As she and others recall in the documentary, there was tremendous social pressure for women to stay home with children: they were told that was "right and proper" even if it drove them literally "crazy."

As a single, working mother, Schultz's experience of workplace subordination bore a striking similarity to the complaints of many women who wrote to the Royal Commission on the Status of Women. As a clerical worker, she remembers, "we trained men who were paid more than us, then became our supervisors." Feminism made her realize just how much women were getting "screwed," how angry they should be: it "made me feel angry about all the things in my life that I didn't like but didn't know I was angry about." The film memoir makes it clear that feminism was profoundly transformative for her, both politically and personally, though she remained a socialist feminist committed to "human" liberation and working-class struggles and especially to the issue for which she became best known: quality, accessible child care for all working parents.

Schultz, Brown, Anderson, and Jewett came from different backgrounds – immigrant, racialized, working class, middle class – yet they shared a sense of suffocating gender prohibitions of the fifties. Others too recall the punishing double standard, the overwhelming assumption of heteronormativity, the limited, gendered job prospects, the dampening of ambition in girls. The sought-after honour in my high school in the sixties was to be crowned beauty queen; high-achieving girls became nurses, never doctors; and "good" girls did not have "premarital sex" (a term we would see as quaint today), not the least because birth control and abortion were illegal, a glaring injustice addressed by the RCSW.

The Royal Commission on the Status of Women

Anderson, Jewett, and Brown all had some connection – as presenters, commentators, advocates – to the Royal Commission on the Status of Women, which represented both the culmination of post-war reformist equality organizing and a transition to new feminist activisms. By 1967, the context was ripe for governmental attention to "the condition of women." More women were working for pay, and feminist reformers were calling for human rights protections and other remedies for social inequality. The select group of women who advocated for a royal commission may have understood gender discrimination, but they also possessed considerable class, race, and political privilege. Liberal cabinet minister Judy LaMarsh pressed Prime Minister Pearson to imitate US president John F. Kennedy's recent commission on women, while Conservative Laura Sabia, president of the Canadian Federation of University Women, put together a coalition of English-speaking women's groups and the Quebec Federation of Women, creating the Committee for the Equality of Women in Canada (CEW). The CEW demanded government action. Sabia sounded militant when she threatened to have two million women march on Ottawa (an idle boast she later admitted), but the CEW's appeal was a measured call for human rights and equal opportunity: the government should "enable women to achieve such excellence in public and private life as meets the standards set by the Universal Declaration of Human Rights."[100] The framing of the equality issue reflected a constituency that was English and French, white, middle-class, and educated, though working-class and labour women had a presence in the CEW through the participation of Canadian Union of Public Employees leader Grace Hartman.

The Royal Commission proved to be significant, not because it offered a radical critique of oppression, but because it legitimized the problem of women's "status," then shaped how that "problem" was defined by the government for some time to come. It was an achievement for liberal, reform-minded feminists, and, in the public eye, a "milestone against which women's equality was measured."[101] For others, it came to represent passé ideas, the neglect of violence against women, and the exclusion of the voices of poor and racialized women.

At the time, Royal Commissions were often mocked as sly efforts to bury contentious issues under mounds of study, with experts testifying at length in stuffy, sleepy meeting rooms. The RCSW, composed of seven commissioners (five women, two men) chosen with respect to region, language, and rural/urban divides, attempted a more popular format in order to hear from the "common" woman as well as the experts. The commissioners travelled the country, encouraged women to come to malls and community centres to speak, solicited countless submissions, and offered anonymous questionnaires in women's magazines. The result was beyond the commission's anticipation: hundreds of briefs, appearances, personal letters, and questionnaires expressed women's views, which jostled with officially commissioned studies claiming more social science–based evidence.

The commission created a public debate about women's "status" unparalleled since the suffrage movement and allowed some women and organizations to air pent-up grievances that challenged the mythical Canada of equal opportunity, affluence, and domestic contentment. Media coverage was initially dismissive: the ghosts of Stephen Leacock and Henri Bourassa stalked the halls of the commission hearings. The commission was nicknamed the SOW commission by smart-alec male reporters who played up testimony they thought was discrediting, trivial, radical, outrageous, and titillating, although a few determined feminist reporters provided more positive coverage. Cartoonists revived the suffrage-era trope of overbearing, hectoring feminists and subservient husbands.

Figure 8.6 (A, B) Echoing suffrage-era cartoons, those portraying the RCSW often stressed hen-pecked husbands and a "humourous" reversal of roles, with men doing domestic labour | A) Len Norris, *Vancouver Sun*, 18 April 1968; B) Everett Soop, cartoonist for *Kainai News* newspaper on the Blood reserve, Alberta. Glenbow Museum, M-9028-1822

The RCSW has been dissected at length, first by its proponents and participants, often keen to justify its value; by feminist onlookers unhappy with its "naive," superficial reformism; and later by academics who have cast a critical eye on its underlying political philosophy, class bias, ethnic and racist assumptions, and cautious reformist outcome.[102] It became known as much for its silences and omissions as its recommendations. Researchers' entry-point into the massive RCSW archive shaped their conclusions. Those who examined official commission documents and briefs have legitimately critiqued these as evidence of its containment within a limited, liberal political discourse of the time. Looking behind the scenes, others have explained why certain political paths were abandoned and the inner ideological tussles between feminist and non-feminist commissioners. Examining women's testimony, still others suggest it opened up a space for women's "civic resistance" to the status quo. I have used women's personal letters to the commission as one window into working women's day-to-day struggles, unhappiness, even outrage; the strong feelings women conveyed revealed the seeds of discontent percolating below the supposedly serene surface of the post-war gender order.[103]

Perhaps the commission can be characterized as a transitional feminist moment, fraught with problems as well as possibilities. As soon as it reported in 1970, the feminist lobby that had demanded it was under critique from other emerging feminisms. The inherent suppositions of the commission about sexuality, the family, and the gendered division of labour would soon be challenged, even within the organization set up to make sure the government implemented its findings, the National Action Committee on the Status of Women (NAC).

Although a primary concern of the RCSW was women's education and employment, a class analysis was never part of its agenda, and labour feminists were purposely omitted as commissioners – a contrast to the similar US commission. Yet, within a few years, women were unionizing in increasing numbers, becoming a force for change. Many commissioners on the RCSW had absorbed prevailing social science ideas about the inescapable "culture of poverty," yet those ideas were discredited with vigour in New Left and Marxist writing of the late 1960s. Also, the commission put immense emphasis on changing sexist ideas and removing barriers to professions, yet, by the early 1970s, other feminist viewpoints urged a more thoroughgoing critique of the racial/ethnic and sexual division of labour.

A lack of class analysis was not the only shortcoming of the RCSW. As Jane Arscott points out, the report took heteronormativity completely for granted, assuming that sexuality was a "private" matter.[104] This, too, would change by 1970. Given statistics showing high labour force participation rates by immigrant women, the report's recommendations for immigrant women were very weak. By using the 1961 census, and assuming most immigrants needed aid "integrating" into the white French-English majority, the report was also soon out-of-date. True, Canadian immigration policy historically favoured white immigrants, barring men and women of colour, but, after the late 1960s, immigration policy altered this long-standing practice. In addition, the report ignored violence against women, yet, within two years, women were setting up shelters for battered women.

Commissioners intentionally papered over class, race, and ethnic differences in the written report, thinking this would create a more positive, unified response from Canadian women. Yet racialized women who testified warned that these divisions could not be ignored. One anti-poverty activist assailed the commission as being run by "well-heeled" women who did not understand how poverty felt. In Nova Scotia, African-Canadian publisher and activist Carrie Best chastised the commission for its failure to reach out to poor, "Indian," and Black women.[105] "Visible minority" women were not visible in the recommendations. The RCSW, critics later pointed out, took whiteness for granted. This inability to think beyond the dominant experiences of white, Anglo and francophone women, and to critically reflect on its own "universalist" concept of gender, became a touchstone of later judgments.[106]

The commission was more forthright about the need to explore Indigenous women's problems. Its stated intention was to address the lived inequality of "Indian and Metis" women, yet it relied heavily on non-Indigenous "experts" talking about Indigenous women, replicating an anthropological tradition that did not sit well with Indigenous people. Not all such research replicated colonial patterns; anthropologist Julie Cruikshank interviewed Indigenous women in Yukon, relayed their views, and, in her report, rejected the old paternalism of white, social work "helping." Indigenous women, she argued, needed to determine their own priorities. Drawing on New Left ideas about using oral history to give cultural power back to marginalized groups, she and fellow anthropologist Jim Lotz raised the issue of colonialism, as did a few other contributors. The commission avoided that word.

Many Indigenous women did not employ it either, but they did use the hearings to protest abominable conditions in their communities, the lack of employment and hope for young people, and the discrimination of the

Figure 8.7 Florence Bird and Lola Lange speak with Indigenous women in Churchill, Manitoba, while on their northern trip | *Take Thirty*, 17 September 1968, LAC, WO#46904

Indian Act, which removed a woman's Indian status when she married a non-Indian. Seen through the Western prism of "rights," the Indian Act was a point of concern for the commission, which recommended immediate legislative changes. Little did they realize that writing gender discrimination out of the Indian Act entirely would prove difficult: indeed, it remains to this day.

Commission head Florence Bird pressed for hearings in the North precisely because she thought this would help tap into the voices of Indigenous women. The northern trip of two commissioners, however, revealed their overly idealistic, "universalist" view that all women shared an empathetic, female connection. Testimony suggested otherwise. Far more settlers than Indigenous women testified; most did not question their own expertise in defining both the problems of and solutions for Indigenous women. Two solitudes of settler and Indigenous women existed in testimony – occasionally breached by white allies critical of Canada's colonial mindset. Some Indigenous women spoke back forcefully to the commissioners, making it clear that they knew what their communities needed: clean water, decent housing, better education, and protection of their culture for the young, whom they feared were losing their cultural bearings.

For all the commissioners' concerns about Indigenous women, they were stuck in some old patterns. Although the word "colonialism" was not in their political vocabulary, by the late 1960s and early 1970s, it was used repeatedly in more left-wing feminist circles. The RCSW recommendations inevitably focused on what the commission thought the government could reasonably do: reform family law, make contraception available (though complete access to abortion was a more divisive issue within the commission), change ideas about women's education, open up the civil service to equal opportunity. These reflected idealist assumptions – that changing ideas would change society – and policy proposals that fit with a liberal, reform agenda. Yet some were still too much for governments: we are still waiting for a comprehensive, federally funded child care system, one of the RCSW's recommendations.

Conclusion

The first twenty-five years after the Second World War were profoundly contradictory, a time of incremental change with potentially radical consequences. If feminism appeared to be in a holding pattern, there were traces of revolt below the surface of everyday life. Human rights discourses offered promise to African-Canadian women in their ongoing struggle against Jim Crow and for racial equality. For African-Canadian women, subject to the ideological legacy of slavery that cast them as both inferior Blacks and sexually denigrated women, human rights seemed at least a starting point for respect and dignity. However, women, as women, were initially considered irrelevant to the human rights project. Two decades of feminist protests that human rights should include sex discrimination did pay off in the late 1960s, altering both discourse and legislative protections, though cumbersome legal processes could prove frustrating to those interested in radical social change.

The Cold War era had a far more negative influence on feminism. If Canadian McCarthyism took a less visible and violent form than the American version, it nonetheless inhibited progressive dissent of all kinds. It fostered a fear of subverting sexual and gender norms, promoted a confining heteronormative, male-headed family, inhibited collaborations of left-wing women, and cast a pall of suspicion over anti-capitalist feminist politics, even silencing women who stepped out of line by sounding communist. During the war, the labour movement had made some initial noises about women's equality, but these remained subdued, both because labour feminists were hesitant to appear too "feminist," but also because communist trade unions with a platform on gender equality were banished from labour federations, foreclosing debate on these issues.

The Cold War atomic threat of human destruction did reinvigorate feminist pacifism. Over the 1960s, the VOW's theorizing about violence and war developed from moral and maternal calls for nuclear disarmament to more analytical indictments of war and gender, economic, and racial inequality. While every new version of feminist pacifism over the twentieth century was fashioned by shifting politics and global crises, there were threads of continuity from anti-war suffragists during the First World War to the WIL and then the Voices. War raised fundamental questions about patriarchy, masculine militarism, poverty, imperialism, and women's oppression. As they organized against war, feminist pacifists concluded that peace was simply not possible without gender and racial justice. In more than one era, maternalism and anti-war work became the midwife of feminism.

The material reality of women's changing work lives was one of the most potentially unsettling aspects of post-war life. The Fordist economy held out some promise of a male-breadwinner family, but, by the 1960s, more working- and middle-class women with families were in the workforce. Women reminded the Royal Commission on the Status of Women that women had *always* worked, though usually as homemakers with little economic security and even less social esteem. The feminization of the workforce represented a shift in the nature and place of women's labour, a profound one that led to a double day of work for women and growing discontent with the status quo.

Feminists looked for a small measure of economic justice in this new reality, taking up old slogans for equal pay and introducing new demands such as maternity leave. Equal pay was one of the most disappointing feminist reforms ever secured – left-wing critics said so even at the time. Largely symbolic, it did not bolster women's earnings significantly or challenge the gendered and racially segregated workforce. Opponents claimed this very timid reform was unworkable and unnecessary, but the more fundamental problem was its imprisonment within "equal opportunity" liberalism and a narrow legal definition even of that. Even new protections for pregnant and married women proved limited, since they did not cover many un-unionized women nor entail paid leave. If the fifties were conservative, it was not just the image of June Cleaver at fault, but the suppression of more radical ideas, a hesitancy to think utopian thoughts that turned gender and social norms on their head. That was soon to change.

9 Liberating Feminisms

On 31 May 1969, Yvonne Piche erected a teepee in Edmonton's Sir Winston Churchill Square, named for a British imperialist and surrounded by settler state institutions: city hall, the police station, the court house. Piche's reclamation of colonial space was a protest about discrimination against, and the lack of housing for, poor Indigenous women. For twelve days, she lived with her four children in the teepee, with aid from people who brought blankets and took her children to school. Out-of-work and a single mother, Piche came from the Cree Saddle Lake Reserve north of Edmonton. Her protest captured the interest of the national media, and, though she received some positive press, the local *Native Voice* suggested that an Indigenous organization, rather than a "one family" protest, should deal with the housing issue, while the *Edmonton Journal* gave space to landlords repeating racist prejudices against Indigenous tenants. Piche later claimed her protest was about far more – human rights, welfare, educational opportunities, and alcohol abuse – but housing was the most visible symbol of discrimination. Her protest was not a one-time expression of exasperation; she was later involved in Indigenous women's organizing in Alberta with her sister Jenny Margetts, a founder of Indian Rights for Indian Women.[1]

Piche's protest was part of the social upheaval that framed 1960s and 1970s feminism. Her disobedient occupation broke with earlier lobbying methods of the Indian Homemakers Clubs, mirroring instead New Left, feminist, and anti-war protests. It also revealed the heterogeneity of the women's movement. Indigenous women were part of a groundswell of activist resistance that drew discursive support from other feminists but, politically and strategically, stood apart from them, as Indigenous women sought their own pathway to equality, autonomy, and dignity.[2] Their protests against discrimination, racism, and colonialism were coupled with determination to rebuild communities, families, and cultures: Indigenous women's equality could not be addressed outside of this decolonizing project.

Indigenous women were not the only group to create their own pathway to feminism. Professional groups, working-class women, lesbians, recent immigrants, welfare activists, African-Canadian women, artists – and more – all organized equality-seeking efforts that overlapped with, but also disengaged from, other feminist groups. Even seemingly cohesive identity-based groups were not of one political mind, as women debated the why of oppression and the how of liberation.

The mainstream media portrayed feminists as a coterie of loud, demanding, ideologically lock-stepped women. It is true that some concepts were shared, common oppressions identified, and protests joined, and, when resistance was voiced in unison, it might be powerful indeed. But feminism was still fractured, heterogeneous, multiple. Historians often gravitate toward organizations, court cases, lobbying, platforms, events – as I do too. While completely understandable, this misses the many nooks and crannies of local organizing, fleeting events, and private spaces where feminism infiltrated but was not named as such. To trace the upsurge in feminism in the late 1960s, this chapter explores new theories re-animating feminism, the arrival of the women's liberation movement, and a few examples – out of many – of turning points and shifts in feminist organizing.

New Theories, New Movements

Feminist theory – an intellectual framework making women's experiences and subordination intelligible – is a historical process. Theories are created, critiqued, and recreated over time, from Wollstonecraft's eighteenth-century radical liberalism and Engels's nineteenth-century indictment of private property to early twentieth-century anti-war feminist expositions on masculinity, militarism, and violence. By the 1950s, medical and anthropological scholarship was casting doubt on theories of biologically determined gender roles, though the idea of inherent male and female differences still had considerable purchase in popular writing. Feminist theorizing about oppression, however, seemed to have stalled after the Second World War, save for the brilliant but scholastic *The Second Sex* by French feminist Simone de Beauvoir, a book that registered only limited Canadian impact in the early 1960s. American communist writer Mary Inman did develop a new theory of oppression tied to the unrecognized value of women's domestic labour under capitalism, but the Communist Party quickly put a lid on her heresy to their Marxist orthodoxy.[3]

Feminist theory could also take unexpected turns. By the late 1960s, feminists were refashioning explanations for inequality, and, like nineteenth-century socialist feminists who relied on Engels, they understood theory to be implicit in making revolutionary change. Because it defined and analysed the forces sustaining inequality, it inevitably prescribed political choices and activity.[4] Theoretical analysis was also a global, national, and local process; ideas from abroad shaped, but did not determine, the distinctive contours of Canadian feminism. Separating theory from activism is almost impossible, but it is useful to highlight some of the seismic shifts in feminist thought.

Given the cultural reach of the American Empire, US feminist luminaries Betty Friedan, Kate Millett, and Shulamith Firestone had cross-border influence: all three unsettled prevailing ideas about femininity and feminism, creating new explanations for the "social construction of femininity, the psychological origins of patriarchy, and the political nature of sexuality."[5] Betty Friedan's 1963 bestseller, *The Feminine Mystique,* challenged the prevailing assumption that women's primary desire was for motherhood and domesticity; instead, she claimed, the post-war suburban home was a form of stultifying confinement characterized by ever expanding (and unnecessary) housework, suppressed sexual desire, and unfulfilled career ambitions. Friedan assumed a direct causal link between ideas and oppression: women's education, the advertising industry, and Freudian psychology were responsible for fashioning the ideological prison of women's subordination. Her message seemed to be tailored primarily for white and middle-class women, yet the book undeniably struck a political chord with women who were deeply unhappy with prescriptive domesticity – as we saw with Rosemary Brown in the preceding chapter.[6]

Having lived through the Cold War, Friedan hid her "Old Left" communist past, but Shulamith Firestone, a transplanted Canadian active in the American New Left, was of a different generational mindset. If Friedan saw popular Freudianism as a cause of women's oppression, Firestone saw Freudianism as a true expression of the patriarchal nuclear family at the heart of women's oppression. Because women's subordination was grounded in their reproductive role, the link between the nuclear family, women, and reproduction had to be sundered. Women might be liberated from the biological imperative of childbirth through test-tube babies and collective parenting, at the time a solution close to science fiction (one taken up in Marge Piercy's futuristic feminist novel, *Woman on the Edge of Time*), but that was precisely what made Firestone's book so enticingly radical.[7]

Patriarchy was also at the core of Kate Millett's analysis of power and oppression in *Sexual Politics,* a bestseller that made the author a minor celebrity in Canada and the United States. Women's problem was not enforced domesticity but rather patriarchy – the power wielded by men over women and children, encoded in all aspects of life, internalized by women, and expressed, most powerfully, through sexuality. Millett both used and critiqued Freud, suggesting that liberation would occur only when the "psychic structure" of patriarchy was overthrown. Even the supposedly "libertarian" writing of radical male writers, Millett showed, was permeated with misogyny: men's so-called sexual freedom was premised on demeaning, violent depictions of women's sexual subordination.[8]

These three feminist texts, all addressing male domination, were not outlier voices but part of a political continuum and movement milieu. Feminists built on the research of 1950s "sexologists" such as Alfred Kinsey, Virginia Masters, and William Johnson, who had already shown that lived sexuality often fell outside prescribed sexual norms. In women's liberation collections of the late 1960s, feminists extended these insights, contesting all manner of gender, sexual, and familial norms: the vaginal orgasm was a myth; Freud had completely misread women's psychology; heterosexuality and the nuclear family were not the natural order of things. Challenges to sexuality were interpreted variously: the Australian libertarian feminist Germaine Greer, popular in the media, preached individual sexual liberation; others looked for alternatives to the heterosexual, monogamous couple/family, while still others advocated celibate separation from patriarchy. What was later termed "radical-feminist" theorizing about patriarchal power, always stronger in the United States than in Canada, was further delineated in countless studies of rape, religion, and pornography, and expressed culturally in poetry, music, art, and fiction.[9]

Canadians, too, generated new theories of patriarchy and male dominance. Rather than arguing, as Firestone did, that women must be free from biological reproduction, Canadian political philosopher and former midwife Mary O'Brien suggested that women's distinct consciousness was a consequence of their reproductive roles. To be sure, patriarchy was still the problem, but it was a product of men's alienation from human reproduction, their attempt to "transcend natural realities with man-made realities." If male supremacy was universal and transhistorical, O'Brien still drew on Marxism to understand how class and sex oppression were related.[10] Canadian sociologist Dorothy Smith pushed historical materialism in a different direction, fashioning a critique of how "malestream" knowledge was produced, and also contributing to what came to be known as "women's standpoint" theory. Echoing across borders, originating also in the writing of African-American feminists, standpoint theories explored how women's distinct world view emerged from their everyday material realities of productive and reproductive work, as these were interpreted by their own reflection and struggles.[11]

What is indisputable is that women were pushing intellectual boundaries, creating the terrain that came to be known as feminist theory. The cross-fertilization of theories was common. The analytics of patriarchy, for instance, were grafted onto socialist theory, and there was renewed feminist engagement with Marxism, especially by Canadians, who, like some British and European women, were refashioning a hybrid Marxist feminism. Sexual liberation was linked to socialism in unconventional Marxist writing that equated sexual emancipation with the totality of human liberation. New Left guru Herbert Marcuse, influential in Canada and the US, called for a liberation of "mind and body" that went beyond an end to alienated labour, encompassing new social values that endorsed "life as an end itself ... the enjoyment of being, the emancipation of the senses and of the intellect from the rationality of domination." Not surprisingly, Marcuse viewed women's liberation as "perhaps the most important and radical" of 1960s social movements.[12]

Marcuse aside, Canadian women often found other Marxist writing preoccupied with paid, "productive" labour or "side-tracked and mystified" in obscure language intended for a rarified circle of the male intellectual elite.[13] Feminists responded by charting new theories, posing entirely new questions. If Marx saw both the production of material goods and reproduction of the working class as dialectically related, why, they asked, had social reproduction – the intergenerational and daily reproduction of people – been studied so little by the left? Housework, for instance, had long been designated women's "natural" role, but, feminists argued, housework was not inherently female, though it was certainly denigrated and undervalued, falsely idealized as "a labour of love." Friedan thought it mindless non-work, but Marxist feminists had an entirely different set of questions.

Maggie Benston, a chemistry professor and feminist activist at Simon Fraser University, penned "The Political Economy of Women's Liberation" in 1967, an opening salvo in an extensive international theoretical debate (in which Canadian writing figured prominently) about women's domestic labour under capitalism. First mimeographed for the New Left as a discussion paper, then reproduced and circulated internationally, "The Political Economy of Women's Liberation" asked what are the material conditions of domestic labour, how does it relate to the gendered division of paid labour, and does it create measurable economic "value" for capitalism? Benston's theory was that housework was a parallel "mode of production," a holdover from pre-capitalist times, but it nonetheless was a "fit" with, and very profitable for, capitalism, since it encompassed the unpaid work of child rearing and family and "emotional" care necessary to reproduce the working class.[14]

Benston's theory sparked intense debate across borders; in Italy, those influenced by her approach called themselves *Benstonistas.*[15] Her writing was critiqued, revised, and reformulated by subsequent Marxist feminists, including those who linked theory with experience, asking how housewives negotiated and understood their daily domestic labour.[16] The important point, however, was the questions Benston and other Marxist feminists posed. Earlier communist and CCF feminists organized women based on their homemaking labour, but they did not fundamentally challenge such labour as women's work or analyse how it perpetuated women's oppression under capitalism. Marxist feminists now did. Moreover, domestic labour became part of a broader feminist discussion of social reproduction, exploring how women, the family, the state, and social institutions figured in the many activities that reproduced the labouring population, day by day, generation by generation.

Other Canadian feminists were similarly connecting Marxism and socialism to feminism, although they were determined to break away from rigid, discredited Old Left ideas. They avidly consumed Juliet Mitchell's "Longest Revolution," first published in the influential British *New Left Review* in 1966. Although Mitchell's ideas were disdained by some male comrades, such challenges were on the wrong side of theoretical history: her work was part of a revolution in feminist thinking. Mitchell drew on Marxism but expanded the "structures" that explained women's oppression to include production, reproduction, the socialization of children, and sexuality. There were contradictions within these four areas, and connections between them; moreover, without transformation of all these areas, emancipation was not possible. Unlike many feminists critical of Freud, Mitchell suggested that psychoanalysis could be creatively combined with class analysis to explore gendered subjectivity.[17]

Feminist writing ran the gamut from scholarly high theory to popular political pamphleteering, though many feminists read both. How do we understand the "mutually reinforcing dialectical relationship between capitalist class structure and the hierarchical social structuring of patriarchy," asked the academic essayists in one book exploring how these two systems, either parallel or intertwined (that itself a big debate), worked.[18] History was plumbed for answers: Canadian sociologist Roberta Hamilton looked back to the seventeenth century to locate the roots of patriarchal thinking and economic production that created the modern family and women's oppression.[19] Not all writing spoke to the initiated. Short, accessible pamphlets, a long-standing socialist mode of education, laid out debates for activists; Charnie Guettel's *Marxism and Feminism* and Dorothy Smith's *Feminism and Marxism* came at theory differently, but they were both intended for movement activists.[20]

Cultural production mirrored political theory. Both *Never Done,* a popular, illustrated history of women's work, and *She Named It Canada,* a comic on Canadian history written for an international feminist conference of Americans, Indochinese, and Canadians in 1969, were heavily indebted to feminist, Marxist, and anti-imperialist writing. In *She Named It Canada,* modelled on a Cuban popular history, colonialism, the search for profit, class struggle, and women's unpaid labour were portrayed as the "real" history of Canada.[21] In the decade that followed, feminist historians, still interlopers in a male-dominated profession, upended traditional categories of inquiry by inaugurating the study of "women's history," an ongoing project of popular and scholarly reinterpretation of Canada.

History was considered essential to theory making: unearthing the past would both subvert the present and help feminists imagine a different future. No author represented this trend better than Sheila Rowbotham, often cited by Canadian feminists as part of their political education. Her writing recovered women "hidden" from malestream histories, but it also sought insights into the origins and shifting grounds of women's oppression. Written for both academic and movement audiences, *Women, Resistance and Revolution* revealed women already *had* a rich revolutionary history, stretching from the well-known Russian revolutionary Alexandra Kollantai to the unknown Stella Browne, a Canadian immigrant to Britain who campaigned for socialism and birth control in the 1920s. Rowbotham's parallel book, *Women's Consciousness, Man's World* was Marxist, feminist, and humanist in tone. The oppression of women, she argued, was fundamentally social and historical, shaped within capitalism, yet women were active agents, always remaking their own history, though not under conditions of their own choosing.

Rowbotham's personal, ironic, and insightful writing brought theory to life, conveying how oppression was felt as a different consciousness. Feminism (contrary to some later critiques of the "second wave") called up uncertainty and openness; it was an invitation to attempt "a perilous, uncertain quest" that moved tenuously from the abstract theorizing to daily life and back again.[22] Rowbotham also captured the utopianism of the moment. When feminists are asked, "what do you want," they reply to men, "we want to reconstruct a new world with you, where peace and truth will reign, we want justice in every spirit, and love in every heart."[23] Her answer might have come from the mouths of nineteenth-century utopian socialists.

Rowbotham saw some similarities between the oppression of women and the colonized: "the cultural take-over, the economic dependence, the identification of dignity with the oppressor" were similar, but comparisons ended there, since colonizers included women "who enjoyed the spoils of imperial domination and were sometime its most vehement defenders."[24] While radical feminists equated the treatment of women with that of racialized/colonized peoples, Marxist feminists more often sought connections between anti-colonial and feminist thought, particularly in Quebec, where "decolonization" theory was prominent in the late 1960s and early 1970s. Imbibing anti-colonial writers Frantz Fanon, Albert Memmi, and Jean-Paul Sartre, Marxist feminists understood Quebec as part of a global movement for national liberation and against colonialism. Feminists insisted women were fundamental to this liberation movement.[25]

Employing theoretical writing on colonialism, patriarchy, and class, Quebec feminists probed the links between women's oppression, capitalism, and colonial structures of power; they analysed ideology and sexual repression too, not as separate from, but rather integral to the capitalist and colonial experience.[26] Unlike earlier Quebec feminists, they were unwavering critics of the church – the religious repression of Catholicism was a destructive force, encoded in the family, itself "un petit l'état dans l'état" (a small state within a state).[27] Quebec feminists Veronique O'Leary and Louise Toupin recall the political zeitgeist of this moment as one in which colonial/racial and gender oppression were theoretically fused: "a cette époque, nous nous considerons comes les nègres blanc d'Amérique" (at this time, we considered ourselves like "les nègres blanc d'Amérique") and "commes femmes, nous identifions le racism dont les Noirs sont l'objet au sexismme que nous subissons" (as women, we identified the racism of which Blacks were the object to the sexism that we suffered).[28] Yet the notion that French Quebec was colonized was repudiated by Indigenous activists who characterized Quebecers as invaders just like any others.

Beyond Quebec, anti-colonial writing did have some impact; some second-wave Canadian feminists credit anti-imperialist ideas and movements such as Red Power as revelatory, aiding their intellectual pathway to feminism. Indigenous theoretical and experiential writing like *Prison of Grass* and *Halfbreed* opened some feminists' eyes to Canada's oppression of Indigenous peoples – although Indigenous activists did not need colonialism "revealed": they lived it.[29] Still, in the first flush of women's liberation in Canada, race figured less prominently than in the American intellectual and political landscape. Canadians adopted the concept of the "multiple oppressions" of race, class, and gender, developed by the African-American activist Frances Beal; this was translated by Canadian feminists as the "double" or "triple" oppression of Indigenous women.[30] Writing by the African-American Combahee River Collective, which sought to "extend Marxism to incorporate an understanding of the oppression of Black women" by looking at the intersection of race, class, gender, and sexuality, also circulated in Canada, although the collective's definition of "identity" politics did not refer to a sense of self (as it often does today) but rather to an explication of multiple oppressions in which class figured strongly.[31]

New feminist theoretical debates unfolded quickly, often with great ardour, since political analysis mattered to the struggle. However, just as nineteenth-century women did not read Mill or Wollstonecraft and suddenly become suffragists, most feminists in the 1960s did not see the light after reading Millett or Marcuse. (Indeed, some attributed their awakening to the inspiration of novels like Marilyn French's *The Woman's Room*.) Most important, social context mattered: feminists were made at the crossroads of new intellectual flashpoints and women's daily experiences of childhood, home, family, education, politics, and work.

Women's Liberation

As women devoured new feminist theories, they were simultaneously creating a movement. By the late 1960s, it had a name: women's liberation (WL). Yet even those involved in the women's liberation movement did not fully agree on what "liberation" meant. To detractors, it was "women's lib"; women's "libbers" became a perjorative epithet. To the media, fascinated

Figure 9.1 Slogans on signs carried by Toronto demonstrators as part of the Abortion Caravan in 1970 distinguished them from previous maternal feminists | Clara Thomas Archives and Special Collections, York University Libraries, Toronto Telegram fonds, ACS 04612

but prone to sensationalizing, it was a noisy expression of young, middle-class women piqued over beauty contests and other trivial issues. Yet these derisive images of WL falsely assumed that all feminist activity fell under this label and likely exaggerated the homogeneity of WL.

American and British historians now question the assumed social narrowness of women's liberation: in Britain, it "reached across a broad socio-economic and age demographic," taking in various "campaigns, identities and experiences."[32] In Canada, too, the WL movement was a collection of localized groups, with different social complexions and political goals. WL was one thing: it seemed new. Women were addressing an old problem, oppression, but they wanted to do politics differently: eschew bureaucracy and hierarchy, use new feminist theory, and tackle unnamed issues, often doing so with disregard for the niceties of post-war femininity. Doffing hat and gloves to appear respectable, like those in the Voice of Women, was not their style. As one WL placard said, "Don't rock the cradle, rock the boat!"

If WL appeared to explode precipitously, it had roots in changes in social and economic life. Increasing numbers of girls and women entering high school, college, and the labour force in the post-war period created a fertile context for revolt. Women's stymied expectations were one impetus for their radicalization. Both students and women already in the workforce could see that the promise of post-war prosperity, mobility, and equality rang hollow for women still shunted into gendered job ghettos, treated as "until" (marriage) workers, paid less, and harassed more.

Other protest movements also inspired WL. American histories often communicate a linear narrative: young women involved in the anti–Vietnam War, civil rights, and student movements, as well as in the New Left, became disenchanted with male chauvinists arrogantly running the show, and left to create the WL movement. While this greatly simplifies the reality, it is part of the story. In the late 1960s and early 1970s, Canadian women participated in an amorphous radical rebellion that included Red Power, countercultural, student, anti-nuclear, and anti-war causes.[33] This was the 1968 generation, whose hopes were expressed in mass protests by youth and workers across the globe. Some were forestalled or ended tragically in repression and massacre, but 1968, as a metaphor, outlook, or sensibility, had a lasting impact on the political imaginary, though its meaning is hotly debated to this day.[34] Feminists took to heart the slogans written on Paris walls, calling for the transformation of not only the economy, but also sex, love, the family, imagination, life: "Be realistic, demand the impossible; the liberation of humanity will be total or it will not be; power to the Imagination; building a revolution is also breaking all the inner chains."[35]

Some Canadian women of this New Left generation were schooled in internationalist religious and political mobilizations of social conscience in both Quebec and English Canada in the late 1950s and early 1960s. They also cut their teeth on anti-nuclear work, the CCF/NDP, the small Young Socialists/Ligue des jeunes socialistes, the Canadian Campaign for Nuclear Disarmament, and especially the Student Union for Peace Action (SUPA), which promoted an anti-nuclear, non-aligned foreign policy abroad and direct action for social change at home. For SUPA, the global and local were inseparable: the "systemic inequalities foundational to the nation-state" could not be separated from the crisis of war and imperialism in the global order that had brought the Soviet and US power blocs to the brink of destruction.[36] SUPA organized teach-ins on the Vietnam War and campus demonstrations for educational democracy, protesting university administrations steeped in the patrician certainty that they should make all decisions, from setting curriculum to firing radical professors. Off campus, SUPA tackled urban poverty and Indigenous rights in experiential community-based organizing.

Rebellion was not limited to university campuses; young workers also questioned authority, including their own unions, as they disobeyed their leadership and went on an extraordinary number of wildcat strikes.[37] Indigenous women were more likely to gravitate toward Red Power, the "revolutionary" Native Alliance for Red Power on the West Coast, or, later, the Company of Young Canadians, a government-funded "peace corps" directing youth protest into community organizing.[38] Generations overlapped in this radicalizing moment. In the Neestow Project, SUPA students who lived on northern Saskatchewan reserves received advice from Malcolm Norris, a socialist Métis activist since the 1930s, while CYC volunteers were instructed by Odawa educator Wilfred Pelletier. A Halifax SUPA youth project led by African-Canadian activist Rocky Jones was supported by Voice of Women members Muriel Duckworth and Pearleen Oliver. Opposition to the Vietnam War drew old and young into common, if sometimes contentious, collaborations. Despite their different politics, young women's liberationists cooperated with their "metaphorical mothers" in the VOW in protests against Canadian complicity in the war.[39]

When women's liberation burst out of this cauldron of radicalism in 1967–68, most women embracing the label were young or middle-aged and white, though not all came from middle-class privilege. Media reports cast women's liberationists as overly zealous, pampered student radicals; as a Saskatoon feminist lamented, "we are portrayed as bra-burning, man-hating, aggressive, hysterical campus freaks."[40] News reporting in the United States and Canada assumed feminism was limited to white, university-educated, middle-class women. This obscured the many parallel equality-seeking movements of poor, working-class, Indigenous, and Black women.[41] The class background of Canadian feminists was more complex than the media implied. Even in universities, the partial democratization of higher education and the Fordist economy meant that working-class and lower-middle-class women, some from ethnic, newly "whitened" European immigrant families, were first-generation students. Designating all feminists as middle-class also obscures the fact that whoever they began as, they could become someone else, their activism shaped by ideology as well as class background.[42]

Many WL groups that started out on university campuses moved into community organizing, drawing together a wider swath of women who saw gender inequality as the last, ignored oppression in the ideological ferment of the sixties. New Left ideals of independence, liberation, anti-imperialism, and socialism influenced the movement, as did the claim that personal as well as social relations must be transformed.[43] On this count, women gave the New Left a failing grade. The first WL "manifesto" published in Canada, "Sisters, Brothers, Lovers ... Listen," written by SUPA women, situated their discontent in the writing of Simone de Beauvoir and especially the Marxist-feminist writer Juliet Mitchell. The manifesto bluntly assailed male dominance within the left: New Left women were expected to "cater" emotionally to the male leaders and do the typing and pamphleteering, yet their "thoughts were not given serious attention until they were spoken by a male." Men were turned into intellectual "father figures," and women who did not fit the feminine mould were marginalized.[44] If this manifesto registered anger and alienation, it did not abandon hope for a collaborative politics of socialist human liberation: "In order to keep the revolution alive, we must act as though the revolution had occurred by our relationships with one another."[45]

Since many WL groups were influenced by Marxism, they demarcated themselves from reformist feminists by citing their left-wing credentials.[46] In *Women Unite!*, the first Canadian WL anthology, a critique of the Royal Commission on the Status of Women (RCSW) declared that equal rights groups endorse a "civil liberty equality" that works "within the system," while women's liberation believed in "fundamental" social change. Recognizing who had the power was a first step: "women are oppressed by an economic system based on the exploitation of many by a few powerful owners and a social system dependent on racial, national and sexual chauvinism ... A few token women ... in corporate board rooms will not and cannot liberate women."[47] As founders of Winnipeg Women's Liberation recall, "we were the noisy group ... [demanding] historic change." While the "status of women" group was linked to the RCSW, women's liberation was founded in 1969 by those with a "socialist or social democratic" perspective.[48]

Trying to maintain a dual commitment to the left and feminism proved difficult when male comrades superficially sympathized with equality but privately denigrated women's political bona fides. When a sexist parody put-down of women New Left Caucus members in Toronto, who "knitted" and "cluck clucked" throughout meetings was leaked, women confronted the three male authors; they demanded respect, but also appraised the parody as evidence of men's failure to understand Marxism. Their male comrades had forgotten that a revolution entailed the humane treatment of each other; the movement needed "dancing and hugging" as well as theoretical analysis. "What we reject about our role is its specialization," they wrote, "not that we're socialized to be sensitive to emotions, but that's *all* we're limited to."

Women's liberation, they said, had helped them realize the "relevance of personal experience ... Marxist positions need to understand the concrete and existential understanding of contradictions as they happen to real people (Speaking of materialism, gentlemen)."[49]

If some women left the New Left for WL, they did not jettison all its ideas. Many embraced the word "liberation" because of its association with the self-determination of other oppressed groups – Third World and people of colour. The comparison may seem a conceit to us now, but the idea that women had to define their own emancipation was in part a homage to movements they admired, if it also evinced naïveté about how women's liberation was profoundly different. Like the New Left, women sought new political modalities that challenged authority-based political hierarchies, and they developed countervailing strategies: rotating leadership and service roles, consensus decision making, decentralization, and an egalitarian ethos that counted paid staff as equals in decision making. Of course, all of this, too, needed coordination and organization.

Along with this effort to re-centre marginalized voices, WL explored how the "personal was political." This slogan has been mischaracterized as a preoccupation with the self. On the contrary, the personal mattered because what society cast as women's individual problems – what women experienced as inadequacy, unhappiness, or fear – actually reflected systemic oppressions. "There are no personal solutions ... only collective action for collective solutions," wrote the woman who coined the term.[50] Politicizing the personal was associated with consciousness-raising (CR) groups: the "raising" part of CR assumed that talking in small, protective, safe spaces would give women the confidence to confront sexism and inequality in their own lives and recognize that these were shared, social problems. CR pinpointed oppressions felt, but not yet named: sexual abuse, rape, abortion, domestic violence, sexist denigration, sexual harassment, and so on. It was empowering for women to give voice to these traumas, not unlike in the Me Too movement. Montreal Women's Liberation insisted CR was not supposed to be "group therapy" but, rather, show how "common experiences" were part of an oppressive "system and structure of society."[51]

Experience sharing might push women into collective action, but it could stall at the personal, leading to "cliquish and undemocratic" groups unwelcoming to women outside existing networks.[52] Consciousness raising of "like-minded" women also reinforced class and race differences in the movement, reinforcing the image of a predominantly middle-class, white feminism, a problem of "narrowing" vision that seventies feminists were not unaware of.[53] When white women extrapolated from their shared experiences, they failed to understand how differently day-to-day oppression was experienced by women of colour in a society characterized by systemic racism.

Moving from personal experience to political mobilization did underpin other women's mobilizations against economic inequality. Two Toronto single mothers who met at their children's summer camp talked about their experiences with an unjust welfare system, then mobilized more welfare mothers through their networks, creating a female-dominated and -run organization, the Just Society Movement (JSM). Combining public advocacy and immediate aid to those ensnared in the morass of the welfare bureaucracy, the JSM became a militant voice for the "self-empowerment"of the oppressed. The JSM avoided formal structure and membership, opting for a non-hierarchical organization, and incorporating children into their meetings and demonstrations. Like Depression-era anti-poverty activists, their politics combined a discourse of "militant mothering" with a radical critique of the economic system. Allied with the women's movement, they joined demonstrations for abortion rights and peace. The connection between women's reproductive rights and class was highlighted by JSM activist Doris Power in her testimony during the 1970 Abortion Caravan protest on Parliament Hill. Visibly pregnant, she told politicians she had been refused an abortion: "low-income" women often found they could secure an abortion only if they agreed to be sterilized.[54]

Women's liberation groups, like the JSM, often created "pop-up" protests: there was militancy, urgency, and spontaneity to many political actions. Facing exclusion or denigration, women rebelled with immediate action: anger produced a potent "collective power."[55] Women remember tapping into a reservoir of bravado many did not know they had, as they acted out street-corner theatre, gave impromptu speeches, organized demonstrations, and wrote pamphlets. When women art students in the College of Art of Ontario identified sexist exclusion, they simply set up their own non-juried show. To correct the lack of feminist voices in the theatre, six Montreal women created Le Théâtre des Cuisines as an instrument of "education and combat" to oppose "l'exploitation specifique des femmes."[56]

Also in Montreal, forty women marched out of a meeting and blocked the street, chaining themselves together to protest Mayor Jean Drapeau's bylaw prohibiting demonstrations. "In 24 hours, we had 50 women from different sectors ... Word got out fast," recalled trade unionist Nicole Therrien.[57] Ninety-seven of the street protesters were arrested. Francophone women then established the Front de libération des femmes du Québec, expelled the anglophone women's liberationists, and broke up into cells (modelled on the nationalist Front de libération du Québec), one of which engaged in "shock tactics." They organized a rally for abortion on Mother's Day, occupied male-only taverns, and disrupted the witness testimony of Lise Balcer during the trial of FLQ members. "The law is shit," they shouted, pointing out that women were still banned from juries in Quebec.[58]

Swift action made temporary allies of divergent political groups. In Toronto, three groups, Toronto Women's Liberation, New Feminists (NF), and Young Socialists joined a demonstration organized by working women from the Ontario Federation of Labour demanding that sex discrimination be added to the provincial Human Rights code.[59] Supporting striking women workers at the Hanes hosiery mill was one project of the Women in the Labour Force subgroup of Toronto Women's Liberation. Invited by some of the militant strikers to provide backup, the Toronto group found itself in disagreement over tactics, not with the strikers but with a Maoist communist party also on the picket line.[60]

Both Toronto Women's Liberation and the NF picketed in front of the Maclean Hunter Building when *Maclean's* magazine published a piece by the recalcitrant defender of "male superiority," Lionel Tiger. The unsympathetic female *Toronto Star* reporter covering the protest claimed the angry and "militant" women threatened to "lynch" the editor, which a protestor flatly denied in a letter to the editor, saying this was patently untrue: they just asked for space to rebut Tiger.[61] Press coverage of women's liberation was often mocking or dismissive, scolding that "bitter, angry" women's liberationists had gone "too far." A *Toronto Star* editorial agreed that equal pay was a sensible demand, but WL promoted the hatred of happily adjusted housewives and all men: this "lunatic fringe of young women" were nothing more than "hysterical, emotional adolescents" whose main objective was to "downgrade men."[62]

As with the *Maclean's* protest, acting on the moment was critical. In Hamilton, those of us active in the McMaster Women's Centre mobilized community women's groups within a week to protest dangerously dismissive comments made by the police about rape, demonstrating at the police station with banners with the rather obvious slogan "No to Rape." Some actions were decidedly performative. Nine women from the feminist paper *The Other Woman* occupied the Toronto offices of *Guerrilla*, an "underground" community newspaper, demanding the editors do a special issue on International Women's Day. The male editorial response proved the women's point that men, like capitalists, would not relinquish power without a fight, since "they immediately called the police – you know the people they denounce as pigs" to eject the women.[63]

Traditional lobbying might be combined with street theatre. The ever-imaginative Vancouver Women's Caucus delivered a brief to the provincial Human Rights Commission, which had yet to prohibit employment and educational discrimination based on sex. While some women lobbied inside, outside the office three women created a political "tableau," very like the dramatic tableau used by suffragists. One woman representing "1959" was decked out in an apron, chained to a stove; the "1969" woman, wearing jeans, held a sign "Freedom Now"; and the "1979?" woman, wearing a suit, also carried a rifle and ammunition, "suggesting the lengths women might go to secure freedom."[64] The performative, outrageous, and ironic in feminist protests, coupled with WL's disavowal of hierarchy, puzzled RCMP informers and infiltrators. Undoubtedly, they scratched their heads at flash-in-the pan groups like WITCH (Women's International Terrorist Conspiracy from Hell) or the Purple Penis Avengers. Trapped in their long-standing obsession with spying on communists, the Mounties searched diligently for "reds" within the movement, but their reports sometimes contained little more than naïve, homophobic, and inane observations. Still, RCMP infiltration had a more sinister side, disrupting personal lives and destroying movement resources.[65]

Disruptions of beauty contests, seared in the public mind as symbols of WL, were only one of many guerilla-like tactics. Women's Liberation in Winnipeg announced its arrival by disrupting a University of Manitoba beauty contest, while the Simon Fraser University Student Society and Women's Caucus sponsored a feminist participant in the national Miss University pageant in Toronto so she could persuade other contestants to pull out, opting to be "a human being" rather than a "beauty queen."[66] Recent feminist writing has acknowledged that race- and class-based beauty contests (such as Miss Indian Princess or Miss Labour Council) offered marginalized women a sense of self-worth,[67] but most mainstream beauty contests – whether or not they offered scholarships – were, and are, primarily corporate exercises in the objectification of women.

Characterizing second-wave protests of beauty contests as inflexibly "judgmental" oversimplifies; feminists argued that they were not condemning the women participants but rather the "big business" exploitation of women as "products," and the promotion of an unrealistic feminine ideal. Even the term "liberation" was being commoditized by advertisers, they realized; used to sell everything from shoes to cigarettes, the latter marketed with the ubiquitous "You've Come a Long Way Baby" slogan.[68] Feminists also used Remembrance Day to make a political point about the violence and rape inflicted on the female body during war. Women laid flowers and gave speeches decrying violence against women at alternative vigils at the Ottawa and Vancouver armistice events. Scripted outside of official ceremonies, these interventions were not appreciated by those in attendance. This blanket indictment of the military is not something we would likely see today.[69]

There was no cookie cutter women's liberation: each group's priorities reflected the immediate context, potential allies, changing issues, and the local leadership (even if there was not supposed to be any). Regina Women's Liberation prepared an eighteen-page brief for the provincial minister of labour in 1972, calling for equality legislation for working women. Thorough, detailed, and comprehensive, it did not emphasize a revolutionary point of view, though other statements by the group were more radical.[70] Yet in the same province, Saskatoon Women's Liberation was forthrightly socialist; it

Figure 9.2 Women's liberationists staged protests to coincide with November 11th to protest violence against all women during wars | Canadian Women's Movement Archives, University of Ottawa, CA ON0034 10-001-S3-I511

began as an "offshoot" of the local Committee for a Socialist Movement but drew in feminists from the university and downtown women's centres as well as the centre for lesbians and gays. When a critical letter to the *Saskatoon Women's Liberation Newsletter* advised the group to tone down its politics, it responded adamantly that Women's Liberation "has always followed a socialist philosophy."[71]

Reflecting its Prairie roots, the Saskatoon group investigated women and the family farm under siege from "agri-biz," publishing a piece that would have made suffragist Violet McNaughton proud.[72] Other groups similarly defined women's liberation in regional terms. Thunder Bay Women's Liberation was initiated by the Canadian Union of Students at Lakehead University then moved into the city and became a more pluralistic entity: the group included "working-class, middle-class, welfare women, old and young, hippie and straight, political and non-political, university students and some not," remembers an early participant. "We did not realize at the time how unique this diversity was."[73] Northern groups like this one saw their politics through the prism of local needs: they spoke for women who were geographically isolated, and thus had fewer job prospects and inadequate social and health services. Close to many Indigenous nations, they also emphasized the importance of Indigenous women's struggles.

Collaboration between disparate groups was more likely in outpost regions or smaller cities. The Halifax Women's Caucus began as a New Left consortium, but absorbed women from the Dartmouth and Halifax New Democratic Party Youth, the Revolutionary Socialist Movement, and the "Rosa Luxemburg co-op." Aided by student organizer Cathy Walker, the organization drew in more "students, secretaries and professors," with multiple goals: public educationals were organized and a daycare planned, and women studied revolutionary pamphlets sent by the Canadian Union of Students and other WL groups. The Halifax group distributed the "McGill Birth Control Handbook," even where university administrations did not want it – for example, at the local Catholic women's college (where fifty copies disappeared within two hours).[74]

Splintering politics were inevitable in larger centres. In 1969, women broke away from Toronto Women's Liberation to form the New Feminists, claiming that the former group was too Marxist. NF, in contrast, would focus on male dominance and ideologies of women's inferiority, and not be "sidetracked ... to fight anyone else's revolution."[75] "Our [feminist] revolution is the most important revolution in the history of human beings," NF declared rather immodestly, and warned that reformist treatment of the "symptoms" of oppression might camouflage the "real sickness" of patriarchy. Making divorce easier, for instance, foreclosed a full-scale critique of patriarchal marriage.[76] Some women's liberationists saw NF as more attuned to "American" feminism, but happenstance, connections, and occupation might lead individuals to one group or another. Sherrill Cheda, a new American immigrant who was married with children and working, attended a VOW benefit for the Chicago Seven and from there went to a WL group, finding the women "very young." She joined the NF, but her political experiences – consciousness raising, demonstrations for daycare and human rights, and work on non-sexist education – overlapped with WL.[77]

Women's liberation was thus a malleable concept rather than a platform or organization, and exchanges between groups, membership fluidity, and of-the-moment collaborative protests were common. Women's centres, often funded by federal Opportunities for Youth or Local Initiative Program grants, were different. They emerged in the early 1970s as broadly based collaborative ventures offering a smorgasbord of feminist offerings, from consciousness raising for high school girls and carpentry lessons to mini-courses on feminism – the dense reading list of the Toronto Women's Centre course on Marxism and women's liberation indicated how seriously the movement took feminist theory.[78] Along with bookstores, coffee houses, dances, sports teams, and more, women's centres multiplied with velocity. Women were claiming safe, empowering space in a social context rife with harassment, regulation, and restriction: bars that did not allow lesbians, streets that were unsafe, clubs and professional groups closed to women, media that disparaged their movement.

Some women's centres set up feminist-friendly referral and counselling services, establishing a virtual "yellow pages" for women,[79] but women's centres might alienate non-white or poor women by implying that women's interests were primarily gender-based. Yet, women's centres encompassed some ideological diversity; women with revolutionary sympathies rubbed shoulders with those more concerned about social services for women. This caused tensions. In Winnipeg, an activist worried that women's liberation, situated within an amorphous women's centre, "lost its political clout"; meetings, she lamented, became unbearable "Ann Landers therapy sessions." Others disagreed, but the concern that highly directed government grants to women's centres might ultimately compromise a radical project turned out to be prescient.[80]

If WL groups reacted to the local, they also had their eyes trained on the global. Imperialism and war abroad figured often in WL and subsequent feminist newspapers. Saskatoon Women's Liberation publicized the struggles of South African women under apartheid and Spanish feminists imprisoned by Franco's fascist regime, while the Winnipeg group's newspaper included stories about the torture of Chilean women by the military junta. Solidarity work might involve joining a demonstration against US aid to the right-wing regime in El Salvador or setting up a more personal connection between a Regina cooperative daycare and one in a refugee camp for Zimbabweans displaced by an anti-colonial war.[81]

Yet the very word "imperialism" also divided feminists: some did not utter it; others thought it essential to feminism. At the United Nations World Conference on Women in Mexico in 1975, liberal feminists linked to the Canadian government refused to support resolutions that called for the "elimination of racism ... and alien domination and the acquisition of territories by force." Other Canadian grassroots and left-wing feminists vocally disagreed, making clear their alliance with Third World and anti-imperialist women.[82]

Like American feminists involved in Third World work, WL groups focused on the oppression women experienced in specific imperialist contexts while also drawing "intersectional" links between racism, imperialism, and women's oppression.[83] Saskatoon Women's Liberation devoted an edition of its newsletter in 1975 to racism (which does suggest that this was not a regular topic), arguing that race and gender oppression were created by similar cultural and economic forces, both traced to capitalism. Pointing out the insidious "Canadian way" of denying racism, even when it was clearly directed against "Native and Black" populations, the editorial concluded that women had to "recognize the need to fight the battle of sexism, racism and capitalism as one and the same."[84] This proposed united front of opposition, however, may have underestimated the very distinct oppressions experienced by colonized and racialized women.

The iconography of resistance by Black and Third World/colonized women displayed in WL newspapers, American historians hypothesize, was used by feminists as "cultural capital" to stress their commitment to revolutionary ideas and counter the trivialization of feminism in the mainstream press, but one side effect was the "orientalization" of the racialized, "radical Other" by white women.[85] Similarly, in Canadian papers edited by white women, resistance to imperialism might be visually represented by a North Vietnamese woman or anti-racism linked to quotations from Sojourner Truth; this symbolism idealized racialized rebels but problematically overlooked racism within the women's movement itself. However, to stress only these representations, interpreted through contemporary theory, may downplay women's emerging comprehension of the theoretical and political connections between imperialism, race, and women's oppression.[86]

WL newsletters and meeting minutes dispute not only the image of a movement preoccupied solely with gender but also that of a structureless one. One American study famously concluded in 1975 that WL's rejection of leadership led to a "tyranny of structurelessness" characterized by unnamed, informal hierarchies.[87] While this may have some truth, since a smaller group of women often directed the key work, feminists' attempts at horizontal participatory democracy did not throw all organization to the wind. Women took minutes, set up internal caucuses, and organized rotating spokespersons. After all, someone had to secure funds and space, set up phone trees, respond to the media, and organize demonstrations. As caucuses, subcommittees, and action groups multiplied to work on specific forms of oppression, there was a healthy, if sometimes contentious, splintering of energies into multiple causes. By the end of the 1970s, the nomenclature of women's liberation was used less, but WL had already shaken up feminist thinking in profound ways.

Reclaiming the Body

Since the nineteenth century, feminists equated emancipation with women's right to bodily autonomy. How that was imagined changed: nineteenth-century white, middle-class feminists believed in voluntary motherhood through abstinence; interwar socialist feminists argued for married women's access to artificial birth control; and, by the 1960s, women's liberationists called for birth control and abortion "on demand." In addition, the right to *have* children, rejecting the forced sterilization of racialized, poor, and disabled women, was added to feminist platforms in North America in the late 1970s, although Canadians were initially less forthright than Americans in making these connections.[88]

Reproductive and lesbian rights are explored below in detail as examples of women's demands for bodily autonomy, yet feminist body politics encompassed far more, including domestic violence, sexual assault, sexual harassment, sex workers' rights, pornography, censorship, control over birthing, and opposition to the masculinist medical, psychiatric, and pharmaceutical establishments. Even if similar concerns were identified by earlier feminists, both theory and everyday organizing shifted, sometimes profoundly so.

Wife battering, for example, was a "moral" issue for temperance suffragists and later a "welfare" or familial issue for experts in the family court system that feminist reformers had pressed for. Despite the fact that women mentioned it in their letters to the RCSW, the issue was ignored in the report; commission research director Monique Bégin now concedes it was one of the commission's major failures.[89] By the early 1970s, feminists were recasting domestic violence as a pervasive social problem, an expression of male power, and a direct cause of women's inequality. Feminists exposed women's limited ability to escape violent mates and how unsympathetic police and courts were to domestic violence. Making the personal political helped to expose wife battering, and the movement's predilection for feminist-run alternative services sparked the creation of shelters. Transition houses appeared in Toronto and Vancouver in 1972; by the end of the decade, there were 63 shelters across Canada, and 264 by 1987. Even rural and small-town shelters that hesitated to name their "feminist" politics were committed to women's equality and autonomy, providing respite for women with no options for safe space.[90]

Over the next decades, the feminist response was "multi-pronged," including service provision, legal reform, and educational advocacy. Feminist unanimity on strategy could be elusive, especially when choices had to be made between always circumscribed political options. Even changing terminology, from "wife battering" to "domestic violence," incurred debate.[91] Because race and colonialism profoundly structured women's experiences of violence, legal reform could easily disappoint, exposing the class, race, and colonial biases in police practices and the criminal justice system. Yet, feminists could agree that domestic violence was a deeply rooted problem, that it had structural causes and resilient rationalizations, and that short-term social resources were needed to offer women protection and choices.

Pornography was somewhat different. Seldom a defining issue for previous generations of feminists, it became hotly debated and viscerally contentious, not least because it spoke to women's realistic fears of violence. Even defining pornography and its distinction from "erotica" proved impossible. If some feminists thought it obvious that porn encouraged violence by celebrating coercion, female subjection, degradation, humiliation, and misogyny, others argued that the regulation of pornography risked censorship by a repressive state, potentially making common cause with right-wing lobbies more interested in protecting traditional, heterosexual, and marital sexuality. Anti-censorship writing included civil libertarian, socialist-feminist, and LGBTQ perspectives, and even feminists with similar politics had profound disagreements over pornography. Liberal feminist June Callwood remembers she could not even discuss the issue with her good friend Doris Anderson, who did not endorse Callwood's anti-censorship, civil libertarian stance. Alternative "positive strategies" that advocated sexual autonomy, choice, and pleasure for all women were lost in the wider public debate; one historical takeaway is that the mainstream media never captured the political complexity and sensitive introspection of feminists wrestling with pornography.[92]

By contrast, feminists found a measure of common ground on reproductive rights, although race, class, disability, and politics still structured divergent experiences and perspectives. In their efforts to reclaim the body, a new cohort of feminists often chose militant disobedience over slow legal reform. Since the early 1960s, the Voice of Women and the New Democratic Party (NDP) had called for revision of *Criminal Code* provisions that made the dissemination of birth control information illegal. Ignoring the law, the Montreal New Left published a how-to guide, "The McGill Birth Control Handbook," and distributed it across the country on campuses and in high schools. In 1969, criminal law reform followed public opinion, legalizing birth control, but abortions were legal only if a woman could prove her mental and/or physical health were endangered to a therapeutic abortion committee (TAC) of hospital doctors – if there even was one in her local hospital.

The WL movement was dissatisfied with a compromise that mirrored the timidity of the RCSW, which had been divided on if, and how, to legalize abortion. With backstreet abortions still a threat, women's liberationists demanded "abortion on demand" and mobilized to skirt the law, undermine it, and protest it. Women set up counselling services to help women negotiate the TAC process, advised women on how to travel elsewhere (including to the United States) if there were no local services, and formed abortion rights groups. Abortion was a political issue laced with strong emotion, as many women had witnessed or experienced the terror of illegality – women risked injury, sterility, even death, and they were forced to leave school and jobs, isolated in maternity homes, or shamed into "going to an aunt's" to hide their pregnancy. Women simply said, no more.

The Vancouver Women's Caucus (VWC) came up with an imaginative tactic: they organized the cross-Canada Abortion Caravan in 1970, an "On-to-Ottawa trek" that demanded women's bodily autonomy and rights. VWC members set out with a van, outfitted with a coffin on top – a symbol of deadly backstreet abortions – with a loudspeaker blaring "We want our revolution" and with the slogan "Smash capitalism" on the side of the van

Figure 9.3 The Abortion Caravan stop in Calgary during its On-to-Ottawa trek. Cathy Walker in van door | University of Calgary Archives and Special Collection

(the latter causing internal caravan debate until it was removed in Regina). The rhetoric and public performance of the caravan captured public attention and mobilized sympathizers along the way, forging a Canada-wide network of abortion rights activists.[93] Caravaners, many active in the anti–Vietnam War movement, adopted the language of war, declaring they would "no longer sit idly by while women died." "We consider the government of Canada in a state of war with the women of Canada," announced their rousing communiqué. "If steps are not taken to implement our demands by Monday, May 11, 1970, we will be forced to declare war on the Canadian government."[94]

Joined by Quebec and Ontario allies, the women rallied in front of Parliament: pointing to the class inequalities in abortion access, placards read "Just Society Just for the Rich," a play on Prime Minister Pierre Trudeau's electoral sloganeering for a "Just Society." They marched to the prime minister's home, past the RCMP, occupied the lawn, and left behind the coffin full of symbolically horrific instruments of illegal abortions. Women then joined an anti-war protest at the National War Memorial, marking the killing of four student protestors at Kent State University in the United States. The following day, as women demonstrated in unison across Canada, the VWC mimicked a suffragette tactic: disguised as "respectable ladies," they chained themselves to the railing of the visitors' gallery of the House of Commons and began to shout at stunned parliamentarians.[95] Headlines across the country typecast protestors as "strident, irate, screaming, angry" women, but the caravan put the need for access to abortion on the front page.[96]

The caravan was only the beginning. As Beth Palmer documents, inequality and inadequacy of access sparked a movement for free, accessible abortion as part of the provision of state health services – unlike the more "individual rights" American legal approach. Politics and strategy were nonetheless hotly debated. Should abortion be a single-issue project framed within broader reproductive rights? Should abortion rights groups mobilize broadly, even with allies with different politics? While the Canadian Abortion Rights Action League/Association canadienne pour le droit à l'avortement mobilized chapters across the country to lobby for legal access as a fundamental human right, some urban groups like the Ontario Coalition for Abortion Clinics confronted lack of access by setting up free-standing clinics. Both challenged the existing law through the courts, but, as Ontario Coalition leader Judy Rebick noted, socialist feminists placed more purchase in "mass action" and collective political struggle.[97] Despite political differences, there was collaboration. Some feminists raised money and pursued respectable lobbying while others took to the streets, defending abortion clinics. As Palmer shows, the use of multiple strategies was tactically useful, allowing political difference and cooperation to coexist in a difficult, but productive synergy.[98]

Class figured in feminist analyses of the issue. Socialist feminists especially positioned abortion within a broader critique of capitalism: abortion rights had to be accompanied by universal health care, adequate welfare, and free child care; otherwise, "choice" was meaningless. The reproductive choice to have children as well as not have children, in other words, "does not exist in a vacuum."[99] Alliances were sought with unions and immigrant women's organizations. Strategic thinking that truly integrated colonialism and racism into reproductive politics came later. The demand for abortion "rights" was replaced by the language of "choice," yet, for Indigenous women with histories of coerced birth control and sterilization, "choice" seemed to be a "privilege not enjoyed by those whose reproductive lives are shaped primarily by poverty and discrimination." Not until the 1990s did the more inclusive concept of "reproductive justice" emerge.[100]

Still, the 1970s movement for reproductive choice was very different from earlier feminist discussions, which might support birth control for families but avoided any discussion of abortion. Moreover, Quebec feminists, previously hesitant to challenge the Catholic Church, now did so without hesitation. The Quiet Revolution, secularization, and radical social movements transformed their discussion of women's bodily rights. How abortion was won is another question, elaborated elsewhere. A 1988 Supreme Court of Canada decision on the case of Dr. Henry Morgentaler, who operated free-standing abortion clinics apart from hospital TACs, solidified a legal right to abortion, but this simply "moved the debate to new terrain," including the struggle for access.[101] Challenging the law was only one locus of resistance. Civil disobedience, defending clinics, calling for social services, protesting in the streets, petitions, and lobbying were all used, reflecting continuity with sixties feminism, both the reform-minded RCSW and direct action of the women's liberation movement.

Lesbian Rights

Bodily autonomy also entailed women defining their own sexual identity, choices, needs, desires, and relationships. New thinking about sexuality was encouraged by radical-feminist theories of heterosexual oppression and Marxist-humanist ideas of sexual emancipation, as well as the less-than-successful sexual experimentation in the New Left. While many earlier feminists consigned sexuality to the private realm, a new generation insisted it was socially organized, ensnared in unequal power relations that were economic, social, cultural, and psychic. These had to be outed, critiqued, changed. Feminists had to reclaim the body from heterosexist ideology: reproduction and sex had to be separated, sexual activity outside marriage validated, and the privileging of heterosexuality challenged.

Similar ideas of sexual emancipation had circulated in dissident but marginal sexual socialist movements since the nineteenth century; now they were openly, unilaterally, and militantly defended. Largely missing in groups dominated by white feminists, however, was a meaningful activist connection between sexuality and race. Black women wrote of the imprint of slavery's legacy on their bodies; their sexuality was cast as "other," promiscuous, their bodily integrity deemed less worthy than that of white women. Indigenous women made a similar point: white feminists did not experience the racist stereotypes of the promiscuous "squaw," the violence this licensed, the internalized oppression it produced.[102] Indigenous women's alienation from other feminists' "body talk" undoubtedly contributed to their own autonomous organizing.

What became blithely known as a "sexual revolution" included multiple challenges to the status quo. Reproductive freedom was one element, but heterosexuality and monogamy were also contested as prescribed "normality." The critique of monogamy was part of a broader, left-wing indictment of marriage, the family, and the commodification of "true love" as women's only or highest goal in life.[103] LGBTQ culture and organizing flourished as never before. Women's queer sexual subcultures, same-sex desire, and sexual and intimate relationships had always existed. In the post-war period, as more women lived and worked away from families, often gravitating toward urban centres, lesbian subcultures became more visible, though lesbians were still reviled and harassed.[104] Emerging lesbian identity, culture, and movements of the late 1960s and 1970s shattered previous private accommodations to heterosexism and homophobia, and instead publicly demanded dignity, recognition, and rights.

A public announcement of one's lesbian identity with "pride, bravado and considerable nose-thumbing" took courage; lesbians faced not only "social prejudice and heterosexist attitudes" but "state mechanisms (laws, courts, police, school systems)" that prevented them from living freely and without fear.[105] Ancient attitudes died hard. When Parliament debated the decriminalization of homosexuality in 1969, some MPs railed about the "perversions" of homosexuals; even those favouring reform labelled homosexuality a psychiatric problem. The more "open-minded" *Chatelaine* may have hinted at lesbian existence, but also veered toward a psychiatric-pathological analysis of lesbian relationships as "immature, neurotic, maladjusted" oddities that were not "natural."[106]

Lesbian feminist theory and cultural expression provided an exhilarating opportunity to create new identities, communities, and political organizing. Writing on "homosexuality" was not new, but how lesbian feminists rewrote theory and history was. Adrienne Rich's theory of "compulsory heterosexuality" exposed the myriad of informal, institutional, and ideological ways in which society validated, rewarded, reproduced, and pressured women into heterosexuality.[107] In the 1970s, the idea of a "Lesbian Nation" emerged: a subculture once "assigned to debilitating secrecy" now forthrightly announced its presence, fortified by "shared symbols, language, ideology, aesthetics."[108]

Yet lesbians were not politically homogeneous: some self-identified as feminists, some not; some gravitated toward radical feminism, others socialist feminism. Lesbian feminists also disagreed – both within the women's movement and among themselves – over which spaces and protests should be women only. There were tensions, as Julia Creet shows, between those who belonged to "an old gay culture," lesbian feminists, and lesbian separatists who wanted to live autonomously from men.[109] Still, the combination of "visible lesbianism with politics," adds Creet, was a ground-breaking, new phenomenon.[110]

Exactly how lesbians should relate to women's liberation was a pressing theoretical and political question. According to an influential Radicalesbians manifesto, the lesbian, as a "woman-defined woman ... does not define herself in relation to men"; lesbianism was thus "at the very heart of women's liberation for only women can create for themselves a new sexuality, sense of self, a new consciousness apart from men."[111] The connection between feminism and lesbianism was often conceptualized as a continuum of oppression: "as long as any woman can suffer political and legal harassment for how she chooses to live her life," wrote the authors of *Stepping Out of Line*, "then every woman faces the same threat ... [Lesbians'] oppression is a more extreme form of the oppression faced by all women."[112] Some heterosexual feminists declared that they too were "women-defined women," opposed to women's oppression, concluding "a true feminist is a lesbian by definition."[113]

Fine words, but lesbians often found the women's movement could be as hostile as the rest of society; relations between straight women and lesbians became "fraught with tension, suspicion and confusion."[114] Frightened of "lesbian baiting," some feminists claimed sexual orientation was a private issue, something to be ignored – a denial that lesbians understandably saw as homophobia. "Despite our feminist activism, I feel as if we are just tolerated during International Women's Day," noted one Prairie activist, a sad commentary on a day of solidarity.[115] If the women's movement was fearful of lesbian issues, gay rights groups were sometimes simply dismissive.

Lesbian-feminist priorities and allies varied across the country. Queer activism in the prairie West, notes Valerie Korinek, was not a story of linear progress: it "came and went," with "liberationist, progressive, and later human rights strategies" all used, sometimes argued by the same activists.[116] Some political lesbians created alliances with feminist organizations; others opted for separate organizing – their own pathway to liberation. In smaller cities, collaborative work with either gay rights and/or feminist organizations seemed the only practical option.

In British Columbia, feminist resolve to build a new umbrella provincial organization with an inclusive political mission eventually encouraged collaboration, though not without angst, tension, and clashes along the way. Created in 1973–74, the BC Federation of Women's mission was to work for "fundamental social change" to "eradicate sexism."[117] Yet lesbian issues were not even mentioned at the founding convention. Lesbians immediately organized their own caucus and initiated difficult conversations within the federation to convince other feminists that male supremacy, heterosexism, and homophobia could not be separated. Although their efforts created intense "conflict and [an] identity crisis" for the organization,[118] education worked: by the next convention, lesbian issues, including the right to child custody and inclusion in the Human Rights Code, were successfully adopted.

Lesbian-feminist politics might also lead to separate organizing and spaces for lesbian cultural, service, and political efforts, such as the Lesbian Organization of Toronto, whose history is detailed by Becki Ross.[119] The economics of lesbian motherhood were addressed by a smaller group, Wages Due, an offshoot of the international Wages for Housework campaign, which had a strong Toronto contingent. Wages Due presented lesbianism within a larger "struggle against capitalism and patriarchy," arguing that all women needed an alternative to the compulsory heteronormative family. Since housewives' lack of power stemmed from their economic "wagelessness," even though they created "free labour" for capitalism (the domestic labour debate in a new form), they should demand wages for housework. This would not only free lesbians from the restraints of heteronormativity but would also provide all women working in the home with freedom from male control. Wages Due, critiqued by socialists and liberals alike as a backward step, pressing women into homemaking, nonetheless led to other important mobilizations, such as the Lesbian Mothers Defence Fund which aided lesbian mothers facing child custody cases in unsympathetic courts.[120]

"Lesbians are everywhere," announced a banner at an International Women's Day march in Toronto. The slogan challenged heteronormativity and proclaimed women's right to sexual autonomy and self-determination; lesbians refused to return to a maligned, closeted existence. Many gays and lesbians espoused "liberation" as their goal, tying their movement to critiques of war, capitalism, state repression, and all hierarchical sexual and familial relationships. This originating radical "liberation" impulse, argues Gary Kinsman, lasted longer in lesbian than in gay milieux, though it was later overwhelmed by more rights-based organizing and accommodation with neoliberal values.[121]

In the 1960s and 1970s, lesbian organizing marked this groundswell of feminism as boundary breaking. As one participant remembered, "lesbian feminism was about taking feminism and shaking it up."[122] Lesbians and "passing" women, argues Anne Enke, played a central role within feminism

Figure 9.4 International Women's Day march in Toronto, n.d. | Photograph by Diana Marmorek. Courtesy of Peter Marmorek

and beyond, revising the sex/gender dynamics of public space by proudly occupying spaces previously structured around exclusion, sexual danger, and heterosexism. The power of laying claim to dignity and equality indicated the immense influence "of the women's movement beyond those institutional actors calling themselves feminist."[123]

Anti-Colonialism and Feminist Advocacy

Media commentary on the Royal Commission on the Status of Women often assumed the "origins" of Indigenous women's organizing for equality emerged with their efforts to challenge section 12(1)(b) of the 1869 Indian Act, which stripped them and their children of all rights as "status Indians" if they married non-Indians or, more rarely, if their status Indian husbands enfranchised. In a cruel double standard, white women marrying Indian men became "Indian." As Six Nations lawyer Kathleen Jamieson pointed out, this clause had a multiplying, destructive impact: an Indian woman had to leave her parents' home on marriage, and she could not own or inherit property, participate in the band, be buried with her forbearers, or return to her family, even if "she is in dire need, very ill, a widow or divorced."[124]

The testimony of Mary Two-Axe Earley and other Indigenous women before the RCSW placed this discrimination in the public spotlight. Thirty women from Kahnawake crowded into the Royal Commission hearing room, accompanied by supportive NDP leaders Grace MacInnis and Thérèse Casgrain. The women spoke of their fears of eviction and the indignity of having their identity denied. Earley noted that dogs could be buried on the reserve, but she could not, and Charlene Bourque, a brave fifteen-year-old whose mother had lost her status, spoke of being caught between two worlds. She was bussed to a "white" school, where she was not welcome, yet she had no educational rights on the reserve. The Indian Act, she testified, "has made me nothing ... I want my rights, I want my heritage. I am very proud that I am an Indian and that is what I am in my heart."[125]

The RCSW report and feminist organizations called for changes to the "marrying out" section of the Indian Act, but it was Indigenous women's organizing that propelled the issue forward. Court cases brought by Jeannette Corbiere Lavell and Yvonne Bédard became focal points for this anti-colonial, feminist struggle. Corbiere Lavell, from the Wiikwemkoong Nation on Manitoulin Island, launched the initial case. When it reached the Supreme Court of Canada, it was merged with the case of Yvonne Bédard, a Six Nations woman who had lost her status and was not allowed to live in the reserve house bequeathed to her by her mother.

Figure 9.5 Mohawk women presenting a brief to the RCSW. From left, Betty Deer Brisebois, Charlene Bourque, Mary Two-Axe Earley, Cecilia Ouimette | *Ottawa Citizen*, 3 October 1968, Courtesy Post Media

A veteran of the Company of Young Canadians (CYC), Corbiere Lavell, then involved in the Indian Centre in Toronto, was shocked to discover that she had been removed from band membership when she married a non-Indian, even though her history and identity were thoroughly "Indian": "I believe that a person who has been brought up on a reserve, who speaks an Indian language and considers herself an Indian is Indian ... My home, my parents and my grandparents are there and my friends ... They are all my people and they can never take that away from me."[126] Corbiere Lavell and Bédard argued that gender discrimination in the Indian Act contradicted Canada's Bill of Rights. Although the women were encouraged by a win in a lower court, in 1973 the Supreme Court of Canada narrowly declared against them, ruling that the Indian Act was exempt from the Bill of Rights.

Figure 9.6 When the Supreme Court ruled against Jeannette Corbiere Lavell (front left) and Yvonne Bédard's claim of discrimination in 1973, women protested in a number of cities. Edith McLeod is front right | University of Ottawa Archives, Canadian Women's Movement Collection, CA ON0034 10-001-S3 I 1367

Indigenous women's resistance extended far beyond this legal strategy. Focusing too intently on the Indian Act, argues Sarah Nickel, leads to "Indian Act myopia," obscuring both Indigenous women's previous organizing and many other sites of struggle in the 1970s and 1980s. Indigenous women's politics were shaped by their immediate experience, Indigenous cultures, national mobilizations, and transnational ideas, including feminism. It defied easy categorization, for like the broader women's movement, Indigenous women expressed "degrees of multiplicity across organizations, communities and positions," taking in various permutations of anti-colonial, feminist, and maternalist ideas.[127]

Like the New Left, Indigenous peoples were influenced by transnational mobilizations of the late 1960s; ideas about Red Power, personnel from the American Indian Movement, and the Canadian newspaper *Akwesasne Notes* all traversed the forth-ninth parallel. An international Indigenous conference in New Mexico in 1971 connected Canadian Indigenous women to other anti-colonial groups. Indigenous women also received a political education in the Native Alliance for Red Power, the Canadian Indian Youth Council, and the CYC, all of which kindled anti-colonial politics. There was interchange with socialist groups, which had historically paid little attention to internal colonialism, but now could not ignore the importance of Red Power.[128] Even the tamer CYC facilitated rebellion; its Indigenous projects focused on community development, but the "larger plan" was to "confront the elements of white society which have oppressed [Indigenous people] for so long and to change their manner of relating to native people."[129]

Two CYC volunteers helped to set up the Ontario Native Women's Association, and the CYC-sponsored northern Ontario newspaper, the *Kenomadiwin News,* put women's issues at the forefront. Edited after 1969 by Elizabeth Morriseau, the *News* covered the Corbiere Lavell–Bédard case and issues farther afield, including an exposé of reproductive rights and racism that was prompted by an NDP MP accusing the government of the forced sterilization of Inuit women.[130] The Ontario Native Women's Association, open to all Indigenous women, with status or not, was featured in the *Kenomadiwin News* as a major step forward; the group's extensive reform program, focusing on "the home, children and the family" as well as cultural preservation and social rights, was reprinted in full in the paper.[131]

Urban Indigenous women had for many years been involved in essential community-building projects that aided newcomers to the city, preserved identity, and solidified belonging, but their roles now shifted.[132] Since the

1930s, Métis women in Regina and Saskatoon had played an essential but supportive "background" role in Métis organizations, argues Cheryl Troupe, but, by the 1970s, they were "more organized, more vocal," more "involved in political organization," more likely to "assert their own political will," even in opposition to their own Métis organization.[133]

In 1972, the newly established Saskatchewan Native Women's Association navigated its own pathway between feminism, Indigenous rights, and Indigenous women's needs. While rejecting the label "women's liberation," it fought for improved conditions for women – daycare, education, social services – as well as treaty rights. The following year, the organization organized a sit-in of the federal Department of Indian Affairs (DIA) offices to protest its parsimonious refusal to fund women's education in domestic science courses. While the protestors secured DIA funding, they were unhappy that the Federation of Saskatchewan Indians, presumably allies, accepted the DIA's claim that the women stole money and wrecked an office machine. Without even hearing their side of the story, the women complained, the federation agreed the women should be "punished."[134]

Indigenous women on reserves had long played roles as community builders and organizers. After the Second World War, their collective voices for change were quietly nurtured in reserve-based Indian Homemakers Clubs and, in the Maritimes, Antigonish University community development programs for Mi'kmaw women. Established in 1937 to survey and improve women's homemaking skills and harness their voluntary labour, the clubs were a Federal state project of "assimilation, integration and citizenship."[135] By insisting women could "improve" inadequate domestic skills and family life, both the clubs and community development implicitly blamed women for problems that were material, structural, and colonial in origin. Indigenous women, however, used the clubs to generate locally-based knowledge about community needs, preserve Indigenous culture, and advocate for the reform of reserve health, housing, and education. As clubs and community development efforts became sites of "activism and agency," women reclaimed traditional social and political influence, redefined their economic roles, and embraced discourses of rights and knowledge that countered colonial versions of Indigenous womanhood.

As these organizing efforts flourished in the post-war period, they laid the groundwork for a different brand of politics in the 1960s and 1970s. In 1968, for instance, recognizing that the state objected to their increasingly vocal role as a "pressure group," BC Indigenous women created a new British Columbia Indian Homemakers' Association (BCIHA), from existing clubs, and the British Columbia Native Women's Society, a broader coordinating group with both individual and club membership. These organizations were outspoken about the need to rebuild the material basis and cultural bonds of family life, but they did not see "family issues," often equated with women, as divorced from treaty, sovereignty, and Indian Act ones, associated with "male" organizations.[136] The BCIHA newspaper, the *Indian Voice,* condemned the paternalism and neglect of the DIA but, at times, also the failure of some male-dominated Indigenous organizations to understand the day-to-day realities of women and children, including multiple forms of violence.

Indigenous women's engagement with male-dominated Indigenous organizations was often based on both collaboration and critique: collaboration in pursuit of a (sometimes elusive) pan-Indigenous anticolonial unity, yet selective critique of political decisions that discounted mothering, family needs, and gender equality. Although the BCIHA had joined with the BC Chiefs in resolutely rejecting the government's White Paper of 1969, for instance, the Homemakers' and BC Native Women's Society's expansive membership model, including all Indigenous women irrespective of status, meant they were more sympathetic to discussions of revisions of the marrying-out clause of the Indian Act.[137] When the Union of BC Indian Chiefs decided to refuse federal funding in the name of pushing ahead its sovereignty-based project, BCIHA women pushed back, even asking the DIA for help. It would be "innocents" – children, the disabled, the poor – who were "caught in the crossfire" of this rash decision, they claimed.[138] The BCIHA was carving out a distinct politics, rooted in the daily needs of Indigenous women and their communities, critical of both colonialism and those who would deny Indigenous women's birthright.

The BCIHA's dual vision of anti-colonialism and advocacy for women's needs was common in many Indigenous women's groups, but women protesting the marrying-out clause faced criticisms that they were interested only in the latter at the expense of the former. Their demands were equated by some Indigenous men with a liberal, "equal rights" feminism that was Western, individualist, and alien to Indigenous cultures. The National Indian Brotherhood (NIB), representing status Indians, feared the Corbiere Lavell court case would undermine their distinct status recognized by the Indian Act and prevent "Indian" organizations from using it as a "lever" in negotiations with the state, especially at a time when the White Paper threatened their very existence.[139] However odiously colonial the Indian Act was, the NIB argued, it should be altered only with the consent of First Nations;

moreover, since colonialism had caused gender inequality, only decolonization would solve it. Indigenous women countered that this perspective erroneously assumed all pre-contact Indigenous communities were egalitarian, reminding their critics that "tradition," a flexible concept, had also been used to justify gender discrimination.[140]

The debate about revising the Indian Act never aligned simply along male-female lines. Discussion of the "marital issue" was testy at the first two national meetings of the emerging national native women's organization. The Alberta Native Women's Society claimed the patrilineal assumptions of the act did not contravene all Indigenous cultures, while others echoed the concerns of the NIB: the collective will of First Nations should outweigh women's individual rights established by a Canadian court. In 1972, a representative to a national gathering in Saskatoon was critical of women like Corbiere Lavell who made the decision "to marry a white man," then "turned around" and pleaded "discrimination." The real concern was treaty land – adding new members, this critic warned, meant the very existence of "reserves [was] at stake." Corbiere Lavell herself agreed that "preserving Indian land" was a priority, and both sides believed bands should be self-determining, but lobbying the state to alter gender discrimination in the Indian Act was a more divisive question.[141] Tensions filtered down to provincial and local Indigenous organizations. In Alberta, Jenny Margetts, Christine Daniels, and Nellie Carlson, all from Saddle Lake but living in Edmonton, all active in Indian Rights for Indian Women (IRIW), remembered they became further alienated from their home community and encountered daily hostility: "We were followed everywhere, our phones were tapped, our mail was confiscated, our lives were threatened, simply because we said, We are Indian women of Canada and we lost the rights that we were rightfully born with."[142]

Indigenous legal scholar Mary Ellen Turpel, however, believed that relying on Parliament to amend the Indian Act was dangerous: it undercut the cultural autonomy of Indigenous nations, threatened their right to self-determination, and prioritized the individual over the collective.[143] Yet women fighting the marrying-out clause were part of a larger pan-Indian "nationalist" and cultural resurgence; their fight was not for equal rights with other Canadian women, but for the same rights as other "Indians," against a patriarchal colonial order forced on Indigenous nations.[144] Women, like Indigenous nations, had been "dispossessed": they too wanted self-determination, negotiation of treaty rights, cultures preserved, and social investment in their communities, but they argued that Indigenous women's rights were "existing rights," foundational in Indigenous nations, which could not be simply "extinguished" by a colonial state.[145]

In part because discrimination in the Indian Act resonated as an equal rights idea, many feminist groups threw their support behind IRIW (which only confirmed the view that the IRIW represented Western feminism). A *Chatelaine* article lamented that "Indian women" were the most "unequal in Canada," and celebrated women's efforts to change the Indian Act and secure resources such as clean water for their communities.[146] Feminist support did sometimes move beyond the discursive, percolating through actions of support and solidarity. The Thunder Bay Women's Centre raised money to send Corbiere Lavell to a crucial 1971 Edmonton meeting, and, when her court case was lost, they co-sponsored a "National Day of Mourning" at the Indian Friendship Centre to "mourn the death of the Bill of Rights." A funeral procession headed from the centre to city hall to lay a wreath, later appropriately placed at the doorstep of the DIA office.[147] In Vancouver and Toronto, too, settler women demonstrated against the court decision alongside Indigenous women.

After the defeat of the Corbiere Lavell–Bédard case in 1973, Indigenous women refocused their political and legal strategies and redoubled their efforts. Sandra Lovelace, a New Brunswick Maliseet woman from the Tobique First Nation who had lost her Indian status when she "married out," put the issue of the Indian Act before the United Nations Human Rights Committee. Although it took years, the UN duly informed the Canadian government – not surprisingly – that the clause contravened women's human rights. Like earlier Indigenous activists, women used international organizations and meetings to shame the Canadian government, in hopes that this would alter a domestic stalemate.

Indigenous women's political organization blossomed as part of a resurgence of Indigenous anti-colonial activism: from 1969 to 1974, eleven new regional and provincial Indigenous women's organizations emerged, most with a mandate to nurture culture and language, attend to family and children's needs (especially addressing child removal), and work to address women's lack of access to employment, education, and social services. In 1973–74, a new national organization, the Native Women's Association of Canada (NWAC), open to all Métis, Inuit, and First Nations women, was established. The thorny issue of the Indian Act was managed with a smart solution: a separate organization, Indian Rights for Indian Women, was mandated to specifically fight Indian Act gender discrimination, though NWAC and IRIW had some overlapping memberships and leaders.[148]

The proliferation of Indigenous women's organizing reflected new political awakenings, but also channelled women's long-standing responsibilities for community care and advocacy into activist projects.[149] While Indigenous women often described their advocacy as "social" rather than "political," their extraordinary voluntary labour was inherently "political." They often justified this work using the discourse of "Aboriginal motherhood."[150] "Mothers of the nation" countered the derogatory view of inadequate mothers long voiced by the DIA, stood apart from perceptions of Western feminism, and complemented the fight of the male Aboriginal leadership against colonialism. Women's leadership roles, suppressed by racist colonial laws and practices, as well as women's long-standing contributions to cultural survival – whether as clan mothers or community leaders – were being reclaimed."[151] Indigenous discourses of motherhood, as Sarah Nickel so aptly shows, were not of one piece, varying across organizations, individuals, and circumstance. They might reinforce women's familial responsibilities in a very heteronormative, even patriarchal, sense, but they were also employed as feminist critiques of male political dominance in the Indigenous rights movement. Indigenous women underwent their own process of "consciousness raising," strengthening their collective demands for dignity, equality, and Indigenous sovereignty. The concept of motherhood, "folded into their feminism,"[152] was employed strategically, but it also embodied the deeply felt sentiments of Indigenous women – not unlike the combination of strategy and feeling that characterized the VOW's maternalism. Unlike those mothers, however, Indigenous women often had their children taken from them by the state, perhaps making their maternal claims all the more powerful.

If we put too much emphasis on women's legal organizing and national organizations, as important as they were, we can miss the nooks and crannies of local mobilizations that reflected a burgeoning Indigenous women's movement that drew on historical roles but voiced new political goals. In Roseau River, Manitoba, Anishinaabe women organized to address dire living conditions on the reserve and their harmful effects on children. Faced with "apathy and indifference" from those with the "power and money" to change these conditions, women decided to "take action ourselves." Ignored by the band council, they formed the Roseau River Women's Organization and raised funds to build a community centre that would provide resources for children and "hope" for their future.[153]

The Tobique Women's Political Action Group in New Brunswick expressed its loss of faith in both the DIA and local government in more militant fashion. Members occupied the band council office for four months

Figure 9.7 Banners at an International Women's Day march protest the removal of Indigenous children and forced sterilization | Photograph by Johanne Pelletier, Canadian Women's Movement Collection, University of Ottawa Archives, CA ON0034 10-001-S3-I317-I320

after their efforts to address women's substandard housing and homelessness went unanswered. Women's homelessness was exacerbated by the "marrying-out" clause; those women who returned to the reserve after divorce or to escape abuse, often as single mothers, found that they had no housing rights. The DIA could claim that women without status did not deserve assistance, and the band council could point to its lack of federal funding to address the issue; the upshot was women left in an untenable situation. The occupation temporarily created a volatile and divided reserve, but women's plea for action also garnered national attention, which was heightened two years later when New Brunswick women organized a 100-mile walk of women and children from Oka to Parliament Hill.[154] Another long-distance trek, protesting child removal – the "sixties scoop" – was undertaken by BC Indigenous women, along with male allies, in 1980. A Children's Caravan travelled from the Okanagan Valley to Vancouver, demanding that the provincial minister of human resources place child welfare under band control to stem racist child removals and disregard for Indigenous families. First Nations women's experiences made them acutely aware of connections between Indigenous dispossession, the marrying-out clause, and loss of their children, all of which were linked to patriarchal colonialism.

Indigenous women also organized to aid urban women and children escaping violence and homelessness. Despite the best efforts of feminists to redefine domestic violence, they continued to face denials and flippant derision; in 1982, NDP MP Margaret Mitchell faced laughter and jokes in the House of Commons when she spoke about "wife abuse."[155] However, Indigenous women experienced violence differently, in the context of pervasive racism and a history of colonialism. On one hand, assimilationist policies, particularly residential schooling and child removal, had long undermined familial relationships; on the other, Indigenous women contended with a racist society that rendered violence against them normal and acceptable. In its most vicious expression, murder was tolerated and went unpunished.[156] While feminists' new thinking about familial violence was not limited only to a critique of patriarchy, this was one strong theme; yet, for Indigenous women, prioritizing gender conflict over race, poverty, and the Indian Act, did not make sense. Federal Indian policy, residential schools, child welfare, cultural denigration – all these contributed to the violence experienced by Indigenous women.

Indigenous women "applied their own analysis of women's oppression to grassroots service" by and for Indigenous women.[157] Sometimes with the aid of other Indigenous organizations, they organized shelters that recognized the needs of women leaving reserves who wanted to preserve their cultural identification and who worried – with cause – about their children being taken away. In Thunder Bay, Anishinabequek, the local chapter of the Ontario Native Women's Association, established Beendigen, a shelter for Indigenous women and children in crisis. Anishinabequek activists worked with local feminists involved in a parallel shelter initiative, though they nurtured two autonomous projects. If their approaches differed, Indigenous and non-Indigenous women shared common problems: insecure funding and difficulty aiding women disadvantaged by poverty, class, and homelessness. As Nancy Janovicek shows, a similar pattern of separate and cooperative work existed in Kenora, Ontario, where Indigenous and non-Indigenous women organized a conference in 1975 to address racism, race relations, and inequalities between women, and then worked temporarily on a common women-in-crisis project, with the support of the Kenora Native Women's Association.[158]

Indigenous women also linked violence to economic development. Testifying before the Berger Inquiry into northern oil and gas pipelines, they conveyed their strong connection to the land, fears of increased violence against women with an influx of resource workers, and the failure of planners to consider the economic security and jobs of local women.[159] One witness at Fort McPherson, in the Northwest Territories, made the point directly: "I worry about my own girls when I hear that 800 men might be in a camp." Male-dominated governments and businesses, she testified, "make the decisions" about development, but it is women who face the brunt of resource development, including violence, fear for their children and loss of traditional values.[160] Development and "modernization," northern Indigenous women found, were recipes for multiple assaults on women's traditional rights – the violence done to their land-based way of life was coupled with violence against them as Indigenous women. As Patricia Monture was to point out in an influential essay, "violence" may be defined quite differently for Indigenous women, inseparable from the violence of colonial dispossession and denigration.[161]

"Feminism" remains a contested word in Indigenous women's writing. Some critiques of "white feminism" repudiate any concept of emancipation that fails to confront the power of colonialism in shaping both Indigenous and settler women's lives. Other critics equate feminism with a disparagement of mothering and the family, or characterize it as "liberation from male domination," an individualist concept incompatible with Indigenous women's needs and belief systems, and antithetical to the collective project of Indigenous rights.[162] Certainly, critiques of the family associated with the first flush of women's liberation writing did not sit well with Indigenous and other racialized women whose families had historically provided some refuge from racism. The publication of Indigenous women's memoirs and cultural creations in the seventies, including *Halfbreed* and *In Search of April Raintree,* highlighted how different their life experiences were from those of white women, again explicating why they pursued separate political pathways.[163]

Aboriginal feminism, suggests Joyce Green, in a more affirmative vein, offers both philosophical and political means of resistance: "feminism takes gendered analysis seriously as a social organizing process, recognizes multiple feminisms, critically explores women's subordination and uses a feminist analysis to counter colonialism and racism."[164] Since the 1970s, North American Indigenous feminists have drawn selectively on feminist "critical theoretical approaches" while challenging other feminisms to think more critically about colonialism.[165] Indigenous women's cultural, personal, and political excavations chipped away at the dense layers of colonial thought and practice, questioning everything: how Indigenous "tradition" has been used and misused, the collective tissue of heteropatriarchy and colonialism, and the possibility of new histories that "re-feminize [Indigenous women's] original being."[166] Like other feminists, they were engaged in a project of historical recuperation. Sarah Nickel's historical recovery of BC Indigenous women's organizing captures the multiple dilemmas and achievements of their political labour: she acknowledges both the collaborations *and* "fraught" relations with settler feminisms and male-dominated Indigenous organizations; however, her analytical focus is on Indigenous women's refusals, resistance, and demands for recognition as they constructed their own distinct Indigenous feminism.[167]

Despite accusations that feminism was not authentically Indigenous, women's organizing was grounded in both Indigenous cultural traditions and different blends of anti-colonial, anti-capitalist, and feminist ideas.[168] Women were reclaiming status, roles, and rights that had been abrogated by patriarchal colonialism and capitalism, also internalized in destructive assaults on Indigenous women's well-being. For all the Indigenous women's movement's differences from other women's movements, there was a shared sensibility: this was not a politics of either difference *or* equality, but rather a vision of far-reaching social transformation.

Creating a Counterculture: Feminist Newspapers

When five Toronto lesbians founded *The Other Woman* (*TOW*) in 1972, with no resources other than talent and commitment, they were creating both queer and feminist culture. The first edition of *The Other Woman* had two articles on lesbianism, seen as "too much" by some, but part of *TOW*'s mission was to provide space for lesbian and radical-feminist voices. When it was first established, wrote Pat Leslie, one of the founding five, the paper was created with "volunteer labour, paid for out of pocket ... We wanted support from the women's community and women outside women's groups. It was not meant only to be read by so-called radical feminists."[169]

The Other Woman was one of many feminist newspapers, nestled inside a broader cultural project that had historical antecedents yet new dimensions. Like suffragists, feminists used drama, literature, and satire to make their point; like socialist-feminist cultural producers of the 1930s, they connected feminism to class exploitation – indeed, Dorothy Livesay's writing connected thirties radicalism to second-wave feminism. Continuities aside, the explosion of feminist cultural production was remarkable for its breadth, geographical reach, and diversity of form. Music, including women-only festivals, literature, theatre, satire, comedy, documentary and feature films (given support through Studio D, the women's film unit of the National Film Board), newspapers, magazines, comics, calendars, posters, visual art, and more: all were part of a textual and visual project that fused culture and politics in a new movement culture. Culture played a crucial role in creating a "feeling" of feminist resistance: a deep, emotional sense of anger, entitlement, struggle, justice, joy in the face of immense opposition. Feminist cultures of the 1970s provided bonds that tied women together yet also a space that exposed sharp, sometimes irresolvable, differences.

New feminist and left-wing publishing houses multiplied. New Hogtown Press began in 1968 as the "press of choice" for women's liberation and the New Left, issuing short pamphlets on everything from Indigenous protest to the WL movement for as little as ten cents each – political dissemination, not profit, was the goal. Vancouver's Press Gang Publishers, founded as a collective in 1970, became a women-only feminist and anti-capitalist press by 1974. Founded in 1972, Women's Press (previously Canadian Women's Educational Press) produced fiction, graphic novels, scholarly works, children's books, and popular anthologies. Founded just over a decade later were Sister Vision Press, committed to publishing women of colour, and *Tiger Lily: A Journal by Women of Colour,* a magazine for racialized, immigrant, and refugee women. More than one feminist press produced a popular, annual women's pocket calendar/diary featuring "herstory" vignettes to counter "mainstream" male history.

Prioritizing one cultural practice over another is, admittedly, problematic. Feminist filmmaking – including works from Studio D – likely reached a larger audience than poetry or theatre, but were the latter any less important?[170] How do we tease out the linguistic, class, and ethnic variations in feminist cultural expression? Examining one cultural form may occlude the connections between cultural strategies, not to mention the cultural dimensions of political campaigns. One performative strategy of the abortion rights campaign, for instance, was "public testimonials" in which the inadequate law was put on mock, public trial. Street theatre was used in Vancouver: as women marched to the courthouse, they enacted street corner riffs on therapeutic abortion committee meetings, exposing the class bias and hypocrisy of these "private" medical judgments.[171] Guerrilla theatre became an integral part of the Abortion Caravan's cross-country meetings.

Artists mobilized to support feminist campaigns, and activists developed new cultural strategies to invigorate struggles and extend public awareness. During the 1985 Eaton's strike, for instance, an "Eatons Boycott May

(A)

Figures 9.8 (A, B) New cultural production was part of the women's liberation movement. Feminist presses published children's books, graphic comics, day calendars, poetry, political pamphlets, fiction, non-fiction, and more | A) *The Day The Fairies Went on Strike* (Press Gang Publishers, 1981); B) *She Named It Canada* (Corrective Collective, 1971). Thanks to authors Linda Briskin and Maureen Fitzgerald and former members of the Corrective Collective

(B)

Extravaganza" at Toronto's Massey Hall featured countless writers and musicians, including satirical songstress Nancy White, who performed a biting sketch of the unappealing Lady Eaton, while local actors, the Eaton's Part Time Players, embedded with the strikers for a week, producing a short drama from the picket-line point of view.[172]

Since feminist newspapers were regionally, topically, and linguistically varied, they offer a revealing slice of this vibrant movement counterculture. Feminist columnists and commentators in the mainstream media – Michele Landsberg, Lise Payette, and others – were important popular educators for feminism, but there was also a veritable explosion of alternative feminist print culture. By the mid-1980s, approximately forty magazines and papers had been created, offering both an external "public sphere" for education and internal movement space for political dialogue.[173] Feminist papers attempted to rewrite history, create new political networks, incite debate, and forge an "imagined feminist community."[174] In contrast to suffrage-era papers or CCF women's columns, they permitted both sharper internal debate and more intimate, personal narratives. Some were raucously "performative" in nature, pushing the envelope of staid journalistic decorum.

Many feminist papers were committed to a collective, grassroots journalistic practice, consensus decision making, sharing authority, and encouraging women with less privilege to contribute. Run on a financial shoestring, fuelled by love and commitment, they were plagued by budget shortfalls, volunteer burn out, political disagreements, and the pitfalls of structurelessness. Not surprisingly, the average run was only seven years. Although some used government grants to kick-start their operations, this aid was sporadic, faded over time, and could potentially tie their hands editorially.[175] This cornucopia of feminist offerings had one common goal: to be an alternative voice, countering the marginalization, trivialization, sensationalization, and co-optation of women's issues. In the mainstream press, Eleanor Wachtel noted sardonically, women had to be "beautiful, have an important husband, be victimized, show ability as a homemaker or hold 'woman first' status in some area."[176] As a counterweight, the feminist press could unashamedly act as "organizing tool" for the women's movement.[177]

Papers did have varying politics and aesthetic styles.[178] *Kinesis,* one of the longest running, founded by the Vancouver Status of Women, evolved into a vibrant forum for discussion of everything from prison abolition to women's culture, labour history, and violence against women. *Branching Out,* emanating from Calgary, was especially attuned to culture, and was, along with *Herizons* (Winnipeg) and *La Vie en Rose* (Montreal), closer in appearance to the American magazine *Ms.* Founded in 1979, *La Vie en Rose* claimed it would replace earlier "moralistic, ghetto[i]zing, prudish" feminisms with a more welcoming, popular version. It "lightened up" feminism with culture, entertainment, and interviews, though debate and politics were not abandoned. The tone was set on its inaugural cover: a picture of Pope John Paul II wearing red lipstick.[179]

Images: Kootenay Women's Paper, the *Yukon Optimist,* and the Nova Scotian *Pandora* all positioned themselves as women's papers sensitive to regional perspectives. Smaller regional presses often pragmatically accommodated different political projects under one publishing roof. Founded in

1972 in Thunder Bay, the *Northern Woman's Journal* included "different ideological views," though there was a basic commitment to women's liberation: "we recognize different approaches to emancipation, but emancipation is our goal."[180] The paper covered local initiatives for working women, socialist study, divorce and separation, theatre, non-sexist books for children, a feminist library, and birth control, and established an alliance with the Native Women's Association and a municipal progressive reform group. One edition lamented that a feminist film festival had to be cancelled. No wonder: who had the energy after all the other activity?

The Other Woman, established in 1972, more boldly declared it was a "revolutionary feminist" publication. Its revolution included a critique of heterosexual privilege and a validating space for lesbian culture. What does it mean to be a radical lesbian, asked one reader? The answer, "to risk ridicule, comfort, job, fighting in streets, on the job, in the courts, in the jails, mental institutions, and bedrooms of the nation."[181] *TOW* was a welcome countervailing space. Yet, as Pat Leslie has indicated, the paper tried to reach a broad readership, with articles on capitalism, imperialism abroad, colonialism at home, birth control, sterilization, abortion, women in fascist countries, history, class, welfare, work, poverty, feminist organizations, film, book reviews, art, and more.

Given the paper's lesbian-positive focus, it faced homophobia. One woman who claimed to be a lifelong supporter of "women's rights," wrote that she was "disgusted" with the paper and its "vulgar women's libber" content and the material on lesbianism. Another asked, "Are you only a gay paper? Does everyone putting into your paper hate men? You are segregating men and women." She took issue, too, with an article that suggested a vigilante means of "outing" rapists, yet was positive about other articles, including one "on fixing a toilet" (it was actually an article on fixing leaky faucets, and very informative at that).[182] Whatever her misgivings, she sent a donation.

Disagreements over ideas did not mean abandoning an alternative feminist paper. A Thunder Bay reader criticized *TOW* for "too little class consciousness," but admitted that "women's papers are not so numerous in Canada that we can afford not to support one that shows promise." Another reader who "got her start" in the Toronto women's liberation movement in 1968, "but now lived in a small city, contrasted her Marxist views with the "radical feminism" of *TOW,* but added, "communication" was essential: "We need someplace we can turn to for information without the class and sex typing slant of the daily press."[183] Letters came from afar: from a prisoner at

Kingston Women's Prison, from a high school student in rural Alberta doing "research" on women's liberation, and from a mysterious "Emma Goldman" in Montreal who thought *TOW* made up for the lack of radical-feminist outlets in Quebec.[184] A San Francisco lesbian group commended *TOW*'s lesbian manifesto. The editors tried to answer letters and connect letter writers who might have common interests.

TOW and other feminist papers filtered political preoccupations of the seventies, such as Canadian nationalism and American imperialism, through feminist eyes. "I Am Canadian," an article indicting American cultural domination (including in the women's movement), was praised by a group of Quebec anglophone women, who said they talked about it "all week in our house."[185] A letter from a reader in the United States was profane in her opposition; all nationalism was "reactionary," and the Canadian New Left variety made them just "as small as all these American red necks waving precious old glory ... No one is trying to steal your culture."[186]

The private archive of *TOW* letters conveys how close to the bone women lived and felt their politics. Many were printed as debate, exposing the fault lines within feminism. Any image of an unreflectively middle-class movement was shattered in the fallout from a particularly "explosive" conference in which working-class lesbians confronted other middle-class attendees. This working-class women's group assailed the hidden benefits of class in the women's movement. Everything from orthodontists, piano lessons, and decent meals, to education and family to fall back on, shaped middle-class women's confidence and their dominance in meetings. If the assessment of class privilege was apt, the tenor of the debate proved divisive. One *TOW* collective member resigned, claiming that personal denunciations and guilt about class origins, or a "feminist tithe" on income, were not good politics.[187] When *TOW* folded in 1977, feminists recognized the loss of a forum for debate. VOW president Kay Macpherson said she had always liked the paper and sent a donation to aid the payment of debts.

Two other papers launched at the beginning of women's liberation, and also proudly "revolutionary," were more Marxist, New Left, and anti-colonial. *The Pedestal* (later, simply *Pedestal*) was founded in 1969 by the Vancouver Women's Caucus, and *Québécoises deboutte!* was initiated in 1971 by the Front de libération des femmes du Québec (FLFQ), with ties to Quebec nationalist and socialist politics. Both papers made links between class and gender, capitalism and patriarchy; both saw history as a means to recover a forgotten past, understand women's oppression, and inform contemporary feminist theory and politics.

Figure 9.9 Vancouver's *Pedestal,* which began publishing in 1969, aspired to a "revolutionary" point of view | *Pedestal* 3, 9 (October 1971) at RISE UP!, https://riseupfeministarchive.ca/publications/the-pedestal/

Pedestal's coverage of women's history included Canadian middle-class suffragists, but it was more interested in discovering how working-class and socialist women created a revolutionary politics. In 1972, its feature on International Women's Day was a long list of historical class struggles: the British matchgirls' strike of 1888, wives supporting striking miners in British Columbia in 1913, women joining relief strikes in the 1930s, and wartime women workers demanding daycare as well as equal pay.[188] Historical biographies were regularly featured, both international revolutionaries such as Rosa Luxemburg and local socialist heroines such as Helena Gutteridge, whose working-class suffragism – involving orating from corner soapboxes – contrasted favourably with the "afternoon parlour" meetings of middle-class suffragists.[189]

Grassroots education was part of *Pedestal*'s plan to grow women's historical consciousness; workshops were organized so women could learn about the "herstory" lacking in the educational system, and articles asked how women's cultures (plural, not singular) and resistance were mutually determining. "Women and the Blues," for instance, traced the origins of blues to the poverty, oppression, and migrations of African Americans, with women's musical creations linked to their "proud tradition" of resistance, their expressions of "anger and frustration" at the oppressive economic and race structures of American life.[190]

Yet *Pedestal* did not equate feminist transformation with cultural change: challenging workplace exploitation and government policies were also important, as were anti-imperialist struggles. In "Double Oppression," Ellen Woodsworth traced the history of Indigenous women's legal subordination under the Indian Act, and the resulting historical constructions of white femininity and Indian womanhood, the former exalted, the latter denigrated. The pervasiveness of racism in a class society had led to divisions between "white and Indian," and to the "dehumanization and oppression" of First Nations women, who were "fighting a double battle" against social indignities and economic exploitation. White feminists needed to "speak up" in solidarity.[191] What made this piece unusual was the analytical intertwining of race and gender, rather than locating – as many authors did – the struggles of Indigenous and settler women in parallel narratives.

Québécoises deboutte! (*QD*) was similarly shaped by national and international political and theoretical influences, but the struggle for Quebec self-determination was pre-eminent, summed up in the famous slogan "No women's liberation without Quebec liberation, no Quebec liberation without women's liberation." The FLFQ, a consortium of working-class and middle-class women from the arts, trade unions, and schools, had been "touched by the vibrant socialist and nationalist agitations of 1960s Quebec."[192] The paper's explication of women's oppression fused a historical critique of capitalism and colonialism. A three-part series, "Histoire d'une oppression," began with the pronatalist policies of the colonial state and the church, which relegated women to a reproductive, submissive role.[193] The history of native-newcomer contact added a new layer of colonialism; white colonizers, especially the Jesuits, attempted to remake Indigenous egalitarian cultures in their own patriarchal image, encouraging the sexual and social repression of Indigenous women whose "liberté sexuelle" threatened the colonial project. This was a story of sexual repression but also of "genocidal" elimination of Indigenous peoples.[194] In the last installment,

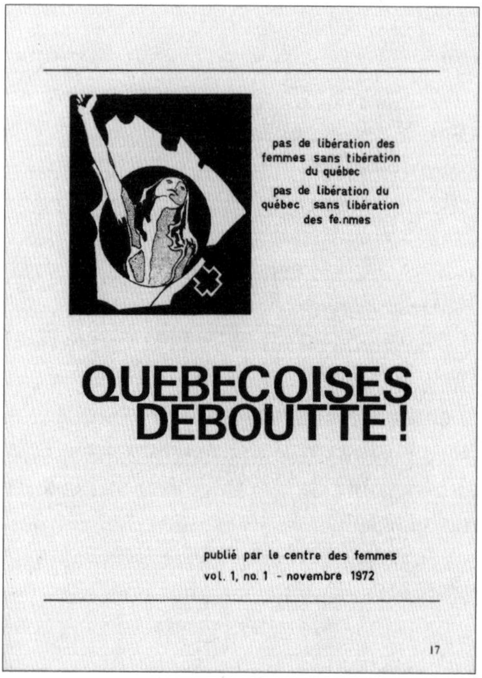

Figure 9.10 Published by Quebec feminists from 1969 to 1971, *Québécoises deboutte!* was a "revolutionary" paper influenced by feminism, Marxism, and Quebec nationalism | *Quebecoises deboutte!* 1, 1 (November 1972), https://numerique.banq.qc.ca/patrimoine/details/52327/3132701?docsearchtext=quebecoise%20deboutte

women's role as insurrectionists, from the 1837 Patriote rebellion onwards, was recuperated to show the historical erasure, but continuing potential, of women as revolutionaries.[195]

QD's definition of oppression, like that of *Pedestal,* was not mired in a Marxism obsessed with the forces of production, as later critics assumed of sixties Marxist writing; connections were made between sexuality, the family, love, religion, and capitalism. In "l'histoire d'amour," sexual repression is explained by the influence of church doctrine and a social order structured around private property and class exploitation. Ideas of private property permeated the family, reinforcing the cult of women's chastity, heterosexual romance, and the institution of marriage. The family was its own patriarchal mini-state, shoring up women's subordination and their internalization of inferiority. Even the alienation of capitalist work contributed to repression, as the family was constructed as an ideological "haven" in a world of endless work. Lessons for the present were clear. Emancipatory political analyses must connect class, colonialism, sexuality, and gender in order to liberate women in both the external world of work and the internal world of desire.[196] Yet, by the 1980s, Veronique O'Leary and Louise Toupin argue, this innovative "second-wave" feminist politics was forgotten, its revolutionary and radical moorings distorted or downplayed in feminist memory by "amnésie des historiens."[197]

New Left-Wing Political Formations

Since the late nineteenth century, socialist parties had claimed they were champions of women's emancipation, although the small cadre of socialist feminists within left-wing parties often struggled to make this commitment a reality. This was true too of the New Democratic Party, the successor to the CCF: one reason women organized the BC Federation of Women in 1973 was their exasperation with the provincial NDP government's failure to enact equality legislation in its own platform. Even Rosemary Brown, an NDP MLA, lamented the party's foot-dragging.

In the 1970s, influenced by the New Left, Marxist-feminist theory, and their own experiences, feminists experimented with new socialist formations they hoped would reflect the ideals of women's liberation and thus be decisively different from old socialist models – whether the Communist Party or the NDP. Although many "new communist" movements and parties declined or collapsed by the 1980s, their attraction, influence, and claims making were part of the "newness" of feminism in the long sixties.

One of these new left-wing feminist formations was the Waffle women's caucus. In a period of intense concern about American domination of the Canadian economy, the Waffle, a lobby group within the NDP, argued that American corporate control endangered Canada's political independence, workers' jobs, and the prospect of socialism within Canada. What was needed was an independent, socialist Canada. The Waffle failed to mention gender equality in its first manifesto, but women members soon changed that. Waffle feminists promoted a combination of Canadian nationalism, socialism, and feminism, not unlike women in Quebec, though promoting a very different nationalism. Feminist Waffle member Varda Burstyn later concluded that the women's caucus provided the "only political formation of any size, substance and vitality [in the early 1970s] where militant feminism really flourished"; it challenged existing NDP "ladies' auxiliaries" and the party's "bland" stance on women's issues.[198] This may overstate: CCF/NDP feminists, who for years had fought for women's equality, would have been offended by their devaluation as "auxiliaries." However, Waffle feminists did nudge the NDP along the road to feminism, helping also to establish women's equality as "a real issue" for unions.[199]

In some provinces, Waffle and women's liberation politics fused. In Saskatchewan, influenced by the energy, style, and politics of the New Left, Marxism, and women's liberation, the Waffle women's caucus pushed for NDP policies on abortion rights, universal child care, equal pay, and female quotas on the party executive. The last demand was contentious, shaking up a male-dominated leadership that, in true liberal fashion, understood its dominance as meritocracy. Waffle women's uncompromising feminism and challenge to the leadership was thus different from earlier CCF women, who felt they must swallow their feminist misgivings in the cause of socialist solidarity. Feminist Wafflers remember vigorously fighting at NDP conventions for demands such as abortion rights. Some union and party stalwarts dismissed them as "radical women's libbers" but feminists took collective heart from the struggle: the "exhilaration of the women's meetings ... the sheer energy," Burstyn recalled, "was a high I will never forget."[200]

Sifting through Waffle women's caucus documents, one is struck by the intense internal theoretical debates. As "analytic socialists," wrote the Moose Jaw Waffle women's group, we need to work through the "theoretical and strategical" decisions to guide our political priorities in our battle against capitalism. In an effort to avoid a "masculine" political style, the women added, "we should not avoid hard debate," resorting to the feminine fall-back of being "gentle and soft spoken ... Not wanting to be like men ... there is no need [for us] to act like women."[201] Newsletters and party documents dissected the connection between gender oppression and class exploitation, putting Marxist-feminist theories to work: some used Engels as a theoretical source; others looked to Juliet Mitchell's Marxist feminism or Margaret Benston's theory on the political economy of domestic labour. Yet most Wafflers rejected the old CCF practice of organizing housewives, dismissing housework as isolating ("worthless and petty," said one group), detrimental to women's class consciousness, and connected to repressive ideologies about female inferiority.[202] They debated where to put their strategic energies – daycare, abortion, working women – as well as potential alliances with women's liberation groups, some Wafflers seeing overlapping goals, others concerned WL had become too individualist or reformist.[203]

Waffle women could agree that the creaky structures of the NDP rested on male dominance and discouraged participatory democracy, but they were also critical of communist traditions, insisting so-called socialist states like the Soviet Union were undemocratic and mired in gender inequality. Echoing turn-of-the-century socialist Bertha Merrill Burns, they warned that socialism spelt only the *possibility* of equality: without feminism too, women's emancipation would remain elusive. When the NDP leadership, using international union muscle, expelled the Waffle in 1972, some women stayed in the party, while others left. Within a short space of time, they had shaken things up. In the 1970s and 1980s, NDP women caucused to strategize for feminist goals, founded their own socialist-feminist magazine, *Priorities,* and worked to give the NDP credence on women's equality issues.

The Waffle represented one link between the New Left and new communist parties of the 1970s; both attempted to revitalize Marxism to explain women's oppression and guide women-centred organizing. In the early 1960s, socialist parties like the League for Socialist Action and the Young Socialists soldiered on with very small memberships, but, in the early 1970s, there was a surge of interest in "new communist" formations. Reading groups, Marxist educationals, alternative newspapers, and bookstores provided popular venues for radical education outside universities, still curricular bastions of establishment thinking. Some organizations like the New Tendency rooted themselves in workplaces and working-class communities by adopting democratic, participatory, and anti-leadership methods, but, more often, parties guided by Marxist and Leninist writing emerged, some oriented toward communist China and Maoism, others sympathetic to the Trotskyist Fourth International. Save for one or two, most distinguished their politics from the failures of Soviet-style Stalinist communism; this was especially true for Trotskyism, which arose as an international, critical alternative to Stalinism.[204]

Unlike the more loosely defined New Left, Marxist-Leninist parties were democratic centralist: political positions were vigorously debated internally, but, once a platform was agreed on, members were expected to defend it in a disciplined manner. Debates within Trotskyist formations in particular were notoriously extensive; recognized "tendencies" (different political views) were hashed out in publications and conferences, and, even after a decision was made, defeated minority positions often had representation in the leadership. Nonetheless, to critics, these parties were dangerously "vanguardist" – that is, a small cadre of leaders with the "correct" political analysis required disciplined members to follow suit. This, of course, left out the "democratic" intention of democratic centralism.

One dilemma for historians is that many of these new communist parties were relatively short lived and left minimal textual traces, not the least because they were infiltrated and monitored by the state, with RCMP "dirty tricks" used to discredit them.[205] Also, former members often became unforgiving critics, including of the left's gender and sexual politics. The organized left, wrote Varda Burstyn in the 1980s, suffered from "institutionalized sexism and heterosexism," having squandering theoretical and organizational creativity for a confining "orthodox" Marxist economism. It was a fairly categorical condemnation. Moreover, for subsequent generations, the harsh internal debates within and between parties, the splintering of groups, even the notion of revolutionary politics, seemed esoteric and inconceivable.[206]

Why, then, did new communist formations appeal to many socialist feminists? With the historical distance of a bystander rather than a member, perhaps it is easier for me to see that feminists made understandable choices rather than inexplicable mistakes. First, revolution was "in the air," as one American participant put it.[207] For the 1968 generation, a radical transformation of society seemed the only answer to the massive inequality, multiple oppressions, and contradictions of advanced capitalism. Moreover, momentous revolutions were happening across the Third World.

Second, feminists who experienced unstructured, "horizontal" organizing in the WL movement saw some benefit in more directed, disciplined mobilizations; political parties also offered a sense of solidaristic camaraderie in struggle. Moreover, being in a party did not mean abandoning women's liberation; it might entail participation in feminist and working-class mobilizations, including reproductive rights, unionizing, anti-racist and LGBTQ movements, trying to persuade other women that a revolution was precisely what was needed.

Third, a broader socialist-feminist milieu surrounded this revolutionary project. Reading groups, working women's caucuses, and feminist unions constituted an informal outer circle that gave Marxist-Leninst parties hope: evidence that women were looking for a socialist home. In Vancouver alone, multiple study and action groups like Bread and Roses were mulling over what Marxist feminists should do politically. Even if they were critical of new communist parties, they were searching for a rapprochement between socialism, working-class organizing, and feminism. An increasingly vocal working-class feminism also elicited revolutionary hope. Militant strikes of women workers, women's union caucuses, feminist alliances with labour – described in the next chapter – forecast a sharpening gendered class consciousness that might be harnessed to a socialist project.

Fourth, the theoretical analysis of women's oppression promoted by revolutionary parties simply made sense. Socialist feminists were developing new Marxist-feminist theories intended to counter the shortcomings of the Old Left's analyses that had simplified gender oppression as a mere corollary of class, discounted sexual liberation, and idealized the heterosexual family. Marxism, writes Meg Luxton, "taught me how to think critically and gave me a political analytic framework for understanding capitalism," while the women's liberation movement "revealed as systemic the sexism and misogyny I had experienced." Her intellectual and political metamorphosis, she recalls, took place in listening, reading, and thinking, in the Third World bookstore, the Marxist Institute, the Women's Press collective, and the Cinema of Solidarity, as well as in the "doing" of politics: while occupying a University of Toronto building to demand campus child care, "we provided shelter for refugees fleeing the 1973 [Chilean] coup," explored ideas about non-sexist child rearing and imagined how "collective living and socialism" might work. For women experiencing both a transformative political education and the "inspiring solidarity of collective action," these were "both politically and intellectually heady times."[208]

Finally, while Maoist parties were not very sympathetic to autonomous feminist organizing and gay and lesbian struggles, Trotskyists made women's and gay/lesbian liberation at least a *stated* priority. From its founding in 1973, the Trotskyist Revolutionary Marxist Group (RMG) (not yet a party), claimed that women's liberation was integral to its politics. One reason to create a new organization, they claimed, was the left's perennial failure to "integrate women's oppression into all aspects of its work."[209] The RMG's revised Marxist analysis foregrounded social reproduction, the family, and sexuality, while not ignoring women's super-exploitation in the workforce. Like the Old Left, it assumed women's paid labour might encourage a socialist consciousness, but, unlike the Old Left, it criticized the idealized, patriarchal, heterosexual family, a profoundly "conservatizing" force that stood in the way of women's liberation.

RMG publications drew on the cultural feeling and language of both the New Left and women's liberation: by supporting women's liberation, they ventured, they might play a "decisive role in the struggle for the liberation of [all] humanity."[210] Although capitalism was the overarching context for women's oppression, ideologies of "female inferiority" and sexual repression were critical impediments to women's emancipation. The sexual revolution promised by the earlier New Left, it acknowledged, had not materialized, at least not for women, but sexual oppression could not be attacked in isolation; freedom was not possible until social relations premised on profit, commodification, and alienation were also swept away.

The Revolutionary Workers League (RWL), founded in 1977 by a number of Fourth International groups including the RMG, similarly claimed both "homosexuality" and women's emancipation as their political priorities. Copious internal critiques – sharp and lengthy – from women within the party tried to hold it to account, insisting gender equality should be placed more forthrightly at the core of its work.[211] Internal party critiques always abounded, whether it was over feminism, gay and lesbian issues, anti-racist strategies, or trade union work, as party members integrated into working-class jobs – another story in itself. The RWL was one among many new communist parties more open to LGBTQ and feminist struggles, but it ultimately faltered in the face of internal criticisms.

Within the women's movement, new communist parties had to combat suspicions that they acted only for their party, not feminism. A war of words between the League for Socialist Action (LSA), a Trotskyist group committed to legalizing abortion, and *The Other Woman* (*TOW*) showed relations at their most hostile. *TOW* denounced the LSA as vanguardist, male-dominated, authoritarian, and trying to "infiltrate" women's groups, while the LSA countered (though not in *TOW*, where they were seemingly not welcome to publish) that this was old-fashioned anti-communist "red baiting," daring critics to brave a real debate over the LSA's socialist-feminist ideas.[212]

More measured reflections came from non-party socialist feminists. Women in the Vancouver Women's Caucus worked with LSA women, but felt that the latter's adherence to strict party priorities inhibited vibrant discussion and open-minded strategizing. Another Vancouver socialist-feminist study group published a pamphlet discussing its encounters with the "far Left": they shared a Marxist perspective but feared that new communist parties did not fully comprehend women's day-to-day experience of oppression, including within the family.[213] Socialist feminists could be supportive of various party projects, but critical of their methods, especially of Leninism. A widely circulated critique of vanguard parties from a socialist-feminist point of view, *Beyond the Fragments* registered a strong impact on feminists across borders.[214]

Not all communist encounters with feminists were hostile. Women in new communist parties could be dedicated activists in International Women's Day committees, unions, abortion rights campaigns, and queer organizing. I worked with the RWL on a labour solidarity campaign for striking miners, and, while I knew the league had an agenda, including recruiting new members, I also respected their analysis, dedication, and sacrifices. The few Fourth International groups that survived past the 1980s maintained a commitment to feminism (though some have recently fallen apart over such issues), but most new communist parties closed up shop by the late 1980s. Internal implosions were often feminist in nature; vanguard parties were criticized as undemocratic and male dominated, failing to fully embrace women's equality and gay liberation. Sexist sexual politics and the limitations of parties' working-class strategies were also faulted.

However, the subsequent political trajectory of "new communist" women is revealing. If some abandoned politics, many more were dedicated to reproductive rights, trade unions, social movements, LGBTQ organizing, women's studies, and many more political projects. The momentary turn of feminists to revolutionary politics was not, perhaps, something to apologize for, but should be seen in context. By the late 1980s, revolution was no longer in the air, but, sadly, capitalism was no tamer, and the ideology of the right, that "there is no alternative" to the cruel austerities of neoliberalism, might have been more insidious than a "naïve" hope in socialist revolution.

Conclusion

Between the time the RCSW was created in 1967 and its 1970 report, the political landscape shifted dramatically. LSA women who testified before the RCSW proposed a plan for the "fundamental" transformation of society: twenty-four-hour daycare so women could be "freed" from traditional responsibilities, reproductive freedom, equality in the workforce, educational opportunity, an end to ideologies of women's inferiority. They also laid the "cause of women's inequality" at the doorstep of capitalism.[215]

These women were dismissed as wide-eyed radicals by the media covering the RCSW, but, by the early 1970s, they did not look so wide-eyed compared to emerging women's liberation groups. The Abortion Caravan rejected the timid compromises of the RCSW; the Corbiere Lavell–Bédard case was in motion; lesbian women were organizing for rights and recognition; wife battering had been outed; and a new feminist counterculture, with Marxist, anti-colonial, and radical-feminist sensibilities, was being born.

Seeing so much activism, it is difficult to avoid imagining a wave. There was resurgence and refashioning of older feminist concerns – such as equality at work – but also entirely new visions of equality. Feminism was redefined theoretically, politically, and organizationally, rapidly and enthusiastically so. A new cohort of feminists claimed they had broken with history, positioning "women's liberation" against more tepid varieties of feminism. This un-self-reflective progress narrative could irritate older feminists who had, after all, celebrated International Women's Day for decades, tried to organize white-collar workers, and mobilized against wars and imperialism. A favourite slogan of anti-war activists in the 1960s and 1970s – "Let the military hold a bake sale" – was actually coined by the earlier Women's International League for Peace and Freedom.

Continuities were evident: the VOW was already organizing against the Vietnam War; socialist feminists had long organized within social-democratic parties; alternative feminist countercultures existed on the margins since the nineteenth century. But "something was happening here" that was exciting for those in the mix of it. Perhaps this upsurge is better imagined as part of ongoing streams of feminism, ebbing and flowing over the twentieth century, with this moment a groundswell of multiple rebellions. Or, in Nancy Hewitt's terms, part of ongoing feminist "radio waves" – multiple, overlapping, with different frequencies and channels.[216] In the late sixties, the volume definitely went up.

Whatever the metaphor, we need to acknowledge what was divergent in this upsurge of resistance. The 1970s were not simply the 1950s: material and social changes, especially in women's work lives, provided fertile grounds for discontent and other radical movements of liberation awakened women's consciousness of oppression. The New Left, anti-colonial movements, and anti-war activism were incubators of feminist dissent. They raised questions about class, race, and imperialism that led women *to* feminism, they provided examples of autonomous organizing, and they offered novel approaches to socialism – even if women then critiqued the very movements that had inspired them.

The winding down of the Cold War was important to a changing feminism in which Marxist and socialist ideas constituted ingredients of one stream of activism. Even if the RCMP was spying on you (and they were), state repression did not work as effectively as it had in the 1950s: feminists and leftists simply thumbed their noses at McCarthyism. Some feminists experimented with new forms of communism, and though former participants are critical of the Left's failure to live to up feminist aims, one can see how theory and politics in global context fused to create revolutionary hopes.

Given the impact of socialist and anti-imperialist ideas, as well as challenges to heteronormativity within this feminist cohort, I don't believe these feminists were unaware of "differences" between women, though many focussed particularly on the intersection of gender and class. Women's political awakening, Frances Wasserlein points out from her interviews with women's liberationists, pushed them from "liberal idealism to socialist idealism," or social democratic to "socialist and communist" politics.[217] They were also a more variegated group than privileged, white, middle-class students the media – and subsequent commentators – imagined. Many white Canadian feminists, however, were far less cognizant of "race" and institutionalized racism, and although the feminist press and organizations consistently pointed to Indigenous women's oppression, they were not well connected to Indigenous women's movements. Discursive recognition of other oppressions may exist, but not necessarily translate into deep understanding, communication, and working coalitions.

When women's liberationists used the slogan "sisterhood is powerful" (actually an American term), they were not referring to women claiming the same experiences, but rather the power of common action. But common action might be difficult when women defined their oppression differently or were following distinct pathways to equality. Like some LGBTQ activists who opted for separatism, Québécoises who supported self determination or working-class women who self organized, Indigenous women created their own movement that saw women's dignity and equality as inseparable from decolonization. Still, however heterogeneous and fractured the women's movement was, these multiple streams of feminism added up to a significant groundswell of rebellion.

10 Feminist Organizing in the 1970s and 1980s

In 1979–80, women telephone operators in the Communications Workers of Canada led a strike against one of Canada's most powerful corporations, Bell Telephone. For decades, Bell had constructed a workforce in which women were limited to lower-paid clerical and operator positions, hired for their "polite" and accommodating demeanour. The strike shattered any notion that politeness equalled submissiveness. Fighting for a first contract with improved wages and working conditions, strikers blocked entrances in the January cold; called out strikebreakers; protested in front of management offices; tied up the switchboard, which was staffed by managers, with fake inquiries; and even threw a few eggs at scabs. Strikers identified the transformative feeling of a new sense of self-esteem: "the strike has given us backbone," said a thirteen-year veteran operator. "We may have been a submissive bunch of women in the past, but after this strike, we'll be a force to be reckoned with."[1]

While many strikers did not self-describe as feminists, feminist organizations backed their strike as an important equality struggle, and some strike leaders redoubled their commitment to the women's movement. "Walking in the International Women's Day Parade," recalls Joan Roberts, "was one of my clear[e]st memories [of the strike] ... I got to walk up front [carrying] my picket sign 'Help Crack Bell.' I was the lucky one ... everyone else was too frightened to walk with women's libbers. I was honoured and had called myself a feminist since I was thirteen."[2] Feminists were made in a multitude of struggles like this one: women trying to make a decent living, raise families, secure more workplace dignity, expand their social rights, control their bodies and sexuality, as they came face to face with the structures and ideas that sustained a profoundly unequal and unjust society.

The Bell strike required daily, detailed, precision organizing: strike committee meetings, communicating with picket captains, developing a strategy, putting out a newsletter, contacts with the press, appeals to the public, managing a dwindling strike fund. This organizational efficiency seems to contradict the image of women's liberation as a more spontaneous, militant, unstructured form of protest. Yet, both modes of resistance existed in the 1970s, and both extended into the 1980s. Periodizing feminism by decades can be misleading, producing overly general narratives of progress and decline that simplify the complex texture of feminist resistance. Still, changing social contexts did reshape feminist thought and organizing by the end of the 1980s. Feminists faced different challenges: neoliberalism was eating away at social welfare and wage gains made in the post-war period, and the state was incorporating some tamer elements of feminist protest, while discrediting other demands. That is the negative side of the ledger. On the plus side, feminist organizations proliferated, and some issues were emerging from the shadows of public consciousness. When MPs laughed at Margaret Mitchell's comments on wife battering in 1982, a media furore ensued in which her immature, sexist colleagues were taken to task for ridiculing violence against women.

This chapter samples feminist organizing, briefly alluding to the National Action Committee on the Status of Women (NAC), an important but already documented story, and focusing instead on local Status of Women Action committees, labour mobilizations, and immigrant women's and anti-racist struggles. Other feminist efforts also thrived, including cultural, anti-violence, and anti–sexual assault work; LGBTQ organizing; prison abolitionism; family law reform; the development of women's studies programs; campaigns adressing abortion rights, pornography, and sexual liberation (and more). Sites of struggle were seldom siloed; working women pushed their unions to make abortion rights a trade union demand, and immigrant women stressed that violence was experienced differently by new immigrants and particularly acutely by racialized women. By the mid-1980s, feminists identified a threat that crossed class, race, and gender boundaries: right-wing organizing against racialized immigrants, trade unions, feminism, and LGBTQ rights. Threatened by small feminist gains, fearful of an altered family, this conservative backlash was met with new efforts to create feminist alliances in the face of a politics of retrograde reaction.

Organized and "Institutional" Feminisms

For good reason, NAC has been discussed at length. It was a remarkable effort to create a national feminist organization bridging region, generation, culture, race and ethnicity, language, and ideology; yet it was also a difficult, fractured project that faced immense obstacles to unanimity.[3] Determined to see recommendations from the RCSW implemented, the reformist Committee for Women's Equality sponsored a Toronto "Strategy for Change" conference in April 1972. With Royal Commission on the Status of Women (RCSW) instigator Laura Sabia, a Progressive Conservative, in the chair, thirty-one women's organizations represented, five hundred attendees, political affiliations from left to right, "radical" women caucusing on their own, it was a tumultuous two days.

The outcome was not pre-ordained. A hefty liberal and Liberal Party presence pushed for a government-appointed, ongoing monitoring Advisory Council on the Status of Women, but the radical caucus pushed back. Trade unionist Madeleine Parent made the point that carried the day: "what we need is not an advisory council responsible to parliament but a parliament responsible to the women of Canada."[4] NAC was born as an autonomous entity, quickly moving from a narrow focus on the "status of women" to a broader range of equality issues. Its platform evolved over decades, shaped by the political culture, economic context, other social movements, as well as the unexpected in political life.

The young NAC juggled multiple feminisms under one roof. Women's liberationists were critical of NAC's top-down "institutional" style, as opposed to a bottom-up, grassroots feminism.[5] Some NAC women favoured polite insider lobbying of politicians; others thought that political action packed more clout and feared that a platform designed to suit all groups would co-opt the radical edge of feminism. However wide-ranging NAC's equality agenda, it accepted certain rules of political engagement: it concentrated on federally focused research, lobbying, and education, developing a strategic but still limited "parliamentary activism."[6] Nonetheless, NAC had mobilizing potential, by virtue of its newsletters, meetings, local groups, annual general meetings, and its claim to speak for all women's interests.

NAC's rapid growth led to institutionalization: it hired staff, had a powerful executive and many subcommittees, held annual general meetings, published a national newsletter, and so on. Such expansion was possible due, in part, to subsidies from the federal government. Inevitably, contradictions surfaced. Should NAC concentrate on lobbying or offer a larger vision of transformation? How could one have democracy and transparency in a complex, structured organization with no individual voting membership? Would government funding for NAC compromise its independence? How could the need for leadership be balanced with membership control? How could NAC hire dedicated, overqualified feminist staff and then *not* expect them to unionize and demand better working conditions?

To optimists, NAC's very existence signalled a groundswell of feminist activism and hope that a strong coalition might command political influence across the country. Canadian feminists were used to negotiating regional and linguistic divisions; a belief in "undivided sisterhood" historically had never been "very marketable in Canada."[7] While women still used mainstream political parties, especially the Liberals and NDP, to advance feminist goals, they invested tremendous energy in NAC as a non-partisan coalition.[8] NAC's longevity, "ideological diversity and ability to bridge generations of feminists" was praised as evidence of a uniquely Canadian version of feminism. Jill Vickers, Pauline Rankin, and Christine Appelle characterize NAC's outlook as "radical liberalism": it was committed to political dialogue, the democratic and parliamentary process, the welfare state, and optimism that state interventions could remedy injustice.[9]

This assessment may be too homogenizing. While NAC incorporated elements of radical liberalism, it also validated collectivist solutions. Over time, it moved leftwards, as it concentrated more on the concerns of working-class and poor women. The parliamentary activism of NAC made it a voice for reform, not revolution, but the participation of socialist feminists and trade unionists ensured the presence of an anti-capitalist point of view and ties to labour organizations.

While some praised NAC's ability to navigate ideological diversity, it did not initially embody racial and ethnic diversity. NAC newsletters in the first decade tackled contentious economic issues that pitted liberal against more left-wing feminists. However, race and systemic racism were not incorporated into these discussions, although Indigenous women's struggles received consistent attention. Internal and external pressures forced NAC to address the marginalization of women based on race and ethnicity as well as sexual orientation and disability within its own organization. An unquestioning acceptance of Canada's multicultural mythology, argues Mary Jo Nadeau, meant that a hegemonic "white mode of feminism" initially dominated NAC. NAC wrestled with both its failure to develop an anti-racist politics and its automatic assumption of a universalized white Canadian nation/womanhood. By the late 1980s, there was a pivot to a more "integrative" understanding of race and a more explicit anti-racism, in no small part because of the voices of women of colour and "visible minority" women within and outside NAC.[10]

NAC's initial concern with building bridges with the "internal Other" had to do primarily with Quebec and, secondarily, with Indigenous women.[11] Bicultural links with Quebec women were a high priority, a reflection of political preoccupations with Quebec's claim of colonial alienation and new articulations of French-Canadian nationalism. Historically, English-speaking and Quebec feminists had tried to bridge religious, cultural, and linguistic differences by finding some common political ideals. The scenario was now entirely new: many Quebec feminists wanted to leave confederation entirely.

Granted, Québécoises' feminism was plural. As discussed in the preceding chapter, one amorphous group – the Front de libération des femmes du Québec – espoused a revolutionary vision of feminism tied to independence for a socialist Quebec. Naturally, revolutionary-left *indépendantistes* were not going to spend their time debating federal state policy with anglos. Another "autonomous" feminist tendency, loosely associated with the journal *Têtes de pioches,* developed a critique of patriarchy, heterosexism, and Quebec's historic pronatalism. Yet a third tendency was grouped around the Fédération des femmes du Québec (FFQ), NAC's primary organizational connection to Quebec.[12]

Founded by former suffragist Thérèse Casgrain in 1966, the FFQ built on the liberal modernizing tradition associated with Quebec's Quiet Revolution. Reformist, pragmatic, policy oriented, it employed advocacy, lobbying, and education, urging political action in the service of an "egalitarian feminism." As Diane Lamoureux notes, it reflected an optimism that, once women's oppression was documented with irrefutable evidence, feminists could secure redress through the state.[13] Like NAC, it was an umbrella organization, a "melting pot" of political views,[14] with strong representations from liberal, labour, and social-democratic feminists, whose demands for wholesale changes to work, family, and social rights (including, after some initial division, abortion rights) were still quite transformative.

Nationalism was essential to the "identity and self-assertion" of feminism in Quebec,[15] though debate and differences occurred between more revolutionary currents that linked feminism to left nationalism and reformers who placed more hope in the provincial state as a protector of their culture, language, and progressive social programs. When the Parti Québécois held a referendum on independence in 1980, Quebec feminists were divided. The FFQ wisely declared neutrality. A year later, as the national constitutional brouhaha began, it was difficult to find a meeting of Quebec and English-Canadian feminist minds.

The constitution was an unexpected issue NAC could not have foreseen in 1972. The Liberal federal government's plan to repatriate the constitution in 1980–81 shook up feminist alliances. If there was to be a charter protecting human rights, reform-minded feminists asked, should women not demand a clause ensuring gender equality? Indigenous and Quebec feminists had another question: How would legal protection for *all* women affect the distinct oppressions defining *their* lives? The Black Canadian Women's Congress noted that constitutional gender protections might not address the "equality rights of black and women of colour."[16] NAC, not of one mind, took a backseat, while a hastily convened cross-party Ad Hoc Conference of Canadian Women on the Constitution (AHC) assumed leadership – though with some NAC overlap.

The AHC was aided by the clumsy decision of the Liberal government to cancel an Advisory Council on the Status of Women's constitutional conference, fearing delegates might not fall into line with the government's agenda. Advisory councils had been established by federal and provincial governments in the 1970s to provide expert advice on the implementation of gender equality – an extreme example of the institutionalization of feminism. As government appointees, they were constrained, sometimes beholden to their government overlords, though some did important research essential for the movement.[17] Doris Anderson, president of the federal advisory council, was no Liberal handmaiden; she very publicly resigned when the conference was cancelled. Her protest galvanized feminists determined to secure *Charter* rights.

Penney Kome has written a blow-by-blow account of the AHC's successful campaign to secure a gender equality clause (section 15) and a statement (section 28) that "notwithstanding" anything else in the *Charter*, all rights applied equally to men and women.[18] Canadian women seemed to have won what eluded American feminists: a constitutional guarantee of equal rights. Over time, the *Charter* became a useful legal tool; aided by the feminist Women's Legal Education and Action Fund (LEAF) and, initially, government funds for legal cases, it scored some successes, though it has also proven limited in terms of more substantive economic equality.

Subsequent attempts to bring Quebec into the constitution proved divisive. In the 1987 battle over the Meech Lake Accord, the FFQ resigned from NAC when the latter did not endorse the accord, which recognized Quebec as a distinct society.[19] Feminists outside Quebec worried that

Meech, offering strong provincial powers, endangered both *Charter* equality rights and strong federal standards on social welfare. Conversely, Quebec feminists, shaped by "different histories, traditions" and recent political experiences, saw provincial powers as an essential protection for their culture and nation.[20] NAC's support for Indigenous organizations' demand for protection of their sovereign rights was dicey, when the Native Women's Association of Canada (NWAC) was not even at the constitutional table, shut out by male-dominated Indigenous organizations. Later, both NAC and NWAC unified in opposition to the final repatriation effort, the Charlottetown Accord.

Although the FFQ would later return to NAC, divergent nationalisms – French, English, Indigenous – and different cultures, experiences, and aspirations were a check on feminist unity, especially since Anglo-Canadian nationalism dominated, and hostile politicians whipped up anti-NAC feeling by misrepresenting their constitutional views, which were always more complex than the media allowed.[21] In the 1990s, even the FFQ moved toward self-determination for Quebec, a sign not of drifting but of quite distinct nations. Successful temporary alliances of English and French feminists, such as the Bread and Roses march in 1995, were crafted as cross-border versions of solidarity rather than as tight institutional alliances – perhaps more realistic strategies.

Constitutional debates – intricate, complex, and passionate – have faded in memory, but they reveal the complexities of forging a national institutional feminist presence. Reconciling French and English nations heading in different directions was difficult, and, within NAC, hegemonic racial assumptions and class privilege divided women. The process of developing one platform or policy statement on an issue belied the very different interests of women based on class, race, and colonialism. Unlike the protest of Thunder Bay feminists, marching with Indigenous women and men to protest the Corbiere Lavell–Bédard decision, longer term institutional alliances were more challenging.

Local Status of Women Action Committees

Like assessments of the new communist parties discussed in the previous chapter, we look at NAC through retrospectively critical eyes, detailing its deficiencies or defeats – not all of their own making. As former NAC president Judy Rebick has argued, it was a brave experiment, and one that shifted over time to a more activist feminism attuned to grassroots activism, class, and race inequality.[22] Government funding aided face-to-face exchanges of women – even those without resources – from across the country, as meetings thrashed out research, policies, and politics touching on all areas of women's lives. Most women attached to NAC, however, did not attend its AGMs, described by one jaundiced participant as argumentative affairs with no compensatory "fun,"[23] but, rather, participated in municipal, regional, and provincial action groups, responsive to local issues and political cultures. As with earlier feminist mobilizations, regional organizing often defined the day-to-day political experiences of feminists.

Provincial Status of Women Committees, sometimes called Status of Women Action Committees (SOWCs), offered a convenient hook on which to hang local feminist concerns, a more grassroots alternative to government-appointed advisory committees. SOWCs' ostensible origins lay in follow-up on RCSW recommendations, but many women were simply looking for a new organizational conduit for their activism. SOWCs were lobby, educational, and action groups, constituted primarily by white working and professional women, albeit encompassing some ideological diversity. Though situated within a reform tradition, the labour feminists involved in SOWSCs kept class issues on the agenda, and those with socialist and women's liberation backgrounds often harboured more radical hopes of social transformation.

The Nova Scotia Women's Action Committee (NSWAC), founded in 1975, is a good example. Emerging from International Women's Year events, it referenced the RCSW in its origin story, expressed concern that NAC have Maritime representation, and sent delegates to NAC meetings, but its focus was on local matters. In 1980, it sponsored a public workshop on constitutional issues, but NAC's political crisis was a mere line in their minutes packed with other pressing concerns. Over the next decade, the NSWAC dealt with daycare, unemployment, equal pay, human rights legislation, non-traditional jobs, abortion, occupational health, sexism in education and CBC programming, workers' rights, violence, and women on provincial boards, among other issues.

The NSWAC was nonetheless distinct from the local women's centre, which was a clearinghouse for every imaginable local women's group. The NSWAC promoted political action and had the courage to address issues other women's groups in the province avoided, such as abortion. Its call for more women on provincial boards and commissions (and there were pitifully few) replicated an issue dear to the earlier mild-mannered Nova Scotia Business and Professional Women. Using a grant, the NSWAC hired a summer student to create a "resource bank" of prospective candidates so governments would stop claiming there were no qualified women.[24] On the other hand, the NSWAC's position on "community-based, free, universal, 24 hour" child care, with immediate attention to better wages for workers, was more in line with the NDP and socialist groups of the time.[25]

Knowing that it could not do everything, the NSWAC sought allies. It wanted to pursue sexism in the educational system and so suggested that a committee work with the teachers' union to examine school texts and press for a women's coordinator in the Department of Education. If other activist groups, such as Action Daycare, were on the scene, the NSWAC offered support. Short-term actions were mounted to protect women's day-to-day social needs; protest was registered, for instance, over changes to a local hospital that would compromise maternity care. Although primarily based in Halifax, the NSWAC advertised feminist initiatives further afield, such as Reel Life, a media collective of feminist cultural workers that toured small towns in Nova Scotia and New Brunswick in a van, collecting information on women's local concerns and providing films, art, slides, and books on women. Like many cultural projects in the seventies, women were eager to correct history with new "herstories," especially by addressing the lives of ordinary women. Reel Life also made videos about social activists and staged cultural interventions, including a "Toad of Your Choice" contest to counter the Miss Teen Halifax pageant (the toad with the best warts won).[26]

The NSWAC organized public educationals; sponsored election debates on women's issues; chastised politicians with numerous letters of protest (many penned with suitable indignation by historians Linda Kealey and Tina Simmons); and prepared and delivered briefs to all political parties. Government apathy and weak provincial legislation were both in its line of fire; it insisted that human rights protections should include marital status and have valid enforcement measures and that the "fifteen" major flaws in the proposed matrimonial property bill be rectified.[27] On the latter issue, the NSWAC echoed feminists across the country. In 1973, the Supreme Court had ruled against Irene Murdoch, an Alberta farmer who tried to secure a share of the family ranch in her divorce. Despite twenty-five years of unpaid labour (while enduring physical violence), she had, according to the judge, made merely "normal" wifely contributions: the husband kept the ranch.[28] NAC demanded reform to ensure women's ability to leave marriages without facing poverty. Marriage, said SOWCs, had to be seen as an "equal partnership," and women's "unpaid work within the family seen as vital to the unit as paid work."[29]

The NSWAC was especially concerned with labour (work, pensions, daycare), and women's bodily autonomy (violence and reproductive choice). Equal pay for work of equal value was just one provincial struggle. Most feminists of all political persuasions agreed that existing equal pay laws had been dismal failures; a solution was equal pay for work of equal value (or "pay equity") legislation, which would require employers to compare occupations of men and women based on knowledge, skill, effort, responsibility, and working conditions. The ideal outcome would be wage adjustments upwards so female daycare instructors who cared for children were not paid less than men who looked after toilets.

On pay equity and other issues, the NSWAC often began at ground zero, trying to secure recognition that a problem was actually a problem. Nova Scotia politicians, the reigning Liberals in particular, were completely dismissive of pay equity. When the premier gave a speech denouncing the concept as "idealistic and impossible to enforce," the NSWAC issued a press release, fighting back with facts and figures: the government's *own* Advisory Council on Women had recommended it; women earned a shocking 60 percent of male wages; and the current law was toothless. The problem of economic discrimination, NSWAC insisted, is "not [changing] poor attitudes but profit [made] using women as cheap labour."[30] Even the NDP, supposedly a natural ally, might be unsupportive. When the provincial NDP leader condescendingly dismissed the NSWAC's "righteous indignation" and labelled it just another "interest group," feathers flew in the NDP milieu.[31] His attitude was so egregious that the federal NDP women's coordinator apologized to the NSWAC. Securing support for even small improvements for working women, in other words, was an uphill battle.

The NSWAC made public issues of passing conflicts as well as organizing around longer-term problems. When the provincial "Michelin bill" was passed, restricting the right to unionize, NSWAC members signed a letter of protest; in 1977, they threw their support behind a hospital workers' strike. Concerns about rising unemployment led to a Halifax Coalition of Support for the Unemployed; NSWAC members joined and organized a panel to discuss women's unemployment concerns. To build longer-term links with working women, they collaborated with local trade unions, sponsoring a public meeting with Madeleine Parent, designed to bring more women into the labour movement. Conferences on sexual harassment and occupational health were organized, the latter packing a hall.

Women's access to safe and legal abortions was also an NSWAC priority. The flaws in the 1969 *Criminal Code* reforms were unambiguous in the

Figure 10.1 The NSWAC panel on women and unemployment, in Halifax in 1978 included economist Martha McDonald, union organizer Linda Michaels, historian Linda Kealey, Sharon Reilly of the Metro Coalition for Support of Workers, and sociologist Pat Connelly | Dalhousie University Archives, Nova Scotia Women's Action Committee fonds, newspaper clippings

Maritimes; in Prince Edward Island and New Brunswick very few hospitals had therapeutic abortion committees (TACs). Women simply could not get abortions, a situation that arguably worsened in the 1980s.[32] Although Halifax did have a TAC, timely referrals and immediate access to abortions proved difficult. The NSWAC may have preferred to see abortion decriminalized, but it had to deal with immediate threats to further limitations on access. Tina Simmons explained that women faced an intimidating environment: the "reactionary" climate of "so-called Right to Life" organizing "weighs heavily" on women's "ability to take control" of their reproductive choices. Lack of public education about birth control and abortion and the "conservatism" of TACs led to delays for desperate women. Requiring women to secure written permission of husbands or parents, warned the NSWAC, would set up another roadblock, "subordinating decisions about women's health" to another person.[33]

Every SOWC was slightly different. Some pursued a few local issues, others federal and provincial ones. The Corner Brook SOWC protested the local beauty contest, which it believed "marketed" women's bodies for money,[34] while the Saskatchewan SOWC advertised a long list of causes relating to work and reproductive rights. If the Saskatchewan committee's concern with family property law seemed liberal in nature, its radical daycare platform mimicked a socialist playbook. The Ontario SOWC, initiated by Lynn McDonald, a McMaster sociology professor, was a united front of women in Liberal Party politics as well as NDP and labour feminists who were organizing working-class, immigrant women. The Ontario SOWC politely lobbied banks and Air Canada, urging them to change their sexist treatment of women workers, but it also supported militant picket lines, including strikes at Fleck Manufacturing and Dare Foods, where women combated strikebreakers and police violence.[35]

SOWCs were about reform, not revolution, and their membership was not racially diverse. Some avoided more contentious issues such as LGBTQ rights. Even so, their ambition to correct the "most demonstrable discriminatory treatment" of women might still be unwelcome in the highest levels of provincial governments.[36] The Ontario SOWC presented its first brief, with the usual unassailable facts and figures detaling women's inequality, to Premier Bill Davis in 1972. Chomping on his cigar, feet on the desk, he was visibly unimpressed. He blasted the women with his own gender query: Why were women not school principals? Clearly, women lacked ambition: case closed for feminism. Successive governments, the women recall, would not be so dismissive.[37]

Other SOWCs endured continuing hostility. The Alberta Status of Women Action Committee (ASWAC) was initially solicitous of the provincial Conservative government, inviting the Deputy Premier Henry Horner to its inaugural conference. Horner went on the offensive in a thoroughly "condescending" speech. Women were already equal, he lectured, and, if not, they should put some elbow grease into their own bootstrapping. His government believed in less government, certainly not a new minister responsible for a women's portfolio, and, if feminists tried impolite tactics, he warned the government might become more antagonistic – though it was hard to imagine anything more hostile.[38]

Alberta's political climate, remembers a former ASWAC staffer, was not welcoming: the press routinely made anti-lesbian comments and denounced the ASWAC as extreme "radical feminists."[39] The ASWAC's newsletter had an eclectic, pluralistic reach, no doubt to create a coalition of the beleaguered, though, like many SOWCs, the Alberta group was primarily white, with working-class and middle-class representation. In one year, technology at work, violence, abortion, Nicaragua, disarmament, paid work, Indigenous women, and criminal justice were all covered in ASWAC messaging. In the early 1980s, sexual assault, violence, and pornography assumed some priority, but, in 1983, the ASWAC's International Women's Day message zeroed in on the unfolding economic crisis, warning that it would lead to budget cuts hurting women and right-wing efforts to "push women back into their place."[40]

Long-term planning by SOWCs might be waylaid by local crises demanding attention. More than once, the ASWAC protested when Alberta judges made egregious sexist and racist comments. In 1984, at the request of the Northwest Territories Native Women's Association, the ASWAC publicized Judge Michel Bourassa's lenient sentencing for multiple assaults on a thirteen-year-old Indigenous girl. The (Indigenous) men did not consider it wrong in their culture, the judge rationalized, as "they were living their lives in a normal fashion in the way life is lived in the high Arctic." His assumption that violence was the norm in "native culture" was assailed as ridiculous by Inuit writer Minnie Aodla Freeman in the *ASWAC Newsletter*.[41] Another commentator reminded readers that Bourassa's remarks were not one-time problems. Judges "again and again" excused violence against women (for example, claiming a husband was provoked by a "shrew" of a wife), and, when women protested, the state offered "empty and useless justification, absurd explanation, predictable double-talk."[42]

Institutional, organized feminism, then, extended far beyond NAC. Just as in the United States, where local chapters of the National Organization for Women had different political complexions, SOWCs experimented with different versions of reform feminism, moulding their goals to the local political economy and culture. Depending on the city or region, the SOWC might play a dominating presence or simply be one of many organizational choices. In Toronto, for example, the International Women's Day Committee, a large umbrella coalition, likely commanded more strategic importance. Beginning in the 1970s, International Women's Day (IWD) in some cities moved from a one-day event to a year-long feminist organization.[43] In 1979, the Toronto committee declared itself a socialist-feminist organization committed to mass action, whereas the Calgary IWD was more cautiously pluralistic in its politics. Vancouver's IWD reflected the strong "left coast." In Halifax, by contrast, one participant remembers her trepidation joining a small march of a couple of hundred women; even still, the NSWAC complained of police harassment of the marchers.

Labour Feminism and Organizing Women Workers

Paid labour was a political priority for many feminists, in no small part because the workforce had undergone a radical transformation after the Second World War; in the course of a generation, women went from being working daughters to becoming working mothers. As the nature and place of women's labour shifted from the home to the workplace, many women faced a double day – wage labour by day, domestic labour by night. Although there were differences based on region, class, immigrant status, ethnicity, race, and age, the trend was universal. Many working-class families needed a second income to prosper; women in professional occupations were bucking efforts to fire them on marriage; and younger women expected paid labour to be a permanent part of their lives.

Yet, many women struggled to support themselves and their families on second-class wages, with little recognition of the importance of their labour. Most women were limited to lower-paid "female-typed" jobs, while the very few professional women faced deeply entrenched sexism. A "second tier" of immigrant, racialized, and Indigenous women workers were channelled into contingent, super-exploited occupations.[44] Despite a transformed workforce, tenacious myths persisted: as members of the Canadian Union of Public Employees told the RCSW, women were considered secondary, temporary earners; if they had young children, they were told they should not work at all. Women experienced the contradictions between a male-breadwinner ideal and a female-breadwinner reality with acute frustration, voicing their ire in hundreds of private letters to the RCSW. Single mothers who could barely support their children on "women's wages" complained about an economic system that denied their role as breadwinners and a familial ideology that portrayed their children as "third-class oddities" because they were not in a *Leave It to Beaver* family.[45] These glaring contradictions in women's daily lives fuelled their resistance to the status quo.

The strength of Marxist feminism and socialism in the seventies women's movement also made paid work a priority for activists. In the tradition of Bertha Merrill Burns and Rose Henderson, socialists believed feminism would be meaningless unless it eliminated patriarchal-capitalist work relations. Both socialist and labour feminism, overlapping but distinct, shaped women's workplace organizing. Labour-feminist projects to enhance women's equality, dignity, and economic autonomy derived inspiration, energy, and direction from socialists, but labour feminism was more politically diverse. Socialist feminists, with roots in women's liberation, new communist parties, and Marxist-feminist thought, had a more thoroughgoing critique of the systemic oppressions of class, gender, race, and sexuality. They saw capitalist patriarchy, entrenched and legitimated in structural and ideological forms, in need of root-and-branch transformation. Labour organizing was a way station, not the final destination.

Labour feminist methods were multiple: organizing women into unions, creating women's caucuses within unions, establishing independent feminist unions, gaining access to non-traditional work, pay equity coalitions, daycare mobilizations, human rights protections, anti–sexual harassment groups, and many cultural explorations of women's labour. There were long-running campaigns with tangible reform legacies, such as pay equity, as well as fleeting efforts, such as a 1977 Waitresses Action Committee, protesting an Ontario government proposal to cut back on servers' wage entitlements.[46] While pay equity echoed similar feminist demands going back to the turn of the century, other issues were ignited by new feminist thinking about power and sexuality. Campaigns against sexual harassment exposed an old problem, empowering women to make new demands for dignity at work. The post-war conception of daycare as a "welfare" issue was challenged by women's liberationists, who claimed it as an equality "right" and a means to rethink the nuclear, patriarchal family. As Lisa Pasolli shows, these challenges were translated into militant tactics: occupations of university and community spaces, cooperative experiments, and uncompromising lobbying of governments.[47]

It is important to recognize continuities. Before women's liberation burst on the scene, working-class women were stirring the pot, pushing for maternity leave and contesting the sacred shibboleths of separate male/female seniority lists and the male-breadwinner ideal. Ontario women autoworkers organized their first women's conference in 1964; Ontario Federation of Labour women followed in 1965. Both addressed women's second class-status in the labour movement, if gingerly so. Avoiding the label "feminist," women were encouraged to forward equality claims based on the labour movement's historic commitment to "fairness" on the job. In the late 1960s, women autoworkers campaigned for human rights legislation to prohibit sex discrimination in the workplace. In a decisive shift, says Pamela Sugiman, "they began to view gender equality as a specific goal, not a residual gain in a universal working-class struggle."[48] They worked with the Voice of Women and younger women's liberationists on these issues, absorbing their feminist ideas and, in turn, influencing them.

Nor were autoworkers alone in rethinking gender hierarchies. Grace Hartman, later president of the Canadian Union of Public Employees (CUPE) and NAC, recalled the sexism she endured in a white-collar union of municipal workers; men dismissed her activism as not "bad for a woman" or, worse, needled her with reminders that married women belonged in the home. Speaking to fellow women unionists in British Columbia, she urged them to fight back and fight harder for their rights, reminding men in the audience, "Women are not going back to the kitchen ... so this is your fight too."[49]

Despite continuities in working-class feminism, there were "radical ruptures" in labour organizing.[50] New rebellions were encouraged by socialist feminists who reinvigorated a left-wing presence within the labour movement that had been suppressed for some time. The pathway from women's liberation to workplace organizing was exemplified by the Vancouver Women's Caucus (VWC). The caucus initially promoted reproductive rights, created feminist curricular materials for teachers and students, and educated themselves with a hefty reading list; it also created subgroups, including the Working Women's Association. The association moved quickly from theoretical discussion to actual practice, supporting strikes, leafleting unorganized workplaces, and sponsoring educationals for working women. No workplace was too insignificant, no group of women dismissed as a lost cause.

In an interview, former VWC members conveyed the exhilarating feeling that fuelled labour and socialist feminism: this sensibility combined a sharpened awareness of oppression with a political optimism that the course of history might be altered by radical action. They came to feminism through different pathways, some through student activism or anti-war work, some with progressive parents or unconventional working mothers, some already versed in labour and socialist struggles, some not. Whatever the original spark, these women shared common outrage about social inequalities and women's oppression, an unbounded sense of intellectual and political discovery, and a camaraderie that comes from taking on the impossible. Inaction was out of the question; the only debate was whether they were "revolutionaries" or mere socialists. Their worldview was shaped by the "spirit of 1968," anti-capitalist and "anti-imperialist" movements of the time. Perhaps most evocative was their sense of *possibility:* as one joked, "I guess we thought we could change the world."[51]

One of the many projects the Working Women's Association initiated was a daring attempt to set up an independent, socialist-feminist trade union, the Service, Office, Retail Workers Union of Canada (SORWUC). SORWUC tackled what Canadian Labour Congress (CLC) unions claimed were near-impossible targets: banks, stores, restaurants. Shaped by New Left, socialist, and women's liberationist ideas, SORWUC was a union dedicated to women's equality *and* class mobilization: women's liberation, it insisted, was possible only when "we put an end to women's economic inferiority."[52] As a first step, unions should set aside Cold War anti-communism and

Figure 10.2 SORWUC organized bank, service, and daycare workers other unions had failed to unionized. In 1977, Vancouver SORWUC servers at the Bimini's restaurant went on strike | Rare Books and Special Collections, UBC Library, SORWUC Local 4 fonds, box 15, file 21

political timidity, combining unionization with movements for universal daycare, rent controls, and welfare provision.

SORWUC integrated grassroots decision making, rank-and-file democracy, and gender equality into its union practices. Members were given full control over bargaining, all positions were elected, and any paid officer could not receive more pay than a normal worker. Equal pay and anti–sexual harassment provisions were contract priorities. SORWUC was centred primarily in British Columbia, where, as Julia Smith shows, it had remarkable success. It organized twenty-three bank locals in Vancouver by 1977, as well as gaining a foothold in restaurants, daycares, and social services. SORWUC contradicted the pessimism of the CLC, which saw these feminized jobs as almost "unorganizable," and it revealed the immense appeal of a working-class feminism stressing dignity in the workplace, equality for women, and a more compassionate, equitable society.

Smith also pinpointed the causes of SORWUC's decline in the 1980s. First, employer opposition was unrelenting, with strikebreakers used to shut down organizing. The damage done by CLC unions, which raided SORWUC locals and refused to honour their strikes because SORWUC was outside the "official" house of labour, was considerable. The labour law regime also worked against small units trying to establish first contracts, even though SORWUC pioneered a major legal victory for the whole union movement by arguing successfully that each bank branch could be organized as a unit. But government-appointed labour relations boards were mystified by this feminist union, dismissing it as a women's liberation group rather than a trade union. In fact, it was both.

SORWUC was not the only experiment using democracy and decentralization to foster workplace feminism. Another BC union of clerical workers, the Association of University and College Employees (AUCE), experimented with grassroots control, elected leaders, a vibrant shop-steward system, and a non-hierarchical organizational model. The result: women's demands – equal pay, maternity leave, and rethinking gendered job classifications – bubbled up from the grassroots as union priorities, earning AUCE the label "feminist union," although many locals were mixed gender.[53] These experiments benefited from a vibrant feminist counterculture in which paid work *mattered,* and was being retheorized and reimagined. Women's labour history and employment issues were prominent in feminist newspapers like *Kinesis;* Marxist-feminist writing analysed productive and reproductive labour; filmmakers documented women's work; and women's presses featured how-to-organize manuals as well as books on unions, organizing, and working women's oral histories.[54]

Feminists also participated in campaigns arising from nationalist dissatisfaction with international unions headquartered in the United States, which were preoccupied with American research and political priorities. New Canadian unions were created as alternatives, some committed to democratic control, socialism, and feminism. The Canadian Textile and Chemical Union (CTCU), led by Madeleine Parent and Kent Rowley, was perhaps the best example. In the 1950s, Parent and Rowley had abandoned their positions in an international (American) union over internal corruption and turned their organizing energies to marginal workplaces, often with immigrant, women workers. Labelled communists, they were ostracized by the CLC, yet the CTCU scored a series of organizing coups. Giving women workers the experience and confidence to become activist leaders was part of Parent's agenda. So too was pushing the union to take a firm stand on feminist issues: the CTCU endorsed a pro-choice position before other unions and participated in the Ontario Equal Pay Coalition.[55]

Parent, like the unionists in SORWUC, saw class struggle as a vehicle for women's emancipation. Women's equality and dignity were integrated into CTCU labour struggles, including major strikes at Texpack in Brantford and Puretex in Toronto, where the union exposed the egregious video surveillance of women workers, also taking it up – unsuccessfully – with the Human Rights Commission. Learning how to organize from Parent was itself a feminist experience. The CTCU created important cross-generational connections for labour feminists. True, some older labour feminists in the CLC were irritated with "women's liberationists" like SORWUC for ignoring their earlier attempts to organize white-collar and bank workers. Seventies feminists, they pointed out, did not suddenly invent equality issues. However, in the case of the CTCU, Parent's political acumen inspired a new generation of socialist feminist labour activists, including Lynn Kaye, a labour lawyer and later NAC president, and Laurell Ritchie, a union organizer, later Canadian Auto Workers staffer.

When Grace Hartman warned that women were not returning to the kitchen, she might have added they were heading straight for public sector unions. Once the public sector secured the right to unionize in the late 1960s, its heavily female workforce became a power to be reckoned with and a conduit for feminism: nurses, teachers, hospital workers, child care workers, civil servants, and more used unions to advance a gender equality agenda. It was no accident that CUPE, with a large female membership, advocated for child care, daycare workers lobbied for pay equity, and teachers' unions called for non-sexist education. The militant, illegal strike of nurses in Alberta in 1988 bore the unmistakable imprint of feminism. A feminist analysis framed their objection to the devaluation of their caring labour and their opposition to the male-dominated patriarchal power structures of the hospital.[56]

By the late 1970s, women were also mobilizing within their unions in informal networks, caucuses, and regular conferences, each with different degrees of autonomy, though all intent on purusing gender equality. One school of thought saw women's committees as a "deficit" strategy, giving women the confidence and tools to become active; another stressed their united voices in support of feminist demands and a more female-friendly union culture.[57] Women's caucuses also became allies for anti-racist and LGBTQ organizing within unions. While ostensibly created to rectify the paucity of women leaders, caucuses encouraged forms of participatory democracy that aided grassroots feminism and militancy. The "interconnected web of militancy, democracy and gender," as Linda Briskin comments, "was the ground on which feminist reimagining of labour organizations took place."[58]

Labour feminism encountered some resistance from entrenched masculinist ideas and men who "had long controlled the movement."[59] Women's separate organizing, demands for access to non-traditional jobs, and affirmative action challenged traditional union definitions of equality as sameness. Differential treatment, feminists countered, might be required when power and privilege were already distributed unequally. Feminism was slowly accommodated, even if the road was a bumpy one. As late as 1990, a controversy blew up when the CLC conference on "empowering women" included separate men's and women's workshops. In the face of the public displeasure of male unionists, CLC vice-president Nancy Riche stood her ground. Defending female-only spaces, she offered men some pointed advice: perhaps they should use their workshops to contemplate ways to support women in their struggle for equality.

Labour feminism also fuelled campaigns for legislative change relating to human rights, pay equity, and employment equity, the latter concept developed by the 1984 federal Abella Royal Commission on Equality in Employment, which recommended proactive measures to facilitate equality for Indigenous peoples, the disabled, visible minorities, and women.[60] Provincial pay equity coalitions were often alliances created from the bottom up; in Ontario, the Pay Equity Coalition drew together twenty-five organizations, including liberal feminists from Business and Professonal Women's Clubs, trade unionists, social reformers from the YWCA, and "left of NDP" socialist feminists.[61] Despite its admirable intention to combat systemic wage discrimination, some feminists doubted its potential: pay equity would not redress the racial division of labour; it still sanctioned some wage hierarchies (not a very socialist vision); and it relied on job-evaluation models in which employers had a (biased) say.[62] As provincial pay equity campaigns unfolded, women also had to manage the nitty-gritty of legislative detail, compromise, negotiation, and engagement with mainstream parties. Reformist legal strategies in general elicited debate; they might be co-opted, contradictory, produce unintended consequences, and fail to address the underlying economic basis of systemic inequalities. Still, the hope of addressing glaring pay gaps of impoverished women enticed labour feminists into the legislative route.

The Ontario Pay Equity Coalition scored a significant win in 1987, when a pay equity bill covering the public and private sector (the latter a first) was passed under a Liberal-NDP accord. Critics from the left saw this as a "partial labour feminist" victory, but even this "partial" bill provoked hyperbolic opposition from business and neo-conservative, anti-feminist lobbies.[63]

Figure 10.3 Laura Sky, filmmaker and feminist activist, speaks from a pick-up truck during an Equal Pay Coalition demonstration, Toronto, ca. 1980–82 | Canadian Women's Movement Archives, University of Ottawa Archives and Special Collections, CA ON0034 10-001-S3-I361

Feminists were well aware of the legislation's limitations – it left out some women with no male job comparators, and it might require costly litigation – but, nonetheless, they believed it raised potentially radical questions: What is the underlying basis for women's economic subordination? Why is a systemic undervaluing of women's labour integral to capitalist social relations? Moreover, the gendered labour market had implications beyond the workplace: it was linked to the ideology of masculine superiority, the family wage ideal, and women's subordination in the family.

Piecemeal legal reforms in a capitalist wage economy inevitably pose dilemmas for feminists. Do limited gains aid or suppress more radical resistance? Does the process of organizing – even with flawed outcomes – encourage a bolder alternative vision? The changing economic context also shaped the fate of pay equity. In supermarkets, women gained little, as global restructuring led to a proliferation of part-time jobs that were impossible "moving targets" for evaluation.[64] New hopes, it is true, shape resistance.

When a Conservative government was elected in Ontario in 1995, it promptly repealed key elements of the *Pay Equity Act,* ended the funding of pay adjustments and eliminated the Pay Equity Legal Clinic – along with other anti-labour and anti-equality measures. Labour feminists fought back with pressure campaigns and lengthly legal battles to regain what had been lost.

Labour feminism also found an outlet in new autonomous pressure groups like Saskatchewan Working Women (SWW), Hamilton Working Women, Edmonton Working Women, and Organized Working Women (OWW) in Ontario. Open only to trade union members, OWW assumed that reshaping the workplace through collective bargaining was "inseparable" from the fight for "women's equality." If OWW could "facilitate women's increased activism within unions," this would "strengthen the trade union movement" and result in unions integrating "women's demands" into contracts.[65] OWW was union-centred but had an expansive understanding of alliances; it worked with other social movements as well as women from unions (like the CTCU) shunned by the mainstream labour movement – despite pressure to the contrary from CLC unions.

The Edmonton, Hamilton, and Saskatchewan groups were open to all working women, though they were still predominantly white, urban working women. SWW was one of the most active and longest-lasting groups. Emerging from a 1978 Saskatchewan Federation of Labour meeting, SWW drew in recruits from the Waffle, new communist parties, the labour movement, the NDP, and unorganized women workers. It had multiple commitments to "political action, the labour movement and party politics."[66] It also hoped to spur unionization of the unorganized. SWW based its constitution on SORWUC's democratic, feminist principles and initially tried organizing bank workers, though the three Saskatchewan locals did not survive.

Some SWWers were seasoned unionists disenchanted with timid union leaders "suspicious and unfriendly" toward feminism: "They were afraid of everything that was political or radical," recalled one member, "and women's liberation was like, Oh My God" – beyond the pale.[67] Even women's caucuses within the labour movement, they astutely feared, would be absorbed and co-opted into the union leadership, losing their radical vision. As an autonomous labour *and* socialist-feminist group, SWW could operate outside and inside the trade union movement. It promoted a radical critique of capitalist patriarchy but also worked on immediate reforms; it was critical of unions' sexist culture, while still firmly supporting labour causes.

SWW theorized expansively about multiple forms of labour sustaining the oppression of women: the links between unpaid domestic labour and

Figure 10.4 Saskatchewan Working Women at a Saskatoon City Council meeting, January 1979 | Photograph by Tammy Tampalski, City of Saskatoon Archives, Saskatoon Star Phoenix fonds, S-SP-A-11283-001-1

paid work; the isolation of farm women labouring without pay; the super-exploitation of immigrant labour. In an agricultural province, it wanted to build links with rural women, but its educational and organizing efforts were focused primarily on urban life, class struggle, poverty, and, later, racism. By the 1980s, the group was engaged in solidarity work with Third World groups protesting imperialism abroad, particularly in Latin America and apartheid South Africa. Temporary, issue-based collaborations with Indigenous women were also attempted; SWW supported a daycare for Indigenous children in Regina, met with Indigenous groups to listen to their needs, then provided workshops on Indigenous issues. Even if SWW's political analysis took account of race and colonialism, its primary lens was class, its membership predominantly white. Indigenous women, the majority still living on reserves, organized autonomously.

Socialist feminists in SWW were committed to labour causes, but the two strands of feminism were distinct, overlapping, sometimes existing in tension. In the 1980s, Linda Briskin identified the conundrum of socialist-feminist practice as a balancing act between "mainstreaming" (working within the system) and "disengagement" (critiquing the entire system); there was no magic recipe for balance, only continued struggle to bring socialist-feminist ideas "to labour institutions and public consciousness."[68] Yet, many women of colour argued that neither labour nor socialist feminists had an adequate anti-racist analysis, a charge socialist feminists acknowledged as they turned a critical eye on their own movement.

Immigration, Race, and Ethnicity

In the 1970s, Saskatchewan was an overwhelming white settler province, with minimal in-migration. In the next decade, though, SWW joined with immigrant women's organizations to demand legislative protection for domestic workers on temporary visas. Similar alliances emerged elsewhere. After the late 1960s, declining European immigration and Canada's labour force needs resulted in the partial liberalization of immigration policy; a points system, ostensibly race-neutral, replaced long-standing racist "white preference" practices. Systemic and subjective gender and race biases did not suddenly evaporate since "liberalization" was essentially a new "rationalization for the primacy of labour market principles" that encoded race and gender inequalities. Still, new rules did produce demographic, cultural, and political change as more immigrants from Asia, Africa, the Caribbean, and Latin America settled in Canada.[69]

The RCSW had paid scant attention to immigrant women. Extrapolating from existing census trends, it assumed newcomers would "assimilate" into the Anglo or French majorities: a white, European population was again equated with nation building. In feminist journalism of the 1970s, "immigrant women" and "race" were often uttered in one breath: articles decried racism against immigrants and urged more attention to Indigenous, racialized, and immigrant women as a "group." The equation of "immigrants" with "race" was in one sense illogical, since immigrants had diverse social and geographical origins. Yet increasing numbers of immigrant women of colour, or those without English or French, did encounter the most "adverse" immigrant experience, including racism.[70]

In the 1980s, the designation "visible minority women" was used to distinguish women of colour, but it too was problematic. Himani Bannerji's critique disassembled the term: if all people have visibility, she asked, "how are we more visible than others?" The assumption is that "there is something peculiar about these people" – in other words, normal equals white, abnormal equals women of colour. The term homogenizes all nonwhite people from diverse cultures, languages, and states; they are categorized by their "visible" bodies into a "social zone that is also a prison."[71] President of the Congress of Black Women of Canada (CBWC) Glenda Simms used, but was critical of, the "visible minority" label: the "problem is not that we are a minority," she said, but rather that "we live in a racist society."[72]

Figure 10.5 Jean Augustine, Liberal MP, speaking at Congress of Black Women of Canada, Hamilton meeting, n.d. | Kenny Photographic Productions, Clara Thomas Archives and Special Collections, York University Libraries, Jean Augustine photo scrapbook

Some anti-racist feminists nonetheless utilized "visible minority," in part because this vocabulary was institutionalized in organizations, committees, and caucuses that dealt with racism, sexism, as well as the immigrant experience, such as the National Organization of Immigrant and Visible Minority Women, founded in Winnipeg in 1986. Immigration and anti-racist activism ran in parallel *and* overlapping tracks, though there were debates over priorities: anti-racist groups wanted "racism named, prioritized, addressed," while immigrant groups saw this "folded into" their mandate, along with sexist immigration policy and cultural discrimination.[73]

Immigration and race issues came together over time in groups like the CBWC, formed in 1973 out of the Canadian Negro Women's Association. Alienated from a predominantly white women's movement and a male-dominated Black "nationalist" movement, women in the CBWC built a parallel movement of advocacy, education, and reform, though it forged coalitions with other feminists on specific issues.[74] Black women, they argued, faced ongoing "racial discrimination in employment and other areas," but they were simultaneously affected by "sexism": both shaped Black women's lives "from the time slaves were first brought to Canada."[75]

Often led by professional women, the CBWC convened annual meetings that explored issues ranging from familial concerns about health, violence, and youth to workplace inequality, daycare, and retraining for women. Not unlike earlier organizations of African-Canadian women, the CBWC acted both as community builders for Black dignity and advocates for women's equality. Racism in the school system was tackled as was the "triple oppression" of class, gender, and race in the labour force. By the 1980s, the CBWC was more vocal on immigration and refugee issues, delivering briefs on the needs of refugee women and responding with public campaigns that highlighted instances of racial discrimination and violence directed against newcomers. Together, CBWC leaders hoped, all groups of Black women might create a powerful solidarity enabling the organization's advocacy of "human rights and liberties for Black women."[76]

Newer organizations like Women Working with Immigrant Women (WWIW), founded in the mid-1970s, were premised on women's immigrant rather than cultural or racial identity, though WWIW too addressed racism. Immigrant women's interests were sometimes "subsumed" under the voices of "male immigrant community leaders," but women's marginality was also embedded in immigration policy.[77] "Family class" or "sponsored" immigration, for instance, assumed women were dependants in a patriarchal, male-breadwinner family, even though immigrant women participated disproportionately in the workforce. They were denied language training and pushed into low-wage jobs, making them more vulnerable to underemployment and poverty. Sponsorship overdetermined women's fate in the face of violence or marriage breakdown; they feared ostracism or deportation if they left families, and existing sexual and domestic assault services were geared toward the needs of white, English-speakers.[78] Women refugee claimants who faced violence in their own countries were also ignored: "well-founded fears of rape," feminists pointed out, were not valid rationales for refugee status.[79]

By the 1980s, grassroots, community-based organizing through immigrant women's resource centres was common in urban areas. Organizations serving immigrant women often crossed into political advocacy. How could they not, when women's daily problems resulted from sexist policies, racist ideas, and employment discrimination? However, state funding for ostensibly "helping" organizations also created political constraints. Proactive advocacy might include defensive campaigns supporting women for whom existing laws proved useless, or worse, who were targets of the state. Their personal stories advertised the immigrant realities of racism, sexism, and class bias. INTERCEDE, a group advocating for the rights of foreign domestic workers, went public with the case of a Toronto domestic worker who quit a job paying a shocking $50 a week, only to face deportation because her paperwork for a new job could not be completed. Once the *Charter of Rights and Freedoms* was enacted, INTERCEDE used that too to challenge discriminatory labour laws.[80]

Similarly, the Women's Issues Committee of the Coalition of Black Trade Unionists rallied behind a South African health care worker in Sudbury who won a human rights case for discrimination, only to find that the job she had secured was abolished; she was left mopping floors. The message was clear: don't complain, don't demand your rights.[81] Unions co-sponsored these public protest meetings, though unions also developed institutionalized, internal methods of addressing racism: anti-racist campaigns, departments, committees, and staff positions.[82] A more comprehensive point of resistance was on-the-ground organizing to alter the legal basis for exploitative employment practices, such as the temporary domestic worker program. In the 1950s, small groups of Caribbean immigrants were admitted only to fill service and domestic service jobs. An expanded temporary visa program followed in the 1970s. As more women joined the workforce, the state did not invest in child care but rather encouraged the use of temporary labour of less affluent women from abroad. Yet these women were denied both the protection of labour laws and a pathway to citizenship.

In Vancouver, no fewer than four coalitions protested the temporary work program: the Labour Advocacy and Research Association (LARA); the British Columbia Domestics Association, which campaigned for provincial legislative reform; the Committee for the Advancement of the Rights of Domestic Workers, targeting federal reform; and the Domestic Workers Union, a trade union that grew out of an international committee against racism. LARA, originally concerned with visa farm workers, provided space for Caribbean women domestics to congregate to discuss common problems. And they were plentiful: ill treatment on the job, including unending hours, sexual harassment, and lack of living space; problems negotiating visas; fears that any complaints about ill treatment would lead to deportation; and racist stereotypes about women's "natural affinity" for caring or subordinate labour.[83] LARA, SORWUC, and the BC Domestics Association pressed for new provincial labour standards to protect domestics against rampant exploitation. They secured a minimal victory: domestics were included in the regulation of minimum wages and holidays, but many other inequities, such as hours of work and overtime, were left unregulated.[84]

Literary and journalistic writing was an important part of visa worker campaigns, exposing the class, race, and gender relations of paid domestic labour. Makeda Silvera's *Silenced*, for instance, commanded political and cultural attention. Reprinted three times, *Silenced* made the personal political by recounting domestic workers' life stories, their day-to-day humiliations and exploitation, as well as desperate efforts to aid their families at home.[85] A journalist for the Black Canadian paper, *Contrast*, Silvera covered the campaign to support seven Jamaican domestic workers threatened with deportation in 1977. Coached by immigration authorities to omit any mention of children at home on their initial visa applications, they were later threatened with deportation when they applied to bring their families to Canada. With the support of African-Canadian, immigrant, labour, and women's groups, the Committee against the Deportation of Immigrant Women secured reprieve, but this was but one victory in a much larger battle.

Ultimately, activists looked to Ottawa to change a system that domestic workers argued was a "form of bonded slavery."[86] In 1980, a national campaign of domestic workers and feminist and labour allies, with the apt slogan "Good enough to work, good enough to stay," used lobbying, briefs, and public demonstrations to push the state to alter a system that held domestics hostage to a modern version of indentured labour. Success was again partial. The government allowed women to apply for landed immigrant status after two years, though it employed subjective measurements of their "suitability" for self-sufficiency. Women with children were still assessed more critically: the government wanted their temporary labour, not their families.

By the mid-1980s, Canadian governments were concerned about newcomers who were politicized by their experience of immigration and racism. Increasing immigration, "revolutionary movements" abroad (and some at home), and the "popularity of women's issues" made immigrant women of colour a constituency to be watched, enticed by the state into "appropriate" politics to "neutralize" tensions building up.[87] Linda Carty and Himani Bannerji point out that the designation "visible minority women" originated with government-sponsored conferences in the early 1980s on the problems of immigrant women, including racism and the workplace. Since the state had a hand in shaping the political agenda of these groups, "visible minority" women were constructed as an undifferentiated group, with class differences obscured.[88]

In a similarly critical vein, Tania Das Gupta notes the "problematic and contradictory, beneficial and regressive" nature of organizing visible minority

Figure 10.6 Campaigns in the 1980s for reform of immigration rules for temporary domestic workers used the slogan "Good enough to work, good enough to stay," which is still used today | Photograph courtesy of Tania Liu, United Food and Commerical Workers (UFCW), reprinted on https://rabble.ca/blogs/bloggers/policyfix/2015/04/temporary-foreign-workers-face-unjust-crackdown

women under the umbrella of the state's institutionalized multiculturalism. The federal government made every effort to manage the agenda and choice of spokeswomen for consultations and government-sponsored events, with the result that more critical reflections on the systemic and structural nature of racism were curtailed and grassroots groups sidelined. To boycott such events seemed a dead end, as state-facilitated visible minority and immigrant women initiatives did offer space for anti-racist work, particularly urgent since the 1970s witnessed increased racist assaults on people of colour, and countervailing political resistance from small groups to this violence.[89] But they were also a means to integrate selective middle-class elements, co-opt anti-racism as "race relations," and promote individual "solutions" of immigrant adjustment, education, and aid, endorsing superficial change.[90]

Such state-facilitated organizing had contradictory effects, but there were many bottom-up mobilizations of immigrant women addressing the intersection of race, class, and gender inequality. Some were connected to critiques of imperialism. Latin American refugees displaced to Canada by reactionary, American-sanctioned military coups, for instance, processed gender issues through the prism of anti-imperialist work. Haitian women who fled the American-backed dictatorship of "Baby Doc" Duvalier exemplified grassroots efforts linking feminist, class-based, and anti-imperialist politics. Montreal émigrés joined Maison d'Haiti, embracing its critique of imperialism; they also used its newspaper to protest the exploitation of female domestic workers as "slaves."[91] Rally for Haitian Women emerged out of Maison d'Haiti in 1973. An anti-Duvalier cross-class coalition that was feminist and socialist, Rally for Haitian Women argued that the struggles for feminism and democracy were inextricably linked. It cooperated with Canadian groups like the CBWC as well as international women's organizations, including communist ones. As anti-imperialists, these émigré feminists valued global alliances of women who had experienced dispossession and dislocation in the face of colonial and dictatorial regimes.

Nègès Vanyan, a second feminist Haitian organization, organized Quebec émigrés as "single mothers, immigrants, blacks." Both the local and the global mattered. Internationally, Nègès Vanyan created alliances with other global and national feminist organizations, pressing the case for a new democracy in Haiti that included women's rights. In Montreal, it organized around women's literacy, work, education, and health needs, speaking to Creole women in their own language, often derided as a dialect of the very poor. Spokeswoman Adeline Chancy was an effective public educator, speaker, and organizer, sharing her analysis of the intertwined gender and racial inequality shaping immigrant women's lives. Understanding the historical roots of these structures, she argued, was critical: these "date from a [Canadian] past marked by conquest, massacres, subjugation to slavery and missionary crusades."[92]

Visible minority and immigrant women's organizations with an anti-racist agenda looked to other feminist organizations as allies but were routinely disappointed, angry, and frustrated. Women of colour were critical of an overwhelmingly white women's movement for its failure to comprehend how pervasive racism was and to reflect on their more privileged identities. Within NAC, for example, observers claimed a misplaced ideal of "multicultural diversity" exercised an ideological grip that hampered its ability to deal with racism.[93] Yet racialized women were well aware that whiteness was "exalted" and "people of colour" were perceived as "outsiders" coming into "an existing nation."[94]

An internal NAC Visible Minority and Immigrant Women's Committee, established in 1984, offered space and means to name and challenge racism – both in society and within NAC. In 1985, a group of Ontario women publicly contradicted the NAC president's claim that NAC truly opposed racism, disputing NAC's prerogative to speak on behalf of all Canadian women. The Visible Minority and Immigrant Women's Committee prioritized an anti-racist agenda and secured enhanced representation on the NAC executive and committees for Indigenous women and women of colour. "It took a lot of fighting on our part, a lot of challenging to get NAC to listen to what we were saying," recalled one member. "From 1986 we have had to push and challenge and insist and get angry and call people racist, but at least when people come out they don't only see white faces on the stage, which is also very important."[95]

Many histories suggest difficult discussions, white feminists' defensiveness, and slow change within organizations. Some histories claim a symbolically important ideological shift circa 1986, when the International Women's Day event in Toronto featured racism as its key issue with the slogan "Women say No! to racism from Toronto to South Africa." Aside from this being a Toronto-centric view, the Toronto Black Women's Collective disputed the full commitment of the IWD Committee to anti-racism, pointing to its reluctance to allow Black women to "assume leadership and authority." The

Figure 10.7 International Women's Day anti-racism poster, Toronto, 1986 | Poster design by Sunday Harrison, courtesy of the author

committee took the critique to heart, asking why socialist feminists had not incorporated a systemic analysis of race into their practice.[96]

Toronto was not alone: in Calgary, both the 1986 and 1987 IWD events featured a dialogue about race.[97] There is something of a "progress" narrative in these reflections, in which a white, middle-class feminist movement reluctantly realizes its own privilege. Second-wave feminist theory and organizations, the argument goes, "assumed there was a singular experience of gender" until these ideas were "shattered" in the mid-1980s, when "anti-racist" feminists asked "how race intersected with gender."[98] We should, perhaps, be wary of linear narratives, especially those that essentialize "black" or "women of colour" feminism (and "white" feminism, for that matter), also congealing class and race together.[99] In the 1990s, some feminist writing juxtaposed a new wave of enlightened feminism that recognized differences among women to a simplistic sixties and seventies feminism concerned with gender. The story is more complicated.

Fighting the Right

Racism was linked to the rise of new right-wing organizations in North America in the late 1970s and early 1980s. Anti-racist, LGBTQ, and feminist organizations understood them as a potent threat to the small gains they had made and the possibility of further reform. Feminists encountered a changing social context by the end of the eighties. An economic downturn, which had begun in the mid-1970s, resulted in cuts to health, education, and social services; the federal and provincial governments initiated coercive measures to curtail labour's bargaining rights, and a neo-conservative revolution, symbolized abroad by Ronald Reagan and Margaret Thatcher, had echoes in Canada's conservative government of Brian Mulroney, elected in 1984.[100] This counter-revolution marked the consolidation of neoliberalism, a form of capitalism prioritizing individualism, the market, government deregulation, and the rights of capital across borders. In reality, government regulation was not abandoned; it was redirected to favour business interests as they attempted to reverse falling profits, solve resource problems, and put a lid on working-class demands for "more," including those voiced by women and racialized workers who had never been an equal party to the "Fordist accord" of the post-war period.

Just as women and racialized workers were demanding a more equitable share of the pie, the pie was carved up with a smaller slice going to working people. Successive Western governments blamed budgetary deficits on social welfare, health, and education spending and on unrealistic wage demands, a myth repeated so often it became "truth." This ideological offensive was perhaps the most insidious side of neoliberalism. Thatcher's claim that "there is no alternative" to austerity (for workers) and deregulation (for capital) began to become "common sense," even permeating social democratic and labour parties.

Feminists identified multiple ideological tentacles in the New Right. While situated in a material reality of slow economic growth, unemployment and stagflation, the right included groups hostile to feminism, LGBTQ rights, and racialized immigrants. Opposition to abortion, as Judy Rebick pointed out, was a centrepiece of the right's agenda.[101] Calling for feminist organizing against a reconstituted right in 1981, Sara Diamond in Vancouver and Amy Gottlieb in Toronto pointed to a renewed Ku Klux Klan presence and police violence against both racialized immigrants and gays.[102] Organizations linked to evangelical Christianity, others merely fascist makeovers, were conduits for the New Right. Fascists in the Western Guard and Nationalist Parties peddled the usual toxic mix of racism, anti-Semitism and white supremacy, while evangelicals claimed to be protectors of the traditional family and a mythological domesticity that had never existed for many immigrant, working-class, and racialized women.

More lesbian and gay public visibility and feminist demands for equality had created a "crisis of legitimacy in the traditional family"; patriarchy and heterosexuality no longer simply went unquestioned.[103] The mainstream media uncritically relayed anxieties about the supposed disintegration of the "traditional" gender order: typical headlines included how "women's lib is driving men to counselors" and "how feminism became a dirty word" (which quoted a woman calling feminists "a bunch of ugly dogs"). Men's rights groups also secured a public hearing for their allegation of reverse discrimination. Apparently, feminism led to their oppression.[104]

Homophobic American right-wing proselytizers against women's equality, such as Anita Bryant, were welcomed to Canada by new organizations like Renaissance International, Positive Parents, and Right to Life. United in their opposition to gay civil rights and women's reproductive choices, they smeared politicians who championed gay issues, railed against abortion, and portrayed lesbians as a menace to society. Lesbians in caring and teaching professions feared a new target on their backs as the right claimed they should not be in positions to "indoctrinate" the young.[105] Feminist and LGBTQ groups in urban centres pointed to policing problems: law enforcement intelligence officers infiltrated gay and lesbian organizations and looked the other way when LGBTQ people were harassed on the streets.

Propping up an imagined "traditional" family was especially important to REAL (Realistic, Equal, Active for Life) Women, founded in 1985. While vehemently anti-choice, the group also opposed "no-fault divorce, universal free child care, enforced affirmative action, equal pay for work of equal value, and prostitution." Combining economic, social, and sexual conservatism, it claimed the wage gap between men and women was simply evidence of different "career" choices. In any case, married women's "real" role should be homemaker and mother, a helpmate to the (male) head of the household.[106] The appeal of REAL Women, as Karen Dubinsky wrote at the time, lay in the same difficult material conditions and gendered vulnerability that had nurtured feminism. Women's second-class wages, rising divorce rates, more single-mother households, and the threat of violence were realities that some women thought could be staved off with protection within a "traditional" family.

Claiming to exalt women's mothering, right-wing groups put their finger on a reality: this *was* devalued work. This appeal bore a strong resemblance to women's anti-suffragist arguments in the early 1900s. REAL Women buttressed the anti-abortion movement, itself a threat in the 1980s, as abortion providers and clinics faced attacks that became more violent and murderous in the 1990s. REAL Women's animus was also focused on NAC, derided as an unrepresentative collection of radical extremists. REAL Women demanded government funding (and got some from the Mulroney government), although its goals contradicted Canada's and the United Nations' equal rights commitments.

Socialist feminists saw ideological connections between right-wing groups and called for robust alliances of workers, lesbians and gays, the racialized, and women. Feminist tactics were multiple: they joined in fleeting mobilizations, created longer-term alliances, established their own anti-right-wing groups, and defended local SOWCs and NAC. In 1978, feminists and the LGBTQ community orchestrated a large public protest of Anita Bryant's visit to Toronto and other cities, laying the foundations for anti-right organizing, though also exposing political tensions between lesbians and gays.[107] By 1982, a wide coalition of social movement groups in the same city organized a May Day "Fight the Right" festival to educate, raise the alarm about the right, and talk about collaborations. Anti-racist, feminist, gay and lesbian, and immigrant organizations participated along with anti-imperialist groups who saw the right's hand in Reagan-Thatcher aggressions against other countries, particularly in the Global South. Women for Survival connected the right to the ascendant power of "hawks," nuclear arms

Figure 10.8 In 1978, feminists and the LGBTQ community orchestrated a large public protest of Anita Bryant's visit to Toronto. "Freedom of Press" refers to *The Body Politic* magazine | Courtesy of Charlie Dobs, http://onthebookshelves.com/abryant.htm

build-ups, the profiteering arms industry, and intervention in Third World venues such as Latin America.[108]

By 1981, the Bread and Roses socialist-feminist collective in Vancouver put "fighting the right" and "anti-racism" on its agenda; it suggested working within feminist coalitions such as the British Columbia Federation of Women and with groups "not officially part of the women's movement," such as unions and welfare groups already battling rearguard actions to cut existing entitlements.[109] Two years later, a Social Credit provincial government put right-wing ideas into legislative action. It announced a sweeping package of twenty-six bills that constituted a comprehensive attack on the post-war "accord" and social and human rights protections secured over the last three decades. The bills rolled back collective-bargaining rights in the public sector; stripped fired employees of recourse; weakened employment standards; disbanded the Human Rights Commission; abolished rent controls; and privatized some medicare services. Organizations like Vancouver Women's Health Collective, providing birth control information, were defunded; women's shelters were impoverished by cuts. Women workers and those on social assistance would be especially hard hit, but it was an all-out attack on workers, the poor, the disabled, and the marginalized.

Feminists kick-started the Lower Mainland Solidarity Coalition and helped to build the later province-wide Solidarity Coalition, both remarkable, widespread popular mobilizations against the Social Credit proposals. Women workers participated as union members, but separate feminist groups were pivotal. Women against the Budget (WAB) raised awareness about the devastating, differential impact cuts would have on women. Ignoring the advice of trade union leadership, who were more sympathetic to "respectable" protest, WAB organized a "stone soup luncheon with Gracie," held in the wealthy enclave of Shaughnessy, in Vancouver, at the home of human resources minister Grace McCarthy. The labour leadership also disapproved of the occupation of government offices, another effort WAB joined. Like many of the dissident constituencies making up the Solidarity Coalition, WAB was eventually done in by the leadership of organized labour, which

Figure 10.9 Handbill issued during the Solidarity campaign in British Columbia. Women against the Budget highlighted the harmful effects on women of Social Credit budget cuts | Simon Fraser University Archives and Records Management, Kate Braid fonds

controlled the overarching Operation Solidarity. It narrowed demands to a few collective-bargaining issues, manipulated calls for a general strike, and eventually "sold out" the whole Solidarity mobilization in an infamous private meeting between the premier and union leader Jack Munro.[110]

Other anti-right mobilizations were more identity specific. In 1981, Toronto women founded Lesbians against the Right (LAR). Some had participated in GLARE (Gays and Lesbians against the Right Everywhere) but found it "male dominated"; lesbians, they decided, had to deal with their own "invisibility," their "intertwined oppression as women."[111] The Toronto group hammered out a statement of principles: they were lesbian feminists, women-identified-women who opposed lesbian oppression and saw lesbianism as an integral part of the struggle for women's liberation. It birthed the new group with a public educational that addressed LAR's links to other struggles: trade unions, the gay movement, the women's movement, and the anti-nuclear and environmental movement. The right, as Lorna Weir told LAR, had multiple facets: the economic right wanted to deregulate the economy, but the religious right wanted to reregulate women's sexuality and reproduction.[112]

Lesbian feminists situated their struggle within global and local contexts. They recognized that both capitalist crisis and challenges to patriarchal legitimacy had stoked a North American right-wing movement, but, locally, they tackled immediate concerns such as police harassment. A Canadian network of groups similar to LAR sprang up; contacts in Calgary, Victoria, Vancouver, and Montreal sent their coordinates to the newspaper *Lesbian/Lesbienne* in order to facilitate national communication. The Vancouver group laid out an ambitious strategy involving "grass roots organizing in communities, schools, unions, women's organizations, speaking to groups, outreach to lesbians who are not involved in the lesbian movement; education of our potential allies such as the immigrant communities, women's groups, unionists, gay men; media watches of right wing activity; articles for local papers; appearances on talk shows." This exhaustive list enumerated by Sara Diamond reflected the view that the right was engaged in a multi-pronged attack, so the response also had to be multi-pronged. Out of a national meeting came the decision to set aside an annual country-wide day of "cultural, artistic, political" actions against the right.[113]

Feminists in immigrant and anti-racist organizations also protested right-wing policy shifts. Proposed changes in immigration policy to do away with the live-in caregiver program, so closely associated with women of colour, encouraged "business-class" immigrants, and enforced a costly entry fee of

Figure 10.10 GLARE (Gays and Lesbians against the Right Everywhere) mobilized against a renewed right in the late 1970s and 1980s. International Women's Day demonstration, Toronto, ca. 1982 | Photograph by author

$975 dollars – a new "head tax" – mobilized groups in fierce opposition. INTERCEDE opposed the abolition of the caregiver program, as this would "systemically discriminate against women who do women's work in the home, against poor women who do this work, and against women of colour who have made up the majority of workers."[114]

Both local Status of Women Action Committees and NAC joined the battle. As NAC moved toward a more activist stance, from lobby to "protest" group,[115] it faced the federal government's intensified neoliberal agenda and REAL Women's anti-abortion crusade. NAC's opposition to the government's constitutional plans further angered the federal Conservatives, as did its campaign against free trade with the United States. As long as NAC spoke to recognizable "women's issues" such as daycare, remembers NAC vice-president Marjorie Cohen, its voice was accepted, but when it talked about the budget, privatization, trade policy, "we were going too far."[116] Feminist labour critics charged that capital would be the free trade winners, working-class women the losers. Cohen produced a blistering feminist critique, showing women's manufacturing jobs would be lost, service jobs downgraded, social programs impacted, standards of environmental and labour protection watered down. When she spoke at the picket line of hosiery workers in Toronto in 1987, she pointed out that this employer's excuse for lowering wages was a forewarning of what free trade would bring – and she was not wrong.[117]

Adding to NAC-government antagonism, in 1989–90 the Conservatives attempted to move backwards, restricting legal access to abortion. Feminists' mobilization to protect women's reproductive rights paid off, as the bill was defeated in a tie vote in the Senate, but this was a battle simply to hold to existing gains. NAC's more left-leaning, social democratic agenda and persistent criticisms of government policy made it persona non grata with the Tories (though it would have irked neoliberal Liberals too). NAC's government funding was cut drastically, wounding its organizational abilities. In 1989, Conservatives boycotted the annual Parliament Hill lobby organized by NAC since the 1970s. NAC held its standard Q & A with the other parties, then performed a satirical skit to ridicule the Conservative no-shows, substituting a mock government of women leaders for the absent Tories. CCF playwright Elsie Gowan would have appreciated the role reversal similar to her play *You Can't Do That*. Perhaps the suffragists would have enjoyed this reborn mock parliament. The media might have praised feminists for having a sense of humour. Instead, they downplayed the "embarrassing" and "confused" presentation.[118]

Conclusion

By the end of the 1980s, feminism prospered, yet was under attack. NAC secured a national televised election debate on women's issues in 1984, signalling that feminism had "arrived" politically. Human rights and pay equity laws had secured support. In 1985, federal legislation altered the marrying-out clause in the Indian Act. Yet this revision only partially reinstated

Indigenous women, and, if (some) MPs realized violence was no (public) laughing matter, it remained a foreboding threat to women's lives, multiplied exponentially for murdered and missing Indigenous girls and women. A recent inquiry has labelled this unrelenting violence a "genocide."[119] As right-wing forces gained momentum, hatred against feminists manifested itself in violence. In November 1989, sixteen women students at L'École Polytechnique in Montreal were murdered by a misogynist gunman who declared that he "hated feminists." As my seven-year-old daughter and I placed candles at a vigil that night, I wondered whether continuing feminist struggles could possibly protect her from such violence.

While this chapter begins and ends with NAC, organizational feminism was far more regionally and politically complex than can be captured in one national organization, nor can institutional feminism be easily separated from grassroots feminism. Feminist activities coalesced around regional SOWCs, IWD coalitions, city-wide alliances, and many temporary and longer-term organizational efforts relating to welfare, abortion, work, immigration, anti-racist, anti-imperialist, anti-nuclear, LGBTQ rights, pornography, child care, and environmental groups. Although a former NAC president remarked that the eighties were characterized by the pursuit of "single" feminist issues,[120] women did attempt to connect those campaigns, both intellectually and practically, as exemplified by LGBTQ, labour, racialized, and feminists' anti-right mobilizations.

In this organizational mix, some feminist priorities persisted from the 1960s through the 1980s. Paid labour was an ongoing priority, though how feminists analysed and tackled it shifted in light of anti-racist movements, exasperation with existing unions, grassroots efforts to shatter the entrenched sexual division of labour, and legal and ideological campaigns to challenge the undervaluing of women's work. Working women, dissatisfied with the status quo, experimented with new organizations: INTERCEDE, SORWUC, SWW, union women's committees, and more were constructed by and for working women, sometimes as counterweights to existing institutions that had failed them. SORWUC used an older tactic – unionization – combined with new ideology and strategies that doubled as a fundamental critique of what the labour movement had become – politically and organizationally timid, without a comprehensive vision of feminist and socialist change. While the former became increasingly important within the labour movement, the latter did not.

Some feminist concerns that had significantly heightened in the 1960s and 1970s, such as Canadian and Québécoises relations and nationalisms, faded somewhat with time. Immigration and anti-racist organizing, on the other hand, assumed a greater presence. Demographic and political shifts challenged white feminist assumptions about what and who the nation was. If feminists in the early 1970s explored the linkage of gender and class oppression and critiqued imperialism, by the 1980s, feminist debates focused more on the intersections of race, gender, and class. This is not to argue that political changes were smooth sailing. Racialized women felt a deep disconnect between their experiences and those of white women; challenging power relations within feminism proved exacting, perhaps because white women clung to an idealized view of Canadian feminism as a haven of equality in an unequal world.

How ideological differences within feminism related to organizing is difficult to disentangle, but it is necessary to attempt to do so. Separating feminism into abstract categories – liberal, anti-racist, radical, Marxist, LGBTQ, socialist, and so on – carries the risk of assuming these streams were internally coherent, stable, perhaps with institutional expressions that were counterposed to other institutions. Yet, as this chapter shows, SOWCs were politically polymorphous, and on-the-ground organizing often involved coalitions, alliances, break-ups, and tensions that belied easy categorization. Even living one's life might involve different kinds of feminist labours, at work, intellectually, at home, in political organizing.

Nonetheless, feminist mobilizations of the 1970s and 1980s *were* demarcated by ideological difference, lived out as debate, fracture, disagreement, and the constitution and reconstitution of organizations. Feminist critique defined praxis. Marxist anti-racist critics opposed the organizational assumption that all "visible minority women" had similar interests, seeing this as class politics of liberal mystification. Socialist feminists argued against the notion that working women needed only equality of opportunity, as this strategy belied structural inequalities endemic to capitalism. Some reform feminists endorsed parliamentary strategies that equated the election of more women to office with gender progress, while others did not see this as an urgent priority, arguing that "more" representation did not necessarily produce feminist outcomes. The distinction between a liberal faith in reform within the system and a socialist-feminist critique of the entire system continues to enable different, if mutually engaged, currents of feminism.

When it came to issues such as violence or reproductive rights, defensive unities might be forged across partisan lines: in such cases, perhaps greater female political representation mattered. It was a female Conservative senator who cast the strategically critical vote on the abortion bill in 1990, helping to defeat it. But support for neoliberal policies of economic retrenchment was another kettle of fish. Conservative Party and socialist feminists would not see eye-to-eye on the economy, for neoliberalism was fundamentally a capitalist, class project, with a few women rising to the top, while others faced intensified social reproductive labour, exploitation, poverty, and a stagnating standard of living. Those were to prove some of the economic challenges the next generation of feminists faced in the coming decades.

Afterword
The 1990s and Beyond

Ending this history circa the 1990s is not an endorsement of a declension narrative that assumes feminism disappeared into a trough of indifference in the 1990s and after. Nor were the 1990s a "post-feminist" age. That term was coined by sceptics who claimed feminism had achieved its goals and outrun its usefulness: it was *history*. If feminism was spent, no longer needed, it followed that feminists still promoting it were stuck in the past; they were unreasonable, angry, misguided, bitter women – the standard anti-feminist tropes.

Post-feminism was fashioned in popular culture as liberation achieved, at least in an individualist sense. Women's freedom, ambition, autonomy, and independence were taken for granted, especially in media designed for a new generation; savvy and sexy women professionals and rebellious "girl cultures" proliferated.[1] They had appeal: after all, who would not prefer feisty female detectives and Buffy the Vampire Slayer to June Cleaver? Since freedom had arrived, women could participate in sexualized displays or self-deprecating, desperate mate-seeking that earlier feminists would have torn out their hair over, but were now claimed as consensual, ironic, humourous, liberating. This was "enlightened sexism," and it often counterposed an older, strident, dated feminist to her younger, fun-loving opposite: again, anti-feminist tropes.[2]

A few women who commanded media attention precisely because they claimed the feminist movement was passé and peddled outdated victimology accepted the label "post-feminist," but feminism was not dying. It persisted in the 1990s and after, albeit in new forms, and with new theories, issues, and strategies. Nor should we assume the standard story of historic feminist shifts by decades – the radical sixties, gender essentialist seventies, the more theoretically sophisticated eighties, and so on. Such decade-specific narratives often become overly generalized stories of progress, loss, recovery.[3] All end points are somewhat arbitrary. Mine comes after a century of feminist history, but it also recognizes that the next political generation faced an extremely challenging economic, social, and political context.

By the 1990s, the economic picture was bleak for those with a feminist critique of capitalism, and a significant section of the Canadian women's movement had some such critique, ranging from thoroughgoing Marxist to mildly social democratic. While the emergence of neoliberal capitalism can be traced back to the 1970s, it had solidified its dominance by the 1990s, drowning out the remaining defenders of a Keynesian economic order. Freeing up markets, opening borders to investors, deregulating capital, lowering direct taxes on the wealthy, governments and business claimed, would trickle down into economic benefits for all – even though wealth was clearly streaming up. A select group of feminists benefited from this new economic rationality: there was new opportunity and upward mobility for a small number of women, often white, educated, professionals, the benefactors of previous feminist battles and gains.

For the majority of women, neoliberalism did not signal expansive opportunity. Those already economically and socially marginalized by class and race were hit especially hard by shifts in social provisioning and paid and unpaid labour. Neoliberalism did not just undermine the welfare state by eroding benefits and programs, it also destabilized the very principles that underwrote feminists' equality demands. Feminists had been critical of a gendered, post-war welfare state, and a partial one at that, based on a male-breadwinner model, but there was still the possibility of speaking up for women's equal rights and entitlements as mothers and as citizens.

This language of rights was under attack as universal programs and entitlements were jettisoned by both Conservative and Liberal governments in favour of selective care for the "deserving." Poverty was not to be tackled through wealth equalization; it was a problem to be solved by providing "a leg up" to the deserving or simply blaming the undeserving. Decentralization of social welfare responsibilities to provincial and local governments encouraged more means-tested, cost-cutting measures. Social problems were individualized. Self-blame, self-discipline, or self-help became mantras of politicians and policy-makers, and it was not only Conservatives and Liberals, but some labour and social democratic governments that acquiesced in various ways to these ideas. When progressives capitulated, they closed off alternatives and opposition, giving neoliberal ideology a freer rein.

Women's paid and social reproductive labour was inevitably reshaped by neoliberalism. The post-war accord, promising secure, pensioned jobs, was evaporating; businesses no longer saw this bargain as being in its interest. Precarious, insecure work was always part of capitalist economies; the post-war compromise was more the exception than the rule, but it had raised expectations, especially for women and racialized workers, who hoped for a small slice of economic security. But paid labour was instead becoming more insecure, exacerbating gender and race divisions; women of colour, for example, were overrepresented in service jobs especially liable to precariousness. Employment in the public sector was contracted out, younger workers – even unionized ones – were forced to settle for two-tier contracts with reduced pay and benefits, and labour law protections were scaled back by some governments.

In business parlance, this was "flexibility," even innovation. Insecurity was rebranded as liberation; the new economy supposedly allowed workers to experiment, be creative, and not be tied down to a position. Like the more recent sharing and gig economy, the payoffs accrued primarily to the very few. The percentage of those unionized declined, limiting one long-standing activist avenue for women's equality-seeking. The labour movement was weakened by sustained assaults from the state and business, and, without an internal left, it tended to hunker down in defensive mode.

Social reproduction, involving all the work required for the generational and daily reproduction of humans, also changed. Most families needed multiple breadwinners, yet women's domestic labour still outpaced men's. Health, education, and community services aiding this familial labour were curtailed, privatized, or recast as an individual/family responsibility. In Ontario, for instance, an Early Years program encouraged parents to learn parenting skills, yet there was no increase in funds for public child care.[4] When social services were inadequate, whether it was for care for the elderly, disabled, or children, women were expected to pick up the slack. Yet they were monitored more closely by the state to make sure they were providing good care![5] As workers, mothers, and caregivers, women protested, but many governments became "less democratic" and responsive as policy migrated from elected, public, visible entities to backroom deliberations of politicians and bureaucrats.[6]

This new "political rationality" was more than an economic shift: it was an entirely "new way of seeing and truth telling."[7] Feminist organizing was inevitably affected by profound ideological changes in how the gendered order of public and private responsibilities was imagined, even how values like freedom and equality were defined.[8] One outcome was governments' forthright undermining of some feminist groups. The Stephen Harper government removed the words "equality" and "advocacy" from Status of Women Canada's terms of reference (its original raison d'être) and abolished the court challenges program, which had aided *Charter* challenges by groups without resources. The latter had been a thorn in the side of the Tories, irking Harper's chief of staff, who believed it favoured "as stringent a feminist interpretation of the Equality section as you could possibly have ... [They fund] the gay rights side, the feminist side, the pornography side, the abortion side."[9] Many governments not only defunded but "delegitimized" feminism, so much so that gender equality goals were "virtually erased from public discourse."[10]

There were exceptions. After the massacre at the École Polytechnique, feminists successfully drew attention to the pervasiveness of violence and achieved advances such as the reform of sexual assault laws. However, the longer term impact of neoliberalism on anti-violence work was more contentious. State funding for services came with a price tag: more oversight, institutionalization, professionalization, and bureaucratization of rape crisis centres and shelters. New laws and policies that took violence seriously altered public perceptions of violence for the better, but might have unintended consequences. Feminists always stressed that violence was embedded in social, gender, and racial power relations and thus needed tackling on multiple fronts; women required comprehensive supports such as child care, legal aid, housing, retraining, welfare, counselling, and so on. State solutions for domestic violence, however, increasingly narrowed to a "law and order" agenda focusing on criminal punishment, though blame for violence was still meted out to marginalized women not considered "ideal victims."[11]

The problematic relationship between feminism and the criminal justice system became a debate within the women's movement: Did criminalizing violence really help poor and racialized women or lead to unhelpful state interventions in their lives and the over-incarceration of poor and racialized men? "Carceral feminism" emerged as a term of critique, with some feminists admonishing others who had abandoned "social justice for criminal justice" and supported incarceration and deportation as solutions for sex trafficking and violence, strategies that evaded the underlying causes and might draw feminists into alliances with social conservatives.[12]

The neoliberal agenda *was* challenged. Significant gains made over previous decades on reproductive, sexuality, legal, and workplace issues, for instance, were defended by feminist, labour, LGBTQ, and anti-racist groups. Essential, day-to-day work, like keeping sexual assault centres and shelters afloat, took immense practical energy, and, despite the pressures of institutionalization, women running shelters continued to define their work as "social change" and pro-equality advocacy against systemic violence.[13] Other feminists mobilized to maintain a flawed welfare state they were once critical of as it threatened to become even more deficient, disproportionately hurting women with the fewest economic options. As working women faced austerity and anti-union measures, their attempts to build alternative unions were replaced by integration into existing labour structures they had long criticized – some union was better than no union.

Many organizations, including the National Action Committee (NAC), were engaged in self-critical soul searching, altering its earlier failures to effectively differentiate women's lived experiences in terms of race and colonialism, in the process creating new platforms and alliances. Many of these organizations stepped up quickly to protest neoliberal austerity policies undermining the rights and livelihoods of women, workers, and racialized and poor Canadians. During the presidency of Sunera Thobani, NAC recognized that alliances with labour and community groups were essential to a unified opposition to retrogressive governments. In Ontario, after the election of Conservative Mike Harris in 1995, NAC activists immediately formed the "Embarrass Harris" coalition, and, only eighteen days after the election, mobilized two thousand protestors, staking out ground against his agenda to roll back pay and employment equity gains and make massive cuts to social services and education. Ontario child care workers, anticipating cuts to hard-fought-for user and wage subsidies, were the first to organize an "illegal" strike against the Harris government.[14] These protests, often coorindated with other community and labour groups, reflected feminist strengths accrued over the 1970s and 1980s.

Resistance throughout the 1990s and after was hampered by the decline of the left globally and a rightward shift in many labour and social democratic parties; in Canada, the NDP, which had built up a strong feminist presence and platform, nonetheless hid from the word socialism and suppressed grassroots efforts to challenge its centrist drift in foreign and domestic policy. Many former socialists fell into pessimism and resignation:

Figure A.1 Days of Action protest in Peterborough, Ontario, 24 June 1996. Women protested Ontario Conservatives' neoliberal cuts to social spending and education and the rescinding of gender equality legislation | Photograph by author

some retreated to liberalism, claiming it was the only refuge in the face of right-wing threats. A litany of former radicals – particularly, though not exclusively, American – renounced their misguided socialist youth. Imagining an entirely different world of social and personal relationships based on collective mobilization and transformative structural change seemed much harder. Rather than embracing the Paris '68 slogan, "Be realistic – demand the impossible," the impulse now was "Forget the impossible – settle for realism."

Even in difficult times, new equality strategies, alliances, and mobilizations emerged; feminism – as shown in this book – was always plural, innovative, constantly changing. NAC struggled on, and, after its demise, new organizations bubbled up from the grassroots. Young women founded ReBelles, resolving to fight the "right in the state and in our minds" with "new energy, fresh ideas and activist commitment ... to defend womyns's rights."[15] Collaborations between labour and feminists, such as the Bread and Roses protests, were crafted, significant human rights gains were made for the LGBTQ community, and some services, such as shelters for battered women, were widely accepted as necessary, even if they were underfunded.

Figure A.2 ReBelles poster | Courtesy of the author

Indigenous women's activism gained momentum, from the grassroots to national organizations like the Native Women's Association of Canada; anti-racist writing flourished; and anti-poverty organizations militantly defended the few welfare benefits women had. Web and zine production replaced feminist newsletters and newspapers, and, facilitated by the revolution in technology, pop-up protests might become globalized resistance. Recent "slut walks" originating in Canada, for instance, quickly became international, exposing the never-ending women-blaming by police for violence against women.

The intellectual focus of feminism also altered course. Improved access to higher education and the professions was one significant legacy of the "second wave." Still, some worried that academic feminism – institutionalized in women's studies programs and universities – substituted on-the-ground politics for lofty, alienating, incomprehensible theorizing. The marginality, edginess, and outsider perspective of feminism born in struggle was supposedly compromised by the comfort of educational privilege; new feminisms were conceived through "texts not political practice."[16] Feminism did secure some credibility in academia, though it was hardly favoured, and the distinctions between researching, writing, and activism were exaggerated. Feminist politics, identity, and scholarship were usually interwoven.[17] Feminists had for some time debated how theory was created; preferably, it was not the product only of esoteric academic discourse but also of reflections on women's experience, history, social movements, organizing, writing, and action.

Nonetheless, there were significant shifts in feminist thought: post-structuralism and postmodernism (here abbreviated to "post" thinking), post-colonialism, and queer theory expanded the repertoire of feminist ideas meant to change the world. Feminists used post-structuralist Michel Foucault to analyse the disciplining of the female body, applied feminist writing on gender fluidity to LGBTQ organizing, and deconstructed notions of difference and identity. They also rethought how race, class, and gender were related, using theories of "intersectionality," a concept focusing on the simultaneous, intersecting relations of race, gender, and class that had its origins in Black feminist writing of the 1970s. None of these theoretical frameworks were without antecedents, none lacked internal debate, but they offered novel insights into feminist politics.

While it is impossible to discuss these shifts without sharp simplification, by the early 1990s, post-structuralism and postmodernism dominated discussions of feminist theory, reflecting a parallel ascendance of Western, especially American, academic influence. Long-standing issues – violence, racism, inequality, sexuality – were still of concern, but "post" feminism diverged from positivist research and was also quite distinct from Marxist feminism. Post-structuralists pronounced the "master narrative" of Marxism to be politically and intellectually deficient; as a result, scholarly attention to class and labour contracted. If Marxists were concerned with the social and material contexts structuring women's experiences, post-structuralists were more interested in the discursive constructions of experience – indeed, some declared truly "authentic" experience simply impossible to validate, an unsettling proposition for racialized and working-class women whose experience had long been disregarded. In much post writing, too, claims to absolute truth – including categories such as injustice, oppression, and exploitation – were shifting and contested, not fixed. These challenges to truth claims, scepticism about a search for origins and causation, as well as an emphasis on identity, fluidity, border crossing, and contingency, differentiated feminist politics under the influence of post theories.

Emphasizing both the discursive character of power and the multiple aspects of identity construction productively buttressed existing writing on race and intersectionality penned by feminists of colour, opening up discussion, for instance, of how Canadian feminism was implicated in nation-building discourses of reform, empire, race, and a privileged whiteness. There was concern, however, that the actual living, breathing, suffering woman could disappear into discourse, her agency discounted in favour of a postmodern human subject imagined as "fragmented, unstable ... constituted in the ebb and flow of conflicting meanings generated by various discourses."[18] Some post writing also unproductively implied a linear version of feminist history in which previous feminist theory uniformly presumed the existence of a singular, universal "woman," a charge of simplistic gender essentialism repeated so often that it became taken-for-granted in much academic discourse. While feminists had long questioned what was validated and valued as knowledge, post writing assumed it interrogated these claims in a far more thoroughgoing, complex manner, with an eye to the deconstruction of all categories of knowledge.

Post thinking permeated much feminist theory and extended beyond to popular culture, policy-making, and political discourse. There was still both theoretical hybridity and debate. Some post-colonial and critical race theories, for example, drew on postmodernism while still employing concepts of structural and systemic class and race domination. However, critics of this theoretical turn worried that post thinking created a new version of "identity" or cultural politics that risked disengagement from structural analysis and questions of economic redistribution. Describing power in Foucauldian terms as an ever-proliferating, decentred "web," critics also countered, ignored the reality that power *did* concentrate in certain "headquarters."[19] Perhaps most damning, if postmodernism was the cultural logic of "late capitalism," was it then quite compatible with capitalist ideology? The emphasis on border crossing, fluidity, flexibility, and post thinking's penchant for relativism seemed a fit with neoliberalism and the post-Fordist economy, not a challenge to it.[20]

These theoretical shifts were linked to the decline of the global left, but they also became intertwined with a self-designated "third wave" of feminism, a term coined in 1992 by American Rebecca Walker. While much third-wave writing was American, related, though less extensive, Canadian discussions followed. Third-wave writing emerged in a specific intellectual and material context. Post theories were extremely influential, particularly discussions of difference and identity, and radical technological change offered the prospect of global, instantaneous political exchanges – though we have also seen the internet captured for powerful forces of reaction. The consolidation of neoliberal, globalized capitalism based on gendered and racialized divisions of labour, painted a bleak picture of younger women's economic prospects, even while popular culture celebrated their new autonomy and freedom.

Media-savvy third-wave writers experimented with innovative techniques of communication, and many debated "pro-sexuality" freedoms they saw as lacking in earlier feminist discourse. The expressive, "fun" aspects of popular culture were reimagined as liberating, if contradictory, in contrast to a supposedly stifling, prescriptive "political correctness" of the second wave. Culturally, performative politics and the personal narrative as a form of introspective liberation writing resonated. Intersectionality was declared an influence, though, unlike post thinking, intersectionality – at least strands originating in Black feminist thought – placed more emphasis on "groups exploiting other groups" and relational structures of oppression.[21] While not necessarily attributable to a "third wave," the 1990s explosion of trans activism and writing about trans experiences, politics, and theories was significant, and fundamentally disrupted heterosexual "normalcy" beyond earlier feminist imagining, challenging not only the binaries of femininity and masculinity, but the feminist and lesbian movements, too. Destabilizing binary categories of women and men, lesbian, gay, bisexual, and creating a trans politics of refusal and resistance, entailed another "radical rupture" in liberation thinking.[22]

Much self-declared third-wave writing also insisted it encompassed a more inclusive "multicultural" feminism, truly attentive to race and ethnicity as well as embracing a stronger appreciation of a "profusion of gendered subjects,"[23] sexual choices, and freedoms unexplored by second-wave feminists. Walker, among others, declared the third wave a new brand of feminism that allowed younger feminists to "be real and tell the truth with complexity and ambiguity."[24] In Canada, too, self-described third-wave feminists claimed debts to queer theory and more attention to race and ethnicity; their feminism, open to ambiguity and multiple "positionalities," represented political heterogeneity and "multivocality."[25]

An implicit emphasis on women's individual "self making" in third-wave writing, however, invited consternation. Was there not an intellectual overlap between third-wave writing and post-feminism, with its celebration of women's power, choices, and individual lifestyle? Assuming the infinite ability of women to transform their lives was an individualist "free for all," critics argued, ignoring the structural bases of women's exploitation and oppression.[26] If third-wave writing claimed it built upon the foundation of the previous women's movement, it often sketched out a linear narrative of historical progress: it had moved above and beyond the seriously flawed second wave – not unlike 1970s feminists who criticized the limited vision of previous feminist generations. The most triumphant claimed that third-wave feminism had superseded "white, middle-class" second-wave feminism, which had "collapsed" under the contradictions of its own "essentialism, universalism, naturalism." Not only were these feminists obtuse about class and race, third-wave critics claimed, but they boxed sexuality into "politically correct" categories and overreacted to popular culture with singular disapproval.[27]

It is hard to imagine a more unflattering assessment. Feminists who became politically active in the 1960s and 1970s saw this progress narrative as historical amnesia: their concerns about race, class, and imperialism had been "airbrushed out of history."[28] Multiracial feminisms and anti-racist white feminism, American scholars argued, had also been part of the second wave.[29]

An evolutionary narrative of discrete "waves" of ever-improving political awareness did elide historical complexity.[30] Previous feminist critiques of socially imposed femininity and sexuality took root in very different ideological and social contexts – and should be assessed as such. Streams of socialist feminism traced throughout this book did not focus only on gender oppression, and racialized women had for many years developed unique political projects linking racial and gender equality. Writing by women of colour in the 1970s challenged the "whiteness" of feminism, redefining it in the light of a critical race theory and class analysis,[31] even if this writing was also claimed by the third wave. The impulse to inhabit a generationally new, more progressive feminism, to tackle what feminists had failed to conquer in the past, understandably appealed, but, as I have argued throughout this book, distinguishing waves characterized by universalized, undifferentiated feminist ideas is a problematic template for women's history.

An age-specific third wave was not ideologically homogeneous, nor were all its concerns without precedent. Women generationally within the third wave worried that *declining* attention to social class as a structure belied the actual economic disintegration of neoliberalism. Perusing third-wave publications, one Canadian feminist asked why there was no attention to "McJobs," capitalism, and attacks on welfare: after all, this was the economy many young women faced.[32] Feminist organizing also continued along separate pathways as Indigenous women, for instance, built new mobilizations specific to their experiences of the violence of colonialism. Debates about sexual liberation and the "pleasures and dangers" of sexuality were raging long before the 1990s in "sex wars" over pornography, sex work, and censorship. While some feminists in the 1980s endorsed reining in violence with sexual regulation, others promoted a "sex-positive" feminism and opposed censorship.[33] The "do-it-yourself" anti-rape strategies challenging police and woman-blaming identified as particularly "third wave" bear similarity to previous feminist grassroots protests.[34] The distinction between so-called second- and third-wave discussions of sexuality, in other words, was likely more blurred than it was portrayed.

If anything, internal debates and separate pathways to equality within a new cohort of feminists, whether a "third wave" or not, was very much within the tradition of Canadian feminism. As I have tried to show, feminism was heterogeneous, polyphonic, and hybrid. Different experiences and voices created distinctive versions of equality, dignity, and independence; multiple streams of feminist activity ebbed and flowed over the nineteenth and twentieth centuries; and feminism was often linked theoretically and practically to other equality and emancipation movements. Women's different pathways to feminism were to some extent connected to changing historical environments and their social location – how they experienced gender, class, race, and colonial relations. But feminism was also a political, intellectual, ideological *act,* a form of personal transformation, and, most important, a commitment to make collective change. Seeing society with newly acquired feminist eyes might invalidate all that one took for granted, unsettling what was expected, accepted, and familiar and, in the process, redefining definitions of justice, equality, truth, as well as gender.

Capturing this complex texture of feminist activism in the past alerts us to how limiting some contemporary currents designated as feminist advancement are. The recent popular recasting of equality as "lean-in" feminism, defined by female corporate success stories, including women who have found the magical work-family balance (with live-in nannies, of course), contributes to a faulty progress narrative. Moreover, this superwoman story recasts feminism as individual/familial happiness rather than a collective search for equal rights and social justice.[35]

More than one American writer has argued that second-wave feminism was "seduced" into a partnership with neoliberal capitalism that persisted into the twenty-first century. The "affinity" between feminist and neoliberal values, expressed through a common emphasis, for instance, on women's integration into the labour force, supposedly provided ideological cover for crushing austerity policies and obviated the more radical, egalitarian feminism of the second wave.[36] While it is true that some forms of feminism stressing individualism, opportunity, and upward mobility have an affinity with liberal democratic capitalism, this symmetry manifested itself long before neoliberalism. It was the stuff of sharp critique by early twentieth-century socialist feminists and was integral to debates in the second wave. "Success" stories of individual women made good magazine copy over the entire twentieth century. Lean-in feminism may be offensively self-interested, but the concept is not entirely new. If some streams of feminism were routinely incorporated into the ruling power groups, others were, and remain, more radical, critical, and marginal. We should not forget these outsider views, making them part of the amnesia problem.

Outsider feminism periodically included flashes of utopian desire and hope. Utopian impulses often emerged in periods of intense activism of overlapping social movements, in certain groups, particularly the left, or with intellectual shifts in feminist thought. Flora MacDonald Denison – democrat, feminist, suffragist, and Walt Whitmanite – thought feminism had truly transformative potential: it might be a revolutionary solution to the spiritual alienation, material deprivations, and violence of her time. When socialist feminists spoke of the "New Jerusalem" in the 1930s, they articulated a desire to build an ideal society on earth, as did Prairie activist Nellie Peterson, who described her world of cooperation and peace as nothing less than "a dream" to aspire to.

New forms of utopian-feminist writing blossomed again in the 1970s. While earlier fictional feminist utopias were often "blueprints" for perfect societies that assumed the inevitable progress of Western modernity, "critical" feminist utopias of the seventies included debates, flaws, contradictions, and uncertainty. Their ideal future was not preordained or perfect, and might be attained only by political resistance in the here-and-now. Incorporating some of the zeitgeist of the sixties and seventies, utopias like Marge Piercy's *Woman on the Edge of Time* were hybrid critiques that linked gender oppression to imperialism, ethnocentrism, homophobia, racism, economic inequality, and environmental destruction.

However other-worldly, feminist utopias are inevitably circumscribed by the cultural context in which they were created. By the 1990s, feminist scholars influenced by both postmodernism and a new "pragmatism" claimed that second-wave utopias were falsely optimistic, idealizing, essentialist, and lacking self-reflection. Feminists should move to "higher ground," one feminist philosopher wrote: "pragmatism," educated discussion, and evolutionary change were preferable to utopianism, for "realism is more likely to lead to optimism." Without utopianism, feminism becomes a more "dynamic, ... richer and possibly more enduring foundation for feminist thought," she concluded.[37] Or, poorer, depending on your point of view. After all, if there is no imaginative risk taking, passion, and high, even "unrealistic" expectations, will we not be reduced to the daily grind and disappointments of accommodation, resignation, and the repetition of limited reforms?

There is some truth to the lament that, by the 1990s, the retreat of the left from "castles in the air" to a "watery liberalism, ameliorative change and modifying the market," threatened to suppress the utopian spirit.[38] Debates about utopian visions, however, never disappeared, even if feminists like Piercy felt compelled to pen dystopian warning novels in the 1990s. Utopianism, she mused, is born of "hope for a better future, but when people are fighting very hard to stay in the same place, to retain the rights they have already won, and are losing ... hope evaporates."[39] In our time, the word "utopian" is increasingly suspect, used pejoratively to suggest impossible, unreasonable, unrealistic goals.

As someone who came out of a socialist-feminist tradition, I assume that utopianism should not be smothered into acquiescence. We need transformative visions that imagine the possibilities of something that does not exist – namely, the elimination of all subjugation, alienation, and exploitation. Utopian thinking is other-worldly precisely because it involves critique of the nightmare of our current world, in which capitalism, oppression, racism, colonialism, and environmental destruction weigh heavily on humanity. If feminist history is a project of gaining a better understanding of the past in the present, in the hope of a creating a better future, then one question we should not abandon is how – even in bleak times – we can continue to nurture utopian feminist impulses.

Notes

INTRODUCTION

1 Joan Wallach Scott, quoted in Catherine Rottenberg, "Happiness and the Liberal Imagination: How Superwoman Became Balanced," *Feminist Studies* 40, 1 (2014): 166.

2 Rachel Blau DuPlessis and Ann Snitow, "A Feminist Memoir Project," in *The Feminist Memoir Project: Voices from Women's Liberation,* ed. Rachel Blau DuPlessis and Ann Snitow (New York: Three Rivers Press, 1998), 7.

3 Yasmeen Abu-Laban, "Keeping 'em Out: Gender, Race and Class Biases in Canadian Immigration Policy," in *Painting the Maple: Essays on Race, Gender and the Construction of Canada,* ed. Veronica Strong-Boag, Sherrill Grace, Avigail Eisenberg, and Joan Anderson (Vancouver: UBC Press, 1998), 70.

4 Ruth Levitas, *The Concept of Utopia* (Syracuse, NY: Syracuse University Press, 1990), 169; Angelika Bammer, *Partial Visions: Feminism and Utopianism in the 1970s* (London: Routlege, 2012), 3.

5 Astrid Henry, *Not My Mother's Sister: Generational Conflict and Third-Wave Feminism* (Bloomington: Indiana University Press, 2004), 7.

6 Robyn Wiegman, "Feminism's Apocalyptic Future," *New Literary History* 31, 4 (2000): 809; Henry, *Not My Mother's Sister,* 25.

7 Nancy Hewitt, introduction to *No Permanent Waves: Re-casting Histories of US Feminism,* ed. Nancy Hewitt (New Brunswick, NJ: Rutgers University Press, 2010), 8.

8 Joan Sangster, "Radical Ruptures: Feminism, Labor, and the Left in the Long Sixties in Canada" *American Review of Canadian Studies* 40, 1 (2010): 1–21.

9 Wiegman, "Feminism's Apocalyptic Future," 811.

10 Henry, *Not My Mother's Sister,* 5.

11 Veronique O'Leary and Louise Toupin, eds., "Pourquoi ne pas toujours repartir à zéro," in *Québecoises deboutte!: Une anthologie de textes du Front de liberation des*

femmes (1969–1971) et du Centre des femmes (1972–1975), Tome 1 (Montreal: Centre des femmes, 1982), 9.

12 Susan Friedman, "Making History: Reflections on Feminism, Narrative and Desire," in *Feminism Beside Itself,* ed. Diane Elam and Robyn Wiegman (New York: Routledge, 1995), 11.

13 Linda Gordon, "Comments on *That Noble Dream,*" *American Historical Review* 96, 3 (1991): 685.

14 Terry Eagleton, *After Theory* (New York: Basic Books, 2003), 136.

15 *Never Done* was a popular history of women's work: the Corrective Collective, *Never Done: Three Centuries of Women's Work in Canada* (Toronto: Canadian Women's Educational Press, 1974).

16 Paraphrasing "Men make their own history but they do not make it just as they please: they do not make it under conditions chosen by themselves." Karl Marx, "The Eighteenth Brumaire of Louis Bonaparte," in *Karl Marx and Frederick Engels: Selected Works* (Moscow: Progress Publishers, 1968), 97.

17 Fredric Jameson, *The Political Unconscious: Narrative as Socially Symbolic Act* (Ithaca, NY: Cornell University Press, 1981), 9.

18 Quoted in Lynne Segal, *Why Feminism?* (New York: Columbia University Press, 1999), 20.

19 Wiegman, "Feminism's Apocalyptic Future," 815.

CHAPTER 1: SPREADING THE WORD OF WOMEN'S EMANCIPATION

1 Andrée Lévesque, *Freethinker: The Life and Works of Éva Circé-Côté,* trans. Lazer Lederhendler (Toronto: Between the Lines, 2017), 52, 252.

2 Afua Cooper, "Acts of Resistance: Black Men and Women Engage Slavery in Upper Canada, 1793–1803," in *Rethinking Canada: The Promise of Women's History,* 7th ed., ed. Lara Campbell, Tamara Myers, and Adele Perry (Toronto: Oxford University Press, 2016), 94–103; Mary Anne Poutanen, *Beyond Brutal Passions: Prostitution in Nineteenth Century Montreal* (Montreal and Kingston: McGill-Queen's University Press, 2016); Constance Backhouse, *Petticoats and Prejudice: Women and Law in Nineteenth Century Canada* (Toronto: Osgoode Society, 1991), chap. 7.

3 Eileen Hunt Botting, *Wollstonecraft, Mill, and Women's Human Rights* (New Haven, CT: Yale University Press, 2016), 15–16.

4 Kate Soper, "Naked Human Nature and the Draperies of Custom: Wollstonecraft on Equality and Democracy," in *Mary Wollstonecraft and 200 Years of Feminism,* ed. Eileen Yeo (London: Rivers Oram Press, 1999), 208.

5 Mary Wollstonecraft, *A Vindication of the Rights of Woman* (Cambridge: Cambridge University Press, 1995), 112.

6 Barbara Taylor, *Mary Wollstonecraft and the Feminist Imagination* (Cambridge: Cambridge University Press, 2003).

7 Botting, *Wollstonecraft,* 75.

8 Ian Ward and Clare McGlynn, "Women, Law and John Stuart Mill," *Women's History Review* 25, 2 (2016): 234.

9 Soper, "Naked Human Nature," 208.

10 Botting, *Wollstonecraft,* 164–65.

11 Thomas Paine published *The Rights of Man* in 1791, the year before Wollstonecraft's *Vindication*. Paine defended the French Revolution and the right to overthrow despotic governments.
12 Sarah Knott and Barbara Taylor, introduction to *Women, Gender, and Enlightenment*, ed. Sarah Knott and Barbara Taylor (London: Palgrave Macmillan, 2005), xviii.
13 JoEllen DeLucia, *A Feminine Enlightenment: British Women Writers and the Philosophy of Progress, 1759–1820* (Edinburgh: Edinburgh University Press, 2015), 7.
14 Ibid., 8.
15 Taylor, *Mary Wollstonecraft*, 57. See also Silvia Sebastiani, *The Scottish Enlightenment: Gender and the Limits of Progress* (London: Palgrave Macmillan, 2013).
16 John Robertson, "Women and Enlightenment: A Historiographical Conclusion," in *Women, Gender, and Enlightenment*, 692–704.
17 Sankar Muthu, *Enlightenment against Empire* (Princeton, NJ: Princeton University Press, 2009), 277.
18 Botting, *Wollstonecraft*, 168.
19 Soper, "Naked Human Nature"; Botting, *Wollstonecraft*.
20 Karen O'Brien quoted in Sebastiani, *The Scottish Enlightenment*, 17.
21 Emily Stowe, "The Movement in Canada," *Woman's Tribune*, 2 March 1889.
22 Stowe, "The Work Advancing in Canada," *Woman's Journal*, 19 April 1890.
23 Thomas Paine, *Rights of Man*, ed. Henry Collins (Baltimore: Penguin Books, 1969), 250.
24 Jennie Foulds, "Canadian Women's Suffrage Association," *Women's Suffrage Journal*, 2 July 1883.
25 On Brewster, see Lara Campbell, *A Great Revolutionary Wave: Women and the Vote in British Columbia* (Vancouver: UBC Press, 2020), 67.
26 Jane Rhodes, *Mary Ann Shadd Cary: The Black Press and Protest in the Nineteenth Century* (Bloomington: Indiana University Press, 1998). I use "African Canadian" and "Black" interchangeably. The latter designates "descendants of Africa during the slave trade, black loyalists, refugees, fugitives, settlers who immigrated during the American Civil War and those who immigrated mostly from the Caribbean and Africa after the Second World War." See Joseph Mensah, *Black Canadians: History, Experiences, and Social Conditions* (Halifax: Fernwood, 2002), 21.
27 Shirley Yee, "Gender Ideology and Black Women as Community-Builders," *Canadian Historical Review* 75, 1 (1994): 53–73.
28 Mary Ann Shadd, "Women's Rights," *Provincial Freeman* (*PF*), 2 August 1854.
29 Shadd, "Female Education," *PF*, 7 June 1855.
30 Dolly Bangs's [likely a pseudonym] reply to "Henrietta," *PF*, 29 April 1854.
31 Shadd, "The London Convention," *PF*, 24 March 1853.
32 "Editorial," *PF*, 30 June 1855.
33 African Canadians were clustered primarily in Nova Scotia and Ontario. Research has focused on Ontario, but there may be similar examples in the Maritimes and also the West.
34 Afua Cooper, "'Doing Battle in Freedom's Cause': Henry Bibb, Abolitionism, Race Uplift and Black Manhood, 1842–1854" (PhD diss., University of Toronto, 2000),

165; Julie Roy Jeffrey, "Permeable Boundaries: Abolitionist Women and Separate Spheres," *Journal of the Early Republic* 21, 1 (2001): 79–93.

35 Lorene Bridgen, "'Lifting as We Climb': The Emergence of an African-Canadian Civil Society in Southern Ontario (1840–1901)" (PhD diss., University of Waterloo, 2016), iii, 55.

36 Samuel Ringgold Ward, quoted in ibid., 55.

37 Ibid., 58. See also Peggy Bristow, "Whatever You Raise in the Ground You Can Sell It in Chatham: Black Women in Buxton and Chatham, 1850–1865," in *We're Rooted Here and They Can't Pull Us Up: Essays in African Canadian Women's History*, ed. Peggy Bristow et al. (Toronto: University of Toronto Press, 1994), 69–141.

38 "Five O'Clock Tea," *Wives and Daughters* (*WD*), 1 January 1892.

39 Helen Santmyer, quoted in Heather Murray, *Come, Bright Improvement! The Literary Societies of Nineteenth-Century Ontario* (Toronto: University of Toronto Press, 2002), 106.

40 Ibid., 108.

41 Sarah Curzon, "Sweet Girl Graduate," *Grip Sack*, 1882; Céleste Derksen, "Out of the Closet: Dramatic Works by Sarah Anne Curzon, Part Two. Re-Dressing Gender Inequality – *The Sweet Girl Graduate*," *Theatre Research in Canada* 15, 2 (1994), https://journals.lib.unb.ca/index.php/TRIC/article/view/7198.

42 "University College Petition for the Admission of Female Students," *Globe*, 31 January 1883, quoted in Tarah Brookfield, *Our Voice Must Be Heard: Women and the Vote in Ontario* (Vancouver: UBC Press, 2018), 58.

43 J.W. Bengough, "Mr. Stotinbottle on Woman Suffrage," *Grip Sack*, 1882.

44 "Women's Franchise in Canada," *Women's Suffrage Journal*, 1 November 1883, 200.

45 Lottie McAllister, *Clipped Wings* (Toronto: W. Briggs, 1899), 19, 25, 142.

46 She would have embraced the label "literary artist." Misao Dean, *A Different Point of View: Sara Jeannette Duncan* (Montreal and Kingston: McGill-Queen's University Press, 1991), 58.

47 Sara Jeannette Duncan, *A Social Departure*, quoted in Thomas E. Tausky, *Sara Jeannette Duncan: Novelist of Empire* (Port Credit, ON: P.D. Meany Publishers, 1980), 60.

48 Dean, *A Different Point of View*, 78.

49 Marjorie Lang, *Women Who Made the News: Female Journalists in Canada, 1880–1945* (Montreal and Kingston: McGill-Queen's University Press, 1999).

50 Janice Fiamengo, "Baptized with Tears and Sighs: Sara Jeannette Duncan and the Rhetoric of Feminism," in *ReCalling Early Canada: Reading the Political in Literary and Cultural Production*, ed. Jennifer Blair et al. (Edmonton: University of Alberta Press, 2005), 268.

51 Ibid., 266, 277.

52 Sara Jeannette Duncan, "Unions for Women," in *Sara Jeannette Duncan: Selected Journalism*, ed. T.E. Tausky (Ottawa: Tecumseh Press, 1978), 40–41.

53 Dean, *A Different Point of View*, 69*n*13.

54 Lorraine McMullen and Sandra Campbell, introduction to *New Women: Short Stories by Canadian Women, 1900–1920*, ed. Lorraine McMullen and Sandra Campbell (Ottawa: University of Ottawa Press, 1997), 1–18.

55 Jean Blewett, "The Experiences of a Woman Bachelor," in McMullen and Campbell, *New Women,* 141–56.
56 Jean McIllwaith, "The Assimilation of Christina," in McMullen and Campbell, *New Women,* 293–306.
57 Edith Eaton, "Story of One White Woman Who Married a Chinese," in McMullen and Campbell, *New Women,* 228. On Eaton, see Mary Chapman, *Becoming Sui Sin Far: Early Fiction, Journalism and Travel Writing by Edith Maude Eaton* (Montreal and Kingston: McGill-Queen's University Press, 2016).
58 Ethelwyn Wetherald, "Some Queer Husbands" and "A Very Soft Sex," in *Thirty Years of Storytelling: Selected Short Fiction by Ethelwyn Wetherald,* ed. Janet Friskney (Ottawa: Tecumseh Press, 2011), 246, 13.
59 Letters, *WD,* September 1891. One woman insisted Prime Minister Gladstone was her ideal of "moral courage."
60 Ethelwyn Wetherald, "Browsing in the Library," *WD,* 1 April 1892.
61 Wetherald, "Ignorance and Womanliness," *WD,* 1 June 1891.
62 Untitled article, *WD,* 1 December 1890.
63 Lévesque, *Freethinker,* 23.
64 Chantal Savoie, "La page féminine des grands quotidiens montréalais comme lieu de sociabilité litteraire au tournant du XXe siècle," *Tangence* 80 (2006): 128.
65 Lévesque, *Freethinker,* 71.
66 Ibid., 251.
67 Ibid., 15–16.
68 Ibid., 23, 24.
69 Ibid., 60.
70 Ibid., 51.
71 Ibid., 49.
72 Diane Thibeault, "Premières brèches dans l'idéologie des deux sphères: Joséphine Marchand-Dandurand et Robertine Barry, deux journalistes montrélaises de la fin du XIXe siècle" (master's thesis, Université d'Ottawa, 1980), 112–14; my translation.
73 Ibid., 111.
74 On Dandurand, see Sophie Doucet, "Joséphine Marchand-Dandurand ou 'Le Laurier féminin': Une journaliste féministe, moderne, libérale and nationaliste (1861–1925)" (master's thesis, Université de Montréal, 2003); on Barry, see Sergine Desjardins, "Robertine Barry (Françoise)," *Canadian Encyclopedia,* 14 November 2016, http://www.thecanadianencyclopedia.com/en/article/robertine-barry-francoise/.
75 Murray, *Come, Bright Improvement!,* 119.

CHAPTER 2: THE ORIGINS OF SOCIALIST AND LABOUR FEMINISM

1 Letter from Bertha Merrill Burns to Margaret MacDonald, 29 April 1907, Library and Archives Canada (LAC), J. Ramsay MacDonald fonds, MG 30-109, box 1, file 1-2.
2 Bertha Merrill Burns, "Woman and the Social Problem," *Western Clarion* (*WC*), 13 August 1904.

3 Burns, "Women and Socialism," *British Columbia Federationist* (*BCF*), 31 October 1913.

4 Burns, "Women and the Social Problem."

5 Jonathan Beecher, *Charles Fourier: The Visionary and His World* (Berkeley: University of California Press, 1997). The idea that the condition of women was the measure of humanity's progress was an Enlightenment idea. See Silvia Sebastiani, *The Scottish Enlightenment: Gender and the Limits of Progress* (London: Palgrave Macmillan, 2013), 170.

6 Donald Pitzer, ed., *America's Communal Utopias* (Chapel Hill: University of North Carolina Press, 1997); Chris Jennings, *Paradise Now: The Story of American Utopianism* (New York: Random House, 2016).

7 Barbara Taylor, *Eve and the New Jerusalem: Socialism and Feminism in the Nineteenth Century* (London: Virago, 1983).

8 Sheila Rowbotham, *Hidden from History: 300 Years of Oppression and Women's Fight against It* (London: Pluto Press, 1973), 43. See William Thompson, *Appeal of One Half the Human Race, Women, against the Pretensions of the Other Half, Men, to Retain Them in Political, and Thence in Civil and Domestic, Slavery* (London, 1825).

9 Quoted in Jane Rendall, "Clio, Mars, and Minerva: The Scottish Enlightenment and the Writing of Women's History," in *Eighteenth Century Scotland: New Perspectives*, ed. Tom Devine and J.R. Young (East Linton, UK: Tuckwell Press, 1999), 60.

10 Donald Wilson, "Matti Kurikka: Finnish-Canadian Intellectual," *BC Studies* 20 (1973): 57.

11 Donald Wilson, "Matti Kurikka and A.B. Makela: Socialist Thought among Finns in Canada, 1900–1932," *Canadian Ethnic Studies* 10, 2 (1978): 9–21.

12 Varpu Lindström, *"I Won't Be a Slave": Selected Articles on Finnish Canada* (Beaverton, ON: Aspasia Books, 2010).

13 Diana Chown, introduction to *The Stairway*, by Alice Chown (Toronto: University of Toronto Press, 1988), ix.

14 Linda Kealey, *Enlisting Women for the Cause: Women, Labour and the Left in Canada, 1880–1920* (Toronto: University of Toronto Press, 1998), 95.

15 "The Kingdom of the Home," *Citizen and Country*, 13 April 1900.

16 Heather Brown, *Marx on Gender and the Family: A Critical Study* (Chicago: Haymarket Books, 2013); Martha Gimenez and Lise Vogel, "Marxist-Feminist Thought Today," *Science and Society* special issue 69, 1 (2005): 5–10.

17 June Hannam and Karen Hunt, *Socialist Women: Britain, 1880s to 1920s* (London: Routledge, 2002), 17.

18 Frederick Engels, *The Origin of the Family, Private Property and the State* (New York: Pathfinder Press, 1972), 68.

19 Eleanor Leacock, introduction to ibid., 28.

20 August Bebel, *Woman under Socialism* (1904; New York: Schocken Books, 1971).

21 Mary Cotton Wisdom, "Socialism and Ignorance," *Cotton's Weekly* (*CW*), 20 May 1909.

22 Wisdom, "The Status of Women," *CW*, 4 May 1911.

23 Wisdom, "Women's Rights," *CW,* 1 April 1909.
24 Mary Jo Buhle, *Women and American Socialism, 1870–1920* (Urbana: University of Illinois Press, 1983); Ellen Carol DuBois, "Woman Suffrage and the Left: An International Socialist-Feminist Perspective," *New Left Review* 1, 186 (1991): 20–45.
25 Bertha Merrill Burns, "Women in the Case," *WC,* 20 August 1904.
26 Mary Cotton Wisdom, "Motherhood and Socialism," *CW,* 11 November 1909.
27 Bertha Merrill Burns, quoted in Janice Newton, *The Feminist Challenge to the Canadian Left, 1900–1908* (Montreal and Kingston: McGill-Queen's University Press, 1995), 57.
28 Nora Tutty quoted in Campbell, *A Great Revolutionary Wave,* 161.
29 Bertha Merrill Burns, "Women and the Social Problem," *WC,* 13 August 1904.
30 Ibid.
31 Campbell, *A Great Revolutionary Wave,* 43–44.
32 Resina Mawani, *Colonial Proximities: Crossracial Encounters and Juridical Truths in British Columbia, 1871–1921* (Vancouver: UBC Press, 2009), 120.
33 Nora Tutty, "The Suffrage Movement News and Views," *Vancouver Daily World,* 2 July 1913; Karl Marx and Frederick Engels, *The Communist Manifesto* (1848), https://www.marxists.org/archive/marx/works/1848/communist-manifesto/.
34 Peter Campbell, "The Great Are Only Great Because We Are on Our Knees: Dialectical Thinking, the Commodification of Labour Power, and the Legacy of the Socialist Party of Canada," *Labour/le travail* 87 (Spring 2021).
35 Donald Avery, *"Dangerous Foreigners": European Immigrant Workers and Labour Radicalism in Canada, 1896–1932* (Toronto: McClelland and Stewart, 1979).
36 See Angus McLaren, *Our Own Master Race: Eugenics in Canada, 1885–1945* (Toronto: Oxford University Press, 1990) and his "What Has This to Do with Working-Class Women: Birth Control and the Canadian Left," *Histoire sociale/Social History* 14, 28 (1981): 435–54.
37 Janice Newton, *The Feminist Challenge,* 140. [Parenthesis added.]
38 Catherine Cleverdon, *The Women's Suffrage Movement in Canada* (1950; Toronto: University of Toronto Press, 1974), 88.
39 J.H. Hawthornthwaite, "The Women's Franchise Bill," *WC,* 10 February 1906.
40 J.H. Hawthornthwaite, quoted in Campbell, *A Great Revolutionary Wave,* 152.
41 *WC,* 26 September 1908.
42 "Home Truths," *WC,* 14 November 1908.
43 Edith Wrigley, "Three Women Jar Loose," *WC,* 12 September 1908; "A Woman's View," *WC,* 5 September 1909.
44 Bertha Merrill Burns to Margaret MacDonald, 29 April 1907, LAC, MacDonald fonds, box 1, file 1-2.
45 Enjolras [T. Phillips Thompson], "Women's Rights," *Palladium of Labor,* 20 March 1886.
46 Veronica Strong-Boag, "Only the Brave or 'Canada's Daughters Shall Be Free': Respect, Redistribution, and Suffrage in Women's Struggle for Canadian Democracy," 2 November 2016, Women Suffrage and Beyond: Confronting the Democratic Deficit, https://womensuffrage.org/?p=22830 (accessed 20 November 2019).
47 Gregory Kealey and Bryan Palmer, *Dreaming of What Might Be: The Knights of Labor in Ontario, 1880–1900* (New York: Cambridge University Press, 1982), 143–44, 319.

48 Craig Heron, "Labourism and the Canadian Working Class," *Labour/Le Travail* 13 (1984): 45–76.
49 May Darwin, "Woman and Socialism," *Daily Mail and Empire*, 9 November 1901. On Darwin, see Wayne Roberts, *Honest Womanhood: Feminism, Femininity and Class Consciousness among Toronto Working Women, 1893–1914* (Toronto: New Hogtown Press, 1976), 43–45.
50 Helena Gutteridge, quoted in Kealey, *Enlisting Women*, 148.
51 Helena Gutteridge, "The Reverenced Helplessness of Women," *BCF*, 21 November 1913.
52 Irene Howard, *The Struggle for Social Justice in British Columbia: Helena Gutteridge the Unknown Reformer* (Vancouver: UBC Press, 1992), 113.
53 "Short Stories," *The Sunset of Bon Echo* 1, 1 (March 1916): 16–18, unsigned but likely written by Flora MacDonald Denison, https://archive.org/details/SunsetOfBonEcho/echo-1-1/mode/2up.
54 Michael Kimmel and Amy Aronson, introduction to *Woman and Economics: A Study of the Economic Relation between Men and Women as a Factor in Social Evolution*, by Charlotte Perkins Gilman (1898; Berkeley: University of California Press, 1998), xiii; Jill Rudd and Val Gough, eds., *Charlotte Perkins Gilman: Optimist Reformer* (Iowa City: University of Iowa Press, 1999).
55 Flora MacDonald Denison, "The Open Road towards Democracy," *Toronto World* (*TW*), 28 May 1911.
56 Olive Schreiner, *Woman and Labour* (1911; New York: Dover Publishing, 1998).
57 Denison, "The Open Road," *TW*, 26 March 1911.
58 Denison, "Women's Suffrage, Canada and Beyond," University of Toronto, Thomas Fisher Rare Book Room (UT, Fisher), Flora MacDonald Denison fonds (Denison), Ms Coll. 51, box 8 (a), Suffrage clippings, n.d. Flora MacDonald Denison used her newspaper column to expose Schreiner's mistreatment at the hands of British troops during the Boer War, suggesting some anti-imperialist sentiment on her part. The troops burnt Schreiner's house to the ground, in the process destroying her book manuscript.
59 Helena Gutteridge, "Women's Work," *BCF*, 16 January 1914.
60 Denison, "Men, Women and Work," n.d., UT, Fisher, Denison, box 8(a).
61 Denison, "The Open Road," *TW*, 19 June 1910.
62 Carole Gerson, "Marie Joussaye Fotheringham: Canada's First Woman Labour Poet," *Canadian Notes and Queries* 44 (1991): 21; Carole Gerson, *Canadian Women in Print, 1750–1918* (Waterloo: Wilfrid Laurier University Press, 2010).
63 Lindsey McMaster, *Working Girls in the West: Representations of Wage-Earning Women* (Vancouver: UBC Press, 2008), 46–48.
64 Marie Joussaye, *Songs That Quinte Sang* (Belleville, ON: Sun Printing and Publishing, 1895), 66–67.
65 Ibid.
66 "Canada Moving," *Woman's Column* 20, 6 (1893).
67 Gerson, *Canadian Women in Print*, 156.
68 Marie Joussaye, *Selections from Anglo-Saxon Songs* (ca. 1920; Cambridge: Proquest Information and Learning Company, 2005).
69 Janice Fiamengo, *The Woman's Page: Journalism and Rhetoric in Early Canada*

(Toronto: University of Toronto Press, 2008), 39.

70 Katja Thieme, "'The Grim Fact of Sisterhood': Female Collectivity in the Works of Agnes Maule Machar, Nellie L. McClung, and Mabel Burkholder," in *Diversity and Change in Early Canadian Women's Writing,* ed. Jennifer Chambers (Newcastle upon Tyne: Cambridge Scholars Press, 2008), 100–17. See also McMaster, *Working Girls,* 6.

71 Thieme, "The Grim Fact," 109.

72 Joussaye, *Selections from Anglo-Saxon Songs,* 66–67.

73 Isabel Ecclestone Mackay, *House of Windows,* quoted in McMaster, *Working Girls,* 169.

74 K. Jane Watt, "Passing out of Memory: Georgina Sime and the Politics of Literary Recuperation" (PhD diss., University of Alberta, 1997).

75 J.G. Sime, "An Irregular Union," in *Sister Woman,* ed. Sandra Campbell (1919; Ottawa: Tecumseh Press, 2004), 55.

76 Sime, "The Bachelor Girl," in ibid., 192.

77 Sime, "Motherhood," in ibid., 62–73.

78 Sime, "Munitions," in ibid., 26–32.

79 K. Jane Watt, "Cadences of Canada: Georgina Sime's *Sister Woman,*" in *Sister Woman: A Critical Edition,* ed. Sandra Campbell (Ottawa: Tecumseh, 2004), 283–92; see also Watt, "Passing Out of Memory," and Gerald Lynch, "Fabian Feminism: Sime's Short Story Cycle," in Gerald Lynch, *The One and the Many: English-Canadian Short Story Cycles* (Toronto: University of Toronto Press, 2001).

80 Bertha Merrill Burns, "Women and Socialism," *BCF,* 31 October 1913.

CHAPTER 3: WOMEN, DEMOCRACY, AND SUFFRAGE

1 Rarihokwats, *How Democracy Came to St. Regis and the Thunderwater Movement* (Rooseveltown, NY: Akwesasne Notes, 1974), 6.

2 James Youngblood Henderson, *First Nations Jurisprudence and Aboriginal Rights: Defining the Just Society* (Saskatoon: Native Law Centre, University of Saskatchewan, 2006), 121. Consent and participation is of course also a theme in European democratic thought. See John Borrows, *Recovering Canada: The Resurgence of Indigenous Law* (Toronto: University of Toronto Press, 2002).

3 Marie Battiste and James Youngblood (Sa'ke'j) Henderson, *Protecting Indigenous Knowledge and Heritage: A Global Challenge* (Saskatoon: Purich Publishing, 2000), 42.

4 Mary Ellen Turpel, "Aboriginal Peoples and the Canadian Charter: Interpretive Monopolies, Cultural Differences," *Canadian Human Rights Yearbook* 3 (1989–90): 6.

5 Marlene Brant Castellano, "Women in Huron and Ojibwa Societies," *Canadian Woman Studies* 10, 2–3 (1989): 46.

6 Carol Cooper, "Native Women of the Northern Pacific Coast: A Historical Perspective, 1830–1900," in *Canadian Women: A Reader,* ed. Wendy Mitchinson et al. (Toronto: Harcourt Brace, 1996), 89–118. On the community reform work of Christian Six Nations women, see Alison Norman, "Race, Gender and Colonialism: Public Life among the Six Nations of Grand River, 1899–1939" (PhD diss., University of Toronto, 2010).

7 Jean Barman, "Indigenous Women and Feminism on the Cusp of Contact," in *Indigenous Women and Feminism: Politics, Activism, Culture,* ed. Cheryl Suzack, Shari Huhndorf, Jeanne Perreault, and Jean Barman (Vancouver: UBC Press, 2010), 94.

8 Donald Smith, "Catherine Sutton (Nahneebahwequa)," *The Canadian Encyclopedia,* 4 February 2008, https://www.thecanadianencyclopedia.ca/en/article/catherine-sutton.

9 Cook's support for and criticisms of *both* Indigenous and colonial law indicate the need to historicize the complexities of Indigenous women's political protests. See Leslie A. Robertson with the Kwagu'Ł Gixsam Clan, *Standing Up with Ga'axsta'las: Jane Constance Cook and the Politics of Memory, Church, and Custom* (Vancouver: UBC Press, 2012), 194, 17.

10 Duncan Campbell Scott quoted in Andrea Catapano, "The Rising of the Ongwehònwe: Sovereignty, Identity, and Representation on the Six Nations Reserve" (PhD diss., Stony Brook University, 2007), 114.

11 Ibid., 84, 89.

12 Gail Landsman, "The 'Other' as Political Symbol: Images of Indians in the Woman Suffrage Movement," *Ethnohistory* 39, 3 (1992): 254.

13 Matilda Joslyn Gage, quoted in Sally Roesch Wagner, *Sisters in Spirit: Haudenosaunee (Iroquois) Influence on Early American Feminists* (Summerton, TN: Native Voices, 2001), 48.

14 Matilda Gage, *Women, Church and State* (1893; Watertown, MA: Persephone Press, 1980), 10.

15 Pauline Johnson, "The Iroquois Women of Canada, by One of Their Own," in National Council of Women of Canada, *Women of Canada: Their Life and Work* (Ottawa, 1900), 442.

16 Catapano, "The Rising," 114. Indian Superintendent Duncan Scott could barely contain his contempt for these "meddling" women, Evelyn Johnson included.

17 Sherene Razack, *Looking White People in the Eye: Gender, Race, and Culture in Courtrooms and Classrooms* (Toronto: University of Toronto Press, 1998), 23.

18 Tarah Brookfield, *Our Voice Must Be Heard: Women and the Vote in Ontario* (Vancouver: UBC Press, 2018), 19–23.

19 John Garner, *The Franchise and Politics in British North America* (Toronto: University of Toronto Press, 1969), 156; Kim Klein "A Petticoat Polity? Women Voters in New Brunswick before Confederation," *Acadiensis* 26, 1 (1996): 71–75.

20 Bettina Bradbury, "Widows at the Hustings: Gender, Citizenship, and the Montreal By-Election of 1832," in *Women on Their Own: Interdisciplinary Perspectives on Being Single,* ed. Rudolph Bell and Virginia Yans (New Brunswick, NJ: Rutgers University Press, 2008), 82–114.

21 Quoted in Jan Noel, *Along a River: The First French-Canadian Women* (Toronto: University of Toronto Press, 2013), 225.

22 Gail Campbell, *"I Wish to Keep a Record": Nineteenth-Century New Brunswick Women Diarists and Their World* (Toronto: University of Toronto Press, 2017), chap. 13.

23 Sarah Carter, *Imperial Plots: Women, Land, and the Spadework of British Colonialism on the Canadian Prairies* (Winnipeg: University of Manitoba Press, 2016).

24 Brookfield, *Our Voice Must Be Heard,* 24. Gérin-Lajoie convinced anti-suffragist archbishop Paul Bruchési that French women should vote locally to prevent anglophones from dominating local politics. Denyse Baillargeon, *To Be Equals in Our Own Country: Women and the Vote in Quebec* (Vancouver: UBC Press, 2020), 52.
25 Veronica Strong-Boag, "The Citizenship Debates: The 1885 Franchise Act," in *Contesting Canadian Citizenship: Historical Readings,* ed. Robert Adamoski, Dorothy Chunn, and Robert Menzies (Toronto: University of Toronto Press, 2002), 69–94.
26 George-Étienne Cartier, quoted in Colin Grittner, "A Statesmanlike Measure with a Partisan Tail: The Development of the Nineteenth-Century Dominion Electoral Franchise" (master's thesis, Carleton University, 2009), 62.
27 Canada, House of Commons, *Debates* (*Debates*), Mr. Wright, citing John Stuart Mill, 16 April 1885, 1145; Mr. Mulock, 28 April 1885, 1427.
28 Ibid., Mr. Wright, 16 April 1885, 1144.
29 Ibid., Mr. Charlton, 27 April 1885, 1390.
30 Ibid., Mr. Landerkin, 24 April 1885, 1356.
31 Ibid., Mr. Edgar, 17 April 1885, 1400.
32 Ibid., Mr. Dupont, 17 April 1885, 1235.
33 Julie Evans, Patricia Grimshaw, David Philips, and Shurlee Swain, *Equal Subjects, Unequal Rights: Indigenous Peoples in British Settler Colonies, 1830–1910* (Manchester: Manchester University Press, 2003).
34 *Debates,* Mr. Weldon, 1 May 1885, 1493.
35 James Daschuk, *Clearing the Plains: Disease, Politics of Starvation and the Loss of Aboriginal Life* (Regina: University of Regina Press, 2013).
36 For example, "Indian Murderers to Vote – Patriot Volunteers Not to Vote," *Globe,* 2 May 1885.
37 *Debates,* Mr. McCraney, 2 May 1885, 1541.
38 Ibid., Mr. Charlton, 1 May 1885, 1523.
39 Ibid., Mr. Landerkin, 2 May 1885, 1540.
40 Ibid., Mr. Sutherland, 2 May 1885, 1526; see also Mr. McCraney on "disgraceful feasts," 2 May 1885, 1541.
41 Veronica Strong-Boag, "Independent Women, Problematic Men: First- and Second-Wave Anti-Feminism in Canada from Goldwin Smith to Betty Steele," *Histoire sociale/Social History* 29, 57 (1996): 1–22.
42 Stephen Leacock, "The Woman Question, 1916," in *The Social Criticism of Stephen Leacock: The Unsolved Riddle of Social Justice and Other Essays,* ed. Alan Bowker (Toronto: University of Toronto Press, 1973), 55.
43 Goldwin Smith, "Woman's Place in the State," *Forum* 8 (January 1890): 519.
44 Mgr. Paquet, "Le féminisme au Québec" (1919), Marianopolis College, Quebec History, Documents of Quebec History/Documents de l'histoire du Québec, http://faculty.marianopolis.edu/c.belanger/quebechistory/docs/LefeminismeauQuebec-MgrPaquet.html, n.p.; my translation. See also Marie-Aimée Cliche, "Droits égaux ou influence accrue? Nature et rôle de la femme d'après les féministes chrétiennes et les antiféministes au Québec 1896–1930," *Recherches féministes* 2, 2 (1989): 101–19.
45 Susan Mann Trofimenkoff, "Henri Bourassa and the 'Woman Question,'" in *The Neglected Majority: Essays in Canadian Women's History,* ed. Susan Mann Trofimenkoff

and Alison Prentice (Toronto: McClelland and Stewart, 1977), 109; Baillargeon, *To Be Equals,* 74.
46 Sheila Eileen Powell, "The Opposition to Woman Suffrage in Ontario, 1872–1917" (master's thesis, Carleton University, 1987), 107, 115.
47 Cheryl MacDonald, *Adelaide Hoodless: Domestic Crusader* (Toronto: Dundurn Press, 1986); Brookfield, *Our Voices Must Be Heard,* 117.
48 On membership in the Toronto Anti-Enfranchisement League, likely linked to the AOWSC, see Wayne Roberts, "'Rocking the Cradle for the World': The New Woman and Maternal Feminism, Toronto, 1877–1914," in *A Not Unreasonable Claim: Women and Reform in Canada, 1880s–1920s,* ed. Linda Kealey (Toronto: Women's Press, 1979), 26.
49 Michael J. Smith, "Female Reformers in Victorian Nova Scotia: Architects of a New Womanhood" (master's thesis, Saint Mary's University, 1986); William Blair, quoted in Shannon M. Risk, "Against Women's Suffrage: The Case of Maine and New Brunswick," *American Review of Canadian Studies* 42, 3 (2012): 391.
50 Toronto Suffrage Association letter to Sir James P. Whitney, n.d., scrapbook, Victoria College, E.J. Pratt Library, Augusta Stowe-Gullen fonds (Victoria, Stowe-Gullen), box 1.
51 Marilyn Lake and Henry Reynolds, *Drawing the Global Colour Line: White Men's Countries and the International Challenge of Racial Equality* (Cambridge: Cambridge University Press, 2008).
52 Marilyn Lake, *Getting Equal: The History of Australian Feminism* (St. Leonards, NSW: Allen and Unwin, 1997), 20.
53 Georgina Taylor, "Ground for Common Action: Violet McNaughton's Agrarian Feminism and the Origins of the Farm Women's Movement in Canada" (PhD diss., Carleton University, 1997), 313.
54 On Gérin-Lajoie, see Margaret E. McCallum, "Marie Gérin-Lajoie, née Lacoste," *The Canadian Encyclopedia,* 9 May 2014, https://www.thecanadianencyclopedia.ca/en/article/marie-gerin-lajoie-nee-lacoste; on the FNSJB, see Micheline Dumont and Louise Toupin, eds., *La pensée féministe au Québec* (Montreal: Les éditions du remue-ménage, 2003); Karine Hébert, "Une organisation maternaliste au Québec: La Fédération nationale Saint-Jean-Baptiste et la bataille pour le vote des femmes," *Revue d'histoire de l'Amérique française* 52, 3 (1999): 1–29, DOI: https://doi.org/10.7202/005467ar; Marie Lavigne, Yoland Pinard, and Jennifer Stoddart, "The Fédération Nationale Sainte-Jean-Baptiste and the Women's Movement in Quebec," in Kealey, *A Not Unreasonable Claim,* 71–88.
55 Gérin-Lajoie quoted in Cliche, "Droits égaux," 109; my translation.
56 Hébert, "Une organisation maternaliste," 21; my translation. Hébert refers to the "l'artificialité des frontières qui existaient entre les sphères privée et publique."
57 Judith Fingard, "The Ritchie Sisters and Social Improvement in Early 20th Century Halifax," *Journal of the Royal Nova Scotia Historical Society* 13 (2010): 1–23.
58 This appears to be the only such group in Canada. Lara Campbell, *A Great Revolutionary Wave: Women and the Vote in British Columbia* (UBC Press, 2020), 161.
59 Irene Baros-Johnson, "Emily Stowe," Dictionary of Unitarian and Universalist Biography, 18 September 2004, http://uudb.org/articles/emilyjenningsstowe.html, and "Ladies Make a Raid on the Old Building," *Globe,* 9 February 1889.

60 "Pioneer Woman MDs" undated newspaper clipping, scrapbook, Victoria, Stowe-Gullen, box 1.
61 Augusta Stowe-Gullen, "Woman as Physician," in *Woman, Her Character, Culture and Calling*, ed. Rev. Principal Austin (Brantford, ON: Book and Bible House, 1890), 123.
62 Sharon Cook, *Through Sunshine and Shadow: The Woman's Christian Temperance Union, Evangelicalism, and Reform in Ontario, 1874–1930* (Montreal and Kingston: McGill-Queen's University Press, 1995); Ian Tyrell, *Woman's World/Woman's Empire: The Woman's Christian Temperance Union in International Perspective, 1880–1930* (Chapel Hill: University of North Carolina Press, 1991).
63 Campbell, *A Great Revolutionary Wave*, 28.
64 Richard Allen, *The Social Passion: Religion and Social Reform in Canada, 1914–1928* (Toronto: University of Toronto Press, 1971).
65 Campbell, *A Revolutionary Wave*, 23.
66 "Why Justice Cannot Be Left in the Hand of Men," *The Champion* (*TC*), July 1915.
67 Maria Gordon Grant, letter, *TC*, May 1915.
68 "Political Equality League Statement," *TC*, January 1914.
69 Ibid. On British justice, see the letter of D. Davis (a PEL organizer), *TC*, August 1912. Especially, but not only, in British Columbia (which had a large British immigrant population), "British" history was often invoked as an argument for suffrage: it was claimed that women in "ancient Britain" were the "political equals of men" (Florence Hall, "Suffrage and Morals," *TC*, September 1915), and British liberal icon and prime minister William Gladstone was quoted to indicate congruence of suffrage with his ideas ("Correspondence," *TC*, August 1912). Yet the concept of British liberty was not universal; it was exclusionary in terms of race and nationality.
70 Mrs Arthur Murphy, "What Knowledge Will Do towards Betterment of Social Conditions," *Western Woman's Weekly*, 10 July 1920.
71 Ryan Eyford, "Lucifer Comes to New Iceland: Margret and Sigfus Benedictsson's Radical Critique of Marriage and the Family" (paper presented to the Canadian Historical Association, Saskatoon, May 2007).
72 Mary Kinnear, "The Icelandic Connection: *Freyja* and the Manitoba Woman Suffrage Movement," in *Canadian Woman Studies: An Introductory Reader*, ed. Nuzhat Amin (Toronto: Inanna, 1997), 87.
73 Eyford, "Lucifer Comes to New Iceland," 3.
74 Margret Benedictsson, "The Widow," in *Writings by Western Icelandic Women*, ed. and trans. Kirsten Wolf (Winnipeg: University of Manitoba Press, 1996), 74–79.
75 Sarah Carter, "'Daughters of British Blood' or 'Hordes of Men of an Alien Race': The Homesteads-for-Women Campaign in Western Canada," *Western Plains Quarterly* 29, 4 (2009): 76.
76 "Getting Down to Realities," *Grain Growers Guide*, 28 October 1914 and "Destitution," *Grain Growers Guide*, 18 November 1914, reprinted in Barbara E. Kelcey and Angela E. Davis, eds., *A Great Movement Underway: Women and the Grain Growers Guide, 1908–1928* (Winnipeg: Manitoba Record Society, 1997), 121–25.
77 Tracy Kulba and Victoria Lamont, "The Periodical Press and Western Woman's Suffrage Movements in Canada and the United States: A Comparative Study," *Women's Studies International Forum* 29, 3 (2006): 265–78.

78 Janice Fiamengo, *The Woman's Page: Journalism and Rhetoric in Early Canada* (Toronto: University of Toronto Press, 2008), 159, 164.
79 Lynne Segal, *Radical Happiness: Moments of Collective Joy* (London: Verso, 2017).
80 Fiamengo, *The Woman's Page,* 162.
81 Speech on political equality, Suffrage file, University of Toronto, Thomas Fisher Rare Book Room, Flora MacDonald Denison fonds (UT, Fisher, FMD) coll. 51, box 8b.
82 Denison, "Under the Pines," *Toronto World* (*TW*), 1 May 1910; Fiamengo, *The Woman's Page,* 160.
83 "Women's Suffrage in Canada and Beyond," clipping, UT, Fisher, FMD, box 8a [emphasis added]. Denison's belief that the vote should be used to create social democracy – a more humane, compassionate, egalitarian society – was similar to later arguments of women in the Co-operative Commonwealth Federation. Just before her death, Denison was at the founding convention of the Canadian Labour Party.
84 Denison, "The Report of the Robert Burns Dinner," *TW,* 25 January 1914.
85 Stanley McMullin, "Walt Whitman's Influence in Canada," *Dalhousie Review* 49, 3 (1969): 361–69.
86 *The Sunset of Bon Echo* 1, 1 (March 1916): 18, https://archive.org/details/SunsetOfBonEcho/page/n13, 8.
87 Michael Robertson, *Worshipping Walt: The Whitman Disciples* (Princeton, NJ: Princeton University Press, 2008), 10.
88 Ibid., 21.
89 "Democracy," *Sunset of Bon Echo* 1, 1 (March 1916): 26.
90 Sir John Cockburn, "The Vote beyond the Seas," *TC,* August 1912.
91 On the Victoria parades, see Campbell, *A Great Revolutionary Wave,* 104; on suffragists in Labour Day parades in Ontario, see Sangster, *One Hundred Years,* 160–62.
92 Francis Marion Beynon, quoted in Catherine Cleverdon, *The Woman Suffrage Movement in Canada* (1950; Toronto: University of Toronto Press, 1974), 65.
93 Robin Brownlie, "Living the Same as White People: Mohawk and Anishinabe Women's Labour in Southern Ontario, 1920–1940," *Labour/Le Travail* 61 (2008): 41–68.
94 Catapano, "The Rising of the Ongwehònwe," 225.
95 Ibid., 298, 209, 325.
96 Post–Second World War, status Indians were were added to provincial and territorial voting lists: British Columbia (1949), Manitoba (1952), Ontario (1954), Saskatchewan (1960), New Brunswick (1963), Prince Edward Island (1963), Alberta (1965), Quebec (1969), the Northwest Territories and Yukon (1960). After 1951, Indigenous women could participate in band council elections. *The Canadian Encyclopeadia,* https://www.thecanadianencyclopedia.ca/en/article/indigenous-suffrage.
97 *Debates,* Mr. Brown, 15 June 1948, 5259.
98 Ibid., Mr. Croll, 15 June 1948, 5267.
99 Ibid., Hon. Ellen Fairclough, 9 March 1960, 1915, 1912.
100 Big White Owl, "The Vote Is a Powerful Tomahawk," *Native Voice,* April 1960; "The Indian Magna Carta," *Native Voice,* February 1960.
101 *Debates,* Mr. R. Leduc, 10 March 1960, 1933.
102 Ibid., Mr. J.A. Habel, 10 March 1960, 1936.
103 Ibid., Hon. J.W. Pickersgill, 9 March 1960, 1914.

CHAPTER 4: REFORM FEMINISM AND WOMEN'S RIGHT TO WORK

1 Halifax Business and Professional Women Club Minutes, 4 February 1938, Provincial Archives of Nova Scotia (PANS), Halifax Business and Professional Women's Club fonds (HBPWC), vol. 711, file 1.

2 Some focused their energies on imperialist organizations, others on reform causes, including the BPWC. A few were influential in policy debates. Charlotte Whitton and Emily Murphy, two high-profile examples, would not have limited themselves to tea making. However, despite the request by some women in the Conservative party for more attention to their views, the party as a whole did not promote gender equality in its practices and platform.

3 "Modernization, 1920–1981," *A History of the Vote in Canada,* Elections Canada, https://www.elections.ca/content.aspx?section=res&dir=his&document=chap3&lang=e#a321.

4 A.S.M Hutchinson, *This Freedom* (London: Little, Brown, 1922).

5 Martha Ostenso, *Wild Geese* (1925; Toronto: McClelland and Stewart, 1961).

6 Louise Rethwich, "This New Freedom," *Canadian Forum* (*CF*), 13 February 1933, 172–73.

7 Veronica Strong-Boag, "'Men Want to Hog Everything': Women in Canadian Legislative Politics after Suffrage Victories," Active History, 17 May 2017, http://activehistory.ca/2017/05/men-want-to-hog-everything-women-in-canadian-legislative-politics-after-suffrage-victories/.

8 Grattan O'Leary, "Is Women's Suffrage a Success?" *Chatelaine,* September 1930, 12, 52.

9 "Women Drivers Irrate," *Toronto Daily Star* (*TDS*), 20 May 1936; "A Little of Everything," *TDS,* 23 October 1939.

10 "Finds Women Acted Much Like Children," *TDS,* 12 March 1934.

11 "I'm No Torch Bearer," *TDS,* 12 December 1932.

12 Terrence Crowley, *Agnes Macphail and the Politics of Equality* (Toronto: James Lorimer, 1990), 48.

13 Agnes Macphail, "Men Want to Hog Everything," *Maclean's,* 15 September 1949.

14 Helen Gregory MacGill, "Are Women Wanted in Public Life?" *Chatelaine,* September 1928; Mrs George Hollis, Miss Mildred Low, Miss Beatrice Brigden, Miss F.S. Greenwood, and Mrs. Donald Macdonald, "Why I Failed to Be Elected," *Chatelaine,* October 1930, 17, 37; "The Confessions of a She-Politician," *Maclean's,* 1 June 1922.

15 Larry A. Glassford, "'The Presence of So Many Ladies': A Study of the Conservative Party's Response to Female Suffrage in Canada, 1918–39," *Atlantis* 22, 1 (Fall/Winter 1997): 19-20.

16 Sylvia Bashevkin, "Independence versus Partisanship: Dilemmas in the Political History of Women in English Canada," in *Rethinking Canada: The Promise of Women's History,* 2nd ed., ed. Veronica Strong-Boag and Anita Clair Fellman (Toronto: Copp Clark Pitman, 1991), 415–45.

17 "A Woman's Party," *Western Woman's Weekly* (*WWW*), 28 March 1918.

18 Veronica Strong-Boag, *Labour Lady: The Life and Times of Mary Ellen Spear Smith* (Vancouver: UBC Press, 2021).

19 C.B. Robertson, "The Challenge of Freedom: An Interview with Hon. Irene Parlby," *Chatelaine,* November 1929.

20 Nellie McClung, quoted in Bashevkin, "Independence versus Partisanship," 424.
21 Robert Clarke and Patricia McMahon, *The Persons Case: The Origin and Legacy of the Fight for Legal Personhood* (Toronto: University of Toronto Press), 2008.
22 "Toronto Authoress Writes Great Feminist Critique," *TDS,* 7 March 1936.
23 Margaret Lawrence, *The School of Femininity: A Book for and about Women as They Are Interpreted through Feminine Writers of Yesterday and Today* (Toronto: Nelson, 1936).
24 "Advertising – New Life," *Toronto Star,* 9 May 1939.
25 Gwethalyn Graham, "Women, Are They Human?" *CF,* 16 December 1936, 21–23.
26 Helen Gregory MacGill, "Are Women Wanted in Public Life? And the Important Question Is, 'Are They Really Needed?'" *Chatelaine,* September 1928, 1, 4, 50.
27 Madame Edmond Brossard, "Causes de la déchéance morale des familles," *La bonne parole* (*BP*), June 1932; "Le féminisme," *BP,* November 1938; "Le suffrage féminin à Québec," *BP,* April 1927; Yvonne Letellier de Saint-Just, "Les droits de la femme sont nés de ses devoirs," *BP,* March 1932.
28 Letellier de Saint-Just, "Les droits de la femme"; Florence Fernet, "La formation sociale à l'École Normale," *BP,* May 1917; M.C. Pesche les-Couvin, "L'éducation de nos filles," *BP,* March 1935.
29 Karine Hébert, "Une organisation maternaliste au Québec: La Fédération nationale Saint-Jean-Baptiste et la bataille pour le vote des femmes," *Revue d'histoire de l'Amérique française* 52, 3 (1999): 23.
30 "Women and the Vote in Quebec," *Jus Suffraggi* (*JS*), May 1922, 117.
31 Denyse Baillargeon, *To Be Equals in Our Own Country: Women and the Vote in Quebec* (Vancouver: UBC Press, 2020), 86.
32 Hébert, "Une organisation maternaliste," 19.
33 Baillgeron, *To Be Equals,* 129.
34 Diane Lamoureux, "Idola Saint-Jean et le radicalism féministe de l'entre-deux-guerres," *Recherches féministes* 4, 2 (1991): 50.
35 Thèrèse Casgrain, "L'attitude de la femme envers les parties politiques," *BP,* January 1928. My translation of "beaucoup de modération, de mesure et de sérénité."
36 Lamoureux, "Idola Saint-Jean," 50; Walter Martin, "Quebec's Woman Warriors," quoted in Catherine Cleverdon, *The Woman Suffrage Movement in Canada* (1950; Toronto: University of Toronto Press, 1974), 293.
37 Marie Gérin-Lajoie, "Entre nous," *BP,* December 1917. My translation of "on a foi dans la justice de son jugement, l'expérience fournie par ce que j'appellerai sa spécialisation dans les problèmes domestiques; en un mot la femme vote en raison de son merité et de la dignité de sa function sociale."
38 Anne-Marie Sicotte, *Marie Gérin-Lajoie: Conquérante de la liberté* (Montreal: Remue-Ménage, 2005), 126.
39 Baillargeon, *To Be Equals,* xi.
40 Andrée Lévesque, *Making and Breaking the Rules: Women in Quebec, 1919–1939* (Toronto: Oxford University Press, 1994).
41 Susan Mann Trofimenkoff, "Henri Bourassa and 'the Woman Question'," in *The Neglected Majority: Essays in Canadian Women's History,* ed. Susan Mann Trofimenkoff and Alison Prentice (Toronto: McClelland and Steward, 1977), 113.

42 Isabella Scott, "Quebec's Unjust Laws to Women," *JS,* December 1922, 39–40. See also "Women are Intelligent Enough, but..." *JS,* March 1922, 83 and "Quebec and Woman Suffrage," September 1922, 180.
43 Baillargeon, *To Be Equals,* ix.
44 "Discours d'Idola Saint-Jean diffusé sous les auspices de l'Alliance canadienne pour le vote des femmes du Québec," Bibliothèque de la Ville de Montréal, Collection Gagnon.
45 Éva Circé-Côté, "Le suffrage féminine," in *Chroniques d'Éva Circé-Côté: Lumière sur la société québécoise, 1900–1942,* ed. Andrée Lévesque (Montreal: Les éditions du remue-ménage, 2011), 176–79.
46 Baillargeon, *To Be Equals,* 59.
47 Helen Gregory MacGill, "La Place aux Dames," *Canadian Magazine* (*CM*), April 1933; W. Turner, "Where Women Are Children: Quebec Classes Its Married Women as Minors," *CM,* April 1939.
48 Scott, "Quebec's Unjust Laws."
49 British Dominion Women's Citizen Union, annual meeting minutes, 22–23 June 1926 and 30 June–1 July 1927, London School of Economics and Women's Library, British Commonwealth League Papers BDWCU.
50 "When We Have Mothers Pensions," *WWW,* 10 January 1918, 1.
51 Elsie Gregory MacGill, *My Mother the Judge: A Biography of Judge Helen Gregory MacGill* (Toronto: Ryerson Press, 1955), 178.
52 Susie Lane Clark, "Suffrage Has Brought Incalculable Benefits to Women Say Proponents," 23 October 1937, Vancouver City Archives, Leon Ladner Collection, MS 641, "Voters, Women" newspaper clipping file.
53 J.B. Johnson, "How Is Canada Protecting Her Needy Mothers?" *Chatelaine,* November 1930; Maude Petit Hill, "Do Women Want Protection: Yes!" *Chatelaine,* August 1928.
54 Elizabeth Ann Kalmakoff, "Woman Suffrage in Saskatchewan" (master's thesis, University of Regina, 1993), 153.
55 By 1930, five of the nine provinces had some form of mothers' allowance/mothers' pension legislation.
56 Barbara Nelson, "The Origins of the Two-Channel Welfare State: Workmen's Compensation and Mothers' Aid," in *Women, the State, and Welfare,* ed. Linda Gordon (Madison: University of Wisconsin Press, 1990), 123–51; Margaret Little, *No Car, No Radio, No Liquor Permit: The Moral Regulation of Single Mothers in Ontario, 1920–1997* (Toronto: Oxford University Press, 1998), xiii.
57 Regena Russell, "Welfare Reform in Quebec: Implications for Single Mothers and Their Children" (master of law thesis, McGill University, 1992), 7–9.
58 Margaret Little, "Claiming a Unique Place: The Introduction of Mothers' Pensions in British Columbia," in *Rethinking Canada: The Promise of Women's History,* 4th ed., ed. Veronica Strong-Boag, Mona Gleason, and Adele Perry (Toronto: Oxford University Press, 2002), 190.
59 Peter Campbell, *Rose Henderson: A Woman for the People* (Montreal and Kingston: McGill-Queen's University Press, 2010), 38; Tamara Myers, *Caught: Montreal's Modern Girls and the Law, 1869–1945* (Toronto: University of Toronto Press, 2006).

60 Amanda Glasbeek, *Feminized Justice: The Toronto Women's Court, 1913–34* (Vancouver: UBC Press, 2009), 172.
61 Constitution, 29 July 1930, Archives of Ontario (AO), Toronto Business and Professional Women's Club fonds (TBPWC), F 2085, box 4. Toronto had the federal charter but relinquished this in 1930.
62 Minutes, annual meeting, 1–5 July 1941, Library and Archives Canada (LAC), Canadian Federation of Business and Professional Women's Club fonds MG 29 I-55 (CFBPWC), vol. 29.
63 CBPWC, *The Story of the Business and Professional Women's Clubs* (Vancouver: Seymour Press, 1951), 5; paper presented by Miss Sarah Shannon, LAC, CFBPWC, box 26, Second Convention, Montreal, 2–4 July 1931.
64 Paper presented by Miss Sarah Shannon, LAC.
65 Scrapbook, typescript of Hamilton history, LAC, CFBPWC, vol. 40.
66 Minutes, 5 February 1918, AO, F 2085, TBPWC, file 5.
67 Minutes, 15 April 1931, AO, F 2085, TBPWC, file 5.
68 Scrapbook, Nora Henderson quoted in "Produce Woman Midway between an Amazon and Moron," clipping, n.d., LAC, CFBPWC, vol. 40. Henderson was addressing the Sixth Convention, Niagara Falls, 11–14 July 1937.
69 Dorothy Cummins, "The First Decade, 1930–32," *The Business and Professional Woman,* September–October 1956, 4.
70 President's address, LAC, CFBPWC, 1935 convention, vol. 43.
71 Transcript of roundtable on vital legislation, Mrs. Smith, LAC, CFBPWC, 1935 Convention, vol. 43.
72 "Women Have Qualities for Business Success Lady Eaton Declares," *Winnipeg Tribune* clipping, LAC, CFBPWC, vol. 40.
73 Margaret Hobbs, "Gendering Work and Welfare: Women's Relationship to Wage-Work and Social Policy in Canada during the Great Depression" (PhD diss., University of Toronto, 1995).
74 On masculinity, see Lara Campbell, *Respectable Citizens: Gender, Family, and Unemployment in Ontario's Great Depression* (Toronto: University of Toronto Press, 2009).
75 Quoted in Hobbs, "Gendering Work," 54.
76 President's report, annual convention, July 1933, LAC, CFBPWC, vol. 43.
77 Gisela Bock and Susan James, eds., *Beyond Equality and Difference: Citizenship, Feminist Politics, Female Subjectivity* (New York: Routledge, 1992).
78 Kathleen Derry, "Women – And Unemployed," *Canadian Congress Journal* 10, 12 (1931): 33–34.
79 From 1921 to 1931, the percentage of married women working for pay went from 7 to 10 percent, and may have increased slightly over the thirties, but this was hardly a large number.
80 Veronica Strong-Boag, *The Last Suffragist Standing: The Life and Times of Laura Marshall Jamieson* (Vancouver: UBC Press, 2018), 98.
81 Gwethalyn Graham, "Women, Are They Human?" *Canadian Forum,* December 1936, 21–23.
82 Helen Gregory MacGill, "The Jobless Woman," *Chatelaine,* September 1930.

83 This was the German fascist slogan for women's proper role: children, kitchen, church. Edith M. Luke, "No Sex Bar," *CM,* August 1935.
84 Agnes Macphail, "Women – What Now?" speech, October 1939, and "Whither Women?" speech, March 1936, LAC, Agnes Macphail fonds, MG 27 III C4 (Macphail), vol. 10, file 23.
85 Médéric Martin, "Go Home Young Woman," *Chatelaine,* September 1933.
86 "M. Martin parle sur la motion de M. Kelly," *Le Devoir,* 8 March 1933; my translation.
87 Ibid.
88 Denyse Baillargeon, *A Brief History of Women in Quebec* (Waterloo: Wilfrid Laurier University Press, 2014), 107.
89 Idola Saint-Jean, quoted in Lamoureux, "Idola Saint-Jean," 54; my translation.
90 "Le travail industriel de la mère et le foyer ouvrier," *BP,* May 1933 (my translation); "Le congrès international sur le travail industriel de la mère, á Paris," *BP,* July–August 1933.
91 Marie Gérin-Lajoie, "Travail des femmes et des enfants dans la province de Québec," *BP,* September 1920.
92 Quoted in Strong-Boag, *The Last Suffragist,* 70.
93 "Support the White Producer," *WWW,* 15 July 1922, 4; "British Progressive League," *WWW,* 11 October 1922, 2.
94 Dionne Brand, "'We Weren't Allowed to Go into Factory Work until Hitler Started the War': The 1920s to the 1940s," in *"We're Rooted Here and They Can't Pull Us Up": Essays in African Canadian Women's History,* ed. Peggy Bristow et al. (Toronto: University of Toronto Press, 1994), 175, 177.
95 Kathryn McPherson, *Bedside Matters: The Transformation of Canadian Nursing, 1900–1990* (Toronto: Oxford University Press, 1996), 211.
96 Jennifer Mills, "A Critical Examination of the Early Years of the Hour-a-Day Study Club, 1935–55" (master's thesis, University of Windsor, 1995), 72.
97 Interview with Pearleen Oliver, transcript, PANS, Nova Scotia Women's Oral History Project.
98 George Elliott Clarke, *Fire on the Water,* vol. 1 (Halifax: Pottersfield Press, 1991), 146.
99 Interview with Pearleen Oliver, transcript, PANS, Nova Scotia Women's Oral History Project. See also Constance Backhouse, *Colour Coded: A Legal History of Racism in Canada, 1900–1950* (Toronto: Osgoode Society for Legal History and University of Toronto Press, 1999), 245–47; Clarke, *Fire on the Water.* Oliver is featured in Doris McCubbin, "The Women of Halifax," *Chatelaine,* June 1954.
100 Halifax Business and Professional Women's Club, annual report, 1956, PANS, HBPWC, vol. 713, file 41.

CHAPTER 5: AGRARIAN, LABOUR, AND SOCIALIST FEMINISM AFTER THE FIRST WORLD WAR

1 Author interview with Sophia Dixon, 1 November 1980.
2 Nellie Peterson, in *Prairie Women,* dir. Barbara Evans, National Film Board, 1987; Author interview with Nellie Peterson, 21 November 1980.
3 Joan Sangster, *Dreams of Equality: Women on the Canadian Left, 1920–1950* (Toronto: McClelland and Stewart, 1989).

4 Reinhold Kramer and Tom Mitchell, *When the State Trembled: How A.J. Andrews and the Citizens' Committee Broke the Winnipeg General Strike* (Toronto: University of Toronto Press, 2010); Reg Whitaker, Gregory S. Kealey, and Andrew Parnaby, *Secret Service: Political Policing in Canada from the Fenians to Fortress America* (Toronto: University of Toronto Press, 2012).
5 Kirsten Marie Delegard, *Battling Miss Bolsheviki: The Origins of Female Conservatism in the United States* (Philadelphia: University of Pennsylvania Press, 2012), 47–51; Erica J. Ryan, *Red War on the Family: Sex, Gender, and Americanism in the First Red Scare* (Philadelphia: Temple University Press, 2015).
6 Georgina Taylor, "Ground for Common Action: Violet McNaughton, Agrarian Feminism and the Origins of the Farm Women's Movement in Canada" (PhD diss., Carleton University, 1997), 349.
7 Naomi Black and Gail Cuthbert Brandt, *Feminist Politics on the Farm: Rural Catholic Women in Southern Quebec and Southwestern France* (Montreal and Kingston: McGill-Queen's University Press, 1999), 27; Yolande Cohen, *Femmes de paroles: L'histoire des Cercles de fermières du Québec, 1915–1990* (Montreal: Le Jour, 1990).
8 There is debate about whether the Ontario WI was feminist, social feminist, or not feminist at all. Monda Halpern, *And On That Farm He Had a Wife: Ontario Farm Women and Feminism, 1900–1970* (Montreal and Kingston: McGill-Queen's University Press, 2001), asserts the WI was feminist, but others are more sceptical about the use of this term: see Margaret Kechnie, *Organizing Rural Women: The Federated Women's Institutes of Ontario, 1897–1919* (Montreal and Kingston: McGill-Queen's University Press, 2003); Linda Ambrose, *For Home and Country: The Centennial History of the Women's Institutes in Ontario* (Erin, ON: Boston Mills Press, 1996).
9 Agrarian feminists might collaborate – or not – with other organized farm women, such as the WI and Homemakers, depending on the province.
10 Halpern, *And On That Farm*, 95.
11 Pauline Rankin, "The Politicization of Ontario Farm Women," in *Beyond the Vote: Canadian Women and Politics*, ed. Linda Kealey and Joan Sangster (Toronto: University of Toronto Press, 1989), 315. There were tensions between the WI and UFWO, which overlapped and competed for members. Some UFWO supporters, including MP Agnes Macphail, saw the WI as far too conservative, limited by the control exerted by the provincial government.
12 James Naylor, *The Fate of Labour Socialism: The Co-operative Commonwealth Federation and the Dream of a Working-Class Future* (Toronto: University of Toronto Press, 2016), 165.
13 Elaine Orvedahl Hamm, "The Ideas of Sophia Dixon" (master's thesis, University of Saskatchewan, 1987), 25.
14 Ibid., 31.
15 Jeffrey Taylor, *Fashioning Farmers: Ideology, Agricultural Knowledge and the Manitoba Farm Movement* (Regina: Canadian Plains Research Center, 1994); Gerald Friesen, *The Canadian Prairies: A History* (Toronto: University of Toronto Press, 1984).
16 Dixon interview.
17 Taylor, "Ground for Common Action," 18.

18 Ibid., 36.
19 Ibid., 13.
20 Margaret Hobbs, "Introduction: The Women's Pages of *The Western Producer,* 1925–1939: Violet McNaughton and Interwar Feminism in Canada," in Canadian Women and Social Movements 13, 2 (2009), special issue of *Women and Social Movements* (Alexander Street Press), https://search.alexanderstreet.com/preview/work/bibliographic_entity%7Cweb_collection%7C2498268.
21 Lori Jones, interviewed in *Prairie Women.*
22 Annie Hollis, "Occupations for Women," *Canadian Forum* (*CF*), May 1930.
23 Hollis, "Home Economics: Why Not Elevate the Kitchen?" *Western Producer* (*WP*), September 1929, quoted in Cathy Holtslander, "Annie Hollis: Organizing Prairie Women with the *Western Producer,*" *Prairie Forum* 29, 2 (2004): 180. Hollis kept up her campaign about the census: "If housework is only open to women, which I don't believe, then it should be recognized as of economic and national value by our own statistics, which simply exclude it." Letter of Annie Hollis to Violet McNaughton, 29 May 1939, Saskatchewan Archives Board, Violet McNaughton fonds, D-27; see also *WP,* 3 September 1936.
24 Veronica Strong-Boag, "Pulling in Double Harness or Hauling a Double Load: Women, Work and Feminism on the Canadian Prairie," *Journal of Canadian Studies* 21, 3 (1986): 32–52.
25 Quote from *Farmers Magazine,* in Monda Halpern, "Such Outrageous Discrimination: Farm Women and Their Family Grievances in Early Twentieth-Century Ontario," in *Framing Our Past: Canadian Women's History in the Twentieth Century,* ed. Sharon Cook, Lorna McLean, and Kate O'Rourke (Montreal and Kingston: McGill-Queen's University Press, 2001), 120.
26 Mary Kinnear, *A Female Economy: Women's Work in a Prairie Province, 1870–1970* (Montreal and Kingston: McGill-Queen's University Press, 1998), 94.
27 Hobbs, "Introduction."
28 Ibid.
29 Quoted in Christina Scowby, "Divine Discontent: Women, Identity and the *Western Producer*" (master's thesis, University of Saskatchewan, 1996), 65.
30 Ibid.
31 James Naylor, *The Fate of Labour Socialism,* 60. By the late 1940s and 1950s, Irvine's ideas were less welcome in a CCF shifting from a socialist to social democratic outlook: Anthony Madiros, *William Irvine: The Life of a Prairie Radical* (Toronto: James Lorimer, 1979).
32 "Her Politics Were Forged by Desperate Conditions," *Edmonton Journal,* 23 August 1980.
33 Nellie Peterson, Radio Broadcasts, 1949, Glenbow Institute Archives (Glenbow), CCF Collection, file 25.
34 Nellie Peterson, interview in *Prairie Women* and interview with Joan Sangster, 21 November 1980.
35 When Notley steered the party in a more social democratic direction, he never wavered in his respect for Peterson as a worthy socialist opponent. Howard Leeson, *Grant Notley: The Social Conscience of Alberta* (Edmonton: University of Alberta Press, 1992).

36 Lori Jones, in *Prairie Women.*

37 Naylor, *Labour Socialism.*

38 Todd McCallum, "Not a Sex Question? The One Big Union and the Politics of Radical Manhood," *Labour/Le Travail* 42 (Fall 1998): 15–54.

39 Laura Jamieson's personal notes, Provincial Archives of British Columbia, Laura Jamieson fonds, collection 311, file 9.

40 James Naylor, *The New Democracy: Challenging the Social Order in Industrial Ontario, 1914–25* (Toronto: University of Toronto Press, 1991), 140–41.

41 Peter Campbell, "The Cult of Spontaneity: Finnish Canadian Bushworkers and the Industrial Workers of the World in Northern Ontario, 1919–34," in *Essays in Northwestern Ontario Working Class History: Thunder Bay and Its Environs,* ed. Michel Beaulieu (Thunder Bay: Lakehead Centre for Northern Studies, 2008), 91–124.

42 Peter Campbell, *Rose Henderson: A Woman for the People* (Montreal and Kingston: McGill-Queen's University Press, 2010), 58–59.

43 Andrée Lévesque, *Freethinker: Éva Circé-Côté,* trans. Lazer Lederhendler (Toronto: Between the Lines, 2017), 298–300.

44 "La loi suffrage," *Ouvrier canadien,* March 1927, 2, 4.

45 Florence Rowe, "It's Time to Get Up Mary," *One Big Union Bulletin* (*OBUB*), 25 June 1925.

46 Rowe, "My Dear Watson I Ask You," *OBUB,* 16 April 1925.

47 Rowe, "On Higgins and Louise," *OBUB,* 9 July 1925.

48 Amelia Turner Smith speeches file, Glenbow, Amelia Turner Smith and Walter Smith Papers (Smith), vol. 9.

49 Patricia Roome, "Amelia Turner and the Calgary Labour Women, 1919–1935," in *Beyond the Vote: Canadian Women and Politics,* ed. Linda Kealey and Joan Sangster (Toronto: University of Toronto Press, 1989), 89–117.

50 Amelia Turner Smith speeches, Glenbow, Smith, vol. 9.

51 David Thompson, "More Sugar, Less Salt: Edith Hancox and the Passionate Mobilization of the Dispossessed, 1919–1928," *Labour/Le Travail* 85 (Spring 2020): 127–64.

52 Ibid.

53 Mary Horodyski, "Women and the Winnipeg General Strike of 1919," *Manitoba History* 11 (1986): 2; Linda Kealey, "No Special Protection – No Sympathy: Women's Activism in the Canadian Labour Revolt of 1919," in *Class, Community and the Labour Movement: Wales and Canada,* ed. Deian Hopkin and Gregory Kealey (St. John's: Canadian Committee on Labour History, 1989), 134–59.

54 Beatrice Brigden Diary, 17 September 1905, Provincial Archives of Manitoba (PAM), Beatrice Brigden fonds (Brigden), box 8; Joan Sangster, "The Making of a Socialist-Feminist: The Early Career of Beatrice Brigden, 1888–1941," in *Educating for a Brighter Day: Women's Organizations as Learning Sites,* ed. Michael Welton (Halifax: Dalhousie University, School of Education, 1992), 116.

55 Letter, Beatrice Brigden to A.E. Moore, 26 July 1919, PAM, Brigden, box 4.

56 Beatrice Brigden, "Boys and Girls Column," *Weekly News,* 8 April 1932.

57 Mabel Aiken, quoted in Allison Campbell, "Beatrice Brigden: The Formative Years of a Socialist Feminist, 1888–1932" (master's thesis, University of Winnipeg, 1991), 131.

58 "Western Canada Labor Women's Social and Economic Conference," *Weekly News,* 22 May 1931.

59 Campbell, *Rose Henderson,* 111, 77. See also Tamara Myers, *Caught: Montreal's Modern Girls and the Law* (Toronto: University of Toronto Press, 2006).

60 Rose Henderson, "The Modern Girl," *OBUB,* 3 February 1927.

61 On relief strikes in Toronto, see Byran Palmer and Gaétan Héroux, *Toronto's Poor: A Rebellious History* (Toronto: Between the Lines, 2016), 196–244.

62 Letter, Bert Robinson to "Comrades," 7 November 1933, University of Toronto, Thomas Fisher Rare Book Room, Woodsworth Memorial Collection, box 9, Socialist Party of Canada file.

63 Elizabeth Morton, quoted in John Manley, "Women and the Left in the 1930s: The Case of the Toronto Women's Joint Committee," *Atlantis* 5, 2 (1980): 118.

64 Elizabeth Morton, "Labour Woman," *Trade Unionist,* 31 July 1931, 3. The paper was published by the Canadian Federation of Labour, a very moderate group of Canadian unions.

65 Ibid., 24 December 1930 and 23 February 1931.

66 Ibid., 28 January 1931.

CHAPTER 6: FEMINISM AND THE PARTY QUESTION

1 Regina Manifesto (1933), Co-operative Commonwealth Federation Programme, Socialist History Project, http://www.socialisthistory.ca/Docs/CCF/ReginaManifesto.htm.

2 Saskatchewan Archives Board (SAB), Saskatchewan CCF Collection (SCCF), CCF–Farmer-Labour Group, minutes, 8 July 1933.

3 Beatrice Brigden, "Have Women Rights?" *Manitoba Commonwealth,* 22 February 1935.

4 Agnes Macphail, quoted in Terry Crowley, *Agnes Macphail and the Politics of Equality* (Toronto: James Lorimer, 1990), 91.

5 Susan Walsh, "The Peacock and the Guinea Hen: Political Profiles of Dorothy Gretchen Steeves and Grace MacInnis," in *The Neglected Majority: Essays in Canadian Women's History,* vol. 2, ed. Alison Prentice and Susan Mann Trofimenkoff (Toronto: McClelland and Stewart, 1985), 149.

6 Interview with D.L., 9 November 1980, quoted in Joan Sangster, "Women of the New Era: The Role of Women in the Early CCF," in *Building the Cooperative Commonwealth: Essays on the Democratic Socialist Tradition in Canada,* ed. J. William Brennan (Regina: Canadian Plains Research Center, 1984), 77.

7 "Memories," typescript, SAB, Gertrude Telford papers, vol. 31.

8 Quoted in Sangster, *Dreams of Equality,* 100.

9 Ontario CCF, provincial executive minutes, 1 October 1943, University of Toronto, Thomas Fisher Rare Book Room (UT, Fisher), Woodsworth Memorial Collection (WMC), box 1.

10 Minerva Cooper address to 1938 provincial CCF convention, Saskatoon, 21–23 July 1938, SAB, SCCF, B7, I-2 Minutes, 1936–52 and II-73. The tussle over voting rights for women's study clubs was ongoing and complex, but it clearly indicated that women did not want just an auxiliary role.

11 Beatrice Brigden "Savings," *Manitoba Commonwealth,* 12 December 1934, Public Archives of Manitoba (PAM), Beatrice Brigden fonds, box 9, scrapbooks.
12 "Fairly Feminine," *New Commonwealth,* 18 May 1935.
13 Ibid., 8 June 1935.
14 Interview of Eve Grey Smith by Joan Sangster, 19 July 1981.
15 Eve Grey Smith, *The Federationist* (*TF*), 28 October 1937.
16 Elizabeth Kerr, "Women's Views," *TF,* 1 December 1938. For a time, Kerr wrote under the pen name of Constance Errol. I have used her own name for consistency.
17 Elizabeth Kerr, "Women's Views," *TF,* 7 July 1938.
18 *TF,* 21 January 1943, 22 June 1946, and 29 July 1948.
19 "Labor Women Attend Conference," *Trade Unionist,* 13 October 1930. Why do I suspect that other women were displeased with her speech? For one thing, they quibbled over her recommendations, not wanting to adopt them, and, second, as soon as she sat down, someone made a motion to limit future speeches to five minutes, considerably shorter than her long speech.
20 Bryan Palmer and Gaétan Héroux, *Toronto's Poor: A Rebellious History* (Toronto: Between the Lines, 2016), 203, 330, 233.
21 Patricia Schultz, *The East York Workers Association: A Response to the Great Depression* (Toronto: New Hogtown Press, 1975), 19.
22 Quoted in Irene Howard, *The Struggle for Social Justice in British Columbia: Helena Gutteridge, the Unknown Reformer* (Vancouver: UBC Press, 1992), 168.
23 Colley, who was involved, along with communist Peggy Harrison, in creating this demonstration, was named "Mother Colley" by the party. Sangster, *Dreams of Equality: Women on the Canadian Left* (Toronto: McClelland and Stewart, 1989), 115–16.
24 H.D. Ainley, "Women in the CCF," *Manitoba Commonwealth,* 29 March 1940; Beatrice Brigden, "Women of the New Era," *Labor Annual,* September 1934. On militant mothering, see Sangster, *Dreams of Equality,* 91.
25 Arthur Cathers, *Beloved Dissident: Eve Smith* (Blyth, ON: Drumadravy Books, 1997), 76.
26 Candida Rifkind, *Comrades and Critics: Women, Literature and the Left in 1930s Canada* (Toronto: University of Toronto Press, 2009), 150.
27 "Mary Wollstonecraft," University of Alberta Archives, Elsie Park Gowan fonds, Acc 87-123, vol. 1, file 18. On Gowan, see Moira Day, ed., *The Hungry Spirit: Selected Plays and Prose by Elsie Park Gowan* (Edmonton: Newest, 1992).
28 William Irvine [and Elsie Park Gowan], *You Can't Do That* (Toronto: Thomas Nelson and Sons, 1936), 7.
29 Mary Reynolds, "And the Answer Is …," *New Frontier,* March 1937.
30 Candida Rifkind, *Comrades and Critics,* 156–57.
31 Mary Quayle Innis, "Schooling," *Canadian Forum* (*CF*), February 1930.
32 Mary Quayle Innis, "Two Ears," *CF,* August 1933.
33 Donica Belisle, "Guilty Pleasures: Consumer Culture in the Fiction of Mary Quayle Innis," in *Consuming Modernity: Gendered Behaviour and Consumerism before the Baby Boom,* ed. Cheryl Krasnick Warsh and Dan Malleck (Vancouver: UBC Press, 2013), 258–73.
34 This is a complex debate, but it has been posed as an "either/or" one, of either Soviet control or local autonomy, with left- and right-wing critiques of Leninism, Stalinism,

and the Comintern mixed up together, and with American historians' typologies of two opposing schools of writing on communism unfortunately repeated by Canadian historians. Two comparative pieces that look at the historiography in a more complex manner are John Manley, "Moscow Rules? 'Red' Unionism and 'Class against Class' in Britain, Canada and the United States, 1928–35," *Labour/Le Travail* 56 (2005): 9–50, and Bryan Palmer, "Re-Thinking the Historiography of United States Communism," *American Communist History* 2, 2 (2003): 139–74.

35 Margaret Gould also published these observations in *I Visit the Soviets* (Toronto: Stafford Printing, 1937). On left-wing political tourism see Joan Sangster, "Political Tourism, Writing and Communication: Transnational Connections of Women on the Left," in *Crossing Boundaries: Women's Organizing in Europe and the Americas, 1880s–1940s,* ed. Pernilla Jonsson, Silke Neunsinger, and Joan Sangster (Uppsala: University of Uppsala Press, 2007), 95–116; Kirk Niergarth, "Gender and the Great Experiment: 'Feminine and Canadian Eyes' See Soviet Women, 1926–1936," *Journal of the Canadian Historical Association* 26, 2 (2015): 139–172.

36 Geoff Eley, *Forging Democracy: The History of the Left in Europe, 1850–2000* (Oxford: Oxford University Press, 2002). A few pieces on women and communism include Beatrice Brodsky Farnsworth, "Communist Feminism: Its Synthesis and Demise," in *Women, War and Revolution,* ed. Carol Berkin and Clara Lovett (New York: Homes and Meier, 1980), 145–62; Wendy Z. Goldman, *Women, the State and Revolution: Soviet Family Policy and Social Life, 1917–1936* (Cambridge: Cambridge University Press, 1993); Elizabeth Waters, "In the Shadow of the Comintern: The Communist Women's Movement, 1920–43," in *Promissory Notes: Women in the Transition to Socialism,* ed. Sonia Kruks, Rayna Rapp, and Marilyn B. Young (New York: Monthly Review Press, 1989), 29–56.

37 Elizabeth Wood, *The Baba and the Comrade: Gender and Politics in Revolutionary Russia* (Bloomington: Indiana University Press, 2000), 216.

38 Florence Custance, "Our Tasks among Women," Central Executive Committee Report, Fifth Convention, 1925, UT, Fisher, Robert Kenny Collection (Kenny), box 1.

39 Margaret Hobbs and Joan Sangster, "Introduction," in *The Woman Worker, 1926–1929* (St. John's: Canadian Committee on Labour History, 1999), 7.

40 Florence Custance, "Cruelty to Women" and "An Interesting Court Decision," *Woman Worker* (*WW*), January 1927.

41 Harold Begbie, "A London Girl," *WW,* August 1926. In the 1920s, again in concert with the Soviet example, communist women were critical of the institution of marriage and its association with the church; some favoured common-law unions instead.

42 "Women for the Senate," *WW,* October 1927.

43 "Why Are Dishonest Masters Not Sent to Prison," *WW,* April 1927; "A Boss Punished for Robbing a Working Girl of Her Wages," *WW,* July–August 1927.

44 Lita-Rose Betcherman, *The Little Band: The Clashes between the Communists and the Political and Legal Establishment in Canada, 1928–1932* (Ottawa: Deneau Publishers, 1982).

45 Andrée Lévesque, *Red Travellers: Jeanne Corbin and Her Comrades* (Montreal and Kingston: McGill-Queen's University Press, 2006), 129.

46 "Comment on procède a la liquidation de la prostitution en Russie sovietique," *L'ouvrier canadien,* April 1931.
47 Mercedes Steedman, *Angels of the Workplace: Women and the Construction of Gender Relations in the Canadian Clothing Industry, 1890–1940* (Toronto: Oxford University Press, 1997), 152.
48 For a critical view, see Ruth Frager, *Sweatshop Strife: Class, Ethnicity, and Gender in the Jewish Labour Movement of Toronto, 1900–1939* (Toronto: University of Toronto Press, 1992); for a more generous one, John Manley, "Communism and the Canadian Working Class during the Great Depression: The Workers Unity League, 1930–36" (PhD diss., Dalhousie University, 1984).
49 Irving Abella, "Portrait of a Jewish Revolutionary: The Recollections of Joshua Gershman," *Labour/Le Travail* 2, 2 (1977): 185–213.
50 Andrée Lévesque writes that Leah Roback was in charge of union education in 1934, though she is not named as an organizer by Steedman. Andrée Lévesque, *Virage à gauche interdit: Les communists, les socialistes et leurs ennemis au Québec, 1929–1939* (Montreal: Boréal Express, 1984), 55.
51 Abella, "Portrait of a Jewish Revolutionary," and Steedman, *Angels of the Workplace.*
52 Steedman, *Angels of the Workplace,* 176.
53 Ibid., chap. 7.
54 Frager, *Sweatshop Strife,* 13. See also Gerald Tulchinsky, *Taking Root: Origins of the Canadian Jewish Community* (Toronto: Stoddart, 1992).
55 Peter Krawchuk, *Our History: The Ukrainian Labour Farmer Movement in Canada, 1907–1991* (Toronto: Lugus, 1999), 366.
56 Charles Roslin, "Canada's Bolshevik Drama," *Saturday Night,* 9 February 1929. See also Joan Sangster, "*Robitnytsia:* Ukrainian Communists and the 'Porcupinism' Debate: Reassessing Ethnicity, Gender and Class in Early Canadian Communism, 1922–1930," *Labour/Le Travail* 56 (Autumn 2005): 51–90.
57 S. Altunin, "Why Workingwomen Should Belong to an Organization," *Robitnytsia,* 15 December 1935.
58 Tymko Izhad, "Do Women Need an Organization?" *Robitnytsia,* 1 April 1928.
59 M. Synooverholets, "Five Years on Thorny Paths," *Robitnytsia,* 15 March and 1 April 1929.
60 Malanka, "And Who Are You?" *Robitnytsia,* 15 January 1929.
61 Member, "Response to Comrade Izhak," *Robitnytsia,* 1 January 1929.
62 T.N., "Do Women Need an Organization?" *Robitnytsia,* 1 June 1928.
63 For notice of the Halifax club, but no information on it, see "New Halifax Branch," *Masses,* July–August 1932. The Vancouver club was especially active in theatre. See Rifkind, *Comrades and Critics.*
64 Symbolized by the title of one of the most famous plays, *Eight Men Speak.* The play was about eight communist leaders arrested for "sedition," most incarcerated, one deported. Plays such as Dorothy Livesay's *Joe Derry* did veer from this mode, using a more imaginative children's chant. *Eight Men Speak and Other Plays from the Canadian Workers Theater,* ed. Richard Wright and Robin Endres (Toronto: New Hogtown Press, 1976).
65 Dorothy Smith, *Feminism and Marxism* (Vancouver: New Press, 1974), 34.

66 Mona Weiss, "My Fellow Stenos," *Masses,* July–August 1932; L.F. Edwards, "McClung & Canadiana," *Masses,* June 1932.
67 Nancy Butler, "Mother Russia and the Socialist Fatherland: Women and the Communist Party of Canada, 1932–1941, with Specific Reference to the Activism of Dorothy Livesay and Jim Watts" (PhD diss., Queen's University, 2010), 277.
68 Marjorie King, "Women Are Mugs," *New Frontier* (*NF*), February 1937; Betty Friedan, *The Feminine Mystique* (New York: W.W. Norton, 1963).
69 Margaret Gould, "Women, Bound or Free?" *NF,* July 1936.
70 Ibid., 21.
71 Ibid., and Margaret Gould, "A Social Worker Looks at the Soviets," *NF,* November 1936, 18.
72 Dorothy Livesay, "Beach Sunday," *CF,* January 1931 and "The Difference," *CF,* May 1931.
73 Dorothy Livesay, "A Girl Sees It!" *Masses,* March–April 1933; Butler, "Mother Russia," 310.
74 Dorothy Livesay, *Right Hand, Left Hand* (Erin, ON: Press Porcepic, 1977), 124.
75 Dorothy Livesay, *Journey with My Selves* (Vancouver: Douglas & McIntyre, 1991), 87.
76 Barbara Foley, "Women and the Left in the 1930s," *American Literary History* 2, 1 (Spring 1990): 162.
77 Larry Hannant, "'My God, Are They Sending Women?' Three Canadian Women in the Spanish Civil War, 1936–1939," *Journal of the Canadian Historical Association* 15, 1 (2004): 153–76.
78 Rifkind, *Comrades and Critics,* 69.
79 Anne Frances Toews, "For Liberty, Bread, and Love: Annie Buller, Beckie Buhay, and the Forging of Communist Militant Femininity in Canada, 1918–1939" (master's thesis, Simon Fraser University, 2009).
80 Some did question the adherence to Stalinism and were expelled. See Jim Mochoruk, "'Pop and Co.' versus Tim Buck and the 'Lenin School Boys': Ukrainian-Canadians and the Communist Party of Canada, 1921–31," in *Re-Imagining Ukrainian-Canadians: History, Politics and Identity,* ed. Rhonda Hinther and James Mochoruk (Toronto: University of Toronto Press, 2011), 331–75.
81 Lisa Young, *Feminists and Party Politics* (Vancouver: UBC Press, 2000), 57.
82 Sangster, *Dreams of Equality,* 110.
83 Walsh, "The Peacock and the Guinea Hen," 144–59.

CHAPTER 7: FEMINISM, WAR, AND PEACE

1 Thomas Socknat, *Witness against War: Pacifism in Canada, 1900–1945* (Toronto: University of Toronto Press, 1987), 31–32.
2 Ibid., 33.
3 James Hughes, *Equal Suffrage* (Toronto: William Briggs, 1895), 31.
4 Nellie McClung, *In Times Like These* (1915; Toronto: University of Toronto Press, 1974), 15.

5 Flora MacDonald Denison, "War and Women," in *Documenting First Wave Feminisms,* vol. 2, *Canada: National and Transnational Contexts,* ed. Nancy Forestell and Majureen Moynagh (Toronto: University of Toronto Press, 2014), 293–97.
6 Melinda Plastas, *A Band of Noblewomen: Racial Politics in the Women's Peace Movement* (Syracuse, NY: Syracuse University Press, 2011), 11.
7 Nellie McClung, *In Times like These,* 14, 17.
8 Ibid.
9 Nellie McClung, "Slacker in Uniform," in *Next of Kin* (Toronto: Thomas Allen, 1917), 147.
10 Suzanne Evans, "Marks of Grief: Black Attire, Medals, and Service Flags," in *A Sisterhood of Suffering and Service: Women and Girls of Canada and Newfoundland during the First World War,* ed. Sarah Glassford and Amy Shaw (Vancouver: UBC Press, 2012), 219–40.
11 The NCWC switched from calls for arbitration in world affairs to declaring the war a time of "opportunity, of national revival and purification." Veronica Strong-Boag, *The Parliament of Women: The National Council of Women of Canada, 1893–1929* (Ottawa: National Museums of Canada, 1976), 291.
12 Editorial, *Women's Century,* April 1918; "Mothers of Consolidation," *Everywoman's World,* April 1918.
13 Constance Hamilton, letter, *Women's Century,* August 1915.
14 Constance Boulton, "Reconstruction for a Greater Canada," *Women's Century,* January 1918, 20.
15 Deborah Gorham, "Flora MacDonald Denison: Canadian Feminist," in *A Not Unreasonable Claim: Women and Reform in Canada, 1880s to 1920s,* ed. Linda Kealey (Toronto: Women's Press, 1979), 47–70.
16 Diana Chown, introduction to *The Stairway,* by Alice Chown (Toronto: University of Toronto Press, 1988), xliv–xlv.
17 Jane Addams, Emily Balch, and Alice Hamilton, *Women at The Hague: The International Congress of Women, April 27–May 1, 1915,* ed. Harriet Alonso (Urbana: University of Illinois Press, 2003), xxiii, xxvii.
18 Quoted in Mary Jean Woodard Bean, *Julia Grace Wales: Canada's Hidden Heroine and the Quest for Peace, 1914–1918* (Ottawa: Borealis Press, 2005), 66.
19 Ibid.; Lorna McLean, "The Necessity of Going: Julia Grace Wales's Transnational Life as a Peace Activist and a Scholar," in *Feminist History in Canada: New Essays on Women, Gender, Work and Nation,* ed. Catherine Carstairs and Nancy Janovicek (Vancouver: UBC Press, 2013), 77–95.
20 Interview with Helen Armstrong's granddaughter in the film *The Notorious Helen Armstrong* (prod. Paula Kelly, Buffalo Gal Pictures, 2001).
21 "Prussionizing Canada," *Canadian Forward,* 12 June 1917.
22 "Martyrdom in Canada," *Canadian Forward,* 25 January 1918.
23 Gertrude Richardson, "Unto This Last, the Mother Cry Is Supreme," *Canadian Forward,* 24 August 1917.
24 "In the Toronto Telegram," *Women's Century,* September 1917.
25 Richardson, "Unto This Last."

26 Richardson, quoted in Barbara Roberts, *A Reconstructed World: A Feminist Biography of Gertrude Richardson* (Montreal and Kingston: McGill-Queen's University Press, 1996), 201.
27 Richardson, "Unto This Last."
28 Gertrude Richardson, "The Call and the Response," *Canadian Forward,* 24 September 1917.
29 Harriet Prenter, "Women's Column," *Canadian Forward,* 24 August 1917. On the Canadian suffragists in the Washington parade, see Joan Sangster, "Canadian Women Marching in the Washington: Feminist Solidarity in Historical Perspective," *Women Suffrage and Beyond,* 20 January 2017, http://womensuffrage.org/?p=22848.
30 Linda Kealey, *Enlisting Women for the Cause: Women, Labour and the Left in Canada, 1890–1920* (Toronto: University of Toronto Press, 1998), and "Women and Labour during World War I: Women Workers and the Minimum Wage in Manitoba," in *First Days, Fighting Days: Women in Manitoba History,* ed. Mary Kinnear (Regina: Canadian Plains Research Center, 1987), 76–99.
31 Helena Gutteridge, *British Columbia Federationist* (*BCF*), 4 September 1914, 2.
32 "Attack by Miss Laura Hughes on Bonar Law and Noted Britishers," *Canadian Forward,* 12 June 1917.
33 Francis Marion Beynon, *Grain Growers Guide,* 12 August 1914 and 25 November 1915, quoted in Barbara Roberts, *"Why Do Women Do Nothing to End the War?": Canadian Feminist Pacifists and the Great War* (Ottawa: Canadian Research Institute for the Advancement of Women, 1985), 12. The modern slogan is credited to the Women's International League for Peace and Freedom, ca. 1965–80, https://www.loc.gov/item/2015649445/.
34 Francis Marion Beynon, *Aleta Dey* (1919; London: Virago Press, 1988), 120.
35 Ibid., 168, 212–13.
36 Lyndsay Campbell, "The War-Time Election Act, Canadian Women's Suffrage and Constitutional Thought in World War I," in *Women's Legal Histories,* ed. Lori Chambers and Joan Sangster (Toronto: University of Toronto Press, forthcoming).
37 Francis Marion Beynon, "Democracy," *Canadian Forward,* 10 December 1917.
38 B. Gould, "Women in the Canadian Election," *Women's Century,* January 1918.
39 Irene Howard, *The Struggle for Social Justice in British Columbia: Helena Gutteridge the Unknown Reformer* (Vancouver: UBC Press, 1992), 99.
40 Tarah Brookfield, "Divided by the Ballot Box: The Montreal Council of Women and the 1917 Election," *Canadian Historical Review* 89, 4 (2008): 490.
41 Kathleen Kennedy, *Disloyal Mothers and Scurrilous Citizens: Women and Subversion during World War I* (Bloomington: Indiana University Press, 1999).
42 The minister responsible for the status of women in Stephen Harper's Conservative government, Kellie Leitch, played a key role in scapegoating immigrants – clearly targeting Muslims – in the 2015 election. Andrew Gee, "Conservatives Vow to Establish 'Barbaric Cultural Practices' Tipline," *Globe and Mail,* 2 October 2015.
43 Rose Henderson, *Woman and War* (Vancouver: Federated Labor Party Publications, 1925), 7; *One Big Union Bulletin* (*OBUB*), 11 November 1926 to 9 December 1926.
44 Henderson, *Woman and War,* 3.
45 Ibid., 19.

46 See Peter Campbell, *Rose Henderson: A Woman for the People* (Montreal and Kingston: McGill-Queen's University Press, 2010), 98, and Plastas, *A Band of Noblewomen*, 19.
47 Chown, introduction, *The Stairway*, lvii.
48 Terry Crowley, *Agnes Macphail and the Politics of Equality* (Toronto: James Lorimer, 1990), 100. Given Macphail's views, both might be seen as "feminist" responses.
49 On the international WIL, see Gertude Bussey and Margaret Tims, *Pioneers for Peace: Women's International League for Peace and Freedom, 1915–1965* (London: George Allen & Unwin, 1965); Harriet Alonso, *Peace as a Women's Issue: A History of the US Movement for World Peace and Women's Rights* (Syracuse, NY: Syracuse University Press, 1993); Linda Schott, *Reconsidering Women's Thought: The Women's International League for Peace and Freedom before World War II* (Stanford, CA: Stanford University Press, 1997).
50 Socknat, *Witness against War*, 108.
51 Margaret Stewart and Doris French, *Ask No Quarter: A Biography of Agnes Macphail* (Toronto: Longmans, Green, 1959), 88, 130.
52 CLWF National Bureau meeting, 15 April 1936, York University Archives (YUA), E.A. Beder fonds (Beder), 1972-001/009.
53 Nancy Boutilier, "Making Peace as Interesting as War: The Educational Strategies of the Women's International League for Peace and Freedom in the 1920s," in *Educating for a Brighter New Day: Women's Organizations as Learning Sites*, ed. Michael Welton (Halifax: Dalhousie School of Education, 1992), 92.
54 Socknat, *Witness against War*, 112.
55 Veronica Strong-Boag, *The Last Suffragist Standing: The Life and Times of Laura Marshall Jamieson* (Vancouver: UBC Press, 2018), 75.
56 Catherine Marshall, C.K. Ogden, and Mary Sargant Florence, *Militarism versus Feminism* (London: George, Allen & Unwin, 1915), 3, 9.
57 Schott, *Reconsidering Women's Thought*, 164.
58 Jane Addams, *Peace and Bread in a Time of War* (New York: Macmillan, 1922), 76, 81.
59 Plastas, *A Band of Noblewomen*.
60 Georgina Taylor, "Ground for Common Action: Violet McNaughton's Agrarian Feminism and the Origins of the Farm Women's Movement in Canada" (PhD diss., Carleton University, 1997). Note that McNaughton later changed her views.
61 Annual reports (proceedings of conferences), 18–20 June 1935, 46, London School of Economics, Women's Library, BDWCU fonds; Fiona Paisley, *Loving Protection? Australian Feminism and Aboriginal Women's Rights, 1919–1939* (Melbourne: Melbourne University Press, 2000).
62 Report of the First Canadian Congress against War and Fascism, 6, 7 October 1934, University of Toronto, Thomas Fisher Rare Book Room (UT, Fisher), Kenny Collection (Kenny), 12.
63 National Bureau meeting, 3 March 1936 and 15 May 1935, YUA, Beder, 1972-001/009.
64 Report of the First Canadian Congress against War and Fascism, 11.
65 Ibid., 10.
66 Ibid., 12.

67 "The people versus war and fascism," CLAWF Proceedings, 6–8 Dec 1935, UT, Fisher, Kenny, 10.
68 Ibid., 11.
69 Socknat, *Witness against War,* 162.
70 James Naylor, *The Fate of Labour Socialism: The Co-operative Commonwealth Federation and the Dream of a Working-Class Future* (Toronto: University of Toronto Press, 2016), 272–73.
71 Dorothy Steeves, quoted in Strong-Boag, *The Last Suffragist Standing,* 127; Howard, *The Struggle for Social Justice,* 214.
72 Howard, ibid., 126.
73 Nancy Knickerbocker, *No Plaster Saint: The Life of Mildred Osterhout Fahrni, 1900–1992* (Vancouver: Talonbooks, 2001), 123.
74 Toronto WILer Edith Fowke likewise transferred her efforts to protecting human rights in an intolerant wartime environment; she worked with the Cooperative Committee on Japanese Canadians (CCJC), which opposed Japanese deportations.
75 Kerr, "Women's Views," *TF,* 23 February 1940.
76 Kerr, "Women's Views," *TF,* 2 May 1940.
77 Kerr, "Women's Views," *TF,* 10 April 1941.
78 Kerr, "Women's Views," *TF,* 30 January 1941.
79 H.D. Ainely, "Women and the CCF," *Manitoba Commonwealth,* 29 March 1940.
80 Kerr, "Women's Views," *TF,* 12 March 1940.
81 Kerr, "Women's Views," *TF,* 30 May 1940.
82 Kerr, "Women's Views," *TF,* 1 February 1940.
83 Muriel Kitigawa, *Letters to Wes and Other Writings on Japanese Canadians, 1941–1948,* ed. Roy Miki (Vancouver: Talonbooks, 1985), 72, 91.
84 Wendy Cuthbertson, *Labour Goes to War: The CIO and the Construction of a New Social Order, 1939–1945* (Vancouver: UBC Press, 2012), chap. 6.
85 Carmela Patrias, *Fighting Discrimination in Wartime Canada, 1939–1945* (Toronto: University of Toronto Press, 2012).
86 Helen Forsey, "Will Women Win the Peace?" *CF,* August 1944.
87 Letter of Avis McCurdy, 25 November 1945, UT, Fisher, Woodsworth Memorial Collection, box 2, Provincial Council file.
88 Gail Cuthbert Brandt, "Pigeoned-holed and Forgotten: The Work of the Sub-Committee on the Postwar Problems of Women, 1943," *Histoire sociale/Social History* 15, 29 (1982): 239–59.
89 Lisa Pasolli, "'I Ask You, Mr. Mitchell, Is the Emergency Over?' Debating Day Nurseries in the Second World War," *Canadian Historical Review* 96, 1 (2015): 1–31; Rianne Mahon, "The Never-Ending Story: The Struggle for Universal Child Care Policy in the 1970s," *Canadian Historical Review* 81, 4 (2000): 582–615; Susan Prentice, "Workers, Mothers, Reds: Toronto's Postwar Day Care Fight," *Studies in Political Economy* 30 (Autumn 1989): 115–41; Annis May Timpson, *Driven Apart: Women's Employment Equality and Child Care in Canadian Public Policy* (Vancouver: UBC Press, 2001).
90 Jamieson quoted in Strong-Boag, *The Last Suffragist,* 150.

91 Jacqui Alexander and Chandra Mohanty, "Introduction: Genealogies, Legacies, Movements," in *Feminist Geneologies, Colonial Legacies, Democratic Futures,* ed. M.J. Alexander and C.T. Mohanty (New York: Routledge, 1997), xxv.

CHAPTER 8: FEMINISM IN A COLD WAR CLIMATE

1 Marion Kerans, *Muriel Duckworth: A Very Active Pacifist* (Halifax: Fernwood Books, 1996).
2 *The Voice of Women: The First Thirty Years,* dir. and prod. Margo Pineau and Cathy Reeves, National Film Board, Full Frame Film and Video, 1992.
3 Brandon French, *Women on the Verge of Revolt: Women in American Films of the Fifties* (New York: Frederick Ungar, 1978); Wini Breines, *Young, White and Miserable: Growing Up Female in the Fifties* (Boston: Beacon Press, 1992).
4 Magda Fahrni and Robert Rutherdale, introduction to *Creating Postwar Canada, 1945–75,* ed. Magda Fahrni and Robert Rutherdale (Vancouver: UBC Press, 2008), 1–20.
5 Alice Kessler-Harris, *Out to Work: A History of Wage-Earning Women in the United States* (New York: Oxford University Press, 1982), 303.
6 Valerie Korinek, *Roughing It in the Suburbs: Reading* Chatelaine *Magazine in the Fifties and Sixties* (Toronto: University of Toronto Press, 2000), 311.
7 Michelle Lasnier, "Le 'Deuxième Sexe,' c'est notre bible," *Châtelaine,* April 1964.
8 Joan Sangster, *Transforming Labour: Women and Work in Postwar Canada* (Toronto: University of Toronto Press, 2010), chap. 1.
9 For example, "Postwar Jobs for All," *UE News,* 19 December 1944; "No Infringement of Seniority," *UE News,* 6 May 1949; UE pamphlet, "Winning the Peace," in possession of author; my emphasis.
10 Veronica Strong-Boag, *The Last Suffragist Standing: The Life and Times of Laura Marshall Jamieson* (Vancouver: UBC Press, 2018), 164. The term "parrot" is from Austin Cross, "Women in Politics Haven't Much Sense," *Chatelaine,* September 1950.
11 Valerie Korinek, *Roughing It,* 369.
12 Doris Anderson, *Rebel Daughter, an Autobiography* (Toronto: Key Porter, 1996).
13 June Callwood, "Let's End the Battle of the Sexes," *Maclean's,* 7 June 1956.
14 Joy Parr, introduction to *A Diversity of Women, Ontario,* ed. Joy Parr (Toronto: University of Toronto Press, 1995), 5.
15 "Agree Women Doers, Men Talkers," *Toronto Daily Star,* 12 September 1958.
16 Joan Sangster, "Queen of the Picket Line: Beauty Contests in the Post–World War II Labour Movement," *Labor: Studies in Working Class History of the Americas* 5, 4 (2008): 83–106.
17 Emily E. LB. Twarog, *Politics of the Pantry: Housewives, Food and Consumer Protest in Twentieth-Century America* (New York: Oxford University Press, 2017), 4.
18 Dean Beeby, "Women in the Ontario CCF, 1940–50," *Ontario History* 74, 4 (1982): 259–83; Joan Sangster, *Dreams of Equality: Women on the Canadian Left, 1920s to 1950s* (Toronto: McClelland and Stewart, 1984), chap. 7.

19 Strong-Boag, *The Last Suffragist,* chap. 8. Jamieson wanted "universal" voting rights for city dwellers. Groups like the Business and Professional Women's Clubs also took up this cause: in Halifax they pressed city hall to end the disenfranchisement of wives of male taxpayers: Jessie MacKnight, "A History of the Halifax Business and Professional Women's Club," Public Archives of Nova Soctia (PANS), Halifax BPWC, vol. 714, file 49.
20 Joan Sangster, "Consuming Issues: Women on the Left, Political Protest and the Organization of Homemakers, 1920–60," in *Framing Our Past: Canadian Women's History in the Twentieth Century,* ed. Sharon Anne Cook, Lorna McLean, and Kathryn O'Rourke (Montreal and Kingston: McGill-Queen's University Press, 2001), 240–47; Julie Guard, "A Mighty Power against the Cost of Living: Canadian Housewives Organize in the 1930s," *International Labor and Working Class History* 77, 1 (2010): 27–47; Brian Thorn, *From Left to Right: Maternalism and Women's Political Activism in Postwar Canada* (Vancouver: UBC Press, 2016).
21 Faith Johnston, *A Great Restlessness: The Life and Politics of Dorise Nielsen* (Winnipeg: University of Manitoba Press, 2006); Sangster, *Dreams of Equality,* chap. 6.
22 Veronica Strong-Boag, "'The Best Version of the Liberal Party': One Feminist Lineage," Active History, 30 April 2019, http://activehistory.ca/2019/04/the-best-version-of-the-liberal-party-one-feminist-lineage/.
23 Jack Pickersgill quoted in Patricia Myers, "A Noble Effort: The National Federation of Liberal Women of Canada, 1928–73," in *Beyond the Vote: Canadian Women and Politics,* ed. Linda Kealey and Joan Sangster (Toronto: University of Toronto Press, 1989), 55.
24 Ibid., 39–62; Monique Bégin, *"Upstairs Ladies!": My Life in Politics and After* (Montreal and Kingston: McGill-Queen's University Press, 2018).
25 Judith McKenzie, *Pauline Jewett: A Passion for Canada* (Montreal and Kingston: McGill-Queen's University Press, 1999), 65. See also Judy LaMarsh, *Memoirs of a Bird in a Guilded Cage* (Toronto: McClelland and Stewart, 1968).
26 Benjamin Isitt, *Militant Minority: British Columbia Workers and the Rise of a New Left, 1948–1972* (Toronto: University of Toronto Press, 2011), 124.
27 Tarah Brookfield, *Cold War Comforts: Canadian Women, Child Safety and Global Insecurity* (Waterloo: Wilfrid Laurier University Press, 2012), 77.
28 One significant anti-nuclear group was the Canadian Committee for the Control of Radiation Hazards. Isitt, *Militant Minority,* 126.
29 Reg Whittaker and Gary Marcuse, *Cold War Canada: The Making of a National Insecurity State, 1945–1957* (Toronto: University of Toronto Press, 1994).
30 Sara Evans, *Born for Liberty: A History of Women in America* (New York: Free Press, 1989), 244.
31 Elaine Tyler May, *Homeward Bound: American Families in the Cold War Era* (New York: Basic Books, 1998); Richard Cavell, ed., *Love, Hate, and Fear in Canada's Cold War* (Toronto: University of Toronto Press, 2004).
32 Gary Kinsman and Patrizia Gentile, *The Canadian War on Queers: National Security as Sexual Regulation* (Vancouver: UBC Press, 2010).
33 Jennifer Anderson, "Propaganda and Persuasion in the Cold War: The Canadian Soviet Friendship Society, 1949–1960" (PhD diss., Carleton University, 2008), 268.
34 Brookfield, *Cold War Comforts,* 84.

35 Letters of Pauline Williams and Mavis Wiley in Library and Archives Canada (LAC), Voice of Women fonds, MG 28 I 218 (VOW), vol. 1, file 1.
36 Christine Ball, "A History of the Voice of Women/La Voix Des Femmes – The Early Years" (PhD diss., University of Toronto, 1994).
37 Frances Early, "A Grandly Subversive Time: The Halifax Branch of the Voice of Women in the 1960s," in *Mothers of the Municipality: Women, Work, and Social Policy in Post-1945 Halifax,* ed. Judith Fingard and Janet Guildford (Toronto: University of Toronto Press, 2005), 254.
38 Frances Early, "Canadian Women and the International Arena in the Sixties: The Voice of Women/La voix des femmes and the Opposition to the Viet Nam War," in *The Sixties: Politics, Passion, and Style,* ed. Dimitry Anastakis (Montreal and Kingston: McGill-Queen's University Press, 2008), 26.
39 Kay Macpherson and Meg Sears, "The Voice of Women: A History," in *Women in the Canadian Mosaic,* ed. Gwen Matheson (Toronto: Peter Martin, 1976), 84.
40 Ibid., 71.
41 VOW's feminist indictment of patriarchal governance was reminiscent of Helena Gutteridge's comment in 1914: if this is the best that "male statecraft" can offer, it is time for women to become involved in the "councils of the nations."
42 Saskatchewan VOW newsletter, May 1970, LAC, VOW, vol. 17, file 6.
43 Pineau and Reeves, *The Voice of Women.*
44 Ibid.
45 Ibid.
46 Early, "Canadian Women," 30; Marilyn Sweet, "Purls for Peace: The Voice of Women, Maternal Feminism and the Knitting Project for Vietnamese Children" (master's thesis, University of Ottawa, 2007).
47 Victoria VOW Brief 248, LAC, Royal Commission on the Status of Women fonds, RG 33-89 (RCSW), vol. 117.
48 Pineau and Reeves, *The Voice of Women.*
49 Victoria Brief 248.
50 Edmonton VOW Brief 159, LAC, RCSW, vol. 13.
51 Montreal NDG (Notre-Dame-de-Grâce) VOW Brief 137, LAC, RCSW, vol. 12.
52 Regina VOW Brief 173, LAC, RCSW, vol. 13.
53 Regina Brief 173.
54 Judy Fudge, "From Segregation to Privitization: Equality, the Law, and Women Public Servants, 1908–2001," in *Privatization, Law, and the Challenge to Feminism,* ed. Brenda Cossman and Judy Fudge (Toronto: University of Toronto Press, 2002), 91.
55 Joan Sangster, "'We No Longer Respect the Law': The Tilco Strike, Injunctions and the State," *Labour/Le Travail* 53 (2004): 47.
56 Women's Bureau statistics quoted in Sangster, *Transforming Labour,* 19.
57 Canada, Department of Labour, Women's Bureau, "Married Women Working for Pay in Eight Canadian Cities," *Labour Gazette* 58 (February 1958): 148–50.
58 Leah Vosko, *Temporary Work: The Gendered Rise of a Precarious Employment Relationship* (Toronto: University of Toronto Press, 2000), 79.
59 Catherine Briggs, "Fighting for Women's Equality: The Federal Women's Bureau, 1945–67, an Example of Early 'State Feminism' in Canada" (PhD diss., University of Waterloo, 2001), 208.

60 Charles Gulston, "The Fallacy of Equal Pay for Equal Work," *Saturday Night,* 17 February 1945.
61 Shirley Tillotson, "Human Rights Law as Prism: Women's Organizations, Unions and Ontario's Female Employees Fair Remuneration Act, 1951," *Canadian Historical Review* 72, 4 (1991): 544.
62 Ibid., 556.
63 Ibid.
64 One study noted some "modest" effect on closing the pay gap in Ontario: Robert Malarkey and John Hagan, "The Socio-Legal Impact of Equal Pay Legislation in Ontario, 1946–1979," *Osgoode Hall Law Journal* 27, 2 (1989), http://digitalcommons.osgoode.yorku.ca/ohlj/vol27/iss2/2. On British Columbia, see Dominique Clément, *Equality Deferred: Sex Discrimination and British Columbia's Human Rights State, 1953–84* (Vancouver: UBC Press, 2014), 89.
65 Briggs, "Fighting for Women's Equality," 227.
66 *Labour Gazette* 67 (January 1967): 18–21.
67 Joan Sangster, "Women Workers, Employment Policy and the State: The Early Women's Bureau in Ontario, 1963–70," *Labour/Le Travail* 36 (Fall 1995): 136.
68 Unlike in the United States, Canadian feminists were not bitterly divided betweeen those wanting complete equality of competition and those wanting protective legislation that recognized women's different work needs because of pregnancy and maternity.
69 Ann Porter, *Gendered States: Women, Unemployment Insurance, and the Political Economy of the Welfare State in Canada, 1945–97* (Toronto: University of Toronto Press, 2003).
70 *In the matter of an Arbitration between Pacific Western Airlines Ltd. and the Canadian Airline Flight Attendants' Association and Deanne Konderat,* LAC, Canadian Labour Congress fonds, MG 28 I103 (CLC), reel H238; Canada, House of Commons, *Debates,* Ernie Winch, 18 June 1965, 2601.
71 *In the Matter of a Dispute between Local 293, United Packinghouse Food and Allied Workers and the Quaker Oats Company of Canada, Ltd.,* Peterborough, 2 September 1960, author's personal collection.
72 On the porters, see Sarah-Jane Mathieu, *North of the Colour Line: Migration and Black Resistance in Canada, 1870–1955* (Chapel Hill: University of North Carolina Press, 2010).
73 Carrie Best, *That Lonesome Road: The Autobiography of Carrie M. Best* (New Glasgow, NS: Clarion Publishing, 1977); Constance Backhouse, "'I Was Unable to Identify with Topsy': Carrie M. Best's Struggle Against Racial Segregation in Nova Scotia, 1942," *Atlantis* 22, 2 (Spring/Summer, 1998): 16–26.
74 Carrie Best, "Editorial," *Clarion,* February 1947.
75 Interview with Pearleen Oliver transcript, PANS, Nova Scotia Women's Oral History Project.
76 Constance Backhouse, *Colour Coded: A Legal History of Racism in Canada, 1900–1950* (Toronto: University of Toronto Press, 1999), 243.
77 Interview with Oliver.
78 Backhouse, *Colour Coded,* 243.

79 Karen Flynn and Funké Aladejebi, "Writing Black Women's History: Where We Have Been and Where We Are Going," in *Reading Canadian Women's and Gender History,* ed. Nancy Janovicek and Carmen Nielson (Toronto: University of Toronto Press, 2019), 79; Marcia Wharton-Zaretsky, "Foremothers of Black Women's Community Organizing in Toronto," *Atlantis* 24, 2 (Spring/Summer 2000): 61–71; Rella Braithwaite, *The Black Woman in Canada* (West Hill, Ontario, 1977).
80 Daniel Hill, *Women of Vision: The Story of the Canadian Negro Women's Association, 1951–76* (Toronto: Umbrella Press, 1996), 62.
81 Letter to the editor, *Chatelaine,* June 1973.
82 Hill, *Women of Vision,* 19.
83 Cheryl Thompson, "Cultivating Narratives of Race, Faith, and Community: *The Dawn of Tomorrow,* 1923–71," *Canadian Journal of History* 50, 1 (2015): 30–67.
84 Rosemary Brown, *Being Brown: A Very Public Life* (Toronto: Random House, 1989), 85.
85 Carmela Patrias and Ruth Frager, "'This Is Our Country, These Are Our Rights': Minorities and the Origins of Ontario's Human Rights Campaigns," *Canadian Historical Review* 82, 1 (2001): 3.
86 "Human Rights," *Canadian Labour,* December 1963.
87 Dominique Clément, *Equality Deferred,* 69.
88 Beatrice Trew, quoted in Sangster, *Dreams of Equality,* 214.
89 Interview with Margaret Mann, ibid., 214.
90 In 1968, the Canadian Labour Congress finally added "no sex discrimination" to its constitution.
91 Clément, *Equality Deferred.*
92 This view is expressed in the United States by those stressing continuity as much as change (e.g., Van Gosse, *Rethinking the New Left: An Interpretative History* [New York: Palgrave Macmillan, 2005]), but is echoed to a lesser extent in Canada by those who reject the concept of "ruptures" in this period: see Lara Campbell and Dominique Clément, introduction to *Debating Dissent: Canada in the Sixties,* ed. Lara Campbell, Dominique Clément, and Gregory Kealey (Toronto: University of Toronto Press, 2012), 7.
93 Brown, *Being Brown,* 88.
94 Ibid., 80.
95 McKenzie, *Pauline Jewett,* 58.
96 Ibid., 86.
97 Ibid.
98 Doris Anderson, *Rebel Daughter.*
99 Quotes, and Pat Schultz's story, are taken from *Worth Every Minute,* dir. Catherine MacLeod and Lorraine Segato, National Film Board, 1987. Some quotes have been slightly altered for readability.
100 Toni Williams, "Reforming Women's Truth: A Critique of the Royal Commission on the Status of Women," *Ottawa Law Review* 22, 3 (1990): 742.
101 Jane Arscott, "More Explosive Than Any Terrorist's Time Bomb: The RCSW, Then and Now," paper presented to the Annual Meeting of the Canadian Political Science Association, 2 June 2010, 1.

102 "Pie in the Sky," *The Pedestal,* January 1971, 8; Caroline Andrew and Frieda Paltiel, ed., *Women and the Canadian State* (Montreal and Kingston: McGill-Queen's University Press, 1997). Another initial critical review was Pat Marchak, "A Critical Review of the Royal Commission on the Status of Women," *Canadian Review of Sociology and Anthropology* 9, 1 (1972): 73–96.

103 Annis May Timpson, "Royal Commissions as Sites of Resistance: Women's Challenges on Child Care in the Royal Commission on the Status of Women," *International Journal of Canadian Studies* 20 (Fall 1999): 1–24; Joan Sangster, "Women's Experience as Evidence: Letters to the Royal Commission on the Status of Women," in *Through Feminist Eyes: Essays on Canadian Women's History* (Edmonton: University of Athabasca Press, 2011); Shannon Stettner, "'He Is Still Unwanted': Women's Assertions of Authority over Abortion in Letters to the Royal Commission on the Status of Women in Canada," *Canadian Bulletin of Medical History* 29, 1 (2012): 151–71.

104 Arscott, "More Explosive," 2.

105 *Victoria Province,* 17 April 1968, LAC, RCSW, vol. 41, newspaper clippings; *Pictou Advocate,* 18 September 1968, LAC, RCSW, vol. 43, newspaper clippings.

106 Williams, "Reforming Women's Truth."

CHAPTER 9: LIBERATING FEMINISMS

1 "Mother Confronts Edmonton Authority," *Globe and Mail,* 31 May 1969; Corinne George, "'If I Didn't Do Something, My Spirit Would Die ... ': Grass Roots Activism of Aboriginal Women in Calgary and Edmonton" (master's thesis, University of Calgary, 2007), 75. Piche was also known as Lillian Shirt. In an interview she said her sister's Indian Rights for Indian Women activism made her unpopular on the reserve and she left, but she had been previously educated in Edmonton (George, "If I Didn't Do Something," 38).

2 For a similar argument in the United States, see Benita Roth, *Separate Roads to Feminism: Black, Chicana and White Feminist Movements in America's Second Wave* (Cambridge: Cambridge University Press, 2004).

3 Mary Inman, *In Woman's Defense* (Los Angeles: Committee to Organize the Advancement of Women, 1940); Avram Landy, *Marxism and the Woman Question* (New York: Progress Books, 1943).

4 Roberta Hamilton, *The Liberation of Women: A Study of Patriarchy and Capitalism* (London: G. Allen and Unwin, 1978), 57.

5 Jane Gerhard, *Desiring Revolution: Second-Wave Feminism and the Rewriting of Twentieth-Century American Sexual Thought* (New York: Columbia University Press, 2001), 82.

6 Betty Friedan, *The Feminine Mystique* (New York: W.W. Norton, 1963). On the impact of Friedan, see Stephanie Coontz, *A Strange Stirring:* The Feminine Mystique *and American Women at the Dawn of the 1960s* (New York: Basic Books, 2011).

7 Shulamith Firestone, *The Dialectic of Sex* (New York: William Morrow, 1970); Marge Piercy, *Woman on the Edge of Time* (New York: Alfred Knopf, 1976).

8 Kate Millet, *Sexual Politics* (Garden City, NJ: Doubleday, 1970).

9 For example, Deborah Babcox and Madeline Belkin, eds., *Liberation Now! Writing from the Women's Liberation Movement* (New York: Dell Publishing, 1971); Robin Morgan, ed., *Sisterhood Is Powerful: An Anthology of Writing from the Women's Liberation Movement* (New York: Vintage, 1970); Germaine Greer, *The Female Eunuch* (1970; New York: Harper, 2006); Susan Brownmiller, *Against Our Will: Men, Women and Rape* (New York: Random House, 1975); Mary Daly, *Gyn/ecology: The Metaethics of Radical Feminism* (New York: Women's Press, 1978). For analysis, see Alice Echols, *Daring to Be Bad: Radical Feminism in America, 1967–75* (Minneapolis: University of Minnesota Press, 1989).

10 Mary O'Brien, *The Politics of Reproduction* (Boston: Routlege and Kegan Paul, 1983), 54. See the special issue on O'Brien: *Canadian Woman Studies/Les cahiers de la femme* 18, 4 (1999).

11 Dorothy Smith, *The Everyday World as Problematic: A Feminist Sociology* (Boston: Northeastern University Press, 1987); Patricia Hill Collins, *Black Feminist Thought: Knowledge, Consciousness and the Politics of Empowerment* (New York: Routledge, 1990).

12 Herbert Marcuse, "Marxism and Feminism," in *The New Left and the 1960s*, ed. Doug Kellner (London: Routlege, 2005), 170.

13 "New Left Caucus: The Knitting Circle," University of Ottawa (UO), Canadian Women's Movement Archives (CWMA), box 66, file 21.

14 Margaret Benston, "The Political Economy of Women's Liberation," *Monthly Review* 21 (September 1969): 13–27; Bonnie Fox, ed., *Hidden in the Household: Women's Domestic Labour under Capitalism* (Toronto: Women's Press, 1980).

15 Bryan Palmer, *Canada's 1960s: The Ironies of Identity in a Rebellious Era* (Toronto: University of Toronto Press, 2009), 298.

16 Meg Luxton, *More Than a Labour of Love: Three Generations of Women's Work in the Home* (Toronto: Women's Press, 1980).

17 Juliet Mitchell, "The Longest Revolution," reprinted in *Women's Estate* (London: Penguin, 1971), 75–122.

18 Zillah Eisenstein, introduction to *Capitalist Patriarchy and the Case for Socialist Feminism*, ed. Zillah Eisenstein (New York: Monthly Review Press, 1979), 5.

19 Hamilton, *Liberation of Women*.

20 Charnie Guettel, *Marxism and Feminism* (Toronto: Women's Press, 1974); Dorothy Smith, *Feminism and Marxism: A Place to Begin, a Way to Go* (Vancouver: New Star Books, 1977).

21 Corrective Collective, *She Named It Canada (Because That Is What It Was Called)* (Toronto: James Lorimer, 1970); Corrective Collective, *Never Done: Three Centuries of Women's Work in Canada* (Toronto: Canadian Women's Educational Press, 1974).

22 Sheila Rowbotham, quoted in Lynne Segal, *Why Feminism?* (New York: Columbia University Press, 1999), 17–18. Segal uses Rowbotham to counter subsequent postmodern caricatures of second-wave feminism as a movement characterized by unquestioned orthodoxies and fixed notions of gender.

23 Sheila Rowbotham, *Women, Resistance and Revolution* (London: Penguin Books, 1972), 133.

24 Ibid., 201.

25 Sean Mills, *The Empire Within: Postcolonial Thought and Political Activism in Sixties Montreal* (Kingston and Montreal: McGill-Queen's University Press, 2010), 63.

26 Joan Sangster, "Never Done: Feminists Reinterpret Their Own History," in *Reading Canadian Women's and Gender History,* ed. Nancy Janovicek and Carmen Nielsen (Toronto: University of Toronto Press, 2019), 203–24.

27 "Sexe et politique: La répression sexuelle – ça sert à qui?" *Quebcoise deboutte!* (*QD*), March 1973.

28 Veronique O'Leary and Louise Toupin, eds., "Pourquoi ne pas toujours repartir à zéro," *QD:* une anthologie 2, 25.

29 Harold Adams, *Prison of Grass: Canada from a Native Point of View* (Toronto: New Press, 1975); Maria Campbell, *Halfbreed* (Toronto: McClelland and Stewart, 1973).

30 Regina VOW Brief 173, Library and Archives Canada (LAC), Royal Commission on the Status of Women fonds (RCSW), vol. 13; "Indian Women: Double Oppression," *Pedestal,* March 1972.

31 Keeanga-Yamahtta Taylor, *How We Get Free: Black Feminism and the Combahee River Collective* (Chicago: Haymarket Books, 2017). Also circulating was Cherrie Moraga and Gloria Anzaldua, eds., *This Bridge Called My Back: Writings by Radical Women of Color* (New York: Kitchen Table, Women of Color Press, 1981), 7–8.

32 Emily Flaherty, "The Women's Liberation Movement in Britain, 1968–1984: Locality and Organisation in Feminist Politics in Aberdeen, Brighton and Hove, Edinburgh and Bolton" (PhD diss., University of Glasgow, 2017), 9. On the United States, see Stephanie Gilmore, *Groundswell: Grassroots Feminist Activism in Postwar America* (London: Routlege, 2013).

33 Lara Campbell, Dominique Clément, Gregory Kealey, eds., *Debating Dissent: Canada and the Sixties* (Toronto: University of Toronto Press, 2012).

34 There is a library of writing on 1968. Two international examples are George Katsiaficas, *The Imagination of the New Left: A Global Analysis of 1968* (Boston: South End Press, 1987); and Kristina Schulz, "The Women's Movement," in *1968 in Europe: A History of Protest and Activism, 1956–1977,* ed. Martin Klimke and Joachim Scharloth (London: Palgrave Macmillan, 2008), 281–94. Canada's 1968 also "symbolized more than [a] singular date": see Bryan Palmer, "Canada's 1968 and Historical Sensibilities," *American Historical Review* 123, 3 (June 2018): 773. For the narrow misconstruing of 1968 as a calendar year see Matthew Hayday and Mary-Ellen Kelm, "Reconsidering 1969: A 'Turning Point' for Canada?"*Canadian Historical Review* 100, 2 (June 2019): 202–4.

35 For slogans, see Red Marriott, "Slogans of 68," 30 April 2008, https://libcom.org/history/slogans-68.

36 Palmer, *Canada's 1960s,* 239.

37 Bryan Palmer, "Wildcat Workers in the 1960s: The Unruly Face of Class Struggle," in *Labouring Canada: Class, Gender and Race in Canadian Working-Class History,* ed. Bryan Palmer and Joan Sangster (Toronto: Oxford University Press, 2008), 369–93.

38 Lee Maracle, *Bobbi Lee, Indian Rebel* (Toronto: Women's Press, 1990); Scott Rutherford, "Canada's Other Red Scare: The Anicinabe Park Occupation and Indigenous Decolonization," in *The Hidden 1970s: Histories of Radicalism,* ed. Dan Berger (New Brunswick, NJ: Rutgers University Press, 2010), 77–96; Kevin Brushett, "Making Shit Disturbers: The Selection and Training of Company of Young Canadian

Volunteers, 1965–1970," in *The Sixties in Canada: A Turbulent and Creative Decade*, ed. M. Athena Palaeologu (Montreal: Black Rose Books, 2009), 246–69. Canadian women were also cognizant of the American WARN (Women of All Red Nations), allied with the American Indian Movement.

39 Liora Proctor, "The Student Neestow Project," *Our Generation* 4 (November 1966): 40; Burnley Jones and James St. Walker, *Burnley "Rocky" Jones: Revolutionary* (Halifax: Fernwood, 2016), 77–78; Frances Early, "A Grandly Subversive Time: The Halifax Branch of the Voice of Women in the 1960s," in *Mothers of the Municipality: Women, Work, and Social Policy in Post-1945 Halifax*, ed. Judith Fingard and Janet Guildford (Toronto: University of Toronto Press, 2005), 253–80.

40 Anne Boulton, "A Feminist in Politics," *Saskatoon Women's Liberation Newsletter* (*SWLN*), April 1975, 10.

41 Bonnie Dow, *Watching Women's Liberation, 1970: Feminism's Pivotal Year in Network News* (Urbana: University of Illinois Press, 2014).

42 Problematically, multiple categories, such as "white" and "middle-class," are inevitably congealed. For a critique, see Radha Jhappan, "Post-Modern Race and Gender Essentialism or a Post-Mortem of Scholarship," *Studies in Political Economy* 51 (1996): 15–63.

43 Palmer, *Canada's 1960s*.

44 Judy Bernstein, Peggy Morton, Linda Seese, and Myrna Wood, "Sisters, Brothers, Lovers ... Listen," in *Women Unite! An Anthology of the Canadian Women's Movement* (Toronto: Canadian Women's Educational Press, 1972), 38–39.

45 Ibid., 37.

46 In their first flush in the United States too, some women's liberation groups were anti-imperialist and anti-capitalist, though this tendency diminished over time, more so than in Canada.

47 "Pie in the Sky," in *Women Unite*, 40–42.

48 Ellen Kruger and Linda Taylor, introduction to *Winnipeg Women's Liberation Newsletter* (2016), Rise Up! A Digital Archive of Feminist Activism, https://riseupfeministarchive.ca/publications/winnipeg-womens-liberation-newsletter/.

49 "New Left Caucus: The Knitting Circle." The three male authors were listed as John Bordo, Andrew Wernick, and Ron Colpitts. There are no signatures on the women's response.

50 Carol Hanisch, "The Personal Is Political," in *Radical Feminism: A Documentary History*, ed. Barbara Crow (New York: NYU Press, 2000), 114.

51 "The Small Groups," *Montreal Women's Liberation Newsletter* 1 (March 1970).

52 Sheila Rowbotham, Lynne Segal, and Hilary Wainwright, *Beyond the Fragments: Feminism and the Making of Socialism* (London: Merlin, 1979), 40.

53 Segal, *Why Feminism?* 19.

54 Margaret Hillyard Little, "Militant Mothers Fight Poverty: The Just Society Movement, 1968–1971," *Labour/Le Travail* 59 (Spring 2007): 179–97; Karin Wells, *The Abortion Caravan: When Women Shut Down Government in the Battle for the Right to Choose* (Toronto: Second Story Press, 2020), 217.

55 Clare Hemmings and Josephine Brain, "Imaging the Feminist Seventies," in *The Feminist Seventies*, ed. Helen Graham, Ann Kaloski, Ali Neilson, and Emma Robertson (York, UK: Raw Nerve Books, 2003), 105.

56 "Théâtre des Cuisines," *The Other Woman* (*TOW*), December–January 1976, 17–18.
57 "In Montreal, Feminists Are Shaking Up Society," *Toronto Daily Star* (*TDS*), 31 January 1970. The temporary group was called the Front commune des femmes québécoises.
58 Denyse Baillargeon, *A Brief History of Women in Quebec* (Waterloo: Wilfrid Laurier University Press, 2014), 177.
59 "Feminists Picket Queen's Park Demanding Equality in Jobs," *TDS*, 29 April 1970.
60 "Women's Liberation," McMaster University Archives (MUA), Revolutionary Workers League (RWL) fonds, box 10.
61 "Angry New Feminists Out-talk Templeton," *TDS*, 2 May 1969. This was written by Helen Worthington, who penned other unsympathetic pieces on WL. Letter to the editor from Marjaleena Repo, *TDS*, 13 May 1969.
62 "Women Are Becoming too Liberated," *TDS*, 10 November 1970.
63 Letter to *Guerilla* from Ms Judy Girard, 26 May 1972, UO, CWMA, box 77, file 5.
64 Frances Wasserlein, "An Arrow to the Heart: The Vancouver Women's Caucus and the Abortion Campaign, 1969–71" (master's thesis, Simon Fraser University, 1990), 73–74.
65 Steve Hewitt and Christobelle Sethna, "Sex Spying: The RCMP's Framing of English-Canadian Women's Liberation Groups during the Cold War," in *Debating Dissent*, 135–54. Of course, the RCMP spied on other sixties movements too. To note one example of the destruction of resources: Toronto Just Society Movement papers were stolen/destroyed in an RCMP theft, after which the building was set on fire: Paul Weinberg, "The Praxis Affair: There's a Reason We Put Limits on Spying within Canada," 1 March 2015, CCPA, https://www.policyalternatives.ca/publications/monitor/praxis-affair.
66 "Human Being or Beauty Queen?" and Margaret Benston, "What Is a Beauty Contest," *Pedestal*, April 1970.
67 Joan Sangster, "Queen of the Picket Line: Beauty Contests in the Post–World War II Labour Movement," *Labor: Studies in Working Class History of the Americas* 5, 4 (2008): 83–106; "Indian Princess Crowned," *Kenomadiwin News*, 30 June 1970.
68 "Beauty Contests," *TOW*, December–January 1975; for shoe photo see Maxine Nunes and Deanna White, *The Lace Ghetto* (Toronto: New Press, 1972), 6.
69 "Women remembered on November 11," *Upstream*, December 1979.
70 Regina Women's Liberation brief, UO, CWMA, box 83, f. 31.
71 "General Meeting Minutes," *SWLN*, January 1975; "To the Editors from Bev Bauer" and "In reply," *SWLN*, January 1975.
72 "Equality in Farming," *SWLN*, February 1975.
73 Joan Baril, "Some Herstory and a Goodbye," *Northern Woman Journal* 7, 1 (1981).
74 Cathy Walker, "The Halifax Women's Caucus," *Pedestal*, February 1970.
75 Letter to the editor, M. Repo, *TDS*, 13 May 1969.
76 "The New Feminist Analysis," UO, CWMA, box 66, file 19; New Feminist statement, LAC, VOW, vol. 8, 1971.
77 Sherrill Cheda, "New Feminists Now," *Canadian Woman Studies/Les cahiers de la femme* 11, 2 (1980): 27–28. One author of "Sisters, Brothers," Myrna Wood, believed that the New Feminists included more ex-patriate Americans than Canadians; the former were more open to a "radical" feminist emphasis on patriarchy.

78 Opportunities for Youth and Local Initiatives Programs were short-term employment projects sponsored by the federal government.
79 "Toronto Women's Yellow Pages," UO, CMWA, box 144, file 19, n.d.
80 "Time for Reassessment?" *Winnipeg Women's Liberation Newsletter,* November 1974.
81 On the daycare link, see "Letters," *SWLN,* August–September 1979.
82 Charlotte McEwen, Marguerite Kluensch, and Helen Ralston, "Are You Listening Sisters: Canadian Women Speak Up," 1 July 1975 and "Affairs of the Moment," 10 October 1975, MUA, RWL, box 10; Sylva Gelber from the Women's Bureau and MP Corine Campbell represented the government, which reportedly worried that the resolution would be used against Israel, criticizing the occupation of Palestinian territory.
83 Post-structuralist theory, some feminists argue, contributed to "amnesia" about feminists' earlier efforts to address race, class, and imperialism: Lisa Vogel, "Telling Tales: Historians of Our Own Lives," *Journal of Women's History* 2 (Winter 1991): 89–101.
84 Editorial, *SWLN,* April 1975, 4. In 1977, with the renewal of the group, the name of the publication was changed to *Prairie Woman: A Newsletter of Saskatoon Women's Liberation.*
85 Agatha Beins, *Liberation in Print: Feminist Periodicals and Social Movement Identity* (Athens: University of Georgia Press, 2017), 138: Judy Tzu-Chun, *Radicals on the Road: Internationalism, Orientalism, and Feminism during the Vietnam Era* (Ithaca, NY: Cornell University Press, 2013).
86 "In Canada, Imperialism Begins at Home," *Kinesis,* September–October 1981, 8–9, linked Western corporate power in South Africa to Indigenous dispossession in Canada.
87 Jo Freeman, *The Politics of Women's Liberation* (New York: Longman's, 1975).
88 Beth Palmer, "Choices and Compromises: The Abortion Movement in Canada, 1969–1988" (PhD diss., York University, 2012), 12. By 1979, you see "no sterlization" in the lists of popular demands relating to reproductive freedom: for example, "Editorial," *Prairie Woman,* March–April 1979.
89 David Gutnick, "'Simple Justice': 50 Years Later, Monique Bégin Reflects on the Royal Commission on the Status of Women," *CBC Sunday Magazine,* 6 March 2020, https://www.cbc.ca/radio/thesundayedition/the-sunday-edition-for-march-8-2020-1.5482636/simple-justice-50-years-later-monique-b%C3%A9gin-reflects-on-the-royal-commission-on-the-status-of-women-1.5482637.
90 Nancy Janovicek, "'If It Saves One Life, All the Effort ... Is Worthwhile': Crossroads for Women/Carrefour pour femmes, Moncton, 1979–1987," *Acadiensis* 35, 2 (2006): 27–45.
91 Jennifer Fraser, "Claims-Making in Context: Forty Years of Canadian Feminist Activism on Violence against Women" (PhD diss., University of Ottawa, 2014), ii.
92 Varda Burstyn, "Beyond Despair: Positive Strategies," in *Women against Censorship,* ed. Varda Burstyn (Vancouver: Douglas and McIntyre, 1985), 155.
93 Palmer, "Choices and Compromises," 33.
94 "Women Declare War," *Pedestal,* March 1970, 2. Myrna Kostash, *Long Way from Home: The Story of the Sixties Generation in Canada* (Toronto: Lorimer, 1980), 176; Shannon Stettner, "We Are Forced to Declare War: Linkages between the 1970

Abortion Caravan and Women's Anti–Viet Nam War Activism," *Histoire sociale/Social History* 46, 92 (2013): 423–41.

95 Frances Wasserlein, "An Arrow Aimed at the Heart."

96 Wells, *The Abortion Caravan.*

97 "Strategy for Choice: An Interview with Judy Rebick," *Cayenne* 1, 2 (1985): 23–29.

98 Palmer, "Choices and Compromises," 323–24.

99 Ibid., 67.

100 Marlene Gerber and Loretta Ross, quoted in Karen Stote, "The Myth of Reproductive Choice: A Call for Radical Change," in *Without Apology: Writing on Abortion in Canada,* ed. Shannon Stettner (Edmonton: Athabasca University Press, 2016), 279. On reproductive justice, see Zikya Luna, "Marching towards Reproductive Justice," *Sociological Inquiry* 80, 4 (2010): 554–78.

101 Janine Brodie, Shelley Gavigan, and Jane Jenson, "The Politics of Abortion: Representations of Women," in *The Politics of Abortion,* ed. Brodie, Gavigan, and Jenson (Toronto: Oxford University Press, 1992), 14.

102 Karen Anderson, *Recognition of Being: Reconstructing Native Womanhood* (Toronto: Second Story Press, 2000), 106, 136.

103 Stevi Jackson and Sue Scott, "Whatever Happened to Feminist Critiques of Monogamy?" in Graham et al., *The Feminist Seventies,* 27–40.

104 I generally use "queer" or "LGBTQ" to reflect later language, but usually use "lesbian" here, since that was the identity claimed at the time. On bar culture, see Elise Chenier, "Rethinking Class in Lesbian Bar Culture: Living 'The Gay Life' in Toronto, 1955–65," *Left History* 9, 2 (2004): 85–112.

105 Becki Ross, *The House That Jill Built: A Lesbian Nation in Formation* (Toronto: University of Toronto Press, 1995), 31; Mariana Valverde, *Sex, Power and Pleasure* (Toronto: Women's Press, 1985), 93.

106 Valerie Korinek, "'Don't Let Your Girlfriends Ruin Your Marriage': Lesbian Imagery in *Chatelaine* Magazine, 1950–1969," *Journal of Canadian Studies* 33, 3 (1998): 92.

107 Adrienne Rich, "Compulsory Heterosexuality and Lesbian Existence," *Signs* 5, 4 (1980): 631–60. The concept is similar to the later "heteronormativity." Stevi Jackson, "Interchanges: Gender, Sexuality and Heterosexuality: The Complexity (and Limits) of Heteronormativity," *Feminist Theory* 7 (2006): 105–21.

108 Ross, *The House That Jill Built,* 16.

109 Julia Creet, "A Test of Unity: Lesbian Visibility in the British Columbia Federation of Women," in *Lesbians in Canada,* ed. Sharon Dale Stone (Toronto: Between the Lines, 1990), 184.

110 Ibid.

111 Racialesbians, "The Woman-Identified Woman," in *"Takin' It to the Streets": A Sixties Reader,* ed. Alexander Bloom and Wini Breines (New York: Oxford University Press, 1995), 329–34.

112 Nym Hughes, Yvonne Johnson, and Yvette Perreault, *Stepping Out of Line: A Workbook on Lesbianism and Feminism* (Vancouver: Press Gang, 1984).

113 Judi Morton, "When I Grow Up I Want to Be a Lesbian," *Pedestal,* June–July 1975, 10–11.

114 Ross, *The House That Jill Built,* 26.

115 Valerie Korinek, *Prairie Fairies: A History of Queer Communities and People in Western Canada, 1930–1985* (Toronto: University of Toronto Press, 2018), 280.
116 Ibid., 404.
117 BC Federation of Women Constitution, UO, CWMA, box 5, file 5.
118 Creet, "A Test of Unity," 184, 191.
119 Ross, *The House That Jill Built.*
120 Christina Rousseau, "Wages Due Lesbians: Visibility and Feminist Organizing in 1970s Canada," *Gender, Work and Organization* 22, 4 (2015): 364–74.
121 Gary Kinsman, "Queer Resistance and Regulation in the 1970s," in *We Still Demand: Redefining Resistance in Sex and Gender Struggles,* ed. Patricia Gentile, Gary Kinsman, and Pauline Rankin (Vancouver: UBC Press, 2017), 58–85.
122 Quoted in Ross, *The House That Jill Built,* 61.
123 Anne Enke, *Finding the Movement: Sexuality, Contested Space and Feminist Activism* (Durham, NC: Duke University Press, 2007), 257.
124 Kathleen Jamieson, *Indian Women and the Law: Citizens Minus* (Canada: Advisory Council on the Status of Women, 1980), 1.
125 "Indian Women Want to Be Indians," *TDS,* 3 October 1968; "Indians Tell of Fears," *Ottawa Citizen,* 3 October 1968, 43.
126 Elizabeth Dingman, "Indian Women – Most Unequal in Canada," *Chatelaine,* February 1973, 39.
127 Sarah Nickel, "I Am Not a Women's Libber although I Sometimes Sound Like One: Indigenous Feminism and Politicized Motherhood," *American Indian Quarterly* 41, 4 (2017): 300.
128 See, for example, Dick Fidler, "Red Power in Canada," *Labor Challenge* (paper of the League for Socialist Action), 23 February, 6 April, 20 April 1970. The interchange is also evident in writing by Indigenous activists – for example, Adams, *Prison of Grass.*
129 Kelly Pineault, "Shifting the Balance: Indigenous and Non-Indigenous Activism in the Company of Young Canadians, 1966–1970" (master's thesis, Trent University, 2010), 131.
130 *Kenomadiwin News,* 4 November 1970, 1. See also Karen Stote, "The Sterilization of Aboriginal Women in Canada," *American Indian Culture and Research Journal* 36, 3 (2012): 117–50.
131 "New Association Formed: ONWA," *Kenomadiwin News,* 30 June 1972, 1.
132 Heather Howard Bobiwash, "Women's Class Strategies as Activism in Native Community Building in Toronto, 1950–75," *American Indian Quarterly* 27, 3–4 (2003): 566–82.
133 Cheryl Troupe, "Métis Women: Social Structure, Urbanization and Political Activism, 1850–1980" (master's thesis, University of Saskatchewan, 2009), 114, 123.
134 "Native Women's Movement" and "Native Women Rap Indian Group," *Saskatoon Star Phoenix,* 24 October 1973.
135 Aroha Harris and Mary Jane Logan McCallum, "'Assaulting the Ears of Government': The Indian Homemakers' Clubs and the Maori Women's Welfare Leagues in Their Formative Years," in *Indigenous Women and Work: From Labor to Activism,* ed. Carol Williams (Urbana: University of Illinois Press, 2012), 227. See also Magee, Kathryn, "'For Home and Country': Education, Activism and Agency in Alberta

Native Homemakers' Clubs, 1942–1970," *Native Studies Review* 18, 2: 27–49; Martha Wells, "Mi'kmaw Women and St. Francis Xavier University Micmac Community Development Program, 1958–70," *Acadiensis* 44, 2 (Summer 2015): 51–74; Lianne Leddy, "Mostly Just a Social Gathering: *Anishinaabe Kwewag* and the Indian Homemakers' Club, 1945–60," in *Aboriginal History: A Reader*, ed. Kristin Burnett and Geoff Read (Toronto: Oxford University Press, 2016), 352–61.

136 Nickel, "I Am Not a Women's Libber," 309.

137 Patricia Miranda Barkaskas, "*The Indian Voice:* Centering Women in the Gendered Politics of Indigenous Nationalism in BC, 1969–1984" (master's thesis, UBC, 2009).

138 "Innocents Caught in Cross Fire," *Indian Voice* (*IV*), June 1975.

139 Jamieson, *Indian Women*, 2.

140 Nickel, "I Am Not a Women's Libber," 318.

141 "Marital Status Crucial Issue," *Saskatoon Star Phoenix*, 23 March 1972.

142 Nellie Carlson, quoted in George, "If I Didn't Do Something," 38.

143 For two different views, see Mary Ellen Turpel, "Aboriginal Peoples and the Charter: Interpretive Monopolies, Cultural Differences," *Canadian Human Rights Year Book* 6, 3 (1989–90) and Teressa Nahanee, "Dancing with a Gorilla: Aboriginal Women, Justice and the Charter," in *Aboriginal Peoples and the Justice System: Report of the National Round Table on Aboriginal Justice Issues* (Ottawa: Royal Commission on Aboriginal Peoples, 1993).

144 Lilianne Ernestine Krosenbrink-Gelissen, *Sexual Equality as an Aboriginal Right* (Saarbrucken, DE: Verlag Breitenback, 1991).

145 Sharon McIvor, "Aboriginal Women's Rights as 'Existing' Rights'," in *First Voice: An Aboriginal Women's Reader*, ed. Patricia Monture and Patricia McGuire (Toronto: Inanna Publications, 2009), 374–81.

146 "Indian Women," 38.

147 "National Day of Mourning," *Northern Woman Journal*, October 1973, 2, 6. Similar demonstrations were held in Vancouver and Toronto.

148 Krosenbrink-Gelissen, *Sexual Equality.*

149 Marlene Brant Castellano, "Heart of the Nations: Women's Contribution to Community Healing," in *Restoring the Balance: First Nations Women, Community and Culture*, ed. Gail Valaskakis, Madeleine Dion Stout, and Eric Guimond (Winnipeg: University of Manitoba Press, 2009), 203–35.

150 Lina Sunseri, "Sky Woman Lives On: Contemporary Examples of Mothering of the Nation," in ibid., 54–64; on the social/political distinction, see Nickel, *Assembling.*

151 Jo-Anne Fiske, "The Womb Is to the Nation as the Heart Is to the Body: Ethnopolitical Discourses of the Canadian Indigenous Women's Movement," *Studies in Political Economy* 51 (Fall 1996): 65–95.

152 Nickel, "I Am Not a Women's Libber," 309; *Assembling*, 63.

153 "Roseau River Women in Action," *Bulletin of the Canadian Association in Support of Native Peoples*, Fall 1978, 13.

154 Janet Silman, ed., *Enough Is Enough: Aboriginal Women Speak Out* (Toronto: Women's Press, 1987).

155 Margaret Mitchell, *No Laughing Matter: Adventure, Activism and Politics* (Vancouver: Granville Island Publishing, 2008), chap. 15.

156 Sherene Razack, “Gendered Racial Violence and Spatialized Justice: The Murder of Pamela George,” in *Race, Space, and the Law: Unmapping a White Settler Society,* ed. Sherene Razack (Toronto: Between the Lines, 2002), 121–56.
157 Nancy Janovicek, *No Place to Go: Local Histories of the Battered Women's Shelter Movement* (Vancouver: UBC Press, 2008), 22.
158 Ibid., 64. The common effort did not last, though sources do not indicate exactly why.
159 Nancy Rudge, “Berger Report: The Plan and the Price,” *Upstream,* May–June 1977.
160 Testimony from Jane Charlie, Fort McPherson, and brief presented to the Berger Inquiry, quoted in ibid.
161 Patricia Monture-Okanee, “The Violence We Do: A First Nations View,” in *Challenging Times: The Women's Movement in Canada and the United States,* ed. Constance Backhouse and David Flaherty (Montreal and Kingston: McGill-Queen's University Press, 1992), 193–204.
162 Grace Ouellette, *The Fourth World: An Indigenous Perspective on Feminism and Aboriginal Women's Activism* (Halifax: Fernwood, 2002), 26. See also the critique of Sandy Grande, *Red Pedagogy: Native American Social and Political Thought* (Lanham, MD: Rowman & Littlefield, 2004).
163 Campbell, *Halfbreed;* Beatrice Culleton, *In Search of April Raintree* (Winnipeg: Manitoba Pemmican Publications, 1983).
164 Joyce Green, “Taking Account of Aboriginal Feminism,” in *Making Space for Indigenous Feminism,* ed. Joyce Greene (Halifax: Fernwood, 2007), 21.
165 Ibid., 30.
166 Lee Maracle, *I Am Woman: A Native Perspective on Sociology and Women* (Vancouver: Press Gang, 2001), xi. See also Emma Laroque, “Violence in Aboriginal Communities,” in Health Canada, *National Clearing House on Family Violence* (Ottawa, 1994), 72–89.
167 Nickel, *Assembing,* 15.
168 In Audra Simpson and Andrea Smith's terminology, this is “theoretical promiscuity,” a mixing of Indigenous and Western theories and thought systems: Audra Simpson and Andrea Smith, introduction to *Theorizing Native Studies,* ed. Audra Simpson and Andrea Smith (Durham, NC: Duke University Press, 2014), 9–12.
169 Letter, Pat Leslie to Helen Worthington, 16 August 1974, UO, CWMA, *TOW* papers, Correspondence, box 77, file 7.
170 Elizabeth Anderson, “Studio D's Imagined Community: From Development (1974) to Realignment (1986–1990),” in *Gendering the Nation: Canadian Women's Cinema,* ed. Kay Armitage, Kass Banning, Brenda Longfellow, and Janine Marchessault (Toronto: University of Toronto Press, 1999), 41–61.
171 Perhaps the precedent was Gutteridge's “soap boxing” on Vancouver street corners for suffrage. See Wasserlein, “An Arrow to the Heart,” 103.
172 “Eaton's Boycott May Extravaganza,” *Cayenne* 1, 3 (1985): 19–21. One of the strike support organizers, Patricia McDermott, later wrote and produced a play in 2014, *Life on the Line: Women Strike at Eaton's, 1984–85,* based on her interviews with the strikers.
173 Barbara Marshall, “Communications as Politics: Feminist Print Media in English Canada,” *Women's Studies International Forum* 18, 4 (1995): 463–74; Eleanor

Wachtel, *Feminist Print Media* (Ottawa: Secretary of State, 1982). Feminist publishing pushed other alternative papers and magazines, especially on the left, to address feminism: see *Canadian Dimension*'s special issue on feminism, June 1975.

174 Beins, *Liberation in Print*, 3, 10.

175 *Kinesis* was an "editorially independent" newspaper that received some government funding but ran into problems about content because of this: Barbara Freeman, *Beyond Bylines: Media Workers and Women's Rights in Canada* (Waterloo: Wilfrid Laurier University Press, 2011), 165.

176 Eleanor Wachtel, *Update on Feminist Periodicals* (Ottawa: Secretary of State, 1985), 7. Suzanne de Rosa and Jeanne Maranda, "La presse feministe est differente!" *Resources for Feminist Research* 8, 1 (1987): 33–34; Margie Wolfe, "Working with Words: Feminist Publishing in Canada," in *Still Ain't Satisfied: Canadian Feminism Today* (Toronto: Women's Press, 1982), 265–75.

177 Wachtel, *Feminist Print Media*, 23.

178 I concentrate here on three early papers. For a more extensive analysis of seventeen papers, see Joan Sangster, "Creating Popular Histories: Reinterpreting 'Second Wave' Canadian Feminism," *Dialectical Anthropology* 39, 4 (2015): 381–404.

179 Micheline Dumont, *Feminism à la québécoise* (Ottawa: Feminist History Society, 2012), 177.

180 Editorial, *Northern Woman Journal*, September 1973, 1.

181 Correspondence, submitted article, *TOW*, UO, CMWA, box 77, file 5.

182 Letters 8 June and 12 October 1972, *TWO*, UO, CMWA, box 78, file 21.

183 Laurie Atkinson to *TOW*, 25 October 1972; Liz Willick to *TOW*, n.d., UO, CMWA, box 78, file 21.

184 Ibid., letter from "Anne," *TOW*, box 78, file 21, 9 October 1972.

185 Ibid.

186 Letter from C. Poissont, 24 September 1974, *TOW*, UO, CWMA, box 78, file 21.

187 "Daughter of Bolton: Three Views," *TOW*, January–February 1977, 10. Both published and unpublished letters are in *TOW* papers, UO, CMWA, box 77, file 5.

188 Barbara Hicks, "Women in the Thirties," *Pedestal*, June 1970.

189 Dodie Weppler, "Helena Gutteridge," *Pedestal*, May 1970.

190 Carol Phillips and Pat Hoffer, "Women of the Blues," *Pedestal*, October 1970.

191 Ellen Woodsworth, "Indian Women: Double Oppression," *Pedestal*, March 1972.

192 O'Leary and Toupin, "Pourquoi ne pas toujours repartir à zéro," 122.

193 "Histoire d'une oppression," *QD*, November 1972.

194 "Histoire d'une oppression: Les Amerindiens-nes," *QD*, December 1972.

195 "Histoire d'une oppression: La conquête et l'insurrection," *QD*, February 1973.

196 "Sexe et politique: La répression sexuelle – ça sert à qui?" *QD*, March 1973.

197 O'Leary and Toupin, "Pourquoi ne pas toujours repartir à zéro," 9.

198 Varda Burstyn, "The Waffle and the Women's Movement," *Studies in Political Economy* 33 (Autumn 1990): 177–78.

199 Gil Levine, "The Waffle and the Labour Movement," *Studies in Political Economy* 33 (Autumn 1990): 191. On the Waffle, see John Bullen, "The Ontario Waffle and the Struggle for an Independent Socialist Canada: Conflict within the NDP," *Canadian Historical Review* 64, 2 (1983): 166–215.

200 Burstyn, "The Waffle," 180.

201 "Waffle Policy on Women" and "Towards a Strategy for Waffle Women," UO, CWMA, box 100, file 70.

202 "Towards a Strategy."

203 Waffle Women's Caucus, UO, CMWA, box 100, file 70.

204 For one example of "autonomist" organizing from below, which also influenced Wages for Housework, see Sean Antaya, "The New Left at Work: Workers' Unity, the New Tendency, and Rank-and-File Organizing in Windsor, Ontario, in the 1970s," *Labour/Le Travail* 85 (Spring 2020): 53–89. "New communist" is a term used by Max Elbaum to make a distinction between the "old" Communist party and the plethora of parties that grew out of the sixties.

205 John Sawatsky, *Men in the Shadows: The RCMP Security Service* (Toronto: Doubleday, 1980). The "dirty tricks department" spied on and tried to undermine those defined as subversive by the RCMP.

206 Varda Burstyn, "The Left and the Porn Wars: A Case Study in Sexual Politics," in *Who's On Top? The Politics of Heterosexuality*, ed. Howard Buchbinder, Varda Burstyn, Dinah Forbes, and Mercedes Steedman (Toronto: Garamond Press, 1987), 14. Another reflection is Catherine MacLeod, *Waking Up in the Men's Room* (Toronto: Between the Lines, 1998). A visceral hostility to "new communist" parties persists. One reviewer of this manuscript was unhappy to see "so much" (3 pages in a 400-page manuscript) on Trotskyism, apparently not an important topic in their view.

207 Max Elbaum, *Revolution in the Air: Sixties Radicals Turn to Lenin, Mao and Che* (London: Verso, 2002). For a discussion of new communist parties, though only in Toronto, see Peter Graham with Ian McKay, *Radical Ambition: The New Left in Toronto* (Toronto: Between the Lines, 2019).

208 Meg Luxton, "How Do We Know What We Know: A Life and Times in Canadian Sociology," in *Canadian Sociology in the First Person*, ed. Stephen Riggins and Neil Mclaughlin (Montreal and Kingston: McGill-Queen's University Press, forthcoming).

209 Revolutionary Marxist Group document, RWL fonds, MUA, box 7, file 2.

210 "Women's Liberation," [1972] RMG series, UO, CWMA, box 145, file 20. This is only one pamphlet/political statement of many. For similar documents, see "Documents of Revolutionary Socialism in Canada," Socialist History Project, 23 April 2019, https://www.socialisthistory.ca/Docs/docs.htm.

211 RWL document, MUA, RWL, box 7, files 5–7.

212 "Infiltration of the Women's Movement by the LSA," *TOW*, November–December 1973, 14. Lis Angus, "Why Socialists Join Feminist Struggles: Reply to Slanders in *Other Woman*," [1974] Social History Project, https://www.socialisthistory.ca/Docs/1961-/WomensLib/Marxism-Feminism.htm. Similar charges of LSA control over abortion organizing came from other cities.

213 Vancouver Women's Caucus History Project, interview with VWC, n.d. My thanks to Pat Davitt for sending me a transcript of this interview. See also, "Women and Socialism: Accounting for Our Experience," pamphlet, n.d., UO, CWMA, box 145, file 10. See also Wasserlein, "An Arrow to the Heart," 112.

214 Rowbotham, Segal, and Wainwright, *Beyond the Fragments.*

215 "The Status of Women in Canada," LSA brief to the RCSW [1968], Socialist History Project, https://www.socialisthistory.ca/Docs/1961-/WomensLib/RoyalCommission68.htm.

216 Nancy Hewitt, introduction to *No Permanent Waves: Recasting Histories of US Feminism,* ed. Nancy Hewitt (New Brunswick, NJ: Rutgers University Press, 2010), 8.
217 Wasserline, "An Arrow to the Heart," 54.

CHAPTER 10: FEMINIST ORGANIZING IN THE 1970S AND 1980S

1 Joan Roberts, *Cracked: How Telephone Operators Took on Canada's Largest Corporation and Won* (Hamilton, ON: Dundurn Press, 2015), 303.
2 Ibid., 287.
3 A few examples: Jill Vickers, Pauline Rankin, and Christine Appelle, *Politics as if Women Mattered: A Political Analysis of the National Action Committee on the Status of Women* (Toronto: University of Toronto Press, 1993); Caroline Andrew and Frieda Paltiel, eds., *Women and the Canadian State* (Montreal and Kingston: McGill-Queen's University Press, 1997); Mary Jo Nadeau, "The Making and Unmaking of a 'Parliament of Women': Nation, Race and the Politics of the National Action Committee on the Status of Women, 1972–1992" (PhD diss., York University, 2005); Nancy Worsfold, "An Organization and Its Discontents: The National Action Committee on the Status of Women" (master's thesis, Concordia University, 1990); Bronwyn Bragg, "Deconstructing 'Hegemonic Feminism': The Emergence of 'Second Wave' Feminism in Canada (1965–1975)" (masters thesis, Ontario Institute for Studies in Education, University of Toronto, 2011).
4 Susan Crean, *Grace Hartman: A Women for Her Time* (Vancouver: New Star Books, 1995), 91.
5 Nancy Adamson, Linda Briskin, and Margaret McPhail, *Feminist Organizing for Change: The Contemporary Women's Movement in Canada* (Toronto: Oxford University Press, 1988), 181.
6 Mary Jo Nadeau, "The Making and Unmaking of a 'Parliament of Women'."
7 Roberta Hamilton and Michèle Barrett, introduction to *The Politics of Diversity: Feminism, Marxism and Canadian Society,* ed. Roberta Hamilton and Michèle Barrett (London: Verso, 1986), 4.
8 Lisa Young contrasts this non-partisan focus with the actions of American feminists, who put more effort into party – especially Democratic – politics at this point. Lisa Young, *Feminists and Party Politics* (Vancouver: UBC Press, 2000), 54–55.
9 Vickers, Rankin, and Appelle, *Politics as if Women Mattered.*
10 Nadeau, "The Making," 12.
11 Ibid., 158.
12 Heather Jon Maroney, "Contemporary Quebec Feminism: The Interrelation of Political and Ideological Development in Women's Organizations, Trade Unions, Political Parties and State Policy, 1960–1980" (PhD diss., McMaster University, 1988).
13 Dianne Lamoureux, *L'amère patrie: Féminisme et nationalisme dans le Québec contemporain* (Montreal: Remue-ménage, 2001).
14 Flavie Trudel, "L'engagement des femmes en politique au Québec: Histoire de la Fédération des femmes du Québec de 1966 à nos jours" (PhD diss., Université du Québec à Montréal, 2009), 230.

15 Micheline de Sève, "The Perspectives of Quebec Feminists," in *Challenging Times: The Women's Movement in Canada and the United States,* ed. Constance Backhouse and David H. Flaherty (Montreal and Kingston: McGill-Queen's University Press, 1992), 116.

16 Presentation on the Meech Lake Accord, York University Archives (YUA), Jean Augustine fonds (JA), vol. 7, file 45.

17 For example, one of the first overviews of wife battering, published by the Canadian Advisory Council on the Status of Women, began to wake people up: Linda MacLeod and Andrée Cadieux, *Wife Battering in Canada: The Vicious Circle* (Ottawa: Canadian Advisory Council on the Status of Women, 1980).

18 Penney Kome, *The Taking of Twenty-Eight: Women Challenge the Constitution* (Toronto: Women's Press, 1983).

19 Micheline Dumont, *Féminisme à la québécoise* (Ottawa: Feminist History Society 2002), 192–93.

20 Barbara Roberts, *Smooth Sailing or Storm Warning? Canadian and Quebec Women's Groups and the Meech Lake Accord* (Ottawa: Canadian Research Institute for the Advancement of Women, 1988), 11.

21 Brian Mulroney, for instance, advertised NAC's view of Meech as "anti-Quebec." Daiva Stasilius, "Relational Positionalities of Nationalism," in *Between Women and Nation: Nationalisms, Feminisms and the State,* ed. Caren Kaplan, Norma Alarcon, and Minoo Moallen (Durham, NC: Duke University Press, 1999), 182–218; Jo-Ann Lee and Linda Cardinal, "Hegemonic Nationalism and the Politics of Feminism and Multiculturalism in Canada," in *Painting the Maple: Essays on Race, Gender, and the Construction of Canada,* ed. Veronica Strong-Boag, Sherrill E. Grace, Avigail Eisenberg, and Joan Anderson (Vancouver: UBC Press, 1998), 215–41.

22 Judy Rebick and Kiké Roach, *Politically Speaking* (Vancouver: Douglas and McIntyre, 1996).

23 Nancy Worsfold, "An Organization and Its Discontents."

24 Report of resource bank project, Dalhousie University Archives (DUA), Nova Scotia Women's Action Committee fonds (NSWAC), box 2, file 2.1 and 2.9.

25 Daycare, perspectives and resources, 18 January 1980, DUA, NSWAC, box 1, file 1.2.

26 Reel Life report, DUA, NSWAC, box 1, file 3.8.

27 Marriage reform, DUA, NSWAC, box 1, file 1.5.

28 Doris Anderson, "Two Cases Where Women Lost Heavily," *Status of Women News* (*SOWN*), June 1973, 6.

29 Joint statement of all provincial Status of Women Councils, DUA, NSWAC, box 1, file 1.5.

30 Equal Pay, "For immediate release," 17 February 1977, DUA, NSWAC, box 1, file 1.4.

31 Letters, Jeremy Ackerman to Christina Simmons, 18 June 1980, and Judy Wasylycia-Leis to Simmons, 29 August 1980 in DUA, NSWAC, box 1, file 3.4.

32 The federal Badgely committee found that two-thirds of the Maritimes outside Nova Scotia had no community hospital access. In New Brunswick, anti-abortion organizing, including by doctors, had immense influence. See Lianne McTavish, "Abortion in New Brunswick," *Acadiensis* 44, 2 (2015): 107–30; Katrina R. Ackerman, "'Not

in the Atlantic Provinces': The Abortion Debate in New Brunswick, 1980–1987," *Acadiensis* 41, 1 (2012): 75–101.

33 Draft letter of Tina Simmons to S.C. Robinson, head, Department of Gynecology, 21 August 1979, DUA, NSWAC, box 1, file 1.1.

34 "Cornerbrook Status of Women," *SOWN,* February 1976, 9.

35 Beth Atcheson and Lorna Marsden, eds., *White Gloves Off: The Work of the Ontario Committee on the Status of Women* (Toronto: Second Story Press, 2018).

36 Ibid., 59.

37 Ibid., 39.

38 "Alberta Women Organize for Action"; "Advocate Comments on Horner Speech," *SOWN,* December 1976, 3–4.

39 Conversation with F. Adams, June 2019.

40 International Women's Day Declaration, 1983, University of Ottawa (UO), Canadian Women's Movement Archives (CWMA), Alberta Status of Women Action Committee, box 2, file 1.

41 Minnie Aodla, "Inuit Law Defended," *ASWAC Newsletter,* August 1984.

42 "N.W.T Women Protest Ruling" and "Here We Go Again," *ASWAC Newsletter,* May 1984.

43 In the Canadian Women's Movement Archives, hundreds of files from International Women's Day committees are a source waiting to be used to flesh out this complex picture of local feminisms.

44 Joan Sangster, *Transforming Labour: Women and Work in Postwar Canada* (Toronto: University of Toronto Press, 2010), 6.

45 Letter from MW, Library and Archives Canada (LAC), Royal Commission on the Status of Women fonds, RG 33-89, vol. 9, Ontario file.

46 Waitresses Action Committee, UO, CWMA, box 101, file 28.

47 Lisa Pasolli, *Working Mothers and the Child Care Dilemma: A History of British Columbia's Social Policy* (Vancouver: UBC Press, 2015), 132–42.

48 Pamela Sugiman, *Labour's Dilemma: The Gender Politics of Auto Workers in Canada, 1937–1979* (Toronto: University of Toronto Press, 1994), 137.

49 Crean, *Grace Hartman,* 76–77.

50 Joan Sangster, "Radical Ruptures: Feminism, Labor, and the Left in the Long Sixties in Canada," *American Review of Canadian Studies* 40, 1 (2010): 1–21.

51 Author interview with Patricia Davitt, Jean Rand, Pat Howard, Elizabeth Breimberg, Anne Roberts, Vancouver, 20 June 1917.

52 Julia Smith, "'An Entirely Different Kind of Union': The Service, Office and Retail Workers of Canada, 1972–86," *Labour/Le Travail* 73 (2014): 38.

53 Jill Stainsby, Honoree Newcombe, Jacqui Parker-Snedker, and Paul Reniers, *AUCE and TSSU: Memoirs of a Feminist Union* (Vancouver: Teaching Support Staff Union Publishing, 1993).

54 Mary Cornish, *Getting Organized: Building a Union* (Toronto: Women's Press, 1980); Jennifer Penney, *Hard Earned Wages: Women Fighting for Better Work* (Toronto: Women's Press, 1983).

55 On Parent, see Andrée Lévesque, ed., *Madeleine Parent: Activist* (Toronto: Sumach Press, 2005).

56 Rebecca Coulter, "Alberta Nurses and the 'Illegal' Strike of 1988," in *Women Challenging Unions: Feminism, Democracy and Militancy,* ed. Linda Briskin and Patricia McDermott (Toronto: University of Toronto Press, 1993), 44–61.
57 Linda Briskin, "Union Women and Separate Organizing," in ibid., 89–100.
58 Ibid., 104.
59 Deidre Gallagher quoted in ibid., 101.
60 Dominique Clément, *Equality Deferred: Sex Discrimination and the British Columbia Human Rights State, 1953–84* (Vancouver: UBC Press, 2014); Carol Agócs, ed., *Employment Equity in Canada: The Legacy of the Abella Report* (Toronto: University of Toronto Press, 2014). The commission's report was authored by Justice Rosalie Abella. While human rights and employment equity are important, here I use only the example of pay equity.
61 Patricia McDermott, quoted in Carl Cuneo, *Pay Equity: The Labour-Feminist Challenge* (Toronto: Oxford University Press, 1990), 9.
62 Judy Fudge and Patricia McDermott, eds., *Just Wages: A Feminist Assessment of Pay Equity* (Toronto: University of Toronto Press, 1991).
63 Cuneo, *Pay Equity,* 153.
64 Jan Kainer, *Cashing in on Pay Equity: Supermarket Restructuring and Gender Equality* (Toronto: Sumach Press, 2002), 244.
65 Organized Working Women pamphlet, "Why a Trade Union Women's Organization?" excerpt from 1976 founding convention. In author's possession.
66 Cara Banks, "Saskatchewan Working Women: Socialist Feminist Struggles with Inclusivity and Diversity in the 1980s" (master's thesis, York University, 2001), 31.
67 Quoted in ibid., 60.
68 Linda Briskin, "Socialist Feminism: From the Standpoint of Practice," *Studies in Political Economy* 30 (Autumn 1989): 102.
69 Sedef Arat-Koc, "Gender and Race in 'Non-discriminatory' Immigration Policies in Canada," in *Scratching the Surface: Canadian Anti-Racist Feminist Thought,* ed. Enakshi Dua and Angela Robertson (Toronto: Women's Press, 1999), 229.
70 Tania Das Gupta, "The Politics of Multiculturalism: Immigrant Women and the Canadian State," in *Scratching the Surface,* 195.
71 Himani Bannerji, "Popular Images of South Asian Women," in *Returning the Gaze: Essays on Racism, Feminism and Politics,* ed. Himani Bannerji (Toronto: Sister Vision Press, 1993), 182.
72 Glenna Simms quoted in C. Mounsey, "We Will Define Ourselves!," *Speak Out: A Publication of the Congress of Black Women of Canada* (Toronto chapter), March 1987, YUA, JA, 1.
73 Das Gupta, "The Politics of Multiculturalism," 201.
74 Jennifer Mills, "Conferencing as a Site for the Mobilization of Black Feminist Identities in the Congress of Black Women of Canada, 1973–1983," *Journal of Black Studies* 46, 4 (2015): 415–41.
75 "Why a Black Women's Organization," *Speak Out,* January 1987, YUA, JA, box 6 file 2.
76 Edmonton chapter, "Who We Are," and Scarborough chapter, "Constitution," YUA, JA, box 3, file 2.

77 Roxana Ng, "Sexism, Racism, Canadian Nationalism," in Bannerji, *Returning the Gaze*, 223.
78 For an overview, see Yasmeen Abu-Laban, "Keeping 'em Out: Gender, Race and Class Biases in Canadian Immigration Policy," in Strong-Boag et al., *Painting the Maple*, 69–83.
79 "Women and the Immigration Process," *Cayenne* 1, 2 (1985): 12.
80 "Rally Protests Order to Deport Young Domestic," and "Appeal to the Minister of Labour,'" 20 May 1986, UO, CWMA, INTERCEDE, box 36, file 14; "Domestics Launch Charter Challenge," *Globe and Mail*, 18 April 1987.
81 Poster for rally for Josie Makotoko, UO, CWMA, Coalition of Black Trade Unionists, Women's Issues Committee, box 70, file 20.
82 Ronnie Leah, "Do You Call Me Sister? Women of Colour and the Canadian Labour Movement," in Dua and Robertson, eds., *Scratching the Surface*, 111.
83 Audrey Macklin, "On the Inside Looking In: Foreign Domestic Workers in Canada," in *Maid in the Market: Women's Paid Domestic Labour*, ed. Winona Giles and Sedef Arat-Koc (Halifax: Fernwood, 1994), 22.
84 Rachel Epstein, "Domestic Workers: The Experience of BC," in *Union Sisters: Women in the Labour Movement*, ed. Linda Briskin and Lynda Yanz (Toronto: Women's Press, 1983), 222–37.
85 Makeda Silvera, *Silenced* (Toronto: Williams-Wallace, 1983).
86 Epstein, "Domestic Workers," 231.
87 Das Gupta, "The Politics of Multiculturalism," 194.
88 Linda Carty and Himani Bannerji, "Visible Minority Women: A Creation of the Canadian State," in Bannerji, *Returning the Gaze*, 207–22.
89 Daiva Stasiulis, "The Politics of Minority Resistance against Racism in the Local State," in *Community Organization and the Canadian State*, ed. Roxana Ng, Gillian Walker, and Jacob Muller (Toronto: Garamond Press, 1990), 214.
90 Das Gupta, "The Politics of Multiculturalism," 187, 194.
91 Sean Mills, *A Place in the Sun: Haiti, Haitians, and the Remaking of Quebec* (Montreal and Kingston: McGill-Queen's University Press, 2016), 177.
92 Ibid., 179.
93 Nadeau, "The Making and Unmaking."
94 Sunera Thobani, *Exalted Subjects: Studies in the Making of Race and Nation in Canada* (Toronto: University of Toronto Press, 2007), 139.
95 Anonymous member quoted in Vijay Agnew, *Resisting Discrimination: Women from Asia, Africa and the Caribbean and the Women's Movement in Canada* (Toronto: University of Toronto Press, 1996), 86.
96 Ibid., 88; Carolyn Egan, Linda Gardner, and Judy Persad, "The Politics of Transformation: Struggles with Race, Class, and Sexuality in the March 8th Coalition," in *Social Movements / Social Change: The Politics and Praxis of Organizing*, ed. F. Cunningham et al. (Toronto: Between the Lines, 1988), 22–47.
97 Calgary International Women's Day events, 1986, 1987, UO, CWMA, box 36, file 33.
98 Enakshi Dua, "Exploring Articulations of Race and Gender: Going beyond Singular Categories," in *Race and Racism in 21st Century Canada*, ed. Sean Hier and B. Singh Bolaria (Toronto: University of Toronto Press, 2007), 175.

99 For a critique of the way in which "whiteness" has become essentialized, rather than being seen as an analytical concept tied to historically based claims and counter-claims, see Vic Satzewich, "Whiteness Studies: Race, Diversity and the New Essentialism," in ibid., 67–84.
100 Sylvia Bashevkin, *Women on the Defensive: Living through Conservative Times* (Toronto: University of Toronto Press, 1998), 3.
101 "Strategy for Choice: An Interview with Judy Rebick," *Cayenne* 1, 2 (1985): 22.
102 Presentation for Lesbians against the Right (LAR), 9 May 1981, UO, CWMA, LAR, box 44, file 6, and letter, Sara Diamond to "Dear Sisters," 12 June 1981, file 4.
103 Introduction to LAR, UO, CWMA, LAR, box 44, file 6.
104 "Post Feminism," newspaper clippings, UO, CWMA, box 27, file 9.
105 Kathy Arnup, "Presentation for Lesbians against the Right," UO, CWMA, LAR, box 44, file 6, 8.
106 Karen Dubinsky, "Lament for a Patriarchy Lost'? Anti-Feminism, Anti-Abortion and R.E.A.L. Women in Canada" (Ottawa: Canadian Research Institute for the Advancement of Women, 1985), 30.
107 Julia Pyryeskina, "'A Remarkably Dense Historical and Political Juncture': Anita Bryant, *The Body Politic,* and the Canadian Gay and Lesbian Community in January 1978," *Canadian Journal of History* 53, 1 (2018): 58–85.
108 Judy Liefschultz, "How Women for Survival Is Fighting the Right," Presentation for LAR, 9 May 1981, UO, CWMA, LAR, box 44, file 8.
109 Bread and Roses minutes, 15 November 1981 and 13 December 1981, UO, CWMA, Bread and Roses, box 4, file 15.
110 Bryan D. Palmer, *Solidarity: The Rise and Fall of an Opposition in British Columbia* (Vancouver: New Star Books, 1987).
111 Sharon Stone, Case Study of Lesbians against the Right, UO, CWMA, LAR, box 44, file 3.
112 Introduction to LAR, UO, CWMA, LAR, box 44, file 6.
113 Letter, Sara Diamond to "Dear Sisters."
114 *Domestics' Cross-Cultural News,* October 1994, UO, CWMA, INTERCEDE, box 36, file 14.
115 Bashevkin, *Women on the Defensive,* 40.
116 Marjorie Cohen, "The Canadian Women's Movement and Its Efforts to Influence the Canadian Economy," in Backhouse and Flaherty, *Challenging Times,* 218; Marjorie Cohen, *Free Trade and the Future of Women's Work* (Toronto: Garamond Books, 1987).
117 "Free Trade Deal Called a Pretext for Low Pay," *Globe and Mail,* 2 December 1987.
118 Worsfold, "An Organization," 146–47.
119 Jeremy Muttall, "Canada has enabled a 'genocide' says report into missing and murdered Indigenous women and girls," *The Star,* 21 May 2019.
120 Rebick and Roach, *Politically Speaking,* 91.

AFTERWORD

1 Angela McRobbie, "Notes on Postfeminism and Popular Culture: Bridget Jones and the Gender Regime," in *All about the Girl: Culture, Power, Identity,* ed. Anita Harris (London: Routledge, 2004), 3–14.

2 Susan Douglas, *The Rise of Enlightened Sexism: How Pop Culture Took Us from Girl Power to Girls Gone Wild* (New York: Henry Holt, 2010).

3 Clare Hemmings, *Why Stories Matter: The Political Grammar of Feminist Theory* (Durham, NC: Duke University Press, 2011).

4 Leah Vosko, "Crisis Tendencies in Social Reproduction: The Case of Ontario's Early Years Plan," in *Social Reproduction: Feminist Political Economy Challenges Neo-Liberalism,* ed. Kate Bezanson and Meg Luxton (Montreal and Kingston: McGill-Queen's University Press, 2006), 145–72.

5 Susan Braedley, "Someone to Watch over You: Gender, Class, and Social Reproduction," in ibid., 215–30.

6 Kate Bezanson and Meg Luxton, introduction, ibid., 4.

7 Janine Brodie, "We Are All Equal Now: Contemporary Gender Politics in Canada," *Feminist Theory* 9, 2 (2008): 149.

8 Judy Fudge and Brenda Cossman, "Introduction: Privatization, Law and the Challenge to Feminism," in *Privatization, Law and the Challenge of Feminism,* ed. Judy Fudge and Brenda Cossman (Toronto: University of Toronto Press, 2002), 3–37.

9 Brodie, "We Are All Equal Now," 158.

10 Melanie Beres, Barbara Crow, and Lise Gotell, "The Perils of Institutionalization in Neoliberal Times: Results of a National Survey of Canadian Sexual Assault and Rape Crisis Centres," *Canadian Journal of Sociology* 34, 1 (2009): 141.

11 Lise Gotell, "The Discursive Disappearance of Sexualized Violence: Feminist Law Reform, Judicial Resistance, and Neo-Liberal Sexual Citizenship," in *Reaction and Resistance: Feminism, Law, and Social Change,* ed. Hester Lessard, Dorothy Chunn, and Susan Boyd (Vancouver: UBC Press, 2007), 127.

12 Loreen Snider, "Criminalizing Violence against Women: Solution or Dead End?" *Criminal Justice Matters* 74 (2008): 38–39; Elizabeth Bernstein, "Carceral Politics as Gender Justice? The 'Traffic in Women' and Neoliberal Circuits of Crime, Sex, and Rights," *Theory and Society* 41, 3 (May 2012): 233–59.

13 Beres, Crow, and Gotell, "The Perils of Institutionalization," 135.

14 Douglas James Nesbitt, "Days of Action: Ontario's Extra-parliamentary Opposition to the Common Sense Revolution, 1995–1998" (PhD diss., Queen's University, 2018), 38.

15 Barbara Legault, "ReBelles: Feminists Fighting with Love and Rage," *Canadian Dimension,* November–December 2010, https://canadiandimension.com/articles/view/rebelles.

16 Clare Hemmings, *Why Stories Matter,* 64.

17 Barbara Winslow, "Three Faces of Trevia: Identity, Intellect, Activism," in *Voices of Women Historians: The Personal, the Political, the Professional,* ed. Berenice Carroll, Eileen Boris, and Nupur Chauduri (Bloomington: Indiana University Press, 1999), 13.

18 Mariana Valverde, "Post-Structuralist Gender Historians: Are We Those Names?," *Labour/Le Travail* 25 (Spring 1990): 228.

19 Nancy Hartstock, "Foucault on Power: A Theory for Women?" in *Feminism and Postmodernism,* ed. Linda Nicholson (New York: Routledge, 1990), 157–75.

20 Rosemary Hennessy, *Profit and Pleasure: Sexual Identities in Late Capitalism* (New York: Routledge, 2000). I am not an impartial commentator. I wrote about these

theoretical debates, and, though I drew on some post-structuralist theory, I echoed warnings of the limitations of an overly discursive, cultural post-structuralism, unanchored to historical and material contexts, and sadly deficient in human agency. For example, Joan Sangster, "Feminism and the Making of Canadian Working Class History: Exploring the Past, Present and Future," *Labour/Le Travail* 46 (Fall 2000): 127–66.

21 Susan Archer Mann and Douglas J. Huffman, "The Decentering of Second Wave Feminism and the Rise of the Third Wave," *Science and Society* 69, 1 (2005): 71, 62.

22 Janice Ristock and Catherine Taylor, "Introduction: Sexualities and Feminisms," *Atlantis* 23, 1 (Fall Winter 1998): 1; Eleanor MacDonald, "Critical Identities: Rethinking Feminism Through Transgender Politics," in ibid., 3–12; Meg Luxton, "Transphobia and Transactivism," *Atlantis* 29, 1 (Fall Winter 2004): 1.

23 Susan Archer Mann and Ashley Suzanne Patterson, *Reading Feminist Theory: From Modernity to Postmodernity* (New York: Oxford University Press, 2016), 357.

24 Rebecca Walker, introduction to *To Be Real: Telling the Truth and Changing the Face of Feminism*, ed. Rebecca Walker (New York: Anchor Books, 1995).

25 Natasha Pinterics, "Riding the Feminist Waves: In with the Third?" *Canadian Woman Studies* 20 (Winter–Spring 2001): 2–3.

26 Ann Braithwaite, "The Personal, the Political, Third-wave and Postfeminisms," *Feminist Theory* 3, 3 (2003): 335–44; Mann and Huffman, "The Decentering of Second Wave Feminism," 74.

27 Stacy Gillis, Gillian Howie, and Rebecca Munford, *Third Wave Feminism: A Critical Exploration* (New York: Palgrave Macmillan, 2004); Astrid Henry, *Not My Mother's Sister: Generational Conflict and Third-Wave Feminism* (Bloomington: Indiana University Press, 2004), 22.

28 Miriam Glucksmann, "V. Airbrushing the History of Feminism: 'Race,' Ethnicity," *Feminism and Psychology* 18, 2 (2008): 405–9.

29 Becky Thompson, "Multiracial Feminism: Recasting the Chronology of Second Wave Feminism," *Feminist Studies* 28, 2 (2002): 336–60.

30 Leela Fernandes, "Unsettling 'Third Wave' Feminism: Feminist Waves, Intersectionality, and Identity Politics in Retrospect," in *No Permanent Waves: Recasting Histories of US Feminism*, ed. Nancy Hewitt (New Brunswick, NJ: Rutgers University Press, 2010), 98–120.

31 Lynne Segal, *Why Feminism?* (New York: Columbia University Press, 1997), 23.

32 Rebecca Ellis, "Second Thoughts about a Third Wave," *Canadian Woman Studies* 20–21, 4/1 (2001): 26.

33 Carole Vance, ed., *Pleasure and Danger: Exploring Female Sexuality* (Boston: Routledge and Paul, 1984).

34 Lise Gotell, "Third Wave Anti-Rape Activism in Neo-Liberal Terrain: The Garneau Sisterhood," in *Sexual Assault in Canada: Law, Legal Practice and Activism*, ed. Elizabeth Sheehy (Ottawa: University of Ottawa, 2012), 245.

35 Sheryl Sandberg, *Lean In: Women, Work and the Will to Lead* (New York: Alfred A. Knopf, 2013). Sandberg is the COO of Facebook. One critique is Catherine Rottenberg, *The Rise of Neoliberal Feminism* (New York: Oxford University Press, 2018).

36 Hester Eisenstein, *Feminism Seduced: How Global Elites Used Women's Labor and Ideas to Exploit the World* (Boulder, CO: Paradigm Publishers, 2009); Nancy Fraser, "Feminism, Capitalism, and the Cunning of History," *New Left Review* 56 (March/April 2009): 97–117. For a critique, see Joan Sangster and Meg Luxton, "Feminism, Capitalism and the Problems of Amnesia: A Response to Nancy Fraser," *Socialist Register*, ed. Leo Panitch, Greg Albo, and Vivek Chibber (London: Merlin Press, 2013), 288–309.

37 Sally Kitch, *Higher Ground: From Utopianism to Realism in Feminist Thought and Theory* (Chicago: University of Chicago Press, 2000), 93, 184. Critiques of the history of utopian writings have rightly stressed their western European biases and neglect of Indigenous dispossession, but those limitations were not part of these feminist critiques.

38 Russell Jacoby, *The End of Utopia: Politics and Culture in an Age of Apathy* (New York: Basic Books, 1999), 16.

39 Marge Piercy, interview with Elton Furlanetto, *Utopian Studies* 25, 2 (2014): 416–30.

Index

Note: "f" after a page number indicates a figure